Eighth Edition

Growth and Development of the Young Child

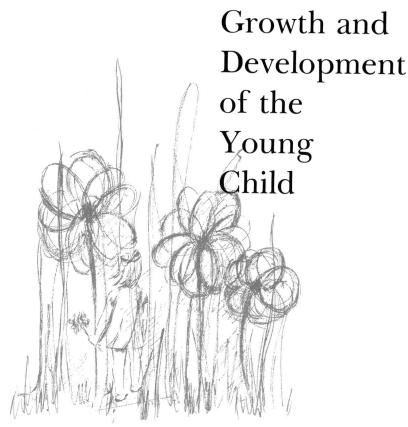

MARIAN E. BRECKENRIDGE, M.S.

Physical Development and Nutrition,
Late of the Merrill-Palmer Institute, Detroit

MARGARET NESBITT MURPHY, Ph.D.
Child Development and Family Life,
Purdue University

W. B. Saunders Company
Philadelphia · London · Toronto

W. B. Saunders Company: West Washington Square
Philadelphia, Pa. 19105

12 Dyott Street
London, WC1A   1DB

1835 Yonge Street
Toronto 7, Ontario

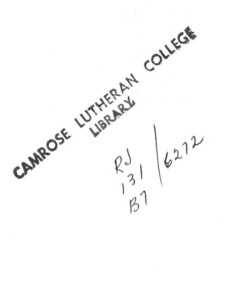

Growth and Development of the Young Child

SBN 0-7216-1937-1

Print No.:   9   8   7   6   5   4   3

Preface

In child development, biological and psychological systems as well as environmental systems outside the person are involved. This book views the child up to the age of five years from many angles in study of his physical, motor, intellectual, emotional and social development in settings within the family and elsewhere. It is written for those interested in thought or ideas related to present knowledge from theory and research. Focus is on relation of concepts, well supported or with limited evidence at present, and "real" children.

Coordination of content on many variables in the child's development is through cooperation of authors from different disciplines. As one of the first textbooks in the child development field, and in each of its revisions, including this eighth edition, subject-matter has been reviewed and selections of material to continue to use and to add have been made by authors specializing in divisions of biology, nutrition, psychology and family development.

In this eighth edition a number of the additions concern the psychological development of the child. Some of the recent research findings which have been included suggest current interest in recognition of variables in bodily and neurological functioning. Others suggest attempts to recognize the child's plasticity in the sense that his behavior reflects experiences of his particular setting and the times of their occurrence. Content has been expanded on subjects such as motivations, attention, language development, concept formation and thought, social responsiveness of the infant, the child and the adult, enrichment of experience, persistence of and change in attributes of the individual during a span of years, family structures, and methods of assessment.

The first chapter concerns concepts of human development to which the student might refer in considering various physical and behavioral changes and their processes. Interactions in the family, heredity and prenatal development are studied in Chapters Two and Three. Chapters Four through Seven refer to a variety of basic needs, physical and psychological. Chapters Eight through Eleven deal with sequences of physical, motor, intellectual, emotional and social development in time and seek explanations of their variations. Chapter Twelve is on phi-

iii

losophy of adult-child relations. Continuity and change in attributes of the individual over a period of years are considered in Chapter Thirteen on predictions of future development.

Although this book covers only the early part of the life span, many of the concepts discussed and the evidence to support these concepts have relevance for other ages. Also, the past, present and future of the child are so intimately connected that a thorough comprehension of the early years plays a role in understanding later behavior and development.

It is hoped that the material in the book will be used in a flexible manner so that the student's thought draws upon content in one section in considering questions in another section. Also, thought on the part of the individual student can lead to many ramifications through the selection of additional references, the devising of additional means, observational and otherwise, for relating concept and theory with facts and reality.

The authors have been grateful for the soundness of emphases of the authors of the first four editions, Winifred Rand, Mary Sweeny, and E. Lee Vincent. The scholarly and sensitive outlook of Marian Breckenridge is an important part of the fifth, sixth, seventh and eighth editions.

Many persons have contributed to each revision in many ways—with critical reviews of the former edition, with information and photographs, and in the preparation of illustrations and manuscript.

For the eighth edition, Stanley Garn, Chairman of the Department of Growth and Genetics of the Fels Research Institute, reviewed chapters on physical growth. Avanelle Kirksey of the Department of Foods and Nutrition, Purdue University, reviewed and revised the chapter on nutrition. Their participation is appreciated.

The cooperation of the staff of W. B. Saunders Company in the preparation of this edition is appreciated.

MARGARET NESBITT MURPHY

October, 1968

Contents

Introduction 1

CHAPTER ONE

*Current Concepts and Theories of Growth and
Development* 3

    Complexity of the Child 3
    Developmental-dynamic Concept 5
    Concept of Orderly Trends 21
    Concept of Uniqueness of the Individual 24
    Ways of Viewing Individual Differences 25

CHAPTER TWO

*The Home and the Family as Background for Growth and
Development* 31

    Complexity of the Family 31
    The Family as a Growing Organism 32
    Family Members and Their Relations 40
    Family Orientations 51
    The Family and the Community 65
    Methods of Study of the Family 77

CHAPTER THREE

Life Begins 80

    When Life Begins 80
    Planning and Preparation for Children 80
    Adjustments to Pregnancy 86
    Inheritance and Environment 88
    Development of Embryo and Fetus 91
    Recognition of Pregnancy 108
    Maternal Changes during Pregnancy 109

PHYSICAL NEEDS DURING PREGNANCY............................ 113
EMOTIONS IN PREGNANCY.. 117
ATTITUDES OF FAMILY MEMBERS................................ 119
OBSTETRICAL PERIOD.. 122

CHAPTER FOUR

*Physical and Psychological Needs: Warmth, Meeting
Situations without Extreme Stress or Apathy, Dependence
and Independence*.. 129

WARMTH.. 132
MEETING SITUATIONS WITHOUT EXTREME STRESS
    OR APATHY.. 138
DEPENDENCE AND INDEPENDENCE............................... 151

CHAPTER FIVE

Physical and Psychological Needs: Nutrition........................ 158

NUTRITIONAL NEEDS... 159
PHYSICAL EQUIPMENT... 161
NUTRITION.. 178

CHAPTER SIX

*Physical and Psychological Needs: Eating Behavior;
Elimination*... 203

EATING BEHAVIOR.. 203
ELIMINATION... 216

CHAPTER SEVEN

*Physical and Psychological Needs: Activity and Rest;
Social Contact; Other Needs; Personality Components*............ 225

NEED FOR ACTIVITY AND REST..................................... 225
NEED FOR SOCIAL CONTACT.. 235
VARIETIES OF NEED.. 241
COMPONENTS OF A HEALTHY PERSONALITY...................... 242

CHAPTER EIGHT

The Child's Equipment for Growth and Development........... 247

PHYSICAL DEVELOPMENT: EQUIPMENT FOR
    MOVEMENT.. 247

External Dimensions and Weight........................... 247
Skeletal System.. 263
Nervous System... 275
Muscular System.. 279
Body Dynamics.. 281
Endocrine Glands... 287

CHAPTER NINE

Motor Development 294

Development of Control over the Body.................. 295
Development of Hand Skills.................................... 304
Variables in Motor Development............................ 310

CHAPTER TEN

Intellectual Development.. 323

Development of Sensitivity and Perception.............. 324
Development of Language...................................... 342
Development of Concepts, Problem-solving
    Ability and Thought.. 358
Development of Creativity...................................... 373
Measurement of Intelligence in Young Children...... 383

CHAPTER ELEVEN

*Development of Concepts of Self, of Others and of the
World: Emotional-social Sequences and Interactions*............. 389

Concepts of Self, Others and the World as
    Outgrowths of Emotional, Social and Cognitive
    Development.. 389
Methods of Studying Emotional and Social
    Development.. 417
Implications of Emotional and Social
    Development.. 421

CHAPTER TWELVE

Philosophy of Adult-child Relations........................ 429

Aims for the Child and Methods of the Adult........... 429
Use of Ideas about Personality Development........... 432
Attitudes of the Adult.. 441

CHAPTER THIRTEEN

Early Years: Foundation for Later Growth and
Development 453
      Summary of Development 455
      Forecasting the Future 458

List of Films 467

Bibliography 475

Index 513

Introduction

Many people, whether parents, potential parents, teachers, or others associated with children professionally and nonprofessionally, are interested in children. People want to know "how they tick" and why. Most also feel a responsibility to provide a healthy environment for children. Confusion has resulted from the barrage of advice, the fads and old wives' tales, the various theories of child development and the different emphases of research findings. There is a need for more knowledge and understanding so that specific issues can be dealt with, facts and fallacies sifted, and confidence gained in one's ability to meet situations.

A person associated with a child wishes for further understanding of him as an individual and for increasingly satisfactory relations with him. Questions arise about the child's physical, intellectual, emotional, social and spiritual growth: e.g., the child's gain in weight, hours of sleep, play activities, feelings, reactions to adult suggestions, and interest in a world beyond his comprehension. The various phases of growth and development are interrelated in a complex way. Well-founded ideas are important, as is their application to an actual situation with a baby or young child.

A person seeking knowledge for its own sake finds important sources in research, theory and perspectives of well-qualified people working in fields concerned with children and families. The meanings their material conveys can be highlighted by reference to reality. Observations of children may consider not only outward behavior, which is objective, but also what underlies it, which is more subtle. Questions raised will draw upon material read and observations made. Careful consideration of many points, rather than quick solutions, will enter into final conclusions.

What we know about children and their families and what we hope for children and for ourselves in association with them, and why, form a fascinating field of study.

TOPICS FOR STUDY AND DISCUSSION

1. To begin to be more aware of the interrelatedness and complexity of growth and development, briefly report one illustration of physical growth and intellectual, emotional and social development noted in observation of one child or a group of children.

1

2. To begin to clarify your understanding of ways the presence of an adult in a special situation affects a child, report (*a*) what an adult said or did, and (*b*) what circumstances the particular situation provided that you consider related to each of the phases of growth and development listed.
3. List questions about various phases of growth and development of children and factors affecting them that are of interest to you.
4. Consider the quality of observational records you have made in an attempt to begin to discover individuality of several children. Contrast reports of gross behavior and finer details; specific occurrences and generalization; differentiation of objective reporting and interpretation or speculation by an observer.

SELECTED READINGS

Almy, M.: Ways of Studying Children. New York, Bureau of Publications, Teachers College, Columbia University, 1959, pp. 46-51. Three aspects of observation: description, feelings, inferences.

Carbonara, N. T.: Techniques for Observing Normal Child Behavior. Pittsburgh, University of Pittsburgh Press, 1961, iv-25. The observer role, the observing process, techniques for "seeing," excerpts from records, techniques for taking notes and writing observations.

Hartley, R., Frank, L. K., and Goldenson, R.: Understanding Children's Play. New York, Columbia University Press, 1952, pp. 339-350. Aspects to be noted when observing creative activities. Additional questions to be considered in observing use of clay, finger paint, easel paint and blocks.

Kagan, J., and Moss, H. A.: Birth to Maturity. New York, John Wiley and Sons, Inc., 1962, pp. 20-26. Naturalistic observations of the child as one source of data for research.

CHAPTER ONE

*Current Concepts and
Theories of Growth
and Development*

COMPLEXITY OF THE CHILD

Child development is that segment of human development from conception to adulthood. Study of it encompasses the nature and process of changes in structure, function and behavior which occur as children progress toward maturity. Because the study of child development involves various facets of the individual and his environment, knowledge from many fields is drawn upon: biology, psychology, sociology, education, anthropology, nutrition, medicine and psychiatry. The gathering of facts and theories from these fields became of particular interest in the twentieth century. In the 1920's and 1930's much of the research was concerned with the nature of structures, functions and behavior, e.g., progressive changes in height and weight, and motor, sensory and language responses. In the 1940's emotional aspects of development received additional attention.

By the 1950's interest in process had increased. Attempts were made to explain behavior by studying motivations. The child, his family and community influences were considered in terms of feelings as well as behavior. Often one activity of the child (e.g., aggression or eating habits) and one phase of his environment (e.g., parent-child relations or relations of brothers and sisters) were selected for study.

By the 1960's interest increased in correlating information about the child, his environment and his interaction with the environment. In some instances the information came from longitudinal studies, in which the same persons are observed at intervals during part of their life span or continuously throughout life (Kagan and Moss, 1962; Stone and Onqué, 1959). In other instances information is from cross-sectional studies, in which measurements are made only once or within a short interval of the person's life. Detail has been assembled from many research reports (Falkner, 1966; Hoffman and Hoffman, 1964, 1966;

3

Mussen, 1960; Stevenson et al., 1963) and from various theories of development (Baldwin, 1967; Maier, 1963).

This correlation of information in the study of child development is necessary because of the complexity of human beings. A *child* is a thinking, feeling, acting person who is growing and changing. His body is his equipment for living. Through it he receives impressions from the world about him. He uses his body both to express his thoughts and feelings and to manipulate (or be manipulated by) his environment. His personality includes those things he knows, as well as his interpretations of himself and his surroundings. In life itself and in his behavior the child reflects his constitution and experience.

Constitution is described as follows (Witmer and Kotinsky, 1953):

Constitution is . . . conceived as the sum total of the structural, functional, and psychological characters of the organism. It is, in large measure, an integral of genetic potentialities influenced . . . by internal and external environmental factors. It is not a biological given, a structure destined to function in a predetermined manner. . . .

What is given is the genotype, the complex of genetic potentialities with which the organism is endowed. Each individual's genotype is a unique physico-chemical system comprising particular kinds of potentialities that have definite limits. . . . The manner in which the genotype functions depends in part upon the environment in which it undergoes development.

A child's constitution is not static, but changing. At any moment it is the result of inherited genetic potential influenced by previous and present environmental factors. Activity and vigor, general and specific sensitivity, tempo and rhythm, body resilience and vulnerability, intellectual endowment and pattern of development are among the genetic potentialities whose interactions with environment are of particular interest in the study of personality development.

Study of the functioning of the person must take into consideration the setting in which he functions. The individual does not live in a vacuum; he functions in a setting. He has experiences, and these provide stimulation for developing his potentialities in many ways. Much of the stimulation of the young infant is of a sensory kind (Casler, 1961). Stimulation of the older child is more likely to be in the realm of knowledge or ideas (Becker, 1962). Experiences of both infants and older children include associations with people as well as things. *Experience* refers to a person's inward and outward responses to events. Stimuli or cues leading to responses may come from the individual's own reactions or from outside the self. Responses may be those characteristic of the human race, whatever the immediate situation, or may vary according to individual genetic endowment, culture and family.

Attempts to deal with a tremendous amount of detail about constitution and experience would be difficult even if methods of identifying and recording them were available. It is more realistic to recognize particular systems, which together make up the whole child. Sigel (1956) refers to the "'whole' child as an organization of a number of systems, which function at varying degrees of autonomy and interrelatedness." He writes:

A starting point . . . may be a tripartite breakdown of *biological, psychological, and exogenous environmental systems.* Within each of these further delineation is possible, e.g., within the biological we can separate skeletal, or neural subsystems; within the psychological such subsystems as cognition, perception can be distinguished. Further identification of smaller units within some of these second order categories can be isolated.

Hopefully, the concern with each of these systems would be with process and with content. Thus, the interest, in psychological systems, for example, would be with the processes, e.g., cognitive process, and with cognitive content, e.g., attitudes, beliefs.

The perspective this book attempts to present is broadly as follows: Human development is related to age, to the biological and psychological systems of the individual, and to external environmental systems. In viewing change in the child and in explanation of such change (aiming for a perspective of child development), attempts are made to coordinate and draw upon research and theory. Different theories of development vary in their emphasis on particular systems (biological, psychological and environmental), but each includes some recognition of the various systems.

DEVELOPMENTAL-DYNAMIC CONCEPT

One way of drawing upon current thought and knowledge from a number of different sources of information pertaining to child development is to refer to a developmental-dynamic concept. This embraces a number of concepts by attempting to consider sequence and interaction, to look for interrelatedness of various aspects and processes, and to recognize biological and psychological systems of the person as well as exogenous influences. Such considerations overlap, but each is more likely to be included in a point of view if clarified separately.

Sequence and Interaction

Basic in a developmental-dynamic concept are ideas about change with time and an interrelatedness in what life includes. Attention focuses on what the person is and what happens to him, and how, as times goes on. Both descriptions and explanations are sought. Description tells what the person is like. Explanation concerns processes through which attributes of the person become manifest.

Figure 1 suggests the many strands in an individual, some more closely connected than others at a particular time and in sequence from earlier to later times. It also suggests interaction of the individual and his environment with an "open-ended" connotation. The many strands from genetic potentialities, constitution at a given time, and immediate setting have an open quality; as they intertwine, the future may change. Certain behavior may emerge in one setting and not in another, or in one combination of endowment, previous experience and current influences, and not in another. John Anderson (1956) refers to an "ongoing manifold."

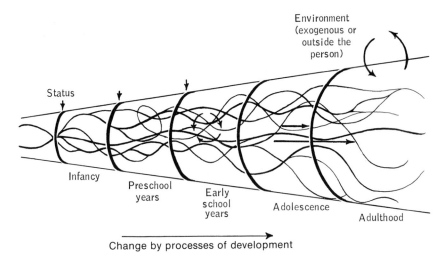

FIGURE 1. *Sequences and interactions in human development.*

In viewing the individual at a particular time, interactions among various aspects and processes can be studied. Explanations of change in the individual can be studied in terms of sequence from an earlier age to a later age and in terms of immediate events.

In considering . . . child development we need some conception of the nature of the growing human person or a theoretical model against which to orient our studies. The growing person is an ongoing manifold moving through time with a multidimensional head much as a tunnel-making machine moves under a river. Viewed from the moving front or the present moment . . . this consists of many irregularly shaped structures of various sizes with a complex series of interrelations. At the boundaries there are complex relations to the external world which involve a continuous intake and outgo on both a physiological and a psychological level, an interchange which maintains a dynamic or ongoing equilibrium.

Viewed as a whole, the system is asymmetrical and open-end. Its basic organization is hierarchical in the sense that as it moves forward in time new properties and qualities emerge at successive levels of integration. These need study and analyses in and for themselves. An analysis at one level, however adequate, cannot explain the properties of a higher level.

Development means the emerging and expanding of the capacities of the individual to provide progressively greater facility in functioning. Development has aspects, elements or content, and also processes. The aspects may be biochemical (e.g., nitrogen content), structural (e.g., muscle or bone), internal responses (e.g., muscle contraction) and behavioral (outward, as in matching colors, and inward, as in attitudes toward one's self).

The term "aspect" can be used at various levels. For example, nitrogen (a biochemical aspect) is a part of protein, which, in turn, is a component of bone which forms the skeletal system. The skeletal system has a structural and functional role in development and is, therefore, a unit of study in the development of the physical equipment of the individual. Another example of the organization of aspects can be seen in perception. Involved in perception are the structure and function of the sense organs and the nervous system, with their chemical and physical properties plus external environment. Thus many aspects are organized to provide a certain behavior which, in itself, can be viewed as an aspect of development.

Processes through which aspects emerge and expand as the child proceeds from one phase to another include growth, maturation, learning, and influence of emotional tone. A process is the means by which change in an aspect takes place. It is a "why" of development. The sequential changes of an aspect resulting from these processes form a pattern. Thus there are patterns of motor development, intellectual development, emotional and social development. The totality of changes as life progresses is called growth and development. *Dynamics* means interactions out of which development comes, both among various aspects and processes at one time and those in the progressive changes in time.

Interrelatedness of Aspects and Processes

Implicit in the idea of sequence and interaction broadly conveyed in Figure 1 is the idea of possible connections between a variety of parts. What in the person is being viewed, the *aspect*, is sometimes called his status, behavior, activity or response. If such aspects as seeking food, utilizing oxygen, having twenty teeth, running or handing a toy to another child are being considered, a variety of possible connections among them is easily imagined. If, instead of a cross section at a particular age, a longitudinal view is taken, one step or stage in the pattern may be seen to be connected with a previous step. The child may go from seeking food by sucking, to putting it into his mouth with his hands or fingers, to using a teaspoon, as he proceeds from infancy to early childhood. Or he may go from giving away a toy he does not care about to letting someone hold a prized possession, or vice versa. Thus he progresses in development. Though attention may be focused on particular patterns, it can be with recognition of relations among them. Study of what occurs (aspects) and how (processes) constitutes the study of development.

Questions as to how change occurs, which go beyond the detail of particular actions or incidents, are partially answered through reference to a broad concept or theoretical position. Some of these concepts and theories have more factual data to support them than others have; some have a more thorough approach on the plane of abstract thought. Knowledge and syntheses of ideas are incomplete. In the search for orderly trends in data and ideas, little is known in comparison with all that one wishes were known. In the points of view of scholars in child development and other fields there is some skepticism; there are also well-founded statements.

Processes refer to explanations of an aspect or pattern. Explanations of many of the aspects and their change tend to be in terms of similar processes. The following paragraphs provide a background for reference to areas considered in later chapters. For example, explanations of phases in language development, sensory changes and others may be sought in processes of growth, maturation, learning, and influence of emotional tone.

GROWTH.   Growth is increase in bodily size or dimensions. As children grow larger, so do their hearts, lungs and other organs. Growth is a product of self-multiplication of cells, and addition (apposition, as in bones and teeth). We can observe growth taking place, its differential rates in various parts of the body, and its consequences, but the fundamental nature of cellular growth is unknown.

The term "growth" is sometimes used in the study of child development according to its precise definition referring to size. At other times it becomes more inclusive and refers to the totality of physical change. In such instances "growth" acquires the same meaning as "development." This has come about because quantitative changes (growth) and qualitative changes (maturation) are closely associated; one seldom occurs without the other. Garn and Shamir (1958) refer to size and development as concerns of physical growth studies. Meredith (1957) could see no significant distinction between physical growth and physical development. In its more inclusive connotation, growth is sometimes used for the sake of brevity as an overall term to mean physical growth, maturation and learning. This use of the term will appear occasionally throughout this book. As used on the title page, the word "growth" serves to emphasize changes in size, while the word "development" includes all changes.

MATURATION.   Maturation is the term used to designate qualitative changes, i.e., changes in complexity which make it possible for a structure to begin functioning or to function at progressively higher levels. Change is due primarily to innate factors, but involves functioning in an environment. As physical structures (such as bones, sensory equipment, the nervous system) become more complex, it becomes possible for the child to feed himself, to acquire voluntary control of elimination, to climb stairs and to acquire many other skills. Change of this kind with age reflects a biological influence, a heritage of the human race. The various patterns of unfolding, due primarily to maturation, tend to be similar from one human being to another. Maturation is characterized by a fixed order of progression, by a tendency to inevitability since it is genetically determined, by irreversibility and by universality in that it is found among all races, in all environments. The pace tends to vary, however, from one individual to another.

Why the cells which comprise bones, teeth, an eye or a nerve go from simpler to more complex forms, and how enzymes are produced which enable cells to carry on their functions, are the focus of research in genetics as well as in other fields. The part that early sensory functioning plays has become of great interest to psychologists.

Although emphasis is on intrinsic factors in considering the maturation process, extreme extrinsic factors can affect rate and pattern. Acheson (1966) says, "Intrinsic factors that determine the rate and pattern of skeletal maturation stem from the genotype. . . . The genetically predetermined patterns and rate of skeletal maturation can be modified by the intervention of environmental influences, either inadequacies in nutrition or ill health."

Physical maturation is most dramatically illustrated by the changes in the first two or three months of prenatal life, during which the organs and systems are laid down from a single cell. Another illustration is that of deciduous tooth development, with the sequence of tooth buds, emergence of structure, calcification, eruption, completion of roots, and then resorption and shedding.

Behavioral change, considered to be due primarily to maturation, is illustrated in certain sequences of motor responses through which most infants and young children proceed. For example a progression of bodily coordination preceding and including walking is as follows:

1. Raises head.
2. Turns over.
3. Sits up with support; without support.
4. Stands with support; without support.
5. Takes steps or walks with support.
6. Walks without support—the first independent steps. Movement is awkward, and the child cannot steer around objects in his path.
7. Walks well enough to clear obstacles, but is still attentive in adjusting to them. Unless he attends to what he is doing, he bumps or falls.
8. Can move in any direction and adapt to obstacles of varying height. Shows no hesitation or need of special attention in skirting objects or climbing over them.

Research related to this sequence is reported in Chapter Nine.

A pattern of unfolding such as this implies parallel changes in body proportions, muscles, nerves and skeleton, as well as their functioning or use. Hebb (1966), referring to what he calls *psychological as contrasted to physical maturation,* considers that both have physiological and nutritive sources, but that the psychological also includes "pre- and postnatal experience normally inevitable for all members of species," which provides what he calls "sensory, constant." "Sensory, variable," pertaining to variations in learning, has as its source differences in experience from one person to another.

Figure 2 illustrates both similarity of pattern and differences in pace, important parts of a concept of maturation.

Among theories or overall statements about development are references to maturational sequences and the maturation process. They pertain to physical aspects and to the development of various abilities. Krogman (1950a) refers to the process of aging as maturation and to its termination as maturity:

In a larger framework of biologic thought . . . maturity is, in a sense, a climax of a biogenetic process; in this vein it may be considered as a never-ending series of climactic events in the life cycle of the organism. Therefore, the definition of maturity must shift with the stage or level of development unfolding that, in broadest aspect, we may call *organic growth.* Maturity, as a biological concept, thus becomes an aspect of the process of physical growth: it may be morphological, physiological, biochemical. It is rarely only one; it is generally all three, well-nigh inseparable.

Baldwin (1955) refers to maturity as increase in *competence.* In his description of the psychological factors underlying the increase in competence of the child, he lists four aspects of maturity:

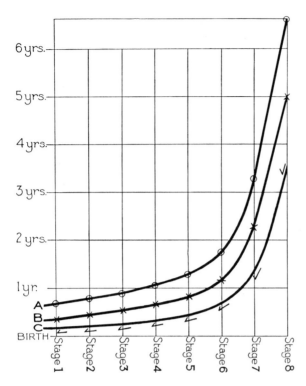

FIGURE 2. Similarity of pattern and differences in pace among individuals in the development of walking.

Three possible channels of development of walking are indicated. Curves show the ages at which 3 different children (A, B and C) attained abilities in bodily coordination summarized in the text.

Abilities in bodily coordination

The first of these, expansion of the psychological world, comprises the child's ability to notice obscure objects, to anticipate consequences, to strive for abstract goals as well as concrete ones, and to strive toward a remote future goal. . . . As he matures, the child becomes able to respond to more and more objects and more kinds of objects.

Secondly, as his psychological world expands, "his perception of the properties of the external world becomes more objective." A third aspect of change is differentiation; as he matures, the child becomes more able to make fine discriminations. "This flexibility of behavioral adjustment is achieved because many . . . actions are independent of one another and combinable in any desired way." A fourth aspect of maturity is emotional stability.

For the significance of feelings of competence, see pages 13 and 14.

Maturity of the child, explained primarily through the process of maturation, is regarded as one basis for the beginning of new learnings.

Maturational readiness is essential to learning. The "never-ending series of climactic events in the life cycle" and the "increase in competence" refer to the child's use of his emerging abilities. In this use he is learning (acquiring behavior through his interaction with the environment of his own body and with that outside himself). *Recognition of the relation of maturation and learning* has gained support from studies relating the child's ease of learning responses to his maturity (Gesell and

Thompson, 1941; McGraw, 1939). Additional research is needed to provide more factual material concerning maturation and ease or difficulty of learning in children. In the light of current, admittedly limited, knowledge, whether the behavior pertains to chewing, walking, grasping, perceiving, using words, adjusting to a group away from home or some other activity, maturity makes possible a particular response; the extent to which the response is well consolidated affects the ease or difficulty with which related learning takes place. When structural and functional readiness is present, satisfaction in learning is inherent. When forced before he is ready, the child simply does not learn, is unskillful, may require a longer time to learn the behavior or may show undue strain. Research attempting to check some of these points of view is indicated on page 12.

The pacing of expectations to natural growth may be illustrated by reference to the young child's learning to feed himself. He does not learn to feed himself until he has achieved such responses as these:

Ability to sit up while making controlled movements of hands and arms
Ability to coordinate hand and mouth actions with fair smoothness
Mastery of sufficient finger control to permit easy holding of the spoon or food
Emotional maturity to permit him to surrender at least part of his complete
    dependence upon his mother.

A *developmental stage* is a phase or step in a sequence or progression. The child's stage of development of a particular ability reflects interaction of the organism and his environment. It is biologically based (has intrinsic factors) and can be affected by experience (extrinsic factors). For example, the child may not achieve his potential for skeletal development because of ill health or undernutrition, or for perceptual development because of deprivations in general experience. Or, by the addition of particular learning experiences, an ability may appear earlier than it would otherwise have done in a particular child. In normal situations there is usually some correspondence of ages and developmental stages. Although order of appearance of stages tends to be invariable for most children, particular experiences can occasionally produce variations.

Knowledge from individual children suggests that the child himself tends to indicate when he is ready for any given experience. One way is by the eagerness with which he seeks new function, seizing with zest on each new opportunity for activity as it is available. McGraw (1943) says:

Whenever any function or aspect of a function emerges, the child exhibits an indomitable urge to exercise it. The baby who has just acquired the ability to roll over can hardly be kept on his back; the infant who has just learned to pull himself up by grasping the bars of the crib does so repeatedly, though once up, he stands and cries, because he has not at the same time achieved the ability to let himself down. . . . I have seen a baby struggle again and again to stand on his feet in order to walk a few steps for a lure, although he could have crept for it with great ease.

Recognition of the part environment plays in offering opportunities for the next stage or phase is implicit in an emphasis on interrelation of maturation and learning.

Statements pertaining to relation of maturation and learning refer to *timing* and to the *influence of stimulation.* According to Baldwin (1955):

> Elapsed time, whether or not it includes practice, is accompanied by improved performance, although not as much improvement as if the time had been spent in practice. In many activities, however, there must be some practice of a skill before a certain point in time if the maturational potentialities are to be realized.

Knowledge of the effects of timing and stimulation on the child's progress from one developmental phase to another is incomplete. Research findings have not yet made it possible to state conclusions on questions such as these: When the infant or child is mature enough to make a particular response, how does it affect his later development in this and other aspects if his practice begins early or late? If he has little practice or a great deal? How and with whom do effects of *general experience* (as the infant and the child respond in the ordinary course of events) and *specific training* (as responses are brought out by encouragement of particular practices) differ?

Related research on questions such as the foregoing is cited later in sections on particular aspects and processes of development: e.g., sensory motor development (White and Held, 1966), sensory conditioning (Lipsitt, 1966), learning to read (Fowler, 1962), development of language and thought in disadvantaged children (Gray and Klaus, 1965; Hess, 1964; Hunt, 1964), emotional and social development (Harlow, 1966).

Recognition of the part both maturation and learning play in the development of a child puts an adult in a quandary when setting the environmental stage. It is possible to swing too far in the direction of doing nothing until the child aggressively seeks an experience, or too far in the direction of forcing adult-conceived ideas upon him, regardless of readiness.

LEARNING.   Learning is influenced by many factors other than maturational readiness. The following definition is considered broad enough to include variations among theorists in the field: "Learning, as we measure it, is a change in performance which occurs under the conditions of practice" (McGeoch and Irion, 1952).

Change may be brought about by practice of a new function with satisfaction; it may also be brought about by dissatisfaction. Infants learn to be skillful in reaching for an object; under one condition of practice they learn more rapidly, and under another condition, more slowly. A child learns by practice to climb stairs with more and more sensory and motor facility. Under other conditions he learns a concept such as "round." He is told that various objects, e.g., a plate, button or watch, are round. Then, when he uses a new set of blocks and picks up a piece he has not seen before and calls it "round," and at the same time rejects or ignores blocks of other shapes, his concept learning is revealed.

In changes in performance such as these, factors usually considered essential in the learning process are operating, i.e., motivation (drive or incentive), cue (stimulus), response (act or thought) and reinforcement (reward) or achievement of a goal.

Acquiring behavior through experience is complex, but we may attempt to distinguish in a particular child's behavior and setting factors contributing to change in performance. The following pages present a few ideas about learning. They appear here with an emphasis on motivations because much of an understanding of the child and his development seems to hinge upon such things as what he really cares about, what he is attentive to, and what his situation enables him to learn.

Motivations have roots deep in the nature of human beings. Although use of terms varies (drives, biologically primitive tendencies, activation and affect, incentive, or motivational variables), there seems to be agreement that strong stimuli which impel action have biological bases. Impelling properties, innate and unlearned, concern food, absence of pain, sex, relatedness to others, and activity and rest. As the individual adds experiences in these areas, the particular stimuli impelling action change and represent elaborations of the earlier ones. Dollard and Miller (1950) say: "Strong stimuli which impel action are drives. . . . While any stimulus may become strong enough to act as a drive, certain special classes of stimuli seem to be the primary basis for the greater proportion of motivation. These might be called the *primary* or *innate* drives. . . ." Motivations which are learned "are acquired on the basis of the primary drives, represent elaborations of them."

Motivation is a part of particular biologically primitive tendencies and also of the more general tendency to be active or to rest. Hebb (1966) refers to particular biologically primitive tendencies (hunger, pain, sex, maternal, and exploratory motivations) and also to the tendency to be active or lethargic. The individual has innate tendencies to seek relief from stress; he also has innate tendencies to activity optimum for him, e.g., in the use of sense organs.

Among the special classes of stimuli which seem to be bases for motivation, some are closer to *bodily functioning* (homeostatic, visceral, tension-decreasing), and others to *cognitive functioning* (sensory, neurological, tension-increasing). Hunt (1966) says, "Although it is quite clear that painful stimulation, homeostatic needs, and sex all constitute genuine motivating systems, a very large share of an organism's interaction with the environment is informational." Recognition of *information processing*, or informational interaction with the environment, as intrinsic motivation, has implications for cognitive learning. The child in his spontaneous play, curiosity or exploration is having informational interaction with the environment. "Slight degrees of incongruity, which can readily be accommodated, lend interest and may provide attractive problems, but the larger ones are repelling and perhaps even devastating" (Hunt, 1960).

Effectance (the production of effects on the environment), resulting in the feeling of efficacy, is motivating. Effectance motivation has been described by Robert White (1960) as a supplement or addition to motivation concerning relatedness to others (psychosexual motivation). It is one of the bases of *competence,* i.e., fitness or ability to carry on transactions with environment.

> Competence is built up out of all kinds of interactions with the environment, including those due to effectance alone and those due to much more complex patterns of motives. . . . We shall not find it profitable to look for the sense of competence as if it were a separate thing in personality; rather, we must become aware of the *aspect of competence in a wide variety of actions and experiences.*

In his many "exchanges" with his setting the infant or young child is forming organizational patterns (schemata) by the processes of *assimilation* (taking in from the environment) and *accommodation* (making adjustments to these assimilations) (Inhelder, 1962) (see also pp. 359-361).

The child's functioning has in it the seeking of pleasantness and the avoidance of unpleasantness. Young (1967), referring to intracranial stimulations, says, "The exact structure of the neural mechanism that mediates affective arousal (pleasantness or unpleasantness) is not known." He refers to affective arousals as "directive, regulative, evaluative," and to responses

> . . . to organize, repeat, and learn adaptive patterns of behavior that maximize the positive and minimize the negative. . . . On the basis of primary affective arousals, organisms develop dispositions . . . variously called habits, motives, attitudes, traits, expectancies. There is considerable evidence . . . that dispositions are organized hedonically during the early stages of development, and . . . that the directive role of primary hedonic processes is taken over gradually by developing cerebral dispositions.

What the child finds appealing, rewarding, providing incentive (*reinforcing*) as he responds may be in his own functioning or from external sources. Sheldon White (1963), discussing the child's ability to learn to choose the correct stimulus in an experimental situation, refers to various types of appeal which may affect this discrimination learning. As for what is appealing, he asks whether the appeal is built into the child (hedonic). Second, he asks whether stimuli have a value not intrinsic, but derived from their association with previous rewards (secondary). Third, he wonders whether the presence of another person supports learning (social). Fourth, "are motives associated with curiosity, stimulation-seeking, and exploration" (stimulation)? Fifth, do manipulation and mastery of the environment (mastery) bring about satisfaction?

The child's learning experience may vary and include one or several *categories of learning.* Whether it is conditioning, discrimination learning or imitative learning, change in the child's behavior comes from stimuli to which he is responsive. Furthermore, the new responses he learns build onto the residue of responses he is already able to make. Processes are associative and selective. Behavior may suggest that mediation is occurring through connecting links in the brain. Language as a mediating factor may operate as the child grows older; memory may operate as he goes from one situation to another. Strategy, growing out of experience as to the probability of occurrence of , sequence, may also operate. A number of writers warn against the assumption that findings from research in one category of learning are necessarily appropriate for other categories.

Carefully designed research contributes to knowledge of a child's learning. Spilker (1966) emphasizing the "endeavor to provide . . . significant behavioral law," says that "systematic observation, careful and explicit definition, rigorous application of logic . . . are the necessities."

In experimental procedures to study learning, particular variables (conditions of practice) affecting change in performance are controlled. An experiment involving children's choice of two stimuli is reported here to illustrate types of variables, designation of elements in learning (such as incentive, stimuli, response, reinforcement) and ways of reporting findings, and also to provide further support for emphasis on *recognition of the complexity of learning processes*. Figure 3 shows that the amount of practice, previous experience, and effort required are among the variables affecting learning.

The *subjects* were forty-two children, twenty-six of whom were already experienced with research apparatus, with an average chronologic age of fifty-seven months, and sixteen were naive or not experienced, with an average chronologic age of fifty-six months. At the preliminary practice with the equipment and before each of two testing sessions, each child was asked to select a toy and was told that obtaining as many marbles as he could in a "game" would win the toy.

The *procedure* included presentation of a deeper or lighter hue of red in a viewing window of the testing equipment. When the deeper color (positive stimulus) was presented, pulling the handle (response) allowed a marble to appear (reward). Pulling the handle in response to the lighter color (negative stimulus) did not bring forth a marble.

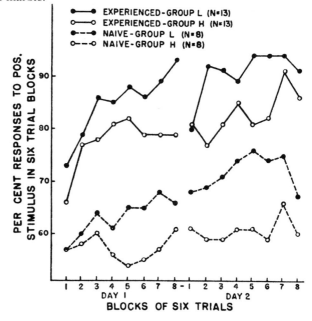

FIGURE 3. Differential conditioning by children as a function of effort required in the task.

Positive stimulus is a deep hue of red; negative stimulus, a lighter hue. In L the lever was adjusted for light or easy effort (requiring a force of one third of the child's maximum previous pull of the handle). In H the lever was adjusted for heavy or more difficult effort (requiring a force of two thirds of the maximum previous pull of the handle). N is the number of subjects. (C. C. Spiker and S. H. White: Child Development, 30:3, 1959.)

The *findings* revealed the influence of three variables: previous experience in a similar situation, effort required and practice on a particular day (with three stimuli which could bring forth the marble and three which could not, i.e., a block of six trials, presented in a series of eight to make a total of forty-eight trials) or from the first to the second day.

Significant differences in percentage of responses to the positive stimuli were as follows: "Group H subjects did not significantly exceed Group L subjects in number of responses given to the negative stimulus ($p > .20$) but did give significantly fewer to the positive stimulus ($p < .05$). . . . Naive subjects did not give significantly more responses to the positive stimulus than did experienced subjects ($p > .20$), but did give more to the negative stimulus ($p < .001$)" (Spiker and White, 1959). In a probability (p) of $< .05$, difference would have occurred by chance alone less than five times in one hundred.

Other variables, not a part of this research design or controlled by it, could, of course, influence the child's learning. This complexity of learning is recognized when the adult in his associations with a particular child attempts to understand the many conditions of practice.

INFLUENCE OF EMOTIONAL TONE. Emotional tone is the term used to designate how a person feels about himself and his world. These feelings concern what matters to him. A feeling of harmony with his world, a relatedness or a lack of it, is a description sometimes used. In some theories of personality development, it is especially important for a child to have, in infancy and in the preschool years, a sense of trust, a sense of autonomy and a sense of initiative. To these, as he grows older, the child adds a sense of accomplishment and identity, and, as he grows into adulthood, a sense of intimacy, a parental sense and a sense of integrity. These components of a healthy personality, in Erikson's theory of personality development, are discussed in detail in Chapter Seven. With these feelings or "senses" more of the individual's responses are of the accepting or pleased kind with regard to himself and his world, rather than the rejecting or displeased kind. Having the greater proportion on the accepting side means having emotional tone conducive to development different from that which might occur if the greater proportion were on the other side.

Feelings such as these seem to be, to a great extent, a reflection of the child's having his basic needs met, including being loved and being given opportunities to use his emerging abilities. This meeting of needs is more likely to happen when the child is "close" to someone, in the majority of instances his mother, soon after birth. The closeness and the feeling of being loved, cared for and understood by a particular person or persons, as he grows older, have subtle qualities in the child and reflect subtle qualities in the persons with whom he is associated. Consequently it is difficult to identify the special practices of parents in infant care which are predictive of particular characteristics in the child (Caldwell, 1964). Key factors seem to involve sensing what the child is ready for. For most infants and young children this involves parents and other family members; for others, a hospital, an institution, a nursery school or a boarding home may be involved.

Those who are close to the child are in a position to sense what he is ready for in terms of basic needs such as food, warmth, activity, rest and elimination. They are also in a position to sense what the child is ready for in terms of elements such as trust, autonomy, initiative and other personality components important for feelings of harmony with the world. They can sense needs for activities which use emerging abilities, and thus can provide opportunities for sensory and motor stimulation and, in the older child, stimulation of use of cognitive powers. This provision for use of emerging abilities is, again, a way of enabling the child to feel in accord with his world.

With attitudes such as these an adult associated with a child is less likely to make stereotyped responses. When the baby cries, his mother tries to decide whether or not it is a hunger cry, and, if it seems to be, she feeds him. If a preschool child wakes at night, the parents try to decide whether or not his sense of trust is concerned, and, if so, they give him the reassurance he needs. When a child indicates that he is seeking sensory responses such as those from a soft toy, or use of large muscles as in climbing, or intellectual discovery as in clarifying what "round" means, someone considers what experiences in play would be related to these interests. Although more self-expression on the child's part goes along with this point of view, it also implies that he is not being the slave of his own whims, but is learning limits and progressing from less mature to more mature behavior.

Overanxiety or apathy can occur when subtle qualities such as these are not present in the child's relations with others and in his exchanges with the physical world.

As the child grows older, more of the complexity in relation of emotional tone to development comes from his demands on himself. Allinsmith (1954) refers to human behavior as representing

. . . a compromise among forces influencing the individual. In the first months of life, there are only two major forces—the child's own impulses, and external reality. After the first few months, a third force begins to affect the individual, and thereafter the three interact to produce behavior. This third force consists of those social demands which were originally part of external reality but which have been *internalized* as part of the person's demands on himself.

Allinsmith continues by saying that in the course of experience the individual learns to make compromises among forces and to use techniques relieving tension which work for him. "The extent to which an individual is symptom-free and capable of meeting life effectively depends upon the ways [he] has learned to solve conflicts in the past, and upon . . . capacity for tolerating anxiety instead of resorting to defensive measures."

The individual's feelings of harmony with his world (as contrasted with lack of harmony) seem to come from various sources: physiological functioning, sensory stimulation, ideas, intentions of others, as well as actual practice. Responses in the very young infant occur by means other than the functioning of the cortex of the brain; bodily functioning plays a great part in his harmony with his world (Pinneau, 1950, 1955a,

1955b). The functioning of the nervous system in the first few months as well as when the higher brain centers are more mature involves sensory stimulation and sensory and motor responses which can provide feelings of well-being (Casler, 1961). Satisfaction can also come from one's own cognition or knowledge (Hunt, 1960; Kessen and Kuhlman, 1962). The feelings from associations with people seem to come from their intentions and feelings and not just from specific practices.

Subtle connections between feelings of the adult and of the child are illustrated by Brody (1956):

> It appears that a mother may choose to breast feed, may try to give good physical support to her infant and may try to feed on a demand schedule—all popular and important criteria for adequate feeding—and yet she may unknowingly offer little satisfaction to her infant in the process. In all of these aspects of a feeding looms the problem of a mother's motives in adopting any of the procedures, and of her consciousness of conflict in this motivation.

Complexity involved in discovering what influences a child's behavior in his relation with another person is suggested in a study by Rheingold, Gewirtz and Ross (1959). They selected vocalizations of infants for study to provide further understanding of the development of social responsiveness as well as of speech. Figure 4 provides supporting evidence that social responsiveness of the adult to particular behavior of the child can increase frequency of the behavior.

In this experiment, responsiveness of the adult was different on different days. At first, and after the days on which particular social variables were added, the adult who leaned over the baby's crib had an expressionless face. But on "conditioning days," whenever the baby made sounds of vocalization, the adult smiled broadly, made "tsk" sounds, and patted the baby lightly, and then resumed her lack of expression. This "complex of social acts . . . resembled those an attentive adult might naturally make when a child vocalizes." On the days of responsiveness of the adult, vocalizations of the babies increased. "The results suggest that the social vocalizing of infants and . . . their social responsiveness may be modified by the responses adults make to them."

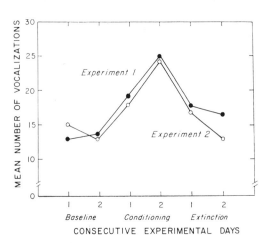

FIGURE 4. Mean number of vocalizations on consecutive experimental days.

On baseline days 1 and 2 the adult's face was expressionless. On conditioning days 3 and 4 the adult's face was expressionless except when the baby vocalized; then the adult smiled, made "tsk" sounds and touched the baby lightly. On extinction days 5 and 6 the adult's face was again expressionless. (H. L. Rheingold, J. L. Gewirtz and H. W. Ross: Journal of Comparative and Physiological Psychology, 52:69, 1959.)

In each of two parallel experiments (Fig. 4) eleven babies were studied. The median age of the infants (one was in both experiments) was three months. All were resident almost from birth in the same institution, with excellent care and multiple caretakers. On the baseline days the experimenter leaned over the crib with her face about 15 inches above the subject's and looked at him with an expressionless face, while an observer tallied vocalizations, out of the subject's sight.

On the two conditioning days the examiner again leaned over the crib with an expressionless face, except that when the subject vocalized, the experimenter made an immediate response of a broad smile, "tsk" sounds and a light touch, and then resumed the expressionless face until the next vocalization. The experimenter's response (a complex of social acts), which was the reinforcing stimulus, was not given on days 5 and 6 (extinction days); the adult's face was expressionless again for the entire time. On each day nine counts of the number of vocalizations in three-minute periods were made. Results of the two experiments agreed: "The analysis reveals no evidence of a difference between experiments. . . . Conditioning raised the rate of vocalizing above the Baseline level, while Extinction lowered it until it approached the Baseline level." Analysis of variance indicated "a difference in the effect of the three two-day experimental conditions (p < .001) and, also, in the effect of successive days within conditions (p < .001)." The study confirmed that the frequency of vocalizing can be increased if an adult makes a social response contingent upon it.

This experiment is thought-provoking as one speculates about the stimuli from within the individual and from his experience which explain change in behavior. The experiment does not seem inconsistent with several explanations of adult influence on speech and other aspects of development.

In investigating key factors in the individual's emotional tone, factors associated with the child and in the child himself, a variety of hypotheses are being checked. Foundations for relatedness with others and identification with a model as the child grows older are of particular interest. Biological bases, learning experiences and power relations receive varying emphasis in theories of human development.

Emphasis on external environment, which statements about adult-child relations sometimes imply, needs the balance of a reminder that "the child is not . . . a simple passive creature molded exclusively by external forces; he is . . . a creature in his own right, moving through his own experiences and creating his own world. This is not to deny the value of nurture in creating the best possible world for children" (Anderson, 1948).

On the constitutional side, theory about the relation of mood and body chemistry has been evolving for a number of years (Cannon, 1933; Dunbar, 1954; Lipton, Steinschneider and Richmond, 1966; Selye, 1956). Is an individual's mood influenced not only by experience, but also by bodily conditions, and, if so, in what manner? How does the autonomic nervous system relate to emotions? What role do endocrine hormones, especially the adrenal hormones, play? How do disturbances in function, as in the case of an allergy, affect feeling? Connections of mood with constitutional aspects, as well as with experience, present another field of interest in research.

The adult attempting to use various elements in a point of view which stresses influence of the child's emotional tone on his development looks for indicators of the child's feelings (see Chapter Eleven). He finds clues in the child's everyday actions over a period of time, as well as from findings of professionally administered tests.

Baldwin (1967), reviewing six theories of child development, refers to the concern with "deep . . . problems of personality functioning" in Freudian theory (including Erikson's interest in sense of identity and self-worth); the "emphasis on operational definitions" and "viewing of behavior of the person from the outside" in stimulus-response theory (including behavior theory and social-learning theory); the interest in "specific problems of conceptual thinking" of Piaget; the attention to "the organization of cognitive structure" of Lewin; the concentrating "on the global problems of development and on discovering how different aspects of the individual's psychophysiological functioning interrelate" of Werner; and the emphasis on "the child's participation in the family as a social system" with "attention to the entire social system as a part of the socialization process" in Parsons.

Recognition of Biological and Psychological Systems of the Person and Exogenous Influences

So far, in thinking of a developmental-dynamic concept, sequence and interaction, or pattern of the person over time, including variables within the person and in his external environment (as suggested in Fig. 1), have been stressed. Processes of growth, maturation (see Fig. 2), learning (see Fig. 3) and influence of emotional tone (see Fig. 4) have been described separately, but have been recognized as interdependent. It now seems important to stress a triple outlook considering the biological, the psychological and exogenous systems whenever possible.

Reference to the biological system or complex organization, with its many smaller units, means reference to bodily structures and functioning. Reference to the psychological system, with its many smaller units, means reference primarily to the nervous system and mental functioning. It is true, of course, that bodily structures and functions, especially of the brain and nerves, are a part of the psychological. Considering the psychological, according to Hebb (1966), means studying "the more complex forms of integration or organization in behavior. It is implied that this includes also the study of processes such as learning, emotion, or perception that are involved in organizing the behavior."

Although the words "biological" and "psychological" frequently overlap, they serve to emphasize an approach implied in the reference to the child we are attempting to study. To repeat, the child is a complex organism, a thinking, feeling, acting person. He is likewise an organization of a number of systems, some closely related, and some not. According to a developmental-dynamic concept, careful consideration of each system, sometimes separately and sometimes in terms of interrelations, is pertinent.

The third system mentioned here, the *exogenous* system, i.e., external environment, has many angles from which its space, time, people and things may be viewed. The give and take of situation and behavior, the context in which responses occur, are pertinent in understanding the child. The values and feelings the child senses, as well as the actions he sees and the words he hears, are included in the exogenous. Furthermore, the knowledge he acquires and the concepts he forms are linked to exogenous influences.

The logic of attempting to recognize the three systems which have been listed, or subdivisions of them, is rarely questioned. The problem seems to be to do it methodically.

CONCEPT OF ORDERLY TRENDS

Systems or complex organizations imply *orderliness*. The idea of orderliness in human development is an important concept. It is substantiated by studies of subdivisions of systems. When growth in its connotation of *increase in size* has been studied, change in height, weight, dental arch and other aspects, with age and in accordance with body structure, has occurred with a regularity which gives prediction some accuracy (see Chaps. Eight and Thirteen). But even in physical measurements, exact predictions for the future of an individual are made cautiously and with a realization that unknown variables may affect status and progress.

When *change in physical complexity due to maturation* has been studied, a usual pattern of unfolding has been identified: e.g., in prenatal sequences from the fertilized egg to the infant at birth (Patten, 1953); in endocrine glands from before birth to adolescence (Watterson, 1959); in the sequence of skeletal development (Greulich and Pyle, 1959). But here, again, knowledge of *external influences* which might modify the sequence, such as x-rays (Stern, 1960), cautions against saying that a particular pattern always occurs.

Support for the idea of orderliness along with a recognition of individual variations has also come from studies of *behavioral change due primarily to maturation*. For example, in the orderly sequences of motor development reported in Chapter Nine, change with age is established. Progressions have also been identified in sensory development, language, thought, creativity, emotional development and social development (see Chaps. Ten, Eleven and Thirteen).

When *behavioral change with age according to constitution or early functioning* has been considered, some order has again emerged. Longitudinal studies of individuals over long periods of time have revealed persistence of some qualities that found earlier, as well as some changes. For example, in intelligence (see pp. 461-462) and in personality (see pp. 462-464), some of the qualities present earlier were also present later, beyond the level of chance alone. Some of the qualities were different, however, at later ages. Explanations of these differences are being sought by study of *other constitutional variables and experience*.

First steps in the identification of other factors in the person and in his family and community setting are mentioned on pages 38-39. It is interesting to note here implications of knowledge of trends related to particular variables. Understanding of orderliness in the nature of human beings and in the patterns of individuals provides many suggestions for the adult in his associations with children.

The idea of a sequential order or pattern provides for a variation in pace and form of growth and development from one person to another. There are slow growers, fast growers and average growers. Some slow growers prove to be dwarfed; some fast growers prove to be gigantic; but many slow growers and many fast growers turn out to be normal, well-integrated people. Individuals arrive at the various phases of physical, intellectual, emotional and social growth at different times. Upright locomotion, or walking (see Fig. 2), is a step along the way toward greater maturity in motor control. Some children arrive at this step at eight months of chronologic age, some at twelve months, and some at sixteen months.

In social behavior most children tend to proceed from infantile self-absorption to more mature social cooperation at different rates and with different goals and responses. Thus, instead of comparing a three-year-old child with other three-year-olds, we study his current pattern of social behavior, review it in relation to his background, and from this decide what social development he has reached.

For example, if we study a child who, upon entering kindergarten, stands around and does not adapt to the other children in cooperative play, judging him only by observation of his behavior and checking this against a chronologic scale, we might conclude that his behavior represents an inability, frequent in two-year olds, to adapt to a cooperative situation. On the other hand, from the standpoint of his own social growth, which can be interpreted only in terms of his constitution and opportunities, we may see him in a different light. He may have shown a quiet responsiveness in early social adjustments to his parents and to the children in the neighborhood and, at the same time, have been somewhat reticent in a larger group of children or with strange children. We see him now as a child who will take a little time to effect a smooth adjustment to the group he faces in the kindergarten, and also as a child who is proceeding in his own orderly way and adjusting satisfactorily. He is a five-year-old who has made satisfactory progress in social growth of a quiet, nonaggressive but adequate pattern.

In *study of orderly trends according to constitution and experience,* control of as many variables as possible is important. Variables in the child's family setting, such as continuity of care (Orlansky, 1949), stimulation of use of abilities (Sontag et al., 1958; White and Held, 1966), and sensitivity, interaction and warmth (Brody, 1956; Lewis, 1967; Sears, Maccoby and Levin, 1957), are just beginning to be identified. Distinct factors and demensions in the child and in the parents' child-rearing attitudes have begun to have more precision (Honzik, 1967; Schaefer and Bayley, 1963). Influence of a brother or sister on a child of the same sex and within a two-year age range has had careful study (Koch, 1960). Such studies provide information on what variables to look for in the child and his environment to understand his pattern of development. Nevertheless orderliness in data can be present without a high degree of predictiveness from one or several variables in the setting or in behavior of the child.

Another kind of study of setting, different from the family or community, is that involved in learning experiments. In Figures 3 and 4 comparable curves are evident from one group of subjects to another. Certain experiences of the children studied, e.g., presentation of a marble for selection of a certain color, had both similar and varied effects on four groups of subjects. Also, in the study of vocalizations, the addition of certain adult influences had similar effects on two groups of subjects, again with some individual variation. Here, in an experimental approach which identified pertinent variables, laboratory controls were possible. In many instances with children and families in natural settings, such controls are not possible.

From the various kinds of evidence of orderly trends in development come the conviction that the concept is sound and a wish to study it further. Hopefulness about finding additional cohesiveness in research data and a realization that progress will be slow characterize current outlooks.

On the subject of early experience (including what is provided and by whom), Martin (1957) writes:

> An admission that the events we study are unique, unreproducible and non-determinable does not preclude scientific activity . . . We first seek regularity and orderliness . . . within the individual event, which for us is the effect of a particular training agent and practice upon a particular individual under given conditions. As we accumulate data about a number of such individual events, it may be possible to discover, through a study of similarities and dissimilarities among them, certain principles or laws, statistical in form, that may apply to all. We will not enhance the probability of discovering such regularities by losing the individual event in a sea of mass statistics.

Both the orderliness and digressions from it speak for a characteristic of man, namely, plasticity or adaptability. He is able to adjust within given limits to his environment and change in that environment, either through bodily adaptation or through manipulation of his environment. Thus during pregnancy the woman's body adapts physiologically to provide for the developing organism. People acquire immunity to certain diseases. By the use of cognitive functions they are able to devise ways of meeting problems the world presents. Modern technology stands as evidence.

On the other hand, plasticity in infancy and early childhood has its hazards, since deviations from a pattern may result from exposure to conditions which interfere with the expected sequence and thus modify development. This can be noted in the development of malnourished children (Dean, 1960), in those emotionally deprived (Caplan, 1961) or in those with cultural variations (Hess and Shipman, 1965).

CONCEPT OF UNIQUENESS OF THE INDIVIDUAL

Knowledge classified according to previous discussions in this chapter suggests a body of content or subject matter useful in beginning to understand what happens and why in human development. This knowledge emphasizes the great variety of components in human beings. Furthermore, it stresses the uniqueness of each person, with his particular combination of variables unlike those of anyone else. Consequently those who study child development attempt to identify detail about the individual. Williams (1956) writes about biochemical individuality:

Each human being possesses a highly distinctive body chemistry. While the same physical mechanisms and the same metabolic processes are operating in all human bodies, the structures are sufficiently diverse and the genetically determined enzyme efficiencies vary sufficiently from individual to individual so that the sum total of all the reactions taking place in one individual's body may be very different from those taking place in the body of another individual of the same age, sex and body size.

The genetotrophic principle [encompasses] the whole of biology. . . . Every individual organism that has a distinctive genetic background has distinctive nutritional needs which must be met for optimal well-being. . . .

If during embryonic development, a particular ovum has needs which cannot be satisfied in the environment provided, then it either dies or its organs and functions fail to develop in a well-rounded fashion. If, during childhood, the individual has nutritional needs which are not fully satisfied, his metabolism is altered accordingly; he becomes a prey to infections and his growth becomes retarded or distorted.

If this principle is valid we may . . . say that it should be possible, theoretically at least, to meet the needs of almost any developing ovum, even though these needs are unusual, *provided the needs are known.* In case these needs are known and can be consistently met throughout life, then development proceeds in a regular fashion regardless of the presence of untoward structures and partial genetic blocks which augment special needs.

Murphy and Murphy (1960) say that theirs is an "individual centered plea. . . . We are concerned . . . not only with the unusual child but with the everyday child whose individual pattern of weaknesses, strengths, talents, limitations, individual drives, and social belongingness requires . . . skilled guidance and understanding." In considering which of the child's potentials to accent at any given time, they say:

Let the child choose. Let us learn from his choices where his interests and talents lie in terms of what he is ready for, can use for growth at a given time, what his pace, potential depth, and range are. He may need support and help in sustaining an interest, in developing the techniques he needs in order to carry it through. But if it is *his* interest, goal, longing, there will be an optimal chance for fullest growth of his potential capacity. . . . The amount of freedom a child can use depends in part on his ability to grasp and to organize situations for himself; the amount of structure or formal organization he needs depends in part on the level of complexity, confusion, or tension which would exist without adult directives and the child's capacity to handle the complexity of confusion constructively. . . . The concept of the child as potential is challenging.

WAYS OF VIEWING INDIVIDUAL DIFFERENCES

The foregoing concepts, which overlap and supplement each other, lead to a wish for *ways of viewing individual differences which recognize each of the previously mentioned concepts.* As a step in this direction, ways most satisfactorily used record increment, channel and relative proportions in the individual's sequence. These details may be viewed against a backdrop or broad picture provided by study of a group of children. But looking from the individual to the group and back to the individual does not imply a conviction that findings about the particular person should or would conform to group findings. It cannot mean this if group findings are presented so that the variety or range in the group is revealed, and not just the average alone.

Increment means addition or increase in quantity or character. Figure 5 suggests increment in a child's ability at different times to use large muscles as he proceeded from walking to tricycle riding. Change in his motor behavior was at a pace different from that in the majority of children. He took his first steps later than many children do. He was able to ride a tricycle earlier than many. The figure highlights the process of going from what the person is and does (in his many aspects)

A   B

FIGURE 5.   *Increase of an attribute in the individual may have fast and slow phases with reference to orderly trends in data on groups.*

A, This child, at 16 months, is taking his first hesitant steps. This is 2 or 3 months later than the average walking age. B, At 22 months the same child is adept on his tricycle. This is 2 or 3 months in advance of the average tricycle-riding age.

to a record of him, not only for research purposes, but also for under-standing of him as an individual. Detail which can be studied as time goes by may be in the form of photographs, observational records or sound recordings. Interviews with parents are another source of infor-mation. The converting of information from such sources to numerical scores is an important part of research. For some aspects of develop-ment, specific measurements, tests or ratings are available that provide numerical information through use of well-standardized procedures; for other aspects they have not been perfected.

A few illustrations suggest many possibilities for use of increment in viewing individual differences. Gains in height and weight are ex-amples of increments. Additional points scored in an intelligence test from one age to another may be considered evidence of increment; items of increased difficulty at more advanced age levels are passed. Decrease in number of incorrect pronunciations, such as decrease in use of w for r (wed for red) could be considered an increment in artic-ulation, a part of language development. Increase in number of correct generalizations or decrease in number of incorrect generalizations could be considered evidence of an increment in cognition and reasoning. Increase in use of words to resolve issues in associations with other chil-dren (and decrease in hitting) could be considered evidence of social development.

In all these illustrations a yardstick or measure with accuracy and objectivity could be or has been devised to record change in the indi-vidual. These measures reveal status and progress. The person who has records of this kind about increments of an individual child may also wish to use information on other children collected through comparable or similar measures. This would mean reference to careful, thorough, well-designed research.

Much of the research today attempts to recognize several variables. Thus increment according to a *channel*, i.e., a subgrouping in the light of which increments are studied, is often preferred when individual differences are being viewed. Figure 6 provides supporting evidence for the idea that increase of an attribute in the individual is more pre-dictable when reference is made to his subgroup or channel in data on groups. The figure shows lines drawn for the narrowest and widest dental arches and at the fifth, thirtieth, seventieth and ninety-fifth per-centiles (rank in 100 of the group studied) and provides channels for classification of individuals with narrow, moderately narrow, average, moderately wide and wide arches.*

---

* The distance between the deciduous or temporary canine teeth (those third from the center) of the upper, or maxillary, and the lower, or mandibular, dental arches was measured in 100 or more children each year from four to eight years of age. Holcomb and Meredith (1956) explain the graph by saying, "The segment designated 'narrow' encompasses the lowest 5 per cent of the normal range, the segment designated 'moder-ately narrow' comprises the next 25 per cent, and the succeding segments include 40 per cent, 25 per cent, and 5 per cent, respectively. . . . It provides a normative field for de-picting individual status in bicanine diameter, specific for sex and dental arch, at any post-natal age between 4 years and 8 years."

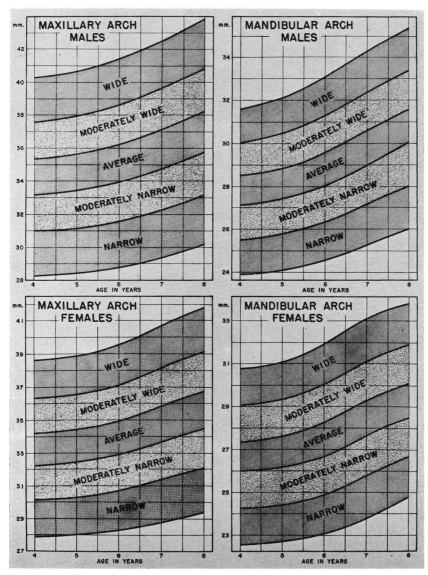

FIGURE 6. *Frames of reference for maximum width between the deciduous canine teeth.*

(Maxillary is the upper dental arch; mandibular, the lower dental arch. Deciduous teeth are the first or "baby" teeth; canine teeth are those third from the center.) The top of the segment designated narrow represents the fifth percentile; moderately narrow, the thirtieth percentile; average, the seventieth percentile; moderately wide, the ninety-fifth percentile. Percentile is rank in 100. Thus 5 per cent of the children studied are in the segment designated narrow; 25 per cent in the segment, moderately narrow; 40 per cent in the segment, average; 25 per cent in the segment, moderately wide; and 5 per cent in the segment, wide. (A. Holcomb and H. Meredith: Width of the dental arches at the deciduous canines in white children 4 to 8 years of age. Growth, 20:169, 1956.)

Figure 7 shows the channel illustrating growth of intelligence in the middle 68 per cent of a group studied (plus or minus one standard deviation from the mean); 16 per cent are above this central group and 16 per cent are below. This way of presenting information uses channels based on group studies, but with emphasis on the child's own change. Bayley (1955), in considering intelligence as measured by tests, suggests trying "to present individual curves of growth in units that will emphasize a child's change in relation to himself. Growth curves will enable us to observe a child's periods of fast and slow progress, his spurts and plateaus, and even regressions, in relation to his own past and future."

Figure 7 also suggests attention to the rate and variability of children's test performances at different ages. Intelligence test performance of two boys over a period of time is plotted on the graph to provide a view of their own performance and increment against a background provided by group study. One boy, 9 M, has a period of acceleration in his curve; the other boy, 8 M, has a lag. Thus Figure 7 supports the idea that increase of an attribute may be viewed by reference to the child's change in relation to himself as well as by reference to normative data.

Another way of viewing the individual is to consider relation of various increments or parts to each other and to a total in terms of *relative proportions*. In physical measurements, proportion of head to total length is an illustration (p. 252); in language development relative amounts of egocentric and social speech are measured (p. 349); in social development, percentage of associations in which the individual approaches others and in which he is approached by others would be an illustration (p. 403). In a study of motivations, or behavioral intentions in terms of goals sought by the child, Martin (1964) considered relative frequency of dependency, nurturance, aggression, control-dominance,

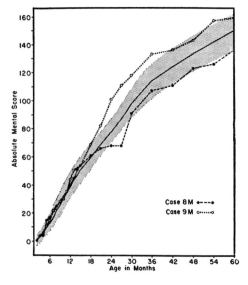

FIGURE 7. Individual curves of growth of intelligence in absolute scale units, showing contrasting patterns.

The shaded part represents the middle 68 per cent of the group studied; 16 per cent are above it and 16 per cent below it. Scores of 2 boys are plotted up to the age of 60 months. (N. Bayley: American Psychologist, 10:814, 1955.)

autonomous achievement, avoidance-withdrawal and friendship-affiliation. Relative amount which a child has in a given category with reference to other categories may be studied for similarities and differences
as he grows older.

However one views particular aspects of the individual's growth
and development, there is often the wish to record *correlates*, i.e., what
accompanies or parallels or, if possible, what causes the increment, in
terms of antecedents and consequents. In many measures of development, increments of one kind parallel increments of another kind, not
because one causes the other, but because maturation is involved in
both. For these, discovery of relative pace of changes is of interest. In
some measures additional parallels, beyond those due to maturation,
have been found in groups studied, more often than would result from
chance alone. In other words, a significant relation has been found.
This does not mean a one-to-one agreement. It may mean that only a
small percentage of the variance in behavior is accounted for by the
variable considered. For a comprehensive view of the individual it would
be useful to have knowledge of his many correlates, some of which
have high connections and some low (but still significant) connections
with growth and development.

Interest in a profile or summary which presents a variety of information about the individual child in the form of a cumulative record
built up with time has existed in the child development field for a number of years. Strengths and limitations in attempts to provide such a
view are suggested in the sections on methods of study of various aspects
of development in the following chapters.

TOPICS FOR STUDY AND DISCUSSION

1. As a focus for study, attempt to clarify distinctions among processes of development
   by stating with precision one idea on each of the following: growth, maturation,
   learning, influence of emotional tone. For clarification of a concept of orderly
   trends and a concept of the uniqueness of the individual, refer to information
   from research in Figures 3, 4, 6 and 7 and to supplementary study which might
   be of interest.
2. Observe several children of similar and different chronologic ages in an attempt to
   record behavior revealing each child's individuality. Consider what each child is
   attentive to, according to your records.
3. As a basis for discussion of learning, observe a child who is suddenly aware of the emergence of a new skill or concept. Record his responses, including indications of
   his feelings. Speculate about motivations, goals and reinforcement.
4. Observe a parent and an infant, noting how each provides for closeness to others and
   for activity (sensory and motor).

SELECTED READINGS

Anderson, J. E.: Dynamics of Development: Systems in Process, in D. B. Harris (Ed.):
The Concept of Development: An Issue in the Study of Human Behavior. Minneapolis, University of Minnesota Press, 1957.
Baldwin, A.: Theories of Child Development. New York, John Wiley & Sons, Inc., 1967,
pp. 587-599. Recommendations for an integrated theory.

Caldwell, B. M., and Richmond, J. B.: The impact of theories of child development. Children, 9:73-78, 1962. Three theoretical systems (social learning theories, maturational theory, and the psychoanalytic approach) have made inroads into the motivating theories of American parents in ways which have implications for today and for future theories.

Falkner, F. (Ed.): Human Development. Philadelphia, W. B. Saunders Company, 1966. Chap. 2. General Considerations in Human Development; by F. Falkner. pp. 16-26. Norms, sampling, data collections, incremental growth, maturity, control of growth, with references to physical growth and development.

Hebb, D. O.: A Textbook of Psychology. 2nd ed. Philadelphia, W. B. Saunders Company, 1966, pp. 156-158. Physical and psychological maturation, constitution and experience are distinguished by reference to genetic, chemical, sensory and traumatic variables.

McCandless, B. R.: Children, Behavior and Development. 2nd ed. New York, Holt, Rinehart and Winston, 1967. Chap 4. Learning and Motivation (maturation and learning, conditioned responses, stimulus generalization, discrimination learning, drive or motivation, and reward and learning).

Murphy, G., and Murphy, L. B.: The Child as Potential; in E. Ginzberg, (Ed.): The Nation's Children. Vol. 2, Development and Education. Published for the Golden Anniversary White House Conference on Children and Youth. New York, Columbia University Press, 1960.

CHAPTER TWO

The Home and the Family As Background For Growth and Development

COMPLEXITY OF THE FAMILY

Much of the thinking about concepts of development of the child suggested in Chapter One can also be used in considering development of the family. Because it changes in size and complexity and has parts functioning distinctly, but also in terms of the whole, the family is sometimes called a growing organism. The family not only has in it several individuals whose sequences and interactions are pictured in Figure 1 (p. 6), but also has a form of its own as a unit or "ongoing manifold" which includes those individuals.

A broad *concept of the family* refers to a basis of close relations by birth or marriage (or adoption); provision of a biological, social and cultural heritage, and an emotional, intellective and physical climate; a nature which includes growth and development of each of its members and also as a unit; and processes which involve orderly change. This listing of important dimensions of a family suggests why its conceptualization is elusive (Broderick, 1967; Hill, 1966; Kirkpatrick, 1967; Parsons and Bales, 1955; Rodgers, 1964). It is also evident why, when so much is involved, parts such as relations of members, economic factors, material possessions or corporate ideas are singled out for consideration in order to make study possible.

The child finds himself in what is sometimes called, for him, the family of orientation. It is a *nuclear family* with ties closer than those of the kinship group of husband and wife. Each member senses his family as a whole; he also connects it with his development as a person. This feeling occurs in both the adults and the children of the family. The subtlety of such an association, of the family as a psychosocial organization, which includes much more than the easily identified items, is suggested by Hess and Handel (1959):

However its life spreads into the wider community, there is a sense in which a family is a bounded universe. The members of a family . . . inhabit a world of their own making, a community of feeling and fantasy, action, and precept. Even before their infant's birth, the expectant couple make plans for his family membership, and they prepare . . . a prospect of what he will be to them. He brings his own surprises, but in time there is acquaintance, then familiarity, as daily the family members compose their interconnection through the touch and tone by which they learn to know one another. Each one comes to have a private transcript of their common life, recorded through his own emotions and individual experiences.

. . . The family members develop more or less adequate understanding of one another, collaborating in the effort to establish consensus and to negotiate uncertainty. The family's life together is an endless process of movement in and around consensual understanding, from attachment to conflict to withdrawal—and over again. Separateness and connectedness are the underlying conditions of a family's life, and its common task is to give form to both.

In considering complexities of the family, several approaches, concepts, ideas or frames of reference are used. One of these, to be used here, is a developmental approach regarding the family as a growing organism, with an implication of some orderliness of change with time and experience. Another approach, using the term "family structure," concerns definable and reasonably stable organization at a given time. Family structure has elements that could be related in various situations as the family changes with time, and includes family composition and relations among members, and also orientation to material elements and setting. In these approaches, attributes of family members, organization of their joint activities, role functions, and values or goals are components to be studied.

THE FAMILY AS A GROWING ORGANISM

Sequences

The family proceeds from one stage to another; even in the brief span of years of the young child the family has ongoing development. Aspects in its sequence may be considered in a number of ways. Selection of an approach represents one set of criteria by which to view the family. Criteria presented here include stage of the family life cycle according to age; developmental tasks of family members and the family unit, and ways of handling them; meeting basic needs of the individuals and the unit; giving and receiving of understanding loving care; and relative emphasis on values or goals and their achievement. Perspectives such as these can be used in considering a particular family or the family as a general field of interest as we study child development.

One way of thinking about aspects of the family's sequence is in terms of its life cycle. *Stages in a family life cycle according to ages* of children and adults are as follows (Duvall, 1967):

Stage I   Beginning families (married couple without children)
Stage II   Childbearing families (oldest child, birth to 30 months)
Stage III   Families with preschool children (oldest child 2½ to 6 years)
Stage IV   Families with school children (oldest child 6 to 13 years)

Stage V   Families with teenagers (oldest child 13 to 20 years)
Stage VI   Families as launching centers (first child gone to last child's leaving
                 home)
Stage VII   Families in the middle years (empty nest to retirement)
Stage VIII Aging families (retirement to death of both spouses)

Stages in the family life cycle are sometimes described by reference to *developmental tasks* of children and their parents. Developmental tasks are actions and feelings important for the person at a particular stage if he is to continue his growth (Havighurst, 1950). In order to emphasize that the individual's adaptation involves complex interpersonal equilibria, forces within himself and in the setting, the term *developmental transactions* is sometimes used (Goodrich, 1961). Many of the tasks or transactions of the infant in his first few weeks and months concern the fitting together of his physiological needs and his environment. At three or four months of age more of his actions and feelings are on an additional plane, because of his ability not only to try out new motor and sensory responses, but also to draw upon organizational patterns which have become modified with experience and coordinated with one another. Distinctive elements capture his attention and affect his assimilation of, and accommodation to, the new. He is discovering which responses to repeat and which to discard. When the child is able to walk and run easily, tasks now added pertain to his broader world. He can investigate more, communicate more and reason more as he proceeds through the preschool years. His actions and feelings concern discovery of meanings of objects, events, himself and other people. Adults can provide him with opportunities to "try his wings" and also to discover reasonable limits.

The National Conference on Family Life (1948) commented on developmental tasks of parents of preschool children:

> Family life . . . never stays put. No sooner has a fence been built to keep a two year old out of the street than he's a three year old, capable of understanding why he must keep to the sidewalk. . . . Teaching the youngster to keep dry is succeeded by . . . helping him to get used to sharing his parents with a new baby. Just as a child has reached a stage when his mental growth has made him an increasingly interesting companion, he is snatched away by the school, and his parents begin to be outsiders, unaware of what is happening to him during a big share of his waking hours.

Some of the developmental tasks of parents pertain to helping the infant and the child to grow and develop in the directions indicated in the preceding paragraphs. Other tasks pertain to new roles, new regimes, relations of wife and husband, assumption of responsibilities for the family unit, maintenance of a sense of self, and relations with relatives and the community (National Conference on Family Life, 1948; Duvall, 1967.

Philosophy and practices underlying achievement of developmental tasks concern a balancing and harmonizing of the needs, responsibilities and joys of each person according to his stage of development and individuality. Furthermore, in the course of time, unforeseen challenges, hazards, crises and problems arise.

Although specific developmental tasks of the family members and the family unit differ at different stages, certain fundamental bases, or threads of continuity, run through the stages. One of these concerns *meeting the basic needs of individuals and of the unit* (see Chap. Four through Seven). The extent to which basic needs are met can be a focus for considering actions, beliefs and feelings throughout the sequence of the family life cycle. This implies that not only the basic needs, but also the understanding loving care which provides for their being met, take different forms at different stages. Warmth, the meeting of situations without extreme stress or apathy, dependence and independence, nutrition, activity and rest, and social contact have qualitative and quantitative differences at various stages of development. Adequate provision for individual needs continues to affect the lives of family members and the preservation of family unity.

Similarly, use of emerging abilities, with different forms at different ages, and personality components (see pp. 242-245) can be considered throughout the sequence. How the family enables each member to gain and to maintain a sense of trust, integrity and other components throughout the years will vary according to the development of the individuals and with changes in the family environment. Personality components are surprisingly appropriate for study of the family as a unit.

Meeting needs such as those mentioned in the preceding paragraphs reflects the *giving and receiving of understanding loving care*. Such care, whether it concerns affection, the learning of values, opportunities and responsibilities, or other aspects, likewise has different forms at different stages, but pertains to life throughout the family cycle. Broad uses of the terms *needs* and *caring*, suggested here, go beyond comfort and cherishing and refer also to quality of outlook, stimulation and response. The extent to which each member of the family group not only receives, but also gives, understanding loving care is of particular interest in any study of the family.

In any study of sequences in the family, focus can also be on *relative emphasis on various values or goals and their achievement*. For example, attention to basic needs may be great or slight. Orientation toward other goals may or may not be evident. What the family strives for at the moment or in its short-term or long-term view may be far on the side of a symbolic environment, which has a different connotation from physical environment.

Values emerge through relatedness of individual and group. For husband and wife, emergence of values of their family unit is linked with their experience together and the personal identity of each. Ackerman (1958), stressing the fact that families vary greatly in the extent to which family functions are oriented to one group of values or another, writes:

From the genetic point of view, the infant, to begin with, has no values. Values emerge only as the child differentiates its separate self from the mother's self. The emergence of values and socialization are parallel processes. . . . The development of value attitudes is organically linked . . . to socialization and the establishment of personal identity. . . . The emotional climate and preferential strivings of one family accentuate the values of love, creativity, adventure and freedom, whereas the qualities of another family are dominated by values of static security, competition, and exploitive aspirations in human relations. . . . There are families where the dominant value orientation emphasizes the inner spiritual life of the family, a dedication to the worth, dignity and personal development of each member. There are others which accentuate the outer facade of the family, its external image in the eyes of the surrounding community. . . . There are some families whose component value trends stress pleasure, the joys of the moment. . . . There are those families in which the dominant value orientation is to power, status, and money.

Whether developmental tasks, basic needs, values or goals or other aspects of the family are considered, it is logical to seek some explanation for the form they take. The heritages of individual members of the family and the processes of interaction of their life together will provide much information.

Heritage

Biologically, family heritage includes *genetic inheritance and biological functioning*. This functioning is the resultant of separate genetic potentialities and transactions. Biological differences, e.g., whether one is fat or lean, have theoretical merit and "should facilitate the elucidation of some practical problems of 'fitness,' as regards both performance capacity and health" (Brozek, 1961). These differences have many ramifications in the family setting.

Susceptibility and response to disease are matters of biological individuality. People differ in their reaction to stress (Lacey et al., 1963; Lipton et al., 1966) and in their susceptibility to both infectious and noninfectious diseases (Stern, 1960). Environmental conditions may precipitate a disease in one person, but not in another. Williams and Siegel (1961) were concerned with "innate susceptibility and resistance" to noninfective diseases. This area of investigation also has ramifications in the family setting.

Biological components of behavior may play a role in the dynamics of the family. Infants at birth differ in their behavior. Some are active, some passive, some cuddly, some relatively unresponsive. The infant's response to being fed or held, and so forth, has effects upon the mother's response and her feelings of being a satisfactory mother. In turn, her response is communicated in her contacts with the infant. Thus the dynamics of mother-child relations are affected by the biological constitution of the newborn.

A relation between behavior and biological function and structure has been demonstrated in genetic studies with animals (Stern, 1960); in the mental retardation accompanying inborn errors of metabolism, e.g., phenylketonuria (Wright, 1957); in the behavior manifested by brain-injured children (Bradley, 1957; Masland et al., 1958); and in disturbance of the autonomic nervous system (Riley et al., 1954). It can be inferred from such studies that a biological component may be present in some of the differences in behavior within the so-called limits of the normal range. It may also be expected that family members differing in their biological make-up, e.g., energy level, may react in different ways in any given family situation.

Williams (1951), a biochemist, sees a possible relation between biochemical individuality and behavior and social relations. He believes that everyone inherits a distinct "metabolic personality" which has implications for understanding behavior.

Plant (1950), a psychiatrist, described a biological basis for difference of one individual from another in *selection of parts of the environment to react to:*

> Between the need of the child and the sweep of social pressures lies . . . a sort of psycho-osmotic envelope. . . . One should never think of this as a tangible, material structure. It is rather a property of that part of the personality which is in touch with the environment. If one must neurologize, then the envelope is . . . to a large extent a cortical structure. . . . It seems to grow in efficiency and complication as the individual grows from childhood — and this at least parallels the growing use of cortical structures. . . . Normally the personality has the ability to shut out large sectors of its environment and to translate those parts that it takes in into usable or understandable material. It is the part of the personality where this selection occurs that I call the envelope.

Presence of roots of individuality at very early ages has been suggested by differences in activity level of infants (Escalona, 1968) and by the relation of temperament of infants to feeding and sleeping and to various behavior disorders (Thomas et al., 1968). For such behavior and for other aspects of personality, the location of biochemical and neurological correlates in the healthy normal person involves problems of research of interest to many, but not yet resolved.

Some writers would emphasize the biological side of behavior in terms of racial and familial stock; others would emphasize the cultural side in terms of learned behavior.

Ideas, beliefs and practices from the past and the present provide a *cultural context* of family heritage. Culture has been defined by sociologists and other social scientists as

> . . . that complex whole which includes knowledge, belief, art, morals, law, custom and other capabilities acquired by man as a member of society. . . . From the standpoint of the child, culture is the social heritage to which he is born and in which he is reared. This social heritage includes the answers which his group has made and is making to the problems of life (Bossard and Boll, 1966).

The child's setting is affected by the attitudes and experiences of the many generations which preceded him. Through the cultural heritage of his parents and the cultural and immediate social situation in which the family lives, the child makes discoveries about himself and his world. Some of these discoveries concern involvement of members of his family within the home and in the community. This involvement, or the family's concern about some thing or activity, may affect family members directly through the work they do or more impersonally through some activity which provides money. In addition to these discoveries about the family and its relations to the community, others (of particular interest to anthropologists) concern attitudes about birth, death, separation, grief, loneliness, responsibility, fun and discipline (Lee, 1962).

> Each group, guided by its beliefs and assumptions about nature and human nature . . . strives to maintain its cherished ways of living by shaping, molding, and attempting to fit the newly born infant, the child, and the adolescent into the kind of personality the group believes to be desirable, if not essential, to its continuance as a people, requiring him to learn its ways of living and conducting his life career (Frank, 1966).

Systematic variations in value orientations exist from one culture to another and within cultures (Kluckhohn and Strodtbeck, 1961). There is a wide range of family settings in which children in different cultures grow and develop. Material equipment, ways of doing things, ideas, habits and interests vary according to where the individual happens to be reared. It is as a part of this culture that social organization can be understood. Again, understanding comes not merely from reference to a particular geographic area, but from knowledge of variations within the particular culture of that area.

Within a particular nation some of the variations in the setting of a particular family come from cultural heritages of the past. Bossard and Boll (1966), stressing that in different regional areas the values transmitted by the family differ, refer to "the child of North Carolina piedmont parentage who is thrust overnight, as it were, into the school and social life of a second-generation Irish or Portugese section in New England. Such a child appreciates, if parents and child behavior students do not, the reality of differences in the regional culture." Parts of the present cultural and social scene that especially influence the child are considered later in this chapter.

These brief references to ways of considering the family over time, and to biological and cultural heritages, suggest the many elements involved in family influence. Interactions between persons include parent-to-parent, child-to-parent and child-to-child reactions. In considering dynamics of family interaction, at a particular time and also in the course of years, Frank (National Conference on Family Life, 1948) refers to "dynamic circular processes wherein each participating entity is at once helping to create and maintain the larger pattern of organization which is also reciprocally directing, influencing, and guiding what he or she is doing."

Interactions

Processes of transmitting a cultural heritage or communicating a particular feeling or idea are crucial in explaining what happens in the family and, consequently, in understanding the family. What, in this association of self and another or others—the personal relationship—causes change in behavior of the family member is elusive. The extent to which processes in the family group and those in associations outside the family, as in the child's associations with his peers and with his teacher, are similar is a thought-provoking question. Also thought-provoking is the extent to which the individual's interactions in the family lay the groundwork for other associations, present and future.

The term *psychosocial* is sometimes used to convey the idea of the individual with his constitution and experience interacting with his social environment. Each of the individuals in the family is discovering who he is and what is his relation to his world. The child is discovering, not consciously, but in his living that he is one who thinks, feels and acts in certain ways; he is also discovering others who think, feel and act in certain ways. He may respond to a given situation in view of his understanding of what others are like by being similar to them or by acting as he would in association with them. Thus *concept of self and of others* emerges; *identity* of self, *identification* of self with others, *images* in the light of which to act, *roles* to play are clarified in the child's early group experience, i.e., his family experience.

Erikson (1956) writes about identity as follows:

> It is this identity of something in the individual's core, with an essential aspect of a group's inner coherence, which is under consideration here: for the young individual must learn to be most himself where he means most to others — those others, . . . who have come to mean most to him. The term identity expresses such a mutual relation in that it connotes both a persistent sameness within oneself (self-sameness) and a persistent sharing of some kind of essential character with others. . . . The term identity covers much of what has been called the self by a variety of workers, be it in the form of a self-concept (George H. Mead, 1934), a self-system (Harry S. Sullivan, 1953), or . . . fluctuating self-experiences described by Schilder (1951).

What matters especially in these processes of interaction of one person with others has been described in various ways. Foote and Cottrell (1955), referring to *identity and interpersonal competence*, recommend research which would attempt to identify important elements and propose hypotheses for investigation. For social research they "set forth a series of reproducible conditions, variation of which in certain interrelated ways is thought to facilitate or retard the development of interpersonal competence." Since personality development depends on interpersonal competence, "every significant other in the family constellation must be taken into account." Abilities possessed by individual family members are listed by Foote and Cottrell as ones they believe should be investigated to discover what qualities distinguish inept from competent performance in interpersonal relations. These components are health, intelligence, empathy, autonomy, judgment and creativity. They pertain to competence, regarded as power, in the sense of ability to produce intended effects.

Hess and Handel (1959) ask, "How shall we understand how [individual family members] fashion a life together?" They study processes which "give shape to the flux of family life, coherence to the extended array of events, perceptions, emotions, actions, learnings and changes which the members experience or undertake." The processes, with excerpts in parentheses to clarify their meaning, are as follows:

1. Establishing a pattern of separateness and connectedness. (This fundamental

duality of family life is of considerable significance, for the individual's efforts to take his own kind of interest in the world, to become his own kind of person, proceed apace with his efforts to find gratifying connection to the other members.)

2. Establishing a satisfactory congruence of images through the exchange of suitable testimony. (Attaining stability amid fluctuation in images family members have of one another and of themselves.)
3. Evolving modes of interaction into central family concerns or themes. (Some significant issue and the general direction of attempted solution.)
4. Establishing the boundaries of the family's world of experience. (How elaborated individual personalities are, how deep or shallow experience is, how much of the world it is important to know about and be interested in, how experiences are evaluated.)
5. Dealing with significant biosocial issues of family life, as in the family's disposition to evolve definitions of male and female and of older and younger. (Certain conventionalized answers are provided by the larger social units to which a family belongs—social class, ethnic group, community. Yet each family provides answers of its own.)

Brim (1960) stresses the variety of learned *roles*. "The 'self' is a composite of many selves, each . . . consisting of a set of self-perceptions . . . specific to one or another major role, specific to the expectations of one or another significant reference group." Role-performance "is something much more complex [than bits and pieces] that is acquired all of a piece; consider the familiar example of the three year old suddenly playing the mother's role almost effortlessly." He suggests that general traits, such as dominance, need for achievement, and others could be considered within a role, though they might differ for the same individual in another role.

Family roles have complementary or reciprocal aspects. Sometimes roles are studied from the point of view of what decreases the complementarity and what restores it. Study of family roles may be in the context of masculine and feminine, the extent to which the person has instrumental (or task) functions, or expressive (or social-emotional) functions (Parsons and Bales, 1955) or the context of the extent to which the person does or does not have power. What a person considers that his role and that of others should or could include can be an influence in the family (Emmerich, 1959a, 1959b).

A person may have in mind roles in terms of mutual expectations, but his definition of them may not instigate role behavior. Baldwin (1961) emphasizes the distinguishing of

. . . role-definition from the psychological mechanisms by which people are led, guided, instigated, forced, or rewarded into . . . complying with the role-expectations. People *do* fulfill role requirements, but . . . in a variety of ways, and by . . . a variety of psychological mechanisms. Sometimes they fulfill them as instrumental acts to avoid punishment or to gain rewards. Sometimes people fulfill the role requirements because they are motivated to conform; for such people, the presence of a standard is sufficient to instigate conforming behavior. Other people—or the same person at different times—may fulfill role requirements because they feel a moral imperative about the behavior itself; for these people it may be unimportant that a certain set of behaviors constitute a social role; for them the actual behavior itself is seen as "something I ought to do." Other people may fulfill role requirements through love, loyalty, or sentiment for another person or for a collectivity. . . . Role requirements may also be met because the actual role behavior is itself a consummatory, rewarding kind of action.

Rose (1962) says that "there are two main streams in interactionist theory, separable although highly interrelated. One is through the study of the socialization of the child, and may be considered social-psychological in focus. . . . The second strain is through the study of social organizations and social processes and may be considered primarily sociological in focus." Obviously, individuals are not mere cogs in a social system. To recognize uniqueness and richness of human personalities and orderliness in social systems will take time.

FAMILY MEMBERS AND THEIR RELATIONS

The young child finds much of his exogenous environment (that outside the person) within the family. Previous sections of this chapter have suggested the complexity of the family environment and have indicated that the family can be viewed as a growing organism with its sequences with time, its heritages and its interactions. From these come material possessions, feelings, practices and ideas which are the setting for growth and development of the child, as well as of other family members and the family as a unit.

The family, when viewed at a particular time, can be said to have a structure, although not with a connotation of rigidity. In reference to *family structure* Clausen (1966) says that the family "at any given time . . . has a definable composition and a reasonably stable organization of joint activities, role relationships and dominant values or goals." These suggest the idea of an "ongoing manifold." Reference is made to them in the following pages to suggest what might be viewed at a particular time. The items selected are such as lend themselves to consideration of the child's setting for growth and development as the family provides it on a particular day or in a particular month or year.

The first components of the family scene to be considered here are climate and composition. *Climate* of the family can be thought of as emotional, cognitively stimulating or not, culturally advantaged or disadvantaged, as well as physical. Family *composition* pertains to the presence of one or both parents, relatives, brothers and sisters, and their attributes and interrelations.

Emotional Climate

Emotional climate in the family, in terms of *love-hostility* and *autonomy-control,* may be viewed by drawing upon findings from a number of studies. Schaefer (1961) suggested this conceptual model for maternal behavior and indicated that several research reports, independently made, have findings which "converge" upon these dimensions. Likewise, in the conceptual model for the child's emotional and social behavior, with love-hostility and extroversion-introversion dimensions, there was a convergence of findings. Although much of the research on parent-child relations has concerned mother and child, it seems possible to use these dimensions in studies on relations of other members of the family. For further discussion related to these dimensions, see page 243 (personality component of autonomy), pages 135-138 (emotional and social development) and pages 151-156 (warmth, dependence and independence).

For the infant, for older children and for adults the forms of behavior, ranging from love to hostility and from autonomy to control, in relations of family members to each other differ according to their maturity. But at every age, acceptance, understanding and support and letting the individual decide for himself when he is able can be sensed. The degrees to which attitudes such as these underlie different forms of behavior provide a range of emotional climate. How the child feels about himself and his world seems to be a reflection of his emotional climate. How the mother and the father feel about the child and about what he does seems to influence this climate more than their specific words or actions.

Parents who want to contribute to the child's contentment and his feeling of harmony with his world do so in settings which are very different. An American pediatrician, Spock (1957), says:

> What good mothers and fathers instinctively feel like doing for their babies is usually best . . . All parents do their best job when they have a natural, easy confidence in themselves. Better to make a few mistakes from being natural than to do everything letter-perfect out of a feeling of worry.

Such naturalness has been dealt with very differently in the literature of both the past and the present. For example, behaviorism, widely accepted by psychologists in the 1920's, stressed regulation of environmental influences on learning and minimized personal closeness (Watson, 1928). Parents were made aware of ways of controlling experience to cause learning and habit formation. About the same time, from the psychoanalytic point of view, which began to be popularized in the 1920's, early childhood emotional experiences, the unconscious, a few drives such as those connected with sex and the will to power, were stressed as basic in the child's adjustment (Adler, 1924; Horney, 1942, 1950; Isaacs, 1946). Parents were made aware of something deep beneath the surface, not easily revealed in behavior. At present some of the literature stresses cognitive elements of experience more than emotional elements (Lipsitt, 1966) or emotional elements as paths toward other abilities (Murphy, 1962). Some of this reflects the selection of parts of development for research rather than disagreement as to the presence of emotional and cognitive elements in a particular experience.

Environmental Stimulation

Another aspect of "climate" of the family concerns settings that facilitate a progression of abilities. What in the environment instigates or evokes use of abilities, and what within the person and in his setting prompts their continued use, are of interest. Gewirtz (1961) says of childhood social learning: "For an analysis of a recurring behavior of the child, we would examine its effect on the environment to determine what consequence sustains its occurrence." Not only food, water, and removal of pain, but also uses of the sense organs, as for touch, sight and kinesthetic sensitivity, are bases for further development in the young infant.

An adult can reinforce these behaviors in a variety of ways, e.g., by near presence, attention, approval, a smile. "These stimuli are incidental to but concomitant with the care [the mother] gives the child, or the other attentive responses she makes to him. Thus the stage is set very early for the conditioning of generalized reinforcers." As the infant develops an attachment to a particular person who takes care of him, usually his mother, he finds in that association "so many different and so many potent reinforcing stimuli . . . contingent on so many of his behaviors, from the earliest learning occasions" (Gewirtz, 1961).

Not only in his associations with another person, but also in his own activities "for the fun of it," the infant or young child is stimulated to proceed further. He is attentive to distinctive stimuli and thus makes discoveries. These depend on the opportunities provided by his setting. After infancy encouragement of a child to be self-reliant in use of abilities seems to be a factor in his later intellectual competence. His attitude of "learning to learn" (as contrasted to being overdependent emotionally on one or both parents for satisfactions from their warmth and approval) tends to accompany gain in mental growth rate. According to Sontag, Baker and Nelson (1958):

> From the years of three to six it would appear that the learning of broad patterns of behavior in relation to parents is of primary importance in establishing a foundation for later interaction with the environment. The child who is emotionally dependent upon his parents during these years would appear to be establishing a mode of behavior . . . not conducive to "learning to learn." . . . However, if the child is learning to meet some of his needs through appropriate aggressive behavior, competitiveness, or individual problem-solving, it would appear that he is laying a groundwork for the kind of motivation characterized in need for achievement, which may operate as a motive in learning experiences. During the elementary school years it is . . . not surprising to see a high need for achievement being related to an accelerated mental growth rate.

The provision of particular kinds of stimulation differs from one family to another. Differences may be in whether things and ideas of the child's environment are appropriately varied according to his abilities, or are meager. Differences may also be in the extent to which others in his environment value or prefer cognitive activities or other aspects of development. Motor abilities, language, knowledge of science, creative activities, self-discipline, and consideration for other people are a few of the areas in which facilitation of development within the family may vary greatly.

Cultural Differences

The family may also be viewed with reference to the extent to which its culture provides bases for that of a broader setting, away from home, into which the child will go. For example, with regard to school, the culturally advantaged child is one whose background has facilitated development of abilities and interests emphasized in school; the culturally disadvantaged child has not had this background.

There are other cultural differences. In ways not concerned with school or with deprivation the child may find the characteristics and values of his family and consequently of his personality different from, or not congruent with, those of the social systems and culture of the community.

Hess and Shipman (1965) discuss the effects of cultural deprivation upon the child's cognitive faculties:

> Children from deprived backgrounds score well below middle-class children on standard individual and group measures of intelligence (a gap that increases with age); they come to school without the skills necessary for coping with first grade curricula; their language development, both written and spoken, is relatively poor; auditory and visual discrimination skills are not well developed; in scholastic achievement they are retarded an average of 2 years by grade 6 and almost 3 years by grade 8; they are more likely to drop out of school before completing a secondary education; and even when they have adequate ability are less likely to go to college.
>
> . . . Behavior which leads to social, educational, and economic poverty is socialized in early childhood—that is, it is learned; . . . the central quality involved in the effects of cultural deprivation is a lack of cognitive meaning in the mother-child communication system; . . . the growth of cognitive processes is fostered in family control systems which offer and permit a wide range of alternatives of action and thought and . . . such growth is constricted by systems of control which offer predetermined solutions and few alternatives for consideration and choice.
>
> . . . The structure of the social system and the structure of the family shape communication and language and . . . language shapes thought and cognitive styles of problem-solving. In the deprived-family context this means that the nature of the control system which relates parent to child restricts the number and kind of alternatives for action and thought that are opened to the child; such constriction precludes a tendency for the child to reflect, to consider and choose among alternatives for speech and action. It develops modes for dealing with stimuli and with problems which are impulsive rather than reflective, which deal with the immediate rather than the future, and which are disconnected rather than sequential.

For further discussion of development of language and thought, see pages 342-373. More detailed consideration of parent-child relations is found in Chapters Four, Seven, Ten, Eleven and Twelve.

Attributes of Individuals and Position in the Family

The climates of each family depend on the personalities of its individual members. A man and a woman bring to marriage two personalities—their biological heritage, health, cognitive abilities and also their potentialities for learning from this new experience. In addition, each person has feelings and attitudes in many areas, including family relations, which may be similar or different. Each brings to marriage his particular expectations of what it should and will be.

Relations of parents to each other affect adjustment of the child.

Baruch (1937, 1939), for example, found tensions in interparental relations coexistent with less satisfactory adjustment of the children.

> The children . . . enter life in an atmosphere created by the two people who are their parents. When . . . the parents have failed to find a measure of happiness, the atmosphere of their home is likely to be quite different from that created by a couple who have found in each other stability and strength. The relationship of one parent to the other is the essence of that climate into which the child is born and in which his primary adjustments to living must be made.

Adults' adjustment in marriage tends to have some relation to their own childhood home (Burgess and Cottrell, 1939; Terman et al., 1938). Happiness of the parents, the affectional bond between parents and children, lack of conflict, happiness of the children, and discipline that was firm but not harsh were found, in early research on the family, to be pertinent when attempts were made to predict success in marriage.

The child's *position in the family* is a factor in his personality development. Particular social situations arise from being the only, oldest, middle or youngest child in the family. For example, the oldest child has had at least a year or so in the family as the only child, after which he was forced to yield part of the attention of his parents to a younger child. As the first child, his associations at each phase of development are with parents who are less experienced.

The youngest child has no occasion to give place to a successor. Because he has less maturity, others may carry more responsibilities for him. Or, with older members of the family not only to wait on him, but also to "boss" him, he may be subject to frequent and inconsistent commands.

The middle child (or children) has neither the position of having been first nor that of having the least maturity in his associations with his parents. As their energies are spent, middle children have a "connectedness" not only with those who are more capable because they are older, but also with those who are more dependent because they are younger.

The only child is in a situation in which the parents' thought, attention and affection are not distributed among several children. He has fewer situations involving the give and take of life which tend to be present in larger families. His experience in adapting to others and being adapted to is more often provided by his parents.

The only boy in a family of girls and the only girl in a family of boys may be, in some degree, selected for special treatment by the other children. Such a child (as well as the others) receives his ideas about masculine and feminine roles from these associations.

Children from families of either boys only or girls only tend to have fewer experiences with children of the opposite sex. Acquaintance with members of the opposite sex, which develops a natural social ease and gives in early childhood the knowledge of differences of the sexes which is frequently of interest to children before school age, may be less likely to occur.

Effects of the child's position in the family on his growth and development are complex. Sears, Maccoby and Levin (1957) interviewed mothers concerning *parental practice in particular ordinal situations.* They reported that in feeding, later-born children were less likely to be breast-fed; in regard to permissiveness for quarreling among siblings, "*older* children were given more freedom than younger ones"; second or later children were more likely to be restricted, particularly "with respect to making noise or interrupting adults at the table." Mothers of only children had a stronger tendency to keep close track of their offspring. Older and middle children were assigned more tasks and chores than were younger children. Sampson (1965) has suggested that the first-born's early concept of himself is likely to reflect parental appraisals, while that of later-born children is likely to reflect peer appraisals.

Characteristics of siblings affect children's personalities. Koch (1955, 1956, 1957, 1960) related ratings of children concerning work attitudes, characteristics of their playmates, attitudes toward their peers, toward adults, toward each other and toward their parents to certain sibling characteristics, such as being the older or younger of a two-child family of the same or opposite sex with age differences of under two years, from two to four years, and from four to six years. Koch refers to "the variable, sex of sib, in relation to sex of child [as] an important conditioner of many of the group differences in personality. . . . The girl with a younger brother, for instance, apparently stimulated by sex rivalry, presents a picture of greater dynamicness than the girl with a younger sister." Koch referred to the two- to four-year spacing as "rather stressful."

Brim (1958) studied effects of siblings on sex-role learning. Traits on which the children were rated were classified as either of the instrumental or task (masculine) role or of the expressive or social-emotional (feminine) role. The data confirmed the hypotheses that "cross-sex siblings will have more traits of the opposite sex than will same-sex siblings, and that this effect will be greater for the younger, as contrasted with the older, sibling." Each child in the study of siblings of different sex had a preponderance of the traits of his own sex. Nevertheless the influence of an older sibling as a model for learning sex-appropriate behavior was suggested.

Clausen (1966) summarizes research on birth order as follows:

Each child has to work out his own identity within the network of relationships and social roles that characterize his place in family, kinship, and neighborhood. Each member of a group of siblings has a somewhat different set of capacities at birth and each finds a somewhat different environment. Certain capacities may be more fully developed in one position within a constellation of siblings; others will flourish in a different position. Insofar as overall development is concerned . . . it does not appear that any position or constellation is to be preferred appreciably to any other. The effects of birth order are, for the most part, indirect, deriving from tendencies toward patterning of psychological environment. But most of these patternings are subject to greater influence from a number of other sources. Even the direct impact of displacement of the first-born is subject to attention by parents who are aware that their preoccupation with a new infant is bound to be resented by the child who has until then had all of their attention. . . . It would appear that the primary value of examining the ways in which birth order may influence personality development is to enhance sensitivity to subtle patternings of relationships within the family. Such sensitivity can increase understanding of the situation of a given child and perhaps permit a measure of modification of potentially harmful influences.

Differences in ability and appearance may produce differences in the child's experience in his family. A less capable child in a family of more capable children, a slow child in a family of children who learn quickly, or a child of less appealing appearance in a more attractive family experiences wider contrasts. Likewise a child who is physically different or exceptionally capable or talented experiences the great variations in what one person can do and another cannot do. The way in which such contrast affects the child's attitude toward himself is a pertinent element in his personality development and in his maximum use of his abilities. Acceptance of self, and interest in doing what one is capable of, reflect family attitudes.

A child seems to like it if he can occasionally be with his mother or father without sharing their attention with other children of the family. Some parents make special efforts to plan occasions when one child has their companionship without the presence of the others. This experience of being alone with his mother or father, instead of being one of a group, can seem especially valuable for the middle child, but has advantages for each child, whatever his position. One child may go along one time, and others at other times, as the mother does her marketing or the father buys supplies for house repairs. A cooperative arrangement with the other parent, a neighbor or a grandparent may be needed for care of the other children, but the extra effort can increase understanding, from the child's, the parent's, the grandparent's and the neighbor's point of view.

A word may be said here about the *adopted child*. A child adopted early in life, preferably in infancy, can be given as much affectional security as natural born children have. Adopted children may even be more secure affectionally than some natural born children, since the adopted child is a wanted child, whereas not all own children are. Adopted children who know from the beginning that they are adopted will not experience shock at this fact. Infants cannot understand this, but the child can grow up aware of the fact that he is an adopted child, cherished by his adoptive parents and by others in the family. Only in this way can one avoid the disaster of the fact of adoption being discovered by accident. Otherwise the child could believe that he was not told frankly and simply about being adopted because there was something to be ashamed of in the fact. Had it been all right, he may reason, they would not have hidden it from him. Open acceptance of the fact of his adoption can reassure the adopted child.

Division of Responsibilities

Within the family there is division of responsibilities (and joys). Sometimes these are discussed; sometimes, not. From one family to another and among members of the same family, the amount of time the child spends with particular members varies. In families in which the mother is not employed outside the home the time she spends at home and with her children varies according to her other responsibilities and interests. Likewise the amount of time the father spends at home and with the children is influenced by a large number of variables. In some families both parents are employed outside the home. "Increasingly, women are carrying out the dual roles of homemaker and employed worker" (Reichert, 1961). Table 1 presents details about working mothers.

Many mothers work because of economic pressures. Their earnings may be the family's only support or are needed to help in maintaining the family. This is particularly true of mothers who head broken homes. The mother's presence at home with her infant or preschool child is considered so important that many social agencies try to arrange it.

In some instances the mother's reasons for working outside the home are not primarily economic. Her own needs, personal and professional, and the needs of the family as she and her husband see them, may lead to such a choice. Emphasis on the quality rather than the quantity of her relations with her children may be a factor in such a decision. To put a premium on the amount of time spent with the child, without reference to what it involves, is open to question.

Arrangements for care which provides a climate conducive to growth and development of the child whose mother works vary greatly. The standard of qualifications can be high for the person who comes into the child's home, or in whose home he stays while his mother is away. Day-care centers and nursery schools as community services, with educational programs for the child and his family when he is away from home, are discussed later (p. 75).

Some mothers of young children find part-time employment outside the home more satisfactory than full-time employment. Others arrange to supplement the family income through business activities which can be carried on at home.

Maccoby (1958) comments on effects upon children of their mothers' employment as follows:

. . . There is no single best way of organizing family life. Some mothers should work while others should not, and the outcome for the children depends upon many factors other than the employment itself. Some of these factors are: the age of the children, the nature of the mother's motivation to work, the mother's skill in child care and that of her substitute, the composition of the family (especially whether it contains a good substitute caretaker), the stability of the husband, and the pressure or absence of tension between the husband and wife.

The mother's self-esteem seems to be a pertinent element in her pattern of child rearing (Sears, Maccoby and Levin, 1957; Yarrow et al., 1962). Among both working and nonworking middle-class mothers, adequacy of maternal behavior was related to their satisfaction with their current status (Yarrow).

A child may be living with *only one parent*. In 1951 about two million children under eighteen years of age were not living with their parents, and nearly four million with only one parent, whether widowed, di-

TABLE 1.   Who Are the Working Mothers?

QUESTIONS	ANSWERS	
Number of Mothers	*In brief:*	*In detail:*
1. How does the present number of working mothers* compare with earlier years?	There were 9.7 million working mothers with children under 18 years of age in March 1965. This was the highest number ever recorded.	The March 1965 figure for mothers with children under 18 years in the Nation's labor force** compares with about 4.6 million mothers in 1950, and 1.5 million in 1940.
2. Of all women workers, what proportion are mothers of children under 18 years of age?	Almost two-fifths at the time of the most recent estimate in March 1965.	Of the total woman labor force in 1950, mothers with children under 18 years of age constituted a fourth. In 1940, their proportion of the total was only a tenth.
3. Do many working mothers have children under 6 years of age?	Yes. Almost 2 out of every 5. More than 3 out of 5 have children 6 to 17 years only.	In March 1965, 3,682,000 working mothers had children under 6 years of age, and 1,696,000 of these mothers had children under 3 years of age. Six million women workers had children 6 to 17 years of age.
Family Relationships		
4. Of the mothers from families in which the husband is present, what proportion work?	If the husband lives in the home, about 3 out of 10 mothers work. The proportion is almost 6 out of 10 for other mothers.	Mothers who are widowed, separated or divorced are more likely to work than others. In March 1965, 48 per cent of the mothers in these categories worked, even when there were children under 6 years in the family. On the other hand, in homes where the husband was present, only 23 per cent of the mothers with young children worked.
5. Of all working mothers, what proportion are	More than 80 per cent of working mothers have	In March 1965 about 8 million working mothers were

Content selected from United States Department of Labor, Women's Bureau, Leaflet 37, Who Are the Working Mothers? 1966. Washington, D.C., U.S. Government Printing Office.

*The term "working mothers," refers to workers who have children under 18 years of age, unless otherwise designated.

**The labor force covers persons 14 years of age and over who are either employed or seeking work.

vorced or away from home. Of thirty-nine million children living with both parents, including adopted parents and step-parents, nearly six million had one parent who was remarried (Midcentury White House Conference on Children and Youth, 1951a).

Rutledge (1960) reported:

... About a third of a million new children a year are affected by divorce or annulment. The number ... orphaned each year is slightly higher than this. However, most divorced and bereaved parents remarry. In 1958 approximately 87 per cent of families with children under 18 had two parents. ... Of the other

TABLE 1. (Continued)

QUESTIONS		ANSWERS
from homes in which the husband is present?	husbands living in the homes.	from homes where the husband was present. The other 1.7 million were widowed, divorced or separated from their husbands for other reasons.
6. Does family income influence a mother's decision to work?	Yes. Far more mothers work outside the home when the family income is low than when it is high.	In families where the husband's income is less than $3,000 the mother is very likely to be in paid employment. In March 1965 this was true of 44 per cent of the mothers with children 6 to 17 years of age only and 29 per cent of those with children under 6 years. When the husband's income was $7,000 or over, the proportions were about 35 per cent and 15 percent, respectively.
7. Is a mother more inclined to seek employment if female relatives are members of her household?	Yes, particularly if she has young children and a female relative is available to look after them during the mother's absence from home.	In families with children under 6 years of age, 32 per cent of the mothers worked when a female relative lived with the family and did not work. This proportion dropped to 23 per cent for mothers who did not have such assistance.

Employment of Mothers

8. Why do mothers of young children work outside the home?	With relatively few exceptions, they need the money their earnings provide.	Many families cannot manage without the mother's earnings. Even if the husband is employed, his salary alone may not be sufficient to meet everyday needs. Of all working mothers with children under 6 years of age, 18 per cent had husbands whose income was less than $3,000, and 29 per cent had husbands with incomes between $3,000 and $5,000. The comparable percentages for working mothers with older children (6 to 17 years of age only) were 13 per cent and 21 per cent, respectively.

13 per cent . . . seven million children [were] living with only one parent or neither parent; 4,100,000 of these with the mother; 600,000 with the father; and most of the others with relatives.

Generalizations on the effect of situations such as these are inappropriate, since much depends on the adjustments of the individual with whom the child lives.

A study by Sears et al. (1946) suggests effects on the young child of the father's absence. Boys three, four and five years of age, from homes from which the father was absent, had much less fantasy aggression than boys from homes in which the father was present. How the father's role contributes toward the sex-typing of boys in respect to their expression of aggression was not discovered. Possible influences suggested are the father's provision of a more aggressive model and a more permissive environment for aggression than the mother provides, and the father's greater aggressiveness operating as a frustration to his son.

According to Stolz et al. (1954), when fathers were away from home at the time of and for more than ten months after the birth of their first child, the children had more difficult adjustments in their early years after the father's return than those in families in which the parents were not separated by war for their first-born's first year.

A home may include three generations of a family. Again, generalization is inappropriate about the effect on the child. Whether the grandparents live with the family or the family with the grandparents, individual characteristics are the most pertinent elements. Ellenwood (1940) suggested that it is necessary for the grandmother

> . . . to be so many people. . . . She is a mother who must gracefully relinquish her authority. . . . In addition . . . she is a mother-in-law, . . . she has to carve a relationship with a person whom fate picked out of the mob . . . Then, she is a grandparent. . . . Always in between Grandma and the baby hover the forbidding parents. . . . And so many rules have completely turned around since Grandma brought her baby into the world!

We have discussed the obvious differences in family patterns (constellations or configurations), such as employment of both parents outside the home, the presence of only one parent or of a grandparent. But greater differences in family structures are in the many aspects and processes indicated in various sections of this chapter. The heritages, interactions, sequences of values, the climate (physical, emotional and in terms of ideas) within the home and outside are the essence of each family. Even though methods of studying orderly trends according to some of these categories are being established, this is not a basis for assuming that a particular family will fit into a certain generalized picture. Sterotyping a family on the basis of particular components is especially questionable, since the interrelation of many variables has not been investigated.

The following observations concerning behavior and practices of individual families are included to emphasize the uniqueness of each group. They also emphasize the importance in sensitivity to a family (as to an individual) of knowledge and thought which go beyond surface responses or material things. Another important consideration is what matters and why, for each family member and for the family as a unit. Such information is not for purposes of judging, but rather for understanding the child's setting for growth and development. A few unique elements in the constellation of the family members are suggested in the following examples.

Mary and Ellen were of similar age. Mary's mother was gay and friendly and had a leisurely manner. Her father seemed matter-of-fact. The children were encouraged to be self-reliant and individual. Mary was the fourth child in a family of five, all girls except the oldest. Her play at home involved attempts to do what the older children were doing; one day football appealed to her; another day, tap dancing.

Ellen's mother seemed quiet and calm. In home management she planned so that routines and activities proceeded smoothly. The father liked logical thinking. He encouraged Ellen's interest in facts, stories and music. From the time she was a baby Ellen's parents took her with them whenever they went out in the evenings. She could sleep at the friends' house and remained in bed until her parents took her home. As the older of two girls, she enjoyed helping her mother take care of the baby.

In these two families some of the aspects usually considered in study, such as socioeconomic factors, education of the parents and place of residence, are similar. Both parents are in the home, and the children are not having behavior difficulties. The two families present details useful in beginning to gain an understanding of the child's setting. Nevertheless the details are not to be labeled as either commendable or questionable.

Unique elements in certain child-rearing practices are suggested in the families described below. Davis and Havighurst (1947) contrast two families with different socioeconomic or social class variables.

"Mealtime" or "bed-time," and other similar restrictions mean little or nothing to the Washington children. They may play on the streets after dark; they do not have to go to bed until the adults go. They eat their meals whenever they wish to and . . . they do not have to eat if they do not want to.

At two years, the Washington twins were crossing the street alone; at three years, they often roamed three or four blocks from home. At three, also, they crossed the carline alone to spend their own pennies at the candy store.

The Brett family, on the other hand, has a diet wide and varied, and each child has his own room and goes to bed at nine o'clock. They have a variety of toys. Mrs. Brett "keeps her children in their playroom or in their spacious yard. Nor does she allow them to stay in the yard after six, even in summer."

Again, without judging, without implying that similar aims or procedures are appropriate for all families, it is possible to consider these facts about the Washingtons and the Bretts and many others in viewing the family.

FAMILY ORIENTATIONS

Other components of the family scene selected for inclusion here pertain to such aspects as space and equipment, health and food practices, home management and routines, housing, rural and urban settings, and socioeconomic elements.

Physical Climate

Consideration of physical climate, as contrasted with emotional, intellective and cultural climate, and with relations of family members, begins to focus attention on material aspects which affect the child's development. These aspects pertain, first, to food, warmth and shelter, and then, secondarily, to opportunities for the individual to unfold in a way that involves use of his abilities. Sunshine, fresh air, opportunities for rest, sleep and exercise, safe milk supply, satisfactory sanitation and protection against disease are of primary importance. The child's use of his abilities is affected by physical climate.

Evidence of the influence of any particular material factor at a level different from one of survival or physical health is not clear-cut. Again, the many differences between families warrant emphasis on the multiplicity of variables affecting growth rather than a cause and effect connection between such factors as specific foods, living arrangements, space, play opportunities and development. Whatever the particular physical aspects of the home, the adult who keeps in mind values which he feels are essential in his family, and uses ingenuity to provide them, has an advantage.

Values of *space* are well known. Until research findings are available in this field, listing possible influences may encourage thought about relation of behavior and situations. A place where he can have fresh air and sunshine and a small area for exercise may be sufficient for the infant, but the child who has begun to explore the world on his own two feet seeks more room. As children grow, they like space that is their own, where they can keep their own things and play their own games without running the risk of hearing frequent complaints because they are under foot. They are sometimes noisy in ways which can be a source of irritation to the family or to the neighbors. Fear of annoying the neighbors or of what they will say may affect a parent's attitude toward his child.

The needs of the adults and children who make up the family differ in many respects. The problem is often one of adjusting to meet the needs of one without totally sacrificing the needs of the others. On the whole, a house is built for adults; much of the furniture and equipment is for adults. Yet children live in that house, and the extent to which it may facilitate their growth and development varies. Respect for furniture and walls is not inherent in children; a child misses something if there is no equipment or furniture which he is allowed to rearrange to make a train or to set up a house or tent by covering it with an old blanket. Imaginative play is too important in a child's life to deprive him of it in his home. But adults' needs are also important. The mother who is in need of quiet rest should be able to get away from eager boys who may play at being various kinds of noisy airplanes.

Whether it be a corner of a room or a lower drawer or shelf, space within reach of the child's arms and assigned to his use enables him to feel that this is his own for his own things. Not only providing the space, but also respecting it and keeping it free from intrusion are important to him. He will not wish to have his things, no matter how absurd they may seem to the unimaginative adult, ruthlessly cleared out. Having no possessions of their own, no space for their own things, and no guidance in respecting the possessions of others may explain some children's difficulties in learning respect for property and for the rights of others.

Equipment of the home can aid in encouraging particular practices.

When the adults of the family begin to emphasize the importance of having clean hands before meals, the child may find that washing before dinner is a matter of a hurried wash at the high kitchen sink at the hands of some grown-up when he comes in from play; or the washing may entail a long trip upstairs to a bathroom where everything is difficult to reach. Convenient arrangements of equipment may provide a way for young children to learn to wash themselves and to reach their own towels, facecloths and toothbrushes. Low hooks or racks, a chair or box to help the child to reach a high bowl, or a separate basin which can be set on a low stool, may facilitate learning. A hook for outdoor clothing that is within the child's reach makes it possible for him to assume the responsibility of hanging up his garments. Tables and chairs appropriate for his size, so that feet need not dangle or arms stretch upwards, may make the difference between his being comfortable and being uncomfortable at meals.

Equipment can make "helping mother" in household tasks pleasurable and within the realm of possibility. The preschool child has the skill, the strength and the interest to help in many ways. He may assist in wiping some of the dishes or use a small mop or broom. He will not give a skilled performance, but he can be learning to share responsibility.

Use of a "grown-up" bed instead of a crib may promote self-reliance. Self-reliance, in a constructive way, may develop if "things" are not too precious in the eyes of the mother or father, if each is able to bear with some serenity some possibly inevitable destruction or marring as family possessions are used by family members. In contrast, if no respect for property is in the child's setting and experience, he has no opportunity to learn it.

With reference to the *economic factor*, extreme poverty or wealth can inject certain difficulties into the family situation that may be among the predisposing factors to a family breakdown.

An income which is so small that it has nothing to allot to recreation (which is re-creation), or which allows no margin for meeting the emergency of sickness or for saving, puts upon those responsible for the care of the children—especially if they are carrying that responsibility conscientiously—a burden which is difficult to bear without worry. Difficulties may arise from wide discrepancies between income and standards of taste and living. Worry creates tension and thereby destroys a certain serenity important to happy life. Wise planning and an ability to differentiate between essentials and nonessentials can do much to alleviate some of the difficulties of maintaining a satisfactory family life in accordance with income. Values to be gained in a family in which there is careful money management may include a spirit of cooperation and helpfulness, self-reliance, a willingness to do without and to give up in order that someone else may have.

The disadvantages of having too little are obvious; the disadvantages of having too much, though less obvious, are nevertheless important. The home in which it is economically easy to provide the child with everything he needs may fail to provide him with opportunities to learn to depend on himself or to feel that what he does needs to be done. He may come to overestimate the importance of self if his every need is supplied and every desire gratified.

It is not possible to translate the term "sufficient income" into dollars and cents, for many factors enter into the calculation. Time and place, the cost of living and standards of living make "sufficient income" almost an individual matter. Children must be sheltered, clothed, fed, protected against disease, cared for if sickness occurs, and educated to meet life as successfully—not only in the material sense—as possible; but individual interpretations as to how this should be done are so varied as to make a definite statement impossible. (See Figures 15 and 16.)

Much of money management is allied with decision-making. Some of the research in this field focuses on what people decide to buy, with an attempt in some instances to discover why (Fitzsimmons and Manning, 1962; Foote, 1960; Wells, 1959). The University of Minnesota Family Study Center began research which uses the developmental approach in a three-generation consumership study (Foote, 1960; Shanas and Streib, 1965).

As in money management, decisions the family makes about health practices, foods and use of time are pertinent to an understanding of the setting it provides. Procedures may be followed in these areas without awareness that a decision is being made, or may be followed after deliberation.

Health Practices

Health practices comprise the daily way of living by which the physical needs of the body are met. Good practices are therefore important in maintaining the health of an individual. Health of each member of the family is important for the group. Healthy parents are in a better position to provide good care for their children. Parents who are hungry, sick or constantly fatigued are handicapped in providing such care. Good health routines will contribute to a state of surplus energy and vitality, characteristics of a healthy person.

When a man and a woman marry, they bring to their new family unit firmly established health habits and attitudes. If these habits are similar, few adjustments are necessary; if they differ considerably, some adjustment must occur. The resulting habits and attitudes become part of the environment and can have a significant effect on the habits and attitudes which will be established by their children.

Habits built up over the years have been determined by circumstances, by understanding of the body's needs and by one's feelings as an individual. Some people are neglectful of their physical needs; some people are overconcerned; others have learned routines which are satisfactory and follow them in a comfortable manner. These last can more easily establish ways of living that will meet the physical needs of each member of the family and create wholesome attitudes toward fulfilling these needs.

Food Practices

Food practices, although a facet of health practices, are dealt with individually (1) because of the importance of food in sustaining life and providing for growth and development, and (2) because of the multiplicity of factors contributing to these habits. An individual's attitude toward food is an expression of his total personality; therefore understanding his behavior in respect to food is related to understanding some of the facets of his personality. A person may tend to be inflexible in eating behavior, or may be flexible and readily accept a variety of foods and new foods. Each person enters marriage with a definite pattern of behavior in respect to food, and the partners set up an environment which can influence the feeling and behavior of their children toward food.

With man, food is not just food; "it is the crossroads of emotions, religion, tradition, and habit. That to which we are accustomed seems natural, while the strange seems unnatural and undesirable" (Graubard, 1943).

Emotions affect what one eats and how one feels about it. People tend to eat what they like. They eat for satisfaction, for relief from hunger, and pleasure from taste or flavor. Generally, this hunger is physiological; however, an unsatisfied psychological hunger is sometimes met by eating. Thus a lonely or unhappy person may use food as a substitute for an unfulfilled need (Bruch, 1957; Rabinovitch and Fischoff, 1952). A person may eat too little or too much when he is anxious or worried. Pleasant or unpleasant experiences associated with a particular food may strongly affect later feelings about it. Food well prepared, served in an appetizing fashion and eaten in good company can create pleasant memories and lead to later enjoyment of the same kind of food. Conversely, food of poor quality, served in unpleasant surroundings or amid unhappy interpersonal relations can lead to unpleasant memories and possible rejection of such food at a later time. Unhappy mealtime experiences may lead to later disinterest in food in general. Thus emotions are a potent force in molding food practices.

Religion, with its taboos and rituals surrounding food, affects the food habits of many. The dietary laws of orthodox Jews, fasting of Roman Catholics during Lent and the exclusion of animal foods by the Hindus are examples.

Tradition, which includes all the social and cultural factors, has a strong effect on the foods selected, food preparation, and behavior associated with eating. Meat, boiled potatoes and vegetables and porridge are acceptable to the British; spaghetti with cheese and a well-seasoned sauce is a mainstay of the Italian diet. American families reveal the heritage of food patterns. Sometimes this cultural heritage has become only a remnant; sometimes it remains as a strong influence.

Food is often chosen because of its prestige value. Certain foods, to some, carry a connotation of wealth and position. In every society some foods are rarer, finer, more delicate, more desirable, more expensive than others. Social groupings tend to express themselves in food. That foods have a status value is indicated by the fact that many families have foods which are served only when guests are present, and others which the family will eat and enjoy themselves, but would be unwilling to serve to guests. The stubbornness with which the American public has clung to white bread, despite the educational campaigns to encourage the use of dark breads, has sometimes been explained by the long history of prestige value of white over dark bread which came from Europe, where white bread, plentiful white sugar and meat every day were symbols of high social status. In addition to foods themselves, the way food is served and behavior at mealtime reflect social heritage and social status.

Custom is a strong force in determining our food habits. The food patterns of an individual who has grown up in a family in which there has been a wide experience with different foods will differ from those of one who has had a narrow experience with foods. A person who has lived in a low-income family will have had experiences different from those of one whose family spent more for food. One who has grown up in a family in which food was merely a means of satisfying hunger will have attitudes toward food quite different from those of one whose family enjoyed food and made mealtime a social time or a time for consolidating family ties. A person who grew up in a family in which the food was planned around someone in the group who required a special diet because of a chronic illness such as diabetes may look upon food differently from another whose family dietary was not thus focused. One person may have learned to look upon food with boredom, another may have acquired a deep interest in food. Thus many patterns result from associations accumulated during the growing years.

The manner in which differences are reconciled at marriage depends on the people involved and the circumstances facing them. In the food pattern they establish for their family, the couple can determine to a large degree how their offspring will feel about food and whether they will be well fed or misfed. For further discussion of cultural influences on food habits, see Lee (1957) and Mead (1950).

Family Food Patterns in the United States

In the United States we live in an affluent society. One characteristic of such a society, a relatively high standard of living, is reflected in expenditures for food and in changes in food patterns and habits. Stiebling (1959) says that food in the United States "costs less in proportion to income than in most parts of the world. Wages for an hour of work in 1959 bought more food, a greater variety of food, and food of a higher market quality than ever before. Middle income groups, both farm and city, spend about one-third of the family budget for food. Low-income city families spend a much larger share." In a 1955 sampling of American households (Murray and Blake, 1959) the low-income group spent 48 per cent of their income on food; the median income group spent 37 per cent; the high-income group, 29 per cent. The low-income families bought less food and paid less for it than the other groups.

In addition to more food in terms of wages, greater variety and higher quality, the American family has more time-saving and work-saving foods, such as ready-to-serve, ready-to-eat, processed, packaged and frozen foods (Miller, 1962).

Among the changes related to food practices taking place in families, Lantis (1962) lists (1) more piecemeal eating, (2) more eating away from home, and (3) greater consumption of liquids other than water.

Piecemeal eating away from home can be observed in the habit of the coffee break; food and drink at recreational centers, including bowling alleys, parks, playgrounds; the popcorn, soft drinks, ice cream consumed at a summer concert; soft drinks purchased at a gas station. The vending machine is encouraging these practices. The physiological effect of between-meal eating upon body composition is being studied (Review, 1961a).

More meals are being eaten away from home in such places as nursery schools and day-care centers, elementary and high schools and restaurants. The working members of the family, usually of necessity, have the midday meal elsewhere; so do many children.

That people are consuming more liquids other than water is documented by the increase in the consumption of fruit juices over fresh fruits and the increase in use of coffee (from 9 pounds per person in 1910 to 16 pounds per person in 1959) and soft drinks (per capita consumption 184.2 bottles in 1955 and 192 bottles in 1960) (Lantis, 1962).

The current practices in food purchasing and the variety available give the impression of increased choice in foods. This, however, according to Lantis (1962), can be "illusory and misleading." The choice at breakfast, for instance, may not be eggs or cereal, but rather of a variety of packaged cereals. Foods offered in vending machines, at drugstores or food concessions are limited. This reinforces a person's timidity in trying new foods.

Food purchased at the store and served at the table or eaten on the run is very remote from that food as it was produced and passed through processing and marketing.

As fewer children have the opportunity to observe the steps by which a food reaches the table or vending machine, as foods become available at all seasons, and as less time is required for preparation in the kitchen, the opportunity to learn the intrinsic value of food is diminished. Lantis (1962) says that "if a child does not feel . . . that a food is precious, one wonders whether the child can readily understand or sense that any specific food, or food element, is vital to him." The responsibility of helping a child to make food choices and to learn to deal with "inducements to buy food and drink," to recognize values for his money, to have satisfactory technical knowledge falls primarily upon the family. This begins in the early years.

Leverton (1967) reports basic nutrition concepts "stated in lay language . . . considered . . . most needed by everyone in making decisions about food that would promote a desirable level of health and growth":

1. Nutrition is the food you eat and how the body uses it.
2. Food is made up of different nutrients needed for growth and health.

3. All persons throughout life have need for the same nutrients, but in varying amounts.

4. The way food is handled influences the amount of nutrients in food, its safety, appearance, and taste.

Thinking of these concepts as "meanings that direct a person's responses and decisions," we can see possibilities for learning, not only by adults, but also by children. Early steps in concept formation in young children are discussed on page 358. Motivations are discussed on page 13.

Home Management and Routines

A woman brings to her marriage certain values for homemaking from her own family. Millar (1961), in a study of three generations in six families, found that all the families shared the goals of home ownership and rearing a family. Most had a high standard for atmosphere in the home. Home management practices, however, tended to be shaped by patterns of each generation.

One of a wife's tasks is the organization of her work as a homemaker. How she does this depends on her training and experience and on the circumstances surrounding her new life. She may have had experience with household tasks; she may continue outside employment; she may share in her husband's work, as in families living on a farm. On the other hand, her only responsibility may be keeping the home and providing for the needs of her husband. Some women are very much aware that this is a time of preparation for the years when the family is growing; others are less aware of it. This is a period of learning to live together. It can be a period of discussion, compromise, sharing and planning from which an agreed way of living evolves.

Division of labor in household tasks often reflects the feeling of the man and the woman about roles in the home, and this, in turn, reflects experiences in their homes as they grew up. These attitudes of the woman and of the man toward their roles provide early orientation for the child concerning masculine and feminine roles. In one study (Hartley, 1959) of children's reports of activities of men and women, approximately two-thirds of the women's activities were in the domestic realm, whereas most of the men's activities pertained to physical strength and stamina and were performed outside the home. (See also pages 39 and 408-409.)

It takes time to perform daily duties. A study in New York state (Warren, 1952) showed that it took the average homemaker 6.3 hours a day for homemaking if she lived in the city and 7.0 hours if she lived on a farm. It has been said that today people are more comfortable and cleaner, healthier, better looking and more stylish. To accomplish this takes more time and much work. The first years of marriage are ones in which the art of homemaking, the learning of effective and easy ways of performing the daily household tasks can be discovered. Learning the easy ways can help to accomplish the work with a minimum of strain on the body and to reduce fatigue with its accompanying nervous tension, irritability and effect on disposition and appearance.

With the growth of the family, time required for homemaking

changes. In the New York state study the average homemaker with children less than eighteen years of age spent 8.1 hours a day in homemaking if she lived in the city and 8.2 hours if she lived on a farm. Work is especially heavy when the children are young. According to Wiegand (1954), in families in which the youngest child was under two years of age the mother spent an average of more than nine hours a day in homemaking. In families in which the youngest child was between four and nine, nearly 7½ hours were used. In families with the youngest between ten and seventeen years the time dropped to less than six hours.

Some couples use certain "tools" for carrying through a plan for family living (Gutheim, 1948). These include a budget, a schedule and a plan for use of the home related to characteristics of the family members. Ways of using money and time for both work and leisure by each person and by the whole family can enter into the plan. These "tools" can be used in such a manner that they do not become the masters of the users, but are a means of providing a smoothly operating family.

Schedules change from time to time, and changes take place as the family grows. Figure 8 shows how a woman's day changes. In the early

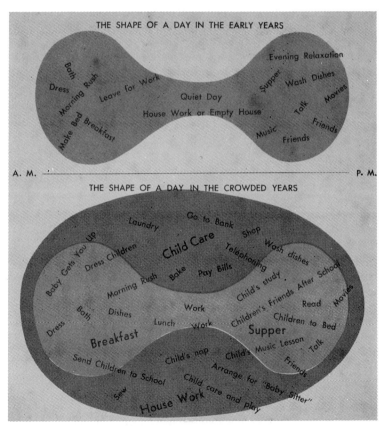

FIGURE 8. *Role functions have great contrasts in the early stages of the family life cycle.*

(Reproduced from F. Gutheim: Houses for Family Living. New York, The Woman's Foundation, Inc., 1948.)

years the crowded times come in the morning and the evening. In the middle of the day the woman is alone to do her housework and any other activities she might choose. When children arrive, the mother is busy all day with child care and housework. She has the care of the children and housework to be synchronized. In addition, if her day can be planned so that she is not fatigued at the end of it, she will have energy for enjoyment of times when her husband is at home.

Gross (1959), reviewing research in home management, states that saving energy is not a concern for many today because of the decrease in energy cost of today's homemaking activities, but that the effective use of the body to avoid strain on muscles and organs needs further investigation. Her review shows "earlier interest in general time management and then in 'energy' management giving way to special problems in the case of these resources."

Paolucci (1966), emphasizing that a concept of management involves conscious direction, suggests that decisions to be made are often social and economic. There may be a conflict in values among family members or between those of the family and other social groups, or decisions may concern limited resources, such as money and physical capacity.

The amount of planning, as well as the ways of performing household tasks, varies greatly from one family to another. Recently stated concepts concerning home management include (among others) the following generalizations (American Home Economics Association, 1967):

1. Decision-making reflects varying degrees of rationality.
2. The decisions of individuals and families reflect differences in the perception of goals and goal achievements.
3. The organization [of activities] of different individuals, and families differs in aim and effect.
4. The perception of available resources may enhance or limit the management potential of individuals and families.

Again, ideas such as these, or others, may have bases in the learning of the young child.

Housing

The place in which the family lives has qualities pertinent to its total well-being. Housing may facilitate family living or cause a strain. Lack of space and privacy for children and their parents can contribute to conflicts and tensions; health hazards are created. These are intensified when lack of space is accompanied by substandard housing and surroundings which not only make it impossible for the basic needs of individuals to be met, but also are breeding places for disease. Children who live in slum areas, with crowding, poor houses and the other deprivations which accompany such conditions and are related to low income, are more likely to have serious health and social problems than children living in other areas. Figure 9 demonstrates that poor housing means poor chances for children. Rates of juvenile delinquency, truancy, in-

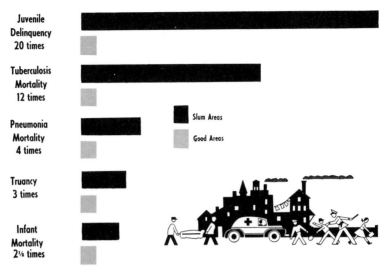

FIGURE 9. *Slum areas have higher mortality and delinquency rates than other areas.*

A graphic presentation of social and economic facts important in the lives of children and youth. Figures from the Chicago Housing Authority. (Reproduced from Children and Youth at the Midcentury. Raleigh, N.C., Health Publications Institute, Inc., 1951.)

fant mortality, and tuberculosis and pneumonia mortality among children are higher in slum areas, according to figures from the Chicago Housing Authority. In Worcester (Macleod, 1961) a higher accident rate was found in deteriorating, overcrowded neighborhoods. In Baltimore (Wilner et al., 1961) accident rates were one-third lower in housing projects than in poor housing areas.

A five-year longitudinal study of housing environment and family was begun in Baltimore in 1954 (Wilner et al., 1960, 1961). The test group, those who were moving to better housing in a housing project, were compared with a control group consisting of those who did not move. All were low-income Negro families. Results after three years indicated lower illness rates and fewer accidents in the test group. The women were interviewed about their experiences at the beginning and again at eighteen months after the change in housing. Those living in the housing project, in contrast to those in the control group, indicated that they liked their apartments. The play space for children was safer; they had more space; they could more easily have privacy when desired; they had more neighborly and supportive interaction and were more apt to form friendships among neighbors. They felt improvement in their social position, but no heightening of aspirations. The test group further expressed interest in activities for keeping up the project, had general pride in it, and expressed favorable views of the project's adequacy as a place to live and rear children in. Both adults and children frequently used the project's community center, but indicated no difference from the control group in items of broader neighborhood or community concern. In psychosocial tests the directional trends in favor of the test group were more likely to be in the area of general morale (optimism, pessimism, satisfaction with personal state of affairs, potency) than in areas involving stressful, inner feelings (mood, control of temper, nervousness).

The basic principles of healthful housing, according to Pond (1946), may be grouped under four broad headings: meeting the physiological and the psychological needs of the individual, protection against contagion, and protection against accidents.

Meeting physiological needs covers the areas of regulation of temperature, ventilation, light, protection against excessive noise, and provision of adequate space for exercise and play for the children.

Meeting psychological needs includes provision of adequate privacy for the various members of the family, provision of opportunities for normal family life, provision for facilities which make possible the performance of household tasks without undue physical and mental fatigue, provision of opportunities for normal community life, provision of facilities for maintenance of cleanliness of the dwelling and the people in the family, and concordance with the prevailing social standards of the local community.

Protection against contagion involves safe and adequate water supply, adequate toilet and sewage facilities, absence of vermin, sanitary conditions in the vicinity, provision of facilities for keeping milk and food fresh, and provision of sufficient space in sleeping rooms to minimize the danger of infection by contact.

Protection against accidents includes a safe dwelling, elimination of fire hazards, protection against the danger of electrical shocks or burns, protection against falls and other mechanical injuries, and protection of the neighborhood against the hazards of automobile traffic. Housing which conforms to these basic principles provides an environment for healthful living.

Beyer (1960), discussing plans for a house, refers to the psychophysiological and social aspects as well as the technical aspects. Under psychophysiological aspects he includes provision for health and comfort, for mental and emotional satisfaction and for personal values. He comments on more considerations of the variables of a house which have an influence on family members through the senses and produce reactions "falling somewhere along a number of continuums—from satisfaction to frustration, from tenseness to relaxation, from interest to boredom, from beauty to ugliness." The social aspects include planning for different kinds of families, i.e., families of various compositions, and their interpersonal relations.

Alterations in the dominant housing values as changes occur in the family life cycle are reported by Douner et al. (1968).

Selection of a home by husband and wife for their family is influenced by elements such as income, availability of houses or sites for renting, buying or building, and personal preferences. They may have little choice because of limiting circumstances, but through ingenuity may make a seemingly impossible spot comfortable. Planning houses for families includes reference to flexibility in plan and arrangement

(Gutheim, 1948). Ideally, it has characteristics such as the following: It changes as the children grow and as human needs change; it changes from time to time with different activities. It is planned to minimize waste of space and to make actions efficient. It includes centers of family living, with places for noise and places for quiet, places for getting together and places for being alone. In other words, the house fits the family needs, whether it be quiet for the father after a hard day, peace of mind for the mother so that she can work and supervise the children, with children's play space near work space, or privacy for the older children when the young ones bother them.

Farm, Rural Nonfarm, Urban and Suburban Settings

Whether a child and his family live on a farm, in a rural, nonfarm area, in an urban or a suburban situation affects experiences family members are likely to have. Stott (1945), in a study of Nebraska families, reported differences between only children who were town and city children and those on isolated farms who had few contacts with children of other families. In Ohio farm families studied by Hoeflin (1954) child-rearing practices with preschool children were more often than not in accordance with currently recommended procedures; no significant relation between socioeconomic status and child-rearing scores was found.

Role patterns of husbands and wives did not vary systematically with residence areas in a comparison of Iowa rural and urban families (Burchinal and Bauder, 1965). Decision-making patterns were relatively similar in the Iowa families. In a comparison of families living on farms near Detroit and families living in the city itself, power relations were relatively similar. Family role patterns differed in activities concerning the family's physical and financial well-being (Blood and Wolfe, 1960).

Barker et al. (1951, 1955, 1961, 1963) studied setting in the sense of the psychological habitat of a child. They considered community behavior and family behavior settings. They emphasized participation in various situations and the richness of this participation in relation to the child's behavior, social action and interaction. The behavior setting unit involved time, place and behavior.

Barker and Barker (1961) reported differences between Kansas and England:

We have been able to describe the behavior possibilities for various age groups within communities by the use of this unit. For example, 52 per cent of the behavior settings of Midwest, Kansas, have no age segregation, i.e., all ages are present in them, while only 23 per cent of the settings of Yoredale, Yorkshire, are similarly unsegregated. . . . Preschool children enter more of Midwest's 579 settings (61 per cent) than of Yoredale's 494 behavior settings (42 per cent). We conjecture that the life experience of a child is quite different if he ranges over more of the community, and if his associates are people of all ages than if he is more restricted to his own age group and fewer settings. . . . Behavior settings coerce the behavior within them so we can at least predict that the wider settings entrance of the Midwest children gives them a larger repertoire of behavior than is possible for the Yoredale preschool children.

This reference to associations which small-town settings provide also seems pertinent to experiences of city and suburban children. Where the child spends his time and with whom gives a wide range in repertoires of behavior from one city child to another.

Frequency with which people move and the directions they go are reported in Figure 12. Figure 13 indicates percentages in central cities, suburbs and other areas.

Socioeconomic Variations

Not only the location, rural or urban, but also the style of life provided is a facet of the family. For variations in this the term "socioeconomic variables" is sometimes used, as is also the term "social class." Hoffman and Lippitt (1960) mention different interpretations of *social class*:

> To some researchers, class represents a way of life; to some, power over resources and persons; to some, reputation or esteem. Some investigators regard class as an objective phenomenon, to others it is entirely subjective; and even those who agree on its subjectivity disagree whether it is a perception of the self or of others. The number of classes in our society has usually been placed at between two and six, although some researchers think of it as a continous ranking system with almost as many positions as there are families to be classified.

Decisions as to which measures to use also vary. After finding that nineteen different indices were highly correlated, Kahl and Davis (1955) concluded that for many purposes the simplest measure was the breadwinner's occupation. Another study (Haer, 1957) found the greatest ability to predict various attitudes and behavior in an index or score which used ratings in several categories. This particular index includes a number of ratings within the following categories: occupation, source of income, house type and area lived in (Warner, 1953).

Child-rearing practices in a particular social class may vary with time. For example, two studies, ten years apart, revealed different relations between social class and child-rearing practices (Havighurst and Davis, 1955). In the 1940's a shift toward more permissiveness occurred among middle-class parents (Bronfenbrenner, 1958). One of the theories which may explain change in parental practice at all social levels refers to the changing relations in the employment situations of the parents.

> Miller and Swanson (1958) offer [an] explanation, which views class differences within the context of larger societal settings they call "entrepreneurial" and "bureaucratic." They contend that the growing complexity of economic organization, the continued increase in urbanism, and the decreased rate of immigration have changed the meaning of social class. Child-rearing patterns have correspondingly changed in such a way that the child's resulting personality will enable him to pursue more effectively an occupation in the family's current setting. For example, risk taking may have been appropriate behavior for the middle class in an entrepreneurial society, but in a bureaucratic society a security orientation is more appropriate. This changed requirement is presumed to be reflected in child-rearing practices, thus fitting the child psychologically for his probable adult occupation (Hoffman and Lippitt, 1960).

In addition to differences in child-rearing practices, differences in families rated according to their socioeconomic characteristics have been reported in social mobility, family routines and rituals, patterns of family work and play, and family reactions to crisis. Less education, a higher percentage of illness and of tooth extractions resulting from neglect, earlier marriage and higher proneness to divorce have been reported for less privileged groups (Duvall, 1967; Koos, 1954). In research on the influences of the family on the child's development, it is difficult to try to determine what qualities in the family members these differences reflect.

The subtlety of socioeconomic influences has been stressed. Allison Davis (Midcentury White House Conference on Children and Youth, 1951c) refers to effects of a family's having been hungry, cold and without adequate shelter and light, to its having been uncertain that basic needs would be met. Then, when these needs have been met, the desire of the child and the adult for much more than adequate provision is explained in terms of a learned fear of deprivation. In families in which anxieties such as these were less pressing the children had more pressures from their families for early and rapid attainment and for conscientious work habits which made them work harder in school.

THE FAMILY AND THE COMMUNITY

A few of the many aspects of a broader world in relation to which families function will be presented here. The families provide some of the trends in communities and are in turn affected by them. Trends in population, size of family, mobility, place of living, employment of women, income, expenditures, absence of the father, and school enrollment are illustrated in Figures 10 through 18. These elements of a changing world, and others suggested here below, are closely connected with situations in which children grow and develop, and to which they will be adapting as they grow older.

A Changing World

Some of the trends in the United States, indicated in Figures 10 through 18, are of course allied with some of the trends of the modern world. Urbanization, industrialization, increased communication, and threat of total war are often mentioned. The large numbers of people, mechanization, the wide variety of experiences and ideas, and the uncertainties on a world-wide scale affect families directly and indirectly (Heilbroner, 1960; Schramm, Lyle and Parker, 1961; Srole et al., 1962). With a realization that the modern world has many other sides, it seems pertinent to add that "Era of Violence" is the title of a volume of the New Cambridge Modern History (1960) which considers most recent times from 1898 to the present.

Text continues on page 72

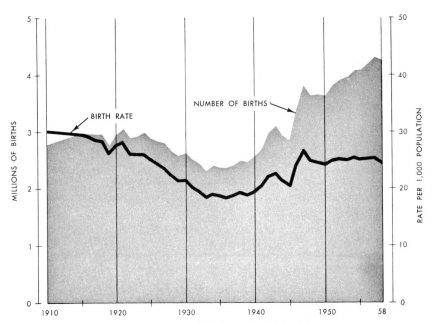

FIGURE 10. **Birth rate and number of births in the United States.**

"The population of the United States is increasing rapidly. This is due partly to decreasing death rates for all ages and partly to increasing numbers of births. The birth
rate itself, which means the number of births per thousand population, is not rising,
because our total population is being made up of larger and larger proportions of
children and old people. But the number of births per thousand women of child bearing age is still increasing and more and more women are having a third or fourth
child." (Golden Anniversary White House Conference on Children and Youth, 1960,
and United States Bureau of the Census.)
    Information from the United States Bureau of the Census is as follows:

	1955	1960	1965
Population	165,069,000	179,323,000	193,818,000
Births	3,923,000	4,288,000	4,169,000
Birth rate	25 per 1000		19 per 1000

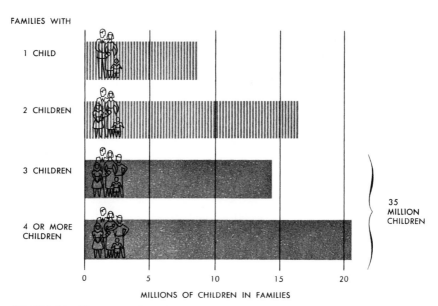

FIGURE 11. *The proportion of families with children under 18 increased from 52 per cent in 1948 to 56 per cent in 1958 to 56.9 per cent in 1960, and was 56.6 in 1965.*

The increase in the number of children per family has been far greater in urban and rural nonfarm families than in farm families. (Golden Anniversary White House Conference on Children and Youth, 1960, and United States Bureau of the Census.)

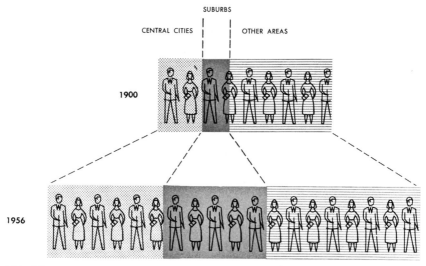

FIGURE 12. *Expansion of suburban population.*

Cities are not growing as fast as their suburbs. In 1956 some 97.5 million people, or about 59 per cent of the total population, were living in 168 metropolitan areas. These include at least one city of 50,000, perhaps other smaller cities, and their suburbs. Between 1950 and 1956 the suburbs grew nearly three times as fast as the population of the entire United States, and over six times as fast as the central cities. In some areas there has been a net loss of population in the core city. (Golden Anniversary White House Conference on Children and Youth, 1960.)

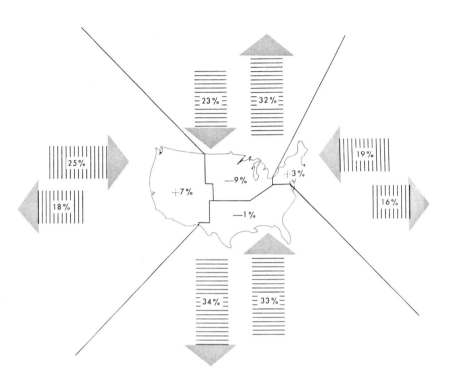

FIGURE 13.   Percentages of people moving into and from 4 regions of the United States. There were 3 million cross-country movers in 1957-58.

"Mobility rates were higher for the non-white population than for the white; about one-fourth of the non-white population moved as compared with one-fifth of the white population. People living in rural non-farm areas were more mobile than people living in rural farm areas or in urban areas. About 16 per cent of the people living in central cities of standard metropolitan areas had moved within the same county during the year. People moving into these central cities, on the other hand, were just as likely to have come from another state as from areas within the same state." (Golden Anniversary White House Conference on Children and Youth, 1960.)

Information from the United States Bureau of the Census for the population 1 year and over is as follows:

	1963 to 1964	1964 to 1965
Total population	185,312,000	187,974,000
Same house	79.9 per cent	79.3 per cent

Different house
    Within a state
    Between states
	3.3 per cent
	3.3 per cent
		3.5 per cent
		3.3 per cent

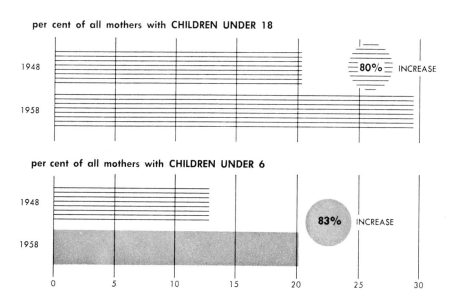

FIGURE 14.   Percentages of working mothers.

In 1958, 7.5 million women with children under 18, about 30 per cent of such mothers, were in the labor force. These include nearly 3 million women with children under 6, or a little over 20 per cent of such mothers. (Golden Anniversary White House Conference on Children and Youth, 1960.)

PER CENT OF TOTAL FAMILY EXPENDITURE OF URBAN FAMILIES

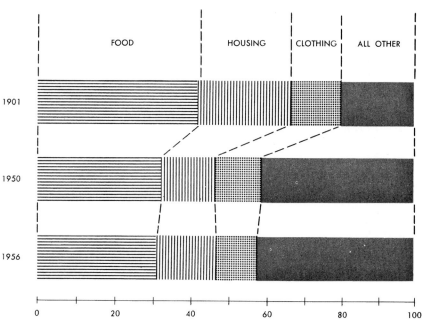

FIGURE 15.   Percentage of total family expenditure of urban families.

Even with increased cost of living, the average city family in the last decade has been able to pay for its food, housing, and clothing with less than 60 per cent of its income, leaving more than 40 per cent for other things. (Golden Anniversary White House Conference on Children and Youth, 1960.)

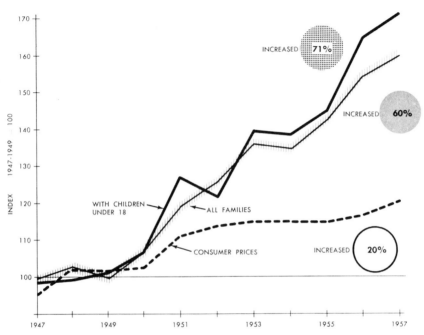

FAMILY INCOME HAS INCREASED

FIGURE 16.   *Increase in family income.*

The median family income in 1957 was $4971, which was 60 per cent above the median family income for 1947-49. During the same period the index of consumer prices rose only 20 per cent.

Very large families tend to have smaller incomes than medium sized ones. The family with 3 children under 18 had a larger income on the average ($5363) than a family of any other size. In 1957 over 39 million children were in families with incomes of $4000 or more, but more than 13 million children were still in families with less than $3000 income. Many of these were in families which had median incomes below the general average — the family headed by a woman ($2763), the farm family ($2490) and the nonwhite family ($2764). (Golden Anniversary White House Conference on Children and Youth, 1960.)

Information from the United States Bureau of the Census on median income of families is as follows:

1947	1950	1955	1960	1964
$3013	$3319	$4421	$5620	$6569

FIGURE 17. *Numbers of children receiving payment under the Social Security Act because of the father's death, absence or disability.*

Most children in the United States under the age of 18 (87 per cent) have a home with 2 parents. But in 1958, of the 25.8 million families with children under 18, 2.8 million (about 11 per cent) were from homes broken by death, divorce or desertion. Although divorce is declining, the number of children involved in divorces has been increasing. Death plays a less important part in the number of broken homes than formerly, as declining death rates have brought about a decline in orphanhood and remarriage rates are high for widowed parents.

An increasing number of children receiving payments under aid to dependent children provisions of the Social Security Act are in families with the father "absent"— separated, estranged, divorced, or never married to the mother, but living. Nevertheless, despite the decline in orphanhood, more children are receiving payments because the father is dead than for any other single reason. A few children also receive benefits because of the death of a working mother. (Golden Anniversary White House Conference on Children and Youth, 1960.)

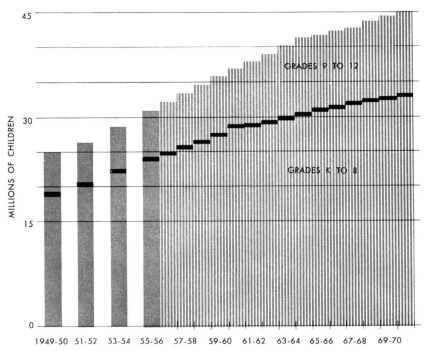

FIGURE 18.   Increasing school enrollment.

The increased number of children means increased school enrollment, and this in turn means a demand for more classroom teachers, more supervisory staff, more desks, more books, more schools. (Golden Anniversary White House Conference on Children and Youth, 1960.)

Information from the United States Bureau of the Census on enrollment of children from kindergarten through high school in public and private schools is as follows:

1950	1955	1960	1965
28,062,000	35,047,000	42,690,000	48,095,000

Influences on the modern American family and the questions they raise for parents and children, suggested by a sociologist, are as follows (Leslie, 1955):

1. The relativity of morals and the search for standards—How to teach the child to be familiar with many standards and accepting of them without leaving him no standards at all?
2. Threat of total war—How to provide children and youth with security which makes them adequate, happy adults at the same time that preparation for war is necessary?
3. Depersonalization of relationships—How to provide satisfying personal relationships when children and parents are in the situation of not really knowing others, or being known by them, even when in a group? How within our kind of society are we going to provide children (and adults) with kinds of intimate personal relationships which make "escapist" behavior unnecessary?
4. Disruption of the kin group—How to enable young unstable families, apart from the example and help of older members of the families, to continue to grow in their security, their moral and ethical values?

For the majority of families there is a continuation of associations with relatives and in-laws with a "kin network" of visiting, mutual aid, and emotional support tending to continue over the life cycle. In relations of the young couple with their parents, a rather recent pattern includes "tacit norms of noninterference" (Leslie, 1967).

Margaret Mead, an anthropologist, stresses rapidity of change in the setting in which families in the United States find themselves today (Midcentury White House Conference on Children and Youth, 1951c):

> American children are growing up within the most rapidly changing culture of which we have any record in the world, within a culture where for several generations, each generation's experience has differed sharply from the last, and in which the experience of the youngest child in a large family will be extraordinarily different from that of the first born. Mothers cannot look back to the experience of their mothers, nor even to that of their older sisters; young husbands and fathers have no guides to the behavior which they are assuming today. So long-standing and so rapid have been these processes of change that expectation of change and anxiety about change have been built into our character as a people. Our homes have become launching platforms from which our children set out on uncharted seas, and we have become correspondingly more anxious that they should be perfectly equipped before they go.

Family Use of Community Services

How the young child feels about his community, what he knows about it and what he does in it are determined to a great extent by his family. Many of his experiences are in the family situation, or in other settings decided upon by family members. How the child feels about his particular heritage and situation has a connection with attitudes of others in his community. His interpretation of their reactions to him and his family will be influenced especially by his parents. The young child who is different, physically or intellectually, whose economic status is above, below or similar to that of the community in which he lives, and the one who belongs to a minority or majority group, will tend to reflect parents' adjustments to these facts. The child's adjustment to the realities and to the reactions of other children and their families to them can depend on what his parents feel, say and do.

Statements such as these suggest the extent to which the family can be influential. Actually, what a family contributes to the child's outlook varies immeasurably. Some of this variation results from differences in resources on which the parents rely, both knowingly and unwittingly. For some, modern means of communication, such as newspapers, movies, radio and television, may be especially influential. For others, use of sources of information in the present and from the past may be more extensive.

Services which the community provides affect the child and his family. Health and recreational facilities, schools, churches, social agencies and special facilities for those with particular problems or difficulties are a few of the community services affecting a large number of families. The form these services take as they attempt to meet the needs of young children and their families varies with the locality.

Community Health Services for Families

The community can serve a family in many ways. It can provide a healthful environment which includes sanitary measures to ensure safe water, sewage disposal, garbage disposal and other public health measures to prevent the spread of disease; abatement of noise; decrease in air pollution; safety measures to prevent accidents; and space for outdoor play and recreation. It can provide shopping facilities with a good variety and quality of foods. It can provide medical care and health education through its physicians, dentists, clinics, public health nurses, nutritionists and hospitals. It can provide a family court or some other means of counseling for families with special problems. Promotion of both emotional and physical health can be incorporated. Many cities have well-organized health centers.

Urban health centers may provide facilities for promotion of child health, care of dental, chest and venereal diseases, eye examination, school services, plus health education, public health nursing, nutritional instruction and certain aspects of communicable disease control. Counties may have mobile units or a center where people can come for help and from which health officers, public health nurses and nutritionists perform their functions. Child health conferences may be held at regular intervals. Associated with some of these conferences are group discussions for mothers (and fathers if they are free to attend them).

Bleiberg and Forrest (1959) described a group in which a pediatrician, a mental health nurse and a public health nurse participate while mothers discuss among themselves problems of rearing their young children. Public health nurses visit in the homes. Often, because she is the only professional contact with the family, the public health nurse acts as a counselor in many ways and assumes the role of a family social worker.

Health insurance plans may provide prepaid maternity care and medical care in case of illness, and, in some cases, health examinations as well.

The concept of family health in which the focus is on the family unit rather than on individuals is receiving increasing attention (Galdston, 1961). The family becomes the unit of health. This concept is being recognized by health agencies. Stitt et al. (1960) reported on a six-year project of a family health clinic offering multiprofessional services for a continuum of pregnancy and early childhood. Its basis of operation was the assumption of a pregnancy, childbearing, child-rearing continuum with its series of challenges and responses which may lead to strengthening or weakening of the family. The professional staff assisted in this progression by acting as technical advisors and helping parents to become good observers, to understand the motion of development of both themselves and their children, and to understand behavior at the moment as a part of this developmental progress. This clinic became an extended family for those attending. Fathers' participation tended to increase family unity. Values accrued not only for the parents, but also for the staff through the cooperation of members of several professions.

Another experiment in family health services is the Family Health Maintenance Demonstration in New York City (Dublin and Fraenkel, 1949; Milbank Memorial Fund, 1954; Silver, 1961), which originated in the Community Service Society and has as its participants the Community Service Society, Montefiore Hospital and the College of Physicians and Surgeons of Columbia University. Families insured under the Health Insurance Plan of Greater New York participate. It is a five-year research program concerned with family health maintenance which includes physical, social and emotional health. An integrated preventive and remedial service is offered by a team composed of a physician, public health nurse and social worker. The program for the family includes (1) an initial inventory, including both an inventory of biological and social characteristics of the family as a group and an inventory of the physical and psychological characteristics of each individual, (2) periodic re-evaluations, (3) guidance and (4) health education which acts as a thread interwoven into the total program. This program provides for a community health service based on the sound concepts of considering the individual as a whole and as a part of an interactive group, the family.

There is also a trend in medical education for students to be brought into direct study and care of families (Clark, 1961), thus encouraging the physicians of tomorrow to see the patient as one of a family group which influences his health or illness.

Day-Care Services and the Nursery School

In the latter part of the last century when it was generally accepted that the mother who was in economic need should work outside her home to support her family, day nurseries sprang up in many communities. Their purpose was to care for the children of working mothers, often from infancy to school age, while the mothers must be at work. Later, questions arose as to whether or not removal from the home was the best solution for this problem.

For a special group another solution was devised through legislation which provided for aid to dependent children and made it possible for the mother to stay at home and care for her own children instead of putting them in the care of someone else for part of the day. This legislation, together with the development of higher standards for day-nursery care, slowed to some extent the rapid increase in the number of day nurseries.

Shortly after World War I the nursery school appeared, from England. The term indicates a place of learning for young children; its program recognizes the period between approximately $2\frac{1}{2}$ or three years and five years as an age when much important learning can take place in a setting planned especially for young children, with opportunities for the child to pursue his own interests and to associate with other children of his own age under the guidance of well-qualified people.

The day nursery was at first principally a custodial institution; the nursery school is primarily an educational institution. During recent years the educational philosophies of both have become similar as teachers and directors have become better trained. Variations in programs reflect differences between the shorter period of time away from home for the child in nursery school and the longer period for the child who is in a day-care center while his mother (or father if he is responsible for the child's care) is at work.

The day-care center has expanded its concept of what care of children means; it has become increasingly aware of its responsibility for the total development of the child and has instituted a more varied program for the children under school age (Child Welfare League of America, 1960). Day-care services for an infant or toddler are sometimes arranged in a private home with a daytime mother in an attempt to meet the needs of a particular child and his family.

Establishment of nursery schools with high standards has contributed to recognition of their supplementation of the child's experience at home. Parents enroll children because of educational advantages; absence of the mother during the day is not the basis for their decision. The school furnishes equipment and activities scaled to the child's size and abilities. Physical activity is provided for. According to the National Association for the Education of Young Children (1948),

> The well-planned nursery school offers . . . opportunities for investigation, experimentation, problem-solving, imaginativeness and creativeness—activities which require children to develop their intellectual powers. . . .
>
> In a preschool group the child spends his time with others who have needs and desires strikingly similar to his own. Furthermore, they express these needs and desires at the same time and in the same ways that he does. Here then, is a rare opportunity for him to learn the importance of the other fellow; to learn to share materials, attention and space with him; to learn how to live in a group that is different in structure from the family group. Here, too, the child learns to accept other forms of authority, perhaps different from those he finds in his family.

Qualifications of the nursery school teacher, health policies, number of adults in proportion to number of children, educational methods and physical setup are a few of the bases for selecting a particular day-care center or nursery school for the child.

A report summarizing information as of October 1965 indicates that among 12,549,000 children in the United States who were three, four and five years old, 27 per cent were enrolled in public and private nursery schools and kindergartens. For each age the number of children and the percentage enrolled in nursery schools and kindergarten were as follows: three years, 203,000, or 4.9 per cent; four years, 683,000, or 16.1 per cent; five years, 2,521,000, or 60.6 per cent (United States Office of Education, 1966).

In the 1930's and again in the 1940's United States Government funds were provided for establishment of nursery schools and day-care centers and for education of teachers. In the 1960's, as part of an interest in providing early health and educational opportunities for children and families who are less likely to have them, government funds have been provided through Project Head Start and other programs. Programs of preschool enrichment of experience are provided in an attempt to decrease cultural deprivation.

Where nursery schools were not readily available, groups of mothers experimented in different ways to provide group experience for their children. For example, a group of rural women who attended an adult meeting once each week arranged to have their children play together on that afternoon under the guidance of a well-qualified nursery school teacher. In many communities three or four mothers take turns having their children meet at different homes perhaps two mornings or afternoons each week. The mother at whose home the children play is responsible for their activities. When cooperative play groups and nursery schools have been established, a trained teacher has given continuity to the program. She has been assisted by parents of the children enrolled. In any of these programs, and also in church school programs, careful study of their quality is an important part of the community's approach to them.

Community interest in growth and development of infants and young children and provision of educational opportunities for parents have sometimes paralleled each other. Preparental and parent education have taken a number of forms and have been provided in a variety of settings.

METHODS OF STUDY OF THE FAMILY

Any consideration of the family, aspects of its structure, and processes of its change with time, points up the necessity for specific information. In one approach longitudinal studies of families are being made. To consider the family from the time of marriage and then to study its development and that of each member seems to be one way to learn more about interrelations. This approach is intended to increase understanding of individuals through time instead of centering on their situation at one cross section of time. Other methods of study are cross sectional. Some experimental research deals with processes in the family and in other situations, such as decision-making. Not one member, but the various members of the family and the family as a unit need to be studied as the family grows. Interest in study of the child and his family has expanded to include interest in the family group and its dynamics.

Hill and Hansen (1960) refer to modern research propositions and define a proposition

. . . as an empirically validated generalization which often takes one of these forms: (1) a *descriptive statement* of observed conditions (e.g., the course of family adjustment to crisis follows a roller coaster pattern of disorganization—recovery attempts—readjustment); (2) an *antecedent-consequent statement* (e.g., if the family has had previous success in meeting crises then there is greater probability that a subsequent crisis will be successfully met); or (3) a *statement of covar-*

iance (e.g., crisis proneness increases as a family's socioeconomic position declines).

To understand the particular family of an individual child means looking for accurate description, considering antecedents and consequents, and giving thought to covariants. The picture of the particular family is then considered in the light of a more general picture provided by knowledge of research propositions.

Study of family influences on the child himself often takes forms similar to those mentioned for study of the family. In attempts to understand a particular family's influence on an individual child, an important method of study involves exploration of possible causal connections between family variables and some aspects of child behavior and development. Such study may mean tentatively considering certain alternatives and knowing that they may need to be discarded and others tried. Leads growing out of thorough study of the particular family and child can be viewed in the light of broader knowledge of trends. Parent-child relations pertaining to particular aspects of development are considered in Chapters Four through Thirteen. Methods of study are reported in these chapters and also in Chapter One.

TOPICS FOR STUDY AND DISCUSSION

1. As a focus for study, how would you clarify the idea that the child develops his concepts of self and of others in his relations with his family? Illustrate by reference to joint activities and role functions which suggest meanings the young child might be learning.
2. After a visit to a home where there is a baby or a preschool child, or both, discuss the child's responses to space, equipment, routines (his and those of other family members) and people, in terms of emotional climate, stimulation of use of abilities and physical climate. If observation in a home situation is not possible, some of the child's responses could be noted in other situations, such as shopping, riding the bus, or arriving at, attending and leaving nursery school.
3. Describe services provided by the community you live in which concern children and their families.
4. Have a panel discussion of three mothers or fathers, one the parent of a young infant, another the parent of an infant and of a preschool child, and the third the parent of preschool and school-age children, in which they discuss a day in their lives — their jobs and their activities with their children.
5. Give vitality to your understanding of variations among individuals in values from heritages and from interactions in the current setting by recording evidence of them in observation of a group of two, three or four children and adults.
6. Select a subject of particular interest to you from among the following or others. For a reference listed here, in the chapter, in the Selected Readings, or elsewhere, indicate qualities of the family or community setting emphasized and support from research and from theory for the ideas presented. *The adopted child* — Brieland, 1959; Carson, 1966; Child Welfare League of America, 1959; U.S. Children's Bureau, 1965; Doss and Doss, 1957; Fanshel, 1966. *Community services for families* — Journal of Marriage and the Family 29:1, February 1967; U.S. Children's Bureau, 1961a, 1962a. *Child-care centers and nursery schools* — Allen and Campbell, 1948; Child Welfare League of America, 1960; Leeper, Dales et al., 1968; Moore and Richards, 1959; Read, 1966; Todd and Heffernan, 1964; National Association for the Education of Young Children, 1948, 1962, 1963; National Society for the Study of Education, Forty-sixth Yearbook, 1947; Swift, 1964; Taylor, 1954. *Family composition and role-relationships* — Burton and Whiting, 1961; Schlesinger, 1966; Toman, 1961. *Family crises* — Arnstein, 1962; Hill, 1949; Rutledge, 1960.

SELECTED READINGS

Bell, N. W., and Vogel, E. (Eds.): A Modern Introduction to the Family. Rev. ed. New York, The Free Press, 1968. Readings from various authors, with Part I, Introduction; Part II, the Family and External Systems; Part III, Internal Processes of the Family; and Part IV, Family and Personality.

Brim, O. G.: Family Structure and Sex-role Learning by Children. Sociometry 21:1-16, March, 1958. Concepts are clarified concerning role learning through interaction, the child's incorporation of the role of another person into his role, and masculine and feminine roles. A number of procedures for collection and analysis of data are described. Findings concerning some relations between ordinal position, sex of sibling, and sex-role learning by children in two-child families are reported. (Also in Bell and Vogel, ibid.)

Child Study, Vol. 34, No. 3. The Man in the Family. Summer issue, 1957.

Christensen, H. (Ed.): Handbook of Marriage and the Family. Chicago, Rand McNally, 1964.

Clausen, J. A.: Family Structure, Socialization and Personality. Chapter in L. W. Hoffman and M. L. Hoffman (Eds.): Review of Child Development Research. New York, Russell Sage Foundation, 1966, Vol. 2.

Deutsch, M.: Facilitating development in the preschool child: social and psychological perspectives. Merrill Palmer Quarterly, 1964, 10:249-263.

Duvall, E. M.: Family Development. 3rd ed. Philadelphia. J. B. Lippincott Company, 1967. Chap. 8, Childbearing Families; Chap. 9, Families with Preschool Children. Discussion of developmental tasks of infants, preschool children, parents and the family.

Golden Anniversary White House Conference on Children and Youth: Reference Papers on Children and Youth. Washington, D. C., White House Conference on Children and Youth, 1960 (32 papers).

——————: Survey Papers. 1960 (30 papers).

These two publications include papers by well-qualified people in a variety of fields who were invited to write concerning the current scene and the child and the community, on subjects such as beliefs and values, child-rearing services, special problems, opportunity, health, education, employment and leisure. Bibliographies are included.

Hess, R. D., and Handel, G.: Family Worlds: A Psychosocial Approach to Family Life. Chicago, University of Chicago Press, 1959. In Chapters 2 through 6, each chapter presents a particular family.

Hoffman, L. W., and Lippitt, R.: The Measurement of Family Life Variables. Chap. 22 in P. Mussen (Ed.): Handbook of Research Methods in Child Development. New York, John Wiley & Sons, Inc., 1960.

Miller, D. R., and Swanson, G. E.: The Changing American Parent. New York, John Wiley & Sons, Inc., 1958. Chap. 3, Interviewing Mothers in the Detroit Area; Chap. 4, Child Training in Entrepreneurial and Bureaucratic Families; Chap. 5, Child Training, Social Classes, and Integration Settings.

Sussman, M. B. (Ed.): Sourcebook in Marriage and the Family. 3rd ed. Boston, Houghton Mifflin Company, 1968.

Waller, W.: The Family. Revised by R. Hill. New York, Holt, Rinehart and Winston, Inc., 1951. Chap. 2.

Walters, J.: A Review of Family Research in 1959, 1960, and 1961. Marriage and Family Living, 24:158-178, May, 1962. Bibliographies classified in 8 categories, including one on the family in other cultures.

Wolfenstein, M.: Fun Morality: An Analysis of Recent American Child-Training Literature. Chap. 10 in M. Mead and M. Wolfenstein (Eds.): Childhood in Contemporary Cultures. Chicago, University of Chicago Press, 1955.

CHAPTER THREE

Life Begins

WHEN LIFE BEGINS

When a new life begins, it both initiates a new life cycle and contributes to the life cycle of the parents. If it is a first child, it initiates a new phase, parenthood; if it is another child, it initiates an enlargement of parenthood.

This new life will have a unique pattern of development which will be determined by the potentialities given by the parents, the conditions in utero, the kind of home into which it is born, the manner in which its needs are gratified, and the feelings and attitudes of the people in its environment. Consequently the home and the parents will have a profound influence upon the development of this child.

PLANNING AND PREPARATION FOR CHILDREN

Rock and Loth (1949) have this to say:

> Nothing in the life of a man or a woman is . . . as important to themselves or to society as their parenthood. . . . Prospective parents should apply at least as much intelligence and foresight to this as to designing a home, buying furniture, planning a vacation or perhaps even choosing a career. Knowledge and thought can be applied to the production of a family with at least as much prospect of success as in . . . any other human activity.

Planning for Children

Planning for children may vary from discussion of how each partner feels about children and what they wish for their children, to a purposeful kind of planning which includes setting goals for themselves as parents, planning how they and their children will fit into a family group, and coming to some decision about the kind of philosophy to have as a basis for family living and the guidance of their children.

The advisability of having children is sometimes in question because of some undesirable trait in the family of either or both husband

and wife. Potential parents with this concern can obtain help by consulting someone who understands the mechanics of heredity and can tell them something of the chances of occurrence of such a trait in their offspring. Physicians informed in the field of genetics can serve as such counselors. Some places have heredity clinics where potential parents can obtain expert information, after which they will be in a better position to make a decision (Reed, 1963). Fears about the transmission of characteristics are often not substantiated by fact, and anxiety may be eliminated completely.

Husbands and wives concerned about infertility sometimes seek medical consultation.

Planning may include decisions in terms of when to begin a family, the number of children, the spacing of these children, and the time of year when they will be born. Economics and health factors are often reasons for such planning.

FACTORS OF AGE, SPACING, MATURITY AND HEALTH. It is presently considered wise to *begin one's family* in the early twenties, i.e., in the early years of physical and emotional maturity. The greatest asset a pregnant woman can possess is youth (Eastman, 1944). A study in Aberdeen, Scotland (Baird et al., 1958), found less risk of difficult labor, stillbirth and inability to establish lactation in mothers having babies in their early twenties than later.

The *spacing of children* is an individual matter, since there are differences in the time required for individual women to recover from the strains of pregnancy and lactation. The interval depends on her general health, nutritional status and the emotional influences in her environment. A woman's physician can determine when she is physiologically ready to have another child.

Pregnancy During Adolescence

There has been an increasing trend for adolescents to marry and have children. The Population Reference Bureau (Population Profile, 1962) reported that in twenty-one states in 1959, 39 per cent of all brides were teenagers compared with 33 per cent in 1950. The percentage for teenage grooms in that interval increased from 7 to 13 per cent. For first marriages, 51 per cent of the brides and 17 per cent of the grooms were in their teens. Eighteen per cent of all first brides were under eighteen years of age. In the same year 36 per cent of the first babies were born to teenagers, an increase from 27 per cent in 1950. Fourteen per cent were born to mothers under eighteen years, an increase from 10 per cent in 1950. Sixteen per cent of all teen-age wives had two or more children. Cook (Population Profile, 1962) commented:

> Today, more women marry in their eighteenth year than in any other, more have their first child in their nineteenth year than in any other. At this rate, the thirty-eight year old grandmother will soon be a commonplace.

Are adolescents ready for pregnancy? Is pregnancy advisable at this age?

Chronologic age is not a good index of maturity because of wide differences in the time of maturing. Biologically, a girl is ready to reproduce when she is capable of producing mature ova which can be fertilized, implanted in the uterus which, in turn, is sufficiently mature to permit the development of the fetus to term.

Gray (1960) stated:

Sexual maturity may be considered to have arrived ordinarily by the age of 18 years, although actually this is not entirely true, because the gradually enlarging and developing pelvic organs continue until the age of 25 years in a large proportion of women. By the age of 18 years young women are considered mature enough to assume the responsibilities of marriage and to bear children, which always hastens maturity of the secondary sex organs. . . . It seems that since women's suffrage a respectable age of marriage, and a not unexpected age for pregnancy, should be considered the dividing line between adolescence and maturity.

Associated with the ability to reproduce is the factor of safety for mother and child, i.e., whether the mother will be able to meet the demands of pregnancy without damaging her health and whether the infant will be well-born at term.

Reproduction is most efficient physiologically when it begins soon after attainment of physical maturity (Cuthbertson, 1958). From an Aberdeen study cited by Cuthbertson some findings indicated (1) greater ease of delivery of the fifteen- to nineteen-year group than among subsequent ages; (2) more success in initiating lactation among the adolescent group. The advantages at these ages may be outweighed, however, by the consequence of poor social environment, poorer growth, impaired general health and poor education. Almost half of this adolescent group came from the two lowest social classes. The pregnant adolescents were shorter and tended to have lower physical ratings, as indicated by a good correlation between height and physical ratings.

Thomson (1957) reported significantly higher rates of prematurity and neonatal deaths among infants born to mothers who were in unsatisfactory health and under 61 inches in height than among infants born to mothers with good general health and a height of 64 inches or more. Hytten et al. (1958) also reported that mothers in lower socioeconomic classes gave up breast feeding more often and sooner than those in upper classes, apparently because of less favorable attitudes toward breast feeding. Poor social environment with its attendant poorer growth, impaired general health and poor education can more than offset the biologic advantages of youth. Many adolescent pregnancies are unwanted, prenuptial, and create an emotional strain on the girl which, in turn, can affect metabolic processes and physical functions at a time when they are adapting to increased demands.

Greenhill (1965) reports that among 500 consecutive deliveries of patients under sixteen years of age, maternal complications occurred in 20 per cent. Eclampsia due to toxemia occurred five times more frequently in the young than in all other pregnant women, and non-convulsive toxemia twice as often.

Aznar and Bennet (1961) reviewed eighteen studies and observed 1139 adolescents, chiefly Negro, sixteen years of age and younger at the time of pregnancy. There seemed to be reasonable safety even though the risk to mother and child was increased, especially among the younger ages. No one, however, believed that such early pregnancy is desirable from a psychological, social, economic, maternal, fetal or obstetric point of view.

Preparation for Children

PSYCHOLOGICAL READINESS. In addition to biological readiness for starting a family, psychological readiness, which includes emotional and social maturity, is also important. This does not necessarily accompany biological readiness. For both sexes the development of a well-integrated personality through the orderly acquisition of successive steps in the process of maturing is important. (See Chapter Seven, pages 225 to 246.) For some adolescents the hazards of childbearing are possibly greatest in these areas. They may not be ready for the responsibilities of parenthood.

PRECONCEPTIONAL PREPARATION. Readiness for children implies continuity of development, and preparation for children, whether done consciously or not, begins long before pregnancy is recognized, even before conception. Thus the concept of preconceptional preparation has emerged. Preconceptional preparation encompasses all that contributes to the creating of a healthy person who has developed to the point of being physically and psychologically ready for parenthood. It means growth and development from birth to maturity in all its phases. It means sound minds in sound bodies. It means providing for needs which will be discussed later. It means also, as Spock (1950b) says, ". . . a fundamental re-emphasis on all childhood education, in which human feelings and family relations will become the core. The result to be hoped for is that the idea of eventually being a father or . . . mother will sound like an exciting aim throughout childhood." It means growing up in homes and communities where children can have love, security, a chance to share and to understand and accept themselves and others; in fact, a wholesome life.

The concept of *preconceptional nutrition* (Stearns, 1958) is a part of the concept of preconceptional preparation. Nutrition can influence the capacity to reproduce successfully (Widdowson, 1955). It is somewhat difficult, however, to demonstrate the effects of nutrition upon reproduction because of the multiplicity of factors in the reproductive process and the difficulty in controlling the many variables in human life. Therefore results are sometimes conflicting.

During the famine period in The Netherlands in the winter of 1944 and the spring of 1945, when women were under nutritional and emotional stress, about 50 per cent of them had cessation of menstruation (amenorrhea) and were presumably infertile (Smith, 1947). Nine months later the number of births fell to about one-third of the usual number. With the return of food the amenorrhea disappeared. In Malaya, however, Millis (1952) concluded that undernutrition in that situation did not affect fertility. Keys and his co-workers (1950), in an experimental study in semistarvation, found that during the period of severe undernutrition the young men produced sperm that were less motile and lived a shorter time. When the diet was restored to meet the needs of the men, the sperm returned to normal. That nutrition may not always be a primary cause of maternal and fetal complications is indicated by the Vanderbilt study (McGanity et al., 1954, 1955). Many factors contribute to complications in pregnancy.

Warkany and his co-workers (1948) demonstrated that certain congenital malformations in animals may result from maternal dietary deficiency. If such a relation exists in man, and if conditions in human mothers bearing malformed infants are similar to those in animals, the first two months, when the organs and systems of the embryo are being formed, are the crucial time, and deficiencies then may result in abnormalities. A woman who waits until she is pregnant to practice satisfactory food habits may be too late, since most women are not immediately aware that they have become pregnant.

The Woman's Preparation.   For a woman a healthy, well-nourished body is important as she approaches her reproductive period, since the physiologic demands on her body during these years will be heavy. Pregnancy is a normal physiologic process to be experienced happily and, for many, with an increased buoyancy of health. It is a period of growth for both mother and child. To provide for this growth, physiologic adjustments occur, and greater demands are placed on all organs and systems of the maternal body. A woman who begins pregnancy with a healthy body, one that functions adequately and whose tissues are well stocked with the necessary nutrients, is well prepared to meet these demands. If she comes to pregnancy with rich stores of calcium in her bones, it is much easier for her to keep, with a good diet, adequate supplies of calcium both for her own and for her child's needs. Experiments have indicated that women who previously had ample calcium in their diets have better retention of calcium (Stearns, 1951). Good nutrition and general health also provide for a good retention of nitrogen (Hummel et al., 1937) from the protein eaten, which is necessary for prenatal growth and later for lactation. The woman who begins pregnancy with a normal hemoglobin level stands a better chance of keeping it normal. Normal body weight for size is another asset. There is some evidence (Tompkins et al., 1955) that a woman who enters pregnancy markedly underweight has a greater hazard of giving birth prematurely than one who is of normal weight or is overweight. Also, although toxemia is less likely to develop than in the overweight woman, when it does occur, it tends to be more severe (Tompkins and Wiehl, 1955).

The woman whose habits of eating, sleeping, exercising, elimination and posture meet her needs has fewer changes to make in her habits in a period that requires a great many adjustments. Buoyant health means better general resistance to infection, fatigue and other physical hazards which may beset her. Because of her good health she may find a good emotional adjustment easier.

Similarly, the woman's intellectual, social and emotional development and habits are of great importance in her adjustment to the chances involved in pregnancy and in the birth and care of her child. If she is emotionally ready for parenthood and, in cooperation with her husband, is ready to give her energies to the creating and guiding of another generation, she will be able to cope with the adjustments required of her. Since the interaction of mind and body is so close, emotional maturity is important for her own physical well-being and consequently for that of her child. It is also essential for the peace and happiness of her husband.

The Man's Preparation. The father's influence on the unborn child is indirect as he contributes to the well-being of the mother. He is important, however, as a member of a growing family. Obviously, good physical health will be an asset for any man with a family. It is also important for a man to have grown psychologically in the development of a healthy personality so that he is ready for parenthood. Such readiness involves the desire for children whom he will regard as a trust and not as an extension of himself.

If he understands himself, has a true appreciation of others and can share with the others of the family in a warm, spontaneous manner, he should be able to meet with confidence whatever problems arise during his wife's pregnancy and lend her the necessary support. Many men are interested in learning what takes place in pregnancy and how the child grows. Equipped with such knowledge, a man can more easily play a supportive role. If there are young children in the family, this is the time for the father, if possible, to participate more actively in their routines and activities, which will relieve the mother and at the same time increase the bond between father and children.

COMMUNITY FACILITIES. In addition to long-range programs of providing for optimum growth of individuals, many communities provide facilities for young people to gain knowledge and receive help with their personal problems, and to gain insight and knowledge which will prepare them for parenthood. Such opportunities include medical and psychological counseling for adolescents, engaged couples and young married couples, high school courses in education for family life, and discussion groups for those anticipating marriage or those recently married. Churches, schools, colleges, social agencies and the medical profession are participating. Thus a couple can enter into parenthood with better understanding of what is ahead and with confidence in their ability to meet the future.

ADJUSTMENTS TO PREGNANCY

Preparatory Adjustments

Whether the pregnancy is planned or unexpected, comes early or later in marriage, and is a first or a subsequent one, both the man and the woman will have to make adjustments. A planned pregnancy may mean that various adjustments have already been made, leaving the couple ready for the adjustments specific to pregnancy. They have had time to anticipate and plan for the changes which may have to be made in their lives with the coming of a baby. Nevertheless many people who do not believe in planning pregnancies make the adjustments with ease. If the woman becomes pregnant very soon after marriage, she will have to make the many adjustments to marriage at a time when she may be undergoing some of the physical disturbances that occasionally accompany pregnancy. This may put a rather heavy burden on both husband and wife. Superimposed on making the early marital adjustments is the realization that there is to be a new member in their family who will absorb a great deal of time and may require an entirely different mode of living from the one currently followed. Nevertheless many young couples manage very well to make the necessary adjustments to a pregnancy in the first year of married life.

In subsequent pregnancies family adjustments will involve the children as well as the parents. The ease of adjustment depends on the emotional maturity of each. Unresolved emotional problems, even if unrecognized before, may well become intensified at this time.

Although the adjustment will differ somewhat in both degree and kind, depending on the circumstances, the planning and preparation can be of such intense and mutual interest as to draw the parents into a closer sympathy and understanding. When both husband and wife have some realization of what adjustments are to be made, they are better equipped to make them successfully and less likely to think of them as difficulties or problems.

Financial Considerations

Among the adjustments to pregnancy is recognition by both husband and wife of the importance of adequate care for the woman and the expense it entails. The selection of the physician who will care for the woman during her pregnancy and at the time of birth is important. The couple will want a physician whose fee for service will be compatible with their income and who at the same time has proper medical qualifications. They will want one in whom they have complete confidence and with whom they can feel free to discuss all problems, both physical and psychological, which may arise. They may be financially able to secure one of the best obstetricians in the vicinity, or it may be necessary to secure the best available obstetrician at the lowest possible cost. Economy may necessitate attendance at a special clinic for pregnant women, thereby securing the services of well-trained physicians at little or no cost, and going into a hospital ward rather than a private room when the baby is born. The important thing is for the husband and wife to choose wisely a physician who they know is well trained, preferably an obstetrician, or a general practitioner skilled in obstetrics. Good maternal care is economical in the end in that it protects the health of mother and child.

Changes in Living Conditions

The arrival of the baby may necessitate a change because the living quarters seem too small to add a third person whose regimen is to be different from that of his parents. It is generally advised that a baby sleep in a room by himself if possible. In this way he can live in accordance with his schedule without interfering too much with the normal activities of the family. Their movements and the lights in their room will not disturb his sleep. Parents also can relax and rest better if the baby is not in their room. When necessary, however, parents who must continue to live in a small apartment or house can, with ingenuity, rearrange the living space to meet the needs of the infant and themselves. With the increased mobility necessitated by work, military assignments, and the like, young families with infants can adapt themselves to a variety of circumstances.

CHANGES IN LIVING HABITS.   For both husband and wife a baby makes a difference in their household. They are not as free to come and go as they did before. Their night's sleep will probably be interrupted because for a time the baby must be fed once or twice during the night. The late Sunday morning sleep may also be interrupted. These adjustments may prove irritating to some people if they do not anticipate them and accept them as part of the experience.

PREPARATION OF PARENTS FOR ADJUSTMENTS.   It is believed that parents will make the adjustments mentioned above, and any others necessary, with much more ease if, before the coming of the first baby, they have had some information about what to expect and some experience in child care. Some prospective parents may receive information and have their questions answered by the physician during the mother's visits to his office. Or the husband may occasionally accompany his wife, or may seek an appointment with the physician alone to learn about pregnancy and the needs of his wife so that he may be more understanding and supportive. Many communities have classes for prospective mothers conducted by public health clinics and sometimes classes for prospective fathers. Discussion groups for both husbands and wives are sometimes available.

Such experimental groups have been conducted at the Merrill-Palmer Institute in Detroit in cooperation with obstetricians. A class consists of patients of an obstetrician and their husbands. The discussions are conducted by the obstetrician and members of the staff of the institute. The department of health in the city, as well as some hospitals, has also established classes for prospective parents. The Visiting Nurse Service of New York conducted a study of their educational program (Mann, Woodward and Joseph, 1961).

Some of the classes in infant care are excellent and many are good, but some give class instruction without observation of babies or associations with them. Thus these classes may engender anxieties in parents by making them aware of all there is to know about infant care, and the hazards of ignorance, without giving them the assurance and security of their own competence. A few generations ago most young people grew up in large families and usually had many associations either with their younger brothers and sisters or, if they were younger children, with their nieces and nephews. Some high school and college students now gain experience in caring for babies through the practice of babysitting for parents who are away for the evening or part of the day. Others gain experience as aides in hospital and community programs.

Prospective parents may also learn by reading, observation of friends who have infants and perhaps participation in their care. In any community there may be other opportunities to gain experience in handling infants while providing a needed service.

INHERITANCE AND ENVIRONMENT

Interaction of Heredity and Environment

All individuals, except possibly identical twins, are genetically unique.* What the individual becomes is the outcome of the interactions of heredity and environment; both are essential. Dynamic interactions occur between the genetic material present in every functioning cell (except mature red blood cells) and its cellular environment. Cellular activity is influenced also by the larger environment both within and outside the whole organism: first, the maternal environment of the fetus and, after birth, the world outside, including not only the physical environment, but also the intellectual, emotional and cultural atmosphere provided by the family, school, church, social class, nation and the "climate of opinion." Thus the uterine environment before birth and the many facets of the external environment after birth play important roles.

Operation of Heredity

At the time of conception the new organism receives twenty-three chromosomes from each parent, for a total of forty-six chromosomes

---

* Differences during prenatal development which may occur for identical twins are considered by Falkner (1966) with reference to mass of placenta or placental part supplying each twin and to placental transfusion.

(except for a few deviations) as forty-four autosomes and two sex chromosomes, XX or XY. The Y chromosome determines maleness. These chromosomes contain probably about 10,000 pairs of genes (Stern, 1960). In all likelihood the substance of the gene is a chemical, deoxyribonucleic acid (DNA), which contains nucleotides of four bases which, in an almost infinite variety of combinations, seem capable of encoding all the characteristics that an organism transmits from one generation to the next. Hence all genetic differences must be produced by differences in physiologic processes of the cells. By means of these processes emerge the tissues and organs and their arrangement into a harmonious whole which bears the unique characteristics of the individual.

Sometimes a person has fewer or more than forty-six chromosomes because of abnormal chromosome behavior in the ovaries of the mother or in the eggs produced by them, or in the sperm of the father (Stern, 1960; Ford, 1960). Certain abnormalities, such as mongolism (Down's syndrome), are associated with this condition. The mongoloid has forty-seven chromosomes and is characterized by specific abnormalities in structure and retarded mental and physical development.

Ordinarily there are two sex chromosomes, XX in the female and XY in the male. But there may be only one (XO) or as many as four or more (XXXY). Abnormalities of chromosomal number are associated with abnormalities of growth and development. In the small percentage of males having an excess of chromosomes, testicular defect and other differences occur (Andersen, 1966; Hunt, 1966). Or, in the female with a single X, skeletal anomalies and sexual immaturity occur (Hunt, 1966).

Genes do not act alone. They react not only with the cytoplasm of the cell, but also with one another. One characteristic may emerge from the action of many genes; the same gene may contribute to many characteristics. Examples of the former include those traits which show continuous gradation among individuals or "quantitative" characteristics such as height, pigmentation, longevity, degree of resistance to disease, scores on mental tests. An example of the latter is an inborn error of metabolism in which a gene is responsible for interference in a regular metabolic process, thus producing a number of divergent characteristics as seen by the excretion of phenylpyruvic acid in the urine, mental impairment and slight pigmentation disturbances of the hair, in a condition known as phenylketonuria.

The expression of a gene may be influenced in various ways so that it is changed, suppressed or modified. Some genes are changed by mutation (infrequently); some are part of the sex chromosomes and produce characteristics that are sex-linked, such as color blindness; some are sex-limited in that they are expressed in one sex only, like the beard; some are sex-controlled or sex-modified, such as baldness. The genic action may be limited by its strength in expressing itself, as in vitamin D-resistant rickets, a condition in which rickets occurs in spite of an adequate vitamin D intake (Review, 1960b). It may not be expressed because the environment has not provided the necessary elements, e.g., dietary habits and diabetes. Again, expression may be modified by environment, as shown in the serial differences in the height of children in the United States and other countries (Tanner, 1962) and in height of Japanese children born and reared in Japan and in the United States (Greulich, 1957), and also in handedness, which has a genetic component, but is often influenced by social pressure (Stern, 1960).

Origins of Traits

Some traits may be either genetic or purely environmental in origin. This is true in mental retardation (Masland, 1958) and also in heavy pigmentation, which can be either inherited or produced by prolonged exposure to sunlight.

To those traits influenced by heredity which have already been mentioned can be added many more, such as blood groups, physical traits, mental traits such as intelligence, physiological traits, certain aspects of personality. Williams (1951, 1956) states that individuals have differing metabolic personalities as a result of physiological differences, just as they have different psychological personalities. These differences are dramatically demonstrated in the inborn errors of metabolism (Review, 1958a, 1959a, 1959b). Knowledge today strongly supports the view that men are not born exactly alike in either body or mind.

The dynamic relation between heredity and environment calls for a realistic rather than a fatalistic approach to heredity, since a concept of a fixed, immutable expression of hereditary tendencies is wrong. Different children thrive differently in the same environment because of different potentialities. What is the best environment for one may not be best for another. Provision for the health and growth of an individual is facilitated if the strengths and weaknesses with which he is endowed are considered.

Race

Knowledge of heredity is helpful in sorting out the facts and myths about race. There is racial diversity, including color of skin and hair, shape of hair, nose and lips, amount of body hair, facial contours, large differences in stature and many other traits. There is no scientific reason for believing that races differ in their innate capacity for intellectual and emotional development. Differences obtained in test results are best explained in terms of factors of social and educational environment (Carothers, 1953; Knobloch and Pasamanick, 1960) and tend to disappear when environmental opportunities of different racial or ethnic groups become similar. Racial bias, however, can influence personality development both in the prejudiced and in the victim (Ausubel, 1957; Proshansky, 1966).

DEVELOPMENT OF EMBRYO AND FETUS

Development of the fetus in utero requires about 9½ lunar months, or 266 days, after fertilization of the ovum. Since exact knowledge of the time of fertilization is usually impossible, an approximate birth date may be reached by counting back three months from the date of the beginning of the last menstruation and adding seven days. For example, if the last menstruation began on April 19th, the birth date might be expected to be January 26th. The majority of babies are born about 280 days from the first day of the last menstrual period. About 95 per cent of all babies are born within two weeks of the 280 days.

During this period the new organism grows from a single cell (the fertilized ovum), which is almost invisible to the naked eye, to an infant weighing about 7½ pounds. During prenatal life the weight of the body increases several billion times, whereas from birth to maturity it increases only twentyfold. Although gains are greater in the later months, the proportionate growth is much more rapid in the early months of fetal life (see Table 2). This increase in size is due to three aspects of growth: increase in the size of cells, increase in the number of cells and increase in the amount of nonliving intercellular material. Increase in size is accompanied by an appearance of a variety of cells and increase in their number, which is called differentiation. By means of this process, tissues, organs and systems and their sequential development emerge.

Development is continuous. The whole process is a smoothly progressive affair; one stage or phase emerges from another without any real line of demarcation. Any such divisions are artificial.

Maturation of Germ Cells

Every cell of the body has in its nucleus forty-six chromosomes which carry the genes, or determiners of heritable traits. This is as true of im-

TABLE 2. Relation of Age and Weight in the Human Embryo

AGE OF EMBRYO	WEIGHT IN GRAMS	RATE OF INCREASE EACH MONTH WHEN VALUE AT START OF MONTH EQUALS UNITY
4 weeks.	0.02	40,000.00
2 lunar months.	1	49.00
3 lunar months.	14	13.00
4 lunar months.	105	6.50
5 lunar months.	310	1.95
6 lunar months.	640	1.07
7 lunar months.	1080	0.69
8 lunar months.	1670	0.55
9 lunar months.	2400	0.43
Full term (266 days).	3300	0.38

Adapted from L. B. Arey: Developmental Anatomy, 1954.

mature germ cells as it is of other cells of the body, but mature germ cells have only twenty-three chromosomes. This comes about by a process of division of germ cells which results in only twenty-three chromosomes in a mature germ cell. The paternal germ cell and the maternal germ cell each contribute twenty-three chromosomes to the new being whose life begins when the ovum, or female germ cell, is fertilized by the spermatozoon, or male germ cell.

While still in the ovary, the ovum divides into two cells, each with twenty-three chromosomes. In the immature cell the forty-six chromosomes are arranged in pairs, and each of the two new cells contains one chromosome from each pair. One of the new cells contains most of the cell cytoplasm and is much larger than the other. These two cells divide in turn, this time with the usual type of cell division in which the chromo-

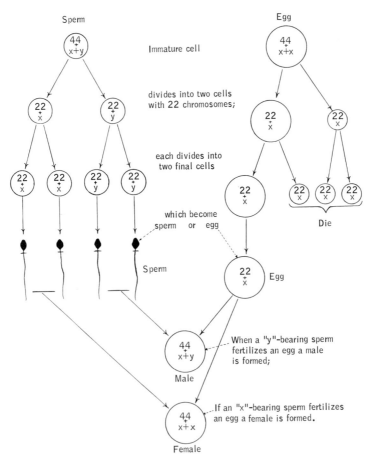

FIGURE 19. *Maturation of sperm (on left) and egg (on right), and their fusion to form a male or female individual. The 46 chromosomes of each immature cell are indicated as 44 plus XY in the male and 44 plus XX in the female. (Adapted from M. S. Gilbert: Bibliography of the Newborn. Baltimore, Williams & Wilkins Company.)*

somes divide longitudinally. Again one larger cell and one very small cell result from the division of the cell which carries most of the cytoplasm of the original immature cell. Thus there results from these two divisions one larger cell, the mature ovum, and three small cells, called polar bodies, which soon die (see Fig. 19). Actually, the larger cell is extremely small, with a diameter of about 1/125 inch.

Division of the immature sperm cell is similar to that of the immature ovum, except that in the division of the sperm cell four mature spermatozoa are formed (Fig. 19). Each of these cells measures only about 1/450 inch in length.

Determination of Sex

Each set of the original forty-six chromosomes (twenty-three pairs) in each of the immature germ cells contains one pair which is responsible for determining sex. In the female the chromosomes of this twenty-third pair are alike and are designated as X chromosomes; thus the mature ovum always contains one of these two X chromosomes. In the male, however, the members of the twenty-third pair are unlike; one is designated as X and the other as Y. Division of the sperm cells will produce spermatozoa with either a Y or an X chromosome. The sex of the new individual, conceived when a mature spermatozoon penetrates and fertilizes an ovum, will depend on whether this spermatozoon carries a Y or an X chromosome. If it carries a Y, the twenty-third pair in the new being will be XY, and a male baby will result; if it carries an X, the resulting pair will be XX, and the new child will be female (Fig. 19).

Fertilization

About every twenty-eight days during the childbearing period of a woman's life, an ovum matures. It is swept into the fallopian tube and passes along this tube on its way to the uterus. If sexual intercourse occurs about the time the ovum is expelled from the ovary, spermatozoa pass through the vagina, uterus and tube to meet the descending ovum. When a spermatozoon penetrates the ovum, fertilization occurs. Although usually only one ovum a month is matured, the possibility of its fertilization is tremendous because there are 200,000,000 to 300,000,000 spermatozoa in each ejaculation. These have long, thin tails which propel them relatively swiftly, and dozens of them may meet the ovum descending the tube. Only one, however, penetrates, and after it has fused with the ovum the fertilized cell repels any others.

Figure 20 illustrates what happens in the uterus and the ovary when fertilization does not occur and what happens when it does.

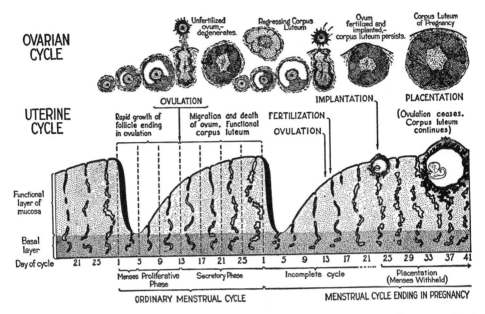

FIGURE 20. *Graphic summary of changes in the uterine mucosa during an ordinary menstrual cycle and a subsequent cycle in which pregnancy occurs. (Modified from Schroder.) The correlated changes in the ovary are suggested above in their proper relation to the same time scale. (Courtesy of B. M. Patten: Human Embryology. 2nd ed. New York, Blakiston Div., McGraw-Hill Book Company, Inc., 1953.)*

Implantation

Immediately after fertilization, as the ovum descends the fallopian tube, the nuclei of spermatozoon and ovum fuse, and rapid cell division occurs, resulting in a clump of cells called the morula, which, in time, changes to the blastocyst. It is probably seven to eight days after fertilization and at the stage of the blastocyst before the ovum begins to implant itself in the uterine lining. The ovum burrows through the uterine lining and embeds itself in the thick decidua, richly prepared for its reception.

Development

EARLY DEVELOPMENT. The single cell, by cell division, becomes a clump of cells (morula) and then a blastocyst, or hollow vesicle, with an outer layer of cells, the trophoblast (the layer through which nourishment is provided), a cavity containing fluid, and an inner cell mass which now undergoes rapid cell division and differentiation (Fig. 21). In this inner cell mass appear three germinal layers, the entoderm, ectoderm and mesoderm, from which develop the tissues, organs and systems of the body. This period of differentiation of cells, during which a human organism is formed, extends from the end of the second week after fertilization until the end of the second month. During this period the organism is called an *embryo*. For the rest of the prenatal period it is called a *fetus*. Figure 22 gives a visual impression of the growth which

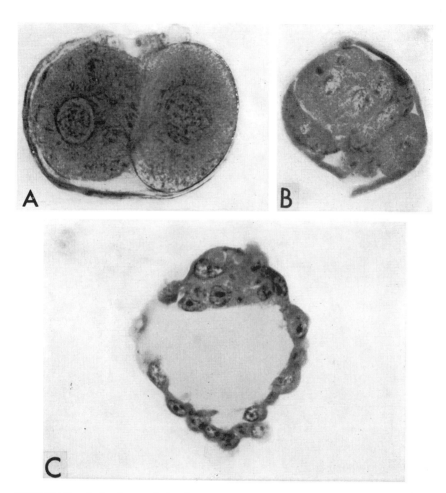

FIGURE 21. *Early stages of development. Human embryos in cleavage and blasto-dermic vesicle stages. (After Hertig, Rock et al.: Carnegie Contr. to Emb., Vol. 35, 1953.) A, Two-cell stage (Carnegie Coll. No. 8698, x500). B, Early morula stage (Carnegie Coll. No. 8452, x500). C, Unattached blastodermic vesicle (Carnegie Coll. No. 8663, x600). (B. M. Patten: Human Embryology. 2nd ed. New York, Blakiston Div., McGraw-Hill Book Company, Inc., 1953.)*

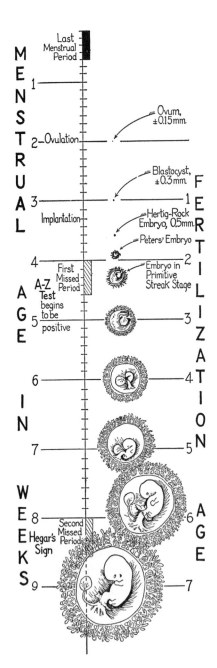

FIGURE 22. *Diagrams showing actual size of embryos and their membranes in relation to a time scale based on the mother's menstrual history. A-Z, Aschheim-Zondek. Heger's sign, softening of the muscle in the lower segment of the uterus. (Courtesy of B. M. Patten: Human Embryology. 2nd ed. New York, Blakiston Div., McGraw-Hill Book Company, Inc., 1953.)*

occurs in the early part of development. Figure 23 shows developmental changes. Note the changes in head and face, hands and feet.

FETAL MEMBRANES. In the very early stages of this period the blastocyst becomes covered with branching projections called villi, and the whole structure is called the *chorionic vesicle.* The developing embryo is connected with the wall of this vesicle by means of the body stalk. As cells covering the villi destroy surrounding tissue in the uterus, walls of the blood vessels in the decidua immediately surrounding the chorionic vesicle are broken down, and the vesicle is bathed by maternal blood which gradually assumes a definite course of flow. Late in the second month of pregnancy some of the villi degenerate, leaving only about one-fifth of the chorion covered. Those remaining, together with tissue developed from the decidua, develop into the *placenta,* or after-birth (see Figs. 23, 24, 25). The body stalk becomes greatly elongated, and through the resulting umbilical cord run three blood vessels; two of them, arteries, carry blood from the infant to the placenta, and the other, a vein, carries oxygenated blood from the placenta to the infant.

The *amniotic sac,* which appears early in gestation as a transparent, nonvascular membrane, completely envelops the embryo except where the umbilical cord projects through it to the placenta (see Figs. 23, *A, B;* 24, 25). The amniotic fluid has important functions. It acts as a buffer to protect the embryo and the fetus from jars and shocks experienced by the mother and allows free movement of the fetus. It provides a liquid medium which is necessary for fetal growth, prevents pressure on the cord, reduces the impact of fetal movements on the mother, provides an even temperature for the developing organism, and plays a role at the time of labor (Greenhill, 1965).

The precise origin of this fluid is unknown. There is support for the belief that the amnion plays an active and perhaps fundamental role in the exchange of amniotic fluid. It is known that both the mother and the fetus participate. There is an exchange of water and electrolytes between the maternal plasma and the amniotic fluid. The fetus swallows fluid, and urine is found in the fluid (Greenhill, 1965).

LATER DEVELOPMENT. Size and Form. During the fetal period, except for a few parts of the body such as differentiated external sex organs, hair, fingernails and toenails which develop during this time, most of the change consists in growth in size (from a length of 7 cm. at three months to 50 cm. at birth), change in body proportions (from the head being half of the total length at two months to about one-fourth at birth) (Fig. 26) and increase in function.

By the end of the third month the fetus resembles a human being, with the head large in proportion to the rest of the body (see Figs. 23, *G;* 27). By six months the body is lean, but in better proportions. At this time the vernix caseosa, a mixture of cells flaked off from the skin and fatty substance secreted from the sebaceous glands, which presumably acts as a protective covering to the skin, begins to form. By seven months

(Text continued on page 102)

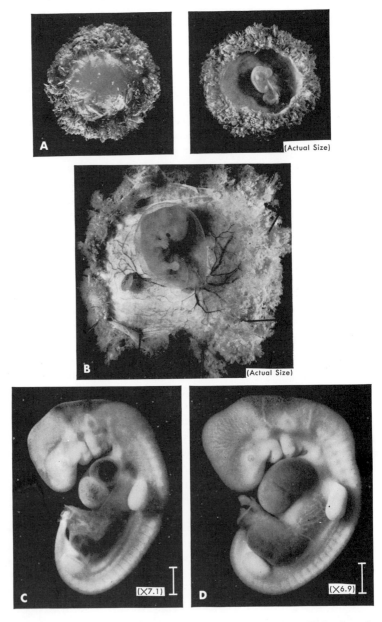

FIGURE 23. *Embryonic development from 28 to 56 days. White lines in C through H indicate actual lengths of embryos. A, A 28-day human embryo. Left: With chorion intact. Right: With chorion dissected to demonstrate embryo in situ in amniotic cavity. B, A 39-day human embryo. Chorion has been opened and pinned back to show embryo in intact amnion. C, A 30-day human embryo. Actual length—7.3 mm. D, A 31-day human embryo. Actual length—7.8 mm. E, A 34-day human embryo. Actual length—11.6*

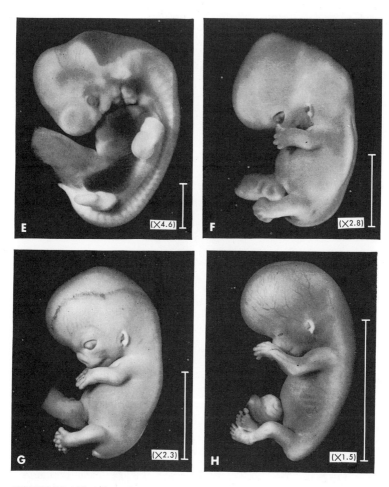

FIGURE 23 *(Continued).*
mm. F, A 40-day human embryo. Actual length—19 mm. G, A 44-day human embryo. Actual length—23 mm. H, A 56-day human embryo. Actual length—37 mm.

(Photographs by C. F. Reather from the Department of Embryology, Carnegie Institute of Washington, Baltimore, Maryland, in Medical Radiography and Photography, Vol. 28, No. 1, 1952. Eastman Kodak Company, Rochester, New York.)

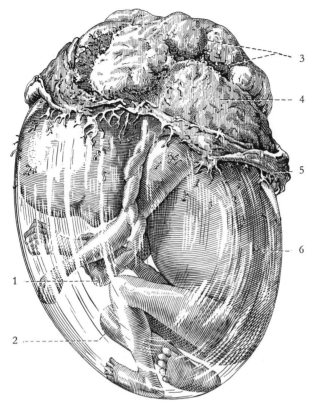

FIGURE 24. *Fetus and fetal membranes, showing amnion, placenta and umbilicus. 1, Umbilical cord; 2, fetus in the amniotic sac; 3, 4, 5, placenta; 6, amniotic sac. (From E. Bleck-schmidth: Stages of Human Development Before Birth.)*

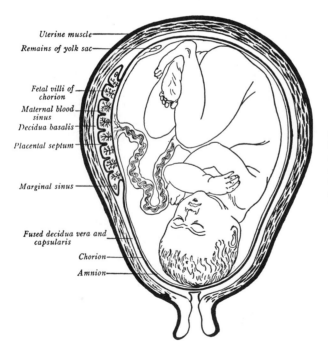

Uterine muscle

Remains of yolk sac

Fetal villi of chorion

Maternal blood sinus

Decidua basalis

Placental septum

Marginal sinus

Fused decidua vera and capsularis

Chorion

Amnion

FIGURE 25. *Diagrammatic section of uterus illustrating relation of advanced fetus to placenta and other membranes. (Anfield, reproduced in L. B. Arey: Developmental Anatomy. 6th ed. 1954.)*

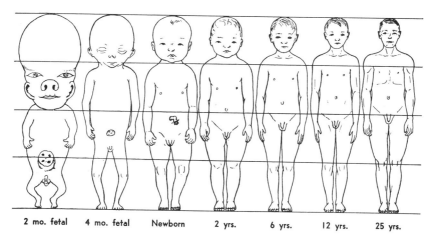

2 mo. fetal   4 mo. fetal   Newborn   2 yrs.   6 yrs.   12 yrs.   25 yrs.

FIGURE 26. *Two fetal and 5 postnatal stages drawn to the same total height to show the characteristic age changes in the proportions of various parts of the body. (Redrawn from Scammon, in B. M. Patten: Human Embryology. 2nd ed. New York, Blakiston Div., McGraw-Hill Book Company, Inc., 1953.)*

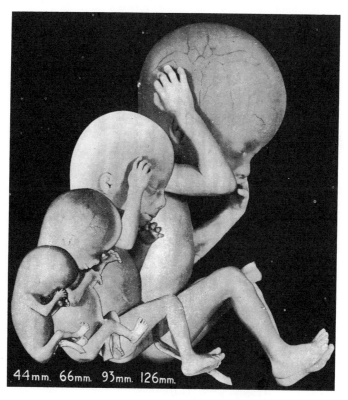

44mm. 66mm. 93mm. 126mm.

FIGURE 27. *Superimposed photographs of fetuses between the third and fifth months of pregnancy (original). (W. J. Hamilton, J. D. Boyd and H. W. Mossman: Human Embryology. 2nd ed. Cambridge, W. Heffer and Sons, Ltd., 1962.)*

the fetus resembles a "dried up, old person with red wrinkled skin." In the eight month subcutaneous fat begins to be deposited, and this continues so that the body continues to round out until birth. Within the body framework, bones begin to calcify toward the end of the second month. Enamel and dentin of the teeth begin to form early in the third month.

Physiological Functions

During the greater part of fetal life all the organs carry on to some degree the processes that will be necessary for the maintenance of life after birth, even though these functions are not essential until birth. From an early age the fetus swallows amniotic fluid, and this is absorbed from the walls of the digestive tract. Enzymes are secreted into the digestive tract; the liver secretes bile; there is some peristaltic activity.

The kidneys secrete urine. Meconium, consisting of waste products, accumulates in the intestines, but normally is not eliminated until after birth. The endocrine glands begin to function, and there is an exchange of hormones between mother and fetus through the placenta. The beating of the heart begins during the first month as pulsations in a rudimentary heart. Fetal circulation is established early.

The fetus makes respiratory movements, and amniotic fluid has been demonstrated to have been taken into the lungs, but there is no constant respiratory movement as there is after birth (Smith, 1959c). Hooker (1952) cites as the precursors of true respiration contraction and expansion of the chest and contraction of the abdomen. These begin rather feebly and increase in vigor. Along with this reflex activity the development of the lungs and especially their elastic tissue is essential. Hooker reported that no fetus in their study could be resuscitated before $23\frac{1}{2}$ weeks. At twenty-seven weeks one premature lived.

Behavior

The beginnings of behavior seen in the newborn are rooted deep in the prenatal period. The development of this behavior follows an orderly, sequential pattern, provided the environment is appropriate.

The development of reflex behavior, typical of the neonate, has been demonstrated in studies begun in 1932 in the Department of Anatomy at the University of Pittsburgh School of Medicine and reported by Hooker (1952). Of 131 fetuses from $6\frac{1}{2}$ weeks (menstrual age) to postmatures at forty-five weeks, which were delivered surgically because of maternal conditions or were born spontaneously, eighty-four are reported. Age was assessed by length. Reflexes were tested by stroking the skin with a hair. The earliest response was noted at $7\frac{1}{2}$ weeks. The results were as follows:

1. Activity develops in an orderly sequence. Several sequences were reported. One of these leads to the swallowing and sucking reflexes. Stimulating the lips resulted first in momentary lip closure, then a firm closure, later pro-

trusion of lips and pursing of the mouth and then sucking at twenty-nine weeks. Swallowing appeared after the ability to respond to stimulus by a firm closure of the mouth at $14\frac{1}{2}$ weeks.

Another sequence was that leading to the grasping reflex, which consisted of (1) partial finger closures between $10\frac{1}{2}$ and eleven weeks, (2) complete closure of fingers with thumb apposition at $13\frac{1}{2}$ to fourteen weeks, (3) closure maintained for a brief time at fourteen weeks, (4) true grasp at $18\frac{1}{2}$ weeks, (5) grasp supporting the weight of the body at twenty-seven weeks. Grasping with both hands comes around the time of birth. This sequence is the same as that of the postnatal acquisition of the function of prehension on a voluntary basis (Halverson, 1937, 1943).

2. The sequence of activity followed a cephalocaudal direction. The earliest response to tactile stimulation was to that in the face, later the palms of the hands and the arms and even later the legs. In the face area, response was limited to the lip and nose areas at $7\frac{1}{2}$ weeks and gradually increased to include the whole face. Responses appeared in the sequence of neck, upper trunk and arms, lower trunk, legs.

3. The proximodistal direction of development of movement seen in other animals was only partially present in these human fetuses.

The first movement of the arms at eight weeks was noted at the shoulder, but prior to that age quivering of the arm and fingers was observed, which no doubt was preliminary to the shoulder movement. Hooker remarks, "It may be that a greater number of sensory endings per unit areas in the hand of man has led to the earlier development of its reflexes."

4. Total pattern responses were gradually replaced by local specific responses.

5. Quality of responses changed from mechanical and stereotyped to gainful, flowing movements.

6. Muscles grew stronger, and reflexes became more and more mature.

Fetal activity in utero generally begins to be felt by the mother about the sixteenth to eighteenth week. The fetus has periods of activity alternating with periods of rest. Studies in which mothers observed and reported fetal activity, both spontaneous and after external stimulation, have shown that the activity, from the sixth month, increased with fetal age up to the last fetal month (Newberry, 1941), varied from day to day (Kellogg, 1941), was more pronounced at the close of the day than in the morning (Harris and Harris, 1946), varied among women, some fetuses being very active and others relatively quiet (Newberry, 1941) and differed in type. Three types of activity—squirming, kicking and a rhythmic series of quick convulsive movements, termed hiccups—have been described (Newberry, 1941). Kicking was the largest component of total activity, and hiccuping the smallest. Maternal fatigue and emotion stimulate fetal activity (Bernard and Sontag, 1947; Schmeidler, 1941; Sontag and Wallace, 1935). Increase in fetal activity is associated with increase in maternal basal metabolic rate (Richards, 1938).

Need of Maturity for Survival

The fetus must have achieved a certain degree of maturity to survive at birth. Organs and functions must have become sufficiently mature to meet the demands of postnatal life. If the fetus is immature, it may not survive, depending upon the degree of maturity (a fetus of seven months or less seldom survives), or it may survive only when specially fed, provided with special warmth, protected carefully from possible infection and given additional oxygen to breathe. It is now recommended, however, that oxygen be used in minimal amounts to meet clinical needs, since oxygen in too large quantities is associated with retrolental fibroplasia, a condition in the retina of the eye which may affect sight (Guy et al., 1956; Kinsey, 1956). Since immaturity is a hazard for the newborn, it is important that a fetus develop fully before birth and not be born prematurely.

Nesbitt (1966), classifying fetal growth by age, designates a fetus of age twenty-nine through thirty-six weeks as viable (premature), with weights from 1000 to 2499 gm., and a fetus of age thirty-seven through forty or more weeks as mature (full-term), with weights of 2500 or more gm. (average, 3000 to 3400 gm.).

Prenatal Influences

The old concept of the fetus as a parasite, living a well-protected life and taking from the mother, at her own expense if necessary, all that is needed for its development has been replaced by the concept of a dynamic relation in which there is an interchange between mother and child and in which the well-being of the mother has an effect on the development of the child. Thus some discussion of prenatal influences is essential in understanding fetal development.

The health of the child is bound up with that of the mother. Maternal difficulties during pregnancy are often associated with conditions of the infant at birth or later. Lilienfeld and Pasamanick (1954) and Kawi and Pasamanick (1959) formulated a hypothesis that a continuum of reproduction casualty is associated with certain prenatal and paranatal conditions. This continuum extends from a lethal component consisting of abortions, stillbirths, neonatal deaths and a sublethal component consisting of cerebral palsy, epilepsy, mental deficiency and behavior disorders in children, including some of the reading disorders. Toxemia and bleeding during pregnancy were found to be largely responsible for this association.

Ingalls (1960), discussing congenital malformations, calls attention to the important factor of timing of environmental impacts, the most vulnerable time being that period when an organ is forming, during the first two months of development. For example, the limb buds are first developing at four weeks, and the primary fibers of the lens of the eye are being laid down at five to six weeks. Time, he says, registers its impact in three ways: fetal age, maternal age (the "human incubator" becomes less efficient with advancing age) and secular hazards such as epidemics, atomic bombings.

In appraising the effect of various factors on the health of mother and child one must consider their multiplicity and place each in proper relation to the others.

Nutrition influences the development of the child. In some instances nutrition may be a limiting factor in the development of a healthy new-born; in others it may be a contributing factor; in some the limiting factor may be solely of a non-nutritional nature. Hence studies differ which attempt to evaluate causal factors in development. Conflicting results may arise from differences in the subjects studied, different circumstances of their lives, time of the study or varying ways in which the data are analyzed.

Studies which have attempted to determine the role of nutrition as a prenatal influence include those in which women on self-selected diets were observed, those in which supplements were given to improve a poor diet, and observations of mothers and infants during periods of severe food shortage. In such studies, birth weight, prematurity and the health status of the infants observed by a pediatrician were investigated. Birth weight was found to be reduced in The Netherlands during the famine months of late 1944 and early 1945 (Smith, 1947) and during the period of food shortage in Germany after World War II (Dean, 1951). In the United States a group of underweight mothers had significantly lighter and shorter infants than mothers of approximately standard weight (Tompkins et al., 1955). On the other hand, no relation between birth weight and maternal diet during pregnancy was found in the Vanderbilt Cooperative Study of Maternal and Infant Nutrition in Tennessee (Darby et al., 1955). It would appear that severe deprivations are necessary to affect the size of the child. Prematurity occurred more frequently among the infants of the underweight subjects of Tompkins et al. (1955). There was a positive relation between poor diets and the incidence of prematurity in Boston (Burke et al., 1943) and Iowa (Jeans et al., 1955), while Dieckman et al. (1951), Darby et al. (1955) and McGanity et al. (1954) found no correlation between the two. Supplementation of poor diets in England (People's League of Health, 1946) was followed by a reduction in premature births. On the other hand, obese women tend to have large, fat babies (Widdowson, 1955).

Poor nutrition, whether due to excesses or deficiencies, can affect the condition of the infant. Obesity, which is a great concern in this country, may create a hazard to mother and child, for obese women are more prone than nonobese women to disorders of pregnancy, e.g., toxemia, which may affect the fetus (Greenhill, 1965; Tompkins et al., 1955).

Deficient nutrition, if severe enough, may contribute to the condition of the infant at birth. The Department of Maternal and Child Health at the Harvard School of Public Health found that the weight and composition of fetal livers may reflect the maternal diet (Smith et al., 1953). Burke et al. (1943, 1949) found in 216 cases in which diets of the mother were evaluated that every stillborn infant, every infant who died within a few days of birth (with one exception), the majority of infants with severe congenital defects, every premature and every "functionally immature" infant was born to a mother with poor or very poor diet. Dieckman et al. (1951) found that pediatricians' ratings of infants correlated highly with the protein intake of their mothers during pregnancy. Supplementation of inadequate diets in England reduced stillbirths and neonatal mortality (Balfour, 1944). During the siege of Leningrad in 1942 under such conditions as severe food restriction, the necessity to do heavy work and the emotional stress of the bombardment, many mothers gave birth to infants who showed lowered vitality (Antonov, 1947). In contrast to this evidence, the Vanderbilt study (McGanity et al., 1954) found no relation between the mother's diet and stillbirths or neonatal deaths.

In spite of the fact that nutrition was not found to be a primary cause of obstetric difficulties in the Vanderbilt study, the authors point out that diet during pregnancy is important. They also indicate that adding to an already adequate diet will provide no additional benefits. It is suggested that the *lifetime dietary history* of a woman is equally important as diet during the nine months of pregnancy, if not more so (Stearns, 1958; Thomson, 1957).

Other factors influencing a woman's health have a bearing on the welfare of the infant. Hirsch (1931) found that *hard work* during the last months of pregnancy increases the number of prematurely born infants and infants of low birth weight. Hard work was one of the conditions affecting mothers in Leningrad during its siege.

Evidence tends to show that maternal experience of deep *emotions* can affect the child. Although the old wives' tale of the effect of maternal impressions such as birthmarks from being frightened by a cat or longing for strawberries or the like is not true, deep and prolonged emotions can alter the body's chemistry. In Chapter Four is a discussion of the body's adaptation to stress. When stress becomes too severe, this adaptive mechanism breaks down. Thus in times of long, intense emotional disturbances during pregnancy the body chemistry of the mother could be so changed that the growing organism would be affected (Ausubel, 1957). Sontag (1941) reported increased fetal activity when mothers were under deep emotional stress. The more active fetuses tended to weigh less at birth and had minimal amounts of fat storage. Some of the infants born to mothers subjected to such stimuli had feeding difficulties during the first month after birth. Richards and Newberry (1938) showed a positive relation between fetal activity and performance of the Gesell test items at six months of age. Whether increased fetal activity has any effect on later development has yet to be determined.

Viral infection in the first six to ten weeks of pregnancy may interfere with normal fetal development. Infants with structural abnormalities have been born to mothers who had German measles (rubella) during the first two or three months of pregnancy. Blattner (1959) reported that 10 to 12 per cent of the babies born to mothers who had rubella during the first three months were affected. Michaels and Mellin (1960) reported that the younger the fetus, the greater the chance that maternal rubella will produce congenital malformations. They found 47 per cent affected at one to four weeks, 22 per cent at five to eight weeks, 7 per cent at nine to twelve weeks and 6 per cent at thirteen to sixteen weeks.

The *maternal and fetal endocrine systems* have a complementary action. A maternal deficiency of endocrine secretions may affect the development of the fetus. For example, if a mother has inadequate thyroid function, part of the secretion of the fetal thyroid will be used to support the "poor relation." Children of hypothyroid mothers have been known to have enlarged thyroids at birth (Sontag, 1941). Similarly, maternal diabetes affects the fetal pancreas, and its function at birth is greatly accelerated (Sontag, 1941). Maternal diabetes also produces hazards for the infant (Dekaban, 1959b; Dekaban and Baird, 1959) and affects its size (Fischer and Moloshok, 1960).

Incompatibility of an inherited blood substance, the *Rh factor* (Smith, Vaughan and Diamond, 1964), between mother and fetus will cause anemia in the late fetal months if the mother has been sufficiently sensitized to have produced antibodies which, in turn, will reach the blood stream of the fetus and cause destruction of the red blood cells. This can occur when the mother has Rh-negative blood and the fetus has Rh-positive blood. Sensitization of the mother may occur through blood transfusions with Rh-positive blood or through gradual sensitization by the fetus. This sensitization will usually not be sufficient to affect the first child. Later children may or may not be affected.

Deep *x-ray* treatment during the early months of pregnancy can affect fetal development. *Radiation* affected fetuses in Nagasaki (Yamazaki et al., 1954) and in Hiroshima (Plummer, 1952). The infants of Nagasaki women who showed definite radiation signs from the atomic bombing had higher morbidity and mortality rates than those of mothers who were beyond the radiation center. Fetal mortality was 23.3 per cent in contrast to 2.7 per cent among the controls; neonatal and infant mortality was 26.1 per cent, controls 3.6 per cent; mental retardation was 25 per cent and 0. It was concluded in Hiroshima in a study of anomalies occurring in children exposed in utero to the atomic bomb that central nervous system defects can be produced in the fetus by atomic bomb radiation, provided exposure occurs approximately within 1200 meters of the hypocenter. No effective shielding, such as concrete, protects the fetus from direct irradiation. Seven of eleven children of mothers within 1200 meters had microcephaly with mental retardation. Nine of these eleven children had head circumferences that fell below one standard deviation of the mean for Japanese children.

Certain *drugs* have deleterious effects, as was dramatically proved in Germany when congenital abnormalities of the limbs, hands and feet were traced to a new sleeping tablet and tranquilizer, thalidomide, first marketed in 1958 and withdrawn from the market in 1961. The sensitive period for damage to the embryo from the drug was from the thirtieth to the sixtieth day after the last menstrual period (Dunn, Fisher and Kohler, 1962; Taussig, 1962).

Endocrine therapy has been found to have attendant hazards for the fetus (Wilkins, 1960).

Anoxia (insufficient oxygen) is a specific cause of congenital deformity in mice (Ingalls, 1950, 1953). Mice were subjected to conditions similar to transporting them to the top of Mt. Everest for five hours (Ingalls, 1956). The nature of the defect is determined by the degree of anoxia and the time during pregnancy at which the mouse is exposed. Some fragmentary clinical and epidemiologic facts are beginning to indicate that the experimental findings in mice may apply to human subjects (Ingalls, 1953). Ingalls pointed out that it is an oversimplification to say that lack of oxygen causes defects. Both genetic factors and environmental stress combine to form a specific defect at a particular stage of development.

The fetus may be subject to the risk of anoxia, even though its oxygen needs are less than after birth. Lack of oxygen can produce neurologic damage which can be reflected in behavior. Psychologic, neurologic and behavioral defects have been demonstrated in monkeys with asphyxia (Windle, 1960). The infant after birth may exhibit behavior suggestive of neurologic damage due to anoxia. Graham and her associates (1957), in a study of the significance of anoxia as a perinatal experience, showed an association between maternal complications in pregnancy and scores on a behavior test for newborns. Infants whose mothers had had complications in pregnancy which are believed to lead to fetal anoxia had poorer performance than those whose mothers had had no such complications.

Conditions unfavorable to the growing organism occur relatively infrequently. "Once implantation is well established the odds are overwhelmingly in favor of a normal delivery and a healthy baby" (Corner, 1944).

RECOGNITION OF PREGNANCY

A number of signs and symptoms indicate a probability of pregnancy; others are positive. Probable signs include cessation of menstruation, changes in the breasts, increased frequency of urination, nausea and vomiting, basal body temperature, progressive growth of the uterus, and biologic test results. The positive signs are fetal heart sounds and fetal movement.

Probable Signs and Symptoms

If a woman in good health who has previously menstruated regularly ceases to menstruate, there is a strong probability that she is pregnant. Many causes other than pregnancy can account for cessation of menstruation; conversely, it is not uncommon for a woman to have one or two menstrual periods, usually very short, after conception has occurred.

Some enlargement of the breasts accompanied by a tingling or burning sensation may occur as early as the fourth week. The breasts continue to enlarge throughout pregnancy. The nipples become darker and more prominent, and the areolae (the dark circles around the nipples) increase in size and also darken. Change is more pronounced in women pregnant for the first time than in those who have had previous pregnancies.

Early in pregnancy the bladder becomes more irritable; there is an increased frequency in the desire to urinate because of changes in the position of the uterus which stretch the base of the bladder. This causes a sensation like that of a full bladder during the first trimester (three months). It cannot by itself be considered a sign of pregnancy, since the need of frequent urination is often a sign of some nervous tension.

A tendency to nausea, often with vomiting in the morning, may appear about the fourth week. About one-third of the women have none, about one-third have much nausea, and about one-third have it occasionally and slightly (Greenhill, 1965). It usually ceases when fetal activity is felt. This sign, however, unless accompanied by other symptoms, is of no diagnostic value, since it may also be a symptom of many other conditions.

The pattern of basal body temperature (rectal temperature taken on waking), if taken daily before and after conception, can serve as a helpful diagnostic procedure early in pregnancy. A level of 98.8 to 99.9°F. sustained for more than sixteen days after ovulation is highly suggestive of pregnancy. Such a diagnosis is correct in at least 97 per cent of cases (Barton and Wiesner, 1945; Palmer, 1942).

The uterus changes in form, size, consistency and position. These changes, when noted by an experienced examiner, are highly probable indications of pregnancy.

Most of the biological tests used for indications of pregnancy depend upon the appearance of large amounts of chorionic gonadotrophin in the blood and urine early in pregnancy. Its biologic effect on the ovaries of rodents or on the gonads of amphibia is tested. Results become positive within two weeks after the first missed menstrual cycle. These tests have an accuracy of 95 to 98 per cent in early pregnancy (Greenhill, 1965). The Aschheim-Zondek, the Friedman, the ovarian hyperemia and the male frog and toad tests are used.

Positive Signs

Detection of the fetal heartbeat by a physician is an absolute sign of pregnancy. Fetal heart sounds are first heard in the fifth month.

About the sixteenth to eighteenth week a woman will begin to feel fetal movement. Active movements may in some cases be felt, seen or heard by a physician as early as the twelfth week, but generally are first recognized about the fifth or sixth month.

MATERNAL CHANGES DURING PREGNANCY

Providing for the needs of a growing organism places increased demands upon the woman during pregnancy. These demands are met by structural and functional adaptations of the body, including uterine changes, development of the mammary glands, development of the placenta with its nutritional and endocrine functions, increased demands on all parts and functions of the body, and physiologic and nutritional adaptations.

Increase in Weight

An average, normal woman increases her total weight during pregnancy by about 24 pounds (Greenhill, 1965). About two-thirds of women can be expected to gain from 13 to 35 pounds. This increase represents the weight of the fetus, the placenta, the membranes and the fluids, the growth of the breasts, and some gain in the other tissues of the body. About 40 per cent represents fetus, placenta, amnion and amniotic fluid; 60 per cent represents changes in various tissues. Most women ultimately lose these gains in six to twelve months (Clements, 1961). During the first third of pregnancy a woman gains about 2.5 pounds; during the second third, about 10.8 pounds; during the last third, about 11.2 pounds (Greenhill, 1965). The gains in the first two-thirds of pregnancy result chiefly from gains in the tissues of the mother; in the last third the gains are due chiefly to the growth of the fetus and the uterus. Excessive gains may mean retention of fluid in the tissues, which is a warning of possible danger. Many obstetricians consider 20 pounds an appropriate gain.

Tompkins et al. (1955) point out that too little gain may also be a hazard. They found that failure to gain an average amount, especially in the first two-thirds of pregnancy, increased the likelihood of premature birth. Premature births were nearly three times as frequent among women who gained less than the average, from their first visit to the clinic to the end of the second trimester, as among the women who had an average or greater than average gain. The authors concluded that early metabolic and physiologic stabilization of a woman, with a steady gain in weight at an average rate, can contribute significantly to a reduction in premature labor, the highest single cause of infant loss.

The Uterus

This organ, situated within the pelvis, stretches from a small, almost solid organ, shaped somewhat like a pear and approximately 3 inches long and about 1.5 ounces in weight, into a large muscular sac, weighing about 1.5 pounds, which will hold a 7-pound or larger baby, a placenta weighing about 1.25 pounds, about 20 inches of umbilical cord, and an amniotic sac containing a quart or more of amniotic fluid. The uterus increases in capacity from 2 cc. to 4000 cc. in order to do this. Through hypertrophy of its muscle walls the uterus must be able to expel infant and placenta at the time of delivery. A woman, to accommodate herself to the change in size, weight and position of the uterus and its contents, sometimes noticeably changes the way she carries herself, tending to throw her head and shoulders back.

Because the uterus is attached to ligaments fastened to the pelvis and is not fixed in a stationary position, it pushes upward into the abdominal cavity as it grows. By three months it is halfway to the umbilicus, by five months at the umbilicus, and by nine months it reaches the tip of the sternum. During the last two or three weeks of gestation the uterus drops back toward the pelvis, and the change in the contour of the body indicates that the end of pregnancy is near.

The Placenta

The placenta is the connection between the maternal and fetal organisms. It performs many functions. Through it the fetus receives nourishment, eliminates wastes, receives a passive immunity which provides protection against diseases to which the mother is immune until the infant, after birth, is capable of elaborating his own antibodies. The placenta serves as a source of hormones, and after the first three months the hormones of this organ maintain pregnancy. It serves as a fetal lung. By selective interchange it transfers the nutrients to be used in providing energy and building blocks for the fetal tissues. It contains enzymes which function in intermediary metabolism.

The placenta begins to function in the third week and attains its maximum size early in pregnancy. From the seventh or eighth lunar month it shows signs of physiologic aging (Greenhill, 1965).

The Mammary Glands

Another change is development of the breasts, or mammary glands. These are skin glands which have undergone highly specialized development. The early cell mass undergoes a process of multiplication and ramification into a fairly complex duct system. Later, secreting glandular cells develop. One of the first signs of oncoming puberty in the girl is increased activity in the breasts, with increased growth in the duct system, due to increased ovarian secretion and increased deposits of fat. Relatively little growth of glandular tissue, or the secreting alveolar cells, occurs until pregnancy, when an extensive differentiation of the glands occurs. This development and the subsequent secretion of milk involve an interaction of the hormones of several endocrine glands— the pituitary, ovaries and placenta, and, indirectly, thyroid, adrenals and pancreas—because of their effects on energy metabolism. Figure 28 demonstrates the hormonal factors that participate in the development of the mammary glands and lactation. In addition to the interaction of hormones, complicated neural and nutritional mechanisms are involved in milk secretion.

By the twelfth week of pregnancy, colostrum, a yellowish fluid, may be secreted. Lactation, however, does not occur until after delivery.

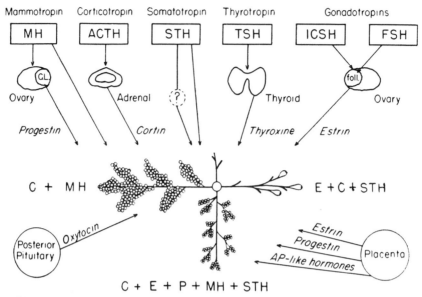

FIGURE 28. *Hormonal factors operating in lactation, according to Lyons and associates. The presence of estrogens (E), corticosteroids (C) and somatotropin (STH) is necessary for duct proliferation (as indicated in the right-hand portion of the schematic puberal mammary gland). The addition of progesterone (P) and prolactin (MH) brings about full alveolar development in the prolactational mammary gland of pregnancy (below). The discharge of milk from the alveoli requires the additional presence of oxytocin in the lactating gland (left). (W. R. Lyons, C. H. Li and R. E. Johnson: Hormonal control of mammary growth and lactation. Rec. Progr. Hormone Res., 14:219, 1958.)*

Physiological Changes

Physiologically, a woman is quite different during pregnancy than before or after. Leitch (Clements, 1961) says that a woman builds up a new way of life to a climax at thirty-six weeks and then undoes most of it in the six weeks after the infant is born.

The fact that she can produce at term an infant weighing 5 to 10 pounds without much relation to her own gain in weight testifies to her physiological adaptability. The body works harder and adapts itself to the added demands. The heart has a greater volume of blood to transport. Because of this increase in blood volume, the hemoglobin count is lower, though the actual amount of hemoglobin circulating in the blood is not reduced. The kidneys excrete more waste products of metabolism; changes in the mechanism of oxygen and carbon dioxide transport occur; sweat and sebaceous glands of the skin increase their activities; skin pigmentation increases. The endocrine glands become more active. Hormonal changes are responsible for maintaining pregnancy and for many metabolic alterations. Macy (1958) pointed out that loss of appetite, reduction in food intake and disturbed gastrointestinal equilibrium in the period before implantation and during the early stages of embryonic development may be the result of the greater hormonal secretions and of the changes in the digestive tract which they produce. Thus alterations in all functions of the body and possible instabilities in functions occur. It is clear that any structural or functional weakness of the maternal organism may become apparent under these conditions.

The basal metabolic rate increases as the thyroid gland becomes more active. Nutritional adaptations take place (Beaton, 1961). Evidence supports this concept for protein, calcium and iron. The pregnant woman retains more protein, more calcium and more iron. Iron is also conserved by the cessation of menstruation. Whether an adaptive mechanism exists for the vitamins is not known.

PHYSICAL NEEDS DURING PREGNANCY

Nutrition

A woman takes with her into pregnancy her whole nutritional past. Her body reflects that past, her food habits and attitudes. In fact, some believe that nutrition prior to pregnancy is of greater importance than nutrition during the period of gestation. If the woman acquired habits and attitudes toward food that have provided her with the essential nutrients and energy in amounts appropriate for the maintenance of a healthy body, she will need no change other than a quantitative increase as the demands of pregnancy increase. Women in a better economic position or with more education tend to have better food habits (Payton et al., 1960).

It is the aim of the maternal nutriture (1) to provide adequate amounts of essential nutrients for the maintenance of the mother so that her tissues will not be depleted, (2) to provide for growth and development of the fetus during the forty weeks of gestation, and (3) to protect both mother and fetus from complications during and after the reproductive cycle. To aid the metabolic and physiologic changes and provide more efficient utilization of nutrients, the placenta permits a differential level of nutrients in the blood of mother and fetus to meet the greater fetal needs. Iron, ascorbic acid and vitamin B_{12} have higher fetal than maternal levels. The mother, however, greedily appears to take for herself vitamins A and E. Iodine shortage may produce congenital cretinism. Riboflavin deficiency in animals may produce a congenital deformity without appreciable effect in the mother (Wishik, 1959), but whether this is true for human beings is not known.

Although there are women who enter pregnancy nutritionally unprepared and go through it with insufficient nutrients or are obese, the *average* American woman has a satisfactory nutritional status and food intake, if the findings of the Vanderbilt study are widely applicable.

The Vanderbilt study (McGanity et al., 1958) included 2338 pregnant white women who attended the outpatient clinic over a period of years in Nashville, Tennessee. Their incomes fell in the lower brackets ($1200 to $3000). These women were followed through pregnancy, the birth of the child, and for ten weeks after delivery. Records were kept of their obstetric performance, clinical assessments of complications, dietary and biochemical assessments, and the condition of their infants. Observations were made during each trimester (three times during pregnancy) and at the postpartum examination. Seventy-three per cent of the women received no dietary supplement. Obstetric complications were similar to or less than in the average obstetric population in this country. No clinically recognizable deficiency disease appeared.

Although not all levels were equal to the recommended allowances of the Food and Nutrition Board, the nutrient intakes were not disturbingly low and had considerable individual variability. An approximate 200-calorie decrease was noted, associated with a similar decrease in most of the nutrients between the second and third trimesters. The diets showed frequent consumption of basic nutrients supplied by milk and eggs, green and yellow vegetables, and citrus and other fruits.

The nutrient levels in the blood and urine were consistent with expectations in a healthy population. Some decreased during pregnancy and rose again after delivery; some rose during pregnancy and fell after delivery. Hemoglobin, serum protein, vitamin A and the urinary excretion of thiamine and riboflavin followed the first pattern; serum carotene, tocopherol and the urinary excretion of N-methylnicotinamide followed the second pattern. Serum ascorbic acid level decreased except when the intake reached 80 mg. The absorption and utilization of iron increased. These changes, except for ascorbic acid, were not related to the intake of these nutrients.

Although for the average woman the findings revealed a satisfactory state, some women were underweight, some overweight, some ate poorly, some excessively, some had low serum and urinary levels of nutrients, and some had obstetric difficulties, and also some infants had difficulties.

The underweight group (less than 85 per cent of standard weight) had the highest dietary intakes (which decreased with parity), increased prematurity and fewer neonatal deaths and congenital malformations. Conversely, the overweight group (more than 120 per cent of standard weight) had the lowest dietary intakes (perhaps some of this under direction of a physician), more stillbirths, three times more toxemia and lowered frequency of puerperal morbidity. High weight gains, which were found in women of all groups and all ages, occurred especially in the second trimester and in those who had more toxemia.

Of all the subjects, 11.3 per cent were classified as having low hemoglobin (less than 10 mg. per 100 ml.). In the total group only 4 per cent showed iron deficiency. Those who received iron supplements remained significantly lower than the unsupplemented group during pregnancy. The input hemoglobin levels were about the same for both high and low hemoglobin levels in mothers.

Comparisons on the basis of high (3250 calories) and low (1000 calories) dietary intakes showed no advantage for the higher intake in calories or protein in the number of fetal or obstetric complications, birth weight or length of the infants or with physical or biochemical changes. When the intake of calories was less than 1500 and protein less than 50 gm., positive correlations were found between diet and certain obstetric and fetal complications, but the conditions appeared to be responsible for the lowered intakes, and not the reverse.

This study indicates that nutrition is important in the life of the pregnant woman, that the range of adequate intakes is not narrow but wide, that physiologic and biochemical changes during pregnancy need to be evaluated not only in terms of diet, but also in terms of the body's adaptation to pregnancy, and that, for most women, a diet that will provide the essential nutrients is attainable normally without need for supplementation.

Daily Dietary Needs

The woman who enters pregnancy with an adequate, well-balanced diet need not increase her food intake until the second half of pregnancy, when needs of the fetus for growth become important. According to the recommended allowances of the Food and Nutrition Board (Table 3), the pregnant woman increases her calorie intake by 200 calories, protein intake by 20 gm., calcium by 0.5 gm., iron by 5 mg., vitamin A by 1000 I.U., thiamine by 0.2 mg., riboflavin by 0.3 mg., niacin by 3 mg. equivalent, ascorbic acid by 30 mg., and includes 400 I.U. of vitamin D. Table 3 shows the comparison of the allowance recommended before pregnancy, during pregnancy and during lactation. These allowances provide for a margin of safety, taking into consideration individual differences. They can be attained with a variety

TABLE 3. Recommended Daily Allowances for Women During Reproductive Rest, Pregnancy and Lactation (Designed for the Maintenance of Good Nutrition of Healthy Women in the United States)

NUTRIENTS	WOMEN: AGE 18–35 YEARS WT. 128 LB., HT. 64″	PREGNANT (2nd AND 3rd TRIMESTERS)	LACTATING
Calories	2100*	+200	+1000
Protein (gm.)	58	+20	+40
Calcium (gm.)	0.8	+0.5	+0.5
Iron (mg.)	15	+5	+5
Vitamin A (I.U.)	5000	+1000	+3000
Thiamine (mg.)	0.8	+0.2	+0.4
Riboflavin (mg.)	1.3	+0.3	+0.6
Niacin (mg. equiv.)	14	+3	+7
Ascorbic acid (mg.)	70	+30	+30
Vitamin D (I.U.)		400	400

From National Academy of Sciences—National Research Council: Recommended Daily Dietary Allowances. Report of the Food and Nutrition Board, revised 1964. Publication 1146, 1964.

*Calorie adjustments must be made for variations in body size, age, physical activity and environmental temperature.

of foods which will provide other nutrients for which requirements have been less well defined.

For most women no supplementations are necessary except vitamin D (but not in excess; see p. 190), and iodine in the form of iodized salt in regions such as the Great Lakes area, where iodine is not available from natural sources. If salt is restricted during pregnancy, another iodine supplement may be necessary for women in such areas. Nutrients in excess of these allowances provide no extra benefits, as indicated in the Vanderbilt study. Burke (1965) points out that a minimum of 2000 calories is needed to meet the increased needs for nutrients. On the other hand, excess of foods high in carbohydrates and fats is likely to lead to excessive gain of weight, which is undesirable. Thus it may be necessary to readjust the dietary habits of those who have a fondness for high caloric foods.

Elimination

Elimination is an important aspect of the nutritional cycle. Waste products are eliminated through the bowels, kidneys, lungs and skin. All these avenues of elimination are important in pregnancy because of the increased loads they carry. Adequate fluid, a diet containing plenty of fruits and vegetables, exercise, regular habit of bowel movement and bathing will contribute to satisfactory elimination.

Exercise and Rest

The balance of activity and rest, which varies somewhat with individuals, changes to some degree during pregnancy in that more frequent rest periods are necessary to prevent fatigue. The amount of rest through the day will vary with the woman and her activities. Exercise which stimulates circulation, promotes digestion and elimination and keeps muscles in good condition may include housework and some exercise out of doors. Walking is an activity in which all can indulge. The strenuousness of exercise is a matter of a woman's customary activities and her physician's decision. Every woman can work out a regimen which meets her particular needs. If a woman has not acquired the art of relaxation, she can be helped to learn it (Rathbone, 1957; Thoms, 1950). Excessive exercise during late pregnancy can lead to premature labor.

Special exercises in breathing, relaxation, and contraction and relaxation of the pelvic floor muscles, which will help the woman to cooperate at the time of delivery, can be practiced during pregnancy (Thoms, 1950; Thoms and Roth, 1950). For instruction in these she can consult her physician or the clinic she is attending.

Teeth

The old wives' tale, "for every child a tooth," has no validity. Although the tooth is a dynamic structure and there is an exchange of calcium and phosphorus in both enamel and dentin, as indicated by isotope studies (Armstrong, 1955), this exchange is much slower than that in bone. It can be said, therefore, that the bones rather than the teeth provide the calcium for the fetus should adequate amounts of calcium be lacking in the mother's diet. Moreover, studies of the incidence of dental caries (Klein, 1935; Ziskin and Hotelling, 1937) indicate that pregnant women have no more dental decay than other women of like age. It is recommended that necessary repair work be done and regular trips to the dentist be continued. The old idea that dental work causes miscarriage has no basis in fact. Lack of dental care during pregnancy and lactation can contribute to tooth loss.

EMOTIONS IN PREGNANCY

Pregnancy is an experience with closely intertwined psychological and physical components. Feelings and attitudes contribute to physical well-being or distress; on the other hand, the physiological changes of pregnancy may act as a trigger in arousing new anxieties and fears and in reactivating dormant ones. Many women at this time have some anxieties and fears, and their feelings may vary. A woman's attitude toward pregnancy is intimately related to her emotional maturity, to her past and present experiences and to her personal adjustment. Her reactions will be a function of her personality. Her behavior, feelings and thoughts may reflect her emotional needs, relations within the family, reasons for having children, feelings about children, feelings about having this particular child, and her cultural background with its traditional customs, superstitions and possible fears.

Emotional manifestations appear along with physiological ones. Caplan (1960) states that pregnancy is a "biologically determined period of psychological stress." Emotional manifestations probably stem from two main areas: namely, the dynamic relation between body and feelings in which physiological and metabolic changes play a role and in the area of psychological dynamics. Among the former changes, emotional lability, and irritability, sensitivity, passivity and introversion, swings of mood, can be placed. Among the latter are the emotional changes that relate to personality.

Both the central nervous system and the autonomic nervous system become more labile during pregnancy, and endocrine and metabolic changes occur. These changes are accompanied by wide swings in mood, overreaction to stimuli and greater sensitivity. The autonomic nervous system loses its usual stability of control. Blushing tends to occur more readily; sometimes hot flashes and sometimes fainting are noted. Nausea may have both a physiological and a psychological element. These may constitute feelings of insecurity, fear and anxiety if not understood, and certainly call attention to bodily functions. This may lead to self-consciousness and undue attention to body functions such as breathing or heart beat which go on automatically. Minute analysis of feelings and a tendency to introspection may lead to misinterpretation of conditions and sensations which are normal to pregnancy.

A woman may change temporarily from an outgoing person actively concerned about others to one who chooses to be a receiver rather than a giver. She may suddenly tend to focus attention on herself, become passive, seek more love and affection; in fact, she may enjoy having attention lavished upon her and being "spoiled." The true meaning of such changes has to be understood by husband and family. Caplan (1960) is of the opinion that indulging her at this time helps in her preparation for motherhood.

Changes in sexual desire and performance may be anticipated at varying phases of pregnancy. Conflicts which were concealed from consciousness may come to the surface and may or may not be handled successfully. Attitudes toward pregnancy and the coming child vary. It is natural for women during pregnancy to have moments of doubt and uncertainty mixed with feelings of pleasure and happy anticipation. These ambivalent feelings can be accepted and dealt with more easily by the woman if she can express them to an understanding listening ear, perhaps her husband, her mother or a friend.

For some time there may be an initial rejection of pregnancy which later turns to acceptance. Caplan (1960) observed that approximately 85 per cent of women of the lower middle and upper lower socioeconomic classes showed some rejection in their first pregnancy; 85 to 90 per cent of those rejecting pregnancy had accepted it by the end of the first trimester.

Emotional change unfolds during pregnancy. Manifestations appear along with physiologic development. Certain emotional behavior will appear early in pregnancy and later disappear; some appears during the middle trimester and some toward the end. Examples may be found in early rejection and later acceptance; concern about herself; passivity, which may begin around the end of the first trimester and reach a peak around the seventh or eighth month; and sexual desire, which may diminish in the middle of pregnancy.

Feelings about their pregnancies and the birth of their babies were investigated (Newton, 1955) in a comparison of a group of women who complained with a group who reported that they felt fine during pregnancy. Two hundred and forty-six mothers of newborn babies were interviewed in the rooming-in wards of Jefferson Hospital in Philadelphia. One hundred and twenty-three interviews on the first or second postpartum day were used in the statistical analysis. Rooming-in was compulsory for all healthy ward patients. The majority of the group were married, Protestant, Negro multiparas; some unmarried or separated mothers with first babies, white and Roman Catholic women were included. No significant differences were found between Negro and white mothers in their expressed feelings toward their biologically determined role, but significant differences were found between different age and socioeconomic groups.

Women who were negative toward pregnancy were more likely to wish to be men and were apt to have fewer motherly desires. Women who were positive toward pregnancy were more apt to be motherly and were less likely to wish to be men. . . . The women who were negative toward the pregnancy . . . were most likely to terminate their pregnancies with easy childbirth.

. . . Other research studies suggest that feelings about pregnancy may change from rejection to acceptance as pregnancy progresses, and that feelings of nausea during pregnancy may be related to undesired sexual experiences and excessive dependence on the mother.

In comparing women who felt that childbirth was hard with those who felt that it was easy, Newton also found differences which, in general, indicated the following:

Women who felt negatively about birth were more likely to be physically less motherly women. They had fewer children, and were more likely to dislike breast feeding and rooming-in care of their babies. Women who felt positively about birth . . . were more apt to want to breast feed and almost always enjoyed the rooming-in care of their babies. They had more babies.

. . . The experiences of childbirth sometimes caused severe emotional trauma and, conversely, . . . psychological influences can affect the experiences of labor.

Freedom from Emotional Strain

To permit a smooth course in pregnancy, freedom from emotional strain goes hand in hand with a satisfactory physical regimen. Emotional strain may be generated within the person or be created by outside circumstances which are in no way under her control. The former need not occur if the woman is emotionally mature, is ready for pregnancy and has a means of allaying the fears and anxieties which may arise at this time. Many of the latter can be prevented if the members of her family are understanding and likely to create an atmosphere in which mutual understanding, self-control and happiness predominate. A woman can meet the unavoidable situations with less emotional disturbance if she has strength within herself and support from others. The day-to-day changes in her feelings may be kept at a minimum if her physical, social and emotional needs are met. Social activities and other interests help to prevent self-centeredness.

Briefly, a pregnant woman can expect to live a normal, wholesome life, taking precautions to avoid mishaps. On the whole, she can live about as any married woman who lives healthfully, avoiding excesses of any sort, but carrying on her ordinary work and play and living a life which is emotionally and sexually satisfying to her. Husband and wife may profit by having someone to whom they may go for counsel about pregnancy and the needs it engenders, and for personal guidance. An understanding physician is in a good position to provide this assistance.

ATTITUDES OF FAMILY MEMBERS

The woman ordinarily has nine months in which to make plans for the arrival of her baby and to make the necessary readjustments in family life. If there are other children, they can be prepared in such a way that they will welcome the new baby into their midst. Reactions of other children may be influenced by age and comprehension, and by attitudes of adults in the family, as well as by preparations made for the birth. Regardless of his position in the family, each child's adaptations will be to another who must for many months, at least, absorb a large portion of the mother's time.

It is not unusual for a young child to have feelings and behavior ranging from love to hostility in his relations with the new baby. The intensity of these feelings seems to depend to a large extent on the understanding of the mother and the ways in which she uses her understanding in making the older child feel comfortable. She can prepare herself for this eventuality by realizing that some jealousy may occur and that the child may express it overtly in his behavior toward the baby or by reverting to infantile behavior such as wetting himself or seeking the same attention that is given to the baby.

Informing the Children

Children often long for a baby sister or brother and welcome the news of an expected arrival, but they can also have erroneous ideas. Their knowledge of a baby may be so limited that they may picture the advent of someone who will immediately begin to play with them. If they know that the baby will be little and helpless, will need much of the mother's care, must be treated gently, and may be a brother or sister, they have ideas to which the new experience can be related more easily. Pictures of young babies or of themselves when they were babies, and visits to see very young babies can enlarge the children's store of knowledge.

Children can be told the truth about reproduction in simple but correct terms. They can accept naturally the statement that the baby is growing inside the mother's body in a special place meant for a baby to grow in, called the uterus, if one wishes to give it its name. They have a wholesome normal interest in the matter and can accept fact in contrast to fiction. If the mother is to go to the hospital when the baby is born, the children can know it. If the hospital is nearby, if they see it or some other hospital, they may have a feeling of familiarity about hospitals which engenders a sense of security. Otherwise they could have the shock of wakening some morning to find that their mother has disappeared in the night and gone to some strange place of which they know nothing.

Children's Concepts of Roles

Fear that children will talk may cause some parents to hesitate to answer their questions correctly and may induce them to hush the questions as if it were not right for the children to ask. But young children can begin to discover with whom a subject is to be discussed. Also, if they find their parents hesitant to reply to their questions, they may inquire from others who could provide untruths and unwholesome descriptions. The way in which parents answer their children's first questions about sex may have something to do with the child's early attitude toward sex, and those first patterns may possibly affect the individual's outlook on sex and all its ramifications in later life. Furthermore, the parents' own attitudes, even when there is little discussion with the child, provide information for him about masculine and feminine roles.

Answering the children's questions about birth correctly pertains not only to the accuracy of the child's information, but also to his concept of his parents as consistently telling the truth. Questions about the birth of a baby or of animals, which are usually asked at an early age, may be the first questions which parents are tempted to answer untruthfully. This may be partly because they themselves are embarrassed and so find it difficult to answer such questions simply and naturally without emotion, and partly because they have not sufficient knowledge to give them the correct vocabulary or enough background to answer the questions in a simple but truthful way. To reduce scientific truths to simple terms which a child can grasp and which can be given in the amounts he is ready to receive presupposes a sense of assurance which comes from having a sound basis of scientific knowledge at one's command.

Whatever the cause for the untruths or half truths which parents may give in answer to these first questions about sex, the fact remains that this may be the first time when parents fail to be honest with their children. A child thwarted in his normal desire for information may be less likely in the future to go freely to the parent with his queries. Children of preschool age do not easily grasp the idea of a long time

FIGURE 29. New roles can be learned early.
This older brother asked to assist in taking care of his baby sister.

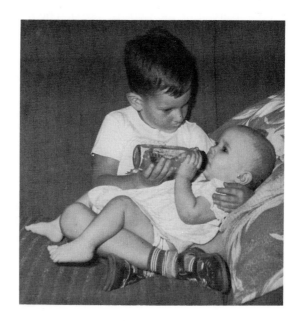

interval. Therefore it may be decided to wait to tell them of the new baby until the latter part of pregnancy. Several months of waiting could seem unduly long to a child. Then, too, since there is always some possibility of a miscarriage, unnecessary disappointment to the children may result.

The children can have some part in the preparation for the baby and his care after birth (Fig. 29). If there is to be some readjustment of space, they can help in making the change. They can join in the preparations for the new baby's clothing and for the place where he is to sleep, and thereby learn something about infants and about family attitudes.

OBSTETRICAL PERIOD

Medical and Nursing Care

With increased health services available to prospective mothers during pregnancy and at the time of birth, increased medical knowledge and broader education in the needs of mother and child, mothers and children today are better protected than they were formerly. This is indicated in the changes in mortality rates. The maternal death rate dropped from 60.8 per 10,000 live births in 1915 to 8.3 in 1950 to 3.7 in 1959 (United States Bureau of the Census, 1961). In 1963, 1964 and 1965 the maternal death rate dropped from 3.58 to 3.33 to 3.05 (United States Public Health Service information in Pocket Data Book, U.S.A., 1967). The average mortality rate for nonwhites, 10.2 per 10,000 in 1959, was greater than that for whites, 2.6 per 10,000 (United States Bureau of the Census, 1961). The principal causes of maternal deaths are hemorrhage, toxemia and infection.

The United States has also succeeded, through good prenatal care and public health education, in greatly reducing its infant mortality rates. The rate for the first year dropped from 99.9 per 1000 registered live births in 1915 to 38.3 in 1945, to 26.4 in 1959 (United States Bureau of the Census, 1961); the rates in 1960, 1963, 1964 and 1965 were 26.0, 25.2, 24.8 and 24.8 (United States Public Health Service information in Pocket Data Book, 1967). The drop in mortality of infants during the first month of life (twenty-eight days, to be exact) has been considerably less than that of infants between one month and one year of age. In 1959, with a mortality rate for the first year for all races in the United States of 26.4, the rate for infants under twenty-eight days of age was 19.0, and for those between twenty-eight days and one year, 7.4 (United States Bureau of the Census, 1961). These figures suggest the need for more extensive research on the causes of death in the first days of life. It has also given considerable impetus to the growing awareness among obstetricians and professional workers in related fields that adequate obstetric care involves both preconceptional and prenatal care if the life and health of the infant as well as those of the mother are to be protected.

Most infants in this country are born in hospitals (Corbin et al., 1962). The trend toward hospitalization has advanced rapidly in recent years. In 1940, 56 per cent of the births occurred in hospitals; in 1958, 96 per cent. The proportion of nonwhite mothers who had their babies in hospitals tripled in the same interval. This has meant for more women aseptic conditions with less chance for infection, and the facilities for handling any difficulties which might arise. With this increase, pressures on hospital facilities and personnel have also increased.

The dilemma today is not to persuade women to have their infants in hospitals, but rather to provide sufficient facilities and personnel so that there will be no compromise in quality of services. With more women to be served both in hospitals and in prenatal clinics, service may become impersonalized so that sympathy, understanding, interest and thoughtful consideration of the mother by both physicians and nurses in the prenatal period and in the hospital may diminish. This may be one of the factors responsible for the decline in prenatal care concomitant with the upward trend in public maternity care that is seen in many large cities where the lower socioeconomic groups are replacing the upper socioeconomic groups, who have moved to the suburbs (Corbin et al., 1962).

Plans for the Children During the Mother's Hospitalization

During pregnancy parents make plans for the care of the older children while the mother is to be in the hospital. The selection of the person to assume responsibility for the care of the child or children will depend on circumstances. It may be a relative, someone employed to be present under the supervision of the father, or a friend. Some fathers plan their vacation at this time and themselves take over full responsibility for the older children. If these plans are made fairly early, the children are prepared for the time when the mother will be out of the home. Before the birth of the baby the father can, if circumstances permit, take over some of the care of a child, have the child with him as he works about the house, and participate in his play more than formerly. The child can be shown the hospital and be given an explanation, in terms he can understand, of the reason why the mother will be there for a time.

Satisfactory plans for communication between mother and children while she is away can be made. Women have used various devices for keeping in touch with their children. One mother who had a telephone in her hospital room called her child each day. Another mother wrote notes each day. Yet another had a series of packages containing some daily surprise for her child. One mother arranged for her husband to bring the children to the hospital grounds, and she appeared at the window to wave to them.

Beginning of Labor

When the baby is ready to be born, the uterine muscles must begin to contract at diminishing intervals until the baby is expelled, a process called labor. Greenhill (1965) states that there is no single cause for the onset of labor. It "apparently begins as a result of a gradual accelerating convergence of . . . structural, humoral, nervous, nutritional and circulatory [factors] which, at a specific time for each species and adapted to the morphologic conditions present in each are so associated that they lead to evacuation by the uterus of its contents." When the uterus begins these contractions, the woman knows that the birth process is beginning.

Duration of Labor

Duration of labor varies a great deal. As a general rule the first labor lasts longer than those which follow, averaging ten to sixteen hours (Davis and Rubin, 1962). During the course of labor the neck of the uterus, or cervix, must first flatten and then dilate sufficiently to let the baby through into the vagina. The vagina stretches from the small opening it usually is into a canal wide enough for the baby to pass through. The perineum, a triangular-shaped muscle between the vagina and the anus, must also stretch as the baby's head presses down upon it.

Stages of Labor

Labor is divided into three stages. The first, the preparatory stage, is the longest, lasting from the first sign of labor until the cervix is completely dilated. The amnion usually ruptures at the end of the first stage. During the second stage the baby leaves the uterus and passes through the birth canal into the outside world. The third stage is a brief period of uterine contractions which expel the placenta.

Position of the Baby

The normal position of the baby in the uterus (Fig. 25) is such that the head will be born first. The proportions of a baby's body are very different from those of an adult's body, the circumference of the head being slightly larger than that of the chest or abdomen. Hence if the birth canal is large enough to let the baby's skull through, it is large enough to let the rest of the body pass. One provision for facilitating the birth of the baby's head through the pelvic opening is that, unlike an adult skull, which is rigid and resistant to outside pressure, the bones of the fetal skull have spaces which permit a certain amount of molding of the head by overlapping of the bones as the baby goes through the birth canal. Because of this malleability, which permits adaptation of the skull to the opening through which it must pass, the head of a newborn frequently seems to have a queer shape, which might be alarming to one who did not understand its cause and realize that within a short time the skull will assume its normal shape.

Role of the Mother During Labor

Childbirth is called labor because it requires hard work on the part of the mother.

Analgesia and anesthesia* were introduced into obstetrics in order to alleviate pain. Pain-relieving drugs are powerful and may create a risk to the health of mother and child. Concern over what might be an excessive use of these drugs with possible attendant risks has led to a search for another way of relieving the pain of childbirth. In addition, the importance of the psychological as well as physical status of the woman is recognized more and more, as is also the effect which the experience of childbearing has on the relations within the family unit. More women have also come to express a desire to be aware of and participate in the birth of their babies.

From these concerns have emerged some psychophysical methods for the relief of childbirth pain and for making childbearing a positive experience. Buxton (1962) made a study of these methods, which include (1) the Pavlovian conditioned reflex method, or the development of a conditioned reflex which will "either shut out or sublimate the painful sensation," (2) natural childbirth, or the breaking up of a fear-tension syndrome, (3) "autogene" training, or a kind of autosuggestion by which a woman may create for herself an atmosphere of calmness and relaxation, and (4) hypnosis, which eliminates the possible dangers of drugs, but does not permit active cooperation of the mother in the process of labor and delivery with its attendant psychological advantages. These methods, except for hypnosis, have in common (a) some education with classes of one sort or another which are generally small groups so that a group feeling develops, and (b) support during labor affording sympathetic and understanding care. They differ in their basic assumption in the purposes of the educational programs and in the rationale and content of any exercise program.

The important aspects of any childbirth training program are educational enlightenment, the feeling that the woman is doing something herself, and the support of sympathetic, understanding physicians and nurses who convey interest and thoughtful consideration. An accurate objective evaluation of these methods is, as Buxton points out, practically impossible because of the nature of what is being observed. It is believed that much of the fear and tension regarding childbirth would never develop if ignorance and faulty knowledge were remedied by education at the secondary school level in the physiology of reproduction.

---

*Analgesia is relief of pain; anesthesia is loss of sensation or feeling.

In this country natural childbirth (perhaps cooperative childbirth is a better term) is the method best known. "Natural childbirth is best described as intellectual, physical, and emotional preparation for childbirth, to the end that mothers realize their potentialities and in so doing enjoy the bringing forth of their babies" (Goodrich, 1950). Stuart and Prugh (1960) say that natural childbirth is a broad concept, not a method: namely, the way the husband, wife, physician and nurse view the whole event of pregnancy.

Preparation during pregnancy includes knowledge of the nature of pregnancy and of the birth process, the woman's role in it, and how she can expect to feel during it. She also learns about hospital procedures and the role of the physician and nurses. This may help to alleviate anxiety or fear of childbirth. Through a series of exercises she learns how to relax and strengthen the muscles involved in parturition. These exercises, plus the elimination of fear, result in reduced pain and, therefore, less need for medication. When labor begins, and throughout the procedure, she is kept informed of her progress. Someone is with her throughout to give assurance and help when needed and medication when desired. It is sometimes possible for the husband to remain with his wife during the first stage of labor. Throughout the birth process she participates actively, and can see and hold her baby while still in the delivery room.

The exact procedure at childbirth will vary according to the individual and will be decided by the obstetrician in light of the circumstances.

Role of the Husband

What role the husband plays at this time is a matter decided by the couple and the physician. For some husbands it will be a waiting role, for others support and perhaps assistance in the first stage of labor; for some who can be calm and confident under the circumstances, being present during delivery. Fundamentally, his role concerns giving support to his wife in a manner appropriate to both. If both are emotionally mature, his participation could serve to consolidate the family unit and strengthen husband-wife relations.

Postpartum Care

After childbirth it is important that the mother have rest. Indeed, for six to ten days, of which about five are usually spent in the hospital, most women are content to be quite lazy, and interruption for meals and nursing their infants prove enough diversion. Even visitors, other than husband and mother, can prove fatiguing.

It is the custom in many hospitals, because of the danger of infection of infants when visitors are allowed indiscriminately in the obstetric unit, to limit visitors to the husband and the two grandmothers, or sometimes to the husband only. Many women have admitted that it was a relief not to have visitors, and at least one study has shown that under such isolation (the husband the only visitor), women were better able to nurse their babies. Darner and Hunter (1943) found, when 100 such women and their infants were compared with a control group of 100 mothers and infants under the same routine of care, but without the ban on visitors, that the initial weight loss of the infants in the rest group averaged 79.3 gm. less than the average loss of those in the other group, and the babies in the first group received on the average 56.7 cc. more breast milk than those in the latter group. While sixty-six mothers in the control group were able to nurse their infants without complementary feedings, eighty-four mothers in the rest group were able to do so.

Women are now encouraged soon after childbirth to get out of bed, for brief periods of time at first, and later to walk about in order to stimulate circulation and improve muscle tone. Moving about helps to promote an early return to a woman's accustomed vitality.

It is the general practice in hospitals for babies to be cared for in a nursery and brought to the mothers at regular intervals. In some hospitals plans are made for the baby to remain with the mother in her room. This practice, in which the mother and her baby are cared for together in the same room, is called *rooming-in*. It brings the family together physically from the beginning and thus can encourage family unity. In such an arrangement a mother becomes acquainted with her baby, learns his needs and how to meet them, and actually participates in his care so that when she returns home she has confidence in her ability to care for her baby. The baby's needs can be met promptly; he can be fed when hungry, diapered when wet, comforted when he cries. The father has an opportunity to share with his wife in becoming acquainted with their newborn and in learning the essentials of taking care of the baby. Thus he can develop a feeling of being a necessary, active member of the family group rather than an onlooker who may feel excluded or rejected, and he can have a background of experience for assisting the mother in assuming her responsibilities after her return from the hospital. Rooming-in is a natural sequence to cooperative childbirth and provides an opportunity for the setting up of a self-regulation program for the infant without delay (see Jackson, 1956).

Such an arrangement is not available to all women, and is not necessarily desirable for all. Again, as in cooperative childbirth, its use depends on the individual and the circumstances. It is considered especially useful for the first child, as an opportunity for the mother to gain experience with assistance from the hospital staff as needed.

Return from the Hospital

When the mother leaves the hospital after five or six days, she is not ready to assume all her former activities. Lactation has not become well established; at this time fatigue and worry may disturb this process. The reproductive organs do not return to normal before six to eight weeks, and most mothers find that they tire very easily during this period. The woman will need adequate rest and a gradual increase in her activities. If there is someone to perform household duties, the mother's strength will not be so taxed, and she will be freer to spend her time and energies on the baby and other children. Need for rest after the birth of a baby is especially great when there are young children at home. The father may be able to take over some of the household tasks. The mother is much more likely to establish sufficient lactation to nourish her baby and will regain her normal energy sooner if she can have some help during this period. Just how promptly she will pick up her usual activities will depend on the advice of her physician.

TOPICS FOR STUDY AND DISCUSSION

1. As a focus for study, clarify your concept of prenatal development, in the embryo and the fetus, by illustrative content on change in size, form, physiologic functioning, and behavior, and illustrative content on influence of the mother.
2. Have students bring to class popular beliefs about pregnancy. Discuss them in terms of current knowledge of prenatal development.
3. Invite to class a nurse or physician who conducts classes for prospective parents. Consider the interests of those who have enrolled.

SELECTED READINGS

Flanagan, G. L.: The First Nine Months of Life. New York, Simon and Schuster, Inc., 1962. Story in words and photographs of prenatal development.

Genné, W. H.: Husbands and Pregnancy: The Handbook for Expectant Fathers. New York, Association Press, 1956.

Guttmacher, A. F.: Pregnancy and Birth. New York, The Viking Press, Inc., 1957. Pocket book edition. Signet Key Book.

Hillman, R. W.: Nutrition in Pregnancy; in M. G. Wohl and R. S. Goodhard (Eds.): Modern Nutrition in Health and Disease. 2nd ed. Philadelphia, Lea & Febiger, 1960. Documented discussion.

Montagu, A.: Human Heredity. New York, The World Publishing Co., 1964.

Rudolph, S. H.: Notes from a maternity ward. Atlantic Monthly, March, 1963, pp. 122-125.

Sears, R. R., Maccoby, E. E., and Levin, H.: Patterns of Child Rearing. New York, Harper and Row, 1957. Chap. 2, Background of Parenthood.

Thoms, H., in collaboration with L. G. Roth and D. Linton: Understanding Natural Childbirth. New York, McGraw-Hill Book Company, Inc., 1950. Explanation of natural childbirth for parents, with illustrations.

CHAPTER FOUR

Physical and Psychological Needs: Warmth, Meeting Situations Without Extreme Stress or Apathy, Dependence and Independence

The concept of human beings as having basic needs, i.e., states requiring supply or relief for well-being and development, can be used in considering a variety of "exchanges" of the individual and his setting. In this consideration it is recognized that knowledge of those conditions requiring supply or relief and of factors affecting them is incomplete. Needs, both physical and psychological, selected for discussion in this and the following chapters as basic to the child's well-being and development are (1) warmth, both physical and close personal warmth or love, (2) meeting situations, both physical and psychological, without extreme stress or apathy, (3) dependence and independence, (4) nutrition, (5) activity which includes movement itself and as it provides a means for exploration of the environment, (6) rest and sleep, and (7) social contact.

The particular importance of each of these needs and the manner in which they are met vary according to the developmental level of the child. The newborn needs to have hunger and thirst satisfied, to excrete the waste products from his body, to sleep, to be active (though involuntarily), to be warm and to feel secure. Although he is independent in being able to suck, swallow and digest his food and thereby satisfy his tissue needs for nutrients and energy, to excrete his waste products of metabolism, and make involuntary movements, he is dependent upon others for food, warmth and security. As he matures, these needs continue, but the way in which they are met changes from time to time. Movements come under voluntary control and are used to explore the environment, and he relates to others in degree and manner in keeping with his development. With increasing competence and experience, the combination gradually shifts from more dependence toward more independence, and, finally, to a more complete independence and responsibility at maturity. Thus the concept of progression as a part of the developmental dynamic concept discussed in Chapter One applies to this area of needs and their fulfillment.

The other phase of this concept, that of dynamic relations within the developing child and in his interactions with his setting, also applies. Meeting one need can become intertwined with meeting another. It seems that no one physical need can be met satisfactorily without, at the same time, meeting other physical and psychological needs. To be well nourished, a child needs not only food, but also adequate activity, sleep, elimination and a feeling of security and of being loved. Nourishment and nurture go hand in hand. Activity in play can fulfill the need for activity, for social contacts and for learning about the environment and one's own capacities. At mealtime with the family the preschool child can gratify his needs for nourishment, emotional warmth, security and being a member of a social group.

In addition, the concept of individuality applies. Each child is an individual with his own physiological rhythms, his own speed of development, his own constitutional factors in personality. Thus he responds uniquely to his environment. Some children grow fast; some, slowly. Some have few respiratory infections; some catch colds easily. Some have a small capacity for food; some, a large capacity. Some have unbounded energy; some tire easily. Some are phlegmatic, taking changes and adjustments to routines, accidents and other events in stride. Others tend to be more excitable or to be more easily thrown off balance by changes and the need to adjust to new situations. Such examples indicate individual variability in the intensity of needs and differences in satisfactory means of meeting those needs.

Individuality is also reflected in the child's family, its characteristic mode of life, habits and attitudes, traditions and customs, the complex of the personalities of the parents and children. How the child's needs will be met will depend upon the family and the circumstances in which it lives.

The needs discussed in this and the following chapters reflect an interest in recognition of biological, psychological and exogenous systems referred to in Chapter One.

The term *basic need* as used here refers to a base, essence, fundamental or foundation requiring supply or relief for well-being and development. An example of a state (or need) whose urgency or necessity (or basic quality) requires supply or relief is the human being's need for oxygen. Too great deprivation means death; an oversupply can have disastrous effects; adequate provision means not just survival, but well-being and development. Likewise, for other nutrients a minimum is necessary for survival; when additional amounts are supplied, well-being and development can occur, but certain excesses can be harmful. The range of individual requirements is great. These concepts apply to the need for rest and sleep and for activity. But when we discuss the needs basic to mental well-being, there is no ready acceptance of any particular listing because our knowledge in this area is limited.

Agreement seems general that mere meeting of physical needs is not enough to produce zest and sparkle in the infant, young child or person of any age. In the 1920's, when institutions supplying physical care for infants had higher mortality rates than occurred for infants at home with their own families, physicians, psychiatrists and psychologists began studies to try to discover why (Baker, 1925; Lowery, 1940; Bakwin, 1949). Since then, love, affection, continuity of care, mothering, nurture, closeness or relatedness to others, and sensory stimulation have been studied as relations fundamental to the continued thriving of infants and children. Emotional deprivation and sensory deprivation continue to be investigated. The adult's provision of relations with sensory and affectional elements was at one time called tender loving care; it is now often called understanding loving care. This suggests more recognition of the difference in relations which the age of the child will dictate. For example, in the first few months of life understanding loving care may mean recognition of the influence of visual, tactile and auditory variables. At later ages it may mean recognition of autonomy sought by the individual. This idea also suggests more recognition of research findings which indicate that physiological functioning, use of abilities and associations with other persons contribute to the child's well-being and development.

The seven rather inclusive basic needs selected for discussion here seem to have connections with a number of primary drives or biologically primitive tendencies. For example, the need for nutrition provides conditions or stimuli calling into action the primary drive for food, but it also calls into action several other biologically primitive motivations, such as those for activity and for closeness to others. As the child grows beyond early infancy, learned responses play an important part in meeting his needs. As this happens, we wish that we knew more about the child's selection of certain stimuli to which to respond. His needs may conflict; among the opportunities offered for meeting several needs, one evokes a motive and another does not. Reasons for this have not been determined in many instances. One child who needs rest may continue his active play; another may find a sheltered spot and curl up and relax. Or the child whose felt cowboy hat makes him very warm may insist on wearing it, even after someone has shown him how hot it makes his forehead. It has not been determined to what extent the child who is not unduly pressed in other directions will tend to seek what he needs basically as contrasted to seeking what he needs more superficially.

Needs less fundamental for development will be discussed later, e.g., a whim or mood of the moment. Until more evidence is available about an individual's seeking what he needs, it can be said that some discrimination within him is suggested by his thriving more in some settings than in others.

WARMTH

Physiological Warmth

Warmth is necessary to provide an internal environment for satisfactory bodily function and a sense of comfort. The steadiness of warmth is maintained by man's adaptability, which includes his physiological adaptability, or temperature regulation, and his ability to create environmental temperatures by artificial heating and cooling systems and to protect himself as much as possible by appropriate clothing.

Temperature regulation is one of the mechanisms which operate to keep the environment of the body cells in an optimum state. This maintenance of physiological stability has been termed "homeostasis" (Cannon, 1933). The preservation of homeostasis is largely due to the integrative and correlative abilities of the nervous and endocrine systems.

The body must maintain its equilibrium within certain prescribed limits with respect to temperature and other aspects even in the presence of changes in the external environment or in the activity of parts of the body (Cannon, 1933; Shock, 1952). Relative constancy of body temperature is essential (Brobeck, 1960), since overheating or chilling below a physiological minimum affects essential bodily activities. Enzymes, which control metabolic processes, are sensitive to changes; their activities are inhibited when the temperature falls a few degrees or are irreversibly inactivated at a high temperature. Further, the cells of the central nervous system cannot function normally at a temperature above 106°F. The load on the cardiovascular and respiratory systems is also increased heavily by the increase in the rate of metabolism as body temperature rises.

Temperature constancy is maintained in spite of heat production and heat loss. Heat is produced by metabolic processes in all tissues, but especially in skeletal muscle tissue. It is obvious that muscular activity in the form of work or exercise has a warming effect when the body is chilled. Involuntary shivering has a similar effect. The basal heat production may be more than doubled by this involuntary activity of muscles (Brobeck, 1960). Heat production in newborn infants has doubled or more than doubled from vigorous crying (Smith, 1959c).

Heat is lost principally at the surface of the skin and the lining of the respiratory system by physical and physiologic mechanisms (Brobeck, 1960). The physical processes are radiation, conduction, and vaporization of water. Their relative importance varies with circumstances. The body radiates heat to relatively cool objects nearby, such as walls, furnishings of a room, bodies of water. Conduction, less important than radiation, is the transfer of heat to substances in contact with the body, such as air (which covers the skin), clothing, and food and water taken into the digestive tract. Vaporization of water removes heat from the skin and respiratory membranes by evaporation.

Internal warming and cooling are further influenced by physiological mechanisms. Constriction and dilation of surface blood vessels permit conservation and dissipation of heat. When the body is chilled, the blood vessels at the surface constrict; thus heat is prevented from escaping, and heat loss is reduced. Conversely, when the body is too warm after exercise or exposure to heat, the surface blood vessels dilate, and heat is dissipated. An additional cooling effect is provided by evaporation of perspiration from the sweat glands.

All the bodily processes which affect heat production and heat loss are regulated by the hypothalamus (located at the base of the brain stem) through two centers, one of which is responsible for protection against heat and the other for protection against cold. The hypothalamus acts as a thermostat, with a "receptive mechanism" to note the temperature and an "executive mechanism" to regulate it (Benzinger, 1961; Patton, 1960). It receives impulses from cutaneous thermoreceptors which send sensory stimulations from the skin, mucous membranes, and so forth, and from centrally located receptors which respond to internal, particularly intracranial, temperature. In response to these stimuli it brings into action all the appropriate motor mechanisms of temperature regulation without changing the central temperature of the body. Other pathways for messages from the thermoreceptors lead not to the hypothalamus, but to the thalamus and cortex of the brain, and thus form the basis for conscious sensation of temperature which provides a clue for seeking a more comfortable environment (Patton, 1960). The cortex of the adrenal gland and the thyroid gland also play a role in these activities (Hardy, 1961).

Temperature regulation in infants and young children differs from that in adults. Sudden fluctuations in temperature may occur under conditions such as a change in external temperature, an emotional disturbance or exercise. For example, an increase of 1 degree may be found immediately after active exercise (Prugh, 1964). Infants and young children also frequently respond to infections with a sudden rise and fall in temperature out of all proportion to the change that would occur under similar circumstances in an adult. This instability can be attributed to the stage of development of various systems of the body and to the relative inefficiency of the homeostatic mechanisms.

Temperature regulation is unstable at birth (Smith, 1959c; Watson and Lowrey, 1962). The infant's relatively greater surface area permits relatively greater loss of heat; immature sweating and shivering mechanisms provide poor means for losing body heat; delicate skin and meager subcutaneous fat provide poor insulation; the thermoregulatory system is immature. The premature has greater instability than the full-term infant.

The newborn may be protected from chilling by provision of a warm, even environmental temperature. If he is born in a hospital, he will be kept in a warm nursery, or, if he stays in the room with his mother, the temperature of the room will be carefully regulated. During infancy a temperature of 68 to 72°F. is considered satisfactory until he is running about. By that time, because of his almost constant activity, he can thrive well in an environment of 65 to 68°F. Some homes are equipped with heating facilities which provide a steady, even temperature. Babies and children can be kept comfortably warm by the kind and amount of bedding and clothing used and the regulation of their use according to temperature changes.

Clothing should be planned according to the climate. For example, in a tropical or semitropical climate the baby may need no clothing except a diaper, and the toddler and the young child may need only a sunsuit. Where warmth is needed, a child can be kept warm enough without being so warm that he will perspire and later become chilled. Most clothing for infants and children today provides warmth and still is light enough in weight to permit freedom of movement. Even outdoor winter clothing can be warm and light in weight. The qualities of lightness and protection from cold are influential at all ages.

The infant's temperature at birth is presumably the same as that of the mother. After an immediate drop of 2 to 5 degrees it rises to 98 to 99°F. (rectal) in about eight hours (Smith, 1959c). By one month the rectal temperature, according to the Bayley and Stolz study (1937) of a group of healthy infants and young children followed up from one month to three years, is 98.96°F., by eight months 99.76°F., by two years 99.66°F., and at three years 98.95°F. Thus body temperature tends to increase during the first seven months, remains fairly constant to two years and subsequently falls. Only two of these averages approximate the so-called average rectal temperature for adults, i.e., 99.6°F. (Brobeck, 1960).

Adults have a diurnal or rhythmic change in temperature during the day and night, with a characteristic individual pattern (Kleitman, 1944, 1963). Infants and young children slowly acquire this daily rhythm, with temperatures lower early in the morning, rising during the day and falling again later. This rhythm is related to the daily routines and is fully established by the time the child is walking and being very active (Kleitman, 1944, 1963). These diurnal fluctuations tend to be greater in young children than in adults; this was demonstrated in a study of two- to five-year-old children (Jundell, 1959).

In addition to wider diurnal fluctuations, changes in temperature from day to day in the same child and large differences among children of the same age document temperature instability and lack of conformity to a norm (Bayley and Stolz, 1937). The individual variability of the children at some ages, as measured by the standard deviation, was greater than the so-called adult normal range (99 to 100°F.) (Brobeck, 1960). At other ages the spread for the children was higher or lower than that for adults. There is some evidence (Bayley and Stolz, 1937) that healthy children may have consistent tendencies toward high or low temperatures which are normal for them. It would be unreasonable, therefore, to expect all young children to have a constant temperature at the usual norm for adults (99.6°F. rectal or 98.6°F. oral).

It becomes apparent that infants and children are affected by care in maintaining an environment compatible with their ability to keep themselves warm. This means providing an environment with appropriate warmth and protecting the infant or child from too great and too sudden environmental changes until he reaches the age when the body can adjust easily to such changes.

Psychological Warmth

It is interesting to try to parallel discussion of the child's need for physiological warmth with discussion of his need for psychological warmth. As does his physical state of body temperature, his psychological state of "emotional temperature" requires supply or relief for well-being. The mind, or behavioral system, must maintain its equilibrium within limits (not yet established) with respect to *feeling warmth instead of coldness from other people*, even in the presence of changes in the external environment or in the activity of parts of the body and of the mind. The emphasis is on the child's own feeling that warmth is present (see Fig. 30). But, as in the case of body temperature of the newborn, meeting the need comes through influences of people in his environment as well as through his own powers. Because the child's feeling of warmth instead of coldness seems closely tied up with his association with other people, the following discussion concerns warmth of others toward him.

Degrees of temperature in an infant or child, or in a room or out of doors, are easily measurable. Attributes or dimensions of love or affection of a person, or of the part of it called warmth, are elusive. Using the broader term *affection,* one group of students trying to put into words what mattered in relations of adults and children listed the following:

FIGURE 30. *Autonomy, achievement and warmth seem interrelated.*

This child was absorbed in her own activity, and then, after accomplishing it, turned with an expression of warmth toward another person. She seemed to know that the adult's response would be one of warmth and to find it easily, although nothing was said as the adult smiled and nodded her head slightly.

1. Loving the child for himself (for what he is which is different from anyone else)
2. Being natural, understanding, sincere and consistent
3. Realizing that children respond to interest and companionship and not to words, demonstrativeness or gifts alone
4. Not being overprotective and stifling independence, but showing a readiness to help when needed
5. Letting the child feel sure of affection whether he is good or bad

Warmth, in the sense of being one of several parts of affection or love, was identified as one of seven distinct clusters, traits or factors in the child-rearing practices of mothers. Sears, Maccoby and Levin (1957) say:

Mothers who were high—toward the warm end—can be described as follows:
1. Much affectionate interaction with the baby
2. High affectionate demonstrativeness toward the child
3. Found ample time to play with the child
4. Reacted acceptingly to child's dependency
5. Praised the child when he showed good table manners
6. Used reasoning as a method of training

Maternal coldness was associated with behavior difficulties as reported by mothers in interviews, and "with the development of feeding problems and persistent bed-wetting. It contributed to high aggression. It was an important background condition for emotional upset during severe toilet training, and for the slowing of conscience development."

Warmth, on the other hand, according to Sears, Maccoby and Levin (1957),

. . . may play several roles. A warm mother spends more time with her child. She offers him more rewards . . . and gives him more guidance. He develops stronger expectancies of her reciprocal affection, and thus is more highly motivated to learn how to behave as she wants him to. He becomes more susceptible to control by her, for he has more to gain and more to lose. It seems likely, too, that he gets proportionately more satisfaction and less frustration from his growing desire for affection.

Maternal warmth is associated with several forms of behavior in the child. Schaefer and Bayley (1963) found emotional involvement and expression of affection to be among the responses of mothers related to positive behavior or happiness, or both, of daughters at thirteen to thirty-six months, and to friendliness at twenty-seven to thirty months. For boys the mother's expression of affection at an earlier age was correlated with cooperativeness at sixty-six to seventy-two months. Data on the mothers' behavior came from observations in test situations during the children's first three years, recorded in the form of extensive notes immediately after the children were seen in the test situations. Ratings of the children were also derived from observations of overt behavior.

When ratings of the mothers' emotional involvement and expression of affection were included with other ratings to provide a love-hostility dimension, this dimension correlated with behavior of the children. "The correlations of early maternal behavior with sons' behavior between 27 and 96 months . . . reveal that friendliness, cooperativeness, attentiveness and facility show a consistent pattern of correlations with variables of the love-hostility dimension of maternal behavior," and for daughters, "loving behaviors again tend to correlate positively and hostile behaviors negatively" with the forms of behavior indicated for boys.

In the infant the smiling response, with intent visual regard and vocalizing, is a form of early social behavior. In development of the smiling response he differentiates between people and things, and seems to smile more frequently at people after approximately four months of age. Rheingold (1966) refers to "the development of the smiling response . . . as an example of the principle that the infant's social behavior is modified by the response of people to *his* social behavior. . . . The infant's positive social responses evoke responsiveness in kind from others in his environment."

A few *social acts*, which seem to be a part of warmth for the infant, were included in a research experiment by Rheingold, Gewirtz and Ross (1959). On days when the experimenter's smile, pat and "tsk" sounds (as contrasted to his expressionless face) followed the infant's vocalization, the number of vocalizations increased (see Fig. 4, p. 18). The activity of the infant which was measured, i.e., amount of vocalization, increased when these stimuli from the adult, which did not involve taking care of the baby, were a part of his day. By the fifth day, when the adult response was not being added, the number of vocalizations was about the same as on days preceding the addition. Another experiment with three-month-old infants (Weisberg, 1963) contrasted effects, such as these, when the adult's responses were contingent on the infant's vocalizing, with effects when the adult's social responses occurred at random. The infants with the social behavior reinforcing their own vocalizing were the ones who made considerable gains in rate of vocalization. Among others with whom the adult remained impassive and the sound of a chime was contingent upon the vocalization, comparable gains were not made.

Withdrawing a few social acts, some of which seem to be a part of warmth for the older child, was practiced in a research experiment by Hartup (1958). Subjects ranged in age from three years, ten months to five years, six months. In the control group during the first five minutes and the second five minutes of an experimental session while the child played with toys, the experimenter's behavior "rewarded, encouraged, supported, or showed affection to the child." For what was called a "nurturance-withdrawal group" the experimenter in the second five minutes "ceased to interact with the child, withdrew from his proximity, and did not reward any of the child's supplications beyond telling him that she was 'busy.' . . . Children in both experimental groups were then asked . . . to learn two tasks, the reward for which was the verbal approval of the experimenter." One of the tasks concerned selection of a certain block from an arrangement of blocks, and the other, copying from memory a row of cubes of different colors. Learning was faster in the girls of the nurturance-withdrawal group. "Highly dependent boys (who may be assumed to be generally anxious concerning their relationships with adults)" also learned more efficiently when the experimenter withdrew her nurturance. Boys with low dependency learned faster in the group with constant nurturance.

In thinking about the influence of warmth on the child it is appropriate to stress the importance of taking into account many circumstances. Gewirtz (1961), referring to the stimulation an immediate situation provides, says:

> In order to understand the development of human social motivation under both normal and deficiency conditions of stimulation, it is not sufficient simply to focus on which, or on how many, stimuli are provided the infant. . . . We must take account of the circumstances under which given stimuli are made available to him, and . . . whether these stimuli are functional, and with his behaviors enter effective contingencies for learning.

Sears, Maccoby and Levin (1957), referring to a broader setting which a family provides, say: "We do not mean to imply any disrespect . . . for either the single variable or the underlying traits revealed by factor analysis. Both are of importance. . . . But there is still a place for the careful teasing out of relationships that involve interaction between one or two or three operationally defined measures of child rearing." Their reference is to information on percentage of emotional upset from severe toilet training (scolding and punishing) in children whose mothers were warm and in children whose mothers were cold. "Over half of the most severely trained children showed some disturbance, while not more than a sixth of the least severely trained showed it ($p < .01$; $r = .47$)."* Mothers who were warm in their relations with their children and severe in toilet training had fewer children who were emotionally upset (23 per cent), whereas mothers who were cold and severe had more children who were emotionally upset (48 per cent) (p .01).

MEETING SITUATIONS WITHOUT EXTREME STRESS OR APATHY

In meeting situations without extreme stress or apathy, the individual draws upon his resources to deal adequately with his world—a world which may at times have physical or psychological disturbances in it. When this rather inclusive need for the person to encounter and handle

---

* The symbols p and r are used to indicate probability of a result due to chance alone and correlation coefficient, respectively. Thus $p < .01$ means that probability due to chance alone is less than 1 in 100. For the correlation coefficient the amount of variability in one factor which is controlled by another may be obtained as r^2. Here .47 times .47 is 22.09. Thus 22 per cent of the variance of emotional upset is accounted for by severity of toilet training; 78 per cent of the variance is unaccounted for.

what occurs, or to cope with it, can be met, he has security through his own abilities as well as through provisions of his setting.

There is *physical* security, as exemplified by the security of a body which is functioning adequately and smoothly and by safety from hazards which may interfere with health and development. *Psychological* security comes from feeling loved and wanted and living in a world that gratifies needs in a consistent, dependable manner and from being assured instead of overanxious through one's own activities.

Physical Health Protection

The *security of a smoothly functioning body* is furthered by the homeostatic mechanisms which maintain stability in the cellular environment throughout the body. Homeostasis includes such things as regulation of body temperature, acidity, amount of available oxygen, water, salts, glucose in the blood. Most of the mechanisms are immature at birth, and thus the body is more variable in its physiological state at that time than later. "Such things as the salt and sugar content of the blood, the water content of the body, the basal metabolic rate and the heart rate are changed by relatively small changes in diet and in external conditions. It takes as many as five years for the child's body to settle down to something like the physiologic stability of the adult" (Havighurst, 1950). This is one justification for protecting infants and young children against too great and too sudden environmental changes. As the physiological adaptive mechanism becomes more mature, a child is able to cope with changes in the environment with increasing ease.

Stress, which is a daily part of life for everyone and can be a bit of the spice of life or a deterring or weakening force, calls adaptive mechanisms into action. It can be of physical origin, as, for example, cold or disease, or of psychological origin, in the form of anger, fear or anxiety. Selye (1950) describes the defensive reactions of the body to stress which he calls the General Adaptation Syndrome. This consists of three stages: (1) the alarm reaction, (2) the stage of resistance, and (3) the stage of exhaustion. Most stress involves only the first two stages; i.e., the person may be disturbed, but his body accommodates to it. Even exhaustion need not be irreversible, as, for instance, physical exhaustion produced by vigorous activity. The nervous and endocrine systems operate in the body's resistance to stress. The pituitary gland is stimulated to produce ACTH (adrenocorticotrophic hormone), which in turn stimulates secretion of the hormones of the adrenal cortex. Thus stress, if not severe and prolonged, can be managed physiologically; but prolonged or severe stress can strain the adaptation mechanisms beyond their capacity. In such an extreme, harmful physiological reactions occur which may eventually lead to disease (Selye, 1950, 1956; Wolff, 1952). Individuals differ in their response to stress; some react vigorously, some less intensely (Lacey and Van Lehn, 1952).

Protection against disease is another aspect of physical security. Illness is both a physical and a psychological hazard for the infant and the young child. It interferes with the regular processes of the body, may interfere with development (Valadian, 1960) and produces stresses and strains in parent-child relations. Diseases which leave permanent handicaps make it difficult for the child to lead a normal and happy life, although this can be achieved under the guidance of wise parents and physicians.

Protection against disease comes both from without and from within. Protection from without involves the removal from the environment of hazards to health. Eradication of specific organisms, as, for example, the parasites causing malaria or parasitic worms, is the responsibility of the community, as is the provision of safe water and food (including pasteurized milk) and facilities for health education. Protecting young children from those who are ill and from other sources of infection is primarily the responsibility of parents.

The child has inner resources of protection. A sound, healthy body offers good general resistance to disease. In addition, bodily functions are integrated to form a general mobilization against disease, as in any stressful situation. Then, too, certain systems offer specific protection, e.g., the skin and the lymphatic system.

The skin protects the underlying parts from injury, from invasion by foreign organisms and from drying.

The lymphatic system also protects against invading organisms. It consists of (1) lymph, which, in general, originates as tissue fluid (the fluid surrounding all cells), which, in turn, has reached the cells from the capillaries of the blood-circulation systems and consists of blood constituents which pass through the capillary walls, plus elements added to it by the tissues; (2) complex networks which collect the lymph in the various organs and tissues; (3) an elaborate system of collecting vessels which conduct the lymph from the capillaries to the large veins of the neck, where it is poured into the blood stream; (4) lymph nodes which are interspersed in the pathways of the collecting vessels, filtering the lymph as it passes through them and contributing lymphocytes to it. These lymphocytes, a type of white blood cell, destroy bacteria. Lymph, in addition to manufacturing lymphocytes, removes worn-out blood cells and other kinds of debris from the body fluids and is the principal source of antibodies.

The importance of the lymphatic system to normal development seems to be indicated by changes during the growing years. Lymphoid tissue is abundant at birth and increases rapidly in infancy and childhood. Lymph ducts are more numerous and lymph nodes larger and more prominent in childhood than in later life. Lymph tissue during infancy and childhood responds to infection by rapid and excessive swelling and increase in size. With advancing age this response becomes less dramatic.

Tonsils and adenoids, which are lymphoid tissue, follow this pattern of increase and decrease in size. Kaiser (1957) found that tonsils of infants were usually small. They increased in size in the second and third years, reaching maximum size at four or five years of age, and then decreased so that between eight and ten years of age they had an insignificant appearance. Tonsils are not commonly removed today. Their maximum development at the time when acute infections of the respiratory and alimentary tracts are most common would seem to indicate that they are part of a natural defense mechanism.

IMMUNITY AND IMMUNIZATION. The child acquires *immunity to specific diseases* either through exposure to them or through artificial immunization. Immunity is an extremely complicated mechanism. "In its broadest biologic sense, [it] comprises all those physiologic mechanisms which endow the animal with the capacity to recognize materials as foreign to itself and to neutralize, eliminate or metabolize them with or without injury to its own tissues" (Smith, 1960). The substance distinguished as foreign is an antigen; the substance produced, antibodies. Antibodies are carried in the gamma globulins of the blood.

The infant is born with a passive immunity to some diseases because antibodies from the mother's blood have passed through the placenta to the fetal blood. Thus if his mother is immune to measles, diphtheria, tetanus, mumps, smallpox, poliomyelitis and the common cold, the newborn infant is also immune to some degree for a brief time to these diseases. Premature infants have less protection than full-term infants. This passive immunity, plus careful shielding of young infants from contact with infections, serves as protection until the infant is capable of manufacturing sufficient antibodies. Before this passive immunity has disappeared, active immunity can be stimulated by artificial immunizing procedures. A program of immunization is set up according to the prevalence of specific diseases.

Newborns produce some antibodies (di Sant 'Agnese, 1949; Osborn et al., 1952), and this ability improves rapidly during the first two months and thereafter more slowly. Osborn et al., from their experimentation with diphtheria and tetanus toxoids, stated that it is possible that the physiological maturity of forming antitoxins of diphtheria and tetanus is reached by about three to six months.

Although newborns have some inborn immunity to several diseases, they are usually not immune to whooping cough, which is especially serious in infants and in the malnourished child. Deaths from whooping cough occur mostly in the first year (United States Department of Health, Education, and Welfare, 1961). Early protection, therefore, is important. Protection against diphtheria is also important, for fewer babies may have passive immunity to it than formerly because of the lower incidence of diphtheria in adults (di Sant 'Agnese, 1949). Where programs of immunization are in effect, the drop in the incidence of these diseases is striking.

The American Academy of Pediatrics (1961) recommends that all infants be immunized against whooping cough, diphtheria, tetanus, poliomyelitis and smallpox. Administration of a triple vaccine of whooping cough, diphtheria and tetanus, plus separate poliovirus vaccine, is begun some time between $1\frac{1}{2}$ and two months. A vaccine containing the four components has been investigated. Two additional doses are given at intervals of one month, followed by booster shots at twelve months, at two years for poliovirus vaccine only, and at four years for all four vaccines. Smallpox vaccination is recommended at six to twelve months and again at six years.

RADIATION.   Radiation as a hazard to health and development has received increasing attention since the dropping of the atomic bomb during World War II and the subsequent study of fall-out in connection with the testing of nuclear weapons.

The sources of radiation include (1) natural or background sources from cosmic rays, radioactive elements of rocks and soil, minute quantities in body constituents, and (2) man-made radiation from fall-out of nuclear explosions with its resultant contamination of air, water, soil and food; medical and dental x-rays; waste from atomic energy plants; industry and research; and miscellaneous sources such as luminous-dialed watches, shoe-fitting machines and television, especially color television (Braestrup and Mooney, 1959; Forbes, 1960; Reynolds, 1960; Robinow and Silverman, 1957; Wallace and Dobzhansky, 1959).

The likely consequences of man-made radiation include excessive defects at birth, smaller birth weight and stature, reduced intelligence, aging, premature death and lessened fertility.

Radiation effects are produced by direct action on germ cells and on somatic or body cells. Radiation of germ cells causes mutations, a qualitative change in a gene which causes it to cease to function, or to function at a different rate or in a different manner, thus altering its role in cellular function and in its contribution to health and development (Stern, 1960; Wallace and Dobzhansky, 1959). Such a change in the germ cells is passed on to future generations as a part of heredity. Although the evidence that radiation exposure induces mutations comes from experimentation with plants and animals, geneticists agree that radiation exposure induces mutations in man (Neel, 1958; Neel and Schull, 1956; Stern, 1960; Wallace and Dobzhansky, 1959).

It is generally accepted that (1) a linear relation exists between the amount of gonadal radiation and the degree of mutation; (2) even the smallest dose may have genetic effects; (3) consequences are cumulative; (4) there is no recovery; and (5) mutations are generally harmful (Reynolds, 1960; Stern, 1960; Wallace and Dobzhansky, 1959).

Body cells, tissues and structures are also affected. The more active the cell, the more responsive it is to radiation. Thus fetal susceptibility is high during the period of differentiation of the organs and tissues of the body (Hicks, 1953; Robinow and Silverman, 1957), and the young, more actively growing tissues of the child are more affected than the relatively less active tissues of the adult (Weber and Hetznecker, 1961).

Radiation injures tissues, thus producing malfunction and disease such as changes in the blood cells and the bone marrow which may lead to anemia and leukemia. Studies on the relation of leukemia in children to earlier therapeutic radiation vary, probably because of differences in methodology. The weight of evidence indicates that ionizing radiation can be a source of leukemia and other neoplastic diseases in children (Weber and Hetznecker, 1961). Strontium-90 replaces calcium in bone. Among other possible damages are cancer, cataracts, loss of fertility, shortening of the life span, and sterility (Glass, 1956; Robinow and Silverman, 1957).

It would seem, according to present knowledge, that there are no completely safe levels of exposure to radiation. It would be wise, therefore, to view all sources as suspect and thus control the amount of radiation as far as possible. This means avoiding unnecessary radiation and taking all possible precautions in its use. This would include elimination of fluoroscopic shoe-fitting machines and the like; careful scrutiny of the use of x-rays for diagnostic and therapeutic purposes; protection in such situations by use of the best equipment, properly installed and regularly checked; attention to the details of procedure, including protection of the gonads; adequate knowledge and training of those using the equipment; protection of workers who may be exposed to radiation or radioactive materials; and watching for pollution of air, water and food from radioactive fall-out and from industrial waste (Price, 1958). No change in food habits is indicated, including the use of milk in the diet (Comar, 1959; Forbes, 1960; Morgan, 1961).

SUPERVISION OF THE YOUNG CHILD'S HEALTH. Parents need the guidance and support of a physician in their care of the child, supervision of his progress, and care for him when it is needed. This physician should be a well-informed general practitioner or a pediatrician who has knowledge of the growth of well children as well as of disease mechanisms. Since one of his obligations will be the establishment of good relations with the child, he needs to like children, understand their psychological development and needs, and have ability to apply this knowledge in dealing with the child. This physician will observe the child regularly to check both his health and growth and to carry out an appropriate immunization program. Many communities have clinics for well babies and children where families who cannot afford a physician may obtain such care.

The routines of washing and bathing can also be included under health protection. Many babies are given a daily bath. In hot weather, baths twice a day may add to the baby's comfort. Many hospitals eliminate both the initial and daily care of the newborn in order to reduce handling or rubbing of the skin and thereby the possibility of irritation and infection. The danger of heat loss from evaporation of moisture from the infant's relatively large surface area is another reason for omitting the bath. Many physicians claim that until the infant is creeping and actually getting dirty, bathing only three times a week is better, both because it is less drying and irritating to the infant's skin and because this regimen gives his mother more time for adequate rest.

Whatever the bath schedule, if the room is warm, the baby can have freedom from blankets and clothes and can kick and exercise, and the person giving the bath can feel no need to hurry the procedure. The baby is more apt to be relaxed and to enjoy the bath if the hands handling him are skilled and unhurried. As soon as the infant learns to reach out and grasp things he will want the washcloth. He may like having an extra cloth that he may hold. Later he may want to have the soap, and still later to dab at his knees with the cloth. When he becomes aware of the stopper, he may want to pull it out and to put it in again. Thus, gradually, he can learn to take over some of the bath procedure for himself.

Bathtime can be fun for child and parent, whether father or mother. Routines of bathtime, like other routines, may become a sort of ritual, and to many young children the conditions surrounding the bath and the order of procedure are extremely important. Bathtime may be a happy time if the routine is followed; it may become a struggle if the routine is changed.

The washing of hands before meals seems more likely to be established as a routine if it has pleasant associations. If facilities are accessible, the child can learn to do this for himself, but may frequently need to be reminded to do so. Young children can learn to use their own towel and washcloth if they can reach them easily.

The early *recognition of physical defects* of eyes, ears, posture, and so forth, also protects health in that it permits correction or prevention of serious impairment.

One of the big health problems in this country is *dental caries*. Those caring for young children need to be cognizant of this problem not only because of the importance of repairing caries in the deciduous teeth, but also because the permanent teeth are forming during these years. Available information on its incidence indicates that dental caries of the deciduous teeth frequently begins soon after their eruption and increases dramatically thereafter (Finn, 1952). In a report of the 10 per cent of children under five years of age who visited the dentist, only one out of three was free of untreated carious lesions; one out of ten had eight or more cavities (Young, 1961).

Dental caries is produced by the etching of the enamel of the tooth and further decalcification of the inorganic portion, accompanied or followed by disintegration of the organic substance of the tooth. This decalcification is caused by acid in the mouth resulting from bacterial action on orally fermentable carbohydrates, namely, sugars and starch (American Academy of Pediatrics and American Society of Dentistry, 1959; Shaw, 1961). The physical nature of carbohydrates, the frequency of their consumption (Bibby, 1961) and prolonged contact of the teeth with fermentable carbohydrate (Review, 1966b) appear to influence cariogenic activity (see p. 198). The amount of acid in the mouth is also influenced by the saliva and components of food other than carbohydrates. Caries tends to occur in areas where bacteria and food adhere to the teeth and are not easily removed (Massler, 1958).

Some persons are more susceptible to caries than others. The susceptibility in some and resistance in others are believed to have genetic and metabolic components (Paynter and Grainger, 1961; Shaw, 1961; Turner, 1960). The structure of the tooth apparently results from an interaction between inherited characteristics and metabolic conditions prevailing during tooth formation. Turner (1960) suggests another possible genetically determined factor, that of the enzyme system necessary for the breakdown of starch in the mouth. Caries-free children differed from caries-prone children in the "biochemical profiles" involved in the breakdown of starch (Turner, 1960). Caries tends to run in families (Klein, 1946, 1947), a fact which suggests both a hereditary influence and one of family food patterns.

Prevention and control of caries, substantiated by experimental evidence, include a balanced diet during the years (prenatal, infant and preschool periods) when teeth are developing; limitation of carbohydrates, especially sugars (American Academy of Pediatrics and American Society of Dentistry for Children, 1959) and in forms that adhere to the teeth (Bibby, 1961); limitation of the length of time the teeth are exposed to sugar, especially the longer exposure that occurs when sugars are eaten as snacks; and the inclusion of small amounts of fluorides in the drinking water (Ast et al., 1956; Blayney, 1960) or topically applied to the teeth (Jordan, 1960; Law et al., 1961).

In a ten-year study (Ast et al., 1956) of the effect upon the incidence of caries of adding a small amount of fluoride to the drinking water, Newburgh children, who drank fluoridated water, had less dental caries than Kingston children, who drank fluoride-free water. In Newburgh six- to nine-year-olds had 57 to 58 per cent less caries in their erupted permanent teeth than did the children of corresponding age in Kingston. Kingston children had lost eight times as many six-year molars because of caries as had Newburgh children. No harmful effects on the health of the Newburgh children were noted (Schlesinger et al., 1956). Maximum effect is achieved when fluorides are ingested from the fourth month in utero to eighteen years, which covers the time of the development of teeth and the susceptible years. In 1959, 26 million people in the United States were drinking artificially fluoridated water (American Academy of Pediatrics and American Society of Dentistry for Children, 1959). Fluorides may contribute to bone formation as well as caries resistance.

In addition, cleansing of the teeth by finishing a meal with a hard, detergent food such as apples, whole orange, celery or carrot and cleansing by regular brushing with a toothbrush are valuable. Some believe that for young children the "natural toothbrush" or detergent cleansing type of food is often more effective than the artificial toothbrush. In adults, however, brushing is considered more effective than foods. Regular visits to the dentist can begin at twenty-four to thirty months; brushing of teeth, at two years.

Providing a balanced diet with "detergent" foods at the end of the meal, reducing the intake of candy, ice cream and other sweets, especially between meals, providing an adequate amount of fluorides in the drinking water, teaching children to brush their teeth and providing dental supervision all contribute to the prevention of tooth decay.

ACCIDENTS. Accidents are the cause of many injuries of young children and the most frequent cause of death in children beyond infancy. They are responsible for the deaths of over one-third of the children between one and fourteen years of age each year in the United States. Over half of all fatal accidents in children occur before the age of five years. The peak of these accidental deaths occurs in the one- to two-year group (Dietrich, 1959).

In the years up to five the principal causes of accidents in the United States, in order of frequency, in 1959 were motor vehicles, burns, mechanical suffocation, drowning, falls, poisons. Many of these occur in the homes. In fact, in 1958, 68 per cent of all accidents of children under five years of age occurred in the home (Jacobziner et al., 1960).

Accidents have multiple causes, including inexperience, physical and emotional immaturity, an unsafe environment and inadequate supervision. Young children with their rapid but imperfect neuro-muscular development and lack of experience and knowledge of the world about them get into hazardous situations without caution and recognition of danger.

Accidental poisoning is a serious aspect of health protection. According to Jacobziner (1959), children under five years of age, comprising 8 per cent of the population of New York City, accounted for 46.2 per cent of poisonings. Half of these poisonings were caused by drug ingestion, barbiturates and aspirin being the chief offenders. The clever disguising of a drug to make it look and taste like candy can lead to an overdose of such a drug. Poisoning may result from normal curiosity, or from the response of testing the world with the mouth, or from past experiences of receiving praise for eating or drinking a variety of substances.

Some persons seem to be accident-prone or accident repeaters. Studies of such children indicate a complexity of causes, which include physical, psychological and intrafamily factors. Comparing repeaters with children having no accidents, Wehrle et al. (1961) found the poisoned group to be more active and mischievous, more likely to experience falls, to have more of a tendency to rebel against disciplinary measures, more frequent separation experiences and more of a tendency for mother's response to minor injuries to involve physical contact and even medication. In the study of Marcus et al. (1960), of six-to thirteen-year-olds compared with a nonaccident group, the accident-prone children had more emotional problems. They were more active before and after birth, had earlier motor development and good coordination and tended to express their tensions through motor activity and differed in their relations with parents. "In terms of learning theory, accidents would be a response to emotional disturbance, a stimulus which under other circumstances might evoke a different response. The conditions under which this behavior would occur include hyperactivity which may be constitutional, a tendency to express tension through physical activity, and disturbed family relationships."

Prevention of accidents involves protection and education. During the first year of the child's life it is entirely protection. Between one and five years the child is learning to protect himself. He may learn by parental example, supervised experiences and being taught specific procedures. His own cognitive abilities change in these years, and he becomes more able to have gradually diminishing protection.

The young child's development is not such that he can assume the responsibility of providing a safe environment and guarding against accidents on the street. A safe environment is one free from the hazards of fire, burns, poisons—including medicines and cleaning materials—small objects which can be swallowed and cause choking, "stumble-traps" such as toys on stairs or scattered about, knives and other sharp objects. A safe environment also provides protected stairways and a safe space for outdoor play. The mother's busiest time is that period when the infant is beginning to walk and is investigating everything around the house. In England, Rowntree (1950) found, by questioning mothers of children under two years of age, that accidents were associated with the period when the children began to walk and before they had developed "heat sense." Stumbling and falling, with accompanying injuries, generally occur less frequently with children who are skillful in the use of their bodies. Happy, self-reliant, self-confident children, free from worry, tend to have fewer accidents than dependent, disturbed, unhappy ones.

Helping a child to learn to protect himself from accidents can be paced in accordance with his speed of maturation and with his ability to comprehend, to respond and to assume responsibility. Safety can be taught the positive way: e.g., "Toys go back in the playbox when you are through with them." "We stand a foot back from the curb until the light turns green."

During the early years the child is learning much about the world around him that pertains to protecting his health. With guidance he can have safer experiences as he learns that hot objects are to be avoided, that matches and stoves are to be manipulated only by adults, that father's tools are to be used under his supervision. He can learn how to cross a street, but cannot always be trusted not to run out after a ball that has rolled into the street. He can learn that cuts and scratches heal faster when treated with antiseptic and bandaged. He has acquired motor skills which enable him to use his body skillfully, and thus he has fewer falls. Even with all this change in knowledge and abilities, health protection of the child as he reaches the time of going to school still lies chiefly in the hands of his parents and the community.

Psychological Responsiveness

Smooth functioning on a physiological plane in feeding, sleeping, elimination, sensory and motor activity is an important part of the young infant's security. The baby receives from his mother food, physical comfort and sensory stimulation as he is held and cared for. Evidence that these matter to him is provided in the change from crying and uneasiness to more peaceful behavior which occurs when they are provided. The infant's being at ease comes as primary drives or biologically primitive tendencies concerning food, absence of pain, elimination, rest and activity, including sensory activity, are satisfied. In sensory activity, use of sight and hearing in response to people and things, as well as use of the sense of touch and kinesthetic sensitivity, occurs. These various satisfactions and a relatedness or closeness to another person often occur together.

In trying to identify particularly important influences on the infant's security, some writers have emphasized the baby's own vigor and his satisfactions in physiological functioning (Aldrich, 1939; Pinneau, 1950, 1955b). Some have stressed the importance of physical contact with the mother as the infant is cared for (Ribble, 1943; Bowlby, 1958); others have stressed the importance of early sensory stimulation, not necessarily from the mother (Casler, 1961). Others emphasize what is sometimes called emotional interchange between child and mother (Brody, 1956; Escalona, 1953; Horney, 1942; Soddy, 1956). A smoothly functioning body, sensory-motor stimulation, affectional ties of mother and child, social responsiveness of others and of the infant himself all seem to enter into the infant's development of organizational patterns with reference to self, others and a world of things. The patterns can mean *being assured instead of overanxious with regard to self, others and the physical world.*

Aldrich et al. (1945a, 1945b) found evidence that a combination of these influences *decreased crying* among newborn babies. For those in the hospital nursery, before they had been taken home by their parents, the attention of a nurse who gave additional care at the time they seemed to need it decreased the amount of crying. Likewise, after the baby had gone home, providing care when he showed signs of hunger, discomfort or an apparent desire to change position decreased his crying.

Variations among mothers in ability to accommodate to the needs of their infants were accompanied by variations in behavior of the infants (Brody, 1956). Feeding experience was considered a measure of infant and mother relations. When mothers' feeding practices were "conspicuous for their ability to accommodate to the needs of their infants" (as in group A of the following list), the infants showed "mature *social responsiveness* and/or superior *confidence in bodily movement* and/or a high quality of *interest in and concentration upon the mastery of objects.*" In this ability to accommodate to the needs of their infants, Brody found that mothers could be grouped as follows:

Group A: These mothers were sensitive, consistent and attentive.
Group B: These mothers, in general, followed closely the pattern of the group A mothers, but fell short of the mark in each index. They were less sensitive, less consistent, and somewhat overactive or overattentive.

Group C: These mothers were insufficiently sensitive, moderately inconsistent, but adequately attentive.

Group D: These mothers were hypersensitive, very inconsistent, and hyperactive.

Variations in sensory stimulation from environment and in the consequent perceptual stimulation in the infants were accompanied by differences in behavior. Casler (1961) studied infants under six months of age in institutional settings without their mothers and reported less *interest and competence* among those who had deficiencies in visual, auditory, tactile, postural and other kinesthetic experience. "Recent neuroanatomical findings, especially those concerning the reticular formation [help] to explain why perceptual stimulation is so important for normal development." It is suggested that the early months of the infant's life may be a critical time for the activation of the brain stem and thalamic reticular systems by sensory stimuli.

Some of the elements in the infant's environment which have been identified as related to his behavior are personal care, the mother's ability to accommodate to needs, and sensory stimulation. Influence of continuity in the infant's care, as contrasted to emphasis on a particular practice, has received support from reviews of studies of infants reared in different cultures (Orlansky, 1949). For example, some are carried on the mother's back; some are weaned early; some have fathers who play vigorously with them. Patterns of development do not seem to result from any single type of treatment. A break in the continuity of care that the infant's mother, or substitute mother, provides is considered especially serious at certain critical times—after eight months (Bowlby, 1951) or at the end of the first year (Stendler, 1952). By this time the child has preferences for the familiar, as provided by a particular person; furthermore, he is at the stage of beginning to try to locate in the world outside himself, people and objects to count on. Along with his preference for the familiar, he can also be responsive to novelty if it is not excessive.

Questions often arise about lasting effects of extreme anxiety in infancy, such as that of separation from the parent. Evidence is incomplete. Significance of infancy and also resiliency of human beings are recognized in the following statement: "We conclude that the rigidity of character structuring during the first year or two of life has been exaggerated by many authorities, and that the events of childhood and later years are of great importance in reinforcing or changing the character structure tentatively formed during infancy" (Orlansky, 1949).

Beyond infancy, responses of the individual and elements in the setting already mentioned continue to be relevant. The idea that change without undue stress is also a part of security at all ages can be described as *accommodation to incongruities*. In this way, distinctions between undue stress for the individual and stress which can be stimulating may be made. An "incongruity-dissonance principle" may be used to explain variations in uneasiness among different persons in similar settings. According to the person's previous experience, a new experience may seem incongruous and so make him overanxious, or congruous enough so that accommodation may be made easily.

Hunt (1960) refers to a study by Jersild and Holmes of fears in children of preschool age. In this study, getting toys to play with meant going into a dark room, taking them from a chair near a woman "dressed in a large floppy black hat and a long gray coat," or climbing along a plank. Some children started immediately for the toys. Others hesitated, but ultimately went ahead on their own. Some would go only if accompanied by the examiner. Others refused to go at all. Hunt suggests that the children who were less fearful were "likely to have had the wider experience with the sorts of situations used . . . to evoke fear" and that some of these experiences may have been painful. But these children had, in their residue from past experience, associations, "cerebral circuits," or "sequential organizations," which could accommodate to the new. In processing information from the new situation their perceptions and thoughts motivated actions of seeking the toys on their own; the perceptions and thoughts were responses which served as reinforcing stimuli prompting this action. Hunt regards systematic theories of psychology of Hebb (1966) and Piaget (1952, 1954) as supporting the idea that limited incongruities can "lend interest and may provide attractive problems," but that "incongruities which extend beyond the child's capacity for accommodation instigate withdrawal or fear and even terror."

Statements such as these provide a frame of reference for considering security in the individual as he finds himself in familar and new situations throughout the years. Residues of experience concern particular events; they also concern more inclusive feelings about self, others and the physical world. The child has many opportunities to discover his own powers and those of others. These experiences provide weight on the side of trust or distrust of himself, of others and of the physical world.

Figure 31 illustrates behavior of children in a situation in which play equipment was new. Their expectancies of each other as they wait to try using it, the confidence of the child who is adjusting a piece so that it will move along the spindle, the attentiveness of those who are watching it, all suggest residues of past experience, "cerebral circuits" which can accommodate to the situation. Many circumstances, including the sensitive, attentive attitude of the adult, seem to be a part of this learning situation.

A thread of well-founded self-esteem and esteem of others has run through this discussion of security. Consequently, information concerning self-esteem of the mother is of interest. Sears, Maccoby and Levin (1957) identify a factor in child-rearing practices which they call general family adjustment, "a dimension that involves the mother's acceptance of, and confidence in, both herself and her husband."

The mother's self-esteem was an important correlate of her ability to feel and express warmth toward the child, especially when he had reached kindergarten age. A similar relationship held true with respect to her esteem for her

FIGURE 31. *Being assured, instead of overanxious, with regard to self, others and the physical world can occur in a variety of settings.*

These children, 4 to 5 years of age, were learning to place parts of a color spindle—a new piece of play equipment. A number of circumstances under which the equipment was presented seemed to prompt responsiveness on the part of the children.

husband. On the average, those mothers who held their husbands in high esteem were much warmer in their relationships to their children than were those who felt less enthusiasm and respect for their husbands.

It is clear that security comes not merely from the elements discussed here, but also from the meeting of the various needs discussed in Chapters Four through Seven. Assurance which comes through knowing what to do and what not to do is considered in the following section.

DEPENDENCE AND INDEPENDENCE

Listing a need for both dependence and independence represents an attempt to recognize that *control both in others and in self* requires supply or relief for well-being and development. On the physical side, dependence concerns material help from others for life's necessities in the area of physical needs; independence concerns one's own way of showing that they are needed, responding to and seeking what the world offers. On the psychological side, dependence concerns cognitive help (as in the acquiring of knowledge) and emotional help (as in warmth, attention, reassurance and approval of socially acceptable behavior) from others; independence concerns one's own way of showing need and of responding to situations. No one can be completely independent of others, but each likes to decide for himself that which he is able to decide instead of feeling "pressed" by another.

This sensing "that he is an independent human being and yet one who is able to use the help and guidance of others in important matters" (Witmer and Kotinsky, 1953), i.e., the sense of autonomy, develops in a variety of situations. The child pictured in Figure 32 is having one of many experiences in which he is a person making choices. In selecting and completing a puzzle, and then selecting another, he is responding in his own way, with independence. Such independence does not preclude dependence. The same child can also be responsive to, or sometimes seek, warmth, approval, attention or reassurance.

As the child grows beyond infancy the trend is toward more independence. He continues to be both controlled and controlling, to be in the power of others as well as to have his own power, and to have external authority to which he adjusts, as well as his own inner authority or conscience. But the trend is in the direction of greater self-control, which becomes more possible as he grows older. This adding of resources within himself is suggested by the following illustrations.

The infant has to have material help from others in order to survive. Yet he has his pattern of being hungry and sleepy and of elimination; he has in himself physiological controls pertaining to food, rest and activity, and elimination. The older child is just beginning to learn to identify some of these physical cues and to act accordingly. For example, a $2\frac{1}{2}$-year-old who is thirsty may go willingly when someone offers to take him to the kitchen for a drink of water; at another stage he may ask to be taken; later he goes alone. The three-year-old who

FIGURE 32. The child can be very interested in an activity to be accomplished alone.

This boy continued with the puzzle until it was completed and then selected another. There were no children or adults nearby.

sees an animal new to him may listen if an adult volunteers its name; later he may inquire its name; when he is older, he may add to his knowledge and answer his questions about it through books he can read. The child who is trying to pull a shovel out of the hands of another child may hear his father shout, "No!" and then say, "Ask him for it." He may then ask for it and get it. At another stage, about to snatch the shovel, he may see his father nearby and ask for it instead of taking it by force. Later he will probably ask for it whether or not his father is present.

These illustrations include steps in *growth toward self-discipline*, or self-control, which involve proceeding from being told what to do by another person, to being influenced by the presence of the other person, to responding when the other person is not present because of something within oneself.

In many situations the child's need for both dependence and independence can be recognized. Thus he has help in learning what to do and what not to do, what to say and what not to say in his rapidly expanding world, but he has the feeling of proceeding at his own pace and in accordance with his stage of development, and also of wanting to do what is expected. Control of this kind, in the relations of parent and child or of another adult and child, can take a variety of forms. Some of the forms of parental control are permissiveness and strictness, or restrictiveness, punitiveness, and involvement of the adult, in terms of degree and of affect, or emotional tone.

Permissiveness and *strictness* are factors in child-rearing practices. Sears, Maccoby and Levin (1957) refer to "a quality of child rearing that has, for one extreme, an attitude of tolerance of changeworthy behavior and a low level of pressure for conformity to adult standards. At the other extreme it has a suppressive and unaccepting attitude toward early childhood impulses, and a high insistence on the adoption of more mature forms of behavior." The factor concerns the parent's permissiveness and strictness regarding such behavior as play in the house and with furniture, table manners, noise, being neat and orderly, toilet training, strict obedience, doing well in school, dependency, aggression, immodesty, masturbation and sex play, as well as the parent's use of physical punishment and the parent's punishment of the child's aggression toward his parents.

Permissiveness and strictness concerning the feeding, sleeping and toilet training of the young child have been the subject of a number of studies. Of particular interest has been the parent's adjustment of schedule and expectations to the child's own patterns, which in these instances are physiological patterns. The phrase "self-regulatory schedule" suggests a schedule in which there is recognition of the child's patterns of response.

"Bed-wetting and feeding problems are associated with forms of non-permissiveness" (Sears, Maccoby and Levin, 1957). Evidence of effects on the child of various degrees of parental control within a range seems to point to significance of something in the personality of the parent and not to mere presence or absence of a definite schedule or expectation. McCandless (1967) says:

> About the specifics of feeding . . . mothers who are well-meaning and who try relaxedly to do what they sincerely believe is best for their children — particularly when this is in harmony with the cultural ways of the community with which they are most closely associated — obtain the best results with their children. . . . The rigidity with which toilet training is carried out is related to a number of other child-rearing practices, almost all of which may be thought of either as restrictive or as indicative of insecurity and low self-esteem on the part of the mother. . . . Clinical evidence and hypotheses about the effects of sex training abound, suggesting that both harsh and restrictive sex training and overly permissive training . . . may leave the child sexually disturbed.

Thus we find little that lends support to extreme permissiveness or extreme strictness. The important factors seem to be the intentions of the parent, the parent's personality, as well as absence of a relation which makes the child feel ignored or unduly restricted. Caldwell (1964) concluded:

> . . . the ideal study will be concerned with attitude plus practice, with the inherent characteristics of the child as well as his immediate reaction to the process, and with the multiplicity of subsequent experiences through which the specific practice must be filtered before coming to rest as a significant influence in the child's life. Only when such studies are available can the definitive review be written on the effects of infant care.

Aggressiveness and *punitiveness* represent another form of parental control. The mother strong in this factor, according to Sears, Maccoby and Levin (1957), seems to have a high level of aggressiveness displayed "in her punishment and in her attempts to get the child to be aggressive" toward other children. She is permissive concerning the child's aggression toward other children. "At the same time, she will not tolerate aggression toward herself." When the mothers were high in aggressiveness and punitiveness, their children were more often aggressive. It should be added, however, that another pattern of behavior in the mother was also a source of aggression in the child. When mothers were permissive for aggression, but not aggressive and punitive themselves, this was a source of continuing aggressive behavior in their children.

> Our measures of punishment, whether of the object-oriented or love-oriented variety, referred to levels of punitiveness in the mothers. . . . The amount of use of punishment that we measured was essentially a measure of a personality quality of the mothers. Punitiveness, contrasting with rewardingness, was a quite ineffectual quality for a mother to inject into her child training.
> . . . Mothers who punished toilet accidents severely ended up with bed-wetting children. Mothers who punished dependency to get rid of it had more dependent children than mothers who did not punish. Mothers who punished aggressive behavior severely had more aggressive children than mothers who punished lightly. They also had more dependent children. Harsh physical punishment was associated with high childhood aggressiveness and with the development of feeding problems.
> Our evaluation of punishment is that it is ineffectual over the long term as a technique for eliminating the kind of behavior toward which it is directed.

On the subject of consequences of parental discipline, Becker (1964) writes:

> The . . . studies, while containing some unresolved complexities, suggest that one "consequence" of a punitive approach to discipline is aggression. In trying to understand the meaning of this relationship, we are faced with difficulties. First, a series of studies . . . provide rather overwhelming evidence that hostile parents have aggressive children. . . . Hostile parents also tend to use more physical punishment and less reasoning and praise. We are faced with a situation where certain techniques of discipline and certain emotional attitudes of the parent tend to occur jointly and have similar consequences for the child. Thus, we do not know for sure that the obtained relation between physical punishment and aggression is primarily a result of the kind of discipline used, a joint effect of hostility and type of punishment, or primarily an effect of the parents' hostility. . . . The only direct evidence on this question is not very conclusive. Sears and associates (1957) used partial correlations to show that maternal coldness and physical punishment contributed about equally to aggression in the child.

In order to recognize permissiveness-strictness or restrictiveness, and also emotional quality in the parent-child relation, dimensions or continua for both can be used, e.g., *autonomy-control and love-hostility*, or *laissez-faire-involvement and love-hostility*. Schaefer (1961) provided a conceptual framework or model for viewing a variety of parent-child relations. His circumplex model for maternal behavior uses two intersecting lines to form four quadrants. One dimension is love-hostility; the other, autonomy-control. When variables that had high intercorrelations were placed adjacent to one another, democratic and cooperative behavior was in the quadrant formed by the ends of the lines for autonomy and love; overindulgent, protective indulgent and overprotective behavior was in the love and control quadrant; authoritarian, dictatorial and demanding antagonistic behavior was in the control-hostility quadrant; neglecting, indifferent and detached behavior was in the hostility-autonomy quadrant. The love-hostility dimension of the mother was predictive of behavior in the child (Schaefer and Bayley, 1963). The autonomy-control dimension of the mother (with ratings of behavior on intrusiveness, concern about health, achievement, demand, excessive contact and fostering dependency) did not show a clear pattern of relation with behavior of boys at twenty-seven to ninety-six months, and the pattern for girls was not consistent across age levels.

Laissez-faire versus involvement was the dimension used, along with love-hostility, in another study of mother-child interactions. Hatfield, Ferguson and Alpert (1967) found reward of independence and reward of dependency among the variables in the love-involvement quadrant, seeming to represent positive involvement with the child; restriction and punishment of independence were in the involvement-hostility quadrant, seeming to represent negative involvement. Punishment of dependency in the hostility-*laissez-faire* quadrant seemed to imply rejection. Focus in this study was on certain aspects of personality development in the child and the socialization process as portrayed in mother-child interaction observed in several test situations. For boys, dependency was positively related to the mother's warmth and to her responsiveness to her son in a test situation in which she was busy. It was also related to her pressure for achievement and independence. For girls, dependency was related to the mother's rewarding of dependency and lack of concern about neatness, again in the test situations.

Additional precision has been suggested for the form of control called *democratic-autocratic*. Crandall and Preston (1955), reporting dimensions of maternal behavior, called one cluster of items "coactive control," and another, "coercive control." Mothers high in coactive control were those who justified their policies of handling their children to the children, endorsed and used democratic policies, explained things and were understanding of their children. In coercive control the mother was quick in enforcing demands or suggestions and severe in her penalties. When effects on the children of different kinds of democratic, autocratic and *laissez-faire* procedures have been studied, findings have concerned a great variety of procedures of adults and responses of children. The importance of considering goals or values of the parents, as well as techniques or forms of control for achieving them, has been emphasized by Baldwin (1955), who says:

> Analysis of the cases falling in the *democratic* group makes it . . . evident that neither a democratic philosophy nor democratic techniques applied in the training of the child can provide an automatically optimum environment. Parental goals are as important as the techniques used in attaining those goals, and healthy personalities in the parents are a prerequisite for a healthy child.

Knowledge of the ramifications of the child's dependence and independence is incomplete. It has been suggested that overdependence occurs in the child who is not feeling nurtured, in the sense of being with adults who reward, encourage, support or show affection. Hartup (1958) refers to "the hypothesis that non-nurturance by an adult is more strongly associated with the occurrence of *dependency behavior* in young children than is nurturance alone. . . . The naturalistic studies of Sears, et al. (1953), Beller (1955), and Smith (1953) all contain data which show a positive relationship between amount of parental frustrations (non-nurturance) and the frequency of dependency behavior observed in young children." Sex differences in relation of warmth of the mother and dependency of the child have been reported (Hatfield et al., 1967).

Adult attributes or dimensions related to the child's need for both dependence and independence might be stated as follows: recognition of what matters to the child deeply as contrasted to superficially, and also recognition of his ability to add new forms of behavior without great frustration. Specific ways of encouraging the child's *growth in self-discipline* or *self-control* might include the following:

1. Recognizing what the child is and is not able to do and enabling him to do for himself what he can
2. Enabling the child to learn what to do, instead of merely what not to do
3. Making plans for constructive activities
4. Being open-minded and relaxed, willing to discuss reasons and reconsider
5. Respecting as an adult aims emphasized for the child

6. Praising when it is justified
7. Expecting "good" behavior and making it interesting, but not always entertaining
8. Being logical; attempting to have the sequence of events related whether commendable or questionable behavior is involved; trying to avoid arbitrary punishment
9. Being honest

TOPICS FOR STUDY AND DISCUSSION

1. As a focus for study, reply to the question: What knowledge of an "antecedent-consequent" type do you find in the literature (research and theory) concerning warmth, security, dependence and independence?
2. Observe several settings provided for young children. Record detail concerning the extent to which they do or do not show recognition of (*a*) characteristics of temperature regulation in infants and young children; (*b*) procedures for health protection and accident prevention; and (*c*) physical care adapted to the individual child.
3. Provide observational detail suggesting the child's warmth, his meeting situations without extreme stress or apathy, his dependence and independence; show the interrelation of the child's own behavior and the setting in providing these.
4. Attempt to differentiate degree of control in the adult by using a high involvement *laissez-faire* continuum. Place illustrations of behavior of the adult and the child along a 5-point scale. Then attempt to add a 1 to 5 rating on a love-hostility continuum to each of these illustrations. For illustrations of behavior draw upon observations of infants, toddlers, children of other preschool ages, and older children.

   What have you begun to discover about attempts to judge degree of control and of love-hostility in the adult? about variations in adult behavior according to the particular practice of the child?

SELECTED READINGS

Aldrich, C. A., and Aldrich, M. M.: Babies Are Human Beings. 2nd ed. New York, Macmillan Company, 1954. Chap. 5, Babies Are Different.

Becker, W. C.: Consequences of Different Kinds of Parental Discipline; chapter in M. L. Hoffman and L. W. Hoffman (Eds.): Review of Child Development Research. New York, Russell Sage Foundation, 1964, Vol. 1, pp. 169-208.

Brody, S.: Patterns of Mothering. New York, International Universities Press, Inc., 1956. Chap. 1, Mother and Infant: The Unit of Study. Chap. 2, Maternal Behavior: The Literature. Chap. 3, Infant Growth: The Literature.

Harlow, H. F., and Harlow, M. K.: Learning to Love. American Scientist, 54:244-272, 1966.

McCandless, B.: Children, Behavior and Development. 2nd ed. New York, Holt, Rinehart and Winston, 1967. Effects of Infantile and Early Childhood Deprivation, pp. 153-168.

Rheingold, H. L.: The Development of Social Behavior in the Human Infant; in H. W. Stevenson (Ed.): Concept of Development. Monographs of the Society for Research in Child Development, 1966, 31, No. 5 (Serial No. 107), pp. 1-17.

Rheingold, H. L., Gewirtz, J. L., and Ross, H. W.: Social conditioning of vocalizations in the infant. J. Comp. & Physiol. Psychol., 52:68-73, 1959.

Stuart, H. C., and Prugh, D. G. (Eds.): The Healthy Child. Cambridge, Harvard University Press, 1960. Chap. 2, The Characteristics of Childhood Illnesses and Immunity.

Wallace, B., and Dobzhansky, T.: Radiation, Genes and Man. New York, Henry Holt & Company, Inc., 1959.

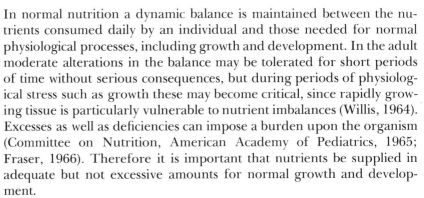

CHAPTER FIVE

*Physical and Psychological Needs: Nutrition**

In normal nutrition a dynamic balance is maintained between the nutrients consumed daily by an individual and those needed for normal physiological processes, including growth and development. In the adult moderate alterations in the balance may be tolerated for short periods of time without serious consequences, but during periods of physiological stress such as growth these may become critical, since rapidly growing tissue is particularly vulnerable to nutrient imbalances (Willis, 1964). Excesses as well as deficiencies can impose a burden upon the organism (Committee on Nutrition, American Academy of Pediatrics, 1965; Fraser, 1966). Therefore it is important that nutrients be supplied in adequate but not excessive amounts for normal growth and development.

The influence of nutrition in early life on physical growth is well documented (Jackson, 1966). Animal studies have shown that severe restriction in the maternal diet during pregnancy can affect the growth and development of offspring (Chow and Lee, 1964). During the first few weeks of life rats can be imprinted by extreme dietary restriction to the extent that their total subsequent growth and development are affected, with development of degenerative diseases and early death (Widdowson and McCance, 1963). In the human being it also appears likely that nutrition affects not only stature and weight, but also other aspects of development, including even intersensory organization (Cravioto et al., 1966). Evidence is accumulating to indicate that permanent impairment of the central nervous system may result from severe dietary restriction or imbalances during critical periods in the first four years of life (Coursin, 1965; Cravioto et al., 1966). Although published data concerning the boundaries of nutritional deprivation and imbalances which produce long-term impairment in learning behavior are limited, animal studies indicate that severe nutritional con-

---

*This chapter was reviewed and revised for this edition by Avanelle Kirksey of the Department of Foods and Nutrition, Purdue University.

ditions may not be essential for such impairment (Barnes et al., 1966). Future studies of the relation of malnutrition to central nervous system development may pose issues of great importance to the study of child development.

In the past the goals of infant nutrition were to keep the infant alive and to promote growth. Barness (1966) has expanded the goals to include, in addition to the preservation of life and adequate growth, freedom from deficiency, ability to repair physical injury, freedom from infection and adequate immunity, social and mental development to full genetic potential, and inhibition of degenerative disease. Griffith (1967) includes among the goals of nutrition neuromuscular coordination and neurological and psychological stability. The importance of adequate nutrition in infancy and childhood is evidenced by the possibility that nutrition conditions many facets of the well-being of a person throughout his life.

NUTRITIONAL NEEDS

Meeting nutritional needs for oxygen, water, protein, fats, carbohydrates, vitamins and minerals implies interaction between the child and his environment. The child's role in the interaction is his acceptance of and physiological ability to utilize the substances provided. This role changes as the child matures, and may also vary from child to child. The environment provides nutrients in varying amounts dependent upon the bounty or scarcity of the particular environment and the recognition of their importance by those responsible for the child's care. The environment also provides a psychological climate which influences the child's role in the interaction.

The substances listed in the foregoing paragraph contribute to a satisfactory nutriture, namely, the condition of nourishment essential for the normal functioning and well-being of a person in a particular environment (Griffith, 1967). Nutriture depends upon metabolism, the series of processes which coordinate to build cells, tissues and organs, and to provide for their proper functioning. Seven processes are involved: (1) ingestion (the intake of food), (2) digestion (the breakdown of food), (3) absorption (the entry of nutrients into the blood or lymph), (4) excretion (the disposal of waste products), (5) circulation (the distribution of nutrients to cells), (6) respiration (the supplying of oxygen and elimination of carbon dioxide), (7) oxidation (the process by which the nutrients are used to build tissue and to produce heat and energy for useful work). The maturation of the nutriture and the systems concerned with these processes will now be considered.

Indications of Maturation of the Nutriture

During fetal life the food supply is elemental—calcium, iron, phosphorus, protein. All nutriment must be in a form which can be transferred from the mother's blood stream to that of the fetus across a cellular barrier, the placenta.

At birth the way in which the infant obtains food suddenly becomes different. The mouth becomes the portal of entry for nourishment. The immaturity of the mouth and other parts of the digestive tract at birth necessitates a highly simplified food, namely, breast milk. When this is not available, nourishment is provided through a satisfactory substitute. During the first few days of transition from fetal existence to that of an independent organism the newborn receives colostrum, the first secretion of the mammary glands and a highly specialized product adapted to his needs.

As the child grows he needs essential substances which breast milk does not furnish in adequate quantities. This is the first transition from complete dependence on food from the maternal body to utilization of other food. Vitamin D is administered in some form to ensure the utilization of calcium and phosphorus in bones and teeth. Vitamin C intake is supplemented generally with a concentrate of the vitamin, orange juice or a juice fortified with the vitamin. Although reliable indications of nutritive maturity are unknown, digestive response to increasingly complex foods is believed to be one of the soundest gauges of nutritive maturation.

The next stage in maturation of the nutriture allows the use of semisolid foods, such as cereals and puréed vegetables and fruits. These supply the increasingly complex food elements the body can use. Purée-ing of foods reduces their complexity, some simplification still being demanded at this stage of the child's nutritive maturity.

Toleration of well-chopped foods might be designated the "premature" nutritive stage. This slight simplification of food is necessary because the child has not learned to chew and has an inadequate number of teeth to masticate his food satisfactorily.

The child moves into the mature stage when he can eat solid, nonsimplified foods. Intact, natural forms of foods are prepared for digestion and reduced to their simple form within his body.

It may be said that there are six stages in the maturation of the nutriture: the fetal, newborn, infant stage I, infant stage II, "premature," and mature (Table 4). These six stages, it is believed, can be de-

---

TABLE 4.   Stages of Maturation of the Nutriture

Fetal stage	Nourished from nutrients supplied by maternal blood
Newborn stage	Simplified and highly specialized food (colostrum) supplied by the mammary glands and adapted to needs of the newborn
Infant: stage I	Infant dependent on mother's milk (or a substitute); essential substances added which are not supplied sufficiently by mother's milk; begins to be independent of his mother
Infant: stage II	Infant diet has semisolid, puréed food added
"Pre-mature" stage	The diet is increased in complexity by adding well-chopped food
Mature stage	Solid, nonsimplified foods, prepared for digestion by mastication and reduced to simple form within the child's body

tected by observing the concurrent maturational changes of oral activities related to the ingestion of food.

The *rooting and sucking reflexes*, present at birth, are the infant's mechanism for finding and taking fluids into the mouth. Some time later a *biting reflex and salivation* appear. The infant bites and begins drooling. This is an indication for introducing puréed food. The next oral indicator includes two kinds of behavior which appear close together: the *ability to swallow small lumps* and *destructive biting*. Now the infant can manage chopped foods. The final oral indication is *chewing*, by which the infant is able to reduce food to a consistency that can be swallowed. This requires at least the first molars. By this time the child can eat solid, nonsimplified foods. These and other nutritive indications provide a better understanding of the reasons underlying individual differences in nutriture which are not explained by age alone. It seems possible for a child to be two years old chronologically and immature nutritively.

Lags in nutritive maturation seem most commonly due to environmental factors such as illness, accompanied by poor appetite, and are correctable under ordinary circumstances. Also, children may be physiologically ready for the later stages, but psychologically unready.

PHYSICAL EQUIPMENT

Various parts of the body participate in providing for its nourishment: namely, the digestive system, respiratory tract, blood-vascular system, senses of taste and smell, the teeth and jaws, the endocrine and nervous systems. All but the last two will be discussed here; the endocrine and nervous systems will be discussed in Chapter Eight.

Digestive System

The digestive tract is the body's equipment for utilizing food. Through its activities of motility, secretion, digestion, absorption and excretion, food is changed to substances which the body can use; these substances are made available to tissues, and what the body does not retain is excreted. These activities are made possible through finely regulated mechanisms in which nervous and chemical elements participate.

The digestive tract consists of the mouth, pharynx, esophagus, stomach, and small and large intestines. The tract varies in size at different levels and functionally consists of two parts: (1) the alimentary canal, through which food passes and within which digestion takes place; and (2) accessory glands (salivary glands, pancreas and liver), which produce secretions vital to digestion and absorption of food.

The alimentary canal is a musculomembranous structure which, like the heart and lungs, is largely under the control of the involuntary nervous mechanism of the body. It is richly supplied with fluids which soften dry foods, and at vital points the movement of the food through the canal is regulated by circular bands of muscle, called sphincters. The muscular walls are well supplied with blood vessels, and the membranous lining contains specialized types of blood vessels called lacteals through which some digested food is absorbed before being transferred into the blood. The walls also contain glands which secrete substances necessary to the digestive processes, including enzymes and hormones. The muscular walls have layers of circular and longitudinal smooth muscles which make possible a churning movement for mixing food with digestive enzymes, and peristaltic waves for mixing the contents along the tract. The muscles are covered with tough, elastic, flexible connective tissue.

The accessory organs of digestion are of two types: those which are mechanical in function and those which secrete fluids necessary for digestion itself. The teeth (see pp. 173-178) and tongue are the mechanical accessory organs, and the salivary glands, pancreas and liver are the functional accessory glands. Secretions of the accessory glands enter at two points, in the mouth and in the first portion of the intestine.

Secretions into the digestive tract are regulated either reflexly or chemically, or by a combination. The secretion of saliva is controlled by reflexes which can be conditioned by sight, smell or taste of food. Even the thought of food, particularly of a favorite food, can start salivation. The act of chewing will also increase the flow of saliva. On the other hand, the secretion of the pancreas is chemically controlled. Gastric secretion has both elements of control. The reflex aspect of control has significance, since pleasant associations with food can stimulate gastric secretion which aids its digestion. Sight and smell of food as well as the presence of food in the mouth can by reflex control initiate secretion.

By the chemical changes brought about by digestive juices and by the physical changes induced by peristaltic movements of the digestive tract, most constituents of food are converted into soluble substances of smaller molecular size which can pass into the blood. The material must pass across two biological membranes, the alimentary tract and the blood or lymph vessel, if the products of digestion, the salts, water and vitamins are to become available for use by cells of the body. This transfer of dissolved material from the intestines to the body fluids, known as absorption, is never accomplished by open ducts, but is effected by other processes.

Absorption is a complex phenomenon involving osmosis, diffusion and other methods of transport, some as yet incompletely understood, by which certain materials are permitted to penetrate the walls of the intestine and others are withheld (Ham and Leeson, 1961). In addition to physical forces, some absorptive processes involve cellular activity with the expenditure of energy. The products of digestion of protein and carbohydrates move from the intestinal absorptive cells to blood capillaries; fat is absorbed chiefly into the lacteals, a part of the lymph system. These products ultimately are transported to cells, where they are either metabolized and used, or stored or excreted.

Inorganic substances in food are absorbed to a varying extent.

Those which form insoluble salts are not well absorbed. Examples of such insoluble substances are calcium soaps, formed when a calcium compound combines chemically with a fatty acid, and calcium oxalate, formed when calcium combines chemically with oxalic acid (found in some foods).

Absorption of food constituents occurs chiefly in the small intestine. Water is absorbed in the large intestine. The residue of undigested food and a considerable quantity of water ingested with food or derived from the digestive juices passes into the large intestine. Through the absorption of water the residue is changed to a soft, semiliquid mass, the feces. A few times a day, particularly after meals, mass movements carry material to the rectum. The tendency of these movements to take place after the first meal of the day constitutes one of the reasons why children are frequently encouraged to go to the toilet after breakfast.

The centers for control of colon activity are located in the central nervous system, indicating that its activity may be affected not only by local reflexes, but also by habit formation and nervous states. The sigmoid and rectal portions of the colon are very sensitive to distention or irritation. The passage of fecal matter into the rectum gives rise to the sensation which sets in motion the comparatively complex reflex mechanism of defecation.

The feces consist of water, dead and living microorganisms, intestinal secretions and excretions, cellular material from the intestinal walls and food residues. Food residues are generally a small component and depend on (1) composition of the food eaten, (2) capacity for digestion and digestive activity of the stomach and intestine, (3) irritability of the digestive tract, and (4) capacity for absorption. For further details of the mechanics of the digestive tract the student is referred to Carlson, Johnson and Calvert (1961).

DIGESTIVE TRACT OF THE YOUNG CHILD. The *intake of food* in liquid form is made possible shortly after birth by the reflexes of rooting and sucking. Infants less than twelve hours of age are not readily stimulated to suck or swallow, and esophageal response to deglutition is incoordinated (Gryboski, 1965). By the third day sucking and deglutition have been modified by the learning experience provided by feeding, and abnormalities occur less frequently. At the touch of the nipple on the cheek or near the mouth the infant turns his head so that the nipple comes in contact with the area of the lips. Sucking, a neonatal response to tactile stimulation of the lip region, results. This strong reflex is facilitated by a relatively short lower jaw, fat pads in the cheeks and adequate muscles. Later, owing to the maturation of the muscles of the tongue, appearance of teeth and development of the lower jaw, food other than in liquid form can be managed by the infant (Gesell and Ilg, 1937). The amount of food taken at a feeding depends upon the satiety mechanism controlled by a center in the hypothalamus. One of the factors contributing to this mechanism is the capacity of the stomach. This varies widely with size and age and is fixed only by the maximum limit of distention; it approximates 30 to 90 cc. at birth, 90 to 150 cc. at one month, 500 cc. at two years, and 750 to 900 cc. in later childhood (Watson and Lowrey, 1967).

The *infant's or young child's ability to digest food* differs from that of an adult more quantitatively than qualitatively. At birth all the enzymes necessary for the digestion of proteins, carbohydrates and fats are present, but are less in amount and differ in proportion. The salivary glands increase in size and appearance, so that at two years they assume the appearance of those of an adult (Ivy and Grossman, 1952). The amount of saliva is scanty at birth, but increases in the next two or three months. Its flow can be stimulated by the nipple or by the presence of food in the mouth. It has been estimated that by the age of $2\frac{1}{2}$ to three months the infant secretes 50 to 150 cc. of saliva a day; the adult secretes about $1\frac{1}{2}$ liters (1500 cc.) (Ivy and Gibbs, 1966). As saliva increases, drooling is likely to appear because of the infant's inability to swallow it; later, drooling results from irritation of the gums during tooth eruption. The concentration of ptyalin, the salivary enzyme which acts on carbohydrates, increases by the age of one year to that of the adult, representing an increase of fivefold from birth (Ivy and Grossman, 1952).

In the stomach a lower acid level prevails during the early months except for a temporary postnatal increase (Ebers et al., 1956; Smith, 1959c). By four months, however, nearly adult levels are reached (Watson and Lowrey, 1967). Of the protein-splitting enzymes, pepsin, in the stomach, increases in quantity until the age of four months, after which a constant level is reached; trypsin, from the pancreas, is adequate at birth. Amylase, the pancreatic carbohydrate-splitting enzyme, is decreased in infancy, but reaches adult levels in older children. Lipase (the pancreatic fat-splitting enzyme) activity is also low in infancy and throughout early childhood (Watson and Lowrey, 1967). Gastric secretion is stimulated by appetite, which generally begins to appear after four or five months.

Among the vital functions of the liver is the production of secretions important in the digestion of food. The liver is proportionately large in the newborn, occupying nearly two-fifths of the abdominal cavity, and forming 4 per cent of the body weight even though it is physiologically immature (Watson and Lowrey, 1967). By three years it has increased threefold. The relative size of the liver of the infant, compared with that of the adult, indicates its importance in early life.

Thus the newborn infant can digest protein, fat and simple carbohydrates when they are fed to him in an appropriate form, namely, milk or a substitute. As he develops, other foods may be introduced from liquids to finely divided or whole foods which are compatible with increasing maturity of muscles, nerves and teeth. When foods are reduced to a simpler form, e.g., puréed meat, they may be introduced at an early age. Healthy infants and young children appear to have the capacity to digest a variety of foods in reasonable amounts. In fact, the secretory and absorbing surfaces show greater development than the supporting musculature involved in motility.

Motility of the tract is another aspect of digestion. One type of motility which occurs in the stomach is that of *hunger contractions*, which are a part of the mechanism by which the need for food is registered. In the newborn these generally begin two to four hours after feeding (Smith, 1959c). In infants from one to six months of age the average time for onset of hunger contractions is about three hours after a meal (Ivy and Gibbs, 1966). In young adults the time is four to six hours (Ivy and Grossman, 1952). These contractions are accompanied by sensations of hunger.

Another aspect of motility is that by which food and digestive products are transported along the digestive tract. In the mouth, food is prepared for swallowing. In the newborn, liquid food is moved to the back of the mouth by *sucking*, which is accomplished by depressing the jaws, an action which tends to produce negative pressure in the mouth cavity. This cavity in the newborn is very shallow; the hard palate is flat, not having acquired the concave characteristics of the adult palate. In the act of sucking, the gum pads are apart, the tongue is brought forword in a plunger-like position in contact with the lower lip; the mandible (lower jaw) moves forward and backward rhythmically as the cheek muscles alternately contract and relax (Fig. 33). (Figure 33 emphasizes the idea that in sucking, the infant uses a variety of mechanisms. This behavior is of interest not only with reference to his ability to secure food, but also because of possibilities of other ramifications, e.g., sensory stimulation, development of the jaws and dentition, development of motor controls in speech.) Sucking is greatly facilitated by the sucking

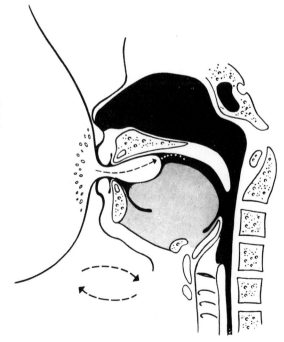

FIGURE 33. In nursing, the infant's mandible moves forward and backward rhythmically, in conjunction with perioral sphincteric action.

The gum pads approximate each other, flattening out the teat. T. A. Graber: Craniofacial and Dentitional Development. Chap. 18 in F. Falkner (Ed.): Human Development. Philadelphia, W. B. Saunders Company, 1966, p. 568.)

pads, small masses of fatty tissue in the cheeks. In the newborn the tongue is restricted in movement, with some curling of the lateral margins, but with no well-defined mobility. By four to twelve weeks there is some backward and forward movement, and the tongue will more or less involuntarily eject food. As the tongue comes under voluntary control it becomes more facile, and food is compressed and shifted about before swallowing.

Before solid food can be consumed, *mastication* must be possible. The beginnings of mastication, which is produced by motions of tongue, palate and jaws, precede the appearance of teeth. Mastication is more effective when the molars have erupted and grinding of the food is made possible. Thus the teeth function in grinding food; the tongue, in mixing it with the saliva and in keeping it pressed between the grind-

INFANTILE (VISCERAL) SWALLOW

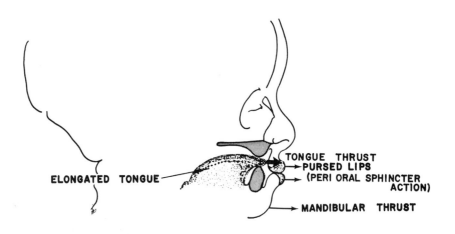

ELONGATED TONGUE

TONGUE THRUST
PURSED LIPS
(PERI ORAL SPHINCTER ACTION)

MANDIBULAR THRUST

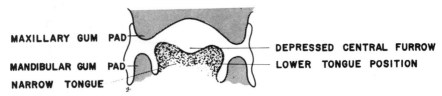

MAXILLARY GUM PAD

MANDIBULAR GUM PAD

NARROW TONGUE

DEPRESSED CENTRAL FURROW

LOWER TONGUE POSITION

FIGURE 34. *Infantile swallowing mechanism.*

Plunger-like action is associated with nursing. Cheek pads flow between posterior gum pads during nursing, unopposed by peripheral portions of tongue. Associated with the tongue thrust is the anterior position of the mandible. The condyle may be felt gliding rhythmically forward and backward during the nursing act. Note the concave midline contour of dorsum of tongue. T. A. Graber: Craniofacial and Dentitional Development. Chap. 18 in F. Falkner (Ed.): Human Development. Philadelphia, W. B. Saunders Company, 1966, p. 572.)

MATURE (SOMATIC) SWALLOW

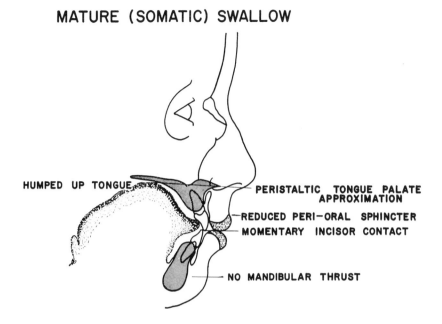

HUMPED UP TONGUE

PERISTALTIC TONGUE PALATE APPROXIMATION

REDUCED PERI−ORAL SPHINCTER

MOMENTARY INCISOR CONTACT

NO MANDIBULAR THRUST

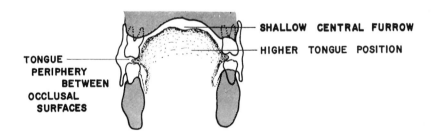

SHALLOW CENTRAL FURROW

HIGHER TONGUE POSITION

TONGUE PERIPHERY BETWEEN OCCLUSAL SURFACES

FIGURE 35. Mature swallowing mechanism.

The dorsum is less concave than in infantile swallowing (Fig. 34) and approximates the palate during deglutition. The tip of the tongue is contained behind the incisors; peripheral portions flow between opposing posterior segments. Anterior mandibular thrust has disappeared. (T. A. Graber: Craniofacial and Dentitional Development. Chap. 18 in F. Falkner (Ed.): Human Development. Philadelphia, W. B. Saunders Company, 1966, p. 573.)

ing surfaces of the teeth. After food has been moistened and lubricated by saliva, it is rolled by the tongue and hard palate into a bolus (rounded mass), and the tongue forces it back into the pharynx.

Swallowing of food consists of three phases localized in the mouth, pharynx and esophagus. The initial phase does not become voluntary until several months after birth (Figs. 34, 35). Until then the infant does not swallow food or liquids put on the anterior part of the tongue, but pushes them out. Therefore, when he is fed with a spoon, the food or liquid should be placed in the back of the mouth. The pharyngeal phase of swallowing is complex and is accomplished by one of the most delicately coordinated reflex mechanisms in the body. Peristaltic waves sweep downward from the upper end of the esophagus to the stomach in a continuous progressive movement. In general, one esophageal peristaltic wave accompanies each swallowing movement initiated in the mouth. Water or semiliquid foods pass rapidly down to the lower end of the esophagus by the action of gravity. The peristaltic waves coming down a few seconds later merely sweep the fluid past the sphincter guarding the entrance into the stomach (Carlson, Johnson and Calvert, 1961).

Figures 34 and 35 indicate that an orderly trend occurs in the mechanism of swallowing as the individual grows beyond infancy. The complexity of the mechanism also suggests how highly individual this neuromuscular behavior could be.

Food is carried from the stomach by waves of contractions of the walls, called peristalsis. Peristaltic activity of the stomach is not so great and is less regular in the young infant than in the child and the adult. This lesser peristaltic activity results from either incomplete development of the neuromuscular mechanism responsible for peristalsis or low tone of the sphincter. The irregularity is probably one of the manifestations of immature homeostasis (Prugh, 1960). During the first three months food is propelled chiefly by a general contraction of the stomach as a whole, somewhat like that of the urinary bladder, rather than through a peristaltic mechanism (Watson and Lowrey, 1967). As the child grows older, peristaltic activity becomes stronger and assumes mature characteristics. The time that food remains in a child's stomach varies widely, being influenced by a number of factors, including the condition of the musculature and the nature and consistency of food.

Food in the intestine is moved by a churning activity, which aids in digestion and absorption, and by a wavelike activity, which propels the contents forward. Slowly and interruptedly the food moves finally into the large intestine. Distention and some irregularities in peristalsis may be expected in the infant, in contrast to the adult, because the supportive structures, the muscular layers, of the intestine are less developed than the mucous membrane. The motility of each segment of the digestive tract is intimately related to that of the other parts.

The time required for passage of food through the gastrointestinal tract varies in different persons. For breast-fed infants the average time is fifteen hours, with a range from four to twenty-eight hours; for the bottle-fed baby it is slightly longer (Ivy and Gibbs, 1966). Residue may remain in the stomach longer if a second feeding is given before the first has left (Platt, 1961). As the child grows and develops, the time increases so that at five years the average time is eighteen hours with a range of eight to twenty-eight hours (Macy, 1942). For most adults the time ranges between twenty and seventy-two hours. In the infant, food moves at a steady rate through the stomach, small intestine and colon. There are no pauses in the stomach, which acts as a reservoir, but there are brief periods of quiescence, which may be prolonged when the child is disturbed significantly during feeding. In the adult, food passes through the stomach and the small intestine at the same pace as in the infant and the young child, but in the colon it may take twenty-four to forty-eight hours longer than in the infant. Slowing up of the passage of food through the colon begins soon after infancy, and in a few years the rate may approximate that in the adult. As the child grows, the sphincters become more vigorous in action. The slower rate of evacuation of the adult colon results from more powerful sphincter control and differently coordinated reflexes (Wolman, 1944).

There is increasing evidence that the intestinal flora has an important role in nutrition and metabolism (Goldsmith, 1965). At birth the intestinal tract is sterile, but within a few days microorganisms begin to appear after inoculation by the oral route. The bacterial species found in the intestinal tract are influenced by a variety of factors, including age, diet — particularly the type of carbohydrate and fat — and interactions among the organisms present. Intestinal bacteria can both synthesize and utilize nutrients. They may synthesize significant amounts of thiamine, biotin, folic acid and vitamin K, and also modify the chemical structure of carbohydrates, lipids, amino acids and other nutrients in the intestinal lumen. Certain flora seem to stimulate the development of antibacterial defense factors in the intestinal wall. Goldsmith (1965) suggested that in view of the many unsolved problems relating to microflora, future investigations should be most rewarding.

Absorption of nutrients in infants and children is adequate to meet their nutritional needs. Even the newborn should be able structurally to absorb appropriate food quickly and easily, since the absorptive surfaces of the small intestine are completely developed and the length of the intestine is relatively greater than later (Smith, 1959c).

Evacuation of waste materials in the infant is an involuntary act. When it comes under cerebral inhibitory control, the mechanism of defecation may be conditioned and the "stool habit" formed (see Elimination, pp. 216-223).

Meconium, which is the first excretion from the colon of the newborn, is composed of bile, mucus, cellular waste, intestinal secretions, fat, hair, and vernix caseosa swallowed with the amniotic fluid. Some is generally excreted within the first ten to twelve hours, and most is evacuated by the fourth day (Sherry and Kramer, 1955; Smith, 1959c). For the next three days the stools are thin, sour, slimy and brown to green, and may carry some remnants of meconium. Thereafter the characteristic infant stool appears, its nature depending on the food he is receiving. As the diet becomes more varied and the relative amount of milk decreases, the feces become more formed and darker; they tend to assume characteristics of the adult stool by two years.

The frequency of defecation varies with individual children. During early infancy bowel movements decrease in frequency and become more regular. By six months an infant generally has one or two movements a day. In a study of 2½-year-olds (Roberts and Schoelkopf, 1951) most of the children had one or two movements a day; an occasional child, however, had one movement every other day. About half the children had movements at approximately the same time each day, and the other half at an unpredictable time. Boys were significantly more regular than girls. This frequency is probably indicative of that for children throughout the preschool period.

Respiratory System

The respiratory apparatus consists of the nose, larynx, trachea, bronchi and lungs, together with the diaphragm and the large and small muscles attached to the ribs which aid in the mechanics of breathing. It is believed that respiratory movements begin late in fetal life, in the absence of actual respiration, and that at birth lung tissue is sufficiently inflated to enable the infant to sustain life. The rest of the lung tissue expands gradually during the next several weeks.

Newborn infants breathe faster (about thirty-four respirations per minute, in contrast to twelve for the adult), less deeply and more irregularly (McKay and Smith, 1964). Restlessness produces irregularity, and crying tends to slow and deepen breathing. In the early days of life different patterns of breathing have been observed among normal resting infants (Deming and Washburn, 1935). No type seemed more efficient than another in providing oxygen, and no infant consistently exhibited a single rhythm. Healthy infants vary their rhythm and speed of breathing from time to time. With increasing age respiration grows deeper, and the mechanism works more economically and shows greater elasticity. According to Watson and Lowrey (1967), the rate for quiet respiration decreases from approximately thirty to eighty a minute for the newborn, to twenty to forty a minute at one year, twenty to thirty at two years, and twenty to twenty-five at five years. The rate varies considerably among children of the same age and size, and in the same child from time to time.

Respiration is important in supplying oxygen to the body for its metabolic activities, and in removing some of the waste products of metabolism, e.g., carbon dioxide, volatile nitrogenous products. The respiratory mechanism must meet the immediate needs of the body for oxygen. The healthy newborn is physiologically able to obtain the oxygen he needs even though his respiratory mechanism is immature. In the first place, the newborn has the unusual ability to withstand degrees of oxygen lack which are intolerable or much less tolerable to the adult (Smith, 1959c). Secondly, breathing of the normal infant, though extremely variable in rate and depth, moves more air in and out of the lungs in proportion to body weight than does that of an adult. On the basis of surface area of the body, the amount of air inspired and expired a minute is approximately the same in newborn infants and in adults. This is achieved by the more rapid and slightly more shallow breathing of the infant. Thus the needs of both infant and adult are met in spite of varying rate and volume and mechanical differences.

The amount of air entering and leaving the lungs with each inspiration increases with age. At one year the amount is 48 cc.; at five years it is 175 cc., less than half the amount in adults (Watson and Lowrey, 1967). The smaller intake is compensated for by more frequent breathing.

The type of respiration changes as development proceeds. At birth and during the first few months respiration is essentially abdominal and diaphragmatic. Changes toward the adult type of thoracic breathing begin when the infant sits up and are rather well developed by two years. Between three and seven years the combined abdominal and thoracic type of respirations is established.

Oxygen, obtained solely through the respiratory system, is essential for the life and activity of body tissues, and for the chemical changes involved in the provision of energy to maintain body temperature, in the functional activities of the several organs, and in electrical exchanges in the body. These chemical changes are the result of oxidation, and their sum total is expressed by the amounts of oxygen taken up by the lungs and of carbon dioxide liberated.

Heat production may be measured by a calorimeter, or oxygen and carbon dioxide may be measured by respiration apparatus and the energy exchange expressed in heat units, i.e., calories produced per hour. When the body is completely at rest, comfortably warm and without stimulating influence of food, the heat generated by the body results from the activities of the internal organs (heart, blood vessels, lungs, glands, and so on) and from the resting metabolism of the cells. This is referred to as basal metabolism, and the heat production may be measured indirectly by the oxygen consumed when the body is resting and relaxed.

Energy metabolism in infants and children differs from that in adults, since it includes an expenditure for growth and is controlled by an immature regulatory mechanism. This latter factor is especially true in the young infant (see pp. 254-255). Other factors that affect energy metabolism are age, size, growth, underfeeding or overfeeding, and subnormal temperature or fever. Basal metabolism is of special significance in the calculation of calorie needs of a child.

Periods of rapid growth, including the first year, are associated with increased heat production. Weight for weight, the infant and the young child are more active metabolically than the adult. The difference increases to a peak at six months. Even at five years the child's basal metabolic rate in terms of weight is double that of an adult (Watson and Lowrey, 1967).

Heat production increases with age as long as growth continues. Individual differences and deviations from the average are greater in children than in adults: the younger the child, the greater the normal variation from the average (Kelley and Bosma, 1966). Knowledge of basal metabolic requirements has provided information useful in establishing recommended calorie allowances for young children and in understanding individual differences in calorie needs. For an evaluation of basal metabolic data for infants, children and youth in the United States, see Sargent (1961, 1962).

Blood-Vascular System

The blood-vascular system consists of the heart, arteries, veins, capillaries and blood. Its functions are transportation to the body of nutriments, oxygen, hormones, disease-resisting substances; collection of wastes, liquids and gases; preservation of conditions essential for normal cell activity; preservation of life through its coagulation mechanism; and maintenance of the acid-base balance.

Before birth very little blood flows through the lungs. The blood in both sides of the heart flows through the general circulation and out through the arteries in the umbilical cord to the placenta for aeration. This is made possible by an opening between the right and left chambers of the fetal heart. When the umbilical cord is cut, this circulation ceases, and the blood is forced into the lungs, where oxygen is obtained as soon as respiration has been established. After pulmonary circulation has become well established, the opening between the sides of the heart closes.

At birth and throughout infancy the blood pressure is low and the pulse weak, but both increase gradually as the child grows older. At birth the heart is slightly large in proportion to body weight. It doubles its weight in two years and by five years has increased fourfold. During the first four years it grows more rapidly than at any other time prior to adolescence. Changes in structure take place that are reflected in functional changes. The heart rate during rest decreases from 100 to 150 beats a minute during the first year to ninety to 125 at the end of the second year, and to approximately eighty-five to 105 at five years (Washburn, 1966). The adult rate is approximately seventy a minute.

Throughout childhood the pulse rate varies considerably. A rapid increase occurs in response to muscular activity or emotional stimulus. During the preschool years the heart sounds begin to resemble those heard in the older child and the adult (Washburn, 1966).

The red cell count drops from 5,000,000 to 7,000,000 per cu. mm. at birth to 3,000,000 to 4,500,000 at six to ten weeks. A rise follows, so that at six months the count is 4,000,000 to 5,000,000; this remains constant throughout the rest of infancy and the preschool years. The hemoglobin level changes from a range of 17 to 25 gm. per 100 ml. of blood at birth to 11 to 15 gm. at six to ten weeks, to 12.7 to 16.1 gm. at six months, and remains the same throughout infancy. During the preschool years the hemoglobin level is 12 to 15 gm. per 100 ml. (Washburn, 1966).

The white cell count is variable in infancy, fluctuating from day to day. These fluctuations decrease during the second year. At birth the count is 15,000 to 30,000 cells per cu. mm., but soon stabilizes to 5000 to 20,000, and during the preschool years is 6000 to 15,000 (adult range 6000 to 10,000) (Washburn, 1966).

Senses of Taste and Smell

The sense organs of taste and smell, called chemoreceptors, are normally stimulated by chemicals in solution initiating an impulse in the nerve fibers responsible for taste and smell. The chemicals must be in solution in the saliva or in the secretions of the nasal cavity. A perfectly dry tongue does not taste, and a dry nasal cavity cannot be stimulated by aromatic substances. These receptors have very low thresholds and can be stimulated by solutions of great dilution (one part in two million).

TASTE. The receptor structures for taste, known as taste buds, occur chiefly on the tongue, but a few are found also in areas in the throat and in the posterior part of the mouth. From available evidence it is believed that the taste buds increase considerably in number during the first year. In the early years they are distributed abundantly on the inside of the cheeks and in the throat, in addition to those on the tongue. Later, during adolescence, they decrease in number, and chiefly those of the tongue remain (Laird and Breen, 1939). Thus, with the same food, the taste sensations of infants and young children may differ from those of older children and adults.

The sensations of salty and sweet are recognized at the tip of the tongue, along with some recognition of sour and bitter; acidity is recognized along the borders, with perhaps some recognition of salt; and bitter is recognized at the base of the tongue posteriorly. Taste buds seem to be fairly well developed at birth, and newborn infants are able to differentiate pleasant and unpleasant sensations. By two or three months taste is so acute that the infant will notice changes in the amount of carbohydrate in his formula and indicate displeasure at substances which are disagreeable to his sense of taste (Watson and Lowrey, 1967).

Feeney et al. (1966) studied the taste sensitivity of fifty-three preschool children and their parents to sweet, salt, sour and bitter. They found no evidence that children's taste buds were more sensitive than those of adults. Many children did not reject the highly concentrated solutions which their parents rejected. Children seemed to enjoy in particular the saturated solution of sugar.

SMELL. Each nasal cavity has small areas of ciliated cells, known as olfactory epithelium. Each is bathed in liquid, and substances to be detected must be soluble in this liquid. The moist receptors lie in the upper portion of the nasal cavity, so that in ordinary respiration the stream of air does not come in contact with them.

No satisfactory classification of smells has been made. The olfactory sense is easily fatigued and may become insensitive for one kind of smell while it is still normally excitable for others. Knowledge of the sense of smell is incomplete. Taste and smell, plus the sensations of touch and temperature in the mouth, combine in varying proportions to give a sense of pleasure in eating. All these sensations are keen in the infant and the young child.

Temporary or Deciduous Dentition

Teeth and jaws, mechanical accessory organs of digestion, are essential for the mastication of food and its preparation for deglutition and digestion. The jaws are essential for sucking. Absence or presence and functional efficiency of the teeth determine in part the form in which food is eaten. Observation of the timing of the stage of maturation of nutriture and of the eruption of teeth reveals that the gradual change from foods requiring no mastication to those requiring biting and cutting and finally chewing parallels to some degree the sequence of eruption of incisors, cuspids and molars.

The tooth consists of a crown, root and pulp cavity which contains nerve fibers and blood vessels. The pulp is covered by three calcified tissues: dentin; enamel, which covers the dentin in the crown; and cementum, which covers the dentin in the root. Each tooth lies in a bony socket, the alveolus, which is part of the alveolar process of the jaws — the upper, or maxillary, and the lower, or mandibular.

Teeth begin to form about the sixth week of fetal life (Watson and Lowrey, 1967). At birth all twenty of the deciduous teeth and the first permanent teeth (six-year molars) are developing. The pattern of development follows the sequence of appearance of tooth buds in the oral cavity. Calcification of primary teeth begins in the fourth to sixth month of intrauterine life (Graber, 1966). Eruption, completion of the roots, absorption of the roots and shedding of the deciduous teeth are followed promptly by the eruption of the permanent teeth. Permanent successors begin their development in the fifth fetal month (Schour and Massler, 1958; Watson and Lowrey, 1967; Graber, 1966).

At the time of eruption the enamel of the crown has completed its development and is without nerve or blood supply; the dentin continues to form until the roots are completed, sometimes after the tooth has erupted. The permanent teeth continue to develop throughout these early years. The deciduous teeth act as guides for the position of the permanent teeth. Tooth development is influenced by heredity (Robinow, Richards and Anderson, 1942; Falkner, 1957; Garn et al., 1960; Graber, 1966), prenatal conditions (Via and Churchill, 1959), illness (Richmond and Massler, 1964), endocrine factors (Massler and Schour, 1958a) and nutrition.

Calcified enamel constitutes a health and nutritional record of the past; soft oral structures, such as the mucosa of the mouth, tongue, lips, gums and periodontal membrane of the tooth, reflect the present nutritional state. The alveolar bone, in which the tooth lies, grows throughout life and responds particularly to changes in mineral metabolism (Massler and Schour, 1958b).

Tooth development appears to be a relatively independent process. In infancy and childhood there is little relation between both tooth formation and eruption and other measures of maturation (Falkner, 1957; Lewis and Garn, 1960; Graber, 1966).

The eruption of teeth follows a regular order with minor deviations. The first teeth tend to be the lower central incisors, followed by the upper central incisors, then the lateral incisors, first molars, cuspids and, last, the second molars. The teeth tend to erupt in pairs with intervening periods of quiescence. Children may vary, however, in this sequence (Robinow, Richards and Anderson, 1942). Ranges of times are used in reporting calcification, eruption and shedding of deciduous teeth in Table 5. All deciduous teeth have permanent successors, whereas the permanent molars have no deciduous predecessors.

The expected age of the appearance of the first tooth is around five to seven months, although this may not apply to a particular child. In one study (Falkner, 1957) no teeth had erupted in any children at thirteen weeks, although all children had some teeth by eighteen months. The period between nine and eighteen months was the most active time. At two years 11.8 per cent of the boys and 10.5 per cent of the girls had completed their deciduous dentition of twenty teeth. At three years every child had all teeth. Nanda (1960) reported that one boy at one year, three months had only one tooth, while another boy of the same age had eight. Rarely do teeth erupt before the age of four months, and sometimes they do not appear until early in the second year. Some children acquire all their teeth in less than one year; others take almost three years (Meredith, 1946, 1951a). Thus in dentition, as in other aspects of development, some children are slow and some fast in their progress.

Little difference between boys and girls is noted in the deciduous dentition (Falkner, 1957; Nanda, 1960; Robinow, Richards and Anderson, 1942). Since siblings often show a resemblance in their tooth development, it is possible that heredity may affect the eruption pattern.

Shedding of any of the deciduous teeth is rare before four years of age (Falkner, 1957). Nanda (1960) reported this phase as beginning at

TABLE 5. Deciduous Teeth: Their Calcification, Eruption and Shedding

	CALCIFICATION		ERUPTION		SHEDDING	
	BEGINS AT	COM-PLETED	MAXILLARY	MANDIBULAR	MAXILLARY	MANDIBULAR
Central incisors	5 fetal month	18-24 months	6-8 months	5-7 months	7-8 years	6-7 years
Lateral incisors	5 fetal month	18-24 months	8-11 months	7-10 months	8-9 years	7-8 years
Cuspids	6 fetal month	30-36 months	16-20 months	16-20 months	11-12 years	9-11 years
First molars	5 fetal month	24-30 months	10-16 months	10-16 months	10-11 years	10-12 years
Second molars	6 fetal month	36 months	20-30 months	20-30 months	10-12 years	11-13 years

From H. C. Stuart and S. S. Stevenson; Physical Growth and Development, in W. E. Nelson (Ed.): Textbook of Pediatrics. 8th ed. Philadelphia, W. B. Saunders Co., 1964. Data adapted from chart prepared by P. K. Losch, who carried out roentgenographic assays of the jaws of 1000 children in metropolitan Boston in 1942 at the Harvard School of Dental Medicine.

five years in girls and five years, six months in boys. Table 5 gives the age as six to seven years.

Occlusion is the relation of the teeth in the maxilla and in the mandible which determines the efficiency of mastication and facial balance. The type of occlusion is dependent upon the degree of synchronous growth of the teeth and their supporting structures and is the result of the interplay of heredity and environment in which heredity is considered a strong component (Sillman, 1942, 1951; Stein, 1956). The pattern of the development of occlusion has individual variation (Moorrees, 1959).

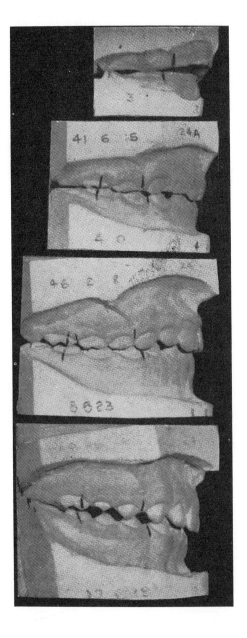

FIGURE 36. *Casts of side view of jaws and teeth of a boy with good occlusion from birth through 12 years of age. Note posterior relation at 3 days; good relation at 4 years 1 month; 8 years 8 months, 23 days; and 12 years, 19 days. (From J. H. Sillman: Serial study of good occlusion from birth to twelve years of age, American Journal of Orthodontics, 37:481-507, 1951, C. V. Mosby Company.)*

At birth the upper jaw is more developed than the lower jaw, as is apparent in Figure 36, which demonstrates good occlusion from birth to twelve years. Good occlusion varies with age. The relative position of the jaws of the infant aids in sucking, and the growth or forward movement of the lower jaw during the preschool years makes good occlusion possible.

During the first three years the pattern of the face is being established. Figure 37 shows the profile of the face at three months, three years, nine months, and nineteen years. The differential growth of the face is illustrated. The cranium grows rapidly and approaches adult size considerably before the face. Growth in cranial depth is most rapid, and width and height follow in that order. In the face, height shows the greatest incremental change, followed by depth and width (Graber, 1966).

Irregularity in the development of the teeth and dental arches may be of the type that corrects itself during development; it may be within the range of normal variation, or may be a type beyond the range of normality which becomes a permanent condition with possible increasing severity.

Premature loss of teeth, through either accident or decay, may affect the alignment of the permanent teeth. Since such loss may prove a hazard to good alignment of the permanent teeth, the care and preservation of the deciduous teeth are important.

Thumb-sucking is considered by some to be one of the causes of protrusion of the upper front teeth (Sillman, 1951). On the other hand, not all thumb-suckers develop malocclusion (occlusion which prevents effective mastication and disturbs the facial balance) (Traisman and Traisman, 1958). A serial study (Sillman, 1951) of a group of children from birth to fourteen years revealed that some thumb-suckers have malocclusion and some do not. Occlusal damage before three years of age is usually temporary, provided the child starts with a normal occlu-

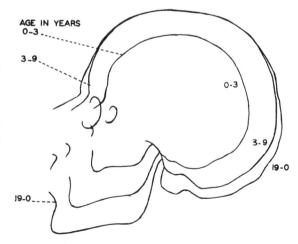

FIGURE 37. *Profile of the face drawn at 3 months, 3 years, 9 months, and 19 years, showing changes in the proportions of the face taking place before 3 years, 9 months. (J. K. Bamba: Longitudinal cephalometric roentgenographic study of face and cranium in relation to body height. J. A. Dent. A., 63:776-779, 1961.)*

AGE IN YEARS
0–3
3–9
0-3
3-9
19-0
19-0

sion. The permanence of the occlusal deformity increases in children who continue thumb- or finger-sucking beyond $3\frac{1}{2}$ years (Graber, 1966). Thumb-sucking can displace teeth, but does not seem to affect the relations of the molars. Spontaneous correction tends to occur when the habit is stopped, even after the preschool years (Sillman, 1951). During the period of tooth eruption, biting, which is part of the oral development of the child, may be mistaken for thumb-sucking. Parental interference in thumb-sucking can tend to entrench it, and thus may increase both the length of time it continues and the intensity or force of sucking. Both of these increase the effect on the dental structure. For further discussion of thumb-sucking, see page 414.

Exercise of the teeth and jaws, i.e., sucking in infancy and later chewing, stimulates the development of muscles which, in turn, stimulate the growth of the jaw and the circulation of blood in the gums. Hence the introduction of hard foods such as toast or a carrot stick at the appropriate time, when the child demonstrates an urge for biting (at the time of the beginning of tooth eruption), offers opportunities for this exercise and practice in learning to chew.

It is advisable that the growth and development of the teeth and jaws be watched carefully, that the child be examined by a dentist who understands the development of teeth and their occlusion, and that growth appraisals be made, a history kept, and changes noted and interpreted. It is considered good practice to watch the development of the jaws beginning when the child is about three years old so that the start of any difficulties can be noted and appropriate action taken.

NUTRITION

The body needs energy for vital life processes and to provide for activity. It needs substances for cellular repair, for processes of metabolism and for growth. These are provided through oxygen, water and foods containing the nutrients: namely, proteins with their essential amino acids, carbohydrates, fats with their essential fatty acids, minerals and vitamins. Nutritional needs are the same in kind for all ages, but differ in amount and in the form in which they are met. In children these differences depend upon development. Meeting these needs will be discussed in relation to the maturing nutriture and with consideration of the maturation of motor abilities, the child's increasing desire for independence and the gratification of his emotional needs.

Oxygen

The fetus obtains oxygen through the placenta. After birth, oxygen is obtained through the activity of the respiratory system. The natural source of oxygen is fresh air. An abundance of fresh air is therefore desirable at all ages. In early infancy, especially, care must be exercised that provision of fresh air does not also involve exposure to cold.

Water

Next to importance of oxygen is water. Its sources include not only water as such, but also as a part of foods eaten and from the oxidation of food metabolites. Foods eaten naturally by young children are usually rich in water. The requirement for water is relatively higher for infants and young children than for adults, owing to the higher metabolic rate and greater water evaporation from the proportionately larger skin surface of the infant and the young child. The daily consumption of water by the healthy infant is 10 to 15 per cent of his body weight, in contrast to only 2 to 4 per cent for the adult (Hansen and Bennett, 1964). Average water requirements per kilogram of body weight under ordinary conditions were cited as 140 to 160 ml. per kilogram for the three-month-old infant and 40 to 50 ml. for an eighteen-year-old. On the basis of total daily fluid consumption, Walker et al. (1963) found an increase from a value of 700 ml. for newborn infants to about 1500 ml. for ten-year-olds. Tap water accounted for about 40 per cent of the fluid intake of the older children, and milk about half.

As the temperature rises, more water is needed because of increased evaporation from the skin. Walker et al. (1963) found among older children a direct relation between the environmental temperature and the intake of fluids other than milk. Cooke (1952) observed that infants under three months of age, when subjected to heat stress, preferred milk and refused water, sometimes taking excessive amounts of milk in an attempt to obtain needed fluid.

The breast-fed infant who receives enough milk to satisfy his nutritional needs ordinarily obtains sufficient fluid to meet his needs for water. The formula of the bottle-fed baby is planned to include sufficient water. It is thought advisable, however, to give the infant water in a bottle, by spoon or by cup at convenient times during the day. This will meet any additional need that might arise and acquaint the infant with water. Later the child can indicate his desire for water, and still later seek it for himself. The mechanism of thirst, which is not fully understood (Falk, 1960; Review, 1958b), apparently operates efficiently in young children.

Perspective in Infant Feeding

In the first half of this century great strides were made in improving the health and growth of infants and young children through improved diets. As knowledge increased, diets were enhanced. In the United States nutritional deficiencies appear relatively infrequently. Obesity, however, has increased even in childhood, and evidence that nutritional excesses may be harmful has continued to appear (Bakwin, 1961; Review, 1960a; Fraser, 1966). Concern for health at maturity and later is leading to a search for the origins in the early years of later health difficulties. Experimentation with rats shows that those with moderately restricted caloric intake seemed healthier and more vigorous at an advanced age (Review, 1961b) and suggests the need for looking at human nutrition from a long-time point of view in terms of optimum rather than maximum.

Thus the feeding practices of today are being examined in relation to the possibility of overfeeding children (Forbes, 1957, 1958, 1961). Questions are being raised as to the virtues of children being taller, heavier and maturing earlier today than several decades ago (Tanner, 1962), to the value of greater retention of minerals and nitrogen demonstrated in children fed high concentrations of cow's milk (Stearns, 1939), to possible relations between early nutritional experiences and later health and development. These questions can ultimately be answered only by following the feeding and the health development of individuals throughout the life cycle. Many believe that a new perspective in infant feeding is needed.

The Infant's First Food

One of the adjustments the infant makes at birth is a change in the manner of nourishment. He now ingests appropriate food, namely, milk, orally through sucking, digests it and absorbs the necessary nutrients. A vital part of this adjustment is becoming accustomed to the feeding situation, that first intimate mother-child relation through which he obtains his food. In this situation both mother and child can gradually establish a satisfying venture which not only provides the infant with food, but also can be the beginning of a close relation between mother and child (Bakwin, 1964). The infant is believed to derive a sense of security and of belonging in this relation from the warmth of the mother's body and from the comfort of being held. These are different variables from those of the feeding process itself (Guthrie, 1967).

During the first few days the infant becomes proficient in finding the nipple and sucking, and the mother becomes adjusted to the pull on the nipple. At this time the nursing period may be limited to five to ten minutes to allow the mother time to adjust to the pull on the nipples and to help to prevent them from becoming sore. A short nursing time seems to satisfy the infant. During this transition period, colostrum is secreted by the mammary glands. This secretion is admirably adapted to the needs of the newborn. It contains less fat and more protein, ash and vitamin A than does milk secreted later when lactation is completely established. The colostrum period varies with individual women from one to five days. During the next five days the composition changes gradually to that of mature milk. Most authors agree that the principal changes from colostrum to mature milk are completed by the tenth day (Committee on Nutrition, 1960).

When the infant absorbs and digests breast milk or its substitute, he begins the third stage in his progress toward maturation of the nutriture. Human milk, if the supply is adequate, provides the essential nutrients for the early months except vitamin D. The adequacy of vitamins other than D depends upon the mother's diet. The amount of breast milk the infant receives depends on the ability of the mother to synthesize milk and the demands he makes in sucking. The usual amount is about 1 pint after the first week or two, and this increases to about 1 quart a day in the fifth month (Toverud, Stearns and Macy, 1950). The amount he needs at a feeding can be determined by the infant if he is fed when he is hungry (as indicated by rooting, sucking or crying) and permitted to nurse until he is satisfied. He will not necessarily take the same amount at each feeding.

Some infants have a sharp satiety reaction (Bakwin, 1964); when they are satisfied, further attempts at feeding are actively resisted. In others, satiety appears gradually and is preceded by playfulness toward the end of feeding. Bakwin pointed out that some infants do not seem to know when they have had enough food. These infants regurgitate and vomit frequently. Recognition of satiety was indicated as being especially difficult in infants with small appetites.

If the infant is not breast fed, a formula to meet his needs should be prescribed by a physician. Both the nutritional and emotional needs of the infant can be met in bottle-feeding. Standardized interviews with mothers of five-year-old children (Sears, Maccoby and Levin, 1957) showed that the early feeding experience, whether breast or bottle, had no consistent effect upon later behavior such as aggression in the home, "considerable" or "high" conscience, dependency, severe feeding problems, bed-wetting at age five or strong emotional reaction to toilet training. The authors point out that feeding as well as other experiences affect the child, but the effects are specific to each child.

The self-regulation type of feeding program can be followed with bottle-fed infants. One mother, whose baby was bottle-fed and varied his intake at different feedings, met the problem by dividing the milk unevenly among the bottles for the day. This baby was taking 35 ounces. She distributed this in two bottles of 6 ounces, three of 5 ounces, and two of 4 ounces. She found that the baby, after having been asleep, wanted to eat several times at $1\frac{1}{2}$- to two-hour intervals and so took less at those times. When she anticipated that he would sleep four or five hours after a feeding, she gave him 6 ounces. Thus she was able to satisfy the baby without waste of formula or keeping him waiting in the middle of a feeding in order to warm another bottle.

Lactation

Lactation consists of two processes: secretion and "let-down" or flow of milk. Secretion is strikingly increased after the birth of the infant and appears to be caused by a change in the balance of endocrines. The exact mechanisms have not been fully agreed upon (Turner, 1966). The inhibitory action of ovarian hormones is reduced, while the stimulating action of prolactin of the posterior pituitary gland is increased. Hormones of the thyroid and of the adrenal cortex also act in controlling lactation. The "let-down," or flow of milk, is effected by a complex psychosomatic mechanism by which, it is believed, sensory stimuli associated with suckling excite nerves of an afferent arc to the midbrain, which in turn acts to release the posterior pituitary hormone, oxytocin (Linzell, 1959; Lloyd, 1962).

The processes of lactation are influenced by a number of biologic, emotional and social factors which interact one with another. Heredity, size and anatomic structure of the breast (which has a strong hereditary component), food and environmental conditions such as the balance of rest and activity, which takes into account the amount and intensity of work, will affect lactation.

The potentiality for both the quantity of milk and the length of time lactation continues under normal conditions is inherent in the mother (Macy et al., 1930). Various conditions will determine how much of that potential will be utilized; one is the demand by the baby. A hungry baby nursing vigorously, as is likely to be the case of an infant on a self-regulatory schedule, is an aid to lactation. Illingworth and Stone (1952) found that 80 per cent of babies on self-demand feeding in Jessup Hospital for Women in Sheffield, England, were fully breast fed at one month, compared with 65 per cent of those on schedule. This difference was significant.

Food is another factor. Nutrition for lactation begins before the birth of the baby. A study in Australia (Woodhill et al., 1955) indicates a consistent correlation between the duration of lactation and the level of maternal diet before and during pregnancy. After the birth of the infant certain nutrient intakes should be increased above those during pregnancy in order to supply the nutrients required for the elaboration of milk. According to the Recommended Allowances of the Food and Nutrition Board (National Academy of Sciences—National Research Council, 1964), diet during lactation is increased over that of pregnancy about one half in calories, protein, calcium and vitamin A and about one third in thiamine, riboflavin and ascorbic acid. These additions to an adequate diet during the latter half of pregnancy will provide sufficient energy and nutrients (1) to maintain the mother's body and to meet her energy needs, and (2) to provide the essentials for milk and the activity of the mammary glands. The nursing mother will probably find that she desires the additional food. The need for extra calcium, riboflavin, vitamin A and protein indicates a liberal intake of milk. At least 1 quart a day is advisable. Liberal amounts of fruits and vegetables, including citrus fruits, are also indicated. Other foods providing protein and calories can be chosen according to the mother's needs and preferences. Vitamin D can be supplied by fortified milk or a concentrate. (See Table 3, p. 115.)

Physical rest and relaxation are also essential for successful lactation. The flow of milk can be stimulated or inhibited by the emotional state. A mother who dislikes breast feeding, is indifferent to it or has mixed feelings about it, or who is tense from concern about the care of the infant or feels uncomfortable about the nursing situation or is under some emotional strain is less likely to be successful than one who begins the experience with desire and determination to nurse her infant, who is calm and enjoying the experience (Call, 1959; Egli et al., 1961; Newton and Newton, 1950b).

The society in which a woman lives may influence her feelings about breast feeding and her willingness or hesitation to try it. The practice of breast feeding is closely bound to the culture of a society. In the United States the prevailing fashion for some time has been to feed infants by the bottle. This was shown in a survey (Meyer, 1958) in which 21 per cent of mothers were breast feeding their babies when they left the hospital, compared with 38 per cent in an earlier survey (Bain, 1948). American mothers nurse their infants less often and for a shorter time than do women in Europe, Asia or Africa. The practice of most European mothers falls between that of mothers in American and the Eastern countries (Aitken and Hytten, 1960).

The decline of breast feeding seems to accompany increasing sophistication of a community (Jelliffe, 1962). Salber et al. (1959) commented that lactation is certain to be affected when woman's role in society is not clearly defined and there is conflict between her ambitions and her biological make-up.

In spite of the low incidence of breast feeding among mothers in the United States, there is a slight revival among women of the middle and upper social classes (Salber et al., 1958, 1959; Yankhauer et al., 1958). Education seems to be an influencing factor. From a sample of mothers in the Boston area, Salber and Feinlieb (1966) found that only 22 per cent of the total group breast-fed, but that 70 per cent of those married to students, 40 per cent of those in the upper social class and only 14 per cent in the lower social class breast-fed. This difference between social classes in breast-feeding practices, which is the reverse of an earlier period, has also been reported in England (Douglas, 1950).

Many women, especially those having their first baby, will profit by some assistance in understanding the process of lactation and by suggestions of ways it can be promoted. A woman can learn that the reflex which releases milk from the breast is stimulated by the sucking of the infant and by associations with the nursing situation (sight of the baby, time for feeding, breast preparations for feeding) and inhibited by pain and distraction. The following suggestions for aiding this reflex to function, as offered by Newton and Newton (1950a), include (1) feeding the baby when he is hungry to afford more vigorous nursing; (2) no supplementary bottle if possible; (3) avoiding pain, emotional conflict and embarrassment; (4) conditioning the reflex by the use of pleasant stimuli, e.g., favorite food or music preceding nursing, nursing in the same quiet place, stroking the breast with clean tissue, or manual expression of a little milk.

A woman needs guidance while lactation is being established. She may need help in the techniques of nursing. The techniques necessary for successful management have been demonstrated by Barnes et al. (1953) and Waller (1946). Mothers sometimes become concerned because milk is slow to come after delivery. The child may receive almost no milk for the first few days. The mother needs to understand that his needs at this time are small. It is not until the fifth day that transitional or mature milk begins to flow. This may be a crucial time for the mother, since she may be leaving the hospital to return home on the fifth day, before lactation has become firmly established. At this time she faces the responsibilities of the care of the infant and of the home. Unless she has some assistance during this transitional period, lactation may suffer because of fatigue and anxieties. Some knowledge of what to expect in the behavior of the infant and some opportunity to care for babies before the birth of her own may strengthen her confidence in her ability to care for her child. Also, the provision of opportunities for her to become acquainted with her baby in the hospital so that he is no stranger when they arrive home may help. Jackson et al. (1956) found a significantly longer period of breast feeding (up to seven months) among mothers who had rooming-in, and thus had their babies with them, than among mothers whose babies were kept in the nursery. The husband can also be of assistance by giving support to the mother and seeing that she is relieved of some of the household responsibilities.

Although most women are able to breast-feed their babies, some cannot. For those who cannot there is ample evidence that babies can thrive on bottle feedings modified to approximate the composition of human milk. A good bottle feeding is preferable to inadequate breast feeding. Also these mothers can give their babies the essential mothering during feeding time and at other times of the day. No mother should feel inadequate or have any sense of self-reproach because of inability to nurse her child.

VARIATION IN QUANTITY OF MILK SECRETED. As lactation proceeds, the quantity of milk secreted from day to day and from week to week may vary considerably (Macy et al., 1931). The gradual increase in milk flow is evidently peculiar not only to the individual, but also to the particular lactation period. The average daily output of milk in three women from the sixth week through the fourteenth month of lactation was 2602 cc. in one lactation period and 3134 cc. in another period in the same subject, 2366 cc. for one lactation period in another subject, and 1419 cc. for the third subject (Macy and co-workers, 1931). These women produced especially large quantities of milk. The total quantity of breast milk produced during a lactation period was found to depend not only on the women's immediate capacity to produce, but also on the demands placed on the mammary glands and on the duration of the lactation period. The investigators showed that, if augmented milk production is to be secured, the milk should be removed from the breast at regular intervals and as completely as possible. These observations confirm the belief that excessive and heavy work tends to depress maximum output of milk and also that nervous factors such as excitement, fear and anxiety lessen the flow, and that severe shock may cause complete cessation.

Differences Between Breast and Bottle Feeding

There is wide agreement that breast feeding is preferable to bottle feeding, but most infants in this country are bottle-fed (Bakwin, 1964; Maternal and Child Health and Food and Nutrition Sections, 1966). This section presents the similarities and differences of human and cow's milk and the progress of infants receiving each.

When comparing the *content of human and cow's milk* and their relative value in promoting health and growth of an infant, it must be remembered that infants are generally fed not whole cow's milk, but formulas in which the cow's milk is adapted by dilution, addition of carbohydrates, and treatment to soften the protein curd. When comparison of the progress of infants fed the two milks is made, it is important to note the composition of the formula. Grouping all bottle-fed infants as receiving the same food introduces an error which could lead to misinterpretations of observations.

Infants fed breast milk or cow's milk receive, ounce for ounce, different amounts and proportions of certain nutrients (Committee on Nutrition, 1960; Guthrie, 1967; Macy, Kelly and Sloan, 1950) (Fig. 38). Cow's milk contains about three times as much protein as human milk; the proteins of each milk have essentially the same biologic value (György, 1961) and similar ability to promote nitrogen retention (Fomon, 1960). The protein of cow's milk forms a heavy curd in the stomach, whereas human milk, having less casein and more lactalbumin, forms a finely divided, flocculent mass which is easily digested. Milk mixtures used in bottle feeding are treated, however, so that the protein curd is also soft, small and digestible. Cow's milk also contains about four times as much calcium and six times as much phosphorus as human milk. These and some other constituents, when absorbed in excess of bodily needs, must be excreted. Young infants excrete more water with them, since the kidney's function of concentrating urine is immature in the early months (Smith, 1959c). When young infants are fed cow's milk in relatively large proportions, the resulting increase in certain minerals and the metabolic products of proteins to be excreted may tax the water reserve, whereas the breast-fed baby is not subjected to this strain (György, 1961).

Human milk contains three to four times more of the essential fatty acids (Williams, 1961). The significance of this difference is not known. Human milk is about one-third richer in iron than cow's milk. Dietary iron is apparently not utilized during the first four or five months (Smith et al., 1955). After this age the difference in iron of the two milks would be important if the infant were not fed other foods rich in iron.

Human milk is also about one-third richer in vitamin A and more than twice as rich in vitamin C. A quart of human milk contains about 41 mg. of vitamin C (Williams, 1961); a cow's milk formula prepared by boiling and diluting may contain almost none (Stevenson, 1947). Human milk, if the mother's diet is adequate in vitamin C, meets the recom-

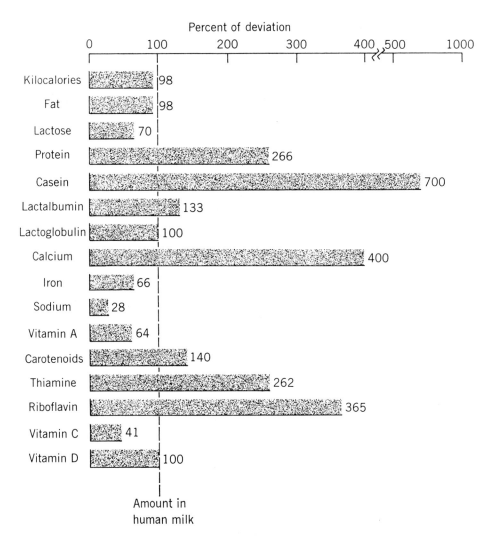

Comparison of nutritive value of cow's
and human milk

FIGURE 38.   *Relative amounts of various nutrients in human and cow's milk.*

*(Based on data from Composition of Human Milk, National Research Council Publication No.
254, Washington, D.C., 1953, National Research Council. (H. A. Guthrie: Introductory Nutrition.
St. Louis, C. V. Mosby Company, 1967, p. 334.)*

mended allowance for vitamin C, but a cow's milk formula falls far short
of it. The niacin content of breast milk is about twice that of cow's milk,
but both milks are a poor source of this vitamin, though a good source
of tryptophan, precursor of niacin, which compensates for the relatively small amounts of niacin. Cow's milk is more than twice as high in
thiamine. But when thiamine in human milk is compared with the
amount an infant receives in bottle feeding, the amounts are similar,

owing primarily to the loss of thiamine in the sterilization process. The riboflavin content of cow's milk is more than three times that in human milk, but the relative utilization of the two milks is not known (National Academy of Sciences – National Research Council, 1964). Cow's milk also is about five times richer in vitamin B_{12} and about four times richer in B_6. The amount in human milk appears to be ample, however. The water-soluble vitamins C and B in breast milk vary with the mother's diet, since these vitamins are not stored. Neither human nor cow's milk contains significant amounts of vitamin D.

The feces of breast-fed infants are acid in reaction; those of bottle-fed infants are neutral or alkaline. György (1961) stated that there is a prevalence of *Lactobacillus bifidus* in the intestinal flora of breast-fed infants and that these bacteria and the acidity in the intestine may be beneficial through the suppression of pathogenic or otherwise harmful bacteria. Human milk contains a fiftyfold greater supply of a factor which stimulates the growth of *L. bifidus* than cow's milk (Williams, 1961).

Weight and weight gains have been used chiefly in the *comparison of growth* of infants who have been breast-fed or bottle-fed. In the United States (Gross and Moses, 1956; Paiva, 1953), the United Kingdom (Levin et al., 1959; Stewart and Westropp, 1953; Thomson, 1955) and Sweden (Mellander et al., 1960) breast-fed infants gain about the same in weight or slightly more than bottle-fed infants from birth to one month or to three or four months. From three or four months on the gains are greater for the artificially fed. When the whole six-month period or the first year is considered, the bottle-fed infants' gains exceed those of the breast-fed. Aitken and Hytten (1960) remarked that the ability of bottle-fed infants to gain almost as well or equally well as the breast-fed in the early months and better in the later months implies a high standard of artificial feeding and hygiene and possibly other environmental conditions. In less favorable conditions results differ, as indicated by studies in a Stockholm children's home (Gyllens884ård, 1960) where the infants breast-fed for at least six months gained more than those bottle-fed, and in Singapore, where Millis (1956), comparing gains in weight of infants breast-fed for only twelve weeks and those breast-fed for more than twenty-four weeks, found that only in the well-to-do Chinese families was the first-year gain greater for infants weaned early.

Progress in weight is not the only criterion a physician uses in evaluating the feeding program of an infant. Gross and Moses (1956) commented that "it would be particularly undesirable to use weight gain alone as a measure of breast feeding." Just what measures physicians use which cause them to advocate breast feeding are not clearly defined. Jackson et al. (1964), studying 599 American infants through six months of age, used at least four length and weight measurements: one at birth, one at six months, and the others at intervals of not less than one month. They found that infants fed various cow's milk formulas and vitamin supplements grew at about the same rate as infants fed human milk with or without vitamin supplements.

Little information about skeletal development of breast- and bottle-fed infants is available. Stewart and Westropp (1953) noted no difference in skeletal maturity at one year. Mellander et al. (1960) observed that girls, but not boys, who were weaned early had significantly more ossification centers at seven or eight months than those weaned late.

Comparison of the incidence of disease in breast- and bottle-fed infants can easily be complicated by environmental conditions under which the infant is fed. The value of breast feeding as a protection against disease is greater in less developed countries (Welbourn, 1958) and in less favored economic classes (Aldrich, 1947) where lack of knowledge and facilities militates against carrying out adequate health measures, or where supervision of the infant's feeding by physicians and nurses is not available. A study of American Indians showed that 95 per cent of infants with severe diarrhea in a group requiring hospitalization were bottle-fed, although only 30 per cent of the infants in the area were being bottle-fed (Maternal and Child Health and Food and Nutrition Section, 1966). Stevenson (1947) found that in a series of carefully supervised infants who were given complements of vitamins considered adequate, there was no significant increase in the incidence of gastrointestinal and other infections in the bottle-fed group. Aitken and Hytten (1960) concluded that "it would appear that under modern standards of hygiene bottle-fed infants suffer no higher overall incidence of infections throughout infancy than breast-fed infants."

Breast-fed infants may have some advantages, however. Stevenson (1947) found that breast-fed babies had significantly fewer respiratory infections during the second half of the first year than those bottle-fed. Stewart and Westropp (1953) found that although the incidence of gastrointestinal and other infections in infancy was not related to the length of breast feeding, it was rare for an infant to have a gastrointestinal infection while receiving breast milk solely. Douglas (1950) found that the difference between breast-fed and bottle-fed infants was not in the number of infections, but in the timing of them. Bottle-fed infants had their peak of incidence earlier than breast-fed infants. The younger the child, the more immature he is and perhaps less well equipped to cope with infections. Whether these differences between breast- and bottle-fed infants can be attributed to qualities in the milk or to conditions associated with the feeding procedure remains to be ascertained.

The existence of viral antibodies in human milk has been known for some time (Valquist, 1958). These antibodies have been considered relatively unimportant in the immune system of the human infant because the quantity is usually low and the absorption slight (Smith, 1959c). Recent studies (Gonzaga et al., 1963; Warren et al., 1964; Review, 1965) indicate that breast-fed infants are more resistant to infection with poliomyelitis virus. This was attributed to the inhibition of virus replication within the intestinal tract by the antibodies in human milk. The incidence of measles has also been reported to be lower in breast-fed than in bottle-fed infants (Review, 1958c). These findings raise the question whether antibodies in human milk may not have some immunologic value and offer some degree of immunity to intestinal infections during early infancy.

The feeding of breast milk virtually eliminates the possibility of a milk allergy. Heiner et al. (1964) reported that clinical sensitivity to cow's milk occurs in 0.3 to 7 per cent of all infants. During the first few months these infants become hyperallergic to proteins of cow's milk. The sensitivity ranges from immediate, anaphylactoid reactions to markedly delayed reactions from chronic low-grade gastrointestinal blood loss. Milk-induced hypochromic microcytic anemia is the best example of the latter.

There are certain psychological components in breast and bottle feeding. Psychologically, both infant and mother gain something in the nursing situation. The infant gains comfort in his close physical contact with another person. He may profit indirectly by the effect of nursing upon the mother. There is some feeling that the greatest psychological advantage accrues to the mother who feels that she is involved in a unique relation with the child and is fulfilling her true maternal role (Guthrie, 1967). Spock (1950a) suggested that breast feeding gives a woman confidence in herself as a mother and that as a result she is more relaxed and effective in her relations with and care of her child.

The bottle-fed infant need not be deprived of close mother-child contacts. Such contacts can be provided in a bottle-feeding situation.

Mothers have various reasons for not breast feeding their infants. Sometimes they are unable to nurse their infants because they cannot produce sufficient milk to satisfy the infant's needs. For many mothers the freedom and flexibility of social life that bottle feeding allows are an important consideration in the choice of the type of feeding. Among fifty-five mothers who had had a satisfying breast-feeding experience, the loss and restriction of their social life were considered disadvantages by twenty-nine of them (Guthrie, 1967). Some mothers cannot breast-feed because they must work; still others may have strong feelings against it (Sears, Maccoby and Levin, 1957). In this event, even if the mother could nurse her infant, the experience would satisfy neither mother nor child. In any case, the mother should have no sense of in-adequacy or self-reproach (Levine, 1951).

Although knowledge of the excretion of drugs in milk is limited, nearly all products ingested by the mother are believed to be excreted in her milk in some form. Knowles (1965) recommends curtailment of unnecessary medication during lactation, but does not discourage breast feeding.

Additional Requirements in Infant Stages I and II

NEED FOR VITAMIN D. Since neither human nor cow's milk is adequate in this vitamin essential for bone mineralization, some source of vitamin D is added. It may be obtained (1) by ultraviolet rays of the sun activating a precursor of the vitamin in the skin; (2) by milk fortified with vitamin D; (3) by fish liver oil, such as cod liver oil; or (4) by a vitamin D concentrate. Milk used in bottle feeding is frequently fortified with vitamin D, as are most evaporated milks. Obviously, for the young infant in the United States the source from sunshine is not usually adequate. He will generally receive his vitamin D in the form of some concentrate prescribed by a physician. The recommended allowance of the Food and Nutrition Board for vitamin D is 400 units (National Academy of Sciences–National Research Council, 1964). Too much as well as too little vitamin D can be given (Bakwin, 1961; Committee on Nutrition, American Academy of Pediatrics, 1965). There is evidence that amounts greater than 1500 units daily will be followed after several months by a decrease in appetite with consequent decrease in calcium retention and in rate of growth (Jeans and Stearns, 1938; Stearns, Jeans and Vandecar, 1936). Fomon et al. (1966), however, found that a daily intake of 1800 units did not interfere with the rate of increase in either length or weight of the infants studied. The dosage of vitamin D should always be considered in terms of units, and recognition should be given to the amounts incorporated in foods.

Because supplementary vitamin D is added to many foods, including dairy products, margarine and certain cereals, people often receive amounts in excess of the recommended daily allowances. When vitamin D is also provided medicinally to infants, their intake can become excessive. Despite increased knowledge of possible toxic effects of excess vitamin D, there is no clear-cut evidence of the maximum safe intake for young children (Review, 1966a). The Committee on Nutrition, American Academy of Pediatrics (1965), reported that one form of mental retardation and one form of congenital heart disease in the fetus were caused by excessive maternal intakes of vitamin D. They endorsed the addition of vitamin D to milk and milk substitutes designed for infants in amounts not to exceed 400 International Units (I.U.) a day. They recommended that enrichment of foods other than milk and infant formula products be discontinued and that products containing vitamin D in excess of 400 I.U. in recommended daily dosage be restricted to sale by prescription only.

NEED FOR VITAMIN C (ASCORBIC ACID).   Next to the need for vitamin D comes that for vitamin C, because shortly after birth the blood level of ascorbic acid in infants begins to fall. The breast-fed baby may be receiving appreciable amounts by the fifth day, provided the mother's diet is adequate in the vitamin. If the infant's diet does not supply a sufficient quantity of vitamin C, as is true of those who are bottle-fed and may be true in some instances of those breast-fed, additional vitamin C must be added to furnish the recommended allowance of 30 mg. (National Academy of Sciences–National Research Council, 1964). C. A. Smith (1959c) recommends a daily supplement of 25 mg. by the second or third week after birth for all bottle-fed infants. Many physicians prescribe ascorbic acid preparations first and introduce orange juice later. Others start with orange juice as the source of vitamin C, beginning with small amounts and gradually increasing the quantity until 2 ounces, the amount which supplies approximately 30 mg., is being taken.

NEED FOR VITAMIN E (TOCOPHEROL). Low levels of plasma tocopherol have been observed in newborns and in bottle-fed infants compared with breast-fed ones (Nitowsky et al., 1956). These findings, in conjunction with the increased requirement for tocopherol when polyunsaturated fatty acid intake is increased, have led to the suggestion that the increased use of polyunsaturated fatty acids in infant formulas could result in a physiological deficiency of vitamin E. Hassan et al. (1966) noted that a syndrome in premature infants associated with low plasma tocopherol levels disappeared rapidly after the administration of vitamin E, and was not observed in infants fed identical diets supplemented with the vitamin. Dicks-Bushnell and Davis (1967) reported low levels of vitamin E in several infant formulas and cereals and considerable destruction of the vitamin content of one cereal by processing. This led to the suggestion that infant formulas may need to be supplemented with tocopherol to give a ratio of tocopherol to polyunsaturated fatty acid similar to that in human milk.

NEED FOR INCREASED AMOUNTS OF VITAMINS, MINERALS AND CALORIES. The infant generally thrives on milk supplemented with vitamins D and C until about three months of age. At this time, because of growth and increased demand for energy, more food is needed. For the first three or four months the iron reserves are adequate. During this time iron acquired during fetal life is being used for hemoglobin. By three months or so additional iron is needed; also, more thiamine than is provided in milk is needed. To meet these needs plus added calories, additional foods are introduced. Many infants today are given solid foods earlier, but the Committee on Nutrition of the American Academy of Pediatrics (1958), after reviewing the evidence, recommended three months as a good time to begin. Meyer (1960) reviewed the evidence for and against earlier addition of solid foods. Of fifteen reports in the literature, six approved or were tolerant of the introduction of solid foods prior to three or four months; nine either condemned or questioned this procedure.

Guthrie (1967) pointed out that the early introduction of solid foods appears to reflect the response of physicians to the demands of mothers to follow a "progressive" procedure rather than any indication that the infant needs the solid food. Among a small sample of infants Guthrie (1966) found no nutritional advantage in the introduction of solid foods before three months and noted some adverse effects such as an increased incidence of food allergy. The principal argument, as yet inconclusive, for the early introduction of solid foods is improvement in food acceptance.

Physiological readiness for more complex foods is indicated by the fact that the three- to four-month-old infant can transfer food voluntarily from the front to the back of the mouth (Committee on Nutrition, 1958). Until the infant can manipulate food from the front to the back of the mouth, the food must be put well back on the tongue. If it is placed on the tip of the tongue, the infant will push it out of his mouth. With physiological readiness for complex foods much "mouthing" activity is occurring, and saliva flows more copiously (as indicated by drooling). Infants readily accepted their first solid foods at $2\frac{1}{2}$ to three months after an earlier period of resistance (Beal, 1957).

Since infants differ in growth and development and hence in their nutritional needs, the time of introduction of solid foods is best determined according to a child's developmental status. Thus some pediatricians use as a criterion for introducing these foods the infant's weight rather than his chronologic age (Meyer, 1960).

Table 6 (p. 199) gives the recommended allowances of the nutrients needed. The foods added include cereals, either whole grain or enriched, fruits, vegetables, egg yolk and meat in sieved or puréed form. The order in which they are introduced generally depends upon the preferences of the pediatrician and those indicated by the infant. With the advent of canned baby foods the introduction of new foods was simplified for the mother. Since it became available sieved meat has been fed at an earlier age with positive results (Leverton and Clark, 1947; Leverton et al., 1952).

New foods are offered to the infant one at a time in $\frac{1}{2}$-teaspoonful amounts, the amount being gradually increased as he learns to like them. He will take an increased amount according to his appetite, which will be the mother's guide to quantity. These foods not only supply the needed food elements, but also help to accustom the infant to variety in the flavor and texture of foods. Pleasant experiences in this feeding situation can assist in establishing a positive attitude toward foods and eating. This is another step in acquiring good eating habits.

Needs of the Child Reaching the Pre-mature Nutritive Stage

The infant's teeth usually begin to erupt some time between five and eight months of age (see p. 173). This is the period when he puts everything into his mouth, and many think that this is the time when he is ready to learn to chew. By this time the pediatrician has usually advised introduction of chopped foods into the daily menu. The child is given a piece of well-toasted white bread, a dry crust of bread or a piece of Melba toast or zwieback. It is important that he be given the opportunity to learn how to chew, because young children who have had only liquid and puréed foods throughout the first year frequently refuse coarser foods when they are offered.

Evidence has been presented that there may be critical or sensitive periods in development, intimately related to maturation, at which time a specific stimulus leads to a characteristic behavior. Illingsworth and Lister (1964) suggest that if children are not given solid food to chew when they are first able to chew, troublesome feeding problems may occur.

By the age of nine months many infants will be taking their food in three meals a day, with perhaps fruit juice or milk between meals. Some children are ready for this routine at an earlier age; with some it is delayed until later.

Importance of Early Experience with Foods

When the child is a year old, he should have become acquainted with and learned to eat almost all the foods that will form the basis of an adequate diet through his lifetime. A time to pay attention to food habits is while they are being formed during the first year. The attitudes established can be of importance in determining whether the future feeding of the child will be easy or difficult, and can thus contribute to the maintenance of health as he develops. (The establishment of good eating habits is discussed in Chapter Six.)

Importance of an Adequate Daily Food Intake

All nutrients needed by the body, although required in widely differing amounts, are equally important. The 8 mg. of iron recommended daily is just as essential to sound health in the young child as the 32 gm. (4000 times the iron allowance) of protein. A variety of foods are needed for adequate nutrition even in the diet of the young child. Overemphasis on any one food, such as milk, eggs, liver, cereals or the vitamins, may interfere with the nutritional adequacy of the diet. Even milk, excellent as it is as a source of calcium, proteins and fats, should not be used to the exclusion of other essential foods. Adequacy can also apply to the quantity of each nutrient; a child can have too much as well as too little. The optimum level cannot be precisely defined for each nutrient.

Meeting Requirements of the Maturing Child

The child matures rapidly during his first year; he crawls, stands, and moves his hands and feet almost constantly when he is awake. He uses more energy, needs larger amounts of food and is becoming increasingly independent. His body structure is maturing; the digestive system that formerly required puréed food can now utilize chopped food. His willingness to change from puréed to chopped foods and to accept new foods is a sign that he is reaching maturity and will soon be ready for foods the family eats.

Children vary widely in the time required to learn that they can eat whole foods. Usually, by the time a child has twelve to sixteen teeth he is beginning to masticate his food satisfactorily and can feed himself (not too successfully from the adult standpoint, but very well considering his stage of maturity). At this stage he may have some meals with the family and can share the family diet. This is, in a certain sense, a transition period from feeding himself part of his meal and being fed the rest by his mother, to participation in a group and becoming independent by self-feeding.

AMOUNTS OF FOOD A CHILD CAN BE EXPECTED TO EAT AT THIS PERIOD. Adults often misjudge the amount of food a child should be expected to eat. Two to 3 level tablespoonfuls may be regarded as a totally inadequate serving, and yet for the young child this may be all he can consume at one time. Some children will eat more than others.* Large children and those who are growing fast will probably eat more than small, slow-growing children. The child's progress, as assessed by a physician, will indicate whether his food intake is adequate for him. Children also vary in their appetite and in their food intake from time to time. Toward the end of the first year the infant's appetite begins to slacken. This is not surprising, since he is now growing more slowly and needs less food for growth. At the same time his motor and social development is accelerating. He becomes preoccupied with the world around him. He shows a strong desire for independence in his activities, including feeding. This is a period of growing independence in self-feeding, expression of choice, replacement of soft foods and specially prepared infant foods with those of coarser texture, and changes in the acceptance of specific foods. Now begins the period of change in appetite and food acceptances which continues into the preschool years.

A longitudinal study of food intake involving an analysis of dietary histories from infancy to five years of age was reported by the Child Research Council for a group of healthy Denver children of the upper middle class (Beal, 1953, 1954, 1955, 1956, 1957, 1961, 1965). This study revealed that children changed in appetite and food intake between one and three years of age. Figure 39 shows mothers' rating of appetite of their children from six months to seven years of age. At six months approximately 85 per cent of the children were reported as having good or excellent appetites, 10 per cent fair and 5 per cent poor. A decrease followed and reached a low rating between three and four years, when 20 per cent were rated good or excellent, 60 per cent fair and 20 per cent poor. Figure 39 shows that decrease in appetite, as indicated by mothers' ratings, tended to occur toward the end of the first year. After four years the ratings improved. For some, intake was gradually lowered (mostly in milk and certain vegetables); for others it dropped abruptly. This change appeared from one year of age to three years. The low plateau lasted for a few months or persisted for two years or more.

Apparently all children can be expected to go through this stage; for some it will be a matter of months, and for others a matter of most of

---

*Individual differences in food intake are demonstrated in the studies of calorie, protein and calcium intakes of children from one to eighteen years in the longitudinal studies of the Department of Maternal and Child Health, Harvard School of Public Health (Burke et al., 1959, 1962).

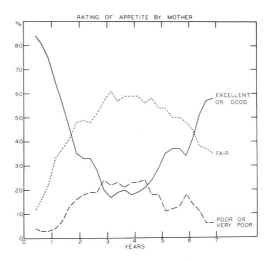

FIGURE 39. *Changes in appetite as rated by mothers. Percentage of the children at each age from 6 months through 7 years whose appetites were rated as (1) excellent or good; (2) fair; or (3) poor or very poor. (V. A. Beal: On the acceptance of solid foods, and other food patterns, of infants and children. Pediat., 20:448-457, 1957.)*

the preschool years. If a generalization may be made from the Denver study, most children will not suffer nutritionally from this drop in appetite (see p. 200). Parents, therefore, can anticipate this and accept it without concern. Parents who are unaware of this may coax the child to eat and in so doing create an appetite problem or the habit of overeating.

The Child's Nutritive Maturity

When the child can eat solid foods which are prepared for digestion and reduced to simple form (ready for absorption) entirely within his body, he is nutritively mature and physiologically capable of utilizing the foods served to the family.

Many children have reached this stage of maturity by their second birthday, although there is no chronologic level to be fixed for the individual child. The mother now can plan one meal for the family. It is not difficult to adapt the family diet to the young child. He can have the lean portions of meat, the fruit out of the fruit pie and perhaps a small amount of crust. Rich gravies and sauces or highly spiced foods can be omitted. Food can be salted mildly, and the adults can add more salt and pepper to their food if desired. Each family plans according to its own food pattern. Patterns differ because of cultural factors, food habits, food preferences and incomes. Children's nutritional needs (see Table 6) can be met within these differing food patterns by including in the daily dietary of each child the following:

3 or more cups of milk and milk products
2 or more servings of meat, poultry, fish and eggs
4 or more servings of vegetables and fruits, including a citrus fruit or other fruit or vegetable high in vitamin C, and a dark green or deep yellow vegetable for vitamin A at least every other day

4 or more servings of bread and cereal of whole grain, enriched or restored
  variety
Plus other foods as needed to provide additional energy and other food values*
(Nutritionists sometimes estimate an average serving for children as about 1
level tablespoonful of meat or vegetable per year of age.)

This framework provides plenty of opportunity for respecting individual differences in amounts and in food preferences. The foods are
natural foods which, in most cases, furnish a number of nutrients. The
use of sugar will be discussed later.

  The lessened appetite of later infancy extends into the preschool
period. In the Denver study (Beal, 1953-1965), corresponding with the
drop in appetite between one and three years of age, calorie, carbohydrate and fat intakes increased slightly, protein intake remained
stationary, and calcium, phosphorus and iron intakes dropped. Thiamine intake maintained a plateau from fifteen months until just after
three years. Riboflavin, like calcium, decreased, and niacin tended to
increase, although children with high intakes during the second year
generally showed a decrease during the third year. Vitamin A intake
from foods rose rapidly to a peak around the first year, dropped, and
then began to increase gradually during the preschool years. Intakes of
all nutrients increased after three years of age. A high peak of vitamin D
intake at four to six months followed by a continuing decrease to five
years could be attributed to both concentrates and the use of fortified
milk. Changes in ascorbic acid reflected the use of ascorbic acid preparations in the first six to nine months; thereafter the diet supplied increasingly large amounts. The changes in vitamin A and carotene reflected differences in plant, not animal, sources. Calcium and riboflavin
values reflected the decrease in milk consumption, which was lowest (16
ounces) between $2\frac{1}{2}$ and three years of age. Niacin intakes reflected meat
intake. The changes in iron intake reflected the change from prepared
baby foods, to which iron had been added, to foods prepared at home.
Even with these decreases the median amount of calories was close to
the National Research Council's recommended allowances, the protein median was above average for the first two years and similar thereafter, and iron was low for most children after $2\frac{1}{2}$ years. Since the hemoglobin levels and red cell counts were satisfactory, the amount of iron
for these children can be assumed to be adequate. Calcium was low also.
The changes in the level of intake of calcium paralleled a theoretic
calcium retention curve formulated by Stearns (1952) for calcium needs
for childhood growth. The recommended allowances of the National
Research Council are maintained at the level of 0.8 gm. from one
through nine years of age. The median for thiamine was slightly higher,
riboflavin tended to be greater, and niacin to be lower than the recommended allowances. The high protein intake probably compensated for
the low niacin, for no niacin deficiencies were evident. Individual pat-

---

*This daily food guide is from Food for Fitness, Agricultural Research Service,
United States Department of Agriculture, Leaflet 424, Revised 1964.

terns of nutrient intakes varied considerably. Some were consistently high, some consistently low, and some varied from time to time. This variability in the food intake of healthy children indicates a need for more information about individual variability in metabolism.

During this period the rate of growth slows, and the relative proportion of body weight accounted for by skeletal muscle increases (Stearns, 1951). The need of minerals for bone is therefore less than at any other time of growth, and that of nutrients for soft tissue is proportionately high. One might expect the calcium intake to be reduced. But with the addition of other foods the increase in undigestible material and a decreased ratio of calcium to phosphorus in the diet tend to decrease absorption of calcium. Also, as the child increases his contacts with other children and adults, the number of illnesses with fever tends to rise. Such illnesses are accompanied by decrease in calcium absorption. The necessary calcium can be supplied by about $\frac{3}{4}$ quart of milk plus calcium from other foods in the diet. A child should not be urged to drink milk. It is better for him to have less milk for a relatively short time than to set up an aversion to it which will operate perhaps for many years. It is better, not only with milk, but also with other foods to serve too little rather than too much. The child will indicate if he desires more.

Sometimes a child tires of a food and refuses to eat it. Some children will eat the same kind of food day after day, year after year, but others like variety. Varying the breakfast cereal, for example, or substituting for it toast, muffins, cornmeal mush or the like may provide a desired change. A food which is refused may be omitted from the diet for a time and reintroduced later. Refusals are generally a temporary matter if the adult accepts them in a matter-of-fact manner.

Little is known about the way in which appetite or food preferences develop. It is apparent that children have preferences for certain foods and that these preferences are in many cases distinctly individual. Diercks and Morse (1965) found that a large percentage of a sample of preschool children disliked vegetables, whereas fruits, meat, milk and bread were relatively well liked. Dudley et al. (1960) observed great variation among preschool children in the acceptance of vegetables prepared by different methods. They suggested caution in generalizing about preferences of children for certain vegetable preparations. Bryan and Lowenberg (1958) found little correlation between food preferences of preschool children and their father's, except a common dislike of foods in the vegetable category. Their data suggested that mothers served infrequently, or avoided, foods which the father disliked.

Many children need a snack between meals because they become hungry before mealtime. Goodenough (1931) found that more outbursts of anger occurred late in the morning and late in the afternoon. At these times children become tired and probably hungry. Easily digested food taken at midmorning and midafternoon may help to alleviate this situation. One study (Keister, 1950) of the behavior of nursery school children demonstrated that a midmorning feeding of fruit juice (e.g., unsweetened pineapple juice) was beneficial in relieving fatigue, in reducing irritability and tension and in promoting a feeling of satisfaction and well-being between that time and lunch, and did not interfere with the appetite at lunch. Another study (Wolman, 1946) of convalescent children in a rest home indicated that milk between meals did not interfere with appetite at mealtime. Yet another study (Munro, 1954) of nursery school children suggested that snacks, when offered early enough in the morning, need not interfere with the noon meal. Eating between meals is advised as a regular procedure at a regular time. Fruit juices or milk and cracker or a piece of fruit may be given at this time. Giving food between meals is an individual matter. An argument in favor of well-chosen snacks is provided by research with obese subjects indicating that smaller, more frequent meals are utilized in such a way that formation of adipose tissue is depressed, while muscle formation is stimulated. This would be desirable during growth as in the prevention of obesity (Guthrie, 1967).

Concentrated Carbohydrate in the Diet

The need to limit the amount and type of concentrated carbohydrates (sugar, candy and sweet beverages) during infancy and early childhood seems apparent from studies implicating its relation to appetite depression and increased incidence of dental caries.

Macy (1942) found that gastric volume increased rapidly and decreased slowly when sugar was present. This appeared to be the result of osmosis. The effect on stomach volume could explain the sense of fullness and cessation of hunger which follows the consumption of concentrated sweets.

The physical nature of carbohydrates and the frequency of consumption appear to influence cariogenic activity more than the total quantity consumed. A two-year experiment in Sweden (Bibby, 1961) showed that the addition of 50 gm. of sugar to bread eaten once a day caused no increase in caries, but that this amount distributed over four meals resulted in a definite increase. Ingestion of 300 gm. of sugar a day in liquid form with meals did not affect caries, but candy, especially a sticky type such as caramel or toffee, offered four times a day between meals increased caries. In all cases the caries incidence fell to the pretest levels when the candies were withdrawn.

A study of rampant caries among preschool children implicated the comforter or pacifier as a causal factor (Review, 1966b). More of the caries group (37 per cent) than the control group (17 per cent) were still receiving bottle feedings and a comforter bottle (a prolonged bottle feeding once daily). The prolonged contact of the teeth with fermentable carbohydrate provided by sweetened feeding bottles, hollow feeders and dummies was believed to be an important factor in the increase in caries.

Additional sugar beyond that needed to improve the flavor of some food is usually not needed. Those experienced in feeding children know that children do not necessarily crave sweets if their diets are nutritionally adequate (Macy, 1942). Desire for sweet foods may be the result of being conditioned to sweetness earlier, e.g., by the use of an oversweet formula or by frequent experiences with sweet foods in a family that likes and eats sweets often. There is a possibility that children have a lower taste sensitivity to sweet. Feeney et al. (1966) found that preschool children accepted much higher concentrations of sugar than their parents. It may be pointed out that lower taste sensitivity may have some advantage in overall food acceptance. Korslund and Eppright (1967) found greater food acceptance and enthusiasm for food among children with the lowest taste sensitivity.

Recommended Allowances

Table 6 shows allowances in terms of nutrients needed during infancy and early childhood. These quantitites are allowances and not requirements and therefore allow for a margin of safety in meeting nutritional needs. They are based on metabolism studies, plus the opinions of those experienced in child nutrition. They are revised from time to time in

TABLE 6. Recommended Daily Allowances for Infants and Young Children

	Age (years)		
	0-1*	1-3**	3-6**
Weight, kg.	8	13	18
lb.	18	29	40
Height, cm.	—	87	107
in.	—	34	42
Calories[+]	kg. × 115 ± 15	1300	1600
Protein, gm.	kg. × 2.5 ± 0.5	32	40
Calcium, gm.	0.7	0.8	0.8
Iron, mg.	kg. × 1.0	8	10
Vitamin A, I.U.	1500	2000	2500
Thiamine, mg.	0.4	0.5	0.6
Riboflavin, mg.	0.6	0.8	1.0
Niacin, Equiv. mg.[++]	6	9	11
Ascorbic Acid, mg.	30	40	50
Vitamin D, I.U.	400	400	400

Taken from Recommended Dietary Allowances. Revised 1964. A Report of the Food and Nutrition Board, National Academy of Sciences—National Research Council. Publication 1146. Washington, D. C., 1964.

* The calorie and protein allowances per kg. for infants are considered to decrease progressively from birth. Allowances for calcium, thiamine, riboflavin and niacin increase proportionately with calories to the maximum values shown.

**Entries represent allowances for the midpoint of the specified age periods, i.e. column for children 1-3 is for age 2 yrs; 3-6 is for age 4½ yrs.

[+]The calorie allowances cited are for infants and children of average activity and are proposed as average and approximate allowances for groups. More appropriate allowances for the individual infant and child may be derived by observation of growth, appetite, activity and body fatness of the individual.

[++]Niacin equivalents include dietary sources of the preformed vitamin and the precursor, tryptophan. Thus 60 mg. tryptophan represents 1 mg. niacin.

order that the latest scientific knowledge may be utilized. Students are therefore advised to watch for the latest revision. The allowances, with the exception of that for vitamin D, can be met by foods provided in a balanced diet.

Facts to Remember When Feeding a Young Child

Nutritional allowance tables are to be used in a flexible manner as a guide for the individual child's intake in relation to children in general. The results are to be interpreted in terms of the child, his size, activity and growth. Children vary in structure, function and metabolic patterns. They also live with a variety of families. Therefore food intake varies widely from one healthy child to another.

The child has needs for the present, but is also building for the future in terms of body structure and food habits. A famous nutritionist's comment of long ago is still true (Rose, 1929): "One year of good feeding at the beginning of life is more important than ten after forty, and a baby's needs are not to be judged by an adult's inclinations. Feeding must be a matter of principle and not impulse; the reward will be partly in the present—much more in the future."

Early childhood is an important period for establishing a normal appetite, good attitudes toward food and good food habits. The adult is responsible for the choice of food offered the child and the way in which it is prepared.

The child's needs for nutrients are higher in relation to his size than those of an adult, and his digestive tract is still immature. Therefore foods providing a variety of nutrients are to be preferred to those containing a few, and foods which can be easily digested are selected. Foods that may irritate the lining of the digestive tract, such as those high in roughage or highly seasoned, are avoided.

Consider the whole child. He needs "psychological vitamins," a term Frank (1951) applied to love, affection, tenderness, patience and understanding. He needs these for appetite, digestion and absorption of food, since emotions influence the activity of the digestive tract and the desire to eat.

Young children frequently go on food jags. A child may eat large quantities of one food for a time, then taper off or stop eating it entirely for a while. Later he will return to it.

A preschool child's "No" at the table may have one of many meanings, such as lack of appetite, refusal of a specific food, assertion of a sense of autonomy, a kind of communication with an adult, a reflection of conflict with an adult or imitation of another child.

A child's appetite varies from day to day and from meal to meal. One day he may eat like a bear, another day like a bird. Some children eat better at one meal than at another.

The young child is often slow in eating, and dawdles. He may become tired in the process of feeding himself because he is not yet adept at it. A helping hand with the last bites may be advisable. Dawdling may be reduced by keeping the eating process as simple as possible. Utensils can be selected that will facilitate eating. Foods such as soup or soft custard can be drunk from a cup more easily than spooned out of a dish.

A young child sometimes wants to be independent, sometimes to be dependent. This is true at mealtime.

Young children tend to make a ritual of eating, as they do of other routines. Perhaps foods are eaten in a specific order; a particular spoon or dish must be used, or the table must be set in a specific way. When these rituals are respected, mealtime tends to go smoothly; when disregarded, the meal may be disturbed and little or no food eaten.

Adults can have certain expectations of the child at mealtime, provided these expectations are appropriate, understood by the child and used with flexibility.

Young children have preferences. They usually like simple, unmixed foods. A meat patty is preferred to meat in a stew. They are aware of textures. They like a variety of crisp, chewy and soft foods in a meal. Mashed potatoes may be acceptable when soft and fluffy, yet be rejected when sticky and gummy. Young children have difficulty in swallowing anything dry. They prefer food not too hot or too cold. If food is too hot, they may not have the patience to wait for it to cool. They may let the ice cream melt before eating it. They like foods that are easy to eat. "Finger foods," i.e., foods they can pick up, are popular. Carrot and celery sticks, pieces of lettuce, cabbage, and the like, furnish an excellent way to introduce the foods which they will meet later in salads. Some young children in the second year will eat vegetables more readily if they can pick them up with their fingers. A whole string bean may be acceptable, but beans may be rejected when cut up and served with a spoon.

Each child has his particular preferences, which may refer to specific foods or to ways of preparing them. Children vary in the number of foods they like and in the intensity of their feeling about them. Most children like what they are accustomed to having. Hence early experience with a variety of foods is important. It is wise to respect children's preferences. No child need be expected to like all foods. His nutritional needs can be met with various combinations. A healthy, happy child will eat a wide variety of foods to meet his nutritional requirements. For further details the student is referred to a philosophy of child feeding by Lowenberg (1965).

TOPICS FOR STUDY AND DISCUSSION

1. As a focus for study, relate the development of the systems associated with nutrition to the feeding of infants and young children.
2. Observe and compare the respiration of a very young infant and of a four-year-old when they are relatively quiet.
3. Invite a dentist to class to discuss his role in preventive dentistry and to answer students' questions about the dental development of the young child.
4. Observe an infant about six months old, another about fifteen months and a four-year-old at mealtime. Record what each child eats, the quantities and his be-

havior. Write a report of these experiences, making comparisons and discussing the adequacy of the food eaten in terms of food requirements for each age.
5. Talk with a mother of a preschool child about her plan and practices for feeding her child, especially in relation to the family foods and mealtime. This may be accomplished by having the mother meet with the class or by having each student meet with a mother.

SELECTED READINGS

Filer, L. J.: Current problems in pediatric nutrition. Borden's Review of Nutrition Research, *27*:1-11, 1966.

Guthrie, H. A.: Introductory Nutrition. St. Louis, C. V. Mosby Company, 1967. Chap. 17, Infant Nutrition. Chap. 18, Nutrition from Infancy to Adulthood.

Lowenberg, M. E.: Between Infancy and Adolescence; in Food, The Yearbook of Agriculture, 1959. United States Department of Agriculture, pp. 296-302. A discussion of the nutritional needs of the preschool child, foods to meet these needs, children's preferences, meal patterns, parental roles.

Macy, I. G., and Kelly, H. J.: Food for Expectant and Nursing Mothers; in Food, The Yearbook of Agriculture, 1959. United States Department of Agriculture, pp. 273-282. Nutritional needs, physiological processes involved, and foods to meet these needs are discussed.

Maternal and Child Health and Food and Nutrition Sections: Economy in nutrition and feeding of infants. Am. J. Pub. Health, *56*:1756-1784, 1966.

Meyer, H. F.: Infant Foods and Feeding Practice. Springfield, Ill., Charles C Thomas, 1960. A pediatrician discusses in Chap. 3, Human Milk and Breast Feeding; Chap. 8, Solid Food Supplements of the First Year.

Stearns, G.: Infants and Toddlers; in Food, The Yearbook of Agriculture, 1959. United States Department of Agriculture, pp. 283-295. Relates nutrition to the physiological and psychological status of the child and his developmental progress.

Stuart, H. C., and Prugh, D. G. (Eds.): The Healthy Child. Cambridge, Harvard University Press, 1960, pp. 142-176. Burke, B. S.: Maternal Nutrition During the Period of Lactation. Burke, B. S.: The Nutrition of the Preschool Child. Burke, B. S., and Stuart, H. C.: The Nutrition of the Infant from Birth to Two Years. Stitt, P. G.: Principles and Practices of Infant Feeding.

Watson, E. H., and Lowrey, G. H.: Growth and Development of Children. 5th ed. Chicago, Year Book Publishers, Inc. 1967. Organ Development; Energy Metabolism; Facial Growth and Dentition.

CHAPTER SIX

Physical and Psychological Needs: Eating Behavior; Elimination

Attention in this chapter will focus on the child's learning pertaining to eating behavior and elimination. Interest in the child's learning in these areas comes from a concept of individual need for adequate bodily functioning for well-being and development. On the physical side, eating and elimination are relevant to health. On the psychological side they are sometimes considered relevant to personality development. Personality theorists are interested in the infant's eating as an early experience with another person—a situation in which he has satisfactions from the food—and as social experience. Theorists have also stressed particular gratifications in early years as stages in progression toward personality maturity. Furthermore, behaviors in these areas are sometimes regarded as indicators of stress.

Focus in the following pages will be on orderly trends in eating behavior and in toilet habits. In viewing such trends, variables which may affect behavior and development will be suggested. But when the majority of children, rather than the extremes, are considered, knowledge of influence of setting (exogenous systems) on the child's eating behavior and toilet habits is incomplete. Likewise, evidence of effects of variables in the child's biological and psychological systems is also incomplete. This inconclusiveness from research is present also in reviews on the relation of parental practices and attitudes in these areas to personality development of the child (Caldwell, 1964; McCandless, 1967).

EATING BEHAVIOR

Foundations for the development of behavior in eating are beginning to be established when the newborn infant has his hunger satisfied. He is thus conditioned to the natural sequence of hunger, ingestion of food,

203

satisfaction, physical well-being and contentment. *Hunger* in the new-born and the young infant is a part of that generalized sensation of unpleasantness which, with the ingestion of food, changes to generalized pleasure (Hamburger, 1960; Prugh, 1960). It is regulated by the hypo-thalamus in the subcortical area of the brain where there are centers for regulating hunger and satiety (Anand, 1960). The action is believed to resemble that of a thermostat. *Appetite,* or the desire for food, which depends in large measure on pleasant experiences with food, requires the ability of association and other functions of the cerebral cortex. It is believed that the cortex has reached the level of development when appetite is more likely to function about the fourth or fifth month (Hamburger, 1960). Prior to this, it is suggested, the conditioning or imprinting acquired through prompt gratification of hunger and the warmth an infant receives lays a foundation for appetite (Hamburger, 1960). Since it can be stimulated by pleasant experiences or suppressed because of unpleasant associations with or memories of food, the adult can play a part in nurturing appetite by building up pleasant associa-tions.

The newborn and the young infant require immediate gratification of the need for food. This immediacy is an expression of their lack of development of the inhibitory functions of the cerebral cortex and the relatively ineffective physiological homeostatic functioning (Prugh, 1960). When this prompt gratification of the infant's need for food is provided by feeding him according to his physiological rhythm, this is called *self-regulation.* From birth through the first few weeks or months this physiological rhythm will be irregular, but later will usually become regular. The mother adapts the feeding of the infant according to his indications of needs and abilities. Feeding in the early months, when the infant is satisfying his food needs and at the same time those for warmth and security, seems to be preparation for the time when eating becomes a more complex, voluntary act, under conscious control.

When the schedule (or absence of it at first) is self-regulatory, the newborn is fed each time he gives evidence by rooting, sucking or crying that he is hungry. He is permitted to nurse as long as he pleases, except breast-fed babies during the first few days, when feeding time may be limited to allow the mother's nipples to become accustomed to the pull of the sucking infant.

Since the infant operates largely on a reflex basis for about the first three months, and since his reflex cry registers protest against many other discomforts besides hunger, judgment of the adult is involved in determining when the cry indicates hunger. The stomach ordinarily takes two or more hours to empty itself of food. Thus, if the baby has been fed recently, it seems reasonable that something other than hunger is prompting the crying. Aldrich et al. (1945b) investigated causes of crying in a newborn infants' nursery and ascribed it to hunger when it occurred near feeding time and was accompanied by sucking move-ments. For fifty babies observed for twenty-four hours over an eight-day period, crying was ascribed to hunger in 2760 instances, or 36 per cent of the total crying time. Other causes included the need for physical care when wet or soiled or after having vomited. A large number of instances of crying, 3295, was ascribed to unknown causes. Aldrich and his co-workers suggested that a complete list of causes for crying should include the need for fondling and rhythmic motion.

The hunger cry is usually insistent and is not assuaged by any means other than food. The cry of colic, which occurs frequently in babies under three months of age, is also an insistent cry, but is more apt to occur soon after feeding rather than near feeding time. Mothers who have successfully fed their babies on a self-regulatory schedule report that it is relatively easy to learn to understand when the infant is in need of food or of some other attention.

In a self-regulatory procedure, infants tend to adopt a regular schedule early and to reduce their feedings during the first year (see Figs. 40, 41, 42). In one study (Olmstead and Jackson, 1950) frequency of feeding was observed in the first week of life in a hospital. In 100 breast-fed infants on a self-regulation approach the total number of breast feedings rose to a maximum on the fourth day and averaged 8.6 feedings. The maximum number for one baby in one day was seventeen.

Figures 40 and 41 show how rapidly fraternal twins put themselves on a regular schedule and reduced the total number of feedings when they were fed according to their own needs. The female twin took only four feedings on four of seven days as early as the third week. By the eighth week she was well stabilized on the four-feeding day and by the ninth week began occasionally to take only three feedings daily. Her twin brother in the ninth week took only three feedings four days out of seven.

Aldrich and Hewitt (1947) studied 100 breast-fed and bottle-fed babies on a self-regulating schedule for the first year and found (Fig. 42) that babies chose to lengthen their feeding intervals gradually. At one month 10 per cent chose a two-hour interval, 61 per cent a three-hour interval, and 26 per cent a four-hour interval. The peak for the four-hour schedule came at three months, and that for four meals a day at seven to nine months. The schedule of three feedings a day was adopted by some at four months, the number increasing until at twelve months 91 per cent selected this adult feeding schedule. With established regularity of demands for food even by three months, the infant's feeding schedule can be adjusted to fit the mother's convenience.

This self-regulatory procedure, satisfying the infant when he is hungry, is considered to foster "a confidence in the lawfulness of the universe" (Gesell and Ilg, 1943). During the early months of predominantly reflex control prompt gratification of basic needs can result in a conditioning to pleasurable associations with persons, with food and with other things.

For the mother such procedure in the early months and years of the child's life requires adaptations to the activities or signs of need of the child, as contrasted to adaptation to a clock. Management of herself and the child is on a flexible schedule. If her role is one of *anticipa-*

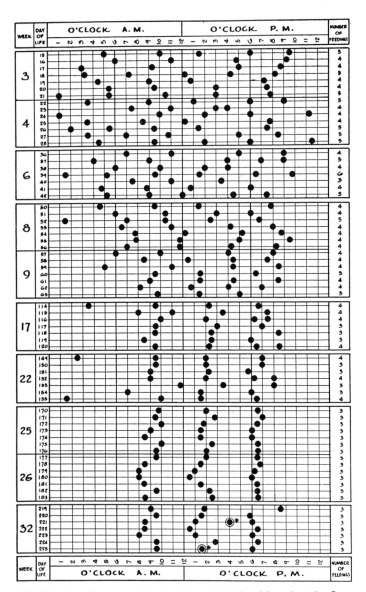

FIGURE 40. *Chart showing feeding schedule of female twin. Cup feeding, on 221st day, given not in response to demand for food, but as educational device to accustom infant to drink milk from a cup. (G. Trainham, G. J. Pilafian, and R. M. Kraft: Case history of twins breast fed on self-demand regime. J. Pediat., 27:97-108, 1945, C. V. Mosby Company.)*

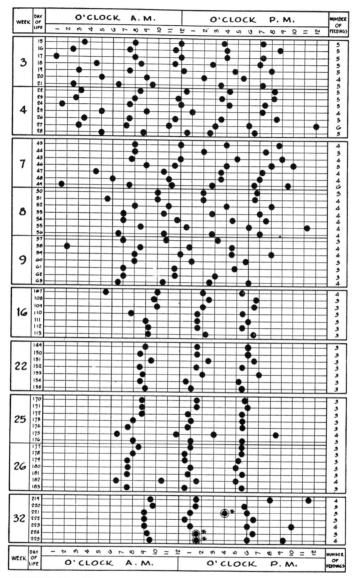

FIGURE 41. *Chart showing feeding schedule of male twin. Cup feeding, on 221st day, given not in response to demand for food, but as educational device to accustom infant to drink milk from a cup. (G. Trainham, G. J. Pilafian, and R. M. Kraft: Case history of twins breast fed on self-demand regime. J. Pediat., 27:97-108, 1945, C. V. Mosby Company.)*

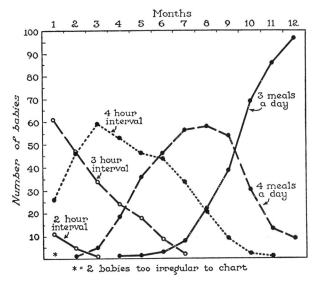

FIGURE 42. *Graph showing increase or decrease, as age advanced, in number of infants on self-regulating schedule who adopted each feeding interval. (C. A. Aldrich and E. S. Hewitt: A self-regulating feeding program for infants. J.A.M. A., 135:340-342, 1947.)*

tory guidance, she is responsive to signs of her child's needs and his increasing maturity, and, on the basis of these, guides him in his environment according to his needs and maturity and the family situation. At times there is some misunderstanding of such an attitude, and an adult-child relation of extreme *laissez-faire* or autonomy occurs. If there is an unduly permissive attitude toward children's feeding programs as in other aspects of their lives, then parents play no positive role in their development. Perhaps such misunderstanding would not exist if the term *adaptive*, meaning adapting to a child's ability, were substituted for "permissive," as suggested by Landreth (1958). A mother can obtain necessary guidance from her own physician and from the one she selects for her baby if she has a pediatrician. The feeding regimen appropriate for mother and child can be determined by the physician after talking with the mother. Many believe that a middle course is most satisfactory for the majority of mothers and babies, i.e., a plan whereby the baby is not put on a rigid schedule, but is guided into reasonable feeding habits.

Research on aspects of infant feeding gratification and personality of the child has been reviewed by Caldwell (1964). In some of this research, self-regulation or feeding autonomy permitted the infant by the mother was predictive of attributes of the child such as assurance and ability to cope with his environment at preschool age (Holway, 1949; Murphy, 1962). In other research extreme adherence to a rigid schedule was associated with an attribute of the mother, e.g., lack of warmth (Sears, Maccoby and Levin, 1957). Caldwell concludes that the relation between infant feeding practices and personality during childhood "cannot be fully described at this time" and suggests that research attempt to give "attention to the infant's individual reaction to various aspects of the feeding situation in appraising the extent of gratification or frustration which he experiences."

In a study in a university community based on interviews with mothers during the first and second years of their children's life, Hubert and Britton (1957) found that 12.5 per cent had a regular feeding schedule, 29 per cent had a semi-demand schedule and 58.5 per cent fed on demand. There was a tendency for those mothers who did not have a definite schedule for household tasks to feed their babies on demand. In another study of middle-class and working-class mothers in two suburbs of a large metropolitan area of New England (Sears, Maccoby and Levin, 1957), 12 per cent followed complete self-demand; 8 per cent, a rigid feeding schedule. The others ranged between these extremes, with varying degrees of scheduling. There was a positive correlation between scheduling and the measure of the mother's anxiety in child rearing.

At the beginning the mother's role is relatively simple. When the feeding regimen is well established, the child, if breast-fed, can be given an occasional bottle, which not only gives him experience with another form of feeding, but also permits the mother some wider freedom. Later, as more functions come under conscious control, the young child has expectations on which he relies; he adapts according to his background of experience. He may have discovered that people of his world provide gratification of basic needs, and also that certain behavior on his part may not receive prompt gratification. It may not be within his comprehension that his parents, after thought and the trying out of several procedures, have concluded that his behavior indicates a whim as contrasted to a basic need. He does discover, however, that satisfactions from the behavior are not forthcoming from the adults. Thus there can be a relation of love and also the beginning of self-discipline.

The child is beginning to fit into the life of the family. Expectations of him in eating can rest upon his degree of maturity and the situation. The adults provide him with his food and the environment in which that food is eaten. They provide examples in behavior and attitudes. By the quality of their guidance they may facilitate the child's development of more mature eating behavior, according to his ability, or relegate him to a kind of "infantile autocracy" in which he is not adapting as a member of the family.

When foods other than milk begin to be introduced, a new element enters the feeding picture: choosing not only the amount of food to be taken, but also the kind. At this time the adults play a role in determining what kinds of foods will be made available to their children. The food practices of the family will strongly affect the developing food attitudes of the young child.

Self-Selection of Foods

It would seem from animal experiments (Scott, Verney and Morissey, 1950) and the experiments of Davis (1928) with newly weaned infants that learning through trial and error is involved in the self-selection of food. Thus factors involved in learning seem to apply to the eating situation. An experiment by Davis (1928) influenced thinking in the late 1920's and 1930's about the feeding of infants and young children. She experimented with a group of newly weaned babies who were allowed to select their own food from a variety of natural foodstuffs. Nothing was done to influence the child's choice, and all pressure and inhibition were removed. The food was natural, unmixed and un-seasoned, and suitable for children. Each child ate alone and had a tray with all the food before him. A nurse helped him to get the food he could not reach. No food was offered either directly or by suggestion. The children ate their food eagerly, in a matter-of-fact way, ate aston-ishingly large quantities, and stopped with an air of finality. From the standpoint of appetite and digestion, optimal results were shown. The children's general physical condition indicated that their nutrition did not suffer, but was well above average.

This experiment demonstrated that under certain conditions with the complete removal of pressure and the granting of freedom in the choice of suitable foods, children's feeding behavior will be adequate for their nutritional needs. Problems sometimes faced by parents would be avoided. The value of this experiment is not so much in the adoption of this procedure in the home, but rather in the application of the principles in various family situations. Davis herself demonstrated (1933) that an adaptation of this method could be used successfully in a private home, as well as in routine feeding of children in a hospital.

A modified self-selection method of feeding for two young chil-dren, one from birth to four years, the other from eighteen months to six years, in one family was as follows (Gutelius, 1948). Three meals were prepared at regular times unless the children asked to eat earlier and it was convenient. Usually they ate at an attractively set table in the kitchen before the adult meal; small portions were served. The mother remained nearby to give help when sought. The children were allowed almost complete freedom in what they ate and how they ate it, in being able to eat as long as they wished, and in eating as much as they wished with the exception of limitations on sweets. At lunch and supper, sweets were limited to one cookie, a small piece of candy or ice cream. Ready-to-eat and nonmessy foods were available at any time of day. Certain restrictions were imposed, such as no sweets between meals, only certain places for eating, food not to be thrown about and wantonly made unfit to eat, children not to annoy their parents while eating. The mother reported that the children had good appetites, their food intake met requirements, and they fussed very little about the limitation of sweets. The variety of selected foods increased. They liked all fruits, almost all kinds of meat, fish, fowl and cereal, and about fifteen vegetables. At five years they showed an interest in adult table manners and had pride in eating what was given them away from home and in being polite. Table behavior at home was unconventional but not objectionable and became more "civilized" with age.

About half or more meals were well balanced. Rarely were milk and citrus fruits omitted. About one-third of their food was taken between meals, and generally consisted of fruit, vegetable or milk. The children generally ate two or three foods at one meal. The author states that such a program presupposes a happy home without emotional tensions and that success depends on the attitude of parents and on the children eating by themselves.

For a great many families such a program might not be considered desirable or feasible. The family can provide eating experiences which make use of a nutritional and a psychological point of view through a variety of procedures. The principles concerning absence of undue pressures, and choice among suitable foods, followed in these studies can be utilized to provide good experiences at mealtime in various home situations.

Introduction of New Foods

A few adventurous infants and young children accept new foods with pleasure the first time they are offered, even foods with such definite flavors as asparagus and cabbage. More often, however, the child learns through repeated experimentation to accept the new food. Thus for most children the introduction of each new food is a learning experience at first rather than a means of meeting nutritional needs. One method is to offer a very small amount of the new food at the same meal with some food which the child already likes. With some children the new food is best accepted early in the meal while appetite is keen. With many others, if the child first satisfies hunger and at least part of his appetite with some food he likes, he may be more responsive to sampling the new food. In either case, if the food is offered with the attitude that it is to be eaten, this can seem to be a part of customary eating procedure.

The esthetic appeal of the food itself can have an effect on the appetite of the child just as it does on that of the adult. The sight, taste and smell of the food served make a direct appeal to the senses. Meals planned to offer contrast of color, flavor and texture can attract children as they do adults. Careful preparation may be especially important when some new food is being offered. Each pleasant experience with a new food can contribute to attitudes of acceptance of other new foods. On the other hand, one serving of burned, undercooked or too hot food provides an unpleasant experience that may occasion a food prejudice requiring months of re-education to overcome. It may also make the child fearful of trying other new foods.

Some children readily accept foods with new consistencies or textures, whereas others require slow education. Thus when the infant goes from puréed foods to chopped foods, it may be necessary to introduce only a small amount of the chopped food, together with a normal serving of the purée to which he is accustomed. Occasionally an infant who completely refuses chopped foods may readily accept whole carrots, beans or other vegetables which he can hold in his hand and feed to himself.

The child who has become accustomed to different types of food can learn to chew properly and use his teeth and gums. Tough foods are not advisable, but vegetables, cooked and raw, certain raw fruits, bread crusts, toast and other foods which offer resistance to the teeth are aids in learning mastication.

Learning Eating Procedures

Steps in learning to feed oneself begin with early neuromuscular development and include (1) putting the hand or thumb in the mouth; (2) cooperation in feeding, i.e., holding the bottle; (3) ability in a sitting position to reach for and convey an object to the mouth with either hand; (4) finger-feeding with food that has to be chewed; (5) ability to drink from a cup held upright; (6) mastery of use of a spoon; (7) mastery of use of other utensils.

The use of each new eating utensil is learned. If this fact is ignored, refusal of the utensil with which the food is offered may sometimes be taken for food refusal. This learning can begin before the infant shows any readiness to use a spoon or cup. Opportunities to hold and investigate these feeding utensils while his mother is feeding him provide the infant with some familiarity with handling the spoon and the cup before he begins to feed himself (see Fig. 43).

Before solid foods are offered to the baby—usually some time

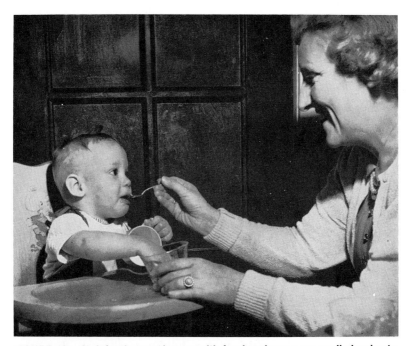

FIGURE 43. *An infant's experiences with food and a cup are preliminaries to feeding himself.*

between two and four months—he can begin to become accustomed to the spoon if it is used several times to feed him his orange juice. In this way, when he is given the new food, he has only one rather than two things to learn at the same time. He is already accustomed to the spoon and now has only to learn to eat the new food. Learning to drink from a cup can also be gradual in that the amount taken at one time can gradually increase as well as the number of times in the day it is substituted for the breast or bottle.

The time of *weaning* from breast or bottle to cup varies according to the rate of development of the child and the setting in which he lives. For most children some time during the last quarter of the first year is a time when other means of eating are greatly increased. Sometimes babies wean themselves. Sometimes, if the mother's attitude is one of anticipatory guidance, she notices indications of the infant's readiness for new steps, and the transition is smooth for both mother and infant.

Weaning is a gradual process; it extends back into the earlier life of the infant, starting with the addition of vitamins, and through the various phases of the additions of new foods with their different tastes, texture, smells, the mouthing of these foods and, finally, the dropping out of sucking and the acquisition of skills of drinking from a cup and the management of whole foods.

If the goal of weaning is to have as little emotional disturbance as possible, it appears wisest to begin the last stages of weaning before the end of the first year or wait until the end of the second year, to prepare the infant for the new mode of feeding and to make the transition as expeditiously as possible (Sears et al., 1957).

Not all infants wean themselves as definitely and readily as this, however. "Fussy" babies who have cried a great deal from birth may be more disturbed during weaning than other babies in spite of gentle weaning procedures (Sears, Maccoby and Levin, 1957). If the mother regards the whole procedure as a gradual learning process and accepts what the baby does successfully, but at the same time shows no impatience because of what he does not do, weaning is usually accomplished easily.

Ausubel (1957) discussed the role of weaning in relation to personality development and the stage of a child's ego development when parents become less subservient to the child and increase their training demands. Thus changes in the dynamics of parent-child relations add their influence to the growing-up process. Lasting effects of weaning on personality development, he believes, cannot be attributed to the manner and time of weaning itself, but rather to the extent to which these factors are characteristic of larger areas of parental behavior.

The age at which the child can skillfully handle his own cup, spoon or fork varies widely. He may go through a period of contentedly allowing someone else to hold the cup. A little later he will put his hands on the cup to assist. Before he acquires the skill to lift, to tilt correctly and to replace the cup, there will usually be a phase in which he insists upon holding the cup himself, but tilts it too far and spills the contents. There are apt to be times, too, when he awkwardly sets the cup down on his spoon or the rim of his tray and spills milk into the tray or, even more trying to his mother, when he drops or throws the cup to the floor.

At first the infant has the spoon manipulated for him. After he has shown an interest in the spoon it may be some time before he is able to fill it and carry it to his mouth without spilling the food. The amount of help given to children by mothers varies considerably. In one study (Hubert and Britton, 1957) during the first year's interview with mothers, 54 per cent of their infants required little help in feeding, 29 per cent required some help, and 14 per cent required much help. In the second year's interview it was found that the mothers who restricted physical activity in the house tended to have given their infants more help at mealtime. At eighteen months children spill food rather frequently. Some children can use a fork at two years, but a spoon or fingers are usually preferred. Often the child tires of manipulation before the meal is completed and welcomes some adult help to finish. The use of a knife and fork together to cut food requires a very complex skill, which begins to appear in the late preschool years. Some five-year-olds can cut food if it is very tender.

In learning to feed himself the child often wants complete independence before he is fully capable of assuming it.

Whether the child begins to eat at the family table as soon as he can feed himself part of his meal or whether he eats alone until he is three or four years old varies according to mealtime procedures and values of the family. It was reported in a study in a university town (Hubert and Britton, 1957) during the interview when the child was in his first year, that 54 per cent of the infants were being fed with the family, 23 per cent sometimes with the family, and 23 per cent were fed alone.

FIGURE 44. Making some of the decisions in serving himself a particular food can contribute to the child's sense of autonomy.

This child, in his fourth year, likes to serve himself.

During the second year's interview it was found that children tended to be fed at the family table when they required little help in feeding. In his associations with family members the child gradually acquires table manners which conform to those of his family. Strang (1951) said, "If at the end of his fifth year a child has made progress in eating quietly, using knife, fork and spoon habitually and resorting to fingers only rarely, very seldom upsetting his milk, using napkin or bib properly, and sometimes saying 'please' and 'thank you' spontaneously, his parents should be content."

Since small children cannot easily sit still as long as adults and their attention span is shorter, some parents do not expect them to remain at the table until the adults have finished. Some families provide opportunities for movement, as the child serves himself or others, pours milk or fruit juice (Fig. 44) or carries something to or from the table.

Variables in Development of Eating Behavior

Information on orderly trends in development of eating behavior of the infant and the young child suggests "conditions of practice," under which learning, or change in behavior, occurs. Motivations are from hunger, a biologically primitive tendency, and also from appetite. Little is known about the ways in which appetite or food preferences develop. But it has been demonstrated that differentiation of taste and differentiation of stimuli in the mouth, as well as conditioning of the sucking response to a loud tone, can occur in the newborn (Lipsitt, 1966). Thus the infant is beginning to form organizational patterns early. The two- or three-year-old, whose nutriture is mature enough for acceptance of a variety of foods, already has bases for congruities or incongruities as these new experiences occur. He seems able to accommodate the new without undue stress if experiences are not too dissonant for him.

Some of the associations of the infant and the child with adults, as hunger is gratified and appetite develops, have already been indicated. Other associations and, consequently, additional organizational patterns of thought in the child may come from his experiences in the kitchen as food is being prepared. The infant or young child, sitting or playing near his mother in the kitchen, grows accustomed to numerous food odors while being "sociable." The preschool child who assists in preparation of food grows cognitively in ways which may concern motivations and satisfactions when the food is served. Informational interaction with his environment, related to his curiosity, or exploration, his production of effects on the environment, and later to his feeling of competence, can contribute to his attitudes toward food. The children in Figure 45 were intent upon preparing eggs for their nursery school lunch. Later at the lunch table, when the scrambled eggs were served, this event was a part of the background of experience they brought to the situation.

At the table, exchanges of the child and his setting may contribute to his comfort or discomfort. The physical environment at mealtime

FIGURE 45. Participation in preparation of food can contribute to attitudes toward food.

(M. E. Sweeny and D. C. Buck: How to Feed Young Children in the Home. Detroit, Merrill-Palmer School, 1937.)

can include a comfortable position in a chair of suitable height and also a place to rest his feet, instead of having them dangling.

A happy, relaxed atmosphere free from emotional tensions, both at mealtime and during the child's preparation for the meal, and a sense of being one of the group can contribute to enjoyment of food, a solid basis of appeal. The mother who encourages but does not urge, who expects success but is not anxious or concerned if the child refuses, and who does not use some foods as a reward for eating others seems to be facilitating her child's development. Attitudes toward food are inextricably bound up with the emotional and social phases of life as well as with its physical side.

Elements considered here tend to parallel those in the discussion of learning on pages 12 to 16.

Differences in specific eating behavior, according to the individual's bodily functioning, were suggested in the discussion of nutrition in Chapter Five. Behavioral differences indicative of individuality, as reported in interviews and also observed, have led to the designation of a number of reaction patterns by Thomas et al. (1963). In these patterns are variables such as degree of regularity, adaptability, intensity, approach or withdrawal, positive or negative mood, low or high threshold of response, distractibility, attention span and persistence. These are among the attributes the individual brings to the situation in learning eating behavior and other forms of behavior.

ELIMINATION

Elimination is necessary for the removal of the end-products of digestion and metabolism. Furthermore, there is a socially dictated need for the child to learn to control his elimination so that he doés it at a time and place deemed appropriate by the society in which he lives. This latter need serves as the basis for the following sections on bowel and bladder control.

Elimination of waste materials is effected through the skin, lungs, digestive tract and kidneys. The skin and lungs carry a smaller yet significant load; the digestive tract and the kidneys the major load. The role of the digestive tract has been discussed earlier (pp. 161-170); the excretory system will be discussed here so that the student will have some understanding of the two systems involved in gaining control of elimination.

Excretory System

There is a constant flow of materials through the human body which, in the process of metabolism, either yield their energy or are subject to more or less complex chemical transformation. When these processes have been completed, the useless or potentially injurious end-products are eliminated from the body. The mechanism for eliminating some of these wastes has been discussed in the section on the digestive system (p. 169). Since elimination and excretion may be confused, it may be well to state the way in which these terms are used in this text. *Elimination* means evacuation of those hollow organs in which waste material has accumulated, and it depends essentially on mechanical changes (such as pressure) which force waste out of the body, e.g., the voiding of urine from the bladder. *Excretion* deals with extraction of wastes from the internal environment, from circulating body fluids, and their passage into temporary waste depositories, into lungs, bladder and gastrointestinal tract. Carlson, Johnson and Calvert (1961) stated:

> In large part, excretion is carried out by cellular activity, involving cellular work and the expenditure of energy by the cell. . . . This cellular activity may be modified by physical forces such as osmosis, filtration, diffusion and electrical force, but cannot be accounted for entirely by them. Activity or work of living cells contributes largely to the phenomena.

KIDNEYS. The kidneys function as excretory organs in removing from the body useless and injurious end-products of metabolism. They also aid in maintaining in the internal environment the conditions necessary for life by playing a part in regulating the composition of the blood. Urine, which is constantly excreted by the kidneys, is stored in the bladder until eliminated.

Before birth the kidneys excrete urine, and some is collected in the bladder. This is relatively little in contrast to the amounts excreted after birth. The kidneys at birth are sufficiently mature to respond remarkably well to the sudden load thrown upon them. In structure the kidney of the newborn appears to be complete, but functional development seems to lag slightly behind (Smith, 1959c; Watson and Lowrey, 1967). Some give four to six months as the age at which function reaches maturity (György, 1961). Until this age the ability to concentrate urine is somewhat immature, so that an infant may have difficulty in handling unusually large loads of electrolytes and metabolic products of protein. It is evident that as the kidneys increase in size, the bladder must make corresponding growth.

Chemical analysis of the urine excreted by the adult kidney shows that it normally contains salts, urea (product of protein metabolism), uric acid (the end-product of nucleoprotein, abundant in cell nuclei), creatinine (from protein and muscle metabolism) and several other materials. Urine is derived from blood; everything in the urine has first been present in the blood, from which the kidneys have "separated" it.

QUANTITY OF URINE EXCRETED.   During the first few days of life the urine is scanty and concentrated, tallying with the small amount of fluid taken and the large water output from the lungs. In contrast to the adult, who excretes approximately 1500 cc. daily, the baby one or two days old excretes 15 to 50 cc. The one- to three-year-old excretes 500 to 600 cc., and the three- to five-year-old 600 to 750 cc. (Watson and Lowrey, 1967). The amount excreted varies considerably, since it is influenced by many factors, such as liquid ingested, the environmental temperature and the state of the digestion or the nervous system.

In the first and second days of life the infant voids urine from two or three up to six times. After this, urination is more frequent throughout infancy, varying from four to six or even thirty to forty times in twenty-four hours. After bladder control has been established the frequency usually varies from six to eight times in twenty-four hours. Roberts and Schoelkopf (1951) found that, at $2\frac{1}{2}$ years, approximately four-fifths of the children had a two- or three-hour interval for urination in the daytime. Urination is never so regular as bowel evacuation. A child will tend to urinate more often when he drinks more fluids, when it is cold or when he is excited or under some other strong emotional tension.

URINATION.   The process of urination is an involuntary reflex act for the newborn and the young infant. Pressure of urine on the walls of the bladder sets up a reflex by which muscles of the bladder contract and those of the sphincter relax. With increasing maturation of the cerebral cortex the young child achieves sufficient neurologic development to learn the skill of controlling urination. The process as described by Muellner (1958, 1960) from fluoroscopic observations of the emptying of the bladder is a complex neuromuscular activity.

Intra-abdominal pressure is created and manipulated by the use of the large skeletal muscle groups of the diaphragm, abdomen and pelvis. Since these finely coordinated activities are complicated, it takes time for a child to learn this control. There is a period of learning when the child tries, is sometimes successful, sometimes not, but gradually improves his skill and finally can urinate at will. In the young infant and the child the bladder has to be full for urination; later, with control, urination can occur with only small amounts of urine in the bladder. The bladder increases in size, doubling in capacity between two and $4\frac{1}{2}$ years, when it is generally sufficiently large to permit the retention of urine during the night (Muellner, 1960).

Nervous Control of Elimination

There appears to be some association with the time of myelination of nerves and their ability to function efficiently, although a nerve can function without complex myelination (see p. 276). Huschka (1942) summarized information on the myelination of the spinal nerves involved in bowel control which showed that this process is not completed until some time between twelve and twenty months of age.

An infant can be conditioned at an earlier age to defecate at a certain time. Watson (1928) demonstrated this with the use of suppositories at six to eight weeks. This is not child control, however, but mother control. Aldrich and Aldrich (1954) remarked that before the beginning of the second year the mother is the one who is trained. This earlier conditioned training breaks down at least temporarily when voluntary participation in the act must appear (Prugh, 1960).

ACHIEVING CONTROL.   Voluntary control of defecation and of urination is governed by the coordinated action of the higher and lower brain centers, those located in the cortical and subcortical regions. Prior to the acquisition of control the infant has experiences which provide a background for this developmental achievement. He has become aware of the sensation of fullness or distention followed by the pleasurable sensation of relief from this fullness which accompanies defecation or urination. He has also become aware of a stool or urine as a part of his functioning. He examines it, is curious about it and receptive to the manner in which it is received by others. Associations according to his behavior and the adult's attitude of casual acceptance or repugnance toward the stool are registered.

The processes of defecation and urination are complex, but bowel control is usually achieved before bladder control, probably because the need to defecate usually occurs more regularly and less frequently than the need to urinate. Maturational readiness and learning experiences operate together to achieve control. As in eating, the mother's role can be one of anticipatory guidance, i.e., watching for clues to the child's readiness for each step (with tolerance for his speed of progress), providing appropriate facilities and creating an atmosphere that will induce in the child a wholesome attitude toward elimination. Within this basic framework the plan adopted by a mother can be governed by herself, her child and the circumstances in which they live.

Children vary in the age of readiness, their responses and the length of the period of learning. For most it begins near the end of the first year or the beginning of the second. Daytime control generally comes first, followed by naptime control and finally by control throughout the night. Night control of urination has usually been established by about $4\frac{1}{2}$ years (Muellner, 1958).

The possible *impact of toilet training on personality development* has received much attention. There are conflicting beliefs, based on theoretical contexts rather than on adequate, balanced, detailed investigation, particularly of a longitudinal nature. Ausubel (1957) offers the assumption that personality characteristics of a child are reflective not of special toilet-training practices as such, but of characteristic and pervasive parent attitudes demonstrated in toilet training. Such values as conformity, punctiliousness, orderliness, cleanliness, self-control, and the like, not only are conveyed to the child through the toilet-training practices, but also are inculcated in endless ways by the parent throughout childhood.

Caldwell (1964), after reviewing research on practices of parents in infant care, which concern elimination training, wrote:

> It appears possible to suggest a relationship between deviant training and pathology when one examines the training history of children showing some type of disorder associated with bowel or bladder function. However, more information about the incidence of similarly deviant training practices used with children showing no overt pathology is essential before such material can be put into perspective. For unselected groups of children it has been difficult to demonstrate broad personality consequences of elimination training practices, although specific reaction to training appears to vary as a function of both age of initiating training and severity of training procedures. Type of training technique used by the mother is related to her own need for order and to anxiety about sex behavior.

BOWEL CONTROL. Toward the end of the first year an infant has motor abilities which enable him voluntarily to release an object he is holding in his hand. About the same time he has motor abilities which could enable him to begin to develop voluntary control of defecation. This readiness for toilet training usually does not appear until near the end of the first year, and with many infants it is later. Sears, Maccoby and Levin (1957) suggested that either of two periods can be chosen with an expectation of reasonable comfort: the second six months of life and after twenty months. The authors offer reasons why a mother may begin toilet training early: advice from her physician, suggestions from a neighbor, traditional custom in her family, tiresomeness of washing diapers, pregnancy, strictness of her attitude toward sex. Defecation is likely after a meal, when peristalsis is more likely to produce an evacuation.

Girls tend to gain control before boys. Sears, Maccoby and Levin (1957) report that gaining of control took longer when begun earlier and came more quickly when begun later. For some children in this group, control was complete in a few weeks; others took as long as $1\frac{1}{2}$ years. Roberts and Schoelkopf (1951) reported that 92 per cent of the girls and 78 per cent of the boys at $2\frac{1}{2}$ years were taking the responsibility for going to the toilet for bowel movements. This difference between boys and girls was statistically significant. For children who resist being placed on the toilet, to discontinue all attempts for the moment and wait a while before trying again seems to be in accordance with knowledge of learning processes. It is considered unwise to start toilet training at the time of another emotional challenge.

The child's feeling toward the routine and the mother's attitude are contributing factors in determining the smoothness with which this learning is achieved. Sears, Maccoby and Levin (1957) found that a child's tolerance for training, as reported in interviews at a later age, had no simple relation to the age at which he began this training. It did, however, have some relation to the severity used in the training process. More emotional upsets were observed in children trained in a severe manner. Fifty-five per cent of the children who experienced severity in toilet training showed emotional disturbance, in contrast to 17 per cent of those whose training was not at all severe, 11 per cent under light pressure, and 26 per cent under moderate pressure. Such disturbances in response to severe training were more frequent among children whose mothers were relatively cold and undemonstrative than among children with warm mothers. The percentage of children who had emotional upsets with severe toilet training was 23 per cent when mothers were warm, 48 per cent when they were relatively cool; the percentage with mild training was 21 per cent when mothers were warm, 11 per cent when they were relatively cool. Thus the mother's personality, as well as severity of training, was related to emotional upsets in the child.

The mother who is warm, is content to let the clues which her child gives guide her, is free from concern and shows pleasure at success, but ignores or minimizes failure, can provide effective assistance to her child in establishing control of elimination.

BLADDER CONTROL. Bladder control generally follows bowel control. It must be learned, like walking. This skill develops in the following manner (Muellner, 1960): (1) the infant urinates automatically without any awareness of the act by reflex contraction of the muscles of the bladder walls when the bladder is full, and continues until the bladder is emptied; (2) he becomes aware of the need to urinate when the bladder is full as a result of the maturation of the autonomic nervous system, and later is able to communicate this need without being able to hold urine (between one and two years); (3) he is able to hold urine for a brief time, gradually increasing this ability so that at three years he generally has bladder capacity sufficient to control urination during the day; (4) he is able to start and stop urination when the bladder is full; (5) he is able to start urination at any degree of bladder fullness, a skill which may be achieved some time between $3\frac{1}{2}$ and six years. According to Muellner, a child with a small bladder capacity is a potential bedwetter.

Thus the time when a child begins to learn this control is determined by his capacity to make appreciable response rather than upon chronologic age. It implies both biological and emotional readiness. Emotional readiness seems to depend upon the child's experiences, especially his interpersonal relations. Prugh (1960) suggested that toilet training begin when the child can hold urine for one to two hours. The child can be encouraged to sit on the toilet seat every hour and a half or so for a few minutes. He can be given the opportunity to observe other children on the toilet. Judicious praise for success can be advantageous, but praise can be overdone and result in too much concentration upon a normal physiological function.

Progress may be steady or irregular. Children react to stress or strain such as illness or fatigue. A child may have diurnal variations, being competent when rested, having accidents when tired. Regressive phases may occur with new interests and adaptations. A child may become too preoccupied in his play to attend to bladder sensations. Accidents may be expected throughout the preschool years, but with decreasing frequency. Girls tend to assume responsibility for urinary control earlier than boys (Roberts and Schoelkopf, 1951).

Age at beginning toilet training has been reported as later with second or third children than with first children. In a study by Hubert and Britton (1957) 14 per cent of the mothers in a university community began training during the first year, 23 per cent around a year, 63 per cent later than a year. Only 7 per cent reported that the child was nearly trained in the second year. Mothers of only children tended to have begun toilet training earlier than one year and claimed that their children had learned a little by that time. Mothers of second or third children tended to delay training and to offer no claim that the child had learned anything in this area. Hubert and Britton state:

> These data suggest that the experience of the first child brought to the mothers a belief that success in toilet training can be achieved only when the child is older; perhaps these mothers of more than one child were also busier and unable or unwilling to devote themselves to this teaching before they knew the child was really ready. They probably were less anxious than mothers of only children. Greater satisfaction was expressed by these mothers with their training methods as compared with that of the mothers of only children.

The case history of E.R., given here, illustrates how the management of a mother contributed to attitudes toward elimination in a child who resisted toilet training for some time. The case history of N.L. illustrates how a working mother carried out a program of toilet training which began in the middle of the second year and proceeded rapidly.

> When E.R. was sitting alone with confidence at thirty-eight weeks, her mother, at the physician's suggestion, tried putting her on a nursery chair. E.R. rebelled, however, and after a few trials her mother wisely gave up the attempt at training. A second attempt several weeks later and another at thirteen months were resisted. At seventeen months she accepted the toilet for bowel evacuation, but again rebelled against the frequency with which her mother took her to the toilet for urination. Again the mother abandoned the effort except for bowel movements. By eighteen months E.R. was saying "toi-toi" long enough before a bowel movement to enable her mother to place her on the toilet seat in time for

this procedure. Although she was having two or three bowel movements a day at this time, E.R. rarely had an accident. By about twenty months she began to be aware of her wet pants and came to her mother to be changed. Within a short time she began with increasing frequency to say "toi-toi" in advance of this function also. By twenty-two months E.R. consistently asked to go to the toilet, even calling her parents during the night when she needed to go. At twenty-six months E.R. went with her family to a cottage on the water. There the many new and fascinating experiences were sometimes so absorbing that toilet needs were forgotten, and there were wet pants occasionally. When this happened, E.R. would say, "Oh! accident, I sorry." After a few weeks in the new environment, however, she was able to stop her play in time to reach the toilet to relieve the bladder pressure. Before thirty months she was entirely reliable in her ability to control this function.

With N.L. this order was reversed, possibly because his mother had no time to observe and take advantage of his natural rhythm in bowel evacuation. Forced to support herself and her son, the mother was teaching in a nursery school which N.L., although under age, was permitted to attend. By the time he was sixteen months old he showed some evidence of discomfort when wet. His mother had a week of freedom from her teaching duties and decided to take advantage of the child's possible readiness for training. The first day she put him on the toilet every hour. This was obviously unnecessary. On the second day she extended the interval to two hours with almost 100 per cent success. By the end of the week she was taking him to the toilet six or seven times during the day at convenient intervals. This was continued when mother and child returned to the nursery school. N.L. readily accepted the procedure and was usually dry during the day, but his mother assumed responsibility. By nineteen months he regularly gave advance notice of his need by pulling an adult toward the toilet. About this time, while sitting on the toilet after breakfast, he began to evacuate his bowels after he had urinated. Soon he refused to get off the toilet after urination if he felt the need to defecate. At twenty-one months he used the term "toitet" to express the need either to urinate or to defecate. At this time he usually slept through the night—eleven to twelve hours—without urinating, or, if he needed to do so, he wakened and called "toitet." In a nursery school with older boys he had opportunity to observe that they urinated while standing. Before N.L. was twenty-four months old he had adopted this posture on his own initiative. At this time his mother reported that he had had no toilet accidents during either the day or night for two months.

TOPICS FOR STUDY AND DISCUSSION

1. As a focus for study, indicate questions of interest to you concerning the child's learning in eating situations; in toilet training. Upon what knowledge could you draw in discussing these questions?
2. Observe eating behavior of a particular child on several different days. What similarities and differences in the setting did you notice? in the behavior?
3. Invite several parents to participate in a discussion of the concept of self-regulatory schedules.

SELECTED READINGS

Caldwell, B. M.: The Effects of Infant Care. Chapter in M. L. Hoffman and L. W. Hoffman (Eds.): Review of Child Development Research. New York, Russell Sage Foundation, 1964. Pp. 9-87. Practices in infant feeding, relation of oral gratification to personality and to oral activities are considered on pp. 19-41; elimination training and its relation to personality, pp. 41-55; "residual" of the review of practices in infant care, pp. 78-82.

Feeney, M. C., Dodds, M. L., and Lowenburg, M. E.: The sense of taste of preschool children and their parents. J. Am. Dietet. A., 48:399-403, 1966.

Read, K. H.: The Nursery School. 4th ed. Philadelphia, W. B. Saunders Company, 1966. Mealtime, pp. 150-158; toileting, pp. 138-150.

Sears, R. R., Maccoby, E. E., and Levin, H.: Patterns of Child Rearing. New York, Harper and Row, 1957. Chap. 3, Feeding; Chap. 4, Toilet Training.

Spock, B.: The Common Sense Book of Baby and Child Care. 2nd ed. New York, Meredith Press, 1957. (Also paperback edition.) Use index.

Stuart, H. C., and Prugh, D. G. (Eds.): The Healthy Child. Cambridge, Harvard University Press, 1960. Contributions of infant feeding experiences to personality development, pp. 220-231, 233-237, 245-247; toilet training, pp. 105-106, 110-111, 210, 246, 257-261, 270.

Watson, E. H., and Lowrey, G. H.: Growth and Development of Children. 5th ed. Chicago, Year Book Publishers, Inc., 1967. Urinary system.

CHAPTER SEVEN

Physical and Psychological Needs:
Activity and Rest; Social Contact;
Other Needs; Personality
Components

NEED FOR ACTIVITY AND REST

Activity, both physical and psychological, and rest are basic needs which have a relation to each other. A person is active, he rests, is active and rests again. Thus he has a rhythm composed of cycles of activity and quietness which is appropriate for him and is influenced by maturational changes and the physical, intellective, emotional and social environment.

The need for physical and psychological activity is fundamental to his development. The waking time of even the young infant, if he is not physically ill or psychologically handicapped, is often occupied with activity. Arms and legs wiggle and jerk in uncoordinated but frequent movement which gradually comes under control and assumes the coordinations of skilled movement. Vocalizations become an increasing part of his life and accompany many of his other activities as he begins his gradual mastery of spoken language. By the time the child is of run-about age he has times of being constantly on the move, running, climbing, poking and prying into many things in the house. His mind is also alert, so that his general bodily and manual activity and his sensory perceptions are providing his intellect with increasing knowledge of the properties of the objects around him. Throughout early childhood this tendency for physical and intellectual activity as well as for rest is persistent and urgent.

Individuality in activity is apparent from birth. Among the behavioral differences in early infancy categorized and documented by Ausubel (1957) are those concerned directly with activity: namely, (1) placidity and irritability, (2) activity level and distribution of activity, (3) tone, length and vigorousness of crying, and (4) differential sensitivity to stimulation of the various senses. Thus a child begins his life as an individual and responds in his own particular manner to his experiences with differences in degree and kind of activity.

The other phase of the cycle, rest, is necessary for well-being since it conserves energy needed for maintenance of the integrity of bodily structures and for growth. When rest is insufficient, fatigue occurs which can be manifested in a child by hyperactivity, emotional instability such as crossness, crying, overreacting to situations, loss of acquired skills and perhaps susceptibility to accidents.

Rest varies in degree from change of one type of activity to another, to quiet play which requires less energy, to relaxation of the whole body while lying in a relaxed position, to sleep wherein the functioning of the body is slowed. The amount of rest and its timing vary with age, the young infant needing more rest and shorter intervals between rest than the toddler, and the preschool child needing more than he does later in the school years. Also, individuals differ in their need for rest. Infants and young children whose environments are not overstimulating are able to rest when they need to. It becomes easier, however, as the child's abilities and experiences widen for emotional and social influences to interfere with relaxation and rest.

Rest and Sleep

SLEEP AS A PART OF A SLEEP-WAKEFULNESS CYCLE. Sleep, which is a part of this balance of activity and rest, is not a negative but rather a positive function of the body. It is not a cessation of bodily activity, but a readjustment of the whole machinery of the body, including the nervous system, which protects the welfare of the organism. The brain is not turned off during sleep, but continues to function, though at a lower level, as indicated by changes in the pattern of brain waves recorded on an electroencephalogram. Other bodily activities such as heart rate, respiration rate and basal metabolism also decrease during sleep.

Sleep is still physiologically and psychologically mysterious. The mechanism or mechanisms by which the body registers the need for sleep, goes to sleep, remains asleep and wakes up are still unknown. Much research is being done on sleep, but much of it concerns experimentation with animals. We are warned by those engaged in this research to be cautious in relating the findings of animal experiments to man, since there are many differences in their sleep characteristics.

Sleep is a part of a sleep-wakefulness cycle, which, according to Kleitman (1963), is an inborn pattern of alternation of rest and activity. It is suggested that the alternation of sleep and wakefulness is due not to two antagonistic centers of sleep and wakefulness, but to the interplay of numerous brain structures in which the reticular formation, which has been demonstrated both to induce arousal of the cortex and to maintain this state of arousal, is a part (Dell et al., 1960).

Children and adults do not sleep "like logs." They move from time to time in a cyclic manner.* They stir, may waken fully or go back to sleep for another cycle (Aserinsky and Kleitman, 1955). The phases of activity and quiet in these cycles are associated with changes in the brain waves as registered on the electroencephalogram. Movement may include much of the body or discrete parts such as a foot, a hand, the head. One discrete movement, that of the eyes with the lids closed, is associated with dreaming (Kleitman, 1960a, 1960b). Why and how this cyclic phenomenon occurs are unknown.

ORDERLY TRENDS IN SLEEP BEHAVIOR.   The maturing of sleep behavior is manifested in the shift of dominance from the sleeping phase to the wakefulness phase. The amount of sleep required decreases with age. The newborn spends two hours of sleep for each hour of wakefulness; the adult, one-half hour of sleep for each hour of wakefulness, thus spending one-third of his time, or about eight hours, asleep. These figures for the newborn agree with those of observations of mothers kept on the second, third and fourth days of life (Parmelee, 1961). These infants slept on the average 17, 16.5 and 16.3 hours, respectively, on the three days. During the first three months, according to Kleitman and Engelmann (1953), there is no change in the total amount of sleep even though a shift to less sleep during the day and more at night has begun. From three to six months (the end of the study) the continued decrease is evenly distributed between day and night.

By the time children are approaching the end of the preschool period they are sleeping, according to the averages in Despert's study (1949), 11¼ hours of the twenty-four. With the lengthening of the wakefulness phase, the cycle becomes synchronized with the periodicity of night and day and is thus transformed into a rhythm which becomes firmly established. The 24-hour sleep-wakefulness rhythm is influenced by physical variations of light and temperature accompanying the succession of night and day, and the "social time-table" of living routines, with its factors of activity, noise, and so on. It is during the second year of the child's life that a 24-hour body-temperature rhythm, in the sense of a regularly recurring variation, becomes fully established (Kleitman, 1963).

As the child matures, a series of changes occur in the pattern of sleep behavior. At first sleep is shallow, and the demarcation between sleeping and waking is not sharply defined. The child awakes because of internal proddings, especially that of hunger. Kleitman (1963) showed that this awakening of the newborn occurs from stimulation at the subcortical level. Environmental stimuli have little effect upon the newborn. There is evidence, however (Kleitman, 1963), of the beginning of enculturation even in the neonatal period by the greater incidence of longer intervals between awakenings during the night when infants are on a self-regulating schedule (Marquis, 1941) and by the somewhat

---

* Motility in sleep has been studied by observation of the subject during sleep, by kymographic recordings of movements by instruments attached to the bed, by electrical recordings of eye movement and by the electroencephalograph.

higher percentage of time spent in sleep at night than during the day-time hours (Gesell and Amatruda, 1945).

As the infant develops he wakes more smoothly and falls asleep more easily. The young infant wakes rather abruptly, often with a sharp cry. Later he wakens more smoothly; his cry is briefer and softer; and even later he wakes without crying. By about sixteen weeks his waking mechanism is functioning efficiently (Gesell and Ilg, 1943).

He is consolidating his sleep periods (Kleitman, 1957). This con-solidation continues throughout infancy and most of the preschool years. The periods decrease from four or five at three months to one by about four years. Figures 46 and 47 show how one child consolidated his sleep periods from the age of three days to four years. Both the decrease in the number of sleep periods and the shift to more sleep in the night hours, an orderly trend stated earlier, can be noted. This child still had one nap a day at four years of age. The changing 24-hour pattern of the individual can have implications for the parent who is interested in a self-regulatory schedule.

Paralleling and associated with this increase in wakefulness are the child's increasing awareness of his environment and his increasing abilities in locomotion and in manipulation of his environment. With omission of the night feeding this period of sleep is uninterrupted. Sleeping through the night occurred at 9.3 weeks in one study (Green-waldt et al., 1960) and between the twelfth and fourteenth weeks in another (Kleitman and Engelmann, 1953). With the constantly increas-ing influence of acculturation, children may establish regular daytime nap periods, at first in the morning and afternoon, and later in the after-noon only. In our society this nap tends to be abandoned before the child is five years of age.

At first going to sleep is under subcortical control; later, when the cortex begins to participate in this function, it may become more dif-ficult. In the first year going to sleep seems relatively simple; later, en-vironmental conditions may have a stronger deterring influence. In the middle of the second year the child may begin to take something to bed — some toy, wooly animal or blanket. He may use some device to help him to go to sleep. Particular routines at bedtime become expected. In a group of $2\frac{1}{2}$-year-olds (Roberts and Schoelkopf, 1951) 90 per cent of the children had definite enough routines that their mothers could describe them. About two-thirds of the routines were simple, such as asking for a drink, a kiss, a special toy or blanket. The other third of the routines were elaborate and ritualistic. Most of the children used some comfort device as part of their routine, e.g., a toy, a bottle, a special blanket. About half of the children used some form of self-comfort such as thumb-sucking, hair-twisting, ear-pulling or rocking. Young children often have a period of calling the parent back, perhaps for a drink, another kiss or a trip to the toilet. Sources of the behavior, in anxiety or in the child's exploration of expectations of the parent, are sometimes discovered through the child's ease of adaptation to various procedures.

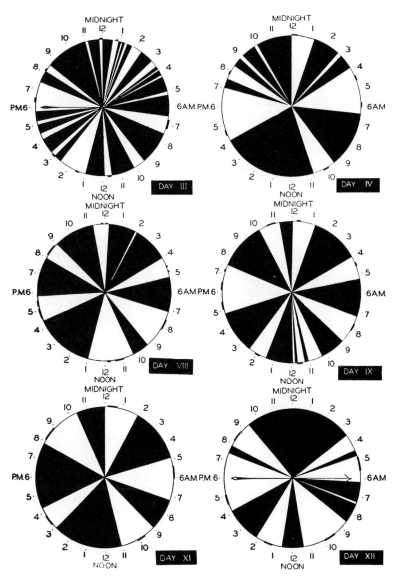

FIGURE 46. *Progressive changes in sleep-wakefulness rhythms show orderliness and individuality.*

Diurnal cycle of behavior of an infant for days 3, 4, 8, 9, 11 and 12. Sleep, awakeness and feeding shown on 24-hour clock dial. Black segments indicate sleep; white segments indicate awakeness. Feedings are shown at margin. (Reproduced from A. Gesell in collaboration with C. S. Amatruda: The Embryology of Behavior. New York, Harper & Brothers, 1945.)

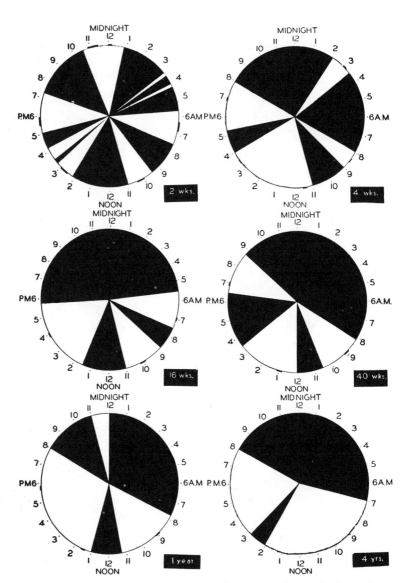

FIGURE 47. Progressive changes in sleep-wakefulness rhythms show orderliness and individuality.

Diurnal cycle of behavior of same child at 2, 4, 16 and 40 weeks, 1 year and 4 years. Sleep, awakeness and feeding shown on 24-hour clock dial. Black segments indicate sleep; white segments indicate awakeness. Feedings are shown at margin. (Reproduced from A. Gesell in collaboration with C. S. Amatruda: The Embryology of Behavior. New York, Harper & Brothers, 1945.)

The motility pattern in sleep changes with age. The cycle of active and quiet phases during sleep increases from about one hour in infancy to about $1\frac{1}{2}$ hours in adulthood, the quiet phase remaining constant and the active phase increasing (Aserinsky and Kleitman, 1955; Kleitman, 1960b). During the night less than one minute of mobility during an hour and a gradual increase in movements per hour through the night seem to be usual patterns of older children and adults. Eye movements also change. Young infants show only slow movements, not the rapid movements associated with dreaming (Dement, 1960).

INDIVIDUAL DIFFERENCES IN REST AND SLEEP. Some children apparently need more sleep than others. Some vary in amount from day to day; others are consistent (Despert, 1949). Spacing of sleep varies; some children sleep less at night and take longer naps, and some have a reverse pattern. Sleep may vary greatly in depth and integratedness among children. Conditions which tend to disturb sleep, such as changes in the digestive tract in the early months, later wetness or some other bodily discomfort, and still later changes in the environment, fear or undue excitement, may affect one child more easily than another.

No general rule about the total amount of sleep can be made, since children vary greatly in their needs and rate of development. Appearance and behavior of children suggest whether or not they are getting adequate sleep. Unusual irritability, hyperactivity, crying easily, and taking longer to go to sleep are some of the indications of the possibility of need for more sleep.

SLEEP REGIMEN. In development of sleeping behavior, as in development of eating behavior, the child can be given opportunity to learn to manage this function basic to his well-being. An infant can develop his own sleep habits if given the setting to do so. Natural fatigue from activity, the satisfaction of relieving hunger, and the contentment that comes from care can be in accordance with the natural rhythm of sleep and wakefulness. Here, as in eating, the adult can facilitate the child's acceptance of bedtime for him according to his attributes. Consistent but not rigid regularity, a definite routine in getting ready for bed and association of bed with sleep by putting the infant or young child to bed when he is sleepy can contribute to learning. Comments by pediatricians indicated that mothers were having more difficulty in establishing children's sleep habits according to need than in the self-regulation of feeding (Ross Pediatric Research Conference, 1957).

Sears, Maccoby and Levin (1957) found in interviews with mothers that putting children to bed at a certain time whether the children were sleepy or not was a common practice. Some mothers reported that their children were ready to go to sleep; others, that the children remained awake for some time, in some instances for as much as two hours each evening after the lights were out. Children were put to bed either for their own welfare or to relieve the parents from the pressures engendered by their presence and to give the parents some privacy.

Hubert and Britton (1957) interviewed mothers in a university community during the first and second years of their children's life and found that during the second year the majority (61 per cent) of the children were expected to remain in bed at bedtime. There appeared to be a relation between leniency on the mothers' part and their feelings about their children's earlier reactions to the introduction of new foods. Mothers who were pleased with their children's reaction to new foods in the first year tended to be lenient with their children at bedtime, allowing them to get up fairly often rather than stay in bed.

Many mothers in their interviews during the second year appeared to consider the naptime important to the point of being strict about it. Only a small proportion of the mothers (9 per cent) allowed their children to omit naps. Half of the mothers kept their children in bed to sleep, while 36 per cent insisted on some rest, if not sleep. Differences in attitude were noted between mothers of one child and mothers of more than one. Mothers of only children seemed contented if their children only rested or played quietly. Mothers of more than one child were stricter about their children sleeping at naptime.

The sleep of the newborn infant seems little affected by sounds in his environment. In a study of crying in a newborn nursery, Aldrich et al. (1945a) found that crying did not seem to be contagious from one baby to another in spite of the fact that hearing in newborns is acute. The vulnerability of sleep to external factors becomes evident later, and elements in the external environment may influence the child's behavior. Although, ordinarily, usual household noises do not disturb the child, he may be affected by loud, penetrating noises.

The emotional climate of the home can affect development of sleep behavior as well as eating behavior. The child who goes to bed after a happy day, secure in the affection of his parents, seems much more likely to sleep well than the child who approaches sleep with some emotional disturbance. Conflicts just before bedtime, as well as just before and during meals, and active and too stimulating play just before bedtime can complicate the process of passing from a state of wakefulness to one of sleep. Information on the influence of television on amount and quality of sleep of young children is incomplete. Attitudes which the parents and other children in the family have toward sleeping may be reflected in the young child's attitude.

Activity

Going from rest and sleep to an eager enthusiasm for the new day seems characteristic of young children. They seem delighted to try out their powers. Long periods of uninterrupted free play, as well as the many experiences in routines such as eating, dressing and toileting, provide resources for further development.

Being alive means being active. During wakefulness the heightened activities in the adjustment of the whole machinery of the body, including the nervous system, provide many stimuli. Need for rest and activity is a condition requiring supply or relief for well-being and development. The infant's eyes follow a moving light; if it is too bright, he turns away. He babbles, making a variety of sounds. He moves his finger over a smooth surface many times. When he is older, he repeatedly makes stepping movements with his feet. Later, even though he often falls, he learns to walk. An older child completes a puzzle and then does it again. He sees a picture in a book and turns back to look at it again. Responses such as these suggest *satisfactions in the child's use of his abilities.* When activities are for their own sake, for the fun of it, this is play. Approval and disapproval of others need not enter into it; furthermore, the child feels well fed and comfortable. His satisfactions are from the activity itself; he has no ulterior motives (see Fig. 48).

In summarizing evidence concerning activity of this kind in animal experiments and in studies of human beings, Hunt (1960) stressed implications of the idea of activity as intrinsic in living organisms for theories of motivation. Exploration, curiosity and stimulation are terms sometimes used when activity for its own sake is being discussed. Gewirtz (1961), discussing learning theory, says:

The highly responsive infant is in active interaction with his environment, regularly and for extensive periods, even when his organic needs are satisfied.

FIGURE 48. Activities the child seeks in play suggest new experiences to which he might be responsive.

Responsive to their child's interest in climbing steps, jumping and sliding, these parents have made equipment for her. The 2-year-old is using the climbing box and sliding board for the first time.

He would seem to behave as if he seeks stimuli which are ever more complex as he moves to each higher stage of development. . . . Reinforcers may be provided by . . . incompletely understood dimensions of environmental change, such as changes in the direction of novelty or complexity (e.g., through approaching, reaching and manipulating, behavior we sometimes call "curious" or "exploratory").

Piaget (1952) emphasized the child's seeking of opportunities to investigate his surroundings. White (1960) recommended recognition of a motive in the child concerning "production of effects upon the environment" which would take into account "activity, manipulation, and exploration." Thus we find much current interest in the child's activity as a basis for further development. Social influences on learning, motivations which came from anxieties, have had frequent investigation. At present this wanting to do something for its own sake is receiving attention.

The interactions of the infant and the child with the environment may be in the form of physical or verbal involvement, or in looking,

FIGURE 49. *The child's responsiveness in a situation may be in the form of observation.*

Some of the visitors continued to stand and watch and to ask questions, with a comparatively long span of attention. Others soon began to play ball with the children who lived on the farm.

observing or perceiving something in the external environment. Furthermore, the child's activity may be in thought, as he attends to something within himself. In Figure 49 some of the children who were visiting a farm were very quiet for a comparatively long time as they looked at the cows. They seemed active, but not in terms of motion or verbalization. Their eyes moved from time to time — to the animals' feet or head, or from one animal to the other.

Influence of setting upon the child's activity is important. Effects of new scenes, materials, people and concepts of self can be viewed from many angles. Some of the elements in the setting which enable the child to be active without undue stress have been considered in discussion of need for security. Personality components, sense of initiative and sense of accomplishment are indicated on page 244. The child's use of his emerging abilities has been considered a part of understanding loving care (p. 34). Factors such as the child's own attributes, the meagerness or enrichment of his environment, which influence development of particular abilities are discussed in Chapters Nine and Ten.

NEED FOR SOCIAL CONTACT

Conditions requiring supply or relief, e.g., needs for warmth, security, dependence and independence, nutrition, activity and rest, all involve the child's associations with other people. As these needs are provided for, and in other associations in the family and outside the family, the child can have a closeness to others and can also learn the ways of the family and culture in which he finds himself. His need for social contact concerns *ties of self and others* (see pp. 243-245). The infant or young child in his experiences with other people discovers his role and the roles of others whom he wants to be like. In this he may lay foundations early for warmth and affection for others and for appreciation of the dignity of his own life style.

Social responsiveness is evident in the infant who is old enough to smile at the sight of another person. Later, after having learned to distinguish one person from another, he shows his pleasure when someone he knows comes toward him. Wishing to be nearby or to do what his mother or father or another child is doing is a part of the social behavior of children of preschool age. They want to be sociable, not all the time, but some of the time, and to different degrees in different individuals; relatedness to others matters to them (see Chap. Eleven).

In the child's *socialization* his social responsiveness comes first, and then control by others which ultimately becomes his own inner control or conscience. It is from others in his world, usually his parents at first, and then other children and other adults, that the child learns what to do and what not to do in his family and in his culture. They provide sanctions and prohibitions concerning specific behavior (reinforcement of particular responses). Changes in the child's behavior occur not only through this *instrumental learning*, but also through *identification* and *role learning*. Parents provide direct training and are also models to imitate. In identification the desire to do what will please another, and consequently oneself, can come through attachments to others. Interest is great in attempting to discover bases for attachment in the very young infant and in the older child. Research suggests that various qualities in interactions of the child with the parent seem to influence the child's assimilation of the parent's role.

Affectional Ties

Mussen and Rutherford (1963) tested the hypothesis that the identification process is "motivated by warmth and affection toward . . . [the like-sexed] parent, whose characteristics and responses are then taken on as a 'total pattern.' " The subjects of the study were first grade children between $5\frac{1}{2}$ and $6\frac{1}{2}$ years of age. Those scoring in the upper half in a test of sex-typing of interests were assumed to have developed a higher degree of masculine or feminine role identification, while those scoring in the lower half were considered to be less identified with the role. Femininity in the girls and masculinity in the boys were considered to be products of the girls' identification with the mother and of the boys' identification with the father. To discover how they perceived their parents, each child was tested in a structured doll play situation. He was asked to complete, in play, incomplete stories about parent-child relations. Scores on the stories (the child's perception of the parents) represented the total number of stories (out of a total of nine) in which the child depicted the father or mother as nurturant or punitive. The power score combined the nurturant and punitive scores. Findings are shown in Tables 7 and 8, which indicate that masculinity or femininity of children is influenced by their perceptions of their parents, in terms of the measurements used. The findings substantiated an earlier study of boys by Mussen and Distler (1959).

As indicated in Table 7, the data "demonstrate that boys with highly masculine interests told significantly more stories involving father nurturance—i.e., scored higher on the average in Father Nurturance (FN) than boys low in masculinity." Thus the particular hypothesis being tested by the research was supported. "There was a tendency (reliable only at the 10 per cent level) . . . for the highly masculine boys to have higher mean Father Punishment (FP) doll play scores than the less masculine boys." This suggests that identification with the father can also be "based on perceptions of him as punitive, threatening, and hostile," but "the evidence . . . was much less impressive." The higher scores on Father Power of the highly masculine boys provided support for the role theory of sex-role identification, "which maintains that sex role learning depends upon the amount of the child's interaction with the identificand (the parent, in this research) and the latter's power or control over the child."

Table 8 gives the findings for girls. Data show that in Mother Nurturance (MN) the mean score of the highly feminine girls was

significantly higher than that of the girls low in femininity. . . . Highly feminine girls, compared with girls low in femininity, regarded their mothers as signif-

TABLE 7. Mean Scores of Boys High and Low in Masculinity on Family Perception (Doll Play) Variables

VARIABLE	HIGH MASCULINITY GROUP (N = 24)	LOW MASCULINITY GROUP (N = 22)	p*
Father nurturance.................	1.3	0.8	0.05
Mother nurturance.................	0.9	1.3	NS**
They nurturance..................	0.3	0.4	NS**
Total nurturance..................	2.5	2.5	NS**
Father punishment.................	2.3	1.7	<0.10
Mother punishment	1.4	1.6	NS**
They punishment..................	0.6	0.6	NS**
Total punishment..................	4.3	3.9	NS**
Father power.....................	3.6	2.5	<0.025
Mother power....................	2.3	2.9	NS**

Adapted from P. Mussen and E. Rutherford: Parent-child relations and parental personality in relation to young children's sex-role preferences. Child Development, 34:595, 1963.

*p represents probability that difference would have occurred by chance alone.
**Not significant.

TABLE 8. Mean Scores of Girls High and Low in Femininity on Family Perception (Doll Play) Variables

VARIABLE	HIGH FEMININITY GROUP (N = 29)	LOW FEMININITY GROUP (N = 28)	p*
Mother nurturance	1.5	1.1	0.05
Father nurturance	0.8	0.5	NS**
They nurturance	0.2	0.3	NS**
Total nurturance	2.6	1.9	<0.05
Mother punishment.................	2.4	2.0	NS**
Father punishment.................	1.9	1.9	NS**
They punishment..................	0.6	0.7	NS**
Total punishment..................	4.9	4.6	NS**
Mother power.....................	3.9	3.0	<0.05
Father power	2.7	2.5	NS

Adapted from P. Mussen and E. Rutherford: Parent-child relations and parental personality in relation to young children's sex-role preferences. Child Development, 34:597, 1963.

*p represents probability that difference would have occurred by chance alone.
**Not significant.

icantly more powerful (i.e., obtained higher scores in M Pow). . . . The highly feminine group's significantly higher Mother Power scores . . . are almost entirely attributable to the higher scores in only one of the components of that score, Mother Nurturance (MN). The two groups of girls did not differ significantly in the Mother Punishment (MP) variable. It may therefore be concluded that the development of a high degree of femininity is importantly influenced by the girl's perceptions of her mother as an important, warm, and gratifying person, but not by the extent to which she is perceived as punitive and threatening.

Relation of attributes of the parents to the sex-role preferences of their children was also considered in this research. For boys, "parents' personality structure and their pressures toward sex-typing [them] were not significantly influential." For girls, "the mothers of highly feminine girls were . . . significantly more self-accepting. . . . Fathers of the highly feminine girls . . . tended to be more masculine and gave their daughters significantly more encouragement to participate in feminine activities."

Imitation of Models Through Observation

Some of the changes in behavior through social contacts of the child come from associations with people other than his parents, perhaps without affectional ties, or under casual circumstances. The child sometimes imitates what he observes. For example, children who viewed a film in which they saw an adult's aggressive behavior toward a plastic doll were later more aggressive toward a similar doll than children who had not seen the film (Bandura, Ross and Ross, 1963). Children who had seen a subdued, nonaggressive model expressed significantly less aggression, in the later, somewhat frustrating test situation, than the other children. Thus we find different behavior occurring, according to the model observed in a film.

FIGURE 50. Children experiment in various roles.

These 4½-year-old girls first walked to the "grocery," then picked up the doll and looked for a particular sweater, and later wheeled the carriage to visit a friend.

FIGURE 51. *Children, in their imitative behavior, select from many models.*

Among these 4- to 5-year-old boys, one was an astronaut listening to his "technician"; another wore a cape similar to that of a television character and also a fireman's hat; a third placed blocks carefully to make a particular building he had seen under construction. Each child continued with his interest, paying little attention to the activity of the others.

The likelihood of aggressive behavior from aggressive movie scenes when similar situations arise in real life, is not easily determined. Maccoby (1964) says:

> All we may safely assume from the experiments . . . is that tendencies toward performing certain actions may be acquired (or augmented) from watching others perform them in the mass media. These tendencies will then enter as one element in the set of behavior tendencies aroused later in some relevant situation, and whether the particular item of behavior will actually occur will be a function of the strength of competing responses and the restraints acting upon the media-acquired behavior.

Thus other attributes of the child, learned as a part of his socialization, will also influence his behavior.

Imitative behavior, frequent in the child of preschool age, is sometimes "exploration" of roles. The child tries out behavior he has observed in children and adults — those with whom he has affectional ties, and others. The girls in Figure 50 were trying out or playing out behavior of adults in marketing and in dressing a baby. Each of the children in Figure 51, who were in the same nursery school group for a second year, was exploring behavior very different from that of the others. Imitation of models and objects the boys had observed seemed to be occurring as one reproduced proportions of a new building, another reflected news of astronauts, and a third was being a television character. Illustrations such as these suggest the diversity of personal attributes which enter into selection of behavior to imitate. They also suggest that the child, in his explorations of roles, discovers their effects. If a hat were snatched away by one of the girls, if a building were knocked down by one of the boys, consequences of one kind or another might occur. The following section refers to effects of negative consequences (positive ones have been considered previously).

Pleasure and Displeasure in Behavior

In the course of his activities the child finds some of his behavior encouraged and some discouraged by the people of his world. He is said to have positive or negative reinforcements, pleasure or pain, reward or punishment, connected with his actions. Positive reinforcements have been considered previously.

Negative reinforcements are not necessarily severe in the sense of harshness or punitiveness; they can let the child know that something is not sanctioned, or is not so well done as it might be, and thus discourage repetition of the particular form of behavior, without being in the vein of deliberate attempt to hurt. Mowrer (1960), considering reinforcement by reward, refers to one type which implies relief (withdrawal of threat) and another type which implies hope (presentation of a promise). For example, a child who is pulling a turtle's leg might be told that it is to be touched gently, but not pulled, or the child who is touching it lightly may be told that that is the way to do it. Each child might handle the turtle gently the next time, and thus have reward in relief from a threat of rebuke or in hope of a favorable reaction.

Attempts have been made to discover when negative reinforcement is most effective. Walters, Parke and Cane (1965) reported a test situation among kindergarten and first grade boys in which there were a number of toys. It was explained that some of the toys were for another boy. "You're not supposed to touch them. So if you touch a toy that is for the other boy, I'll tell you." Each time this occurred the experimenter verbally punished by saying, "No, that's for the other boy." When a child picked up an alternative toy, he was asked to describe it. For some of the children the negative comment was made as their hands neared the toy, but before they touched it, and the adult covered the toy and removed it from the table. For other children the verbal rebuke occurred later, after they had picked up the toy and held it for two or three seconds.

Later, as a second part of the experiment, each child was given a book to look at and left alone in a room with toys he was not to touch. Before he was left alone he saw a film in which a mother left the room after indicating to a child that he was not to play with toys on a nearby table, but was to read. In the film, after she left, the child played with the toys. Different groups of children saw different endings for the film. For some the film pictured the mother returning and handing the child models of the film toys (rewarding him). For some the film ended without the return of the mother. For others the film ended with the mother returning, taking the toy away, spanking and returning the child model of the film to his chair and book (punishing him).

Findings of the research provided support for the hypothesis that children "who observe a model punished for acts that they have been prohibited from performing will show greater resistance to deviation than children who see a model rewarded or receive no punishment for these acts. " Furthermore, with the various film endings, subjects whose own experience was that of the early rebuke showed greater resistance to deviation than those who received the rebuke after they had handled the toy of the other boy for a few seconds. The findings suggest that negative verbal comment at the beginning of a response sequence, as contrasted to after completion of the sequence, is more effective in inhibiting the sequence at another time. Subjects who saw the no-consequence ending of the film deviated as readily and as often as those who saw the child model of the film rewarded.*

Through identification with the mother, father, brothers and sisters, and others, and the learning of roles, and also through learning particular behavior to repeat or to avoid, the child's behavior changes. Sources of change may come through social contact. Ties of self and others may be such that the child becomes loving and responsible and also keeps his individuality, or he can go in other directions. Explanations of how he learns patterns of behavior and internalizes values are incomplete. This learning is discussed further in Chapters Two and Eleven. Behavior is related to basic needs and to immediate elements of the setting.

VARIETIES OF NEED

Baldwin (1955) defined need as "any psychological condition that makes the child more easily motivated by one instigation than another." He referred to moods such as temporary periods of susceptibility to irritation as "short-lived needs because they temporarily sensitize the child to one kind of instigation more than to other kinds. . . . The fact that such psychological states as moods are classified as needs makes it clear that there is no one-to-one correspondence between motives and needs." Specific likes and preferences for one activity over another are examples of needs which may be of longer duration.

Baldwin listed needs in the mature person as (1) general needs, e.g., orderliness, nurturance, cowardice, fastidiousness; (2) attitudes,

---

* For a review of research on effects of mass media, see Maccoby (1964).

e.g., liking, disliking, rivalry, envy, jealousy; (3) objectives, i.e., sensitivity to the consequences of an action. An objective may be a long-range goal, such as becoming a physician or owning a bicycle. When these are obtained, there is a maintenance need "to maintain the status quo or to ward off threats."

Variety in needs of the older person is in contrast to those of the newborn. His functioning then is primarily on a physiological plane. It is a long time before he perceives his hunger, for example, in such a way that he knows he wants food. Other needs may not be perceived, but operate by making the person more easily motivated by one situation than by another. "One of the most perplexing problems in child development is the reason for the development of the various patterns of needs and motives that govern so much of the adult's life."

COMPONENTS OF A HEALTHY PERSONALITY

Personality has been described as "the thinking, feeling, acting, human being" (Midcentury White House Conference Fact-Finding Report, 1951). The individual "varies in his behavior from time to time and from situation to situation. . . . Nevertheless, from an early age, perhaps even from birth, there is continuity in his behavior."

In the development of personality, according to Erikson (1950, 1963), certain feelings, or "senses," are components of healthy personality. These components are (1) sense of trust, (2) sense of autonomy, (3) sense of initiative, (4) sense of accomplishment, (5) sense of identity, (6) sense of intimacy, (7) parental sense, and (8) sense of integrity. A popular version is as follows: (1) sense of trust—that sure feeling: everything is O.K.; (2) autonomy—that strong feeling: I-I-I; (3) initiative—that more clean-cut feeling: my plans and ideas; (4) accomplishment—that feeling of importance: I can do; (5) identity—that new-old feeling: who am I really? (6) those later feelings—I am one with others and I care for others (United States Department of Health, Education, and Welfare, 1952). It seems that the components are more likely to be present if basic needs are met.

How a person feels in terms of these particular senses affects his personality. He struggles to secure them. They matter to him as he grows from infancy to adulthood. If he has more of a sense of trust, autonomy, and the others, then he has more of a feeling of harmony with himself and his world. Certain components are of special importance at certain stages of development. According to Erikson, healthy personality development means the solving of a central problem of a particular stage so that the child can proceed vigorously and confidently to the next stage. For example, after a sense of trust has emerged, the infant continues to need it, but another need tends to predominate (although all the others are also present), and "the struggle for the next component of the healthy personality begins," i.e., the sense of autonomy.

The following quotations from the Midcentury White House Conference Fact-Finding Report (1951) provide clarification of ideas about each component.

SENSE OF TRUST.   The component of the healthy personality that is the first to develop is the sense of trust. The crucial time for its emergence is the first year of life. . . . The sense of trust is not something that develops independent of other manifestations of growth. . . . Rather, the concept "sense of trust" is a short-cut expression intended to convey the characteristic flavor of all the child's satisfying experiences at this early age. . . .

. . . A sense of trust cannot develop until the infant is old enough to be aware of objects and persons and to have some feeling that he is a separate individual. At about three months of age a baby is likely to smile if somebody comes close and talks to him. This shows that he is aware of the approach of the other person, that pleasurable sensations are aroused. If, however, the person moves too quickly or speaks too sharply the baby may look apprehensive or cry. He will not "trust" the unusual situation but will have a feeling of uneasiness, of mistrust, instead.

Experiences connected with feeding are a prime source for the development of trust. At around four months of age a hungry baby will grow quiet and show signs of pleasure at the sound of an approaching footstep, anticipating (trusting) that he will be held and fed. This repeated experience of being hungry, seeing food, receiving food and feeling relieved and comforted assures the baby that the world is a dependable place.

Later experiences, starting at around five months of age, add another dimension to the sense of trust. Through endless repetitions of attempts to grasp for and hold objects, the baby is finally successful in controlling and adapting his movements in such a way as to reach his goal. Through these and other feats of muscular coordination the baby is gradually able to trust his own body to do his bidding.

SENSE OF AUTONOMY.   The sense of trust once firmly established, the struggle for the next component of the healthy personality begins. The child is now 12 to 15 months old. Much of his energy for the next two years will center around asserting that he is a human being with a mind and will of his own. . . .

What is at stake throughout the struggle of these years is the child's sense of autonomy, the sense that he is an independent human being and yet . . . able to use the help and guidance of others in important matters. This stage of development becomes decisive for the ratio between love and hate, between cooperation and wilfulness, for freedom of self-expression and its renunciation in the make-up of the individual. The favorable outcome is self-control without loss of self-esteem. The unfavorable outcome is doubt and shame.

Before the sense of autonomy can develop, the sense of trust must be reasonably well established and must continue to pervade the child's feeling about himself and his world. Only so dare he respond with confidence to his new-felt desire to assert himself boldly, to appropriate demandingly, and to hurl away without let or hindrance.

. . . There is a psychological basis for this characteristic behavior. This is the period of muscle-system maturation and the consequent ability (and doubly felt inability) to coordinate a number of highly conflicting action patterns, such as those of holding on and letting go, walking, talking, and manipulating objects in ever more complicated ways. With these abilities come pressing needs to use them: to handle, to explore, to seize and to drop, to withhold and to expel. And, with all, there is the dominant will, the insistent "Me do" that defies help and is so easily frustrated by the inabilities of the hands and feet.

For a child to develop this sense of self-reliance and adequacy . . . it is necessary that he experience over and over again that he is a person . . . permitted to make his own choices. He has to have the right to choose, for example, whether to sit or whether to stand, whether to approach a visitor or to lean against his mother's knee, whether to accept offered food or whether to reject it, whether to use the toilet or to wet his pants. At the same time he must learn some of the boundaries of self-determination. He inevitably finds that there are walls he cannot climb, . . . objects out of reach, that, above all, there are innumerable commands enforced by powerful adults. His experience is much too small to enable him to know what he can and cannot do with respect to the physical environment, and it will take him years to discover the boundaries that mark off what is approved, what is tolerated, and what is forbidden by his elders whom he finds so hard to understand.

As problems of this period, some psychologists have concentrated particularly on bladder and bowel control. Emphasis is put upon the need for care in both timing and mode of training in the performance of these functions. If parental control is too rigid or if training is started too early, the child is robbed of his opportunity to develop, by his own free choice, gradual control of the contradictory impulses of retention and elimination.

SENSE OF INITIATIVE.   Having become sure, for the time being, that he is a person in his own right and having enjoyed that feeling for a year or so, the child of four or five wants to find out what kind of person he can be. To be any particular kind of person, he sees clearly, involves being able to do particular kinds of things. So he observes with keen attention what . . . interesting adults do . . . tries to imitate their behavior, and yearns for a share in their activities.

This is the period of enterprise and imagination, an ebullient, creative period when phantasy substitutes for literal execution of desires and the meagerest equipment provides material for high imaginings. It is a period of intrusive, vigorous learning . . . that leads away from the child's own limitations into future possibilities. There is intrusion into other people's bodies by physical attack, into other people's ears and mind by loud and aggressive talking. There is intrusion into space by vigorous locomotion and intrusion into the unknown by consuming curiosity.

By this age, too, conscience has developed. The child is no longer guided only by outsiders; there is . . . within him a voice that comments on his deeds, and warns and threatens. Close attention to the remarks of any child of this age will confirm this statement. Less obvious, however, are experts' observations that children now begin to feel guilty for mere thoughts, for deeds . . . imagined but never executed. This, they say, is the explanation for the characteristic nightmares of this age period and for the overreaction to slight punishment.

The problem to be worked out . . . is how to will without too great sense of guilt. The fortunate outcome of the struggle is a sense of initiative. Failure to win through to that outcome leaves the personality overburdened, and possibly overrestricted, by guilt.

SENSE OF ACCOMPLISHMENT.   The three stages so far described probably are the most important for personality development. . . . The fourth stage, which begins somewhere around six years of age and extends over five or six years, has as its achievement . . . the sense of industry. Perhaps "sense of accomplishment" would make the meaning clearer. . . . This is the period in which preoccupation with phantasy subsides, and the child wants to be engaged in real tasks that he can carry through to completion.

SENSE OF IDENTITY.   With the onset of adolescence another period of personality development begins. . . . The central problem . . . is the establishment of a sense of identity. The identity the adolescent seeks to clarify is who he is, what his role in society is to be.

SENSE OF INTIMACY.   After the sense of identity . . . is achieved it becomes possible for the next component of the healthy personality to develop. This is the sense of intimacy . . . with persons of the same sex or the opposite sex or with one's self. The youth who is not fairly sure of his identity shies away from interpersonal relations and is afraid of close communion with himself. The surer he becomes of himself, the more he seeks intimacy, in the form of friendship, love and inspiration.

THE PARENTAL SENSE. "Parental sense" designates somewhat the same capacity as that implied in the words, creativity or productivity. The individual has normally come to adulthood before this sense can develop fully. The parental sense is indicated most clearly by interest in producing and caring for children of one's own. It may also be exhibited in relation to other people's children or by a parental kind of responsibility toward the products of creative activity of other sorts.

SENSE OF INTEGRITY. The final component of the healthy personality is the sense of integrity. . . . The individual . . . "becomes able to accept his individual life cycle and the people who have become significant to it as meaningful within the segment of history in which he lives.

"Integrity thus means a new and different love of one's parents, free of the wish that they should have been different, and an acceptance of the fact that one's life is one's own responsibility. It is a sense of comradeship with men and women of distant times and of different pursuits, who have created orders and objects and sayings conveying human dignity and love. Although aware of the relativity of all the various life styles that have given meaning to human striving, the possessor of integrity is ready to defend the dignity of his own life style against all physical and economic threats. For he knows that, for him, all human dignity stands or falls with the one style of integrity of which he partakes."

A close look at the child's use of large and small muscles, his sensory perceptions, language, cognition, and creativity, his emotions, his awareness of himself, of people, and of the cosmos can shift to a more encompassing look in which their relation to components of a healthy personality is considered. Photographs in this book, indicating behavior of children and situations in which they grow and develop, suggest a number of possibilities for thought on what a situation includes which seems related to personality components.

What, deep within the human being, makes feelings such as those of the personality components matter (whatever they are called) defies complete understanding and certainly complete description. If one meditates about it, he gropes for a *connection between emerging abilities of different stages of development and energies which lead to satisfying action.* The baby, the older child and the adult have needs and seek to satisfy them. To try to answer why has been the concern of philosophers for a great many years. Religions deal with the question. Scientists also have attempted to inquire into it.

TOPICS FOR STUDY AND DISCUSSION

1. As a focus for study, provide support for the following ideas: The child seeks activity and rest. The child's learning in associations with other people is influenced by immediate events, affectional ties, and models. Behavior of the child suggests that particular personality components matter to him.
2. List forms of activity and rest sought by an infant, a two-year-old and a four-year-old,

during similar periods of time. Attempt to classify the information to indicate the child's own decisions or explorations and social influences.
3. Provide observational detail on social experiences of a young child during routines and during free play. How did the adult seem to influence the child's behavior?
4. Indicate distinctions among personality components through illustrations from observation.

SELECTED READINGS

Bandura, A.: The role of imitation in personality development. Journal of Nursery Education, 18:207-215, 1963. Also in W. W. Hartup and N. L. Smothergill (Eds.): The Young Child—Reviews of Research. Washington, D.C., National Association for the Education of Young Children, 1967.

Erikson, E., in an interview with Kathryn Close: Youth and the Life Cycle. Washington, D.C., Golden Anniversary White House Conference on Children and Youth, Inc. Reference Papers on Children and Youth, 1960, pp. 19-26.

Gesell, A., in collaboration with C. S. Amatruda: The Embryology of Behavior. New York, Harper & Brothers, 1945. Chap. 12, The Diurnal Cycle of Sleep and Wakefulness.

Hunt, J. McV.: Experience and the development of motivation: some re-interpretations. Child Development, 31:489-504, 1960.

Mussen, P., and Rutherford, E.: Parent-child relations and parental personality in relation to young children's sex-role preferences. Child Development, 34:589-607, 1963. Also in J. Rosenblith and W. Allinsmith (Eds.): The Causes of Behavior. II. Readings in Child Development and Educational Psychology. Boston, Allyn & Bacon, Inc., 1966.

Sears, R. R., Maccoby, E., and Levin, H.: Patterns of Child Rearing. New York, Harper and Row, 1957. Chap. 8, Bedtime Restrictions.

CHAPTER EIGHT

The Child's Equipment for Growth and Development

PHYSICAL DEVELOPMENT: EQUIPMENT FOR MOVEMENT

All parts of the body are involved with body movement: the digestive tract provides the necessary nutriment; the circulatory system transports it; the respiratory system provides oxygen and removes carbon dioxide; the waste materials are eliminated through the bowel and kidneys; the nervous system is an integrating force; the endocrines regulate various body activities; and, finally, through the skeletal and muscular systems movement takes place. This chapter will contain discussions of growth of the body, the skeletal, nervous and muscular systems, and the endocrines.

EXTERNAL DIMENSIONS AND WEIGHT

Height

Height, or stature, is measured as recumbent length (from the top of the head to the soles of the feet, lying on the back in a horizontal position) until the child is able to stand easily and assume the standard position for measuring height (Krogman, 1950b), generally between two and three years (Falkner, 1962). After that age it is generally measured as standing height.

At birth a baby is generally 19 to 21 inches long. Boys tend to be slightly longer than girls, and the first-born tends to be a little shorter than later babies in the family (Meredith, 1950). Babies of obese mothers tend to be larger than those of mothers of standard weight (Wiehl and Tompkins, 1954). According to norms of Stuart (Vaughan, 1964), 80 per cent of newborn boys range from 18.9 to 21 inches; girls, from 18.8 to 20.4 inches. These norms are based on measurements of a group of healthy white children of north European ancestry living in or near

Boston, for the most part of lower economic status, but all under regular health supervision. It is to be remembered that a norm is a statistical concept and not one of normality. Length at birth, however, gives little clue to ultimate height in adulthood. Tanner et al. (1956) found a correlation between height at birth and in adulthood of 0.25 for boys and 0.29 for girls.

Growth in length is characterized by a rapid but decelerating rate from birth to two years and by a slowly decelerating rate for the preschool years. By three months a baby will generally have gained 20 per cent of his birth length; by one year, 50 per cent; by two years, 75 per cent. By about four years he will generally have doubled his birth length. The slowing down of growth in length in the preschool years is dramatically indicated by the fact that a baby in the first year of life gains about $1\frac{1}{4}$ inches more than he will gain between the ages of two and five years according to Stuart norms.

With this early rapid growth it is not surprising to note that a large percentage of adult height is achieved in the first few years. At two years, according to the Harvard Longitudinal Study cited by Bayley (1962), the mean percentage of mature height for boys was 50 and for girls 53; at five years the percentages were 62 and 67, respectively. Thus girls progress toward mature height faster than boys. Figure 52, show-

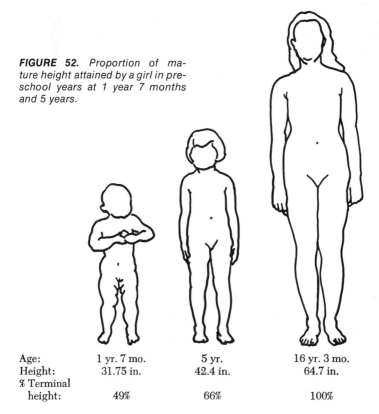

FIGURE 52. *Proportion of mature height attained by a girl in preschool years at 1 year 7 months and 5 years.*

Age:	1 yr. 7 mo.	5 yr.	16 yr. 3 mo.
Height:	31.75 in.	42.4 in.	64.7 in.
% Terminal height:	49%	66%	100%

ing a girl at one year seven months, at five years and at sixteen years three months, illustrates the proportion of mature height attained during the early years. This girl at one year seven months had attained 49 per cent of her mature height, and at five years, 66 per cent.

Children vary considerably in stature. This has been true in all studies of growth. Sex differences have been mentioned above. The early superiority of boys becomes negligible for four- and five-year-olds (Falkner, 1962; Simmons, 1944; Reed and Stuart, 1959). Within the same age and sex children can be expected to show considerable variability. Figure 53, showing two healthy girls of the same age, but of different size and physique, illustrates individual differences in stature. According to Stuart's norms, 80 per cent of two-year-old boys will measure between 33.1 and 35.9 inches; 80 per cent of five-year-old boys, between 40.8 and 45.2 inches. Similar differences can be expected of girls. Children of widely differing backgrounds will show even greater variability.

The pattern of growth in stature for individual children is somewhat stable, as indicated by the Berkeley Growth Study (1954). During the first year the children's stature correlated close to 0.5 and 0.6 with their stature as adults. This correlation increased to 0.83 and 0.85 for boys and girls, respectively, at three years of age, and to 0.86 and 0.84, respectively, at five years of age. Tanner et al. (1956), in correlating

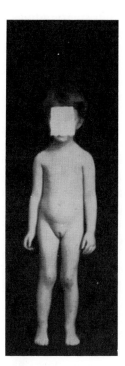 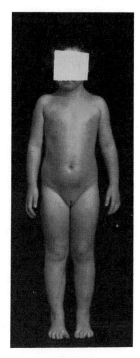

FIGURE 53. *Two healthy girls of the same age, but differing 17½ pounds in weight and 5¼ inches in height.*

Age:	42 months	42 months
Weight:	28.25 lbs.	45.75 lbs.
Height:	38 in.	43.25 in.

early stature with adult stature, also found the correlation at two years to be 0.79 and 0.74 for boys and girls, respectively, and at five years to be 0.77 and 0.81, respectively.

Nevertheless the pattern of growth in stature may vary both in terms of size and pattern of change (Reed and Stuart, 1959) from child to child. Some may be fast-growers from the start; others, slow-growers. Yet others may change their tempo, perhaps by beginning slowly during the first few years and increasing the tempo later. Children in the early years may not resemble their parents in height, but become like them as they grow older. Bayley (1954) found that most children tend to become more like their parents in stature as they grow older. Correlations between the adult stature of the parents and that of the children increased and became significant before they had passed beyond the preschool years.

These studies indicate not only that there are differences in growth patterns, but also that a genetic factor is involved in determining the stature of an individual. In an English study (Hewitt, 1957) the correlation of parent-child height was 0.353. Stern (1960) demonstrated the genetic factor by showing the greater similarity of height and weight of identical twins than of nonidentical twins and siblings.

This family line heredity, which includes race (Garn et al., 1951; Meredith, 1948), is one of the variables that contribute to differences in stature. Environment, which can be said to encompass diet, health, living standards, family surroundings, an atmosphere of contentment or tensions, is also a factor. Behavior delay, as well as delayed maturation and inadequate attainment of size, may be a consequence of protein-calorie malnutrition (Garn, 1966). Young children in a superior environment are generally taller than children of comparable age who live in less favorable circumstances (Meredith, 1951b; Tanner, 1958). Racial differences can be noted by comparison of stature of white children in the United States with Japanese children. Japanese children are shorter than American white children (Krogman, 1950b). These differences cannot be attributed solely to race, however. A strong environmental component is present, as was demonstrated by studies in which comparisons were made of children of the same race living under varying circumstances. Japanese children born and reared in America were found to be taller than those born and reared in Japan (Greulich, 1957). Differences between Negro and white children in the United States can be attributed to a large degree to environment. When American Negro children have been compared with white children of all socioeconomic levels, they have been similar in height (Meredith, 1948). In a study (Scott et al., 1950) of the growth in height and weight of Negro infants from families in the lower middle class, the growth curves of Negro and white infants from comparable economic levels were similar. Growth in length is, therefore, dependent on the interaction of a child's heredity and environment. Heredity sets the potential for growth in height; health and environment determine the degree to which that potential is achieved.

On the subject of developmental genetics of man, E. E. Hunt (1966) writes:

Genetics is the study of the continuity and transmission of life over more than one generation. This continuity can be seen in a series of individual lives, and each life history is a unique combination of a genetic blueprint realized in a unique environment. Even if two individuals differed by only a single gene, that very small difference in their heredity would create distinctive environments for each; indeed, "environment" should be construed so broadly that the genetic background of an individual would represent part of the "environment" for each of his genes. In . . . man, environment includes the circumstances of both prenatal and postnatal existence external to the genes.

Knowledge of how heredity influences the succession of events in normal human physical development is incomplete. One theory suggests that a "time-tally" operation occurs, in a central mechanism, as maturation proceeds, and that actual size of the organism is monitored by means of "an inhibitor substance produced proportionately to the increase of material in body cells" (Tanner, 1963). It is suggested that such a theory or "model" would account for the ability of individuals to "catch up" or have compensatory growth after periods of hormonal or nutritional disturbance (Falkner, 1966; Tanner, 1963). There seems to be agreement (Garn, 1966) that

. . . there is no consistent explanation for variations in size in adulthood, nor . . . a satisfactory explanation for the mechanisms responsible for size variations in childhood. Granting that superior nutrition results in greater growth, the *mechanisms* by which this occurs are not known. Granting the genetic nature of stature, the mechanisms by which the genes make for variations in the length of the body and the size of its individual components are still not known.

Behavioral correlates are being investigated in study of body size. Larger size (lean body mass) and competence in intelligence tests, in school, in social relations, have been found to have slight correlations. Large body size may give the child an initial advantage which he may capitalize upon. Garn (1966) continues: "Typed as a strong man, or leader, the large child may incorporate such successes into the system of devices he utilizes to deal with the world. Nevertheless, there is reason to believe that some of the size-behavior correlates are in fact developmental . . . representing a faster rate of behavioral development in those children who are ahead physically." The explanation is not the simple one, however, that advancement in physical development is associated with advancement in intellectual development.

Variations in Body Growth

A newborn baby obviously differs in body proportion from an adult (see Fig. 26, p. 101). At birth the head comprises one-fourth of the total body length, whereas in an adult the head is about one-eighth of total length. The proportion of legs to total length changes from approximately one-third at birth to one-half at adulthood. The differences in the rate of growth of the different segments of the body during the developmental period are illustrated in Figure 54, which shows that

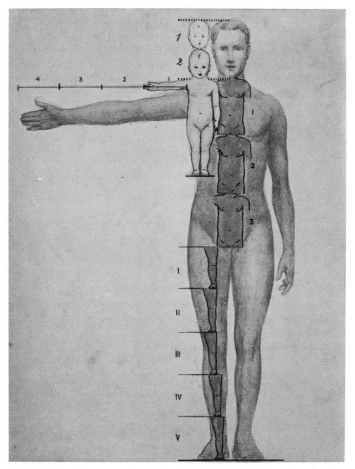

FIGURE 54. *The proportions of a child are different from those of an adult. During the growth period the head doubles in size, the trunk triples its original size, while the arm grows 4 times as long and the leg 5 times as long. (F. Kahn: Man in Structure and Function, Vol. I. Alfred A. Knopf, 1943.)*

during the growing years the head nearly doubles itself, the trunk triples itself, the arms increase about four times in size, and the legs about five times.

During infancy and early childhood relative differences in linear growth are evident. During the first year stem length (measurement from the top of the head to the buttocks when the child is lying in a recumbent position) and total length are increasing at approximately the same rate (Bayley and Davis, 1935). After the first year legs begin to grow more rapidly than the combined head and trunk. By two years the legs are about 34 per cent of total length, and by five years about 44 per cent (from data by Meredith and Knott). By two years a child's legs have doubled their length; by five years they have almost tripled it. In

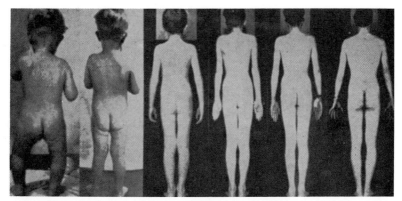

FIGURE 55. *Changes in body proportions with growth shown in photographs of the same boy at 6 ages: 15 months, 30 months, and 6, 11, 14 and 18 years. All are adjusted to the same height. (N. Bayley: Individual patterns of development. Child Development, 27:45-74, 1956.)*

the first two years there is a more rapid increase than between two and five years (Meredith and Knott, 1938).

Stem length is less than doubled by five years of age. About half of the increase during infancy and preschool years occurs before eighteen months (Meredith and Knott, 1938). Thus growth in both stem length and leg length indicates a rapid but decelerating rate in these early years, as was indicated earlier for total length. These changes are illustrated in Figure 55.

Maresh (1959), from longitudinal data, studied the patterns of relative lengths of the bones of the arm and leg (length of bone/height × 100) by means of percentile curves. The majority of the children showed some shift in percentile levels during their growth years. In general, infancy and adolescence were the periods for shifts. From four years to adolescence the percentile positions were usually stable with only minor deviations; the changes were rarely extreme. A short-legged infant did not change to a long-legged adolescent. Also, it was uncommon for the proportions of one child to include very long and very short bone lengths; a spread of three of the five zones was common. Segmental proportions in siblings were more often alike than those in nonsiblings.

Body Weight

The weight of the newborn in the United States varies considerably, but is generally somewhere between $5\frac{1}{2}$ and $9\frac{1}{2}$ pounds. Boys are generally a little heavier than girls. Babies of obese mothers tend to be heavier than those of mothers of standard weight (Wiehl and Tompkins, 1954). The first-born is a little lighter than later babies in the family (Meredith, 1950). According to the norms of Stuart (Vaughan, 1964), 80 per cent of the newborn boys range from 6.3 to 9.1 pounds; girls range from 6.2 to 8.6 pounds.

In the first three or four days, infants generally lose weight. This loss may amount to as much as 10 per cent and is greater among heavy babies than among smaller ones (Stuart in Vaughan, 1964). It represents chiefly the loss of body fluid, which can be attributed to the transition to extrauterine life and attendant adjustments in water metabolism.

Growth in weight during early life is characterized by a rapid but decelerating rate for the first two years, slow deceleration in rate from two to three years, followed by a gradual acceleration for the remainder of the preschool period (Simmons, 1944). When the median of the group studied is considered, an infant tends to double his birth weight by between three and four months and to triple it by age one year; he tends to quadruple it by the end of $2\frac{1}{2}$ years (Vaughan, 1964). The gain in weight from two to five is less than the amount gained in the first year of life.

By two years of age a child is approximately one-fifth as heavy as he will be at eighteen; by five years he has achieved approximately one-third of his weight at eighteen (calculated from median weights of Stuart [Vaughan, 1964]). Girls are slightly advanced over boys in their progress toward mature weight.

There is a wide variability in weight among small children of the same age. Children who are heavier at birth tend to remain heavier throughout infancy and early childhood (Anderson,1953; Illingworth, 1949). Tanner et al. (1956) reported correlations between adult weight and birth weight of 0.38 for boys and 0.42 for girls. At two years the correlation with adult weight was 0.51 and 0.43 for boys and girls, respectively, and at five years, 0.59 and 0.46, respectively. Herdan (1954) reported that about 25 per cent of the variability in children at three years of age can be attributed to birth weight. Boys tend to be heavier than girls, and also there are some differences at the same age for the same sex. According to Stuart (Vaughan, 1964), 80 per cent of boys at two years weigh between 24.7 and 31.9 pounds; at five years 80 per cent weigh between 35.5 and 46.7 pounds. These wide differences are also true of girls. Figure 53 illustrates differences in the weights of healthy children of the same chronologic age.

Factors contributing to differences in weight are family-line heredity, which includes race, emotions and environment.

The resemblance in the early years between parents and children is less for weight than for height. Bayley (1954) found correlations between parent and son to be rather low, but with a tendency to increase with age. The father-daughter correlations indicated some relation by five years, but never reached statistical significance. The mother-daughter correlations showed strongly increasing similarities which were significant by six years of age.

Environmental factors, especially those related directly to nutrition, have a particularly strong influence on weight, as indicated by studies of height and weight of children in time of war. A summary (Keys et al., 1950) of studies provides evidence that during wartime, with its food restrictions, weight and, to a lesser degree, height are affected, the extent of the growth deficit being related to the severity of malnutrition. Nevertheless evidence from World War I and the rehabilitation of Dutch children liberated from Java and sent to Australia in World War II (DeHaas and Posthuma, 1946) indicates that children can recover from periods of deprivation, if not too prolonged, and catch up in growth in weight and height. But children who grow up under substandard living conditions, with inadequate food, will not have the opportunity of rehabilitation and will, therefore, be unable to achieve their potential for growth.

In addition to differences in weight between children, fluctuations in growth in weight occur from time to time in an individual. The curve of growth in weight is not so smooth as that for growth in height. The instability of the pattern of growth in weight has been indicated in the Berkeley study (Bayley, 1954), in which correlations with adult weight were found to be 0.44 for boys and 0.59 for girls at three years and 0.44 and 0.68, respectively, at five years of age. This is to be expected, since weight, which represents body bulk, including muscle, bone, the various organs, fat and water, is fairly easily affected by environment and the health vicissitudes of a child.

Assessment of Length and Weight

The value of learning about growth in length and weight is, for some, its use in understanding the growth of an individual child. The adequacy of growth is determined by assessing both the child's status and his progress. Status is determined by comparing his growth with that of other children; progress is determined by comparing the child with himself from time to time through serial measurements. Population norms or standards provide the means for evaluating status.

The effectiveness of the use of these standards depends to a large degree on the selection of the particular standard and the interpretation made of the comparison. Different standards represent different groups of children, i.e., children of varying hereditary and environmental backgrounds. The standard chosen should be one compiled from a group of children with backgrounds and living circumstances similar to those of the child being studied. Because of the sex differences in growth, standards for boys and girls are separate. A satisfactory standard, in addition, includes not only an average, but also a range, thereby indicating a zone of normality. This zone of normality is sometimes expressed in terms of an average and standard deviation and sometimes in terms of percentile rank.

When averages and standard deviations are used for evaluation of height, approximately 68 per cent of the children measured may normally be expected to fall between plus and minus one standard deviation; approximately 95 per cent will fall between plus and minus two standard deviations.

In a standard based on percentiles, measurements are ranked according to magnitude from the smallest to the largest as they would be found in any typical series of 100 children. The middle point, or median, is represented by the fiftieth percentile. Half of the children may normally be expected to fall between the twenty-fifth and seventy-fifth percentiles, which are equidistant from the median. Eighty per cent of the children may be expected to fall between the tenth and ninetieth percentiles.

Standards are used most effectively when progress and status of a child can be observed concurrently. This can be done when standards are presented as curves which give the pattern of growth of a large group of children over a period of time. Such, for example, are the Iowa curves (Jackson and Kelly, 1945), consisting of three curves, one representing the average and the other two representing plus one and minus one standard deviation for height and percentiles for weight; the Bayley curves (Bayley, 1956a), consisting of curves representing heights and weights of children of accelerated, average and retarded physical maturity based on skeletal assessment and percentage of attained adult stature; and the percentile curves from the Division of Maternal and Child Health in the Harvard School of Public Health (Stuart in Vaughan, 1964). In all cases these curves are drawn on coordinate paper so that actual height or weight can be plotted against chronologic age. When a child's series of measurements are plotted, a comparison can be made between the individual curve and the group curve. See Figure 57.

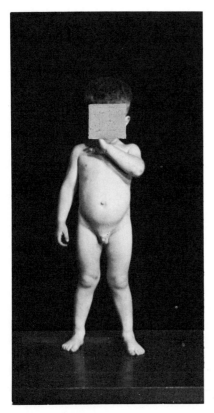

FIGURE 56. *Repeated measurements of the same child at intervals of time (as reported in Fig. 57) provide information on increments in comparable periods of time as well as total height and weight.*

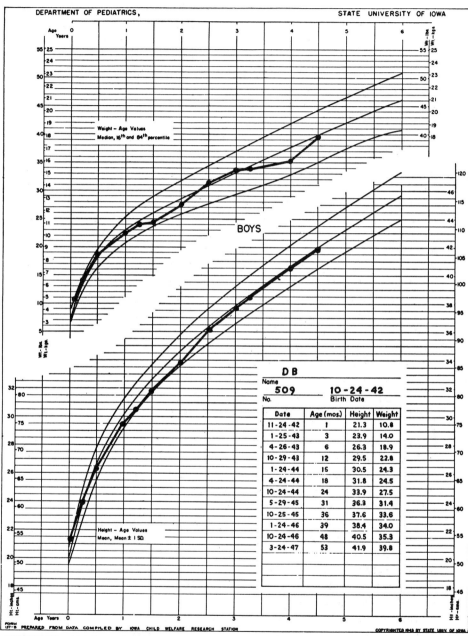

FIGURE 57. *Height and weight of a boy, DB, from 1 month to 5 years of age plotted on Iowa curves.*

Another device for evaluating height and weight is the grid graph formulated and developed by Wetzel (Krogman, 1950b; Wetzel, 1941, 1943, 1944, 1946). There are two grid graphs, the Wetzel Grid and the Baby Grid. The principles of the grid apply throughout the span of human development, from an embryonic weight of 1 gm. to maturity.

The Baby Grid is discussed here because it covers a larger portion of the age span discussed in this text than does the Wetzel Grid. The Baby Grid has two parts to the channel system. One group of channels represents the "sidetracks of infancy," since infants are naturally more chubby than older children. The other group contains the channels of the "main line" of human development into which children return by about school age. The shift from the "side tracks" to the "main line" is indicated in the Baby Grid by the gradual bearing right of the course which infants take in the channel system. This grid is a height-weight gauge of individual progress and status. The channel system on which height is plotted against weight, represents gradations of build from slender on the right to stocky on the left. These channels are crossed at intervals of 10 units by horizontal "developmental level lines" which are, in effect, increment units in terms of size in body surface, which can then be plotted according to age. Another recording system plots these developmental levels against chronologic age with a series of curves (auxodromes) indicating the speed of development for advanced, average and premature infants. Healthy development travels channel-wise and parallels one of the auxodromes.

With the provision of this series of preferential paths for individual children, both in the channels and along the auxodromes, it is possible to evaluate a child's progress in the light of his unique pattern of growth, whether he is stocky or linear in physique and whether the growth rate is slow or fast. A shift in channels or lag in schedule indicates a need to examine the child and his environment in order to determine whether something is preventing the progress which is typical for him. Further study is needed to ascertain what degree of constancy in channel position can be expected of infants and young children, and how wide a deviation from a channel can be tolerated. Studies of the Wetzel Grid (Garn, 1952; Krogman, 1956) indicate that some degree of change in channel may be expected for many children of school age.

Height and weight measurements of the boy shown in Figure 56 are indicated for his first five years in Figure 57. His measurements were plotted on the Iowa curves for height and weight. These curves extend to six years of age. On the Baby Grid the boy reached the limits of the grid at $2\frac{1}{2}$ years. Both methods of assessment indicate that he began as a fairly stocky infant, but changed to a boy of medium build. This was shown in the Grid from a shift to the right into the middle channels, and in the Iowa curves by a comparison of the position of the height and weight curves in relation to the middle curve (mean values for height and median values for weight). He lost status in height during the first and second years, but grew steadily in the following years. In weight he also lost status during the first two years, and again at four.

The speed of development as indicated on the auxodrome panel of the grid indicated a somewhat advanced schedule.

Information on size of a child's parents adds another parameter to age-size standards for children. In Table 9 the columns for boys and for girls are according to midparent values (the average of paternal and maternal statures at the age of thirty years). Thus it is possible to select from these columns parent-specific size standards. For example, if the average of the heights of the mother and the father of a four-year-old boy is short (163 cm.) at age thirty, the average height with reference to which his measurement will be viewed is 99.5 cm. If the average of his parents' heights is closer to the midpoint (169 cm.), the average height would be 102.1 cm. If the parental heights are tall (175 cm.), the average would be 106.3 cm. Garn (1966) says, "There is a large proportion of children, the progeny of tall parents and the progeny

TABLE 9.   Parent-specific Age-Size Tables for Boys and Girls
of Three Selected Midparent Values

	BOYS *Parental Midpoint*				GIRLS *Parental Midpoint*		
Age	*163 cm**	*169 cm*	*175 cm*	*Age*	*163 cm*	*169 cm*	*175 cm*
1–0	73.1	75.1	77.1	1–0	73.0	74.0	74.6
2–0	85.4	87.4	88.9	3–0	84.0	85.5	88.2
3–0	93.2	96.0	98.3	3–0	90.4	93.8	96.5
4–0	99.5	103.1	106.3	4–0	96.8	103.9	103.8
5–0	105.6	110.0	112.7	5–0	103.5	109.1	111.0
6–0	110.9	115.4	118.7	6–0	110.2	115.0	117.3
7–0	116.2	121.3	124.6	7–0	116.5	120.2	124.0
8–0	121.6	126.8	130.4	8–0	122.4	125.8	130.2
9–0	126.9	131.9	136.0	9–0	128.6	131.4	136.6
10–0	132.5	137.4	141.5	10–0	135.1	136.9	143.1
11–0	138.5	143.0	146.8	11–0	141.6	143.4	149.6
12–0	144.7	148.4	152.4	12–0	147.8	150.3	155.8
13–0	151.0	154.9	159.6	13–0	154.2	157.0	161.7
14–0	158.8	161.6	167.8	14–0	158.8	160.4	165.9
15–0	165.8	167.9	174.7	15–0	159.8	162.2	168.4
16–0	169.4	172.8	176.6	16–0	160.5	163.4	169.7
17–0	170.9	175.4	177.8	17–0	160.8	164.0	170.9
18–0	171.5	176.2	178.6	18–0	161.0	164.3	171.8

S. M. Garn: Body Size and Its Implications; in L. W. Hoffman and M. L. Hoffman (Eds.): Review of Child Development Research, Vol. Two. New York, Russell Sage Foundation, 1966.

The values shown are based on fully longitudinal analyses of the statural growth of more than 500 children representing in excess of 12,000 observations in all. The mid-parent value, here the average of paternal and maternal statures, refers to parental size at age thirty. To use, determine the midparent stature and present age of the child in question, reading out in the sex-appropriate column.

Fels Parent-Specific Size Tables for Midparent Categories shown smoothed and arranged by James Eagen. See Garn and Rohmann (1966).

*One inch = 2.54 cm.

of short parents, for whom conventional age-size standards are inappropriate and, in fact, deceptive."

COMPONENTS OF WEIGHT.   Weight is a measure of mass; it reveals nothing, however, about the nature of that mass. What is represented by weight comprises the organs and systems engaged in the body's daily functioning. It is therefore important to know more than merely the weight of a child and his progress in weight.

The components of weight vary in their proportion of the total weight with age and between individual children of the same age. For example, at birth about 25 per cent of the total weight can be attributed to muscle, 16 per cent to the vital organs, and 15 per cent to the central nervous system, whereas at maturity muscles, viscera and the central nervous system represent approximately 43 per cent, 11 per cent and 3 per cent, respectively. The amount of weight attributed to water decreases with age. Tanner (1962) listed the percentages of weight due to water as 75 to 80 at birth, 59 at one year, 63 at three years and 58 at twelve years. The low figure of 59 per cent at one year may be the result of the increase in fat thickness that occurs during the first year. Two children may weigh the same, and yet one may have relatively larger muscles and bones, while the other may have relatively more fatty tissue, or the variation may be the result of a difference in water content.

Sex differences in total body water at birth and in the following months have been reported. Owen et al. (1966) indicate a significant difference between the percentage of total body water in relation to body weight in boys (76.6 per cent at birth, 70.8 per cent at age twenty-five days) and that in girls (74.3 per cent at birth, 65.5 per cent at age twenty-five days) and consider it likely that the mean water content of male infants is greater than that of female infants throughout at least the first nine months of postnatal life. Fat comprises a greater percentage, and water a smaller percentage, of body weight of female than of male infants. The "existence of a sex-related difference in body composition during infancy suggests that fundamental physiologic processes differ between infant boys and girls."

Studies in the growth of muscle, bone and subcutaneous tissue (largely fat) demonstrate differences in the pattern of growth of these tissues with age, between boys and girls and between individuals of the same sex. The use of x-rays has made possible a study of differential tissue growth. By comparison of the shadows of skin and subcutaneous tissue, and muscle and bone at various sites of the body, the relative amounts of these tissues are ascertained. In addition, subcutaneous fat is also measured by the use of skinfold calipers. Figure 58 illustrates the differences in the pattern of growth of muscle and bone and that of subcutaneous tissue during infancy and early childhood.

Muscle growth occurs at a rapidly decelerating rate during the second year and at a more slowly decelerating rate until the onset of the puberal growth spurt (Lombard, 1950; Maresh, 1961). The growth of

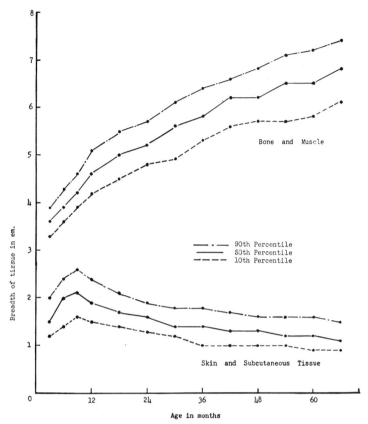

FIGURE 58. *Graphs of breadth of bone and muscle and of skin and subcutaneous tissue, as measured on anteroposterior roentgenograms of the calf of the leg for boys from 3 to 66 months, in terms of the tenth, fiftieth and ninetieth percentiles, illustrating the different patterns of growth and individual variability. (Graphs made from data by Lombard, 1950, and Stuart and Sobel, 1946.)*

muscle tissue lags behind growth of the body as a whole during infancy and childhood (Stuart in Vaughan, 1964) (see pp. 279-280).

Subcutaneous tissue, largely fat, has a different pattern of growth. This tissue tends to increase rapidly in thickness during the first nine months of life, to decrease rapidly from then until 2½ years, and to decrease less rapidly until about 5½ years of age (Maresh, 1961; Tanner and Whitehouse, 1962). At five years it is approximately half as thick as at nine months. Subcutaneous fat thickness that is proper at six months would indicate obesity at six years (Stuart and Stevenson, 1959). This fat pattern contributes to the appearance of chubbiness in the infant and to subsequent loss of chubbiness and gradual emergence of the type of physique which will be characteristic of the child.

Just as there are individual and sex differences in growth in height and weight, so there are individual and sex differences in the growth of tissues. Boys tend to have more muscle and bone than girls; girls tend to have more fat than boys (Lombard, 1950; Maresh, 1961; Reynolds and Grote, 1948). This difference is negligible at birth (Garn, 1958) and slight during the first year (Garn et al., 1956; Tanner, 1962), but from one to six years girls lose fat less rapidly than boys and gain it more rapidly thereafter (Stuart and Sobel, 1946; Tanner, 1962). Among both boys and girls there will be those with larger bones and muscle and those with relatively large amounts of fat.

These differences in the relative growth of tissues indicate that the use of height and weight alone in evaluating growth progress is not enough. What constitutes that weight is important in assessing the health and growth of a child and understanding his behavior.

BODY FORM, OR PHYSIQUE. Body proportions, and the amounts of the three tissues and their distribution mentioned earlier, contribute to an overall body form, build or physique that is a part of the uniqueness of the individual. The child changes from a slender (in proportion to length) newborn infant to a broader, plump infant during the first year, and later to an increasingly slender child up to seven or eight years. Within this general pattern individual physiques emerge.

Most of the studies on physique have been done with adolescents and adults. One study, however, found differences in build between ectomorphs (linear delicacy) and mesomorphs (muscular solidarity) during childhood which pointed to some constancy for these types throughout childhood. Dupertuis and Michaels (1953) studied the growth in height and weight of a group of children followed longitudinally and somatotyped at twenty-one years of age. Between the ectomorphs and mesomorphs significant differences in weight occurred at all ages, and the index $\dfrac{\text{Ht}}{\sqrt[3]{\text{Wt}}}$ was greater for ectomorphs, throughout the period of two to seventeen years, than for mesomorphs.

Some children show consistency in build throughout their growth years, and others show an inconsistency. Bayley (1956b) offers some examples. One child had obese periods in infancy and around the age of thirteen years. One heavy-set boy had a short period in infancy of relative slenderness, while another heavy infant completed his growth as a tall, rather slender adult. One slow-grower remained slender; one fast-grower remained plump. We need further studies in the constancy of physique during childhood.

In a study by Walker (1962) of relation of physique and behavior in a nursery school setting, endomorphy (plumpness), mesomorphy (muscularity) and ectomorphy (slenderness) were correlated with teachers' ratings of behavior. Each of these variables of physique was regarded as a continuum from minimal to maximal and was rated separately. Each showed some relation to school behavior scores. For example, ratings of energetic active and aggressive assertive behavior correlated significantly with boys' and girls' mesomorphy ratings. When total physique pattern (such as mesomorphy or mesomorphy-endomorphy), instead of the three-part scores, was correlated with nursery school behavior ratings, findings showed associations between physique and particular behavior differences. For example, aloofness was somewhat associated with ectomorphy. Endomorphy in boys was associated with aggressiveness, "evidently by virtue of the correlation of both with mesomorphy." Research has not yet provided detail on sources of physique-behavior relations, in bodily conditions such as strength, energy, sensory thresholds, and in learning.

SKELETAL SYSTEM

The body has a rigid framework of bone held together by muscles and tendons, which together with the enveloping skin supports, surrounds, moves and thereby protects the delicate organs essential for the maintenance of health and activity. The framework takes about twenty years to grow and develop its full potentialities. Each organ, if it functions at all, must function to full capacity, harmonious with the changing needs of the growing body. Since the skeleton is a structure which takes a long time to reach maturity, it has characteristics which afford excellent examples of stages of maturity which the individual reaches at various ages. Bone, the tissue which constitutes most of the skeleton, is a living, growing, labile tissue composed of living cells that participate in the functioning of the body and contribute to its well-being. The bones support the structure of the body, determine its stature, and help with overlying soft parts to determine its physique. Any study of the skeleton must contemplate three aspects: bones as supporting structures and agents in locomotion; bones as a source of mineral, particularly calcium; and bones in their role of blood-forming organs through the agency of red marrow.

Functions of Bone

One of the functions of bone is to *support structures* and serve as an *agent in locomotion*. The skull protects the delicate tissue of the brain, the ribs enclose the lungs and heart, and the pelvis supports the abdominal organs. As part of an integrated activity of a group of systems the bones participate in making movement possible. The coordinated action of bones, muscles and nerves makes possible the balance of the body, locomotion, and use of the hands and arms in manipulation of the environment.

The bones not only serve as a framework to support the body, but also are *storehouses of minerals* from which the blood can obtain substances essential for the life and health of the body cells. The spongy part of the bone is a network of trabeculae (rows of cells bridging intercellular spaces), the size of the mesh having a family pattern, but subject to modification in any person from time to time. In health the open spaces of the mesh are well filled with labile mineral, providing a floating store from which the mineral is obtained for blood coagulation, muscle tone, kidney function and functioning of the nervous system. When the body draws upon the bone for mineral, two modifications may occur in the network of trabeculae and the enclosed labile mineral, best described by the metaphor used by Todd et al. (1937):

> . . . snow-covered chicken wire. As the snow filling the interstices melts, the chicken wire mesh becomes more plainly visible and parts that have suffered corrosion stand out as breaks in the mesh. But if the melting snow freezes afresh, the trabeculae become coated with ice. They may not appear thicker but will stand out more clearly and the places where the wire strands of the mesh are intertwisted will appear as nodes in the network. Spongiosa well filled with mineral corresponds to the snow-covered net of chicken wire. Withdrawal of the labile mineral corresponds to the melting of the snow. Breaks in the trabeculae represent a heavier drain on the stored supply. Transformation of labile mineral into the more stable phase corresponds to the ice-covering with knots or nodes in the network.

These changes can be revealed by roentgenograms taken over a period of time.

The degree of mineralization, or the *density* of bone, can be revealed by the depth of the shadow in an x-ray film. Studies of consecutive x-ray films show that in some well children the density of bone varies from time to time. The cause of the fluctuation, undoubtedly associated in some way with calcium metabolism, has yet to be ascertained. An annotated bibliography on bone density has been assembled by Garn (1962). For a discussion of skeletal tissue see Ham and Leeson (1965).

The third function, that of *manufacturing certain blood cells*, is carried on in the red marrow of the bones. The marrow cavity of bone becomes filled with various cells concerned in making red blood cells, some white blood cells and platelets. In the fetus the marrow is distributed widely throughout the bones. During the postnatal growing years the space in bones in which red marrow is found decreases and becomes localized in certain areas such as the diploe of the skull, the ribs and sternum, vertebrae, in cancellous tissue of some of the short bones and the ends of long bones. Diploe is the cancellous layer between the outer and inner tables of the bones of the skull. Cancellous bone is characterized by a lattice structure, as the spongy tissue of bones.

Development of Bones

Most bones develop from a cartilaginous model which is laid down early in utero. This cartilage is gradually replaced by bone, beginning at ossification centers from which it radiates. Through intricate cellular processes the organic matrix of the bone is formed, and minerals, predominantly calcium and phosphorus, are deposited. The mineral salts give bone its hardness and rigidity; the organic material determines its tenacity. Replacement of cartilage by bone begins in early embryonic life and continues until the skeleton has reached full maturity. Bones grow by appositional growth rather than interstitial growth. In other words, growth takes place at the edge of existing bone, not by expansion from within. Bones grow in width by adding new bone at the outer edges underneath the periosteum and dissolving bone (resorption) on the inner surface. Long bones grow in length toward each end of their cartilage models. Bones change in shape by deposition of bone on some surfaces and resorption of bone from others.

In long bones another center of ossification appears at the ends of the cartilage model and is termed an epiphyseal center of ossification, or epiphysis. Note in Figure 60 the middle finger of the hand at age five years. Each bone has a smaller bone at one end. This small bone is the epiphysis. While a long bone is growing there remains a noncalcified area (observable in an x-ray film) between the shaft, or diaphysis, and the epiphysis. New bone is produced by cellular activity at the edge of the diaphysis in this area. At the same time the ossification of the epiphysis continues. Growth of the long bones is terminated when the epiphysis and the diaphysis unite, as seen in the hand of the eighteen-year-old in Figure 60.

Some bones develop in a membranous area rather than a cartilaginous one, e.g., the bones of the vault of the skull. The same cellular processes occur to produce bone, and from ossification centers bony tissue radiates to form the bones of the skull.

Bone development begins by the appearance of ossification centers

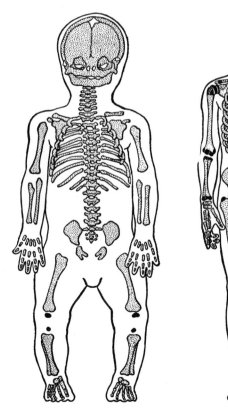

FIGURE 59. *Diagram of skeleton of newborn and adult reconstructed to same height, illustrating stage of skeletal development at birth in contrast to that at maturity. (After B. M. Patten: Human Embryology. Blakiston Co., 1946.)*

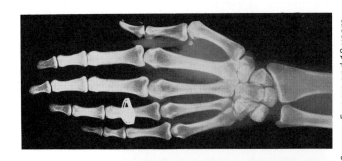
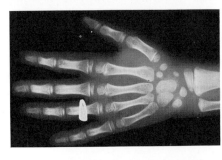
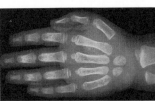
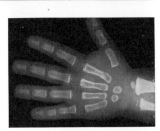

FIGURE 60. X-ray films of hand and wrist showing skeletal maturation of girls at birth, 1 year, 2 years, 5 years and 18 years (mature hand) according to the Greulich and Pyle standards. (Reproduced from W. W. Greulich, and S. I. Pyle: Radiographic Atlas of Skeletal Development of the Hand and Wrist. 2nd ed. Stanford, California, Stanford University Press, 1959.)

at the middle of the sixth week after fertilization and continues throughout the growing years. It is generally not complete until the person is in his twenties. Most primary centers appear before birth; most secondary centers, after birth (Novack, 1954). The skeleton in the early years has many aspects of immaturity and is therefore different from that of an adult. Some of the differences can be observed in Figure 59, which shows the skeletons of a newborn and of an adult. In the young child not all the cartilaginous model has been replaced by bone, and larger spaces between bones exist at the joints of the body. With more space between the ends of bones at the joints, and longer and less firmly attached ligaments, the child has more flexibility in certain movements, all of which gives him the appearance of being double-jointed. Immature bones also have proportionately more water and protein-like substances and less minerals. Thus young bones are less resistant to pressure and muscle pull and are therefore more liable to deformity. Growing bone also has a rich supply of blood. Being more vascular, the bone not only receives a steady supply of bone-building materials, but also will be more readily susceptible than mature bone to any infecting organism which may be carried in the blood stream.

As bones grow they pass through a regular series of changes in form until they achieve their mature size and form. These changes are indicators of the maturational process. "Maturity indicators are those features seen in the radiograph, which because of their regular and irreversible sequence of appearance, mark the development of the bone to its mature form" (Pyle and Hoerr, 1955). X-ray films taken at intervals reveal the maturational progress in skeletal development and the developmental patterns of individual children. Figure 60 shows the bone development of the hand and the wrist that can be expected of most girls, according to the Greulich and Pyle Atlas (1959), at birth, one year, two years, five years and maturity. Note the absence of epiphyses and carpal (wrist) bones at birth, the gradual appearance of epiphyses and carpal bones, the changing of the shape of the bones during early childhood and, finally, the mature hand with complete union of epiphyses and diaphyses at eighteen years.

BONE SCARS. Bone scars may record metabolic disturbances resulting from severe illness and other adverse circumstances and may also appear in the early stages of recovery from malnutrition. Transverse lines may appear on certain long bones, indicating that growth in the length of the bone has been interrupted. Many children show these transverse lines at the distal tibia during growth. Follis and Park (1952) and Park (1954) have a discussion of the processes involved in the formation of bone scars. Some children, after a severe illness, will show bone scars; others, of comparable age and with illness of the same severity, will show none. The reasons for these differences need to be studied. The absence of scars does not necessarily mean that a recent illness or other traumatic experience has not had an adverse effect on a child, whereas the presence of such scars would indicate that it is highly probable that it had done so.

Greulich and Pyle (1959) discussed scars appearing after two widely different kinds of experience. X-ray films of the hands of children in Nagasaki and Hiroshima, taken after the war, showed bone scars in a large percentage of children. The scars were located about the same distance on the radius from the epiphyseal line in children of comparable age. These lines are believed to indicate interruption in growth caused by radiation and other injuries incurred at the time of the atomic bombing. Finer transverse lines have appeared in the radius of some children with severe malnutrition after their diet had been supplemented with milk.

It appears . . . that such transverse lines or scars indicate the occurrence of periods during which the equilibrium between the rate of deposition of mineral and other osseous material and the rate of growth of the bone has been disturbed, either by a rapid deceleration or an interruption of growth or by a sudden increase in the rate of deposition of these substances.

INDIVIDUAL DIFFERENCES IN SKELETAL DEVELOPMENT. Children differ in skeletal development as they do in height and weight, although the process of skeletal maturation is less subject to fluctuations than is growth. Differences between the skeletal development of boys and girls are present at birth and continue as they grow older (Greulich and Pyle, 1959). For example, the fifth carpal bone does not appear in boys until an average age of sixty months, but appears in girls at the average of forty-eight months (Pyle and Sontag, 1943). Hansman and Maresh (1961), reporting on a group followed from early childhood to early adulthood, found that the girls at five years of age had three to seven ossified carpal centers; the boys at the same age had two to seven centers. But 64 per cent of the five-year-old girls had seven centers, while the seventh center was present in less than 5 per cent of the boys. Differences can be expected even among children of the same sex. Hansman and Maresh also found that girls having three carpal centers ranged in age from four months to seven years; boys having the same number of centers ranged from six months to eight years.

Variability is also observed in the pattern of skeletal development. Pyle et al. (1959) studied the patterns of skeletal development of 133 children in the Harvard Growth Study. Some of these children maintained a consistent pattern, but many made one or two substantial shifts in rate from one period to another. The most common shift was a single one occurring after the preschool years, between childhood and adolescence.

Reviewing research on maturation of the skeleton, Acheson (1966) refers to intrinsic factors that determine rate and pattern, which stem from the genotype. "Some are sex-specific and therefore presumably originate from genes on the sex chromosome; . . . some are common to both sexes and so can be taken as having autosomal origin; still others are not sex specific but race specific . . . Variation in chromosome count may also be associated with deviations and aberrations of skeletal maturation." Acheson also reports research evidence of the influence of extrinsic factors of ill health and undernutrition on pattern and rate of skeletal maturation. Consequences of environmentally induced slowing of maturation are considered to reflect the degree of serious or chronic illness, and perhaps variations in susceptibility between centers and in the same center according to its stage of development.

Determination of Skeletal Maturation

Acheson (1966) says that a metamorphosis of the biological and chemical nature of tissue is concerned in skeletal maturation.

> This process must be clearly differentiated from growth, which is the formation of new tissue and which in many limb bones occurs in the epiphyseal growth cartilage plates. In the skeleton of the healthy child . . . growth, or the creation of new cells and tissues, and maturation, or the subsequent consolidation of the tissues into permanent form, proceed . . . the one with the other.

Skeletal maturation can be assessed by x-ray examination of joints of the body and comparison with a standard of the time of appearance of ossification centers, of changes in the shape of these centers and, finally, of union of the epiphysis and the diaphysis. In infancy and early childhood the first two criteria are available. The growth of the bones in the hand and wrist is considered by many to be a satisfactory representative of the growth of the skeletal structure as a whole.* The changes in density of these bones, too, are considered to be representative of the generalized changes throughout the body. Bone development, therefore, can be evaluated by inspection and comparison with a standard roentgenogram of the contours of the ends of bones of the hand, of the wrist bones and the epiphyses, and of the progress toward union of the epiphysis with the shaft of the bone.

The standard generally used in this country is that of Greulich and Pyle (1959), which is a revision and extension of the standards of Todd (1937) and Flory (1936). The degree of maturity is expressed as skeletal age. Greulich and Pyle give each bone an age equivalent, so that comparison of the child's separate bones with the standards makes it possible to assess the age of each bone. These separate ages can then be combined to give the skeletal age for the hand. By assessing each bone it is possible to observe the degree of symmetry of the development of the bones in this area. This procedure calls attention to any imbalance in skeletal development that might be detected in the x-ray film of the hand and prompts investigation of the health history of the child in an attempt to find factors which may be contributing to this imbalance.

The range in the degree of development of the bones in this area can be observed easily by plotting the most advanced age, the least advanced age, and the skeletal age assigned to the hand as a whole. With the plotting of a series of assessments, consistently balanced or unbalanced development or changes can be observed.

---

* An x-ray picture of the infant's foot also gives evidence valuable in interpreting his stage of maturity (Pyle and Sontag, 1943).

Another method of assessment, suggested by Acheson (1954, 1966) and Falkner (1958), considers skeletal maturity in points instead of by skeletal age. These points are based on maturity indicators, or the distinct changes in the shapes of the bones. The measure of maturity is the sum total of the points observed.

A child's progress toward maturity is more important, as emphasized by Todd (1937), than his status at the time of an x-ray examination. If, for example, in six months his skeletal age has progressed six months, then his progress in skeletal age is progressing with his chronologic age. If, on the other hand, he has progressed only two months in skeletal age during the same period, his skeletal growth is lagging behind. If he has gained nine months in skeletal age during this six-month period, his bone growth has been accelerated. A slow rate of skeletal maturing may be the acceptable pattern for one child, just as an accelerated rate may be the acceptable pattern for another.

SKELETAL STATUS AND GENERAL BODY MATURITY.   Some understanding of how a child is maturing physically is needed to understand his development and to appreciate his behavior and needs. Separate assessment of each organ system would be most satisfactory in order to determine general bodily maturity, but is not yet possible. One of the systems which can be assessed is the skeleton. Its role in determining bodily maturity is important because (1) its maturation covers the whole growth period, with maturity indicators distributed throughout this period; (2) the process can be observed by the use of x-rays; and (3) its development is closely related to the development of the reproductive system, which is assumed to be a reliable indicator of general body maturity. This assumption is based on the fact that many changes in tissues, other than those of the reproductive organs, including skin, hair, sweat glands, distribution of subcutaneous fat and muscle growth, occur during pubescence. Thus skeletal development is used as an indicator of physical maturity (Greulich and Pyle, 1959). How much reliance can be placed on this indicator depends greatly on the degree of harmony of a child's development in all its parts.

HEAD AND SKULL.   The circumference of the head of a child at birth measures 12 to 14 inches, being slightly larger in boys than in girls (Washburn, 1966). By one year the head has increased about 33 per cent; by five years, when it closely approximates its adult size, it has increased 48 per cent.

The skull is the bony framework of the head, enclosing the brain and supporting the face. At birth the bones of the skull have not fully developed. Most of the bones have grown enough so that they are separated by "narrow seams" of relatively undifferentiated connective tissues. "An arrangement whereby adjacent bones are joined by connective tissue is termed a *suture*. However, at points where more than two bones meet, the sutures are wide and such areas are termed *fontanelles*" (Ham and Leeson, 1965). Growth of the vault of the skull is appositional growth. Whether the growth takes place primarily at the sutures or on the convex surface of the bones is undecided.

There are six fontanelles at birth, but only two can be seen in a physical examination. The largest one lies in the midline between the two parietal bones and the frontal bone. This diamond-shaped area is called the anterior, or frontal, fontanelle (commonly known as the soft spot). In the midline between the parietal bones and the occipital is a smaller area, called the posterior, or occipital, fontanelle. The posterior fontanelle usually closes between the fourth and eight weeks. The anterior fontanelle usually closes by about one year of age. Aisensone's study (1950) showed that 90 per cent of these closures occur between seven and nineteen months.

During infancy the skull grows rapidly to accommodate the brain, which is increasing steadily in size. At birth the cranial (upper) part of the skull, enclosing the brain (the brain case), has a capacity of 350 cc.; this increases to 750 cc. by one year of age and to 900 cc. by two years. The brain reaches its approximate adult size of 1500 cc. by six years, and in well grown children it may be practically adult in size by $4\frac{1}{2}$ years. Thereafter the increase in the size of the brain case is minor in amount. The early growth of the brain case results in its relatively large size as contrasted with the smallness of the face.

The lower part of the skull, the facial portion, grows relatively faster during the early years than the cranial portion, and thus the face assumes more prominence. The ratio of the face to the cranium at birth is 1:8; at six years it is 1:3; at eighteen years, 1:2 (Moyers and Hemrend, 1953).

Part of the increase in the size of the face during childhood is due to development of the air sinuses. The antrum and ethmoids grow rapidly during the first two years. The average age at which either frontal sinus

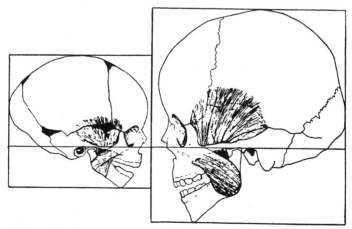

FIGURE 61. *Skulls of newborn child and 6-year-old boy drawn in their natural proportions. (J. C. Brash: The Growth of the Jaws, Normal and Abnormal, in Health and Disease. London, The Dental Board of the United Kingdom, 1924.)*

is definitely evident above the nose and at which it begins to increase in size has been calculated as three years, although this is a difficult evaluation to make, and the age may vary widely (Maresh, 1940).

The development of teeth and their eruption also contribute to facial development in early childhood.

Examination of Figure 61 will aid in recognition of fontanelles and sutures, the relative proportions of cranial and facial parts of the skull, and the changes which occur with growth, such as obliteration of the fontanelles and the increased relative growth in the facial area.

THORAX.   The chest is barrel-shaped in infancy, and the downward slope of the ribs is less pronounced than in later childhood and in adult life; its circumference at birth averages 13.7 inches, slightly less than that of the head. By the end of the first year the chest circumference is 18.3 inches, slightly larger than that of the head (Watson and Lowrey, 1967).

There is considerable individual variability in the time at which a child's chest assumes the adult shape. In the adult the anteroposterior diameter is approximately 75 per cent of the lateral diameter. Some children at five and six years of age continue to have a relatively barrel-shaped chest, whereas in others it is approaching the adult shape (Washburn, 1966).

VERTEBRAL COLUMN.   The spine, or vertebral column, of the newborn is a flexible structure. Before the child is born his head and legs are curved toward the front of the body, and his spine is therefore curved like a "C." When he is born, he must breathe; that requires that his head be raised from his chest, and the cervical spine (neck) begins to assume its individual curvature. As the child learns to sit up and to balance himself for standing and walking, the normal curvatures of the spine develop. From these normal curvatures, as well as the differences in contour and size of the vertebrae, we have come to recognize four spinal regions in man: cervical, thoracic, lumbar and sacral. The cervical and lumbar parts of the vertebral column are free, in that they are not attached to other bones; the thoracic spine articulates with the ribs, and the sacral region articulates in a more limited fashion with the pelvis. The head rests on the cervical spine.

At birth the spine is largely cartilaginous, just as the bones in the arms and legs are, but the spine becomes less flexible as the child grows older, both because the cartilage is replaced by bone and because its motility is limited by its function of maintaining the body in an upright position.

The ribs of the fetus are important. Their ossification begins very early in fetal life, but is not completed until about the twentieth year. They not only enclose the lungs, but also supply attachment for the accessory muscles of breathing as well as the diaphragm. These factors are important in the posture of the body (see p. 281 ff.).

Learning to sit and to walk may put a temporary strain on the muscles and the other soft tissues attached to the vertebrae. Young children may derive such pleasure from the exercise of these new skills that it is necessary to protect them from exhaustion and possible damage.

PELVIS.   The pelvis of the child consists of two sets of three bones (ilium, ischium and pubis), one set on each side, which unite at twenty years to form a single hip bone. The two hip bones, bound together with the sacrum by strong ligaments, form the pelvic girdle, which supports the weight of the body on the legs. This circle of bone lodges the urinary bladder, the lower end of the large intestine, the organs of reproduction of females, and the large vessels and nerves to the lower extremities, and serves as a protection to them.

The pelvic cavity of the newborn is relatively much smaller than that of the adult and is more horizontal in position. In studies of the pelvis during the first year of life and in children between two and nine years, Reynolds (1945, 1947) found that the pelvis as a whole grows more rapidly during the first three months, after which the rate decreases throughout infancy and prepuberal childhood. He found that boys tend to have larger pelvic measurements relating to the outer structure of the pelvis, whereas girls tend to have larger measurements relating to the inner structure, including a relatively larger outlet. From observation of x-ray films of the same children taken at different ages it would seem that a distinctive individuality of shape persists as growth proceeds during these early years. Reynolds found that children who had larger pelves at birth also were longer and heavier and had larger heads. Larger pelves were associated with earlier appearance of the first tooth in both sexes and with advanced ossification of bones in boys. No significant relation was found between pelvic size or shape and time of walking.

The change in gait evident by about the age of three results from a widening of the pelvic girdle and an increase in the relative length of the legs.

EXTREMITIES.   The arms are relatively shorter in the infant than in the adult (see Fig. 54). The clavicle (collar bone), the first bone in the body to ossify, is short and therefore helps to produce the narrow sloping of the shoulders of the infant. The hands of an infant are different from those of an adult; the fingers are relatively shorter and stubbier, owing to slower growth of the last two bones. The hand changes gradually in shape and size as the child grows.

The legs of the newborn are short and flexed, and the soles of the feet are directed toward each other. The legs straighten as the infant grows (see Fig. 62). Growth of the foot (Anderson et al., 1956) in length decreases in rate rapidly from a high in infancy, to four or five years of age, when a plateau is reached. During these years there is no difference in the size of the feet of boys and girls. By five years of age girls have

FIGURE 62. *These twins of 8 months illustrate the body proportions of infants—the relatively short legs and long trunk and head. They also illustrate the chubbiness of infancy and individual differences in size.*

attained between 70 and 75 per cent of the total growth of the foot, while boys have attained between 65 and 70 per cent.

When the growth of foot, stature and length of the leg bones were compared in terms of progress toward their mature size, it was found that the foot was at all times nearer its mature size than either stature or the bones of the leg. For example, at one year of age the feet of the girls were already half as long as they would ever be, whereas these same girls did not attain half of their mature stature until eighteen months, and did not attain half of their mature leg length until three years of age. In boys the same order was true, although the ages were somewhat later.

The infant's foot is characteristic of his stage of development and is flexible, relaxed and more mobile than that of an older child. The arches are much less rigid in infancy than at later periods of growth. In the bottom of the foot is a fat pad which gives the appearance of flat footedness. Even after the child has started to walk, the ligaments are relaxed and the large muscles, not yet accustomed to maintaining balance, are unable to carry out their new task perfectly. The feet are therefore held widely apart in order to widen the base of support, and there is a tendency to toe out, throwing the weight on the inner side of the sole of the foot.

According to Pyle and Sontag (1943), x-ray pictures of the foot of the newborn show two tarsal centers. By five years all seven of the tarsal bones and all the epiphyses of the metatarsals and the toes have appeared. Ossification in the feet of boys lags behind that in girls. For assessment of the skeletal development of the foot the student is referred to the atlas by Hoerr, Pyle and Francis (1962). Soon after walking is established the bones in the arch take on the characteristic individuality of their relative position, i.e., low or high arch. Although much of the bone is still in the cartilaginous state, the adult characteristics of the arch are forecast. Whatever modifications occur thereafter are largely the result of injury or reduction in muscle tonus, and the like. It has been concluded that as early as five years the shape of the arch reveals a strong genetic component (Robinow, Johnston and Anderson, 1943).

NERVOUS SYSTEM

The nervous system, by means of its characteristics of excitability (response to stimuli) and conductibility (the transporting of nervous impulses), is concerned with the correlation and integration of bodily processes, with the reactions and adjustments of the organism to its environment and with conscious life.

The nervous system is composed of two parts, the central and peripheral, the former consisting of the brain and spinal cord, which are continuous with one another; the latter a series of nerves by which the central nervous system is connected with the various tissues of the body—skin, eyes, muscles, internal organs, and so forth. For descriptive purposes these nerves may be arranged in two groups, the cerebrospinal and the autonomic; the two groups are intimately connected and closely intermingled. It is largely through the agency of the central nervous system that all the tissues and systems of the body are integrated into a smoothly operating unit. The functional unit in the central nervous system is the reflex. The nerve impulse is an electrochemical reaction. Because of this property, it is possible to study activity of the brain by means of an electroencephalogram, which records differences in electrical potential from one area to another.

For a complete description of this system in terms of its structure and function the student is referred to other texts (DeCoursey, 1961; Ham and Leeson, 1965; Hebb, 1966; Ruch and Patton, 1965). In this text it can be said that the nervous system performs a role in all aspects of behavior and development. In connection with the need for nourishment, the regulation of food intake is a function of the hypothalamus, where areas controlling appetite and satiety are located (Patton, 1965). In this part of the brain the other autonomic functions are controlled; it plays an important role in the elaboration of emotional or affective behavior.

The cerebral cortex, on the other hand, is the area for conscious thought, the interpretation of sensory experiences, initiation of voluntary muscular activity and control or inhibition of responses, e.g., emotional responses initiated by other centers.

The cerebellum has been called the "secretary" of the cerebral cortex. "It does not initiate motor responses but functions to coordinate muscular movements so that the action will be smooth and efficient instead of jerking and uncoordinated" (DeCoursey, 1961). It is concerned with equilibrium and posture, and muscle tonus.

The reticular formation in the brain stem, which acts as a reflex center in receiving descending fibers from the cortex, hypothalamus and cranial nerves and ascending sensory tracts, appears to play a role in arousal from sleep and maintaining a state of consciousness. "One interpretation of arousal is that sensory impulses excite the reticular system and then gradually diffuse through subcortical areas. When they finally arrive at the cerebral cortex, awakening or a return to consciousness occurs" (DeCoursey, 1961).

These discrete parts of the brain are closely related functionally with one another. Thus brain function is a complex activity involving the interaction of its discrete parts.

Development of the Nervous System

The relation of myelination to function has long been of interest. Dekaban (1959a) suggested that the acquisition of myelin in the various parts of the central nervous system can be correlated with the emergence and differentiation of a particular type of neural activity. Although nerve fibers can conduct impulses before myelination, they do so at a slower pace and with possibly greater diffusion. Myelination seems to be necessary for fibers to conduct nervous impulses sufficiently well to permit muscles to make delicate and precise movements (Ham and Leeson, 1965). It is also believed that increased stimulation can increase the rate of myelination of the nerve fibers involved (Dekaban, 1959a). This assumption is based on experimentation with increasing light stimulation of the eyes of newborn animals.

Larroche (1966), after tracing development of the nervous system before birth, writes:

> Myelogenesis, which begins in the brain stem during the second half of gestation, has hardly reached the level of the hemispheres at term. The afferent nerve bundles are myelinated first, as are most of the cranial nerve roots and the extrapyramidal system. The chief motor pathways are visible approximately at term in the pons and medulla, then in the internal capsule and the subcortical white matter of the central gyrus. Myelogenesis accelerates rapidly after birth.

The central nervous system begins to develop by about $2\frac{1}{2}$ fetal weeks. By birth most of the nerve cells have formed. In fact, after birth few if any new cells appear. Kennedy (1959) stated that cell division in the first six weeks of fetal life accounts for the lifetime quota of 10 billion neurons. Later, prenatal and postnatal development involves development of these cells, their processes and blood supply. The rate of growth of the central nervous system is rapid in the early years; at one year it reaches 60 per cent of its adult weight; at five years, 90 per cent (Tanner, 1961). It does not develop as a whole; its various parts do not grow synchronously. At birth the posterior areas of the central nervous system are further developed than the anterior areas. Thus the cerebral areas are slower in development than the subcortical ones. Even the growth of the parts of the cortex does not progress uniformly. Cell maturation in the cortex is still far from complete at birth, though the sensory and motor areas are in advance of the association centers (Larroche, 1966). Thus, while sensations are registered, the associations become more complex at later ages.

The newborn operates on a reflex level. Among the reflex activities are rooting, sucking, swallowing, emptying the bladder and coughing, all of which are essential for life. Other transient reflexes are present. Since the cerebral cortex is not ready to function to any great extent (Scheibel and Scheibel, 1964), the subcortical centers control early infant behavior. By three months certain reflexes such as the tonic neck reflex, hand grasping, primitive swimming, and so forth, become less definite, preparatory to disappearance, and the occurrence of learned behavior is much more frequent. As an example of the disappearance of a reflex with the emergence of voluntary control, Gentry and Aldrich (1948) found that certain toe reflexes disappeared when voluntary control, as indicated by the use of feet for locomotion, was established. The exception was the Babinski reflex, which disappeared gradually during the first and second years.

This proceeding from generalized motor behavior and innate behavioral devices toward more voluntary control is indicative of maturation of parts of the cortex which inhibit and control activity of the lower centers. By six months control over voluntary movements is considerable. As the cerebral cortex matures to the point of performing a significant role in controlling behavior, the characteristics of cortical behavior become evident, such as a planned element in the mode of reaction, a latency of response and a variety of responses.

This relation between structure and function is further suggested by the possible relation between postural development (standing and walking) and the increase in size and complexity of the cerebellum (Gesell et al., 1940). The cerebellum grows slowly during the first few months, but rapidly in the last half of the first year and first half of the second year. It attains practically full size before five years. Rapid gain occurs at the time when the child is gaining control of erect posture and manual and locomotive activities. Hebb (1966) writes: "The cerebellum is concerned with the coordination of muscular movement, but we have no adequate knowledge of its function (such a large mass must play a bigger part in behavior than our present knowledge suggests)."

Brain Waves

Another change with age is noticed in brain waves. In the waves of the newborn (indicating level of activity of the nervous system, or arousal), as noted on an electroencephalogram, the transition from sleep to waking is not clearly marked, and the differential electrical activity among the different areas of the brain is less marked than later. "The newborn infant shows slow waves as well as faster ones during periods of behavioral wakefulness, which suggests that the infant's consciousness (and that of the sleep-deprived adult) falls far short of what we know as consciousness in the normal waking adult" (Hebb, 1966).

The slow waves of the waking record are of much less amplitude than those in the sleep records, and lack frequencies indicative of the intermediate level of arousal and of active thinking at later ages. As the infant grows older, stays awake longer and pays attention to his surroundings more and more, the smaller, faster rhythms become predominant during wakefulness. By five years of age this latter type predominates most of the time. Changes continue until eleven to fourteen years, when the characteristic features of the adult electroencephalogram appear.

The electroencephalogram reveals not only age changes in brain waves, but also other aspects of brain function and individual variability and is adding to our understanding of sleep and wakefulness.

Need for Oxygen

Oxygen is essential for life and growth and must be supplied continuously, since it cannot be stored for more than a few seconds. Anoxia, or insufficient oxygen, during fetal life produces defects which vary according to the time of occurrence of the deficiency (see Chap. Three). According to Nesbitt (1966), "Animal studies demonstrate conclusively that asphyxia at birth can impair neurologic performance, and the severity of such damage is roughly proportional to the duration of the asphyxia."

Importance of Early Experiences

Much more needs to be learned about the development of the nervous system and its relation to mental functioning. Structure and chemical and electrical function in some way provide a basis for mental activity. The student is advised to watch the ever-expanding research in neurophysiology and its relation to behavior.

The very young infant is not only maturing, but also having experiences which are all-important for mental development. These experiences come from sense-organ stimulation and, as Hebb (1966) points out, do not imply that the infant has neural processes which are sufficiently elaborate to be dignified by the term "consciousness" or "awareness." Early experience, regarded as the pattern of sense-organ stimulation, may be from visual and tactile stimulation, from the infant's own movement of eyes and limbs, and from auditory stimulation perhaps from his own vocalization. While he lies in his crib, moves his arms and eyes at random, makes random noises, is held, is fed, defecates or urinates, has diapers changed or is bathed, he is having a changing pattern of experiences.

Animal experimentation and observations of man deprived of normal early experiences (Casler, 1961; Hebb, 1966) provide substantial evidence that early experiences are determining factors in later perceptions. Theoretically, according to Hebb (1966), "the function of early experience in the mammal is to build up the mediating processes which, once . . . established, make possible the very rapid learning of which the mature animal is capable." Casler (1961), reviewing the literature on maternal deprivation, stated: "Neuroanatomical findings, especially those concerning the reticular formation, help to explain why perceptual stimulation is so important for normal development."

MUSCULAR SYSTEM

Movements of the body are produced by muscular action. Muscular activity is produced not by muscles alone, but by virtue of their structure, their attachment to bones, and their innervation. Muscles are formed of bundles of a special kind of cell which is able to shorten or elongate under nervous stimulation. Muscles under the control of the will, such as those of the arms and legs, are known as *voluntary*; others, such as those of the stomach, are known as *involuntary*. They differ in the nature of the cells that compose them. Muscles cover most of the skeleton and are disposed in all directions, so that a great variety of motion is possible. In most instances muscles are in pairs, so that one counteracts the pull of another. For detailed discussion of the nature and function of muscles, the student is referred to Carlson, Johnson and Calvert (1961).

Growth and maturation of this system continue throughout the developmental period. At birth the muscles represent one-fifth to one-fourth of body weight, in contrast to one-third at early adolescence and two-fifths at maturity (Watson and Lowrey, 1967). The growth of the muscles follows a pattern similar to that of the body as a whole, but lags somewhat behind general growth during infancy and childhood (see p. 260 and Fig. 58).

According to Fomon (1966),

Between 2 and 6 months of age, the increase in volume of the adipose tissue is more than twice as great as increase in volume of muscle. Between 6 and 12 months of age, the increase in volume of muscle is slightly more rapid than that of adipose tissue. Throughout the first year of life bone accounts for a relatively small percentage of the total volume of the four extremities.

Information at the year of peak velocity of growth in height suggests trends in bone, muscle and fat gain from infancy to later ages. For subjects whose roentgenograms were studied by Tanner (1965) peak height velocity was at 12.1 years of age for girls and 14.1 years for boys. For boys a peak in gain per year in area of bone and of muscle occurred at the time of greatest growth in height per year.

Owen and Brozek (1966) write as follows:

In girls, the peak in muscle growth (cross sectional area) was reached shortly after the attainment of peak height velocity. . . . At the time the body grows most rapidly in height, subcutaneous fat increases least rapidly in girls and an actual loss of fat occurs in boys. . . . In general, the subcutaneous fat thickness of girls is greater than that of boys at all ages, although until about 10 years of age the growth of fat tissue proceeds at about the same rate in both sexes. After the first decade the subcutaneous fat thickness of girls shows a continuous, somewhat progressive, increase.

Knowledge of the growth in certain muscle groups has been extended through the study of x-ray films. X-ray films will also demonstrate the density of muscular tissue. Maturation changes have been observed indirectly through tests which measure motor ability and strength. In young children many of these tests cannot be utilized.

It is probable that no new muscle fibers are added after birth.

FIGURE 63. *Muscle development of arms and legs, shoulders and back and neurologic development contribute to coordinated movement of this child, 2 years 4 months of age.*

Changes result from increases in length, breadth and thickness of the fibers, to their structure, to their attachment, and to their control through the nervous system. In the newborn the muscles of greatest development are in the eye and in the respiratory tract. The arm muscles are better developed than those of the leg. During development other muscle groups outstrip those best developed in the newborn, so that in adulthood the thickest bundles are in the leg and in the back. In the early years the large muscles function more adequately than the small, fine muscles. The young child is more skillful, therefore, in activities involving large movements than in those involving precision (see Fig. 63).

The condition of the muscles at all ages depends on the constitution of the person and on his health. In turn, one of the indicators of the health of a child is the degree of muscle tone, which is the condition of constant partial contraction. The tone of the muscles is important, since it affects much of the support that various structures of the body require, such as that which the muscles of the abdomen give to the digestive organs when a person stands upright.

BODY DYNAMICS

Concept of Body Dynamics

Howorth (1946) wrote of posture as follows:

. . . posture should really be considered as the sum total of the positions and movements of the body throughout the day and throughout life. It should include not only the fundamental static positions in lying, sitting and standing and the variations of these positions but also the dynamic postures of the body in motion or in action, for it is here that posture becomes most important and most effective. Posture has a direct relation to the comfort, mechanical efficiency and physiologic functioning of the individual. . . .

Good dynamic posture implies the use of the body or its parts in the simplest and most effective way, using muscle contraction and relaxation, balance, coordination, rhythm and timing as well as gravity, inertia and momentum to optimum advantage. The smooth integration of these elements of good dynamic posture results in neuromusculoskeletal performance which is easy, graceful, satisfying and effective and represents the best in the individual physical activity as well as in the physical activity of the individual.

It is generally accepted that efficient use of the body has a beneficial effect on the general health and physical well-being of an individual, and equally accepted that poor body dynamics, with its accompanying lack of muscle tone, lowered threshold of fatigue, and lessened available mechanical energy, has a detrimental effect on the general health (Tucker, 1960). The body, like any other machine, can be mechanically efficient only when all its parts are maintained in equilibrium.

The body dynamics of a child can be considered in terms of contributing to his physical and emotional well-being at the moment and his continued well-being as he grows and matures. What happens to him in this area in his early life may have significance for him later.

Variables in Body Dynamics

Five factors will be considered here in discussion of the body dynamics of a child: (1) force of gravity, (2) condition of bones and muscles, (3) course of development, (4) personal attributes, (5) exogenous environment.

FORCE OF GRAVITY.   The body is subject to the laws of gravity, and therefore maintenance of good balance with the least muscular effort demands that the body must be, as nearly as possible, arranged symmetrically about a line that passes through the center of gravity. As indicated in Figure 64, when a plumb line passes a little in front of the ankle, just in front of the knee joint, through the hip joint and just behind the ear, posture is considered normal or average (McMorris, 1961). When the body is out of balance, some part is likely to be pushed or pulled out of its normal place or must work under a strain.

CONDITION OF MUSCLES AND BONES.   The condition of the muscles and bones influences balance. The muscles attached to the bones hold the body in position, as well as making locomotion possible. Good muscle tone is therefore important. All the skeletal muscles are arranged in pairs, and, in order to have good balance of parts of the body, these opposing muscles must be of equal strength. When one pair of muscles is strong and the other weak, equilibrium is lost, and that part of the body is thrown out of balance. Forward shoulders illustrate this point.

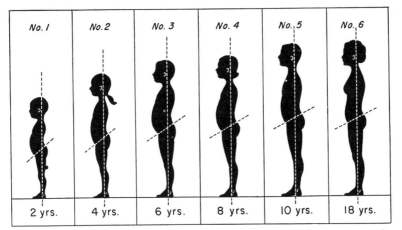

FIGURE 64.   *Silhouette copies of photographs of children of various ages who were considered to have acceptable posture. These illustrations are not drawn to scale. The apparent kyphosis at ages 6 and 8 is caused by scapular winging, which is common at these ages. The relative tilt is illustrated. (R. O. McMorris: Faulty posture. Pediat. Clin. N. Amer., Vol. 8, No. 1, Feb. 1961.)*

INFLUENCE OF COURSE OF DEVELOPMENT. Balance of the body is influenced by the child's growth and development (Phelps, Kiphuth and Goff, 1956). His body is growing and changing in its proportions. Muscles are immature, ligaments loose and relaxed. He has greater mobility and flexibility of joints than adults have. This range of movement in joints is reduced by the gradual tightening of ligaments and fascia and by the strengthening of muscles.

The uterine position persists in the newborn infant. With legs and arms flexed and a convex curve which includes head and body, he is practically a little ball. Much of the first year he is in a recumbent position, and the force of gravity operates horizontally, tending to "unroll" the "coiling" which had been his uterine position. The activity of the infant is also a factor. When the neck muscles become sufficiently mature to hold up his head, the first of the adult spinal curves, the cervical curve, appears. Later, when he begins to stand and walk, the lumbar curve at the lower part of the back appears with a compensating dorsal curve. At the same time the pelvis is tilted forward and the abdomen becomes prominent.

When the child begins to stand and walk, the legs have lost some of the natural curve that may be confused with the condition called bowlegs, which may be one of the characteristics of a rachitic child. During early infancy when he kicks, stretches and stiffens his legs and feet as he cries or anticipates being taken up, he is practicing the shortening of the external rotators of the thigh and exercising the muscles in the abdomen and buttocks. This stretching and adjustment of muscles in the hip, back, legs, shoulder, chest and abdomen are part of his development in preparation for crawling and walking. He will use his arms and legs freely without undue fatigue unless overstimulated beyond the limits of his strength.

A very young child is unstable when he stands because a high center of gravity and a small base make him top-heavy, and immaturity of the nervous system makes it difficult for him to adjust his balance when it is disturbed.

To maintain balance the child, when he begins to stand and walk, stands with everted (toeing-out) feet far apart and with knees flexed. This adds stability by increasing the base on which he stands and lowers his center of gravity. The weight of the body tends to fall on the inner part of the foot, and pronation occurs. Pronation refers to a position of the foot in which the weight in standing is borne heavily on the inner side of the foot, resulting in prominence and sagging of the foot in the area of the ankle; the heel is tilted outwards. The relaxed ligaments and fat pad under the arches give the pronated foot the appearance of being flat. A degree of knock-knee is also present. Gradually, as the rate of growth slows down and relative strength and coordination increase with increased activity, skillful movement becomes as important as weight bearing in the child's balance. With the variety of activity and the resulting muscle strength of the various muscle groups, by six or seven years feet and toes point straight ahead and knock-knees have become straight (Kendall, Kendall and Boynton, 1952). The exaggerated lumbar curve called lordosis, which is still present during the preschool years, but in less degree than during infancy, and the prominent abdomen tend to disappear later. Adult posture, with its upward tilt of the pelvis, does not become established until adolescence.

PERSONAL ATTRIBUTES.   Individuals differ in body dynamics as well as in other phases of development. Some children use their bodies with ease and grace; others apparently use up more energy than most in the daily activities of life; still others, because of their unique body structure, have certain limitations in achieving coordinations.

Because of differences in body structure, children demonstrate differences in body dynamics. The posture of the child in Figure 65 is typical of a young mesomorphic child. The muscular child and the linear child, by nature of their physical endowment, differ in the way they balance the segments of their bodies. For example, a relatively heavy child has more weight to balance, which may affect his leg and foot positions. Certain foot defects may be associated with missing ossification centers. Differences in relative tissue growth, discussed earlier, may contribute to postural differences. Thus there is no one best posture for all children; posture must be evaluated in terms of each child's physical structure and functioning.

A young child seems to express his feelings by the way he uses his body. Preschool children who are insecure and unhappy may indicate their unhappiness by the sagging of shoulders, the tilt of the head, the gait or by lack of activity. On the other hand, children may demonstrate their happiness with a buoyant, vigorous bodily approach to all activities. The child with a focus of infection lacks vigor. A child with a defect such as poor hearing or limited vision may develop a characteristic posture because of this limitation.

EXOGENOUS ENVIRONMENT.   Many environmental factors contribute to posture by their direct or indirect relation to the condition of the muscles and their functioning. Nutrition has been considered in Chapter Five. Balance of rest and activity pertains to fatigue, which can contribute heavily to poor body balance. Young children tend to seek shorter periods of activity than older children and alternating periods of relaxation. It is difficult at times for the adult to remember that sitting erect is a serious physical undertaking for a young child, and that to stand alone is an incredibly complex and delicate mechanical achievement, throwing into new tensions every one of the complicated muscle-bone levers of his body. The infant exerts much energy in these newly acquired skills, and he seems to need time for recuperation.

Generally, the young child, as his skills develop, finds opportunities for all kinds of activity—running, climbing, digging, swinging—thus strengthening all the muscles of his body. Occasionally, however, a child has limited possibilities for use of large muscles. Such a child may become hesitant to try new activities. Some muscles will lack the stimulation of vigorous exercise and may not develop so well as others, which may lead to poor body balance.

Certain aspects of the child's surroundings may affect his posture. If clothing is generally loose and light, activity is not impeded. Socks which are too short cramp the toes. Shoes which fit the foot give both support and flexibility. When an infant is beginning to walk, a proper shoe can both protect the immature foot and aid in walking. Such a shoe has a straight inner border, flat soles and firm heel structures against which an infant can brace his feet in walking. Later, during the pre-school years, laced shoes or oxfords with combination lasts are recommended because of the relatively broad toes and narrow heel of the young child. Some children wear shoes only occasionally. Going barefoot on surfaces that have some resilience, such as sand, grass or a heavy carpet, can provide freedom of movement, but the immaturity of the foot of the young child would indicate the value of supplying support and protection when he is walking on hard surfaces such as pavements or floors without carpet or rugs.

Beds that are flat and firm and chairs that are low enough for feet to touch the floor and shallow enough for the child to sit with his back supported influence good posture. When he sits in a chair too high and too deep, the weight of his dangling feet pulls his shoulder girdle forward and thrusts his head forward.

Parents or other adults can provide the child with an environment conducive to development of coordinated movement and can give him the freedom to explore that environment. Since children tend to imitate, it seems possible that they may imitate the postural habits of adults, especially those of their parents, in activity and in repose. In addition, the adult can provide for regular health examinations by a physician in order to assess the child's progress and detect the beginning of any difficulties. A child also needs protection against illness, as far as possible, and, when illness occurs, protection from fatigue as he is convalescing. The muscles of a child who has been ill have lost some of their tone. Time is needed for their recuperation.

Contrasts in Posture

The beginnings of usual movements and positions of the body occur in the early years. Figure 65 shows a child whose coordination contrasts with that of the child in Figure 66. Muscular relaxation is evident in the latter child. Stuart (Vaughan, 1964) pointed out that functionally poor posture is not surprising in the early years, since children in these years are relatively thin, have loose ligaments and limited musculature, and engage in constant physical activity during the waking hours, characteristics which may lead to chronic fatigue.

Posture which becomes crystallized in later years may have begun in childhood and persisted through the years. This is not inevitable, however. Children with relaxed musculature resulting in poor balance do not always carry that posture throughout life. Figure 67 shows pro-

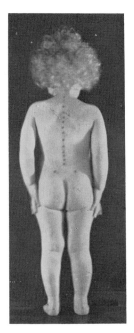

FIGURE 65. *Muscle contraction and relaxation in posture of a 2½-year-old child.*

FIGURE 66. *Relaxed postural pattern of child persisting at different age levels. Note sharp angle of pelvic tilt, prominent abdomen, lordosis, round back, flat chest, forward shoulders and forward head.*

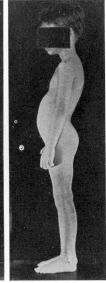

3 years 1 mo.   4 years 9 mo.   5 years 10 mo.

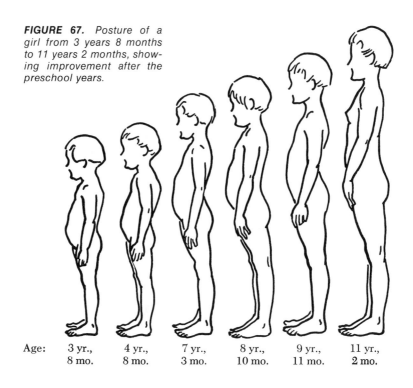

FIGURE 67. *Posture of a girl from 3 years 8 months to 11 years 2 months, showing improvement after the preschool years.*

| Age: | 3 yr., 8 mo. | 4 yr., 8 mo. | 7 yr., 3 mo. | 8 yr., 10 mo. | 9 yr., 11 mo. | 11 yr., 2 mo. |

gression with improvement in muscle tone. Variables influencing the progression are indicated on pages 282-285.

ENDOCRINE GLANDS

Endocrine glands are small glands distributed widely throughout the body that secrete directly into the blood stream complicated chemical substances, called hormones, which are essential to life and to the growth and health of the body. These glands vary in structure and in the nature of their secretions and have the special functions of initiating, regulating and controlling some of the activities of organs and tissues. Although the amount of the secretion of these glands may be almost inconceivably small, they have incredible potency. The glands include the pituitary, thyroid, parathyroids, adrenals, pancreas, ovaries, testes and placenta. (The placenta is discussed in Chapter Three.) The thymus is not classified as an endocrine gland, and there is no proof that the pineal gland has endocrine functions (Williams, 1962).

The functions of these glands are diversified. Because they influence growth and maturation, a discussion of them is included in this chapter. They also play a role in many other aspects of life which have been touched on earlier, such as the body's response to stress (Chap.

Four); maintaining homeostasis (Chap. Four), e.g., regulating the calcium level of the blood; and nutriture (Chap. Five); regulating oxygen consumption and participating in the metabolism of nutrients. They influence sex differences and indirectly, by their physiological effects, moods, feelings and emotions.

The activity of one gland is affected by the secretion of another. Thus the performance of one gland reflects the activity of another. This reaction of one hormone to another can be either antagonistic or synergistic. Growth and development are influenced by at least three hormones: pituitary growth hormone, thyroid hormone, and androgen derived from either the adrenal gland or the testis. All these hormones stimulate protein anabolism, which means the use of protein in tissue building. Much has yet to be learned about their effect on growth and development. Probably each of these hormones manifests its effects at a different period of life and in a different way (Wilkins, 1965).

The thyroid probably exerts its most important influence on growth and development during the first few years of life when development is most rapid. The adrenal androgens are probably responsible for the growth spurt of both sexes at adolescence. The period of life when the pituitary growth hormone is effective is not known. It is probably important during early childhood, since dwarfism can be recognized at this time. Cessation of growth in pituitary dwarfism is not often observed until the third or fourth year (Wilkins, 1965). This fact leads to the belief that the growth hormone is of little importance up to about three years of age. Other glands indirectly affect growth through their part in metabolic processes, thus providing for a healthy body and materials for growth.

This interaction between hormones creates a balance that differs among individuals. Different endocrine constitutions are apparent because of these differing balances. Because of this interaction, the feedback or push-pull (as named by Ham and Leeson, 1965) theory is used to explain hormonal control. This can be observed in the relation of the pituitary gland to the adrenal cortex and the gonads. Pituitary hormones stimulate growth and secretion of the adrenal cortex, and the gonads and hormones of these glands, in turn, affect the secretion of those of the pituitary.

Endocrine glands interact also with the nervous system (Green, 1962; Williams, 1962). Hormones can reinforce nervous system activities, as is noted in intense emotion when the sympathetic nervous system is reinforced by secretion of epinephrine by the adrenal medulla. Hormonal activity can also be initiated by the nervous system, as when the central nervous system stimulates the pituitary to secrete certain hormones which, in turn, affect other endocrine glands. The stimulation of lactation (see Chap. Five) is another example of this relation. The act of sucking stimulates the central nervous system, which, in turn, stimulates the pituitary to secrete prolactin, which stimulates lactation.

Individuals may differ in the amount of hormone secretions and in the response to these substances. A person may have too little, too much or a normal amount of a particular hormone. Thus there is the possibility of three functional patterns produced by each hormone.

Pituitary Gland

The pituitary is a small gland lying in a depression of bone, called the sella turcica, in one of the most protected parts of the head. It consists of two parts, a glandular anterior portion, an upgrowth from the roof of the mouth, and a posterior neural portion, a downgrowth from the brain (Ham and Leeson, 1965). In fact, the posterior lobe is not a discrete endocrine gland, but is a component of the secretory part of the nervous system (Daughaday, 1962b). This gland influences almost every organ of the body either directly or indirectly by way of other endocrine glands; it therefore influences growth and maturation.

The anterior lobe elaborates six known hormones. One, the *growth hormone*, influences the growth of bone and soft tissue. This is called somatotropin because it acts on the soma, or body. An excess of this hormone in the growing years may cause excessive growth in stature. If the excess comes after the growing years (about twenty-five years), the bones become coarser and heavier. If there is a deficiency of this hormone during the growing period, infantile characteristics persist.

Another hormone, *prolactin*, secreted at the end of pregnancy, initiates and provides for the continuation of lactation as it reacts with other hormones (see Chap. Five). Other hormones stimulate the growth and function of many other endocrine glands such as those affecting the thyroid (thyrotropin), adrenal cortex (adrenocorticotropin, ACTH) and sex glands or gonads (gonadotropins). These consist of the follicle-stimulating hormone (FSH), which stimulates the development of mature germ cells, and the luteinizing hormone (LH), which in the male stimulates the growth of the interstitial cells of the testis and their secretion, testosterone, and in women stimulates growth and secretion of the corpus luteum, whose secretion, progesterone, prepares the uterus for the fertilized ovum.

The pituitary is responsible for maintaining equilibrium among the endocrine glands. Ham and Leeson (1965) call the pituitary gland the "chairman of the endocrine society." All the different members report to it regularly about their activity, and the pituitary, in turn, by a series of hormones, has a controlling influence on the structure and function of the various members. This balancing of endocrine activity is explained in the push-pull or feed-back theory. The pituitary thus is affected by hormones of the other glands and also by the hypothalamus of the central nervous system (Daughaday, 1962a; Ham and Leeson, 1965; Talbot et al., 1952). The posterior neural portion secretes two hormones, *vasopressin*, which stimulates smooth muscles of the blood vessels and intestines, and *oxytocin*, which (1) stimulates contraction or increased tonus of the uterine wall so that it may help in expelling the fetus, and (2) seems to participate in the regulation of lactation, i.e., in the "let down" of milk at the time of nursing (Chap. Five) (Daughaday, 1962b).

Thyroid Gland

The thyroid gland, located in the front of the neck, consists of large lobes on either side joined by a narrow isthmus, and secretes a hormone, *thyroxin*. Its development begins early in fetal life. It is one of the first endocrine glands to appear. By the fifteenth week it is well differentiated and begins to secrete thyroxin (Williams and Bakke, 1962). After birth it continues to grow in size until puberty.

Thyroxin has numerous and widespread effects. "It probably stimulates a single basic energy-producing reaction common to most tissues" (Williams and Bakke, 1962). It regulates the rate of oxidation in the body and is therefore related to cellular activity. It influences the rate of growth, development of the bones, the nervous system, circulation, muscles and, in conjunction with the pituitary and gonads, the functioning of the reproductive organs. It also affects the metabolism of nutrients necessary for maintenance and growth. Underactivity of the thyroid lowers the activity of body tissues; overactivity speeds up bodily activities above normal.

A deficiency of thyroxin which begins in fetal life leads to cretinism, a condition in which mental and physical development is retarded. But if thyroxin is given early enough and continued uninterruptedly, the chances for approximately normal physical development are good. Mental development will usually remain somewhat retarded because of possible brain damage during fetal life and early infancy. The mental development attained depends upon the degree and time of onset of deficiency, the length of time between the onset of the deficiency and the treatment and the age at which treatment was begun and its adequacy (Smith et al., 1957; Wilkins, 1965). Overactivity of the thyroid seldom occurs in the early years.

Iodine is a component of thyroxin. When iodine is insufficient to meet the demands for the formation of thyroxin, the gland enlarges. Thus a simple endemic goiter is formed. It is called endemic because it is more likely to occur in areas where the iodine content of water and soil is low. The use of iodized salt in these areas is advisable for children as well as adults.

Parathyroid Glands

These four small glands lie adjacent to the thyroid gland. They attain their maximum growth and mature structure at puberty. Their secretion is essential for maintaining the levels of calcium and phosphorus in the blood that are necessary for regular tissue activity. Through its effect on calcium metabolism, this hormone plays a role in maintaining the integrity of bone structure, in regulating neuromuscular activity, in the conduction of heart impulses, in the coagulation of blood and in the permeation of cellular membranes. Through its regulatory effect upon the availability of phosphate, it can influence body tissues, with special emphasis on bone, many enzyme systems and the regulation of acid-base balance in the body.

The parathyroid secretion varies according to physiological need.

The calcium level in the blood and the parathyroid hormone operate in a push-pull or feed-back mechanism which regulates secretion of parathyroid hormone. When the hormonal secretion is not in accordance with physiological needs, which rarely occurs in children, characteristic symptoms are noticed. Underactivity will result in a reduction in calcium in the blood which limits the amount available for bone formation; if severe enough, this may produce tetany, an abnormally increased reactivity of the nervous system to external stimuli which results in painful muscle spasms. Overactivity leads to decreased neuromuscular irritability so that the muscles of the body are less responsive to stimuli. Demineralization of bone may occur, resulting in spontaneous fractures because of bone fragility (Ham and Leeson, 1965; Rasmussen and Reifenstein, 1962; Talbot et al., 1952).

Pancreas

The pancreas is a gland of both external and internal secretion. It secretes enzymes and pours them through a duct into the digestive tract. It also secretes a hormone, *insulin*, which is produced by the islets of Langerhans. This hormone regulates the use of sugar. When inadequate amounts are produced, carbohydrate metabolism is disturbed, there is a rise in blood sugar, and sugar appears in the urine. The condition is known as diabetes mellitus. The pancreas is not directly concerned with development, but is indirectly concerned, since it controls a source of energy to the cells (Williams, 1962).

Adrenal Glands

The adrenal glands are two very small bodies lying in front of the upper end of each kidney. Each gland consists of an external cortical portion and an internal medullary portion. The cortex is formed from the same embryonic tissue as the reproductive organs; the medulla has its origin in common with that of the sympathetic nervous system. The cortex is highly developed in fetal life as the provisional cortex, which is later replaced by the permanent cortex. A few years after birth the cortex has assumed the characteristics of that of the adult (Forsham, 1962; Ham and Leeson, 1965).

The cortex secretes a number of steroid hormones which perform many functions. They are essential for the maintenance of life. Certain hormones, *androgens*, play a role in the adolescent growth spurt and development. These cortical hormones influence metabolism of sodium, potassium and water, carbohydrate, fat and protein, and the production and maintenance of sex differences. They play an essential role in the body's adaptation to stress (Selye, 1950, 1956). Such a brief statement of the functions of this gland fails to indicate its importance in the various ways its secretions affect the many organs and tissues and the complexities of its activities.

Excretion of adrenal androgens in the urine is low up to the time of puberty (Andersen, 1966).

The adrenal medullary secretions, consisting of *epinephrine* and *norepinephrine*, play a role in responding to emergencies and in the body's adaptation to stress. Although these two hormones combine to produce the characteristic effect of the adrenal medulla, they function differently. Both raise blood pressure, but by different mechanisms. Epinephrine has a greater metabolic effect, e.g., in increasing oxygen consumption and in raising blood sugar levels, than has norepinephrine (Forsham, 1962). They respond differently to emotions (Forsham, 1962; Funkenstein, 1955). Evidence seems to show that anger elicits the secretion of norepinephrine, while fear and anxiety elicit the secretion of epinephrine.

Under normal conditions the secretion is too small in quantity to be of observable physiological significance, but under emergency conditions of emotional stress or danger the secretion is sufficient to cause constriction of the blood vessels, acceleration of heart rate, some delay in fatigue, rise in blood sugar level and increased coagulability of the blood. These effects are similar to those produced by stimulation of the sympathetic nervous system.

The adrenal medulla participates in the body's mechanism of adaptation to stress by participation in a chain of reactions. The hypothalamus stimulates the sympathetic nervous system, which, in turn, stimulates secretion of the adrenal medulla. This secretion, through mediation of the central nervous system, causes the release of pituitary corticotropin (ACTH), which stimulates the secretion of hormones of the cortex (Wilkins, 1965). These hormones function in the body's adaptation to stress (Selye, 1950, 1956). For further detail of the adrenal gland and its function the student is referred to Forsham (1962), Ham and Leeson (1965) and Talbot et al. (1952).

Gonads, or Sex Glands

The testes and ovaries are part of the reproductive system and produce internal secretions which classify them as endocrine glands. In fetal life these hormones are important in sex differentiation. They are relatively quiescent during early childhood. Prior to adolescence pituitary gonadotropins, released by the hypothalamus, stimulate the development of ovaries and testes and their secretions. These hormones are responsible for the changes that occur in adolescence.

The testes produce androgens, which are responsible for bringing about the physical changes of the male incident to maturity. Failure to produce androgens at puberty causes a continuation of growth typical of childhood, thus producing overgrowth with an accompanying failure of sex development. It is thought that testosterone, the principal androgen, is an intermediate product in the synthesis of estrogen (Lloyd, 1962).

The ovaries, also triggered by the gonadotropins of the pituitary, secrete estrogen and progesterone. Estrogen causes the feminization of the child and retardation of growth, thought to be due to the closure of epiphyses. Progesterone is secreted from the corpus luteum when an ovum is liberated. It prepares the uterus for the fertilized ovum and regulates various processes in pregnancy until the placenta takes over. The cyclic changes in the secretion of estrogen and progesterone result in the menstrual cycle. As in the male, if the sex glands fail to produce these hormones, sex development is delayed and childish characteristics continue. An excessive secretion in early childhood will produce precocious puberty.

TOPICS FOR STUDY AND DISCUSSION

1. As a focus for study, select, from each section of this chapter, and phrase with precision, content that you believe you would be most likely to draw upon in considering physical development of a particular child.
2. Plot the heights and weights on the Iowa curves of the two girls whose measurements are given below. Discuss and compare their progress in relation to the standard curves.

	GIRL A		GIRL B	
AGE (in mos.)	HT. (in.)	WT. (lb.)	HT. (in.)	WT. (lb.)
3	23	10.5	22.5	11.9
6	25.6	14.4	25.0	17.0
9	26.8	16.5	27.0	20.0
12	28.8	17.8	28.3	22.2
18	31.4	21.2	31.3	24.3
24	33.8	23.8	33.3	27.0
36	37.0	26.4	37.7	32.1
48	39.7	30.4	39.3	37.1
60	42.8	34.0	43.2	42.9

3. Observe the body balance of a two-year-old and that of a four-year-old in activity and standing. Discuss the way each child balances his body with reference to body proportions, size, muscle tone, coordination of movement. Consider influences of clothing and of physical setting on freedom of movement and on practice of body balance.
4. Discuss the significance of knowledge of bone maturation for students in child development. If possible, have x-ray films or photographs of x-ray films of a boy and a girl of the same chronologic age and of two children of the same chronologic age, but with different skeletal ages, for observation in class.
5. Discuss physical, physiological and neurologic bases of learning to walk.

SELECTED READINGS

Garn, S. M.: Body Size and Its Implications. Chapter in L. W. Hoffman and M. L. Hoffman (Eds.): Review of Child Development Research. Volume Two. New York, Russell Sage Foundation, 1966.

Hebb, D. O.: A Textbook of Psychology. 2nd ed. Philadelphia, W. B. Saunders Company, 1966. Chap. 3, The Nervous System: I. Pathways in Learning and Perception. Chap. 10, The Nervous System: II. Motivational Mechanisms.

Krogman, W. M.: Handbook of Measurement and Interpretation of Height and Weight in the Growing Child. Monograph XIII (3). Evanston, Ill., Society for Research in Child Development, 1950.

Phelps, W. M., Kiphuth, R. J. H., and Goff, C. W.: The Diagnosis and Treatment of Postural Defects. 2nd ed. Springfield, Ill., Charles C Thomas, 1956. Chaps. 1, 2.

Stuart, H. C., and Prugh, D. G. (Eds.): The Healthy Child. Cambridge, Mass., Harvard University Press, 1960. Chap. I, The Principles of Growth and Development. Chap. IV, Physical Growth and Development, pp. 86-116 (development to six years of age).

Tanner, J. M.: The regulation of human growth. Child Development, 34:817-847, 1963.

Watson, E. H., and Lowrey, G. H.: Growth and Development of Children. 4th ed. Chicago, Year Book Publishers, Inc., 1967.

CHAPTER NINE

Motor Development

As the child's body matures, it acquires the ability to function in increasingly complex ways. Thus, along with physical growth, motor, intellectual, emotional and social changes occur. These enable the child to proceed from an uncoordinated, helpless being in the direction of a more smoothly integrated and independent member of his world at the age of five or six. This involves learnings in control of body and about himself, the things and people in his world—what they are and what they are for, what people expect of him and what he does to get along with them. He learns to understand and speak the language of these people in order to find his way about their world. He learns to temper his own feelings and desires to recognize theirs if conflict is to be decreased and harmony found. This is a good deal to achieve in five years; it involves growing as well as learning.

Any summary suggesting the variety of competences which appear in the early years also indicates their hierarchical quality. No child is expected to achieve steps of growth and development at exactly the ages reported in "normative" studies. Some children will move at a pace faster than this in most areas, others at a slower pace. Many will be ahead in some areas, though behind in others. This is the way children grow, and we have less concern with the general speed of a child's development and more about unobtrusively "setting the stage" to enable him to move smoothly along the sequence at his own pace. Particular correlates, established through studies of groups, are not expected to be predictive for the individual child. Rather, they represent variables to be considered when attempting to explain or to facilitate his development.

Having discussed physical growth and development of the body by reference to sequence or pattern, we shall now discuss other development according to additional general categories: motor, intellectual, emotional and social. Organization of material about them in this and the following chapters is as follows: First, a broad concept, theory or idea of an orderly trend of behavioral change over time is presented. Such a presentation, for a particular aspect of behavior and its development, recognizes influences (or explanations) in variables within the

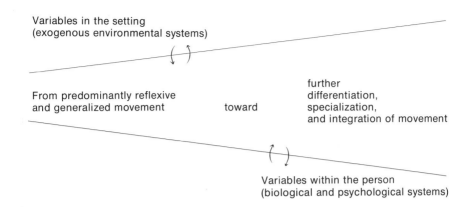

Variables in the setting
(exogenous environmental systems)

From predominantly reflexive
and generalized movement

toward

further
differentiation,
specialization,
and integration of movement

Variables within the person
(biological and psychological systems)

FIGURE 68.   Motor development.

This figure is intended to convey the idea of a trend in motor behavior from the predominantly reflexive and generalized movement of the newborn toward the more differentiated, specialized and integrated movement in the latter part of infancy, preschool years, middle childhood, adolescence and adulthood.

The cornucopia shape suggests the increasing number of organizational patterns of the individual, the larger repertoire of movement, as age increases. The arrows pointing toward the trend in motor behavior suggest endogenous and exogenous influences upon qualities of movements (within the broad trend). The arrows pointing outward suggest influences of qualities of the individual's motor behavior upon other variables within the person and in the setting.

person (biological and psychological systems) and in the setting (exogenous systems). Second, supporting evidence for the broad concept is presented. This factual material is illustrative of current knowledge from research. All this is in accordance with a developmental-dynamic concept, a concept of orderly trends, and a concept of uniqueness of the individual (see Chap. One). Lastly, implications of current thought and knowledge for those associated with children are suggested.

In use of such a method of study a first step, for motor development, is suggested in Figure 68. In some ways this figure represents selection, for more thorough study, of one of the strands of Figure 1 (p. 6). Figure 68 indicates a trend in motor behavior, with recognition of age, and endogenous and exogenous variables. The detail of the figure provides a framework around which to organize content from research on motor development. Both the framework and the knowledge can serve as referrants when considering motor development of an individual child.

In the consideration of motor behavior and its development, the first part of this chapter refers to control over the body in general and pertains chiefly to locomotion; the second part refers to hand skills.

DEVELOPMENT OF CONTROL OVER THE BODY

A broad concept states that the trend in motor development is from predominantly reflex and generalized movement in the newborn toward differentiation, specialization and integration of movement in the older child and the adult. The control the child achieves over his body grows out of the structural and functional readiness of his body for learning. Changes in performance may occur through general experience or through specific practice.

Mechanisms of Control in the Newborn Infant

The most elementary type of response is found in the noncortical capacity of the nerves and muscles (the neuromuscular mechanisms) for reflex and general activity. The more complicated type of response is found in the cortical capacity for learned control of the muscles.

A newborn baby is a fairly efficient living machine. Until he is born, the child's breathing, eating and eliminating have been done for him by his mother's blood stream. At birth he suddenly has to do these things for himself. The birth cry is usually given credit for inflating his lungs and introducing them to the task of respiration. A touch on the infant's lips sets up a sucking movement, a motor response which upon presentation of the mother's breast furnishes the infant with his food. Even though he does these things for himself, he is still entirely dependent upon others for his food supply and his physical needs.

What he can do or feel depends on the development and efficient functioning of his central nervous system. Studies give evidence that the lower (noncortical) centers of the brain, which make possible certain forms of behavior, are well developed at birth, but that development of the higher (cortical) centers is far from complete. Sensory and motor areas of the cortex have been found to be neurologically in advance of the association centers (Larroche, 1966). See pages 275 to 279 for discussion of the nervous system.

REFLEXES PRESENT AT BIRTH.   The newborn is well equipped with many of the neurologic reflex movements common to human beings at any age. He can hiccup, sneeze, cough, blink, yawn and stretch, and he swallows imperfectly (Pratt, 1954). He needs a little longer time before he swallows his saliva routinely. The sucking mechanism is perfected enough to enable him to obtain fluid from his mother's breast, but a little patience is required during the first few weeks, for first sucking is usually slow. Many mothers do not know this, and unless they are under the care of experienced people may become panic-stricken because the baby does not nurse vigorously at once. He regurgitates, urinates and defecates, but he has no control over his sphincters. He has hunger contractions which are sometimes vigorous. The pupillary reflex is also present. In the tonic neck reflex the infant's head is turned toward the right or left side as he lies on his back and the arm of that side extends outward; the other arm is extended upward.

At least three reflex patterns which disappear later are present in most babies at birth. One of these is the *grasp* (or Darwinian) *reflex*, by which the hand closes strongly upon stimulation of the palm. This reflex is distinctly weakened (a sign of maturing) at the end of a month, and in most children is gone by the fourth month—about the time when hand skills are beginning to be learned (see pp. 304-309). The *Moro reflex* is named after the man who described it in 1918. In this reaction, elicited by tapping on the abdomen, by insecurity of support, and the like, the infant spreads his arms apart and then brings them together again in a bow, while the legs make a similar movement (see Fig. 69). This reflex disappears by about three months of age. A third reflex is the *Babinski reflex,* an extension of the toes when the sole of the foot is stimulated. This gives place to the *plantar reflex* (contraction of the toes when the sole of the foot is stimulated, which appears as the nerve centers mature (Richards and Irwin, 1935). The plantar reflex appears in the fourth month after birth in some children, and is present in nearly all children by the eighteenth month. The fourth month is the time when, for most children, the nerves involved become myelinated (develop their myelin sheaths).

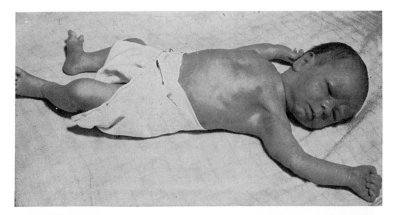

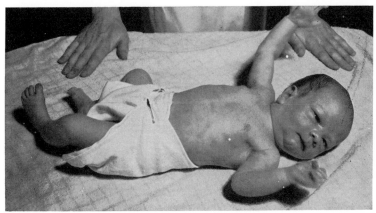

FIGURE 69. *Newborn infant: rest and activity (Moro reflex). (From R. J. McKay, Jr., and C. A. Smith: The Newborn Infant, in W. E. Nelson (Ed.): Textbook of Pediatrics. 8th ed. 1964.)*

GENERAL BODILY ACTIVITY IN THE NEWBORN.   Much of the general activity of the newborn is in response to internal stimuli. His visceral needs direct his behavior. Activity of some infants is greatest just before nursing; for others it is greater after being fed than just before. In addition to activity pertaining to bodily functioning, the neonate is also active in an "attentive" way. He sometimes looks outward or reacts to sound; he is "taking in" from his environment (Rheingold, 1966). His general bodily activity varies when visual and auditory situations have particular characteristics. For example, in a study by Irwin and Weiss (1934) bodily activity decreased as the intensity of the visual stimulus increased within certain intensity ranges of illumination. Decrease in activity also followed initial overt responses when auditory stimuli persisted (Pratt, Nelson and Sun, 1930). In other studies increase in body movement occurred in response to particular stimuli (Lipsitt, 1966), e.g. in the startle response. Reaction to the startle stimulus decreased with repetition of the stimulation.

The early reflex movements, as well as the generalized motion of many parts of the body, are foundations from which the infant proceeds to more complex neurologic functioning and behavior. His use of inherent reflexes and stimulation is a base for further interactions with environment—interactions which have implications for cognitive development (Sigel, 1964).

Development of Control

Within the framework of wide individual differences of maturity rates, development in control of the body proceeds, in most instances, from control of the head through the torso (or trunk) to the legs, and from control of the torso, at the center of the body, outward through the arms and legs (Griffiths, 1954; Shirley, 1931). The full-term newborn and the premature infant who has reached forty-one weeks after a period in an incubator have excellent muscle tone.

In the neck, strong tonus in all muscle groups is evident. . . . The extensors of the head are able not only to straighten the head with the infant in the sitting position, but also to keep it in line with the trunk (for a moment), although the infant has to struggle against a slight tendency of the head to fall back. The greatest change (from the premature stage of 37 weeks) is found in the neck flexors, whose increased efficiency keeps the head in line with the thorax as the infant is pulled up by the wrists. This is a recent achievement. . . . Spontaneous rotation of the head is fairly full (in the full-term newborn) (Saint-Anne Dargassies, 1966).

Even at the end of a month the infant has progressed in his rudimentary and uncertain control over his *head and neck.* By four to six months most children can hold the head up strongly and hence no longer need support of it as they are held. When placed on a hard table, most children of four to six months can lift the upper part of their bodies and, by pulling their elbows under them, can stay up for several seconds. This response is evident in Figure 70. Practically all children

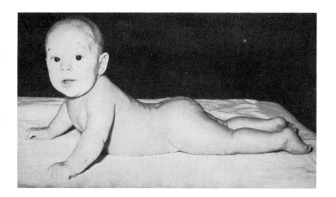

FIGURE 70. **Early motor development includes control of muscles of the head and the torso.**

This 4-month-old infant has the ability to hold up his head and forward portion of his torso.

can do this by nine months of age. If not hampered by clothing, the child growing at the usual rate can *roll* himself over from stomach to back by five to seven months. Sometimes, while lying on the floor on a blanket, he may discover at six or seven months that he can propel himself by wriggling or hitching. There are wide differences in all these rates of motor development, however. Motor items are included in infant test series, such as those of Bayley (1936), Gesell (1925), Gesell and Amatruda (1947) and Griffiths (1954). Revisions of Bayley's Scales of Mental and Motor Development are discussed in Bayley (1965) and Werner and Bayley (1966).

Some children can *sit up* for short intervals at four or five months if sufficiently supported by pillows. The baby shown in Figure 71 has adult help in sitting up. Gesell et al. (1940) found that 20 per cent of the infants they studied were able to sit up with slight support of pillows or

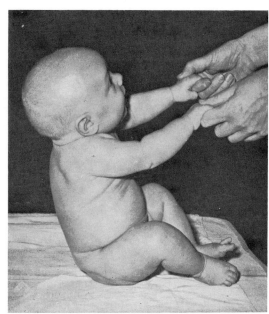

FIGURE 71. **Early motor development includes control of movement of head and back.**

This 4-month-old infant has some control of head, neck and back muscles and can pull up with help, but cannot sit up

blanket at four months; at six months over half sat up in this way, and about 20 per cent sat alone for some seconds. According to Gesell's norms, practically all children of nine months were able to sit alone. Griffiths (1954) and Shirley (1931) corroborated these findings, so that, in general, progression of a baby at six to eight months is such that he sits with slight support, falling over only when he becomes tired or when his wrigglings or a desire to reach something upsets him (Fig. 72).

Stepping movements are usually made at approximately six or seven months if the baby is held under the arms. At eight or nine months he has usually learned some technique or other which serves to get him from one place to another with ease. He may travel on all fours, sit and hitch himself along with his heels or scoot along on one hip, using both hands and the opposite foot for propellers.

Standing with support appears in most children at eight to ten months and is often fully developed by twelve months (Bayley, 1935). Standing without support is almost universal by eighteen months.

The period from nine to eighteen months is one of rapidly increasing facility in locomotion. All investigators agree that this is a time when the child learns to creep, to pull himself up by chairs, to climb, to walk and to control his body as a whole. Rapidly developing children are constantly on the move and may even climb stairs in the creeping position by twelve to fifteen months. If given opportunity for practice on stairs that do not offer too great hazard, many children of eighteen or twenty months can ascend and descend in an upright position with the aid of a banister (Bayley, 1935; Griffiths, 1954).

Dropping from a standing to a sitting position as well as pulling up from a sitting to a standing position may require a practice period for

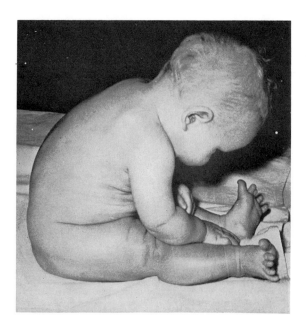

FIGURE 72. Development of coordination is indicated by ability to sit alone.

This 8-month-old infant is able to sit alone, but sitting is still wobbly

learning to control balance and muscle action. Most children have achieved both skills by the time they are a year old. The proportion of the body, the short legs and longer trunk, demands a period of experimentation until the child can adjust the center of gravity of his body so that he can sit, stand and move with the assurance of not falling.

The ease and assurance with which most children learn to walk gives the casual observer no indication of the relation of structure and function, the complex learning that it represents. Controls and adjustments require maturing of skeletal and muscular systems and of the neuromuscular mechanism. Perceptions pertaining to the functions of seeing and hearing and of bodily balance help the child to steer his course to his cherished possessions. All three are needed, since the child not only must learn to place one foot after another; he must also see where he is going and learn to steer around or go directly to objects in his environment.

Crawling and creeping are accessory to the main pattern of development. Most children go through them as a step on the way to walking; some children do not (see Fig. 73).

Walking is a step in bodily coordination developed over a considerable number of months. The coordination begins when the child first tries to lift his head and proceeds when he splashes in his bath with his mother supporting him, around three to five months of age. Bodily coordination proceeds when he accomplishes the sitting posture by himself, then stands up and walks off. By the time he has learned to sit up his visual range has widened, and he turns his head in response to sounds (see Chap. Ten). Initial steps in locomotion usually occur at any time from eight or nine to eighteen months. The average age of walking is cited by many writers at somewhere around thirteen or four-

FIGURE 73.   Motor development proceeds toward more precision of movement of arms, hands and legs.

This 11-month-old child is kneeling and also using eye-hand coordination

teen months, although many children walk before then, and many
others not until fifteen or sixteen months. Most children have taken
independent steps by eighteen months of age (Gesell and Ilg, 1943).

Locomotion continues to develop, proceeding from awkward tod-
dle, flat-footed paddling about, stumbling, running, labored stair-climbing, timid balancing along low inclined boards toward increasingly
complicated adjustments of the body in movement. The walking skill
has been perfected when the child walks and runs with grace and ease
and when he unhesitatingly adjusts to and swings around obstacles in
his path. This behavior of easy motion in any direction and skillful
adaptation to obstacles is achieved by a few children by $2\frac{1}{2}$ years of age;
many children have it by three to four years; most have it by five years.
(See pages 9 and 10 and Figure 2, p. 10.)

As the walking skill becomes smoother and as grace develops, interest in other forms of locomotion is evident. A number of variations
are tried out, such as *standing on one foot, jumping, hopping* and *climbing.*
These, along with learning to ride a tricycle, a two-wheeled scooter
and, finally, a bicycle, all follow as refinements of upright locomotion
and general body balance. Hopping, jumping over low obstacles and
standing on one leg are accomplished by most children before five or
six years of age if opportunity for practice is allowed. In a study by
Gutteridge (1939, 1947) *galloping* was not seen in three-year-olds, but
many four-year-olds practiced it, and many five-year-olds could do it.
Skipping is a later accomplishment for many children.

Much of the factual material on usual sequences in motor develop-

**FIGURE 74. Taking independent
steps enables the child to investigate
more of his world.**

*This 16-month-old child showed body
balance in walking and in leaning
forward.*

FIGURE 75. *Activities involving balance and variation in motor response appeal to young children.*

This child, 3 years of age, repeated the activity of climbing up, walking down the incline, or jumping off, a number of times.

ment is from early research on child development.* Recent interests in relation of motor behavior to other attributes of the individual will be considered in the discussion of variables in motor development (p. 310).

An orderly trend of behavioral change over time in control of the body has been presented (pp. 295-305), and reference was made to related research. Figures 69 through 75 suggest progression from the predominantly reflex and generalized movement of the newborn toward the more coordinated movement of the older child.

In this progression the trend toward further *differentiation, specialization and integration of movement,* which Figure 68 indicated, is evident. Each of these qualities, as seen in movement, seems to be present in the baby of Figure 72, who sits up, but is wobbly, and also in the child of Figure 74, who stands with some balance. But the plane of neuromuscular functioning seems to be more complex in the older child. These qualities and their trend are suggested in photographs of the same child over a period of years (Fig. 76). Thinking of differentiation as making or showing a difference, proceeding from the one to the many; specialization as directing to a specific end or use, concentrating efforts in a special activity; and integration as forming into a whole, incorporating into a larger unit—we can attempt to identify or assess them in the motor behavior of the child shown in Figure 76, *A.* Here, at two years, movement of one hand is differentiated from the other; the functioning of many neck and back muscles provides body balance; specialization is in the concentration of efforts on grasping the cube and on turning to

---

* Reviews of early research on motor development are in Ausubel, 1957; Bayley and Espenschade, 1941, 1944, 1950; Dewey, 1935; Espenschade, 1947; and Fowler, 1962.

FIGURE 76. *Differentiation, specialization and integration of movement occur in simpler and more complex behavior.*

These are photographs of the same child at different ages (2, 5 and 8 years). Distinctions among movements, concentration of efforts in a special activity, incorporation of movements into a larger whole, are evident at each age. Greater complexity in the differentiation, specialization and integration of movement are suggested as she grew older and had more experience.

smile at her father; integration is in her inclusion of these various motor controls at the same time. At the age of five years (Fig. 76, *B*), as she runs down the side of a steep rock, and at eight years (Fig. 76, *C*), as she stands at a height, ready to grasp a rope and board to swing out, differentiation, specialization and integration of movement are again present; increase in the complexity of the organizational patterns (neuromuscularly) is suggested.

DEVELOPMENT OF HAND SKILLS

Differentiation, specialization and integration at different levels of complexity are evident in the child's bodily control and in his use of his hands and his eye-hand coordination as he grows older and also as he has particular opportunities for learning.

Learning to Use Thumb and Fingers

Development in the use of the thumb and fingers is evident during the baby's first months. At birth the hand, though strong enough in the

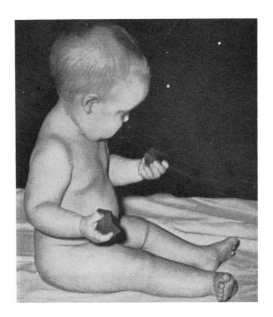

FIGURE 77. Use of thumb and fingers in apposition in grasping represents progression from a palmar scoop.

Sitting with ease at 9 months, this baby has secured 3 cubes and holds them with thumb-finger or pincer grasp.

reflex grip to maintain the body weight, is useless as a vehicle of the will. The thumb lies flaccid and helpless in the palm or fans out uselessly. The hand, however, and especially the fingers are providing, through the sense of touch, some exchange with the outside world. The fingers of the hands may come together, touching, exploring each other as early as one month after birth. Picking up an inch cube with the palmar scoop (an awkward scoop with the whole hand) may be the approach at four to five months. The same technique was used on a small sugar pellet by 50 per cent of the infants studied by Gesell et al. (1940) at six months. By eight to nine months, however, the fingers and thumb work in apposition to each other to make effective the pincer technique of picking up and holding objects (Fig. 77). By one year looking at a small object and picking it up skillfully with the fingers and thumb have become one smooth, coordinated activity (Gesell et al., 1940; Halverson, 1933, 1937, 1943). The greatly increased efficiency of the hand as an organ for grasping when the thumb is in apposition can be seen if the reader will try closing the thumb into the palm of his hand before grasping an object and will then release the thumb so that it can appose the fingers as is normal in adult grasping or in picking up objects.

Hand-Eye Coordination

The development of fine prehension (the act of seizing or grasping) in infants involves integration of visual and neuromuscular components. Reaching and grasping, as the behavior progresses, reflect organizational patterns contingent upon the eye's ability to see and the hand's ability to grasp.

Progression in prehensile behavior and in adaptation to various objects in the environment has been studied from a variety of angles. McGraw (1941) indicated phases proceeding from the newborn's random waving of the hands and reflex grasping to a manipulative and deliberative phase, with sustained attention to the object and effective reaching as long as the child gave undivided attention to it. In the mature phase both the visual and neuromuscular aspects of the performance were reduced to minimum requirements.

Another series for reaching and grasping was described by Shirley (1931) as follows: reaching and missing; reaching and touching; reaching, grasping and not holding; and finally reaching, grasping and manipulating. Shirley found that most of this learning takes place between three and nine months, the process being complete for normal children at nine months.

Gesell and Amatruda (1947) developed a test which suggests sequence in the child's adaptation to materials which interest him. If we present a child of less than six months with a small wooden cube and then with a second, he is more than likely to drop the first in order to take the second. By four months he usually reaches incipiently with both hands, his whole body as well as his hands participating in his eagerness. Such reaching is not as a rule effective, but soon the reaching becomes more nearly narrowed to the use of his hands and becomes more efficient. At six to nine months the greater efficacy of reaching for objects with one hand has been learned, and, as is characteristic of new learnings, the child seems unaware for the moment of other possibilities; so he uses only one hand, dropping one prized object for another. Usually by nine months he uses each hand with enough independence from the other that he can retain the first cube while he reaches for the second (Fig. 77). Three cubes are often too much; he drops one or both to gain a third. Usually, by twelve months he is equal to three, occasionally reaching for the third with his mouth, and by eighteen months he can accept a fourth or even a fifth without losing those he already has.

Development of visually directed reaching has been studied (White and Held, 1966) with reference to a ten-step analysis of responses, including swipes at object (by about two months), unilateral hand raising, both hands raised, alternating glances (hand and object), hands to midline and clasp, one hand raised, torso oriented toward object, hands to midline and clasp and oriented toward object, a Piaget type of reach, and top level reach. In the Piaget type of reach the infant raises one hand "to the vicinity of the object, followed by alternation of glance between hand and object, a narrowing of the gap between them, and then contact. This response and the '*top-level*' reach reflect a return to unilateral function in the fifth month (c. 150 days) of life."

Normative study provided information on range of ages and median age (indicated above) for appearance of these responses. Subjects of the study were infants born and reared in an institution because of inadequate family conditions. In an experimental approach environmental conditions were varied for different groups of infants, as in-

TABLE 10. Comparison of Prehensory Responses Among All Groups

RESPONSE		OBSERVED IN	TOTAL N*	MEDIAN AND RANGE OF DATES OF FIRST OCCURRENCE (DAYS)
				20 40 60 80 100 120 140 160 180
SWIPES AT OBJECT	C+H	13	13	
	ME	11	14	
	MOD. E	14	16	
UNILATERAL HAND RAISING		15	15	
		12	13	
		13	16	
BOTH HANDS RAISED		16	18	
		12	13	
		13	16	
ALTERNATING GLANCES (HAND AND OBJECT)		18	19	
		10	10	
		12	12	
HANDS TO MIDLINE AND CLASP		15	15	
		7	10	
		10	14	
ONE HAND RAISED WITH ALTERNATING GLANCES, OTHER HAND TO MIDLINE CLUTCHING DRESS		11	19	
		5	9	
		7	14	
TORSO ORIENTED TOWARD OBJECT		15	18	
		4	9	
		5	12	
HANDS TO MIDLINE AND CLASP AND ORIENTED TOWARD OBJECT		14	19	
		3	9	
		4	12	
PIAGET-TYPE REACH		12	18	
		6	9	
		8	13	
TOP LEVEL REACH		14	14	
		9	9	
		13	13	

●——● CONTROL AND HANDLED
●----● MASSIVE ENRICHMENT
●—·—● MODIFIED ENRICHMENT

B. L. White and R. Held: Plasticity of Sensorimotor Development in the Human Infant; in J. F. Rosenblith and W. Allinsmith: The Causes of Behavior II. Boston, Allyn and Bacon, Inc., 1966, p. 68.
* N=Number of subjects

dicated in Table 10. Those reared under the usual routine and those to whom nurses gave extra handling each day for twenty minutes from the sixth through the thirty-sixth days are the *control and handled* group of the table. Subjects with *massive enrichment*, in addition to the handling, received from the thirty-seventh through the one hundred and twenty-fourth day, increased mobility (fifteen minutes after each of three feedings they were placed in a prone posture with crib liners removed so that activities of the ward were visible) and also enriched visual surroundings (a stabile with contrasting colors, printed multicolored sheets and bumpers instead of white). Subjects with *modified enrichment* had less modification of the environment than those with massive enrichment. In addition to the handling, they had from the thirty-seventh until the sixty-eighth day two large pacifiers mounted on the crib rails; these had a red and white pattern against a white background. From the sixty-eighth to the hundred and twenty-fourth day these infants were placed in a crib with a stabile similar to that of the other group. The findings, indicated in Table 10, suggest plasticity in human visual-motor development. "Onset of hand regard and visually-directed reaching and the growth of visual attentiveness" were "significantly affected by environmental modification." (See p. 12.) For the group who experienced massive enrichment "it appears that for about a month, starting at day 37, the enrichment was actually ineffective and perhaps even unpleasant. However, once positive responses to the surroundings began to occur visual attention increased sharply." The results were "very much in line with the theory that self-initiated movement with its visual consequences is crucial for visual-motor development." Self-initiated movements were brought forth by elements in the setting.

Learning to Let Go of Objects

Learning to let go of objects seems to involve several steps: simple release and release including bodily balance. An infant's responses at different ages as he drops a cube illustrate these stages. An early step in the "letting go" series is the dropping of objects because the infant has not yet learned voluntary control of the taking-hold and letting-go muscles. He drops the object when his attention and his muscular energy go elsewhere. By six or eight months, however, the letting go is purposeful to the extent that it can become a favorite game to throw a rattle or other object on the floor and have someone pick it up and hand it back.

Hand-Mouth Coordination

Learning to put the hand into the mouth is often one of the earliest coordinations accomplished. As sucking gives way to more mature ways of eating food, we see the development of the hand-mouth coordination for purposes of getting food by the hand method rather than by the sucking method.

Before hand-mouth coordination develops for this purpose of food-getting, however, we often see the infant's fingers or hand getting into his mouth and sometimes being used as a sucking object. This is a reflex-like pattern. In a study of newborn infants during the first five days of life (Kessen, Williams and Williams, 1961) every infant brought his hand to his mouth at least once during five-minute observation periods.

There appears to be another form of hand-mouth coordination that may be relevant to development. This is the use of the mouth as an exploratory organ. The tongue and lips are acutely sensitive touch organs, and children of six to nine months are likely to use them in order to explore everything they can get in their hands. The baby's impulse to explore objects with his mouth provides a way of increasing his knowledge of the many objects that come within his reach. Because of this tendency to put everything into his mouth, he needs some place to play in which offers him freedom yet protection. Opportunity for safe play is to be considered even in the first year of life.

The baby learns not only to carry his hand to his mouth, but also, a little later, to keep his hand (and objects that come into it) out of his mouth. This learning not to put everything into his mouth is called *hand-mouth inhibition*. Hand-mouth inhibition may be regarded as a part of mature hand-mouth coordination; it is present when a child can select the food he wishes and distinguish edible from nonedible substances.

In most children hand-mouth coordination is judged to have begun by around four months, to be dominant at six months, on the wane at nine months, and inhibited at twelve months. This is the exploratory type of hand-mouth coordination and the pattern of waning of the immature pattern. Purposeful, food-getting hand-mouth coordination does not begin until around a year (the time when the immature pattern has waned) and continues in development for several years. By about one year thumb and finger coordination enables the child to be fairly skillful in manipulation of objects. He reaches for the food or spoon during feeding time and thus begins the process of learning to feed himself.

Hand Preference

The question of preference in use of hands arises. Theories concerning handedness differ in the extent to which emphasis is placed on hand dominance or lateral dominance as inherent in the structure of the nervous system and on the extent to which direct and indirect training influences it. It is thought that the side to which the infant faces as he assumes the tonic neck reflex position may be the side for which handedness will develop (Stitt, in Stuart and Prugh, 1960).

Studies provide information on ages in infancy and preschool years at which preference appears. Gesell and Ames (1947) and Ames (1949) found a tendency for alternating preferences in laterality during development and several periods of bilaterality alternating with unilateral reaching and manipulation. Ames says:

> The two hands at the earliest ages work very closely together as though they had not separated off from each other functionally. From 36 weeks through one year a separation and differentiation into an active and a passive hand seems to be working itself out. By 18 months the two hands again move together, but by now in a voluntary simultaneous bilateral grasp by the two hands which are, nevertheless, capable of working quite independently. After two years of age, the passive hand seems to become more passive and to take on more the subordinate role in unilateral behavior.

Hildreth (1948, 1949, 1950) emphasized the gradual settling down to a preference of one or the other hand and the gradual increase of right-handedness with age. A rapid increase in percentage of right-handedness up to three or four years is followed by a gradual increase up to seven or eight years. Hildreth found differences according to activities studied. For example, more children of preschool age ate with the right hand than used the right hand to shovel or to run a toy car.

The exact time to decide whether a child is right- or left-handed is not clear. A child may have a brief or a long period when he seems to use either hand with equal frequency and ease (the ambidextrous period). Some children show definite preference as early as six months, but most children are twelve to fifteen months old before preference is clearly evident. If the child is not markedly left-handed, but seems as late as fifteen or eighteen months to use either hand with equal or nearly equal ease, some parents may encourage the use of the right hand by handing him things toward that hand. Insistence, however, upon the use of the right hand, if the child seems persistently more awkward with the right and more skillful with the left, adds tension, especially if encouragement of the use of the right hand meets with emotional resistance from the child.

A study (E. E. Hunt, 1966) of a population of 10,236 fathers and mothers in New York reported that 3.10 per cent of the women were left-handed and 3.88 per cent of the men. In terms of variability of a symmetrical structure in the human body through X-linked genes, "this difference is not statistically significant and suggests that in this pattern of body symmetry . . . the hypothesis of random X-inactivation seems irrelevant." Sex linkage does not seem to apply as an explanation of handedness.

An anatomic observation with possible relevance to handedness (Benson and Geschwind, 1968) indicates "in a study of fetal and newborn brains . . . that the pyramidal tract from the left hemisphere begins to cross to the right before that from the right hemisphere in most cases. . . . Hand preference may depend upon increased innervation available to one side of the cord, which leads to finer digital control on that side."

The matter of handedness is referred to again in Chapter Ten in connection with the development of language.

VARIABLES IN MOTOR DEVELOPMENT

Influences in Biological and Psychological Systems and Exogenous Environmental Systems

Information on orderly trends in motor development raises many questions on how changes occur. Reference was made in Chapter One to the processes of growth, maturation, maturation and learning, and to the influence of emotional tone. Before these are regarded as explanations of change in motor behavior, it seems appropriate to recall the discussion of the need for activity and rest (pp. 225-235). Activity is characteristic of life itself. At first it is motor and sensory; later it involves complex thought processes. Activity for its own sake produces satisfactions.

Even before birth the individual uses parts of his body, moving his muscles. The newborn has mass movements and also specific responses. As he grows and develops, particular movements of body parts, present earlier or differentiated later, combine in more general and complex movements. Much of the change results from maturation.

In control over the body in general, and in hand skills, approximate chronologic ages at which particular forms of behavior appear seem similar from one child or group of children to another. Similarity of steps through which children proceed gives support to emphasis on the process of *maturation*. Pace in racial groups has been considered in studies of Negro and white children. More advanced skeletal maturation in Negro newborns than in white newborns has been reported (Falkner, 1966). Acceleration in pace of motor development in Negro children has also been reported (Ferguson et al., 1956). Bayley (1965), comparing motor test scores of Negro and white babies during the first twelve months, found the Negro babies more advanced. In other studies, variations among Negro groups have been reported (Dreger and Miller, 1960).

Hebb (1966) differentiates physical and psychological maturation. In physical maturation there are genetic and chemical factors, both prenatal and postnatal, in behavioral development. In psychological maturation these factors are also present, as well as an experiential variable, i.e., "pre- and post natal experience normally inevitable for all members of the species." In another experiental variable the individual has "experience that varies from one member of the species to another." In studies of motor development we find evidence of change of which physical maturation is one part. Psychological maturation is another part, in which "usual experience" is an influence. We also have evidence of specific experiences, i.e., learning under particular conditions of practice, which affect pace of motor progression.

Relation of maturation and learning, as well as the influence of maturation at early age levels, is indicated in studies of twins. Stair-climbing and cube manipulation at a particular level of competence were accomplished in a shorter period of specific practice by a twin who was faced with the situation at a later age (but not very late) (Gesell and Thompson, 1941; McGraw, 1939).

Research by White and Held (1966) (see pp. 306-308 and Table 10) contrasts competencies of institutional infants who had usual routines and handling with those who had massive and modified enrichment. This enrichment included the addition of particular equipment, which encouraged visual and motor responsiveness, change of position and opportunity to look beyond the crib, when crib liners were removed, so that activities of the ward were visible. These "sensory variables" influenced age at which particular prehensory responses were first evident, and median age of their appearance in the groups studied. The infants initiated the sensory and motor behavior.

On the subject of *learning* motor responses, as something different from having them emerge through maturation and general use of the body, whether or not the response is a universal one for human beings and its complexity are pertinent elements. At the later preschool ages when the skill is complex, such as rolling a marble according to a maze pattern, specific practice of it (as contrasted to general practice) assists its development (McGraw, 1939; Mattson, 1933).

Adult attention to one form of behavior in the child and not to another can influence frequency of particular motor responses. In a nursery school setting a three-year-old girl whose behavior included frequent crawling instead of walking upright, and another child whose passive behavior lacked any vigorous play activity, changed frequencies of their responses when adult attention changed. Adult attention "positively reinforcing" to the child was "successfully used to help him achieve more desirably effective behaviors" (Harris, Wolf and Baer, 1964). Another element in the child's learning of motor behavior which may be pertinent is suggested in a review of research on learning of motor skills in adults which indicates that the *individual's knowledge of results* is "the strongest, most important variable controlling performance and learning" (Bilodeau and Bilodeau, 1961).

Anyone who has watched closely two or more children at a particular stage of motor development in some of such human universals as the ability to sit alone, to walk in a mature way or to run, or in some of the skills of this civilization such as cutting with scissors or riding a tricycle, has been aware of variations in the performance of each. Perhaps the observer has wondered about the bases for these variations. On this subject of *individual attributes*, constitutional differences in body build have already been referred to (see Chap. Eight). Individual variations in the amount of bodily activity, even before birth, have been reported. Studies of fetal life (Carmichael, 1954; Newberry, 1941) show that babies differ in the rate of achieving motor developmental patterns even before birth (see p. 102). There are clear individual differences in general impetus to motor activity. Variations are in amount and vigor of activity (Escalona and Heider, 1959; Fries and Lewi, 1938) and in active-passive behavior (Kagan and Moss, 1962). General movement measured by horizontal displacement of hands and feet over five-second intervals varied in a significant way in infants observed and photographed during the first five days of life (Kessen, Williams and Williams, 1961). The more active fetus is likely to be more advanced in behavior

---

FIGURE 78.   *Problem-solving of young children includes motor and sensory behavior.*

These children, $4\frac{1}{2}$ to $5\frac{1}{2}$ years of age, were playing on new equipment constructed by a student (L. Hatfield), using a large "spool" (originally for telephone wire), metal supports and handles. Problem solving for the boy concerned ways of getting to the top, experimentation with ladders of different lengths, and also experimentation in pulling himself up by means of the handle and the open center section. Problem solving for the girls seemed to concern effects of a close and distant view. In their perception of depth, they looked down from the top to the grass below, then climbed down and looked up, several times. They also looked at a beetle from the height and then at close range.

FIGURE 78   (see legend on opposite page)

development as an infant (Richards and Newberry, 1938; Walters, 1965).

It would be interesting to know more about the relation of variations in motor activity to influences within the individual and to external factors. Variations in general activity in the newborn have been connected with the functioning of the alimentary canal (Irwin, 1930; Richards, 1936; Wolff, 1959). According to what we know about learning processes, it seems possible that the strength of these drives or biologically primitive tendencies toward activity and the satisfaction of hunger might play a part in the amount of practice on motor responses and the satisfactions derived from it. When stress is great in his physical or psychological environment, amount and vigor of activity of the individual may change with age (Escalona and Heider, 1959; Fries and Lewi, 1938).

Investigations of the sources of variation in motor behavior would be of interest not only because they would provide a more thorough consideration of motor development, but also because there are possible connections between motor behavior and personality components. A number of the personality components of the early years include reference to motor performance. For example, the child's use of his body in grasping objects is connected with his sense of trust (see p. 243).

Motor and sensory development provides expanding horizons for the child. Through them his cognition increases; he learns about objects of his world and their connections with space, time and causality (Inhelder, 1962; Piaget, 1954) (See pp. 324-342). Figure 78 suggests the variety of abilities used and consequently developed as children try out, through motor behavior, some of their ideas for handling a new situation. Also, motor competence or lack of it affects the child's concept of his body and of himself. Being skillful or lacking in skill influences the child differently at different stages in development of his concept of self. For the child of early preschool years, not being competent may make him hesitate to undertake an activity, but it is considered less likely to affect his self-esteem than in an older child (Ausubel, 1957; H. E. Jones, 1949; M. C. Jones, 1965).

Motor abilities in the infant do not predict later intelligence. Scores on tests predominantly of motor behavior in infancy do not correlate significantly with scores on intelligence tests at later ages (Bayley, 1955). Many of the test items for infants did not differentiate various elements in sensory-motor behavior and muscular coordination; without such differentiation, tests administered during infancy have been found to be poor predictors of later performance in intelligence tests (see pp. 383-386).

Ability to inhibit bodily activity in children of preschool age, in accordance with particular instructions, correlated positively in an experimental setting with measures of intellectual ability. General activity level of children of preschool age whom Maccoby, Dowley and Hagen (1965) studied was not correlated with measures of intellectual ability.

Nevertheless ability to inhibit movement in test situations (in which the child was asked to draw a line slowly, or walk slowly, or lift a jeep slowly by a string on a winch of a toy truck) correlated positively with measures of intellectual ability.

Implications of Thought Concerning Motor Development

RECOGNITION OF FACTORS OTHER THAN MATURATION IN LEARNING BODILY CONTROL AND EYE-HAND COORDINATION. The child's control over his body grows out of the readiness of his body for learning and out of the stimulation his environment provides. This carries a connotation which concerns *enabling the child to feel free instead of hampered in his use of his body.* Implicit in this is a concept of self-discipline. Furthermore, it assumes that the young child who feels free will seek activity which involves the use of his emerging abilities. The following specific factors to be considered when thinking of a child's motor responses are ramifications of this connotation.

Walking is complex, dependent on many inner or maturational factors, and its perfection takes many months. As the child proceeds in this direction at his own pace, one of the influences of the parents, or others, can be in offering him plenty of free opportunity to be as active in general bodily movement as he wishes to be. Later, training in muscular coordination comes through walking, running, climbing, stooping over and standing up, lifting and loading. This may mean climbing up and down steps and over large boxes and pushing loaded wagons, or it may mean using other kinds of equipment.

A case in point is that of Edward. When Edward came into a play group at twenty-five months of age, he had lived always on the second floor of a duplex apartment. There had been no yard or outdoor play space, and he had been carried up and down the steps into the apartment. When out on the street, he was either wheeled in his carriage or led by the hand for a few blocks. Upon entering the group he had had no experience in the coordination of his body in climbing stairs, mounting the jungle gym or climbing on and off a tricycle. All these movements had to be learned. It was several months before he could mount without apparent concern the small ladder by which most children climbed easily and eagerly to the measuring board in the physical growth laboratory. So far as one could judge, this inability to climb was not due to a fear of falling. That his environment was responsible for this condition was suggested by his prompt response to opportunity to use play equipment and the subsequent disappearance of his awkwardness, lack of balance and sense of physical inadequacy.

Parents, or others, can see that the child has *opportunity to practice the motor skills*; they can also consider whether his muscles lack tone or whether he suffers from malnutrition, since, if he has either of these defects, he cannot be expected to support himself in an upright position as soon as a normal child would. If he has been or is ill, he may lack the muscular strength necessary for walking, which, being a new and unaccustomed activity, demands great strength and energy. *Illness* handicaps him also because it curbs his interest in activity and thus deprives him of even the amount of practice his small physical strength might endure. Another influence concerns *space* that is not too slippery, too drafty or too dirty to permit freedom for practice. *Clothing* and *shoes* may be factors in motor development, since the child could be hampered by garments that interfere with free movement or by shoes that are restricting or heavy.

Certain *emotional factors* may affect the child. Severe accidents may produce fear and timidity. Too great anxiety on the part of adults over casual bumps may convince a timid child that he takes too great a risk. Too great enthusiasm over his first attempts may inhibit a self-conscious child. If the parents become overanxious because he does not have a particular skill, the anxiety may be conveyed to the child, and the excessive importance attached to his learning may make him too afraid of failure.

Again, some children have less *motivation* for one form of motor behavior than for another, for reasons not yet discovered. They may have less satisfaction from the thrill of large movements and more satisfaction from certain eye-hand coordinations. It seems logical to let the six- or eight-month-old infant struggle a bit when he has let his rattle drop only a few inches from him. The thrill of recovery can attach satisfaction to his efforts and encourage him to make the effort the next time. When a nine- to twelve-month-old baby has a ball to play with, the urge to pursue it can provide him with a motive for practice in locomotion. In fact, balls of varying sizes and weights illustrate a type of educational play equipment, appealing from a few months of age through the entire period of childhood.

Variations in interest in achievement of a particular skill have not been explained. Why one child persists in learning to use scissors, another in learning to pump on a swing, and still others give up quickly on learning these and other activities are questions yet to be answered.

Development of courage or timidity may be a by-product of motor learnings. If we regard the degree of satisfaction which the child gets from learning to walk as evidence of the innate nature of that act, we can scarcely dispute the innateness of the urge toward locomotion. The thrill of accomplishment which accompanies each new bit of learning seems genuine, as the child throws back his head to show his delight or abandons himself to practicing again and again his new achievement. The number and severity of bumps that some children take without complaint or discouragement in the process of learning upright locomotion suggest intense absorption. The adult who curbs the child's freedom or seems too concerned over bumps during this learning period may be discouraging physical courage. Nevertheless, knowing that sympathy and care will be forthcoming if he is genuinely hurt in a fall can be reassuring to the child.

CHANGE OF ACTIVITIES AS SENSORY-MOTOR ABILITIES INCREASE.
Skill in manipulation of objects develops rapidly from one to two years of age forward (see Fig. 79). Combined with the rapid development of

FIGURE 79. Some play materials lend themselves to use on different levels of difficulty.

Pouring water from the cup into the muffin pan interested this particular child. A younger child might put pebbles or grass into the pan and from there into the tub, and back. An older child might experiment to see whether the pan and cup would float or sink in the tub.

upright locomotion, especially of climbing and running, and associated with a rapidly growing curiosity about things, it can produce behavior disconcerting to some families. The insistent getting into things and the constant handling of everything in the environment sometimes cause sharp conflict between parent and child. Nevertheless the development of hand skill offers something of a balancing interest through absorption in play with blocks, clay, sand and water. Most children do not spend long periods of time seated at this sort of activity, but some of their energy is directed into it.

Our interest includes sequences in activities and not just ages at which a majority have a particular skill. Yet it is helpful to the adult who wishes to encourage the child's use of his abilities to have a few landmarks indicating ages at which many children easily and happily add complex sensory-motor behavior. At two years most children have skills which enable them to scribble, cut gashes in paper with scissors and pile four or five blocks into a tower (Stutsman, 1930). They can string spools on a shoelace and use a fork and spoon, though not without a good deal of spilling. A few children at two become interested in helping to dress themselves. Armstrong and Wagoner (1928), who studied the "functional readiness progress" of children in terms of their ability to dress themselves, reported that at two years of age the children were largely disinterested and indifferent to the activity of buttoning up jackets and seemed not to have the motor control required to manipulate the buttons. Less than half of the children studied by Gesell could put on their own shoes at twenty-four months.

FIGURE 80.   The child's use of eye-hand coordination in settings other than play can be absorbing if he feels unhurried.

This 2½-year-old liked taking off her shoes and socks. She seemed to want autonomy and also help from others when she needed it.

At three years abilities differ in the degree of development. At this age, if they have been given opportunity to learn, most children can accomplish many self-care and other motor activities. They can, for example, copy a circle with a pencil, close the fist and wiggle the thumb, build a high tower with blocks, build simple block houses (Stutsman, 1930). They are able to set a low table if told what to put on it, carry a plate or bowl, feed themselves with a fork, wipe up spilled things without aid, dust, help care for a pet animal and wipe certain dishes. They can also learn to wash themselves, running the water into the bowl, soaping backs and palms of hands, using a washcloth for the face, and wringing it out and hanging it up on their own hook if it is within their reach. They can manage the front buttons of clothing and can undress themselves with the exception of difficult buttons and fastenings and can hang up their own clothing.

These skills by which the child cares for himself depend, of course, on the kind of clothing, the nature of the house in which he lives and the attitude of surrounding adults, as well as his own abilities. Figure 80 shows the interest of a 2½-year-old in using motor skills in an environment which encourages their use.

FACILITATION OF SENSORY-MOTOR DEVELOPMENT THROUGH PLAY EQUIPMENT AND MATERIALS.   Enabling the child to feel free instead of hampered in the use of his body and of his hands has particular meaning for play activity. It suggests the importance of the availability of materials and experiences appropriate to progression in motor development. Equipment and playthings can offer opportunity for sensory and motor practice when the child is ready for various steps. But to provide self-consciously chosen equipment which anticipates every step of development can create an atmosphere of expectancy and resultant tension which would be unwholesome. No amount of equipment can encourage growth for which inner readiness is not yet mature. Too much equipment may tend to rob children of initiative, especially at the age when imagination is developing and when self-resourcefulness can be stifled by an overelaborate set of playthings.

Even if we could bring forth the most mature behavior possible for each child at every stage of readiness, we might question trying to do so, since this in itself takes on the aspect of forcing development. We would not coax him into experiences; we would let him indicate a comfortable pace for himself by letting him seek each experience. Simple toys and play materials, space in which to use them and in which to keep things, and freedom to use them according to his own ideas are pertinent to this emphasis on "leads" which the child himself provides for the adult who is attentive to them.

On the other hand, progression is influenced by the opportunities the adult provides in his setting. For example, in Figure 79 an adult who noticed the child trying to pour water from the large tub into the muffin pan might find a container of a different size from that of the cup the child had been using. Or the child, if he knew where to look for it, might go and get it. Figure 81 suggests that a setting in which the child can proceed from use of ability on one level of difficulty to use on another level can facilitate development.

Variation in use of equipment according to ability is illustrated in play with blocks. In the use of a small set of blocks, for example, the child in one phase of development simply dumps them out of the box, or picks them up one or two at a time and bangs them back into the box to hear the noise they make. Considerably later in development he piles one on top of another, at first achieving a tower of not more than two. About this time he may enjoy putting two or three back into the box with help, as a beginning in learning how to put them away. Later still he can pile several into a tower before it falls over, and he may begin simple bridge structures such as two blocks set a little distance apart with one on top (Stutsman, 1930). Still later, placements are more complex.

In general, play materials and equipment fall into two classes: those which encourage vigorous motion of the whole body, and those which require manipulating an object with the hand or hands while holding the rest of the body motionless. This latter is sometimes called "fine motor coordination," in contrast to "gross motor coordination." It involves primarily a difference in distance range of muscular involvement. "Gross motor" and "fine motor" coordination are somewhat ambiguous terms.

The paralleling of motor development and use of related equipment can be illustrated as follows. For the infant *three to four months old*

FIGURE 81. *Opportunities for choice of level of difficulty enable the child to find motor activity of interest to him.*

All these children were within the age range of 3 years and 3 years 6 months. In spontaneous play activity their selections of equipment varied in terms of type of movement and balance required.

a soft ball or a rattle hung by a cord over the crib will give practice in reaching and grasping, in directing his hand to strike an object, and in coordinating the eye muscles to follow a moving object. If left there all the time, the plaything may cause overstimulation or overfatigue. If it is too close to his eyes, convergence will involve fixating at too short a range and hence tend to turn the eyes inward.

From *three to seven months* control of grasping and holding develops sufficiently to make a string of large wooden beads or spools an appropriate plaything. A piece of crumpled tissue paper makes an intriguing noise when pounded or squeezed and adds opportunity for use of ears as well as eyes—the connection between movements of the hand and the results obtained. Improvised and casual playthings, such as discarded containers, clothespins, ashtrays, clean short pieces of rope or firm cloth, are often more interesting to the child than more elaborate commercial toys. Care is necessary to see that there are no loose pieces or rough, sharp edges to injure the child's eyes, ears or nose, and that no article could be swallowed.

By *nine or ten months* the use of a rubber ball can provide an incentive for wriggling, pursuit and eye-hand coordination. The child, when he first starts to creep, may find his way to the kitchen cupboard, where he likes to pull out the pots and pans and manipulate covers, parts of double boilers and other equipment.

At *twelve to eighteen months* a box of blocks of 1-inch cube size offers practice in handling smaller objects. Larger blocks, 3 to 4 inches, are also favorites at this age. Simple boxes to open and shut, cloth books with heavy bindings showing familiar objects in bright colors, a sandbox with spoons or a small shovel and a sieve and pail all offer opportunity for practice in hand coordination at this age. A small cart or push-and-pull toy will also encourage general bodily coordination.

Around *two years* of age a 10- to 12-inch board several feet long can be set up, at first on a low block, and later on increasingly higher blocks for the child to practice balance and develop surety in use of his own body. Climbing up and down steps and slides, over packing boxes and on climbing bars or jungle gyms or some substitute offers practice in use and development of the muscles of the legs, arms and back and contributes to agility at an early age. Small cars and trucks, interlocking trains and 12- to 15-inch light hollow blocks encourage activity. Dolls and cuddly animals begin to be popular with both boys and girls at this age. Peg boards with large pegs, simple two- and three-piece jigsaw puzzles and other equipment of this kind offer opportunity for practice in hand skill as well as in sense perception.

By *three years* most children are ready for a tricycle, though some children can use one earlier. Transportation toys such as wagons, a train and a dump truck are popular. A place to climb and space for running are important. Blunt scissors, colored paper, crayons, paints and large brushes, clay, a soap-bubble pipe, hammer and nails and simple puzzles are also related to motor and sensory development.

Climbing opportunities, like those for balancing the body and "stunting" or "I-bet-you're-afraid-to-do-this" activities are increasingly sought from the age of *four years* throughout childhood. A trapeze and rings can now be added, as can a turning pole placed just beyond the child's reach so that he can take hold by means of a little jump. Families of dolls or play animals, a costume box, a wide variety of nature specimens, opportunities for creative activities, a blackboard with chalk or simple construction sets are often sought. All these materials become gradually higher, more complex or more challenging as the child grows into each successive stage of greater competence.

In general, equipment appropriate for children from *two to five years* of age is simple. Plenty of space, particularly out-of-door space, with places to run, climb and dig is in accordance with what the child seeks. Materials which he can rearrange and combine for his purposes are of interest to him. Materials and equipment can challenge him to resourceful activity and encourage general bodily activity and sensory-motor activity. Play can also provide for other aspects of development such as those to be considered in Chapters Ten and Eleven.

TOPICS FOR STUDY AND DISCUSSION

1. As a focus for study, select one orderly trend in development of control over the body and in development of eye-hand coordination, and discuss each with reference to functioning of biological, psychological and exogenous environmental systems. Draw upon evidence from research to illustrate influences of physical maturation, exchanges of the child and his setting in general experience and with specific training variables.
2. Use drawings of body proportions and body dynamics (Chap. Eight) to parallel descriptions of bodily skills of one child at different ages, or of several children of different ages.
3. If you are studying an individual child, make a record of his motor responses in terms of (1) bodily controls and (2) hand skills. Attempt to relate what is observed to explanations of sequence in motor development. Comment on environmental influences (e.g., equipment, materials, opportunities for progression to more complex coordinations) which affect the child's motor behavior.
4. Explore the use of a time-sampling method for indicating relative frequency of bodily activity and activity of arms and hands only, in several children in free-play indoors and out of doors, at the same hour on several days.
5. Consider different pieces of play equipment, those which encourage vigorous motion of the whole body and those which encourage use of the hands. Indicate the order in which you would include the equipment in the child's environment, and state the reasons why.
6. The student particularly interested in variations in motor development may wish to note variables emphasized in references such as the following: Bakwin, H. (Ed.): Developmental Disorders of Motility and Language. Pediatric Clinics of North America, 15:3, 1968. H. Bakwin, Foreword; R. S. Illingworth, Delayed Motor Development; J. S. Werry, Developmental Hyperactivity; R. N. Reuben and F. Bakwin, Developmental Clumsiness.

SELECTED READINGS

Harris, F. R., Wolf, M. M., and Baer, D. M.: Effects of adult social reinforcement on child behavior. Young Children, 20:8-17, 1964. Also in W. W. Hartup and N. L. Smothergill (Eds.): The Young Child. Reviews of Research. Washington, D.C., National Association for the Education of Young Children, 1967.

Hartley, R. E., and Goldenson, R. M.: The Complete Book of Children's Play. New York, Thomas Y. Crowell, 1957, pp. 1-38.

Kessen, W., Williams, E. J., and Williams, J. P.: Selection and test of response measures in the study of the human newborn. Child Development, 32:7-24, 1961.

Landreth, C.: The Psychology of Early Childhood. New York, Alfred A. Knopf, 1958. Chap. 4, Motor Behavior (section on factors affecting development of motor skills presents detail from various research).

Maccoby, E. E., Dowley, E. M., and Hagen, J. W.: Activity level and intellectual functioning in normal preschool children. Child Development, 36:761-770, 1965.

Space for Play: The Youngest Children. By Lady Allen of Hurtwood, F.I.L.A., et al. Published by World Organization for Early Childhood Education. Distributed by National Association for Education of Young Children. Washington, D.C., 1964.

White, B. L., and Held, R.: Plasticity of sensorimotor development in the human infant; in J. Rosenblith and W. Allinsmith (Eds.): The Causes of Behavior. II. Readings in Child Development and Educational Psychology. Boston, Allyn and Bacon, Inc., 1966. Also reported in White, B. L.: An experimental approach to the effects of experience on early human behavior. Minnesota Symposia on Child Psychology, Vol. 1:201-225, 1967. Minneapolis, University of Minnesota Press.

CHAPTER TEN

Intellectual Development

In Chapter One the growing person was referred to as a manifold. On the intellectual side of this ongoing manifold are sensory development, language, concept formation, problem solving, thought, creativity and intelligence. In each of these the predominantly sensory and motor activities of the infant and the young child enter into the concepts and ideas of the older child. Intellectual development includes early foundations as well as later use of symbols and abstractions.

When particular aspects of intellectual development (among the many strands of Figure 1 [p. 6] are singled out for study, an orderly trend is evident in each, as well as in their composite. This trend is from few schemata (organizational patterns, in the sense of transposable or generalizable actions) toward more schemata with further differentiation, specialization and integration. This change occurs through mechanisms of motor ability or movement, sensory perception, language, concept formation, problem-solving ability, thought and cre-

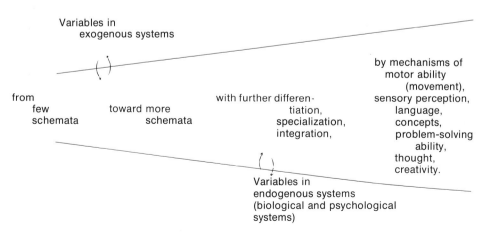

FIGURE 82. Intellectual development.

ativity. In each of these forms of development endogenous and exogenous systems have variables affecting change. Figure 82 attempts to convey this description and explanation of intellectual development.

The newborn and the young infant have relatively few schemata. As the individual proceeds from infancy to preschool years, to middle childhood, to adolescence, to adulthood, his intellectual functioning not only adds associations, but also fits them into previous ones, sorts, combines and recombines them, thus forming more complex organizational patterns of thought. To assess, with some precision, the degree of complexity of the child's organizational patterns (his differentiation, specialization and integration) as revealed by behavior is one of the problems of study of intellectual development. Efforts of various kinds are made to discover change in knowing, i.e., cognitive development. Another problem in study of intellectual or cognitive development is to attempt to discover how change occurs.

DEVELOPMENT OF SENSITIVITY AND PERCEPTION

The child reacts to his world through the *organs of special sense*, and learning for the normal child is largely dependent on the efficiency of these organs.

The organs of special sense may be divided into (1) those of the special senses of taste, smell, sight and hearing, and (2) those associated with the general sensations of heat, cold, pain, pressure, and so forth. What we commonly think of as sense organs are those which have receptors that are stimulated or directly acted upon by some energy change having its source in contact with the surface of the body or nearby as in the sense of touch, or having its sources at a distance, as is true of the eye and ear.

Although the sense organs are structurally well developed at birth, the child comes to use them with greater efficiency and meaning with further development of the nervous system (Scheibel and Scheibel, 1964) and with further experience. At first the newborn and the young infant have sensory reactions in response to the present situation only. Later, a similar situation has many more meanings based on previous experience. *Sensitivity* is present when reaction to stimuli, such as light, form or sound, occurs. When this reaction initiates a series of associations (mediating processes in the central nervous system), *perception* occurs (Hebb, 1966). For example, when the child sees his mother's face above his crib and this initiates associations of comfort, this is perception. Or he may perceive that a cup is to drink from (or to turn upside down) and that a piece of cracker is to eat, whereas a rattle is to be shaken. Or an older child who sees a toy iron on a small ironing board may carefully change its position, placing it on end instead of in a flat position where it might "burn."

Meanings become associated with the things seen, heard, tasted, smelled or touched. As time goes on, perception of the properties of the external world becomes more objective, the child becomes more discriminating in responding to important cues. Increased competence of this kind is an important part of the child's cognition, of his knowing what the world is like.

Gibson (1963) makes distinctions between the variables of sensory discrimination and those of perceptual discrimination. Variables of sensory discrimination are "dimensions like quality, intensity, extensity, and duration, dimensions of hue, brightness, and saturation, of pitch, loudness, and timbre, of pressure, warm, cold, and pain." Variables of perceptual discrimination are

> . . . dimensions of the environment, the variables of events and those of surfaces, places, objects, of other animals, and even of symbols. Perception involves meaning; sensation does not. To see a patch of color is not to see an object. . . . To feel a local pain is not to feel the pricking of a needle. . . . To hear sound is not the same thing as to hear an event, nor is to hear an increasing loudness to hear the approach of a sounding object. . . . (Speech phonemes) are acoustically analyzable . . . but their distinctive nature consists of higher-order variables. . . . Phonemes are the same at quite different levels of pitch and loudness, and hence are phenomenally constant for the voices of men, or women, or children. . . . They are invariant with changes of auditory sensation.

The child perceives the meaning of a word that he hears, although the sound of the voice varies. The child explores and searches and obtains information from the available stimulation. He is an active system of sensitivity. A simultaneous array of many inputs, and also sequence, stream or change in the simultaneous pattern characterize real life situations. By his activity of selective attention the child discovers stimulus variables for perception (J. Gibson, 1963).

In describing a developmental sequence of thought Piaget (Inhelder, 1962) refers to the child's elaborating his schemata:

> The schemata are transposable or generalizable actions. The child establishes relations between similar objects or between objects which are increasingly dissimilar, including relations between those objects and his own body. . . . Each fresh acquisition consists in the assimilation of a new object or situation to an existing schema, thus enlarging the latter and coordinating it with other schemata.

In a stage occupying approximately the first two years, called a sensory-motor period, assimilations are by sensory-motor mechanisms. The child enters into the situation physically. In the next period, which continues beyond the preschool years and is called a period of preoperational thought, assimilations and accommodations are also in a "face to face" exchange with the immediate environment; in addition, there is an increase in symbolic functioning. Being more able to use words and thought, the child more frequently thinks of something without having to try it out in sensory-motor behavior.

Broad concepts or ideas on use of sense organs and perceptual development might be phrased as follows: Sensitivity (reaction to sensory stimuli) is present on the first day of life. Differentiation of stimuli occurs in the very young infant. Behavioral change can occur as a function of how the infant is stimulated; in other words, learning can occur in the very young infant. Sensory stimulation in the first few months of life, as well as later, is important for well-being and development. An orderly trend in development is from simple attention (observing and orienting responses) toward the establishing of relations among dimensions of the environment. Elaboration of organizational patterns occurs through processes of assimilation and accommodation. The following sections include illustrative material related to these ideas.

Sense of Touch

Sensations having their origin in the skin—namely, touch, pain and temperature—have their own *receptors*. These receptors are unevenly distributed over the body.

By means of the sense of touch the child experiences shape, texture, hardness and similar characteristics of bodies with which the skin comes in contact. Certain areas are more sensitive to stimulation than others; e.g., the finger tips are more sensitive to touch than the back of the hand; the lips are more sensitive to heat than the hands. Not all areas of the skin are sensitive to all kinds of stimuli: an object warmer than the temperature of the skin will stimulate only heat spots; a moderately cold object activates only cold spots. Each of these senses undoubtedly has its own special receptor structure which is adapted to stimulation by the definite kind of environmental change with which it is associated. These structures have the same degree of specificity in their relation to the effective stimulating agent as do the rods and cones for light (Carlson, Johnson and Calvert, 1961).

Although the senses of touch and pain are perhaps the most nearly perfect of any of the senses at birth, authors generally agree that newborn infants are not very sensitive to externally applied touch or pain stimuli (Pratt, Nelson and Sun, 1930; Smith, 1959). Within the first three or four days after birth, infants become increasingly sensitive to tactual stimulation (Lipsitt and Levy, 1959). As to pain, even severe scratches or blisters do not seem to cause much discomfort, though most infants have a definite reaction to needle pricks. Even though infants seem thus fairly insensitive to surface abrasions of the skin, they are sensitive to varying temperatures in their bath water or in the room (see p. 133). Infants are probably more sensitive to colder than to warmer temperatures.

The newborn infant begins to use the sense of touch in feeding a short time after birth. His tongue and lips are sensitive to touch at a very early age; later they are used as a means of investigating things in his world. Before the third month fingers are used to produce touch sensations (Bühler, 1930; Shirley, 1931). Babies can be seen at this age lying in the crib carefully touching one hand against the other for the sheer experience of the sensation produced.

Throughout the preschool years touch remains one of the most pleasurable of the child's sensations. He uses it for exploration of almost everything within his reach. Furthermore, the sense of touch adds much to cognition in the early preschool years when exploration of the sensations of hardness and softness, roughness and smoothness, warmth and cold is at a peak. Children of this age are usually alert for opportunities to touch fur, a raincoat, figured goods, starched cloth, silks, the woven pattern of a wicker chair and anything else that offers information about the way things feel.

This running of the fingers over every available surface is really more than the mere seeking of sensations. It is also an exploration of objects as such, an endeavor to learn just what "feel" is associated with what "look" and what "use." The child's reaction to printed silk or to the pattern on linoleum is an example of this. He may have learned in the past to associate change of level with change of line; e.g., he knows that the edge of a table means a drop to the floor line. Now he is interested to discover that in some instances change of line means no change of level; so he runs his fingers over and over the pattern printed on dress or drapery materials and sometimes expresses his discovery by asking why something that looks rough feels smooth.

The young child seems interested in relating the experiences of touching with looking. In this sensory-motor exploration of objects of his world he seeks to add tactual and visual schemata, as well as those from other sensory experiences. In touching an object he adds kinesthetic knowledge which can be "stored" before he has symbols or words. Study of active processes of touching and looking has been of interest in Soviet research on perceptual development. Wright (1966), referring to Pick's (1963) general summary, says that the research "is derived from a 'motor copy' theory of perceptual recognition." For example, "running the fingers around the contour of a block constitutes the image of its shape. . . . Stereometric, three-dimensional objects . . . are more readily discriminable in terms of recognition of size and shape than are two-dimensional pattern stimuli or pictures."

Sense of Smell

Odor reception and discrimination on the first day of life and increased sensitivity to olfactory stimulation in the first four days of life have been noted. Infants reacted to asofoetida (a strong-smelling substance) by increase in body movement and in breathing activity; a nonodorous stimulus in front of the infant's nostrils did not have these effects (Lipsitt, Engen and Kaye, 1963). They reacted to weaker stimuli (had a lower threshold for reaction) on the fourth day than on the first, second or third day. With repeated stimulation within a short time (within minutes) responsivity declined; temporary "habituation" occurred.

In some instances, in early research, when strong stimuli were introduced, reactions may have been of pain. According to Pratt (1954), "newborn infants react vigorously to such stimuli as ammonia and acetic acid, but whether these . . . reactions of the body musculature are to be ascribed to the sense of smell or of pain is uncertain."

Not only the capacity of the newborn to respond to olfactory stimuli, but also his ability to differentiate among stimuli is of interest. Furthermore, if behavior change occurs as a function of how the baby is stimulated, this has interesting implications concerning the human newborn as a learning organism. In an experiment related to these ideas (Lipsitt, 1966), infants became habituated to a mixture of several odors. Response-decrement occurred in a series of trials, with one minute between trials. But when one component of the mixture was offered immediately after this decline of responsivity, the infants were more responsive. These data provide information relevant to an assumption being investigated, i.e., that "recovery" of response to a component "could not be considered a peripheral or sensory fatigue phenomenon but would have to be ascribed to some central process." Thus change in behavior as a function of how the baby is stimulated (a learning process) is suggested. Learning can occur very early in life.

Thorough research on changes in olfactory sensitivity beyond the first few months has not been done (Reisen, 1960).

Smells agreeable to infants are not always considered so by adults. For example, Dearborn (1910) reported that at $11\frac{1}{2}$ months a baby showed no dislike for the bad odor of rancid fish oil emitted by some small fish vertebrae she was playing with, but smelled them repeatedly. He also said that at one year the odor of a fresh marigold was distasteful and caused the child to turn her head away. Preyer (1893) reported that an infant as late as the seventeenth month opened his mouth upon presentation of a fragrant flower. This mistake was not made by this baby after eighteen months of age.

Sense of Taste

Pratt (1954), in a summary of gustatory reactions of the neonate, said: "It is uncertain whether the neonate differentiates all four taste qualities. It appears, however, that in terms of the sucking response salt solutions tend to break up the response, whereas sugar solutions elicit and maintain it. Acid solutions to a lesser extent evoke sucking; quinine solutions seldom do."

Observations lead us to believe that the sense of taste is fairly discriminating after a few months (the taste buds are structurally mature soon after birth). The baby's pleasure in taste, like that in smell, does not always correspond with adult judgment. For example, children accept without objection foods which have high nutritional value, but which adults consider distasteful. Acceptance of a variety of tastes can occur early. Learning that tastes as well as textures vary occurs through a variety of experiences as new foods are introduced in accordance with the physician's recommendation (see Chaps. Five and Six).

In a study of children forty-nine to sixty-one months of age, taste sensitivities to sodium chloride and sucrose solutions were similar to those reported elsewhere for adults. Threshold values were not found for adults for quinine sulfate and acetic acid (Korslund and Eppright, 1967).

Sense of Hearing

The auditory apparatus consists of the ears, the outer, middle and inner ear, and two auditory nerves to convey stimuli to the centers of hearing in the brain. At birth the cavity of the middle ear has almost reached its final size—in fact, the ossicles of the middle ear have reached their mature size in the middle of fetal life—the tympanic membrane has practically completed its growth, and the bony labyrinth of the inner ear has attained its adult size and proportion. Hearing in the newborn is probably established within a few days. In the infant the eustachian tube, the channel connecting the middle ear with the throat, is short, straight and comparatively wide. This may account for the greater incidence of middle ear infections in infancy, bacteria from the throat having easy access to the ear.

Hearing is an important means by which the child relates himself to his environment and is a factor in learning speech.

Stitt (in Stuart and Prugh, 1960) listed three "levels of hearing which contribute to behavior and development in infancy and childhood."

At the most basic level or *primitive* level, sound affords an awareness of movement and change in one's surroundings. In more complicated or *significative* behavior, noises and sounds come to characterize certain conditions, and in turn evoke response; for example, the ring of the doorbell. Perhaps the most complex level of hearing is the *symbolic* level, related to hearing, comprehending and reproducing language. The processes involved are based on interrelationships among auditory, visual, and muscular stimuli and responses, and on integrity of the sensory organs, and the peripheral and central nervous system.

The reaction of the fetus to vibratory stimuli has been reported, and auditory sensitivity in the newborn has been confirmed by a number of investigators. Whether the sound leads to certain reflex reactions or to general bodily activity depends on its intensity and duration. Nearly all writers agree that sharp or quick sounds cause responsive blinking, starting, circulatory and respiratory changes, and sometimes crying during the first few days of life. Some children react to voice sounds before the tenth day (Bryan, 1930; Koffka, 1925). Conditioned responses to auditory stimuli in the first few weeks have been reported (Lipsitt and Kaye, 1964; Marquis, 1931; Wenger, 1936). Several writers mention instances of responses to piano notes, bells and the human voice during the first few months.

Adaptive motor responses to the sound of a voice, ringing of a bell or shaking of a rattle which is out of visual range have been included in a number of infant tests. A large proportion of children turned their heads at the sound at five and six months (Bayley, 1936; Gesell, 1925). A stage of turning the head with eyes remaining ahead was reported as preceding a stage in which the eyes were directed "searchingly to all sides" (Bühler, 1930).

The development of discrimination among sounds is rapid from eighteen months to three years of age. During this period the child learns to. distinguish as well as to identify countless sounds that have not heretofore held meaning for him. He indicates his ability to identify the difference between bird calls and squirrel noises, between his father's voice and Mr. Smith's voice, the special tone which identifies his parents' automobile horn, and so on. Doubtless his growth in the language field makes learning of this kind seem more sudden than it really is. His vocabulary increases rapidly at this time, so that he may appear to be learning for the first time meanings which he has learned before, but can only now express. In any case, he seems to be acquiring understanding of the sound world about him at a spectacular rate.

Sound discrimination is illustrated by an example from Templin's study (1952) of speech development in which the child distinguishes between the words "box" and "blocks" as he hears another person say them and also as he says them.

> In the preschool test, pairs of pictures which were familiar to the children and . . . similar in pronunciation except for single sound elements were presented. An example of an item is a picture of a "box" and some "blocks" presented on a single card and the child is then asked to point to whichever one the experimenter says . . . While both motor and perceptual skills are involved in the production of most sounds, the importance of the perceptual skill probably is increased when the sound is uttered in the proper position in a standard word.

The child's interest in and ability with music also increase rapidly. Although children differ tremendously in capacity to enjoy and to respond to music, most of them in early preschool years have learned to recognize a few simple tunes, can beat a simple rhythm, can detect the difference between high and low notes, between slow and rapid rhythms and between loud and soft intensities in music (see pp. 381-382).

Sense of Sight

To appreciate the discussion of the development in children of the perception of size, shape and distance, knowledge of the physical equipment which makes perception possible is important. Through the sense of sight the child detects light, senses form, recognizes color and perceives depth and distance in space.

The newborn can respond to strong light and objects before his face. This is possible because the sensory cells of the retina, the rods, which detect the intensity of light and make vision possible, function immediately after birth. Later the other sensory cells, the cones, develop, and these ensure recognition of color and contribute to the recognition of form. According to Stuart and Prugh (1960), eye movements begin to coordinate after the first few months and for most are well coordinated by eight to nine months. The eyeball is short and shallow in early life, producing a normal farsightedness, which diminishes as the anteroposterior diameter of the eyeball increases and reaches its adult dimension by six years. The infant can see as well at the periphery as at the center of the eye. Central or "straight" vision develops gradually, reaching adult level around the seventh year. This development depends on practice in seeing objects and focusing upon detail. (For information on development of vision, see Eichorn [1963] and Keeney [1966]).

In considering the child's visual sensitivities and perceptions (as well as those of other sense organs), interest is in stimulus sources to which he responds. What places, things and events give rise to stimuli for him? Gibson (1963), discussing the young child's perception of the environment, refers to "space — that is, the surfaces and edges and places that make up environment" (e.g., behavior in response to depth at an edge and to imminent collision). Other stimuli sources are "objects proper" (detachable solids) and two-dimensional representations of objects (as in pictures), and also unrepresentative and "coded" stimulus sources, such as writing. Much of the study of perceptual development concerns the question: Under exactly what stimulus conditions did this particular differentiation occur?

Looking has been noted in very young infants. Among infants ten hours to five days of age patterned objects, such as a disk with a picture of a face on it or printed matter, were viewed longer when attached to the ceiling above the crib than an unpatterned red, white or yellow disk. Also, infants from four days to six months of age looked more at face-like patterns (one a stylized face and another with features in a scrambled pattern) and less at an oval with a solid patch of black at one end (Fantz, 1961, 1963).

Visual attention ("the state in which the infant's eyes are more than half open, their direction of gaze shifting at least once within any 30 second period") has been studied in terms of percentage of the time it occurred spontaneously during three-hour observation periods (White and Held, 1966). Among infants in an institution, studied from soon after birth through four months, a sharp increase in percentage of time spent in visual attention was reported by about two months of age, "about the same time as the onset of sustained hand regard (visual regard of the hands)."

Visual accommodation ("activity by which the image of a target is focused on the retina of the eye") was not reported prior to one month of age. Flexibility of response, as indicated by "accommodation to targets placed at several distances" and by "capacity to track the target as it moved toward and away from his eyes," was reported as beginning by about the middle of the second month with "performance comparable to that of the normal adult . . . attained by the fourth month" (White and Held, 1966; Haynes, White and Held, 1965). For information on effects of several environmental variables on visual attention and sensorimotor development, see pages 306-308 and Table 10.

Accurate perception of distance and depth is made possible by focusing both eyes on an object at the same time. The two images are perceived as one. This ability to fuse two images into one, known as binocular vision, is an important aid in judging distance. It depends both on coordinated eye-muscle activity and on perceptual experience; it has been reported as achieved by most children at the age of six to eight years (Burch, 1966).

Discrimination of depth has been observed in a test with infants of six to fourteen months, using a "visual cliff" which permitted the infants to crawl on glass with a patterned surface immediately under it or 4 feet below on the floor (Gibson and Walk, 1960). Most of the infants could discriminate depth as soon as they could crawl. They would peer through the glass on the deep side and move away or pat the glass, but refuse to move and cross it. "Of the babies who answered their mother's urging" and left the center board of the platform, most "crawled to her when she stood at the shallow side but refused to come when she called from the deep side." The tendency to avoid a drop-off increased as the depth increased (to 4 feet). "The surface quality of the ground under the infant . .-. controls its behavior in the cliff situation." The textured surface, a coarsely checked pattern, provided cues which a plain gray surface did not provide (Gibson, 1963).

Preference for *color* over gray was reported by Staples (1932) in infants by the end of the third month. The infants spent more time looking at colored disks than at gray ones. By six months of age they discriminated among different colors. Discrimination among colors so that saturated colors can be matched with some accuracy has been reported as fairly frequent by thirty months (Stutsman, 1930). Ability to name accurately primary colors (red, yellow and blue) appears later. Experiments on learning which use cues of hue and brightness of a particular color indicate ability of children of preschool age to discriminate slight cue difference (Spiker, 1956a, 1956b; Spiker and White, 1959) (see Fig. 3, p. 15).

Detail about ages at which particular perceptions of color, size, shape and number usually develop is available in the standardization data of intelligence tests (Stutsman, 1930; Terman and Merrill, 1960). Studies of these perceptions, and others, are reviewed by Gibson and Olum (1960) and E. Gibson (1963).

An interesting question concerns the child's relative attention to color and form. Discrimination of both color and form occurs early. Sigel (1964), discussing the question whether color has a greater attraction than form, suggests that form (as a basis for organization of objects) "usually involves meaningful stimuli and may be essential for communicating the meaning of objects. Color may be less salient in the world of objects because it is less relevant to identification and interaction with objects. The form 'chair' may have more significance for the child than the chair's particular color."

Response to shape, pattern, size or solidity, i.e., *perception of form*, develops rapidly during the preschool years.

Perception of *size* becomes more accurate early in the preschool years, but is still in the process of being perfected so that equipment which has size as a variable is of interest to the child. Madame Montessori (1912, 1913, 1920), as early as 1912, appreciated the interest of children from one to five years in sense perceptions and designed many types of equipment especially adapted to such activity. For example, she found them responsive to equipment for training perception of size, such as the following: sets of cylinders varying in diameter but not in depth, or in depth but not in diameter, or in both dimensions; a set of blocks which, arranged in graded size, builds a broad stair, and another set which, piled in order of size, builds a pyramid.

While riding his tricycle the young child has some accuracy in perception of its size in proportion to the width of an opening through which he wishes to take it. Some months after he has fairly accurate perception of the size of most objects, he may try to sit on a tiny doll's chair and look surprised when it fails to support him. He sees himself least and has less opportunity to judge his own size in relation to other things; he still makes mistakes in judgment of his size even when he is well past his fourth birthday. One very intelligent child of five looked surprised when he failed to step over a 3-foot chicken wire fence with the ease that had carried his father over it.

Discrimination in perception of *shape* progresses rapidly in the preschool years. Gibson and Olum (1960) cite Ling (1941) as follows:

> Infants between 6 and 15 months could learn to choose one of two blocks differing in shape when the "correct" one was sweetened and the other fastened to the board on which it was presented. Change in spatial orientation and size of the blocks had little effect on the discrimination, suggesting that form per se was discriminated. Difficulty was increased by increasing the number of blocks presented. . . . These studies made use of three-dimensional shapes—i.e., objects. Discrimination of two-dimensional shapes or drawings is a different and harder task.

The two-year-old child, as he is introduced to play equipment or test equipment, seems to be just beginning to differentiate between a triangular, a circular and a square block if all are about the same size. If allowed to play with pans in the kitchen, he may try to make a triangular cover fit a round pan, or a square pan fit inside a round one. The child's ability to name "square," "round" or "oblong" is different from his ability to see differences in contour which these terms represent. To perceive shape is one thing; to name it is different. The matching games with cards which four- and five-year-olds enjoy suggest their interest in accurate perception of visual detail.

When *pictorial representations of objects* are the stimulus sources in the environment, eighteen-month-old children reveal some ability to discriminate. For example, the child may discriminate between pictures of familiar animals, and will say "bow-wow" when he sees the picture of a dog, or crow on seeing the picture of a rooster. He recognizes these pictures almost as readily upside down as right side up (Gibson and Olum, 1960).

On the question of whether or not a child reared in an environment without pictures until he could speak could identify pictured objects,

Hochberg and Brooks (1962) tested a child whose vocabulary was taught solely by means of objects. Then, at nineteen months, tests of pictorial identifications were made. The child identified both outline drawings and photographs, on cards, of objects such as toys, shoes, spoon, key, car, mother, sister. "This is strong evidence that ability for pictorial recognition is *not* dependent on association between the picture and the represented object, or . . . between the picture and a verbal or naming response" (Gibson, 1963). Without having had the two occur together—the picture and the object—or the picture and the word—the child was able to make appropriate connections.

In study of *discrimination of letter-like forms* (line drawings of a geometric type) *children's errors in differentiations decreased with age* (Gibson et al., 1962). Furthermore, different kinds of confusion decreased at different rates. Matching identical forms by making topological differentiations between a break and a close (resembling differentiation between O and C) involved few errors even at four years and no errors at eight years. Errors in differentiating transformations of line to curve (as in V and U) and in differentiating rotation and reversal transformations (as in d and b or M and W) were much more frequent at four years, but decreased greatly by eight years. Errors in differentiating perspective transformations (slant to the right or slant back) decreased somewhat, but continued to be frequent from four to eight years. Findings for kindergarten children responding to transformations of letters tended to be in agreement with findings when letter-like forms were used.

On the question why the other transformation types are more difficult to detect at four years, Gibson (1963) says:

> Because, I think, they have not been critical for object differentiation. . . . The errors decrease, after four years, depending on whether they are now critical for letter differentiation. . . . As the child progresses into the early school years, the distinctive features of graphemes (graphic symbols) are detected and confusions with relevant transformation types drop out. . . . How distinctive features of the set of graphemes are picked up by the child now becomes a focal issue. Are they pointed out to him by the teacher? To some extent this happens. . . . But the child probably learns a good deal by himself.

Studies of grapheme-phoneme correspondence, which are also related to reading (as are the grapheme differentiations reported here), have been undertaken (Gibson et al., 1962).

Kinesthetic Sensitivity

Knowledge of the part played by the "position sense" in perceptual development is incomplete. Evidence indicates prenatal presence of this sensitivity to position and movement of the body parts (Carmichael, 1954; Zubeck and Solberg, 1954). Certain head and postural responses in the newborn are elicited by the movement of the body as a whole or in part (McGraw, 1946; Shirley, 1931). In the course of this motor behavior static and kinesthetic stimuli are provided which are considered bases or beginnings of responses in the newborn which will lead to upright posture and walking (Pratt, 1954). "Orienting reactions" are "indicated by autonomic and other involuntary responses when attention is focused on a particular stimulus." Included are "changes of state in the sense organs themselves, changes in the musculature that directs the sense organs, changes in the central nervous system, and vegetative changes" (Wright, 1966). These are considered bases or beginnings of responses which lead to perceptions. (See p. 327 for responses of touching and looking.)

In kinesthetic sensitivity, response is to sources of information other than those from seeing or hearing. For example, in speech development some of the information is proprioceptive through sensitivity to pressures, movements and postures. In other responses, involving motor reactions of limbs and of the body, muscles in movement, tendons and joints provide bases for perceptions.

Variables in Perceptual Development

Having ability to use his eyes and ears and other sensitivities, the infant develops "expectancies" regarding the things he sees and hears; he learns meanings of tastes and touches and pressures. He does this by blending experience of things seen, heard, tasted, touched and smelled. Thus repeated sights and sounds and other sensory experiences represent a repertoire which later events supplement. As he proceeds from one phase of development to another the child's cognition is a result not only of immediate reactions to cues, but also of associations previously perceived, though not part of the present external situation. This suggests the importance of perceptions in the child's thinking as he grows older.

Piaget's discussion (1954) of sensorimotor or practical intelligence in the first two years of development refers to the young infant's "assimilating the external environment to his own activity." In the second phase the "increasing coherence of the schemata thus parallels the formation of a world of objects and spatial relationships; in short, the elaboration of a solid and permanent universe. . . . When sensorimotor intelligence has sufficiently elaborated understanding to make language and reflective thought possible, the universe is . . . formed into a structure at once substantial and spatial, causal and temporal" (see pp. 359-360).

Some of the keys to understanding of variables in perceptual development lie in knowledge (at present incomplete) bearing on questions such as the following: To what in his environment is the newborn attentive? How does the individual select particular environmental sources of stimulation to which to be attentive? How does the richness or variety of early sensory experience affect perception at the time, and cognition in later years? In considering any of these questions, it is important to recall a perspective which recognizes variables within the individual, as well as those in his environmental sources of stimulation. With this perspective, variables affecting perception are considered in the context of (or in relation to) other variables, rather than as separate absolutes.

ATTENTION TO CONTRAST AND DISTINCTIVENESS. Attention is a pertinent element in perceptual learning. As indicated in the previous section, the newborn is somewhat attentive to stimuli in the outside world. When environment has variety in it, the infant selects, from many possibilities, a particular part for attention. With this part, differentiation, specialization (in the sense of selection on particular bases) and integration occur. For example, in Figures 83, 84 and 85, each child is adding schemata which make his perception of a person, a hammering board or goldfish more complex. Furthermore, each is beginning to organize (in neural connections) an overall view, a schema, or a concept for now, which may later be revised.

One explanation of the question why a particular part of the environment absorbed attention is in terms of the *contrast and distinctiveness* of the stimuli for the individual (Kagan, 1967). The individual seeks some variety; he also seeks, in his information processing, to grasp the new. Appealing contrast and distinctiveness have some incongruity, an optimum of neither too much nor too little. Handling this incongruity and straightening it out or "ordering" it, in the sense of accommodating the new to the earlier associations, is satisfying. Thus at an early age (about four months) infants found more of a pleasing contrast and distinctiveness in a test situation, in one stimulus than in another (Kagan, 1967; Kagan et al., 1966). They were not only attentive, but also smiled more in response to a three-dimensional face (a sculptured model) which resembled a regular face; they looked at a "scrambled" face, but smiled less in response to it. The smile suggested perceptual recognition

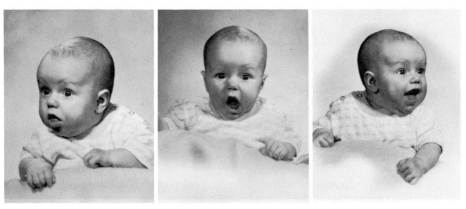

FIGURE 83. *Occasional slight variation in the familiar, and discovery of relation of the novel to the familiar, can be pleasant.*

When these photographs were taken, this 3-month-old boy was being held over the shoulder of a familiar person. Another familiar person stood near the photographer, "jumped up and down" and "made a face." The baby's expression suggests looking, "studying," and then smiling after matching the somewhat different appearance of the person (the unknown) to the known. Photographs courtesy of Vincent Weston.

of the face—a discovery that the new could be fitted into or matched with something already known. "Thus, large cardiac decelerations (a sign of attention) and smiles were most likely to occur to stimuli that seemed to require tiny, quiet cognitive discoveries . . . Sixteen-week-old infants and 8-year-old children smile spontaneously at events that seem to have one thing in common—the event is a partial match to an existing schema and an active process of recognitory assimilation must occur" (Kagan, 1967).

An infant's attention to distinctive elements and his joy in perceptual discovery are suggested by Figure 83.

EARLY SENSORY EXPERIENCE. Deprivation of sensory stimulation in the first few months after birth can have effects not only on an infant's repertoire of associations for perceptual development, but also on his well-being and development in other aspects. Use of neural pathways, as the newborn reacts to sound, sight, touch, taste and smell, means activity in subcortical parts of the brain. This activity, especially of the reticular formation, before there is much cortical functioning, is a basis for further development. This use of sensory equipment and associations with people are a part of the everyday life of most infants. Emotional and cognitive foundations for further development tend to be built together. The one-week-old or the one-month-old may react to light or to a pattern before his eyes; he is also being picked up or talked to, and thus assimilating and accommodating in a world of people as well as of inanimate objects. In the times of quiet wakefulness the infant of one, two or three months of age has a receptivity to events of the external world; his attention goes from one small discovery to another. This occurs when opportunities for contrast and distinctiveness are in his environment.

Casler (1961), stressing significance of sensory deprivation from a neuroanatomic point of view, reviewed studies of infants in institutions. He related malfunctioning at later ages to perceptual deprivation during the first few months of life; emphasis was on lack of early visual, auditory, olfactory and tactile stimuli capable of activating the brain stem and thalamic reticular systems (components of the reticular formations).

Another source of information on effects of early sensory experience is from research on infants and young children for whom specific sensory experiences or training opportunities were added. Some of these enrichments of experience were for children with perceptual deprivation in their background; others were for children for whom deprivation had not been present. Particular competences increased when particular conditions of practice, i.e., conditions for learning, were added. Certain perceptual abilities appeared earlier among those who received specific training or particular opportunities for learning, as compared to a control group. For example, discrimination among sounds and smells, related to experience, was demonstrated in infants in the first few days of life (Lipsitt, 1966).

In other research successful visually directed reaching for and grasping an object above the crib occurred earlier in institutionalized children who received extra handling by a nurse during the first month of life, some novelty (pacifiers in the center of bright red and white targets) during the second month, and additional stimulation of color, design and a view through plastic at the bottom of the crib until four months of age. These babies were able to reach for and grasp an object above the crib earlier than other institutionalized babies who had the stimulating environment in the second month without the transition time of slight novelty. Both groups learned to grasp earlier than the institutionalized babies who continued in the bland environment (White and Held, 1966).

White (1966), discussing effects of different environmental variables on development of prehension (reaching and grasping, which involves eye-hand coordination), refers to a "modified or paced enrichment" as "the most successful match of external circumstances to internally developing structures." In recognizing this plasticity in human visual-motor development, and the variations in effects of different degrees and times of enrichment of experience, he refers to these results as "very much in line with the theory that self-initiated movement with its visual consequences is crucial for visual-motor development." The child in Figure 84 is seeking sensory-motor activities. When equipment for use of his emerging abilities was nearby, he was attentive to it, and initiated activity with it.

When enriched experience was added for children of preschool age, particular competences also appeared earlier than for those who did not receive the specific training. For example, among culturally disadvantaged children, enriched experiences centered around the development of attitudes and aptitudes considered conducive to school achievement (Gray and Klaus, 1965). Teachers of children three to $5\frac{1}{2}$ years of age attempted to "promote achievement motivation, to stimulate language development, to encourage the child to order and classify the objects and events of his world." Control groups did not have this preschool experience. The children who had the special training showed a "modest gain" in intelligence test performance; the control groups, who did not have the special experiences of several summer schools and home visitor contacts, showed losses.

A later report (Klaus and Gray, 1968) indicated gains in intelligence test performance of the control groups after their first year of school (in first grade). Effects of early experiences of the experimental groups "lasted to some extent through 2 years of public schooling . . . [with] still significant differences . . . on . . . major measures. . . . On the other hand, the parallel decline across the . . . [experimental and control] groups in the second year of public schooling" suggests that many variables, in addition to early intervention, are operative.

Another example of special training concerns development of reading ability. Training in form perception, in letters and in words has been introduced early, and reading has occurred early (Fowler, 1962, 1963).

FIGURE 84. *Exchanges between the child and his environment add schemata.*

This 16-month-old child hit the pegs with the wood mallet with accuracy part of the time. He turned the board over and "found" the pegs he had driven down. Sound, touch, sight, disappearing objects, cause and effect connections, were a part of his experience. His mother was attentive, but did not take away from his autonomy. His schemata (organizational patterns) are organizations of particular behaviors relevant to one another

In learning to perceive differences, whether in the everyday events of his life or in special training materials, the child acquires information which he can use in classifying or categorizing, and in forming concepts. As he grows older he becomes more able to use symbols in his thoughts. In contrasting the sensory-motor period from birth to approximately two years with the later preoperational thought period at approximately two to seven years, Flavell (1963) describes the preoperational thought as "a much faster more mobile device which can recall the past, represent the present, and anticipate the future in one temporally brief, organized act."

In Figure 85, focus of attention, exchanges between the child and his environment, grasp of ideas connected with past and present events, and consideration of one attribute at a time seem to be occurring.

Values can also have an effect on perception (Blum, 1957). Gibson (1963) suggests that "needs, likes, and dislikes affect perception by directing attention toward relevant aspects of incoming stimulation." For example, children overestimated weight of jars filled with candy, as compared to sand, but were more precise in judgment when candy was compared to candy (Dukes and Bevan, 1952).

Gibson and Olum (1960), commenting on enrichment of stimulation, refer to Montessori's interest in the "idea of developing 'sensi-

FIGURE 85. The young child learns distinctive features of his world.

This 3½-year-old seemed to be drawing upon meanings established earlier. He gave the fish some food, watched while it was eaten, and then added more. He focused his attention on feeding the fish, watching it swim, looking through the glass and through the water, for a part of each morning over a period of several weeks. He was learning to detect differences. These perceptions of differences could be used in categorizing and in concept formation.

tivity' by providing special opportunities for practice. . . . The 'Montessori Method' specialized in such practice. . . . The procedure was always from 'few stimuli, strongly contrasting, to many stimuli in gradual differentiation, always more fine and imperceptible' (Montessori, 1912). Activity and self-correction on the part of the child were thought very important. Transfer from simple kinds of preliminary training was stressed." The idea of the child's finding a "match" for his readiness for learning if materials to choose from were available was stressed by Montessorri. In some instances, if the adult noted an ability or a lack of it in the child's behavior, the adult then provided appropriate materials. In other instances the child himself selected from materials varying in difficulty, i.e., something he could succeed with or would find a challenge because of the possibility of success. This idea of the "match," related to theory of incongruity-dissonance, is discussed by Hunt in an introduction to *The Montessori Method* (1964).

To deal adequately with current questions concerning encouragement of cognitive development early, information from longitudinal studies which included a number of variables would be needed. Reasons for speed would also need careful thought.

Implications of "Real" as Contrasted to "Vicarious" Experiences in Early Years

Development of sensitivities and perceptions can suggest a variety of implications for the adult in his associations with young children. One concerns *recognition of the importance of free play.* In free play the child tends to let the adult know what he cares about doing or learning. The boy in Figure 86 is learning about a number of realities. Feeling free to manipulate materials, to experiment with them, unhurried and with a minimum of guidance, the child adds meanings which make his perceptions more complete. He is learning through play, as he mixes sand and water, completes a puzzle without assistance, or fits together two blocks to make their length equal to that of one longer block. Furthermore, these sensory experiences and perceptions provide facts to be used in reasoning, ideas to be expressed in language.

Realization of the extent to which the child learns through his senses leads the adult to recognize the importance of *providing a variety of experiences which are real instead of vicarious.* Seeing and hearing a steam shovel at work, touching a fluffy chicken, tasting carrots for which the seeds were planted, smelling vanilla that is put into a pudding are experiences which stories and pictures may supplement, but for which they are not a substitute.

Values in experience with "the real thing" are suggested by the following situations. A city child of school age and his teacher were getting materials ready to take to school for use in the third grade. A younger brother and a sister and neighborhood children of preschool age looked at the exhibit of kernels of wheat, wheat plants that were growing, and flour.

Unwrapping the jar of wheat kernels, Peter asked, "What is that?"
Miss O'Dell: "That's wheat."
Peter: "Kinda like corn."
Billy: "For Wheaties."
Looking at the flour, Connie said, "Flour goes in cakes in the oven."

FIGURE 86. The young child learns through sensory experiences.

The child's use of the sense of touch, sense of sight, and muscular adjustment, as he plays with sand and water, pertains to perceptions of texture, form, color and weight.

Miss O'Dell: "What else can we make from flour?"
Connie: "Bread."
Miss O'Dell: "When we put the bread in the oven, what happens?"
John: "We make toast."
Looking at the wheat plants growing, Jack said, "Some plants take a long time to sprout. My bean plants didn't come up for a long time."

Many possibilities for meaningful experiences are evident to the adult who gives thought to children's responses such as these. Cues concern provision of opportunities for preschool children to have a part in activities such as planting seeds, caring for plants, helping to bake bread or cake. In the course of these activities the children would discover many facts. The older child, of school age, was at another stage of development. His exhibit had meaning for him, but was less appropriate than other experiences for the young children.

DEVELOPMENT OF LANGUAGE

Definition

Language is generally understood to include any and all means of expressing feeling and thought: facial expression and gesture, as well as spoken and written words. Many writers consider that language development begins at birth. Philosophers such as Kant have suggested that the birth cry expresses "wrath at the catastrophe of birth." Psychologists would deny that the newborn baby has enough development to express a particular emotion. Physiologists, however, attribute to even the earliest vocalizations a function in the beginning of developing mechanical control over the vocal apparatus.

Speech is a complex muscular coordination which involves voluntary muscular actions of the abdominal wall, the thorax, larynx, soft palate, and tongue and lips, and is performed without conscious thought. Voice sounds are emitted from the mouth because a regulated expiration of breath forces air past the vocal cords, which vibrate variously in response, on through a passage which can be modified to produce the exact sound desired. From the moment of birth the waking hours of the infant are occupied with vocal activities as well as with activity of the arms and legs and of the sense organs. In the sense that the skills of walking can be said to develop from apparently instinctive beginnings in locomotion displayed in random muscular activity, so the skills of talking can be said to develop from the apparently instinctive beginnings in vocalization displayed in vocal sounds.

For speech as a motor skill and for the development of articulation, "neurophysiological events that are responsible for the normal operation of the healthy mechanisms" are not known (Lenneberg, 1964). "We do not know the neurological basis for speech movements . . . how serially patterned movements get themselves serially organized" (Teuber, 1964).

In studies of *quantitative and normative aspects of language,* frequency of use of various sounds, parts of speech, or functions, have been viewed with reference to changes with age and with particular influences. Much of the information on early vocalizations, comprehension of language and production of language (including words, sentences, sentence structures, articulation, content, and uses of language) is of this sort (McCarthy, 1954; Ervin-Tripp, 1966). The relation of affective aspects of language learning to other aspects of the individual (such as his social behavior) and to environmental influences (such as association with one or two or a number of different adults) has been considered (McCarthy, 1961).

In *linguistic behavior,* as Ervin and Miller (1963) refer to it, focus of study is on language as "a system that can be described internally in terms of two primary parts or levels — the phonological (sound system) and the grammatical. . . . We can study the child's developing language system from two viewpoints, first, the child's own system — a description of his own sound system and the set of rules he uses to form sentences — and, second, progress in the mastery of the linguistic system of the model or adult language." Many studies are "of the rules of individual systems."

"Joan, described by Velten (1943), will serve as an illustration [in study of the system of contrasts]. At 22 months Joan had *bat* (bad), *dat* (cut), *bap* (lamb) and *dap* (cup). In these words b and d can be seen to contrast, in that they signal differences of meanings in otherwise identical words. These four words also illustrate a phenomenon that applied to all of Joan's vocabulary at this time . . . b and d occurred only in initial position, never final, whereas p and t occurred only in final position, never initial." This behavior illustrates a hypothesis about the development of child language: "that the development of the sound system can be described in terms of successive contrasts between features that are maximally different and which permeate the whole system."

In the following section orderly trends in some of the elements of language are reported first. These elements are vocal, grammatical, and in terms of the child's use or intentions. Later, variables affecting development and their interrelations are considered. Again, maturation, or change with age, is one variable. Other variables pertain to attributes of the individual (including motivations) and to opportunities his environment provides for learning.

Early Vocalization

Within the first month or so mothers usually feel that they can interpret the nature of the child's crying. Sounds can express emotional states. They are, in fact, to be thought of as part of a total bodily reaction elicited in exciting or strenuous situations. Variations in voice quality and intensity occur under different circumstances. The actual control of muscles which push air over the voice mechanism and the control of the vocal apparatus which produces crying are present at birth. In the sense that the ability to cry at all is the more mature stage of many complex coordinations, even newborns are mature. Among the earliest non-crying sounds heard during the first month or two are "grunts, gurgles, burbles, or sighs," which are comfort vocalizations (Van Riper, 1950). Categories of vocalization noted in early months include whimper, tremble, cry, scream (Bullowa, Jones and Bever, 1964). "During the first thirteen weeks vocalization categories from most to least frequent are fussing, crying and cooing. Cooing gradually increases in frequency and crying decreases, even during hunger (Lenneberg, Rebelsky and Nichols, 1965; Tischler, 1957)" (Ervin-Tripp, 1966).

Inherent orderliness is evident in the *vowel and consonant* usage in the first 2½ years of life. Irwin (1952) and Winitz and Irwin (1958), in a study of vocalization of infants, reported great expansion in the mastery of sounds during the first six months of life. Newborns have a deficit of back vowels and an absence of consonants formed by the forward mouth parts. The most frequent vowel sound is *ae*; little active participation of the tongue and mouth muscles is required. Only about half of the vowels and few of the consonants are present in the first month of life. Many but not all of the vowel and consonant sounds and sound combinations have been mastered by normally maturing infants by 1½ years.

Ervin and Miller (1963), referring to vocalizations of the infant before he says meaningful words, indicate that "the most striking change . . . is the acquisition of increasing control over volume, pitch, and articulatory position and type, a control manifested by continuity or repetition of these features." They refer to a study by Tischler (1957) of children in contrasting social situations. "There was a gradual increase in the frequency of vocalization. It reached its peak at eight or ten months of age, then declined. Between the eighth and the twelfth month almost all conceivable sounds occur, including some not in the adult language."

A stage of random articulation or babbling precedes speech. Later, when babbling or cooing and language are occurring at the same age, vocal behavior in each differs (Ervin and Miller, 1963).

Most parents talk to their children while bathing or tending them. This parental impulse provides the child with a model not only for rhythm during early infancy, but also for vocabulary as his development progresses.

Language Abilities

COMPREHENSION. Most children have developed a sufficiently discriminating reaction to language to permit recognition of their names by the time they are six to eight months old, and by the time they are eight or nine months old they understand either the word "No" or the tone in which it is spoken when it is used to forbid action. Just how this attachment of meaning to definite words occurs in the brain is not known.

In the development of comprehension, according to Lewis (1951),

. . . the child responds affectively both to the intonational pattern of what he hears and to the situation in which he hears it. . . . He hears a phonetic pattern.

. . . When at last the phonetic pattern acquires dominance so that irrespective of the intonational pattern it evokes the appropriate response from the child, we say that he has understood the conventional word.

In attaching meaning to words heard, the child has perception of speech of another person. From understanding a name, or that "No" means "Stop what you are doing," or some other differentiation, he proceeds rapidly in his comprehension. By twelve to fifteen months most children understand a fairly wide assortment of simple concrete or action words such as "ball," "dinner," "drink" and "bye-bye." Within two or three months of this stage they understand and react to simple sentences such as, "Where is baby's ball?" "Give Mother the spoon." "Want to go bye-bye?" In the earlier stage the response to "Give Mother the spoon" may be an undifferentiated reaction to the single word "Mother" or perhaps "spoon." The baby might have looked at his mother, held out his arms to her or leaned forward expectantly with his mouth open for food. In the later stages he understands the whole sentence and picks up the spoon to hand it to his mother.

The child understands and also learns to speak the simple, concrete words first. He understands simple action phrases and sentences before he can comprehend and react to more complex sentences. Comprehension of prepositions and phrases of relationship such as "in," "on," "under," "on top of," follows later. Although children of two years can understand a wealth of words and phrases and sentences of action and concrete situations, in one study (Gesell, 1925) they understood and reacted correctly to an average of only three prepositions. Even when the contrast between prepositions is known, the child may not distinguish the object of the verb and the object of the preposition. In a Russian study referred to by Ervin and Miller (1963) children were asked to put a ring on a block.

Eighteen of the children, between 26 and 36 months of age, who understood the difference between "on" and "under," . . . when told to put the ring on the block did the reverse half the time. Thus, they could discriminate the semantic contrast between different prepositions but could not distinguish the syntactic difference between the object of the verb and the object of the preposition. . . . Fourteen children 26-41 months of age were relatively successful in this task.

While the child is learning meanings of words he is also learning their structural properties (syntax). These learnings seem to proceed at the same time and to be interrelated. Thus, without being able to identify parts of speech, the young child could hear a new word and "plug" it into a sentence context. According to Brown and Fraser (1964):

Hearing *car* as a new word in the sentence: "See the *car*" a child could use this context as a basis for listing *car* with count nouns (such as *house, barn, table*), and so be prepared to hear and say such additional sentences as: . . . "The *car* is new"; "This *car* is mine." And a multitude of others.

The word *car* has meaning; it also has structural properties in that it is used as a noun.

By three to four years most children understand the basic vocabulary of their native language, although their intellectual capacity to handle complex thoughts is still limited (see p. 358 ff.). They can seem "snowed under" by too much talking.

ACTIVE VOCABULARY.   In addition to development of ability to comprehend language, the young child also develops a variety of competences in his own use of words and sentences. By about one year children already have a fairly wide range of gestures and facial expressions, but their vocabulary of spoken words is seldom more than two or three such simple words as "Ma-ma," "Da-da" or "Bye-bye." Although comprehension seems to develop rapidly from a year of age on, speech may not move forward so long as the child is using his energy in the achievement of upright locomotion. Most children are deeply absorbed in the achievement of the stepping and independent walking stages of locomotion between twelve and eighteen or twenty months of age. Their acquisition of vocabulary is ordinarily slow at this time. Shirley (1931) reported that the children she studied showed a lull in vocabulary increase during the learning of each new motor skill.

Some girls and boys have from ten to 100 words in their vocabulary around eighteen months of age. The average for children in a number of studies is about five words. Some children, more boys than girls, do not have so many as five words in their vocabularies until they are two or $2\frac{1}{2}$ years of age (Bayley, 1933; Gesell, 1925; McCarthy, 1954; Smith, 1926). When upright locomotion is reasonably well under control, vocabulary spurts forward. During the preschool years the child becomes an entertaining conversationalist. But unless he continues to have exposure to vocabularies larger than his own, his vocabulary increases will cease; he cannot learn the meaning of words that he never hears or reads.

Children in an early stage of language learning usually discover that everything has a name. When this happens, their eternal query may be, "What's that?" Often, given the answer, the child repeats the word himself, thus giving himself practice with it.

Children's nouns, in comparison with those of adults, frequently refer to items with characteristic sizes and visual contours, and their verbs often refer to movements (Brown, 1958). Examples are "chair" and "fall down." Although children's words at first tend to refer to the concrete, they may include a variety of objects or persons, e.g., calling a footstool or a bench, a chair.

The echoing of the adult sometimes contributes to the child's confusion about pronouns. He hears himself referred to as "Baby" or as "John." He echoes by referring to himself, "Baby wants a drink," or "John wants to go bye-bye." Correct use of the pronoun "I" appears later. Confusion between such pronouns as "me" and "I," "him," "her," "his" and "hers" may occur at this phase of language development. Among the first words to be acquired, verbs, adjectives and adverbs appear correctly, but articles, conjunctions, the more complicated forms of

verbs and of adverbs and the correct use of pronouns and prepositions appear later.

The impression many people have of preschool children as being
talkative and on the move physically tends to be an accurate one. They
may use as many as 11,000 to 12,000 words in a day at three years of
age and around 15,000 in a day at four years. Although methods of
differentiating words and of estimating totals differ in recent research,
the early reports are of interest because of this volume of words at early
ages which they suggest (Brandenburg and Brandenburg, 1919;
Nice, 1920).

ARTICULATION.   Van Riper (1950), referring to articulation, says:

> Many of the errors made by little children are due to their perceiving words
> as lumps of sound. They often omit the sounds that are of low intensity. They
> say "ike" for "like," "way" for "away," they omit the final *s* sounds from plural
> words; they may even omit a whole syllable if it is unstressed in the word. . . .
>
> The little child tends to use the sounds he knows best, the *w* instead of the
> unfamiliar *r,* the *t* instead of the *c.* . . .
>
> They find great interest in comparing and contrasting words which provide
> a small difference in a larger similarity. They are fascinated by "fee, fie, fo, fum,"
> by "eeny, meeny, miney, mo," by "Humpty Dumpty."
>
> At first, the child prefers exact duplication, but he passes through that stage
> and comes to love rhyming for its own sake. If you eavesdrop on the child play-
> ing with his toys you will hear him practicing his vocal phonics: "Foggie, old
> foggie foggie, you old goggie you, boggy-boggy, boo, boggie-bogguh." This is
> vocal play, but a much more purposive type. . . .
>
> By these activities the child learns to observe all the features of a given
> word. He plays with its beginning, he twists its tail. . . . He comes to attend to
> the way words begin. He notices the first sounds of words when he begins to vary
> them; "teeny-weeny; teeny-weeny." Children who practice such combinations
> in their word play soon begin to correct their initial errors in words they mis-
> pronounce. Children who practice spontaneous rhyming soon stop omitting the
> final consonants.

The advisability of recognizing the length of time that many children need to perfect their enunciation is suggested by Wellman's study
(1931). At the age of five most sounds were given correctly, but some
were still difficult. At three years almost half of the consonant blends
and approximately one-third of the consonant elements were incorrect.

The order in which sounds are articulated correctly and the ways
in which the child uses particular sounds provide information on his
progression in language ability. Vowels and diphthongs are articulated
correctly at an earlier age than consonants, single consonants somewhat
later, and two and three consonant blends still later (Templin, 1952,
1957; Wellman, 1931). Templin (1952) referred to growth in articula-
tion as rapid between $2\frac{1}{2}$ and $4\frac{1}{2}$ years, but then continuing more slowly
until at least eight years of age. Metraux (1950) presented profiles of
what the speech of the child sounds like, i.e., phonetic reports, over the
age range of eighteen months to $4\frac{1}{2}$ years. Irwin (1960) indicated four
types of errors usually reported: substitutions, omissions, distortions
and additions.

Ervin and Miller (1963) suggested that

. . . the more common contrasts (of sound) are both acoustically or visually distinct and easier to articulate. . . . There is probably a relation between the visual cue and the fact that children usually develop a contrast between labial (e.g. /p/) and nonlabial (e.g. /t/, /k/) consonants well before they develop a contrast between dental (e.g. /t/) and velar (e.g. /k/) consonants. . . . Children . . . frequently make substitutions that differ in manner of articulation. Stops replace the corresponding fricative (e.g. "thing" may become *ting*), and semivowels or vowels replace liquids (e.g. "rabbit" may become *wabbit*; "bottle" may become *batto*) . . . Degree of difficulty in articulation is probably the crucial factor. Thus, stops (e.g. /p/, /t/) are usually acquired earlier than fricatives (e g. /f/, /th/), probably because a more delicate adjustment of the tongue is necessary for the fricatives. Caution must be exercised in ascribing articulatory difficulty, because no simple measure of articulatory difficulty exists.

BUILDING OF SENTENCES. "The child's first word normally appears before the first birthday but a year may pass before the child forms his first two-word sentence" (Ervin and Miller, 1963). Often these first sentences are abbreviations of grammatically complete adult sentences. Thus the child may say, "Chair broken," and "That horsie," meaning, "The chair is broken," and "That is a horse." Brown and Fraser (1964) reported that children of twenty-six to $35\frac{1}{2}$ months of age with the lowest mean utterance length form their construction by omitting a form of the verb *to be*. (e.g., "I going"). Children with somewhat higher mean utterance length omit the modal auxiliary *will* or *can* (e.g., "I park the car"). More advanced children speak acceptable simple sentences.

When we consider that command of a variety of sentence forms means that the child's command of the mechanics of language is nearly complete, we can appreciate something of the amount of language learning that has taken place during the preschool years. Written language follows the vocal stage if children are given formal training.

Uses of Language

About the time the child can put together enough words to form a question beyond the simple, "What's that?" he feeds his growing intelligence by asking innumerable questions. Although occasionally for other purposes, his questions are usually a serious effort to extend vocabulary and to gain information. Brandenburg and Brandenburg (1919) found that in a single day a three-year-old child asked 376 questions, and a four-year-old child 397. "What" and "where" questions are more frequent among young children; "why," "how," and "when" seem to be more frequent as age increases (Smith, 1933). Among the questions usual to three- and four-year-olds are those about sex, death and God. "What is the difference between boys and girls?" "Where do babies come from?" "What does it mean to die?" "What is God like?" These are almost inevitable questions during the period of widespread interest in words and facts. When these questions, like all his others, are answered truthfully, simply and without sentimentality or tense emotional accompaniment, the adult's reply tends to reflect the child's purpose in asking. He is *seeking information.*

In some instances the child's use of language seems to be that of thinking aloud. This function is, in some ways, related to classifications described as egocentric and socialized. In egocentric speech, according to Piaget (1926), the child "does not bother to know to whom he is speaking nor whether he is being listened to. He talks either for himself or for the pleasure of associating anyone who happens to be there with the activity of the moment. . . . He does not attempt to place himself at the point of view of his hearer." In socialized speech the child addresses his hearer, considers his point of view, tries to influence him or to exchange ideas with him. This social function is in contrast to monologues which accompany action or verbalize fantasies, and soliloquies which take place either when the child is alone or when he is with others, but are addressed to no one and are not intended to give information or to solicit an answer. Additional study is needed in sequences of language and thought content, egocentric and socialized, in older children and in adults.

The child uses language *to secure information*, e.g., in naming and in asking questions, and *to think aloud* with no desire to give anyone any particular information. In addition, he uses it almost from the beginning *to transfer information and to secure what he wants.* To accomplish these purposes he gives commands and expresses wants: e.g., "Go bye-bye," "Mine," and "Bobby wants a drink."

Soon, however, use of language to communicate goes beyond simple requests and expression of wants and begins *to serve the purpose of simple narration.* The child tries to tell about things that have happened to him or that he has imagined. At first these narratives are extremely simple. A two-year-old child who had witnessed an accident in which there had been a good deal of excitement told breathlessly that "Bobby fell out of the bus," but could give no further detail. His only answer to any question was reiteration of the statement, "Bobby fell out of the bus." At three years these narratives become somewhat more detailed. An occasional three-year-old can tell a fairly well connected story: "I went to Grandmother's house. She lives on a farm. I saw pigs and chickens and a baby cow. Grandpa said it was a calf. It walked funny, like this," with an apt demonstration of a wobbly calf-walk.

Imaginative elements often creep into these narratives: "I saw a big black bear. It was in the yard by the lilac bush." Once the child has achieved a basic language facility, imagination can produce a whole original story. "Once there was a great big engine" can be followed by many details, the engine not only talking, but waving good-bye as well. The tendency to animate objects is characteristic of the imaginative narrations of young children. Creativity in stories and in poetry can occur in preschool years (Baruch, 1939; Read, 1966).

Probably the last use the child makes of language is *expression of complex thought and reasoning.* In spite of the difficulties involved, three-year-old children are beginning to express in language ideas and simple reasoning. A child of three wanted to know, "Where does the milk go when I drink it?" As language skills develop, reasoning or thinking is expressed much more clearly. A four-year-old child stood gazing out of the window on a windy day. After a thoughtful pause he said, "Trees moving, wind blowing—trees moving make the wind blow." This is false reasoning, but clearly expressed. Another four-year-old gave two examples of simple astute reasoning while in the process of washing his hands and combing his hair. He said, "The water is warm and I am cold. It will make me warm." And then, "My tie is green, so your comb must be green, too. It's the same color."

Concept formation, problem-solving ability and thought are discussed on pages 358 to 373. Language ability, with its use of symbols, facilitates these forms of behavior and their development.

The role of speech and language in regulating the child's behavior is of interest with reference to motor behavior and also to higher thought processes. In verbal mediation internal verbal responses help to direct behavior. Zigler (1966), discussing Luria's verbal mediation theory, says,

> For Luria, higher mental functions are developed in the course of social interaction of a verbal nature. To provide empirical support for his position, he has examined the role of both the adult's and the child's speech in regulating, i.e. initiating and/or inhibiting, certain motor reactions of the child. . . . [At first] the child's own speech is insufficient to control his motor reactions, although adult verbal instructions can serve to initiate or impel such behavior and later to inhibit it. In the second stage, the child's own speech begins to play a regulatory role. . . . In the third stage the "impellant" action of speech recedes into the background, and a regulatory function which now includes a system of "significative connections" or meanings becomes predominant. The final stage is characterized by . . . a higher form of internal speech which constitutes an essential component of thought and volitional action.

A child's use of language in ways such as these highlights the close relation between skills in communication and other aspects of growth. Dawe (1947), referring to the significance of experiences in communication, emphasized that language is important for adapting to and controlling one's environment: it is a medium of learning; there is emotional value in being able to express oneself clearly and effectively; conversely, there is frustration if one is deficient in this ability; language habits and personal adjustment seem interrelated.

In addition to its cognitive function, language also functions with reference to emotional development, in that it enables the child to express his feelings and to express them in ways that others understand (as well as contributing to his own understanding) (see p. 421 on emotional and social development). Illustrations of this are in the following "poems" of children about hospitals (Smith, 1962):

By a four-year-old: "The hospitals I don't like because the beds you can't get out of."

By a five-year-old: "I guess the nurses walk more miles than anybody in the whole wide world. They walk up the hall and down the hall and back and up. Every time they hear a crying they have to find out "WHO.""

Variables in Language Development

Only human beings have language, in the sense of a "symbolic system which is learned, which consists of conventional basic units and rules for their arrangement, and which includes a conventional set of arbitrary signs for meanings and referents" (Ervin-Tripp, 1966).

The infant's babbling in the first few months is organically based. It occurs in both deaf and hearing children, whose vocalizations in the first three months are qualitatively virtually identical (Lenneberg, 1964). In the course of his babbling the infant's motor control in his articulation increases; processes of change seem to be in accordance with those of other aspects of motor development. McCarthy (1954) said that changes in early infancy "seem to harmonize . . . with the theory of motor development proceeding from mass activity through control of gross muscles to the finer muscular coordinations."

One of the many questions for which answers are not easily achieved concerns processes by which the child selects particular sounds to repeat. Emphasis seems to be on something in his own functioning and his explorations with it. According to Lewis (1951), "The hearing of the adult word can merely stimulate the child to the utterance of his *own* babbling sounds and . . . from this the child may become trained to respond with a particular sound to a particular heard sound." The child in the first year of life also reacts differently to particular words, as other people say them, which indicates that the words have meaning for him. This increase in meanings of sounds heard seems to be in accordance with processes of perceptual development (see also p. 335).

Later, the child's use of words changes grammatically so that he is cognizant of rules to which no one has specifically called his attention. He learns to add *s* for plurals, to think of *ing* in using verbs, and so on. He may say "gooder" for "better" or "bringed" for "brought," but most of the time these endings would be correct. Children show "an ability, increasing with age, to construct grammatically correct sentences using new words" (Brown and Fraser, 1964).

VARIABLES IN THE BIOLOGICAL SYSTEM. *Age* influences language development. Difference in early speech according to *sex* has been reported. In rate of acquisition of active vocabulary, girls are slightly faster than boys. McCarthy (1954), reviewing data in which girls proceed more rapidly than boys in a number of phases of linguistic development, refers to the sex difference as present but small. Bayley (1968) reported high correlation of girls' vocal-verbal ability as young as one year with later verbal scores at twenty-six years of age ($r = 0.80$); the correlation for boys was low ($r = 0.26$). Differences according to *intelligence,* as measured by intelligence tests, have been reported frequently.

Mental retardation is the cause of retardation in language development in some cases. Studies of mentally deficient children show language retardation, whereas studies of superior children show language acceleration. It is appropriate in this connection to assume that children who talk unusually early are probably superior mentally and that mentally deficient children are always late in talking, but it is not to be assumed that all children who are late in talking are mentally retarded.

There are several physical reasons—in bodily equipment for functioning—why the child proceeds from one stage of language development to another, or may have failed to make a good beginning in such development. Probably the first thing that should be done in seeking a cause for retardation is to examine the child's *hearing*. It is not always easy to be sure whether or not a child is deaf enough to prevent his hearing conversation and hence to prevent his profiting from the guidance of models in his language learning. Children are extremely quick to compensate for defects of eyes or ears and may have serious handicaps for a number of years without themselves or adults knowing that they are different from other children. The child fails to realize his handicap because, never having seen or heard well, he does not realize that he could or should be different. The parent fails to discover the difficulty because the child, being deaf, learns to compenstate for his deficiency by extra alertness in his other senses. Even supposedly expert examiners sometimes have difficulty in diagnosing sensory defects because the special methods for examining very young children are not widely known, nor is the required equipment generally available (Irwin, 1960; Van Riper, 1963).

Defective *vocal apparatus* is sometimes responsible for inability or unwillingness to attempt speech.

Occasionally, trouble lies in the *nerve centers* that control speech. Rarely, the difficulty is one known as *word deafness*—a defect in which, though sounds are heard, the associations necessary to lend meaning to word sounds cannot be formed. (See Bakes, 1966, for review of research on aphasia, including developmental language deficiency and the difficulty of identifying the cause of retardation; Bakwin, 1968, for discussions of developmental disorders of language.)

VARIABLES IN EXCHANGES WITH ENVIRONMENT. Among variables in the psychological system of the child, perceptual differentiations, thought and emotional tone seem especially pertinent to language development. In the exchanges of these kinds with his setting the child is influenced by many variables in his external environment.

Model. Influence of the language model is great, but information on processes by which a particular model becomes influential is elusive. Imitative behavior and affectional ties both seem to be involved. Sometimes children who are with their families are cared for by those who do not appreciate the need of talking, or who, when talking, are limited in expression. Occasionally the model for language is someone who seems to provide too much language. The parents or person who takes care of the child may speak in a way which makes it difficult for the child to isolate from the general flow of conversation any specific and understandable words or phrases.

Some children have more experiences with *restricted* language, or modes of communication, as contrasted to the *elaborated* type. In Bernstein's theory (1962, 1964) language affects what the child learns and how he learns; it sets limits within which learning takes place. In the form of communication code or style of verbal behavior, called restricted, language is limited and condensed, and range and detail of concept and information are slight. In the form of communication code called elaborated, language is more precise, and range and detail provide for more complex range of thought. Bernstein reports more of the restricted code in working-class communities in England.

Hess (1964) states a hypothesis for investigation, as follows:

> In cultural deprivation, the pattern of communication that develops between mother and child has an effect upon the child's cognitive equipment and communication skills which handicaps him when he begins his school program.

A mother's use of a restricted code and of an elaborated code and effects which are to be investigated, are illustrated:

> A child is playing noisily in the kitchen with an assortment of pots and pans when the telephone rings. In one home the mother says, "Be quiet," or "Shut up," or any one of several short, pre-emptory commands. . . . In the other home the mother says, "Would you keep quiet while I answer the phone." . . . In one instance, the child is asked for a simple mental response . . . to attend to an uncomplicated message and to make a . . . response [to comply]. . . . In the other example, the child is required to follow two or three ideas . . . to relate his behavior to a time dimension; he must think of his behavior in relation to its effect upon another person. He must perform a more complicated task to follow the communication of his mother in that his relationship to her is mediated in part through concepts and shared ideas; his mind is stimulated or excercised (in an elementary fashion) by a more elaborate and complex verbal communication initiated by the mother. As objects of these two divergent communication styles, repeated in various ways, in similar stituations and circumstances during the pre-school years, these two . . . children would be expected to develop significantly different verbal facility and cognitive equipment by the time they enter the public school system.

Hess and Shipman (1965) refer to difference in language usage among Negro mothers and their four-year-old children from four different social status levels. The mothers were taught simple tasks, such as sorting toys or copying designs, and were then asked to teach these tasks to their children. Mothers were also asked to tell their children a story relating to a picture.

> The most obvious social-class variations were in the total amount of verbal output in response to questions and tasks asking for verbal response. . . . Mothers from the middle-class gave protocols that were consistently longer in language productivity than did mothers from the other three groups [in lower-class categories]. There were [also] differences in the quality of language used by mothers in the various status groups.

See pages 151 through 156 for references to family systems of control which do or do not offer a wide range of alternatives of action and thought.

Affectional Ties. Reference has already been made to the model's influences, not only in qualities of speech, but also in affectional ties.

In stressing affective aspects of language learning, McCarthy (1961) referred to effects of deprivation, saying:

> There seems to be a gradient . . . related to the amount and kind of contact with the mother. This ties in with the data of Spitz . . . Goldfarb . . . Brodbeck and Irwin . . . and others on the language retardation usually found in children who have suffered prolonged separation from the mother at a critical period in their development and who have no opportunity to identify with the mother who normally serves as a language model.

Infants in an institution who had a single mothering experience were compared with those whose physical care and nurturance came from a number of different people (Rheingold and Bayley, 1959). Vocalization was significantly greater in those with the single mothering experience.

Yarrow (1961) commented on language as

> . . . one function in which severe retardation has been found repeatedly in institutionalized infants and young children. . . . On the simplest level, language retardation . . . can be related to inadequate language stimulation. Lack of motivation for imitative behavior may interact with inadequate reenforcement of speech sounds in determining language retardation.

Immediate Pleasant or Unpleasant Associations. Vocalizations of infants increased on days when social actions were forthcoming from an adult (see p. 18).

Mowrer (1952) theorized about transition from random vocalization to selection of sounds and words:

> Words or other human sounds are first made by infants, it seems, because the sounds have been associated with relief and other satisfactions and, as a result, have themselves come to sound good. . . . Human infants . . . in the course of random activities . . . will eventually make sounds somewhat similar to those which have already acquired pleasant connotations and will . . . have a special incentive for trying to repeat and refine these sounds. Soon, however, the infant discovers that the making of these sounds can be used not only to comfort, reassure, and satisfy himself directly but also to interest, satisfy and control mother, father, and others.

Satisfactions in language are close to its functions or uses. Vygotsky "found that action language (as contrasted to egocentric speech) decreased when there was background noise, social isolation, or lack of full availability of listeners because they were foreign or deaf, and that it increased when obstacles were encountered" (Ervin-Tripp, 1966).

Occasionally children do not learn to talk because they do not need to learn. They receive attention and affection and seem to have little occasion to seek verbal communication; their wants are so thoroughly anticipated that no need arises to express wants verbally. Twins, able to communicate with each other, are sometimes slow in developing aspects of language which enable them to communicate easily with others (Day, 1932).

Variety of Experience. Some children develop enough language to express their wants, but are so limited in general experience that they have little to express in narrative and lack the knowledge of perceptions and judgments which provides material for reasoning. The richness and variety of his vocabulary, the fertility of his ideas and the accuracy of his expression all reflect the child's opportunities for learning. A home that is rich in language model and in varieties of experience provides for further differentiation in language development. Irwin (1960) reported on effects of adding speech-sound stimulation in homes of an experimental group.

In order to increase the amount of speech-sound stimulation in the homes of working-class people, the mothers of a group of children 13 to 30 months of age were instructed to read to them daily for . . . 15 minutes from illustrated baby books. The mothers pointed out objects in the pictures, named them, made up stories about them, and talked frequently to the children. A second group of infants of comparable ages in working-class homes in which no systematic stimulation occurred served as the control. The differences in amount of phoneme (vowel and consonant) frequency between the two groups after the eighteenth month were significantly in favor of the experimental group.

Much practice in language takes place when children play with other children. Although children chatter to themselves when learning language, they do not talk with the same need to be understood as they do when with other children, nor do they talk so much (Williams and Mattson, 1942).

In a bilingual family the child "uses forms from both languages indistinguishably until about the age of three . . . unless a strict separation of situation or speakers produces earlier discrimination" (Ervin-Tripp, 1966). The child who uses one language at home and another at school is likely to develop each according to environmental variables presented here as affecting development of language. Thus, if the school situation emphasizes vocabulary and differentiations, language there proceeds in these directions. Some children have different phonetic systems because of dialectal or second language features (Deutsch, 1964).

Interest in enriched experiences which facilitate the acquiring of language in the preschool and kindergarten years seems to be increasing. Dawe (1952) reported greater gains on tests of vocabulary on home living information and on general science information in an experimental group of preschool and kindergarten children than in a control group; the experimental group had an educational program which stressed training in the understanding of words and concepts, looking at and discussing pictures, listening to poems and stories, and going on short excursions. Van Riper (1963) referred to "speech-play experiences which will facilitate fluency." For example, in a speech-play game the Indians say "Ugh," holding the hand under the chin, and thus practice saying the "g" sound and also feel it. In a kindergarten study (Wilson, 1952) children in an experimental speech improvement group showed greater decrease in articulation errors on sounds included in the program, and also on sounds not included; pictures, stories, cards and articles involving practice of particular sounds were presented to the experimental group.

Ervin-Tripp (1966) reviewed training research by Cazden:

She compared two experimental groups and a control group, composed of Negro children aged twenty-eight to thirty-eight months, given two and one-half hours of treatment per week for three months. The "modeling" group, which heard full grammatical sentences in reply to their own, did best. The expansion group, whose telegraphic utterances were "expanded" to full adult grammatical sentences but with no new vocabulary and only the grammatical structures that would "correct" their sentences, did next best. Both improved over the control group in a series of measures of grammatical development. The results suggest that "richness of verbal stimulation" may be more important than the contingency of the adult's response on the preceding utterance of the child.

Tensions.   Consideration of *stuttering* as an aspect of growth has the following basis. One of the peaks of the curve of incidence of stuttering occurs at the stage in language development when the child has more to say than he has vocabulary with which to say it. A study by Johnson (1955) revealed that 15 to 25 per cent of the words used by young children figure in some kind of repetition. This is at the stage of beginning to say words for many children, of putting words into sentences for many others, or of greater use of language in complex situations for others away from home or parents. The difficulty seems to occur at times of emergence of new abilities. The child is reaching out socially and is discovering the use of language as a medium of social communication. Many children find the urge to communicate ideas to others so great that it outruns their active vocabulary. Stuttering or hesitation and uncertainty about words results. The increase in active vocabulary, being rapid from two years on, soon catches up with the social "expansions," and the stuttering disappears, having lasted from two or three weeks to two or three months.

Disappearance of this sort of repetition is more likely to occur if nagging and anxiety are avoided. It is recommended that no negative emotions or lack of self-confidence be aroused during this temporary uncertainty about words, in order to avoid permanent stuttering. The problem is to keep the child from becoming self-conscious about his speech and to help him to develop the vocabulary and feelings of ease needed to facilitate his social expression. Johnson (1955, 1959) stressed the effect of labeling the child a stutterer and referred to speech and personality disorder as developing after diagnosis. Parental tensions created by the diagnosis create tensions in the child.

Stuttering has sometimes been attributed to attempts to change the child from left-handed to right-handed motor performance. (See pages 309 and 310 for discussion of handedness.) After years of research the relation between handedness and stuttering is still confused (Bakes, 1966; Bakwin, 1968). Several studies suggest that stuttering is associated with handedness and with motor facility in general; others emphasize other influences.

The word "tensions" is frequently used in discussions of the causes of stuttering. Self-consciousness or fear of the listener's response discourages effort and tends to produce silence; or it may provide one cause of stuttering. The motor control which regulates speech is the finest in balance of any motor control in human behavior and is the most easily disturbed. It seems more easily disturbed in boys than in girls, since there is considerably more stuttering among boys, depending on the age. Any tension, whether due to shock, self-consciousness, fear of ridicule or of failure, may upset this balance in motor control. When stuttering is due to such causes, methods of dealing with it take into account the inciting cause.

Enjoyment of Language

One connotation from concepts of language and its development and from its orderly trends and influences upon it is the importance of *facilitating the child's use of speech sounds and language with ease and without self-consciousness.* An additional connotation concerns the importance of *facilitating the child's expanding of his language.* This pertains to phonetic, grammatical and meaningful qualities of language pertinent to communication, and to interest and ability in school subjects, and also to his own enjoyment of reading.

Importance of Stories

A child is very responsive to stories appropriate to his stage of development. He enjoys them "for the fun of it." Hearing and seeing, speech, thought, imagination and sometimes sociability all play a part in his joy when a story is told to him and when he tells it to himself as he looks at the book. The variety of stories and books of quality is great.* There has been discussion as to whether or not children should hear stories with an element of fantasy, unrealistic qualities, or traditional fairy stories. Certain children may be frightened or confused; others may find further material for imaginations already overstimulated. On the whole, however, traditional fairy stories and stories with an imaginative aspect which are well selected provide a great deal of joy. Probably no writer, however, would recommend a steady diet or use of them without discrimination.

Children are too easily entertained by stories from everyday life to permit neglect of this rich field. Simple stories about boys and girls who get up cheerfully in the morning and go on through the routines and other activities of the listener's day or stories about their world will also engage the attention of nearly all children from two to four or five years of age. The effect of an example or moral in a story is difficult to measure; certainly, moralizing can be overdone. In providing books

---

* Books for children of preschool age are listed in Association for Childhood Education, 1965. *The Horn Book,* published six times a year by The Horn Book, Inc., 585 Boylston St., Boston, Mass., reviews new books. Methods of selecting and presenting stories are presented in Arbuthnot, 1964; Association for Childhood Education, 1961; Duff, 1944, 1956; and Frank, 1960.

for the young child the adult may ask: Is the book beautiful, mean-ingful, durable, interesting and individually appropriate?

DEVELOPMENT OF CONCEPTS, PROBLEM-SOLVING ABILITY AND THOUGHT

Development of sensitivities and of perception, as well as of language, presents bases for the child's concepts, problem-solving ability and thought. Development of meanings through use of his sense organs is illustrated in the response of a six-month-old infant to a rattle. He seizes it and waves it about, following it with his eyes, and turning to listen; he smells it; he puts it into his mouth, tasting and touching it; he ex-plores it with every sense at his command. From this he learns about rattles, how big they are, their shape, how hard, how heavy, how near, and what kind of noise they make. More than that, he is associating all these things together.

The development of associations and meanings proceeds rapidly as the child leaves infancy, especially as he acquires the ability to walk, run and climb and thus to widen his horizon. In the course of his language development the child is achieving names for the various qualities of objects now being experienced through the senses. As stated in the discussion of language, the period from eighteen to thirty-six months is one of rapid increase in vocabulary. This association of name with sensory quality is only part of the general interest in associating the proper name with every object and experience. We must not, however, conclude that the ability to sense the quality (e.g., hardness, roughness, heaviness) depends on ability to comprehend or to use the right lan-guage name (Braine, 1962). Children usually learn to detect and to differentiate such qualities accurately before they can name them, con-versely, they often learn the names "big," "long," "loud," "hard," "red," "heavy" before they can apply them accurately to the proper sensory experience.

Concept Formation

Along with motor, sensory and language development comes the de-velopment of concepts, or ideas. The child gradually comes to perceive certain definite aspects or qualities even when they appear in different settings. In concept learning "the members of a set of stimuli must have some feature in common—color, form, texture, size, function, name, material, etc.—and the members of different sets must be discriminable in some respect" (Spiker, 1960). Thus a young child develops a concept of "green," "round" or "four," or of himself.

TRENDS IN CONCEPTS. In development of concepts an orderly trend from early years, through adolescence and into adulthood, is from the concrete to the abstract. Piaget (1954), formulating stages as cognition proceeds in this direction, included a stage of sensory-motor operations, a stage of concrete thinking operations, and a stage of formal thinking operations. Inhelder (1962), who has been associated with Piaget at Geneva for many years, distinguishes these stages as follows:

Stage I. Sensory-motor operations. The first major stage occupies approximately the first 18 months. It is characterized by the progressive formation of the schema of the permanent object and by the sensory-motor structuration of one's immediate special surroundings. . . . One can distinguish . . . substages . . . ; their continuity is assured by "schemata" of action. The schemata are transposable or generalizable actions. The child establishes relations between similar objects or between objects which are increasingly dissimilar, including relations between these objects and his own body (for instance the extension of the schema of graspable objects to that of invisible objects). Thus, a schema can be defined as the structure common to all those acts which—from the subject's point of view—are equivalent. . . .

Stage II. Concrete thinking operations. The second developmental stage extends from the middle of the second year until the eleventh or twelfth year. . . . During their elaboration (until about the age of 7), concrete thought processes are irreversible. We observe how they gradually become reversible. With reversibility, they form a system of concrete operations (after the age of 7). For example, . . . although a 5-year-old has long since grasped the permanence of objects, he has by no means yet any notion of the elementary physical principle of the conservation of matter.

. . . Given two equal balls of plasticine, the child is asked to roll one of them into a long sausage form, to flatten it into a pancake, or to break it into small pieces. He is then asked, in terms adapted to his understanding, whether the quantity of matter has increased, decreased, or remained the same. This experiment and others similar to it have shown that most 5- or 6-year-olds assert without hesitation that each change in form involves a change in the amount of matter. Influenced sometimes by the increase in one dimension, sometimes by the decrease in the other, the child seems uncritically to accept the dictates of whatever aspect of change he happens to perceive. Errors decrease gradually, as the older child becomes more and more inclined to relate different aspects or dimensions to one another, until we finally come to a principle of invariance . . .

After a period of gradual construction, and at about 7 years of age, a thought structure is formed; as a structure it is not yet separated from its concrete content. . . . The various thought operations . . . are carried out simultaneously, thus forming systems of operations. . . .

Stage III. Formal thinking operations. The third stage of intellectual development begins, on the average, at about 11 or 12 years of age and is characterized by the development of formal, abstract thought operations. . . .

. . . The adolescent is capable of forming hypotheses and of deducing possible consequences from them. . . .

In the early part of the stage of concrete thinking operations (sometimes called a period of preoperational thought from two to seven years) the child is beginning to function symbolically. He does not need to try out an alternative; he can draw upon his repertoire of knowledge of it.

Sigel (1964) describes phases of the concrete thinking operations as follows:

During the *preoperational* period (two to four) the child . . . still judges things on face value and is not reflective in his thought. . . . Inability to handle multiple characteristics of objects is one reason that Piaget refers to this time of the child's life as one in which he is operating on preconcepts.

. . . The (four- to seven-year-old) child is still egocentric, dominated by his perceptions with his judgments subjective. Three fundamental operations now make an appearance: the ability to think in terms of classes, to see relationships, and to handle number concepts. The child can classify material on the basis of objective similarity. When presented with a group of squares and triangles, he can classify objects on the basis of triangularity or color. But he is still categorizing on the basis of one of these characteristics. At the same time he is increasingly able to comprehend the meaning of similarity and classification. It is now possible for him to see relationships . . . as a result of the ability to perceive relations as well as to compare and order items. The child is now said to be *intuitive* because he does not necessarily verbalize or indicate awareness of his classification.

In the *concrete operations* phase (seven to eleven years) thought is in logical terms. "The child has to be able to ascertain that certain properties of objects are invariant in the face of certain changes. This awareness is called *conservation.*"

Figures 71, 73, 77, 83 and 84 illustrate cognitive development at earlier ages which provides bases for more complex concepts at later ages. All these illustrations are of sensory-motor actions of children under eighteen months of age. It is in this period that changes in ways the young child deals with situations pertain, according to Piaget (1954), to the development of a concept or idea of an object as connected with space, causality and time.

"Permanence" does not exist for the young infant. This begins when, for example, he prolongs the movements of grasping; it has proceeded further when he searches for objects that have disappeared; and it is more complete when the infant takes account of the change of position outside the field of direct perception (beginning at sixteen to eighteen months). "It is in acting on the external world that, according to Piaget, the child elaborates a more and more adequate knowledge of reality. It is precisely the successive forms of his activity in the course of his development that determine his modes of knowledge" (Inhelder, 1962).

Figures 85 through 88 illustrate forms of activity in the preoperational phase and the intuitive phase of the period of concrete thinking operations. Flavell's contrast (1963) of Piaget's sensory-motor period and the period which follows it is as follows: "Representational thought . . . through symbolic capacity has the potential for simultaneously grasping, in a single, internal epitome, a whole sweep of separate events. It is a much faster device (than sensory-motor functioning) which can recall the past, represent the present, and anticipate the future in one temporally brief, organized act."

In Figures 87 and 88 children of different ages were given materials new to them to play with in the sandbox or at the sand table. In Figure 87 there seems to be sensory-motor functioning in handling the plastic container and representational thought in quickly grasping the possibilities of putting sand where it "does not belong" or in pouring it especially fast. In Figure 88 the five-year-old child, who began spontaneously to measure equal amounts of sand, seems to be responding in ways that

FIGURE 87. *Although the child has a concept of an object, he tends, at first, in thought, to be attentive to only one aspect at a time.*

When these new containers were presented for the first time to 3½-year-olds, the girl spontaneously put a little sand into the container, then her hand, and then looked at her hand through the plastic. She is feeling the plastic while the sand falls out. The one boy put sand into a container, then took it and another container to a seat near another child. Without conversation, the boys' behavior suggested interest in where to pour the sand, and how fast. These children seem to be "elaborating" their ideas of sand play; each seems to be "exploring" a new aspect.

are preliminary to a later grasp of the fact that the amount of sand would be the same, whatever the size of the container (a grasp of conservation). The younger boy, while watching the procedure of measuring, may be organizing thoughts, out of which a different use of the materials will materialize for him.

For a review of research on the acquisition of concepts, such as a concept of object permanence, space and spatial relations, development of concepts of form, color, size, causality, and development of conservation of mass, weight and volume, the reader is referred to Sigel (1964).

The gradual adding of objective details out of which concepts are formed proceeds from greater reliance on sensory perceptions to reliance on words which provide symbols for thought. Early responses suggest a concept without use of words, such as the infant's looking down when something falls. Later, naming may occur, as when the child says, "Ball," and then in another setting, where its size and color are different, he again says, "Ball." Still later he may categorize and think or say, "Rubber." The close lines between perceptions and concepts in the young child are evident as we consider his responses concerning

FIGURE 88. **Complexity of the child's concept is suggested by behavior.**

The five-year-old who is measuring amounts of sand began this activity spontaneously when the new materials were presented. His actions suggest a grasp of ideas about sand play and an interest in a more complex thought structure. If he poured one of the equal amounts from the deep narrow container into the shallow wide container, it would be interesting to know whether he thought he had more, less, or the same amount of sand. Grasp of the principle of conservation of matter usually occurs at a later age. Likewise, it would be interesting to know whether the 4½-year-old who is watching the other boy, and also pouring sand, knows whether it will go over the top of the container. Concept of size (or volume) may be of this accuracy at this age.

distance, weight, number and time. Illustrations of judgments suggest reasons why it may be a long time before the child carries over pertinent ideas, or common features, from one setting to another.

LEARNING TO JUDGE DISTANCE. Some of the more complex perceptions are being built during the years from three to five, including particularly the perception of distance, for which the visual acuity is present (Updegraff, 1930). A three-month-old infant reaches for a proferred toy, but his arm movements and his judgment of distance are not yet coordinated, and so he misses it. He has to make several attempts before his hand closes over the coveted object. An infant soon learns accurate judgment of shorter distances, but at a year he still reaches eagerly for the moon and seems unable to understand why it cannot be obtained. At three years he sometimes forgets that distance diminishes apparent size, so that he comments on "the baby automobile" which he sees at some distance. But from three to five years he makes such mistakes less and less frequently.

Concepts of distance and of space seem to be related. Language responses concerning space have been studied. Ames and Learned (1948) described the one-year-old as using gestures or wriggles for *up* and *down*, and the two-year-old as using such words as *up stairs, up high*. At thirty months more exactness of location is indicated by *way up, in here, in there, far* and *far away. Next to, under* and *between* are reported as meaningful for the 42-month-old child. Again distinction between the perception and the use of words to describe it must be made. Words such as these reveal interest in the perceptions.

LEARNING ABOUT NUMBERS. Interest in numbers, although evident before three years of age, does not occupy the time and attention that it does after three. Even at nine months the baby has an awareness of "two-ness" in contrast to "one-ness," since he can put two objects together in relation to each other and prefers two clothespins to one as playthings (Gesell and Ilg, 1943). Children of eighteen months often lay blocks or beads out in rows of two or three. Children of two can often be heard counting "one and another," or "one and one" or, sometimes, "one, two." Children of two or even of three years usually have little understanding of the meaning of any number beyond "one," "two," possibly "three," and "lots." Although they can be taught to recite numbers "parrot fashion," they do not usually, without excessive coaching, actually count a series of more than four objects until they are nearly four years old mentally, or of thirteen objects until they are nearly six mentally (Terman and Merrill, 1960). Particular cognitive levels of maturity are preludes to the child's learning conservation of number (Wohlwill, 1962). His progression from perception to inference is a dimension of his cognitive development.

LEARNING TO JUDGE TIME INTERVALS. A concept of time develops slowly and is expressed almost invariably through language, so that its actual progress is difficult to measure. Sources of confusion for the child come from situations such as the following: A mother takes her child to call on one of her friends for "half an hour." She is interested and time flies; he is bored and time drags. On another day the child goes out to play for "half an hour," and is called to come inside after what seems almost no time at all. "Half an hour" is a variable quantity to a young child who has not yet learned to judge it with the objective aid of a clock. By the time he is four, however, he has learned that "a few minutes" means less than "an hour" or "several hours." When he is two, there seems no other way of explaining "when Daddy will be home" than to tell him that it will be "after you've had your lunch and your nap and have played a long time"; but at four years he will understand that "Daddy will be home late this afternoon." Questions such as "When is noon?" "How long is half an hour?" "When is tomorrow?" are familiar on the lips of four-year-old children. "Yesterday," "tomorrow," "next week" still puzzle them. It seems probable that such complex time concepts as "last spring," "day before yesterday," "a month ago" and especially "New Year's Eve" are unintelligible even to six-year-olds.

In spontaneous verbalizations of children Ames (1946) found words dealing with the present appearing first, then those indicating the future and, later, indicating the past. Expression of temporal order occurred as early as thirty months, but words implying duration did not appear as a rule until thirty-six months.

Inability to appreciate time units seems related to dallying, which is frequent in preschool years. Sitting indefinitely before distasteful foods and occupying endless periods of time at dressing or picking up toys, or continuing to play instead of getting ready for the next event are responses that may occur because the child does not comprehend that time passes. In some situations, study of what the child goes to (the next event of his day) may provide reasons for his being especially slow. As for dressing and putting away toys, interest in companionship or sociability may be a key to his slowness in a situation for which he has the motor skill.

LEARNING TO JUDGE WEIGHT.   Accurate perception of weight depends on judgment of size and knowledge of the weight of various materials. Young children are often confused because weight varies with the material of which the object is composed as well as with the size of the object. For example, at Hallowe'en one group of three- and four-year-old children, having played for a day with a papier-mâché pumpkin, were presented with a real pumpkin. One of the children reached out his hands to accept the gift, but made a muscular adjustment sufficient to hold only the paper pumpkin and therefore dropped the real pumpkin. Even at four years of age the children had not learned much about judgment of weight.

Two-year-old children are faced many times a day with situations as puzzling as this. They reach to pick up a pail with the same free gesture they have seen an adult use and are astonished that they cannot lift it. They learn about how much muscular pull is necessary to lift a pail of sand and make the same sort of muscular adjustment to lift a rubber ball of the same size. It is not at all unusual to see a two-year-old child upset himself because he has prepared to lift a heavy object, only to find himself lifting a light one. Often he attempts to lift things he cannot move at all. One day he seems to have discovered that big things are the heavy ones and little things light ones, only to find that some big thing upsets him because it is light and some little thing cannot be moved, no matter how hard he tugs at it.

ACQUAINTANCE WITH HIS OWN BODY.   Perception of the extent and contour of his own body occupies the child for some months before he is a year old and seems to be fairly clear to him by the time he is three years old. He lies in his cradle at four or five months, touching the fingers of one hand against those of the other, enjoying the sensation he gets. By seven or eight months he has learned to get his toes into his mouth, but he still has to learn that when he bites those toes he gives himself a different sensation because the feet belong to him. Sometimes he bites a finger or toe, then bites a rattle, learning that toes and fingers are part of himself, whereas rattles are not. Before he is a year old he has begun conscious exploration of his own body, studying its extent and exploring its contour. He pats his head, fingers his ear, and rubs his stomach. Not infrequently he discovers that some parts of his body give one sensation, some parts another. He may discover at a year or at eighteen months, sometimes at two or three years, that patting or rubbing the genital organs produces a particularly pleasing sensation, and he will return to the exploration of this part of his body even more often than he plays with ears or toes.

Concepts of his abilities as he uses his body come from experiences concerning distance, number, time, weight and others, as well as from attitudes of people toward his behavior.

COGNITIVE STYLE. Evidence suggests differences in cues to which individuals respond in forming concepts. Style of categorization differs not only with age, but also from one child to another. According to Sigel et al. (1962):

> Our goal is to study what kinds of cues are used as the basis for perceiving similarity—a process conceived as *a prerequisite to categorization.* . . . We are interested in discovering what aspects, from a polydimensional world, are selected and organized into various categories. Further, we are interested in the degree to which individuals are oriented to deal with stimuli in terms of their manifest dimensions, . . . or are inclined to disregard the manifest explicity, and use inferences. These two approaches can be said to be reflections of *styles,* if styles are defined as "stable individual preferences in modes of perceptual organization and conceptual categorization of the external environment."

Grouping or categorizing may be descriptive of physical attributes by referring to parts of the whole (as by saying, "They all have feet") or by a global reference ("They are men"). Or a second style of categorization, called relational-contextual, may be used more frequently ("A horse is used to pull a stagecoach"). In a third style, called categorical-inferential, grouping is according to inferred characteristics of the stimuli ("These are things to build with," or "tools" or "run by motors").

A study by Sigel, Jarman and Hanasian (1962) of four- and five-year-old children revealed the presence at these ages of these style dimensions, which have also been identified with older children and adults. Children were asked to select from three cards a picture that went with or was like one on a fourth card. For the pictures used, descriptive part-whole responses were the most frequent, followed by relational-contextual, categorical-inferential and, finally, descriptive-global. Data in some instances revealed significant differences according to sex, age and intelligence quotient. Boys four years of age used more categorical-inferential terms than girls of the same age, but there were no differences between boys and girls of five years.

Problem-Solving Ability and Thought

In certain test procedures the child is faced with a situation to be met, or a problem. Problem solving, reasoning, thinking are words used to describe his approaches in this situation. Dispute about whether or not young children reason usually hinges upon the question of what is called reasoning. Some writers have said that reasoning is a complex mental process impossible for young children; others, that it is a mental process which grades in complexity from the simple trial-and-error problem solving of animals through the intricate associations and insight involved in the solution of subtle mathematic and philosophic problems. Anderson (1949) said:

> While some problems are met by pure manipulation of physical objects, most are met by a process called thinking, which . . . is a universal process present in the infant as well as the adult, in the feebleminded as well as the bright. It is closely connected with ordinary living and usually involves symbolic processes. Life, to most persons, is a succession of problems . . . met and solved in work and play.

What the child knows—his cognition—grows and develops as his motor, perceptual, language and other aspects of behavior grow and develop. What the child brings before his mind—his thinking—may be something remembered or newly apprehended. What the child uses with a view to attaining a conclusion—his reasoning—may have more knowledge and thought in it as he grows and develops.

To refer to problem solving in actions and in words is a way to clarify the aspect in which we are interested as we study development of the young child. Bijou and Baer (1960) say that the dimensions of problem-solving behavior have not been adequately worked out. They suggest the following definition as a point of departure for study: "Problem solving may be defined as any behavior which, through the manipulation of variables, makes the appearance of a solution more probable" (Skinner, 1953). We shall include manipulation of objects and also of words in thought.

It is evident that problem solving of a rudimentary sort is within the ability of fairly young infants if we consider the following examples.

Gesell (1925) described how nine- to twelve-month-old infants are usually able to recover a cube which has been covered over by an enamel cup.

> The examiner takes one of the small red cubes and casts it upon the table to entice the child's attention. He may even allow the child to handle the cube for a moment. While the attention of the child is directed to the cube, the examiner swiftly covers it with an inverted enamel cup and placing the handle of the cup at the child's right, he notes first the reaction of the child to the cup. . . . It was most astonishing to find one six month child who solved the situation unmistakably, not only once but six times in immediate succession, exhibiting great zeal and concentration.

Simple, concrete problem solving by infants is illustrated further by their discovery of a number of cause and effect connections. Pulling a coveted object by means of an attached string is common in infants of one year. Nearly all children will use a chair to reach something before they are two years of age. Whether or not young children reason is not an argument of fact, but a dispute over definition.

Most infants of twelve or fourteen months have discovered that they can bring a dish on the table nearer by pulling the whole tablecloth toward them; they have discovered the relation between tilting the bottle and getting more milk; they have made the association between having a hat on and going out of doors. Long before twelve months they have discovered the relation between arm movements and the noise produced by a rattle, between releasing their hold of a ball and its falling on the floor. These are examples of an *association of cause and effect*.

Generalization comes later. One need only watch young children to conclude that their ability to generalize is not well developed. They must meet many specific situations and must be told about numerous specific instances before they are able to draw conclusions from them.

The child who has a horn and lets another child blow it may stop at an adult's suggestion. But he is likely to let another child blow it unless the generalization has been added that the horn should be blown by only one person and the reasons presented so far as he can understand. He may also understand, through discussion, why putting the horn away instead of having it in a group may be desirable.

Attempts to draw conclusions are suggested by the following dialogue:

Lynn: My father doesn't like chocolate pudding.
Debbie: My father doesn't, either. Boys don't like chocolate pudding.
Tommie: I like it. I'm a boy.
Lynn: Yes, you're a boy. Then men don't like chocolate pudding.

Bob: I have ten fingers (after counting).
Bill: I have six fingers (after counting inaccurately). You must be older than me.

The young child may not realize that combs, toothbrushes and washcloths belong to the general class of "personal belongings" and are things that each one uses for himself alone; whereas most chairs, books and other household furnishings belong to the general class of "family belongings" and can be used by any member of the family. Personal belongings are alike in the fact that they are used in the care of the person and are different from family belongings as a class. Descriptive-global and categorical-inferential terms were less frequent among the four- and five-year-olds studied by Sigel, Jarman and Hanasian (1962) than descriptive part-whole and relational-contextual terms.

Barbara's playmate Blanche looked out the window at heavily falling snow and said, "Oh, see the feathers." Barbara said, "They're not feathers, are they?" and received from an adult the answer, "No, Blanche is using her imagination." Barbara was apparently much impressed with the word "imagination" and went about repeating it over and over. Later in the day she said, "If Blanche had said, 'That is snow,' would that have been imagination?"

In another illustration of thought beyond the immediate situation, a four-year-old, who discovered that his neighbors did not have television, quickly asked, "But how do you see the news?" and later, "How do you know about the news?"

In commenting on causal relations, children at kindergarten age are able to give mechanical and logical answers which are more often materialistic than not (Deutsche, 1937). Nevertheless the questions children raise, before school age, suggest attempts to grasp more abstract relations (Navarra, 1955).

Whenever a new situation for which the individual has no established reaction presents itself, he is faced with a problem. As long as life flows along familiar channels where no new or unaccustomed action is demanded, habit may serve. But whenever a strange situation arises, habit is insufficient. A new solution or a new pattern of action is needed. The *steps in* such *problem solving* are usually listed as follows:

1. Identification of the problem and determination of its nature
2. Survey of possible solutions
3. Selection of the most promising solution
4. Trial of chosen solution

These steps are illustrated in the following incident in a nursery school where each morning the children are served tomato juice in small glass cups.

The glasses were being served from a low serving table to children seated in groups of four at individual tables. One child from each table was serving his table. Jimmy, age three, carried glasses from the serving table until everyone in his group had been served. But he did not count correctly and appeared at his table carrying a fifth glass, which had to be returned to the serving table. Meanwhile the children at all the other tables had been served, had drunk their tomato juice and had returned their empty glasses to a serving tray. Upon reaching the serving table Jimmy was faced with a problem. He must return his extra glass of juice to the serving tray, but the tray was full of empty glasses. He achieved step 1 in reasoning immediately: he realized where his problem lay and was able to see exactly what the problem was.

He surveyed the situation (step 2) as he stood holding the glass of juice and trying to figure out what he could do about it. An idea which promised to work occurred to him (step 3). He took the glass by its handle and tried to use it as a pusher (step 4), pushing the other glasses about in an attempt to crowd them a little closer and thus make room for his glass. This solution failed. He returned to step 2, considering other possible solutions as he stood thoughtfully holding his glass. Once more an idea occurred to him, and he tried to pile his glass on

FIGURE 89. *Exploration of problems he invents and solutions he tries out can be a part of the child's play.*

This boy, 4 years 8 months of age, was using play equipment designed by a student (S. Hobson). The frames have square, circular and triangular openings. The felt-covered objects have similar shapes. "Problems" invented by this child concerned stacking of the solid objects, throwing from different positions, seeing similarly and differently shaped forms and spaces in various positions.

FIGURE 89   (see legend on opposite page)

top of one of the empty glasses on the tray. But the handle on his glass caused it to tilt, and threatened to spill the juice. At this point experience with similar situations led him to realize that this solution was a failure because, although putting his glass of juice on top of another glass would get his glass on the tray (one aspect of his goal), it would spill the juice and thus defeat another important aspect of his goal.

Once more he stood holding his glass as he surveyed other possible solutions. Suddenly his face beamed. Apparently he had discovered another possibility. He reached out and poured his juice into one of the empty glasses, thus "saving it," and triumphantly set his now empty glass upon another, thus getting it upon the tray. It could tilt now with no loss of juice. In his own mind he had achieved success in solving his problem.

The repertoire of possible solutions was incomplete for this three-year-old. His adding another possibility for use next time, instead of repeating his solution of this time, would seem to hinge upon his receiving adult guidance of a kind which would encourage further thought on his part.

Exploration of a variety of approaches to a situation can be very absorbing to a young child. In Figure 89 the child, of his own accord, began to experiment with play equipment. First he tried stacking the separate parts. Next, after placing forms in front of spaces they matched in shape, he tossed each one through the space. Later he tried tossing one object through three spaces of three frames he had placed close together. Thus he identified a number of problems and tried out a variety of solutions. Exploration of this kind seems related to concept formation, development of problem-solving ability and thought. Some of this experimentation seems to be an attempt at "ordering" or "arranging" in a growing intellect, still on a plane of exploration or concrete thought, rather than of a grasp of a principle.

Bruner (1964) refers to ability of children five, six and seven years of age to reproduce an orderly arrangement of nine plastic glasses they have seen. But when a particular part was transposed and located in a new position, five- and six-year-olds (with a few exceptions) could not produce a new arrangement based on the rule or principle of the other —a rule based on arrangement by diameter and height. Most of the seven-year-olds succeeded in the transposed task.

Figure 90 shows materials which the child could arrange in a number of different ways. The system of ordering could proceed from simple to complex.

Decision making is an essential part of step 3 in problem solving and, like other aspects of reasoning, seems to depend for its development upon practice and success. It includes steps such as the following:

1. For deciding among choices A, B and C, it is necessary to examine the advantages of each, and also the disadvantages.
2. The advantages inherent in choice A must be weighed against the advantages inherent in the other two choices, and also against the disadvantages inherent in the same choice; the same must be done for B and C.
3. The individual making the decision must choose, knowing that by virtue of his choice he is giving up the advantages of the

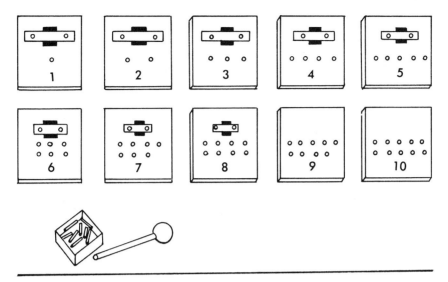

FIGURE 90. *Arranging, ordering, classifying can be on different planes of thought.*

This series of 10 flat blocks, designed by a student (M. Martin), has been used by children in various ways, according to their abilities and interests. Handling the blocks, placement of pegs, placement of pegs by color to match the space, connection of number with the spaces, connection of sound with the number sequence (through the xylophone part at the top of each board) are a few of the possibilities.

    choices he decides against, and accepting the disadvantages of the choice that he decides for along with its advantages.

4. The individual must believe in his decision sufficiently to act upon it.

VARIABLES IN DEVELOPMENT OF CONCEPTS, PROBLEM-SOLVING ABILITY AND THOUGHT. Differences among children in problem-solving ability sometimes concern the child's ability to verbalize his solution. In studies of preschool children in which solution of the problem involved learning the principle, i.e., generalizing, the amount of experience needed for success varied greatly from one child to another. Success in several experiments depended on discovering a basis for securing a doll or toy even when materials were rearranged. For example, in some experimental situations, solving the problem meant learning that the right-hand box contained a doll, or that a certain color or figure was a key to securing a toy. Solving the problem was possible at an earlier age than statement of the principle (Roberts, 1932). An adult's encouraging the child to verbalize his solution seemed to aid in generalizing (Pyles, 1932).

    In Kuenne's experiment (1946) children's ability to verbalize the cue aspects of the stimulus situation, either in response to questioning afterwards or spontaneously during the trials, accompanied far transposition. For example, children who verbalized "always the smaller square for a toy" were ones who also selected the smaller of two squares, even when the size of the pair was far from that of the pair with which training took place (far transposition). When the size of the second pair was near that of the pair used in training (near transposition), children who did not verbalize explicit association of size with success were also successful. The relation between mental age and far transposition was significant, but the relation between mental age and near transposition was low. Most children of mental ages three to six years succeeded in the near test. The percentage of children succeeding in the far test increased as mental age increased from three to six. The mechanisms of discrimination and transposition were considered different in the verbal type of control. Transposition when the difference is near instead of far was considered to resemble mechanisms of animals.

Attributes of the child and encouragement of thought on his part by an adult are variables in development of concepts and of problem-solving ability. Other variables seem to concern particular procedures or attributes of the adult.

In a list of dominative and integrative categories of adult behavior with children, H. Anderson (1939) included "build up," meaning the encouragement of the child to solve his problem without giving him the solution. In a study of college students in association with nursery school children, only 2 per cent of all their integrative contacts (which were more frequent than the dominative contacts) were of this build-up type (Nesbitt, 1943). If a child has caught a wheel of his tricycle while riding between a box and a bench, the adult's comments can help him to select the pertinent facts instead of giving him the solution.

Other variables concern relation of other cognitive processes in sensory-motor, perceptual and language development to more complex processes of thought. How they function in mediation of thought is one of the interests of current research. For a review of research on cognitive development, which concerns intellectual functioning as the structure of understanding and the mechanisms of its achievement, the reader is referred to Wright (1966).

IMPLICATIONS OF INFORMATION CONCERNING DEVELOPMENT OF CONCEPTS, PROBLEM-SOLVING ABILITY AND THOUGHT. A young child learns through opportunity to solve his own problems, to do his own thinking whenever the situation is simple enough to permit a reasonably sound solution from the background of his limited experience, or whenever the risk of a wrong solution is not too great. Guidance in accordance with language ability may be in the form of encouragement of further thought.

Since abilities develop with age and experience, the adult encounters numerous occasions which prompt him to recall that response to specific situations must precede application of general principles. For example, the parent may explain to a three-year-old about keeping floors clean and not tracking mud on them and ask him to remove his galoshes on entering the house. He seems to understand and abides by the request for several weeks. When the weather becomes less severe, however, and galoshes are replaced by rubbers, she is surprised one day when, apparently forgetting the request and his own previous behavior, he appears in the house wearing rubbers and leaving muddy tracks behind him. He is puzzled when asked whether he has forgotten that muddy overshoes are not to be worn into the house, and replies, "But, Mother, you said galoshes. You didn't say anything about rubbers."

Occasions occur which reveal that the individual thinks what he wishes rather than what the situation demands. The child, wearing his rubbers into the house because he has misunderstood the generalization involved, may have thought that rubbers were not included, partly because he wished to think it. Four-year-old Betsy illustrated this type of wishful thinking when, during dramatic play, the "father" wanted a gun which she had found. She carried her point by saying, "No, you can't have it because I'm the mama and mamas carry the guns."

It seems to be in accordance with our knowledge to let children work on problems unaided if there is some appreciable chance that success will come with reasonable effort, but to give aid rather than to allow failure to occur too often. Failure means dissatisfaction and an increasing unwillingness to attempt solution of problems, whereas success, especially that which comes as a reward for one's own effort, is a keen stimulant to further efforts.

Decisions can be adapted to ability. Children have many possibilities in their day for making many decisions apparently trivial to adults, but important to them. "What shall I play now?" "How can I make this tower of blocks stand straight?" "Where shall I keep my doll?" Such decisions can be made by the child himself. When decisions for which he has sufficient experience and judgment are left for him to make, he not only has practice in making decisions, but also feels less "pushed around" or "pressed" by others. In building a sense of autonomy, children seek or need to decide for themselves what they are able to decide; this includes recognition of the greater wisdom of others when it is appropriate.

Quality of play through which the child learns can reflect opportunities provided by adults. The child seems to find satisfactions in functioning as he tries to fit together specific associations and broader concepts. This going back and forth, in his explorations, from the immediate experience to a broader context and then the return to the detail, can have spontaneity.

DEVELOPMENT OF CREATIVITY

Imitation

Children imitate movements they see, sounds they hear, or values of other people. Most writers seem to assume that at least part of the child's tendency to duplicate the behavior and attitudes of those about him is due to a conscious imitation. Close observation of infants may reveal instances of direct imitation of movements before nine months. Gesell and Ilg (1943) say that the nine-month-old and the one-year-old may be prodigious imitators. At fifteen months the child enjoys imitating smoking, coughing, nose-blowing, sneezing and other such activities. By fifteen months also "bow-wow," mewing like a cat, "peek-a-boo," "pat-a-cake," imitative crushing of paper, and throwing a ball are all familiar in behavior. "Bye-bye," imitative combing of hair, kissing a doll, and scribbling with a pencil are also common at this age.

By the time they are two years old most children begin to reflect adult mannerisms. One little girl learned to greet everyone with the same swinging gesture and strident-voiced "How's evabody?" that her father used. Many mothers learn for the first time of the querulous tone which creeps into their "discipline voice" when they hear the three-year-old disciplining her doll in imitation of the adult manner.

From two years onward play time is much occupied with "housekeeping," "traffic cop," "hospital," "shopping" — play in which the child duplicates as faithfully as he can the activities, gestures and tones of adult behavior which have happened to attract his fancy. He is rude with the rudeness of adults whom he admires, or courteous with the easy grace of the fine example of those whom he loves. He speaks clearly and accurately, or mumbles bad grammar and profanity; he is neat or untidy, quiet or boisterous, truthful or sly, at least in some measure according to the examples set for him.

Teaching courtesy involves being courteous before the child and to him; teaching good English involves speaking it to children while they are in the early learning period of language development; teaching attitudes toward health, authority, truth and society are related to the attitudes we ourselves have, since children reflect these subtleties as inevitably as they imitate the more obvious gestures and tones of voice.

The model for imitation will be someone by whom, for some reason, the child is influenced. This will usually be the parent or person who takes care of him and others in his family until the child begins to meet other people. As contacts widen, potential models become more numerous. The strident profanity of a person he meets by chance may appeal to the child as grown-up and prove an attractive model. The pranks of a neighborhood child may receive so much attention and create so much excitement that they appeal to other children for duplication. Investigations of imitative choices are beginning to be made (see pp. 238 and 412). Variables such as arrangements of the setting, sex of the model, and the amount of attention recently received by the child have been studied (Rosenblith, 1959, 1961).

It would not be possible to protect the child from all undesirable models. Furthermore, unless he has some experience in the selection of standards, he can scarcely be expected to use judgment in the matter when he no longer has his parents to assist him. He could be overwhelmed by too sudden or too constant exposure to undesirable models if he were not also exposed to enough attractive and desirable ones, in either life or literature, to keep the balance favorable. Parents, being his first and closest models, have a great balance of power.

Imagination

Just as he imitates the models around him, every child adapts what he takes from his environment not only to his own pace of growth (or maturational patterns) and previous experience, but also to his own individuality. Each child has central orientations of personality or emotional tone which color the ideas that come to him and the manner in which he reacts to the world around him. Thus he creates the world in terms of his own life and absorbs from life the things he needs to fulfill his development. He also expresses back to the world varying interpretations and evidences of his own personality. He is original, in this sense, just as he is in the things he does with paints and clay, with rhythms and bodily movement, and in story telling and dramatic play.

Ability to express himself with any fluency depends on the acquisition of controls over his body, on accumulation of knowledge which will permit him to judge and to handle objects intelligently (sense perceptions and judgments), on language facility and on increasing capacity to have and to use ideas in concept formation, problem solving and thought. It is easy to understand, then, why the child's ability to express himself in what people usually regard as imaginative behavior should increase steadily with age, at least in the early years of life.

Life in our society is such that one cannot give full vent to one's imaginative tendencies. Thus there can be seen in the development of the child's imagination, first the crescendo of increasing ability to be imaginative, or "unrealistic," and to express this, a peak when imagination seems to occupy time and energy along with the world of facts; then a gradual diminuendo as life contributes to the acceptance of the idea of adjustment to the real world of routines and of other people's needs and desires (Isaacs, 1952; Piaget, 1954).

What pattern the crescendo takes and how long it lasts seem to depend on the motor skills, language facility and other requisite abilities of the child and on the ways with which his parents and his world introduce him to reality. The child of preschool age seems able to keep his imagination and inner resourcefulness and initiative, while at the same time learning to cooperate with the necessary routines, to tell the truth and to face facts realistically. In most children's lives, as they live with and adjust to most parents, the expression of imaginative thoughts begins gradually by about one year to eighteen months, mounts rapidly from then to three or four years, and remains at a fairly high point for several years.

Ames and Learned (1946) described a suggestive gradient

. . . which indicates the several threads or general kinds of imaginative behavior which go to make up the total "imagination gradient." These threads are:
1. Possessing an imaginary animal, or human, companion, or "boy or girl" friend.
2. Playing the role of a baby, an animal, a person.
3. Imaginative play with some specific object (animates object, has a specific imaginary object, personalizes object).
4. The various types of imaginative dramatic play and creative story telling and writing, and composing poems and songs.

. . . Any or all parts (of this imagination gradient) . . . may quite normally occur in any one child.

Forms and Functions of Creativity

In trying out the many models of his world, in expressing imagination, as well as in the adding of accurate knowledge, the young child has many resources for recombining the familiar to produce the new. Creativity means inventiveness. Getzels and Jackson (1962), referring to the variety of factors of intellect, identify

. . . two basic cognitive or intellective modes. The one mode tends toward retaining the known, learning the predetermined, and conserving what is. The second mode tends toward revising the known, exploring the undetermined and constructing what might be. A person for whom the first mode or process is primary tends toward the *usual and expected*. A person for whom the second mode is primary tends toward the *novel and speculative*. The one favors certainty, the other risk. Both processes are found in all persons, but in varying proportions. . . . Both have their place, and both must be recognized for their differences, commonalities, interactions, and distinctive functions in the individual's psychic economy. . . .

In general, our tests of creativity involved the ability to deal inventively with verbal and numerical symbol systems and with object-space relations. What most of these tests had in common was that the score depended not on a single predetermined correct response as is most often the case with the common intelligence test, but on the number, novelty, and variety of adaptive responses to a given stimulus task.

In the young child the novel and the speculative, the dealing inventively with his world, are evident in dramatic play, exploration of expanding horizons in creative thinking and use of materials, painting and other graphic experiences, and response to music.

DRAMATIC PLAY.   Many young children discover the fun of living out simple stories by playing that they are the animals of a story or playing mother or father in the role of housekeeping (see Fig. 91). The child's doll becomes a live baby; a row of blocks becomes a train; a child pretends to eat sand pies and cakes with gusto.

Imaginary companions may provide associations when the child is deprived of the opportunity to play with other children at a time when they are becoming important to him. This seems to have a connection with his interests in companionship and in language development. Even in nursery schools, however, imaginary companions are found, since in this way children sometimes provide a baby brother or a parent or a playmate who has attributes the child considers important. Figure 92 suggests possibilities for development of abilities. These children are having "coffee," holding cups, pretending to drink from them, and deciding who will have the cubes that are to be "cookies." Possibilities for being creative, and for other kinds of learning, are present in this play situation. Furthermore, not only the joy of the immediate experience, but also other elements may be present.

Hartley, Frank and Goldenson (1952) stated the values of dramatic play as follows:

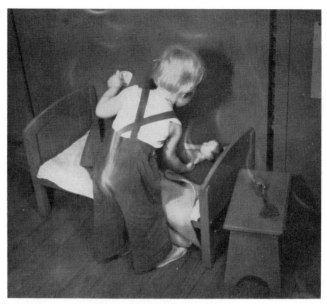

FIGURE 91. Play reflects observed behavior.

This 2½-year-old child enjoyed pretending to be the mother. She also enjoyed having the bed big enough so that some of the time she could pretend to be the baby.

FIGURE 92. Children learn through play.

These children are learning to use different abilities such as hand coordination, perception, language, imagination and social skills.

Through this activity the child is given an opportunity (1) to imitate adults; (2) to play out real life roles in an intense way; (3) to reflect relationships and experiences; (4) to express pressing needs; (5) to release unacceptable impulses; (6) to reverse roles usually taken; (7) to mirrow growth; and (8) to work out problems and experiment with solutions.

WIDENING HORIZONS. Many opportunities for creative thinking are present as children add detail concerning the familiar and experience the new. The children in Figure 93 are adding details of information which may be used in a variety of ways. Adults can play an important part in providing situations in which various abilities of the child may be used.

In considering "science" for young children, adult scientists and others suggest emphasis on the spirit of inquiry as contrasted to emphasis on "bits of knowledge." In making observations, differentiating, sorting or classifying, asking questions, the child is using his problem-solving ability. Furthermore, although there are intellectual qualities in the child's experiences with animals and plants, rocks and shells, there can also be a quality of joy. In Figure 94 the event of having a lamb in the playground had elements for the intellect; it also had elements of affect, or feeling tone concerning widening horizons.

Parents and teachers determine to some extent the opportunities the young child has to express and to value his imagination, to learn new facts about the world, and to use play equipment and creative materials. Russell (1956) describes creative thinking as "problem solving plus." He says that problem solving is usually "more consonant with the facts. Creative thinking is more personal, less fixed. It achieves something new rather than coinciding with previously determined condi-

FIGURE 93.   Science begins with the process of inquiry.

These 4- and 5-year-olds were having opportunities to observe, compare, make distinctions and ask questions.

FIGURE 94. Appreciation of plants and animals includes enthusiasms as well as facts.

The children had a spirit of inquiry concerning the lamb; they also were happy to have it visit their playground

tions." *Originality may be in the thinking, or it may be in the use of materials.* Torrance (1962) defined creative thinking "as the process of sensing gaps or disturbing, missing elements; forming ideas or hypotheses concerning them; testing these hypotheses; and communicating the results, possibly modifying and retesting the hypotheses."

Torrance was interested in assessing creative thinking through

. . . a set of tasks which could be used from kindergarten through graduate school. . . . One task, called the Ask and Guess Test, requires the individual first to ask questions about a picture, questions which cannot be answered by looking at the picture. . . . Next he is asked to make guesses or formulate hypotheses about the possible causes and then the consequences, both immediate and remote, of the behavior depicted.

Another test, called Product Improvement Task, involves common toys and ways of making them "more fun to play with."

An atmosphere of "freedom from time pressure and . . . a playful game-like context rather than one implying that the person is under test" is emphasized by Wallach and Kogan (1965). In such a setting creativity in a particular activity (as a dimension independent of general intelligence) is more likely to manifest itself by a large number of cognitive associations, and by many which are unique, whether verbal or visual abilities are involved.

PAINTING. Sequences through which creative abilities develop are suggested in the development of children's paintings. Given the requisite motor and intellectual maturity, nearly all children enjoy using paints and paper. The joy of handling paints or clay, or of experimenting with a piano keyboard, could be destroyed by the parent or teacher who either insists that the child "stop that messing" or forces him to "copy the bunch of carrots exactly as it is" or to practice the scales. Free experimentation with the various art media can be a part of creative development which is a foundation for later formal teaching. If the child learns to love what he is doing, he may be more likely later to work intensely through the endless hours of developing the techniques which most formal teachers insist on. The children in Figure 95 are discovering the joys of painting.

Many two- and three-year-old children, as well as those who are older, properly covered to protect clothing and in an environment where spills are not serious, will spend long periods at "painting." Given freedom to experiment as they will, nearly all children pass through rather definite phases in their use of this art medium (Beach and Bressler, 1944; Lowenfeld and Brittain, 1964).

First there is relatively uncoordinated scrubbing and sweeping with the brush, spreading color on the page. This may include learning not to drip the paint, not to scrub through the paper, and mastering other elementary factors. Body movements are random. Results are chaotic and are not intended to express anything more significant than sheer joy in color and activity.

Second, body movement is more coordinated. Lines, strokes and distinct color areas appear. An accidental design may develop, and may be the product of an interruption in the work or a disturbance developing from a paint run or a blot or other distracting occurrence. Even a slight shift of the child's mood may seem to change the tone or intention of the activity.

Third, consciously sought design appears. At this stage many chil-

FIGURE 95. *Expression of self as contrasted to conformity can occur in use of materials.*

This child, 3½ years old, is experimenting with paint. Her design was not planned ahead of time. The 2-year-old watches, fascinated, and later asks to try it.

dren fill the whole page before announcing themselves as "done." The design is often conscious in the sense that it develops as the painting proceeds. This is a transition from no design to preplanned design. In this stage certain areas of the painting may emerge and call for a plan of design. The child often plans one area to balance another, accidentally developed area.

Fourth is the stage of preplanned design, in which the child deliberately sets out to paint "a man" or "a house." These two are frequently announced subjects of first consciously planned paintings. Some children arrive at this fourth stage as early as four or five years; others may not arrive at it before six or seven years of age. Inexperienced children of six or seven may scrub in a sky or other large area in their pictures, or may start to paint a scene and lapse into pure design. These children suggest by this that they need more experience in the earlier phases and are seeking freedom to experiment with these phases as they feel a need to do so.

A fifth and mature stage of painting is one in which the idea or feeling is more highly developed, and expression is more purposeful than in the earlier stages.

Children do not move smoothly through these stages; some skip backward and forward. They spend varying lengths of time in each stage. Differences with age and of other kinds are evident in children's paintings and drawings. Analysis of data from color drawings of older children indicated factors of style and motion. "Of the two other factors, which may be interpreted as nondevelopmental components (i.e. independent of chronological age), one emerged as a Style factor, quite closely related also to Shape and Color Use; the other was identified as representation of Motion, strongly sustained by the characteristics of planned Asymmetry and Grouping" (Lark-Horowitz and Norton, 1960).

These methods of studying children's paintings suggest aspects of interest in viewing a particular child's painting. His self-expression, as contrasted to his conformity to standards outside himself, is another element which is of interest.

Creative activities are considered important not only because of the joy the child may have in them, but also because of aspects of his personality they may reveal, and opportunities for personality growth they may provide. Alschuler and Hattwick (1947) warn against attempts at simple diagnosis of a particular child's feelings and needs from his paintings, and say, "In the analysis and interpretation of a given painting it is more often in the interrelationships of several aspects than in any simple characteristic that the distinctive and telling qualities of the child's products are likely to lie." Further discussion of projective techniques is on pages 420-421. Therapeutic values the child gains through graphic arts can be similar to those previously mentioned with regard to dramatic play (Hartley, Frank and Goldenson, 1952).

MUSICAL ABILITY.   Children enjoy singing if songs are presented in the voice range natural to them. Jersild and Bienstock (1934), in a study of the musical ability of young children, found that the number of notes in the voice range increases with age. From two to six years the number of tones in the range of the children studied increased from five through thirteen. This shows a rapid development of range through the pre-school years, and permits the singing of many songs if they are written in the proper range. The two-year range more frequently included D, E, F, G and A above middle C. By three years middle C was included, and at six years the range included the scale from A below middle C to the second G above middle C. Very young children readily sing notes from middle C up to A, and narrow intervals more readily than wider ones.

In a study of three-year-old children Jersild (1931) found that training caused a decided improvement in the number of notes and intervals the children could produce. Updegraff et al. (1937), in a study of three- to five-year-olds, found not only that ability to sing improved noticeably with training, but also that interest, satisfaction and enjoyment increased as ability improved. Training seemed to give the children more self-confidence in singing, more interest in learning and more enjoyment in participating in group musical activities.

Although children differ in capacity to enjoy and to respond to music, most children by three years have learned to recognize a few simple tunes, can beat a fairly good simple rhythm, and can detect the difference between high and low notes, between slow and rapid rhythms, and between loud and soft intensities.

Ability to discriminate pitch, timbre, intensity and interval, as well as skill in pitching the voice, develops quickly if the child has a special ability in this direction and if practice is given. Response to rhythm enables the child to stamp, march or sway in time to simple music. A few can beat drums, clap cymbals or shake a tambourine accurately enough to accompany music. There is temptation to teach children "parlor tricks" in music. Many children of preschool age, having only a slight gift in music, can be taught to sing dozens of nursery rhymes or to dance an entertaining variety of steps to music. Others, if sufficiently coached, can be taught to recognize scores of record or piano selections.

A feeling for music is considered to be of equal importance to the mechanics of performance. Too great an emphasis on academic memory tricks or on mechanical reaction may interfere with true appreciation of music. Children experience music with their minds, bodies and emotions. Letting children hear good music, sometimes listening quietly, sometimes expressing themselves in bodily movement, can provide foundation in appreciation.

INDIVIDUAL DIFFERENCES IN CREATIVE POTENTIAL AND PRODUCTS. Children differ widely in native gifts in the creative areas of intellectual development. Given a reasonable exposure to the possibilities of expression in any one of the areas, the child will reveal what his native gift is by the interest and concentration he displays. Poor teaching will sometimes discourage a child by forcing him into specific patterns of expression, so that occasionally genuinely gifted children may refuse to respond. If the teaching is even reasonably well adapted to his patterns, however, the gifted child seldom needs to be urged to use his abilities in the situation, informal at the preschool age, but still providing opportunity for practice. Children whose abilities are not exceptional also respond almost universally if the setting is appropriate.

Creative potential and creative products are, of course, different. MacKinnon (1962) refers to creativity as "a process extended in time and characterized by originality, adaptiveness, and realization. It may be brief, . . . or it may involve a considerable span of years." In a study of architects who had demonstrated a high level of creative work, he reported a number of distinguishing characteristics. Among these were an openness to one's own feelings and emotions, a sensitive intellect and understanding self-awareness, being perceptive and being intuitive. "Above a certain required minimum level of intelligence . . . being more intelligent does not guarantee a corresponding increase in creativeness. . . . Nor can we be certain that finding these same traits in youngsters today will identify those with creative potential."

MEASUREMENT OF INTELLIGENCE IN YOUNG CHILDREN

Zigler (1966) has this to say of intelligence:

> There is little agreement . . . when the question . . . is raised . . . what is the nature of intelligence? We cannot avoid this question by invoking the very unsatisfying cliché that "intelligence is what an intelligence test measures" since it is perfectly apparent that the test constructor must have some definition of intelligence in mind, either explicitly or implicitly, before he can select test items. However, some consensus can probably be found for the view that intelligence is a hypothetical construct which has as its ultimate referent the cognitive processes of the individual. Given this, we are still faced with the unresolved issue of whether intelligence represents some single cognitive process which permeates every intelligence test or nontest behavior, or whether it represents a great variety of relatively discrete cognitive processes which can be sampled and then summated to yield some indication of the degree of intelligence a person possesses.

Attempts have been made to measure intellectual development in very young children. Gesell (1925) and Gesell and Amatruda (1947) evolved a developmental scale with standards for one month and intervals thereafter. These standards are not, however, a test of intelligence itself; they are, rather, evaluations of the general developmental level the infant has achieved at the time of evaluation. Bayley (1936) developed scales of motor development and mental development for infants, which have been recently revised (Werner and Bayley, 1966). Several other tests or sets of standards for use with infants have been published.

These tests of very young infants cannot be relied on for prediction of future mental ratings. Results of tests on children under two years of age do not correlate closely with tests at later ages, nor do the results of one test agree closely with the results of other tests at the same age. Particularly unreliable are the results of tests of infants under three months of age. After three months of age several of the more carefully constructed tests show consistent, although not high, correlations with each other and with later tests.

We do not know how much of this unreliability is due to the fact that different tests stress different aspects of intelligence, or perhaps to the fact that certain aspects of intelligence do not begin to mature in the earliest months of life and hence do not show up in the tests (Bayley, 1933, 1955). Most of the tests used in earliest infancy contain many motor items which do not tap more than a segment of the development of intelligent behavior. There appear to be two main factors which make up the mental organization of the infant: the motor (nonmental) and the alertness or "mental" (nonmotor) factors. How much of the alertness factor is present to any measurable degree before three months of age is difficult to determine. In proportion as the tests of early infancy are weighted with the motor factor, they will fail to correlate with later tests which are weighted increasingly with the alertness factors.

Werner and Bayley (1966), in a study of eight-month-old infants, report high test-retest reliabilities for mental scale items dealing with object-oriented behavior and low test-retest reliabilities for items requiring social interaction. For motor scale items, high test-retest reliabilities were for items dealing with independent control of head, trunk and extremities; low test-retest reliabilities for items requiring assistance by an adult. The relation of the infant's performance in items such as these to neural functioning is of interest. The prognostic value of neonatal assessments is of interest (Rosenblith, 1966).

Tests of children two to five years of age are somewhat more reliable than those of younger infants, and appear to be increasingly reliable as they involve more alertness and fewer motor items. Several intelligence tests have been widely used at this age level; the lower levels of the Stanford-Binet, the Minnesota Preschool Scales and the Merrill-Palmer Scale of Mental Tests are perhaps the most widely used, in addition to the upper levels of the Gesell Developmental Scale. Intelligence quotient, or I.Q. (ratio of mental age to chronologic age multiplied by 100), is frequently used as a means of scoring test performance. The present scales are not so satisfactory for research and service purposes as may be desired, and further work in the evaluation of the growth of intelligence of younger children is needed.

No prediction is presumed even approximately valid unless the examiner is well trained in the test techniques and has had fairly extensive experience in the testing of young children. Young children require special handling, and the results of their tests require special interpretation. Trained examiners should, and do, refuse to predict with any assurance the future mental development of children from a single examination. Reliability increases if two or more tests are performed and checked against each other, and also if the child is tested again after an interval of several weeks or months. It is particularly helpful in adoption cases to have the child examined by a trained and experienced examiner, then given a trial period of several months in the new environment, followed by a re-examination, if possible by the same examiner.

Influences on Intelligence Test Performance

Whether training influences intelligence is a disputed question. The dispute seems to depend on the interpretation given to test findings and to implications drawn from statistical handling of data (National Society for the Study of Education, 1940). The general implication seems to be that inner factors outweigh environmental training in determining intelligence level, as measured by present intelligence tests. There is reason to believe, however, that seriously limited or sterile environments prevent potential intelligence from reaching its optimum in functioning. It is reasonable, too, that good teaching, if it does not actually raise the level of basic mental capacity, most certainly provides a wider knowledge as material to be used by whatever capacity is present (Jones, 1954).

Pinneau (1961) summarized mental test scores as follows:

> Conclusions as to the stability of mental test scores (relative to age) were based on meager evidence until longitudinal studies were available which covered the life span from early childhood to adulthood. The results of these long-term studies indicate that the stability of intelligence test performance depends on three variables: the age at which the earlier of the two tests is given; the interval between tests; and the intelligence level of the subject. . . . Results . . . also indicate that intelligence is not a homogeneous entity but consists of a number of functions, . . . and that the composition of mentality varies not only from individual to individual but also with the age of the individual. . . .
>
> Theoretical attempts have been made to explain the phenomena of stability and change in the IQ, and studies have been directed at determining how different environmental conditions affect mental test performance. . . . The more detailed analyses of variation in mental test performance have emphasized not merely psychometric factors but also test-taking attitudes, the environment, parent-child relationships, personal experiences, and inherited potentials.

Information from a longitudinal study at the Fels Research Institute at Yellow Springs, Ohio, was reported by Sontag, Baker and Nelson (1958). "Correlations decreased as the age interval between the two tests was lengthened and increased as the child grew older if the interval between the two tests was held constant." For example, the coefficient of correlation between intelligence quotients on the Stanford-Binet test at ages three and four was 0.83; the correlation at ages five and six was 0.87. Correlation between tests at ages five and eight was 0.79. Among children of the superior group in this study, patterns of intelligence quotient change showed individuality. "Some . . . had periods of loss in IQ followed by a gain, other cases had periods of gain in IQ followed by a period of relatively little change, and others had still differing patterns of change." "Learning to learn," not being overdependent on parents, and need for achievement were related to acceleration. Personality predispositions (as inferred from projective test data) for intelligence quotient increase during school years have been described as follows (Kagan, Sontag, Baker and Nelson, 1958):

> Perhaps the most accurate generalization is that for middle-class children with average or above IQ levels, strong achievement, competitive, and curiosity needs may facilitate IQ gains by motivating the child to master intellectual skills.

Current emphases on intelligence tests include more attention to individual patterns, variation in pace among individuals, and influence of experience which stimulates use of ability.

Aspects of intellectual functioning, and consequently methods of assessing them, are more frequently considered according to a developmental-dynamic concept. Numerous concepts pertain to the interrelatedness of various aspects in sequence and in their interactions at a particular stage.

It is hoped that inclusive research on individuals over a period of time will be forthcoming. In the meantime, concepts and theories emphasize looking at the various aspects of intellectual development in an individual child together, as well as separately. Throughout this chapter on intellectual development, in statements of broad concept, in descriptions and explanations of behavior, and in the implications which this knowledge holds for adults associated with children, has run a continuous reference to the potentialities of growth and development within the child in his early years and to the influence of experience. Experience for which the child takes the initiative has qualities different from that imposed by the adult without reference to the child's own pattern. *Provision of a setting which facilitates growth and development* includes almost intangible adult attitudes as well as the more tangible elements.

TOPICS FOR STUDY AND DISCUSSION

1. As a focus for study, select for each aspect of intellectual development one part of particular interest to you. For each of these (concerning sensitivity and perception; language; concept-formation, problem solving and thought; creativity) provide information illustrative of exchange of the individual and his setting. Also, for each, indicate details of behavior which might be studied.
2. For one aspect of cognitive development, devise a means of recording behavior with precision. Try out the method with one child or several children. Classify the data and attempt to draw tentative conclusions.
3. Indicate a few concepts of development you consider relevant to procedures with children in references such as the following:
   Hechinger, F. M. (Ed.): Pre-school Education Today. Garden City, N.Y., Doubleday & Company, Inc., 1966.
   Osborn, D. K., and Haupt, D.: Creative Activities for Young Children. Rev. ed. Detroit, The Merrill-Palmer Institute, 1964.
   Kirk, S. A.: Educating Exceptional Children. Boston, Houghton Mifflin Co., 1962.
   McCall, A.: This Is Music. Boston, Allyn & Bacon, Inc., 1966.
   Wann, K. D., Dorn, M. S., and Liddle, E. A.: Fostering Intellectual Development in Young Children. New York, Teachers College, Columbia University, 1962.

Sensory Perception

1. If you are studying an individual child, record behavior observed indicative of discrimination in use of senses of touch, smell, taste, hearing, sight and kinesthetic sensitivity. Include enough detail on sources of stimulation to provide a basis for discussion of how the child is learning to make various judgments.
2. Discuss a number of pieces of play equipment in terms of the sensory acuity and perception which use of them encourages. Indicate experiences the child might have with the equipment which would be self-teaching. Indicate also variations in activity toward which the child might proceed.

Language

1. If you are studying an individual child, quote what he says to give an indication of different aspects of his language ability (articulation, active vocabulary, grammar, differentiation of meanings, language uses, original stories and poems, response to stories). Consider effects of the situation on his responses.
2. Examine several children's books. Discuss their characteristics by referring to the child's development of sensory perception, language and imagination during the preschool years.

Concept Formation, Problem Solving and Thought

1. If you are studying an individual child, attempt to discover motor and sensory behavior allied with concept formation.
2. Provide an ordinal arrangement, i.e., a sequence of incidents illustrative of problem solving in actions and in words, understanding of cause and effect, generalization and decision making. Indicate effect of the situation upon the child's use of his ability.
3. Describe several incidents pertaining to "science" in which problem-solving ability and thought could be encouraged. Discuss bases for procedures.

Creative Activities

1. If you are studying an individual child, report illustrations of his dramatic play, his use of materials (such as blocks, paint, paper and paste, crayons, clay, wood) and his response to music. Indicate ways of building onto his particular interests.
2. Discuss cues to feelings which dramatic play suggests. Consider implications of understanding of the child gained from this activity.

SELECTED READINGS

Sensory Perception

Church, J.: Language and the Discovery of Reality. New York, Random House, Inc., 1961. Chap. 2, Preverbal Experience: 2. Organism and Environment (egocentrism, behavioral mobilizations, empathy and participation, imitation, learning and schematization).

Gibson, E. J., and Olum, V.: Experimental Methods of Studying Perception in Children; in P. Mussen: Handbook of Research Methods in Child Development. New York, John Wiley & Sons, Inc., 1960. Pp. 318-328, methods of study suited to the abilities of the child; pp. 332-344, research on discrimination of sensory qualities.

Hunt, J. McV.: The Epigenesis of Intrinsic Motivation and Early Cognitive Learning; in R. N. Haber (Ed.): Current Research in Motivation. New York, Holt, Rinehart, and Winston, 1966, pp. 355-370.

Lipsitt, L. P.: Learning processes of human newborns. Merrill-Palmer Quarterly, 12, 1:45-71, 1966.

Language

Bellugi, U., and Brown, R. (eds.): The Acquisition of Language. Monograph of the Society for Research in Child Development. Vol. 29, No. 1, Serial No. 92, 1964. A paper is discussed by N. Chomsky, pp. 35-39; open discussion, pp. 40-42. A section of the paper by R. Brown and C. Fraser is entitled "Evidence that children have construction rules," pp. 45-49.

Deutsch, C.: Auditory discrimination and learning: social factors. Merrill-Palmer Quarterly, 10:277-296, 1964.

Lewis, M. M.: How Children Learn to Speak. New York, Basic Books, Inc., 1959.

Concept Formation, Problem Solving and Thought

Sigel, I.: The Attainment of Concepts; in M. L. Hoffman and L. W. Hoffman (Eds.): Review of Child Development Research. Vol. 1. New York, Russell Sage Foundation, 1964.

Stevenson, H. W.: Piaget, Behavior Theory, and Intelligence; in W. Kessen and C. Kuhlman: Thought in the Young Child. Monograph of the Society for Research in Child Development, Vol. 27, No. 2, 1962.

Creative Activities

Almy, M.: Spontaneous play: an avenue for intellectual development. Young Children, 22:265-277, 1967.

Anderson, H. (Ed.): Creativity in Childhood and Adolescence. Palo Alto, Calif., Science and Behavior Books, 1965.

Getzels, J., and Jackson, P.: Creativity and Intelligence. New York, John Wiley & Sons, Inc., 1962. Chap. 1, The Problem: Varieties of Giftedness in Children. Reference to cognitive abilities different from those revealed by the IQ and other usual measures of intelligence, such as production of novelty, discovering (as contrasted to recalling) and having psychosocial excellence (as in being high in morality and in psychological adjustment).

Hartley, R., Frank, L. K., and Goldenson, R.: Understanding Children's Play. New York, Columbia University Press, 1952.

MacKinnon, D. W.: The nature and nurture of creative talent. American Psychologist, 17, 7:484-495, 1962.

Russell, D.: Children's Thinking. Boston, Ginn & Company, 1956. Chap. 11.

CHAPTER ELEVEN

Development of Concepts of Self,
of Others and of the World:
Emotional-Social Sequences
and Interactions

In this chapter we will use again a developmental-dynamic point of view. The child's concepts of self, of others and of a world beyond his comprehension (a cosmos) can be viewed by reference to status and progress, with attention focused on explanations for change in the child's emotional and social as well as cognitive, development (see Chap. Ten).

CONCEPTS OF SELF, OTHERS AND THE WORLD AS OUTGROWTHS OF EMOTIONAL, SOCIAL AND COGNITIVE DEVELOPMENT

Concepts of self and of others have been considered in Chapter Two, where reference was made to the child's discovering, not in any meditative way, but in his living, that he is one who thinks, feels and acts in certain ways. He is also discovering others who think, feel and act in certain ways. His concept of self and of others begins to emerge; identity of self, identification of self with others, images in the light of which to act, roles to play are clarified in his early experiences (see pp. 38-40). These clarifications proceed along with his emotional and social development. Emotional behavior, in the sense of feelings within the person, as well as exchanges with the environment, and social behavior, in the sense of practices and thoughts with regard to people, change with time and experience. Thus his personality develops.

Emotional Development

BEHAVIORAL EVENTS. In emotion, one class of behavioral events concerns *feelings* (affective behavior) localizable within the individual in

389

internal events, internal changes. Another class concerns *emotional be-havior* (effective behavior) localizable in effects on environment. The two are not easily separated. For example, in emotional behavior the child may be getting out of the way of an angry dog; in other behavior, not observable, i.e., in his feelings, there may be concern about the dog, recall of other experiences and intention to swiftly retreat to a safe place. In addition to these behavioral events of emotion, there are also *physio-logical events*, such as changes in heart rate, blood pressure, secretions of the adrenal glands (see pp. 291-292), the sweating response and muscle tensions.

Jersild (1954) called *emotion* "a label for a vast range of psycho-somatic states." Its *variety* may include feelings, on the subjective side, which are clearly defined or vague; perception or awareness; total re-sponse which is disorganized or organized. Some information on effects of different conditions in the environment upon states such as these has come from carefully controlled experimental research on animals. For example, research has demonstrated greater stress (as indicated by physiological measures) when an unpleasant event occasionally occurs at an unexpected time than when its appearance can be counted upon to occur at a particular time (Brady, 1964, 1966). With regard to develop-ment of affectional systems (as indicated by affectional ties), research has indicated impaired ability to interact socially with age-mates among those deprived in early life of mothering and of contacts with peers (Harlow and Harlow, 1966). Precision in findings such as these, and the leads from understandably different approaches in the study of human beings, tend to have cohesion.

DIFFERENTIATION. One of the trends in emotional development proceeds from generalized feelings and behavior of contentment and acceptance, or annoyance and resistance aroused by comparatively few stimuli, toward particular feelings and behavior with subtle shades aroused by more stimuli. Thus further differentiation occurs. Along with this trend goes a change from greater influence of the immediate setting toward greater influence of thoughts and ideas. As the in-dividual grows older, his emotional behavior varies in kind and amount, depending on his constitution and experience.

Earliest emotion is frequently described as nonspecific. In showing his contentment and harmony with his world, or lack of them, the new-born infant calls into play almost every part of his body. Just what arouses his emotion and just what emotion he shows as the result of specific stimuli are not easily determined, but the majority of writers seem to be in agreement that he becomes emotionally roused by re-markably few types of stimuli and that the number of his emotional reactions is limited. When attention focuses on the behavior of the in-fant, it is evident that he will express emotion vigorously and primitively. When unhappy or frightened, a young infant cries, clutches and strug-gles physically. When he is happy, he relaxes contentedly or, later, coos and laughs to express his joy. He is roused by immediate things. As he grows older, his responses in fear differ from those in anger; his affectionate relations with his parents suggest distinctions between them and other people (Bridges, 1931; Buhler, 1930; Rheingold, 1966).

Variations in expression, as well as in control, come gradually. For example, three-year-olds are normally quite emotional in their reactions to life, being made glad or sad or angry by slight happenings, and expressing these emotions obviously and openly. Yet even at three years the processes of self-control have begun. Most children of this age, when hungry, can wait to eat, having been educated to three meals and two or three snacks a day; crying over trivial hurts has been overcome; and other beginnings in emotional control in relations with people have been made.

Fear. Insight into causes of emotional outbursts and variations in expression and control can be gained by reference to personality components, such as sense of trust, autonomy, initiative and accomplishment, each of which is considered especially important at a particular stage of development. Likewise, extent to which basic needs are met provides an explanation of emotional behavior. (See pages 243 through 245 for a discussion of personality components, and Chapters Four through Seven for discussion of the meeting of needs, and pages 358 through 362 for development of concepts and quality of thought.)

Fears in response to noise and agents of noise, and to strange objects, situations and persons, are among those decreasing with age (Jersild and Holmes, 1935). These situations may arouse fear in the infant in whom a sense of trust of his tangible world is not yet well established. The fears of the older child who has established trust in material things have more of an imaginary angle. Fears of the dark, of being alone and of imaginary creatures in the dark are among those increasing during the preschool years. Imagination is increasing in these years Cognition is also increasing, but along with it comes a realization of unknowns beyond immediate experience and comprehension.

Thus gradually extending the grasp of the known is one way of decreasing fear (connected with the possibility of being injured and with avoidance behavior). Then, in some instances, caution, in contrast to intense emotion, may be the outcome. Gaining competence and skill, finding practical methods of one's own for dealing with the feared situation, and having, by degrees, active experience with, or successful directed participation in, the feared situation provide new responses as ways of overcoming fears. When schemata are already present, to which the new or different or startling event can be accommodated, fear is less likely to occur. In this way of considering fear, great incongruity is an explanation (see pp. 149 and 150).

Anger. Findings about anger (connected with annoyance at persons, animals or things and with behavior which strikes out physically or verbally) seem allied to knowledge about personality components, basic needs, concept formation and quality of thought at certain stages. For example, at two years anger outbursts related to establishment of routine and physical habits and to conflicts with authority seem connected with the child's need for a sense of autonomy (Goodenough, 1931). Although his social difficulties of the next few years are related to his need for time in learning to associate with other children, they may also be a reflection of his seeking trust, autonomy, initiative or achievement. Difficulties in social situations and disagreements with playmates were most frequent sources of provocation of anger between the ages of three and four. Although outbursts were less frequent by the age of four, social situations were still the most frequent source (Goodenough, 1931). The influence of a sense of achievement in decreasing anger is suggested by Keister and Updegraff (1937). Anger was one of the outcomes in situations in which the child was called upon to perform difficult tasks. His anger in response to a particular event decreased as he gained skill in handling it.

The influence of adult disapproval in decreasing aggressive behavior (hurting or causing anxiety to others) is suggested in a study by Hollenberg and Sperry (1950). Children in a doll play situation, for whom verbal disapproval of aggression was added by an adult, manifested fewer and less intense aggressive responses in later doll play sessions than the control group, for whom disapproval was not expressed. Children in the control group increased in their aggressive behavior as sessions continued.

Joy. Joy is connected with pleasure at behavioral events and with behavior which makes for a "deeper immersion in, or continued contact with, the activity or thing" (Hebb, 1966). In this sense, joy and love (affection) are sometimes regarded as similar. "Distinction between the different emotions is found in the ideas that go with them, and the actions that these ideas (mediating processes) give rise to." Thus hostility, disgust and sadness indicate different ideas.

Affection. Affection for others is shown in the first year of life. Jersild (1954) referred to the fact that "there is very little systematic information concerning the development of affection, concerning the way in which the child's capacity for loving, and the range or scope of his affections, wax and change in the process of development."

A report from animal research suggests the following stages in the infant-mother affectional system: the reflex stage, the stage of comfort and attachment, the security stage and the separation stage (Harlow and Harlow, 1966). In these stages the infant proceeds in his relations with his mother from reflexive physical adjustments for survival toward responses which are more voluntary (connected with eating, sensory behavior and some imitative behavior), with affectional bonds. In the next stage, called "security," the infant, in the presence of his mother, is more likely to explore his inanimate and animate world. Later, "age-mate associations" gain preeminence over infant-maternal relations. These stages seem in accordance with trends in human behavior, in which greater variety and complexity occur. For consideration of bases for trends such as these, see pages 19 and 20 for references to theories in which relative emphases on biological, psychological and exogenous explanations vary.

The newborn infant responds on physiological and sensory planes. He feels his own world of sensations; he finds comfort when cared for, but has no respect for the comfort or well-being of others. This is expected from tiny infants. As time goes on, this self-centered being has potentialities and experiences which can enable him to develop an ability to consider others, to feel sympathetic toward them, to be happy at their happiness or sad at their sadness, and to enjoy contributing to their happiness and well-being (Murphy, 1937).

As the child's feeling of closeness to others develops, certain patterns can be seen through which nearly all children grow. At first, for both boys and girls, a close attachment to the mother is characteristic in infancy (Bowlby, 1958; Brody, 1956; Soddy, 1956). She is the source of food, comfort, sensory and motor associations, affection and sociability. Gradually the child includes his father and others besides his mother in the circle of his expanding affections. When the child enters school, he develops a more casual, less dependent attitude toward his parents, and yet is likely to cling still to the intimate moments at bedtime or other times when comfort and assurance are needed.

Social Development

In the infant's or young child's status and progress in behavior with the people of his world, one trend is from a dependent to a more independent relation. Another trend is from self-centeredness toward increased awareness of others; still another is one of gradual assimilation of concepts (values) of his family and his culture, with change in behavior reflecting degree and type of accommodation to these additions. The social relations themselves, and their emotional and cognitive ramifications, contribute concepts of self, of others and of the world. Variables affecting the development are endogenous, in the biological and psychological systems of the individual, and exogenous, in his immediate setting and also in his culture.

DISPOSITIONAL SYSTEMS. In order to view qualities in social behavior at a particular time and at different times as a trend proceeds, some frame of reference is needed. One way to provide a focus is to consider the individual's position on two continua, *love-hostility* and *introversion-extroversion*, as suggested by his behavior. Schaefer (1961) proposed a hypothetic conceptual model for social and emotional behavior which includes these two reference dimensions. In this approach the individual's disposition toward others (his tendency, mood or inclination) is viewed according to whether he is more accepting than not, and more likely to turn toward involvement outside of self or toward involvement with ideas. It is possible to look for position along these continua (or in these quadrants) in considering a number of different forms of social behavior.

Another focus in considering a variety of social behavior concerns *power* (ability to get things done) (see pp. 13, 38). Whether the individual is controlled or controlling and whether he finds himself in a given situation voluntarily or involuntarily can be the perspective (Ausubel, 1957). In this approach the individual's disposition toward dependence or independence, autonomy, coping with his world on his own or otherwise, interest in achievement are involved.

In the child's social behavior it is not that he has only one inclination or the other, but rather that relative proportions can be noted. Also, in considering orderly trends, as the child develops, changes in relative proportions in his dispositional systems, as well as in particular forms of behavior, can be noted. These changes in proportions of dependence and independence are discussed in Chapter Four. Changes in self-centeredness and awareness of others and in values will be considered in the following pages.

POSITION WITH OTHERS.   Social development implies the facets of self and of others. For example, there would be the infant's position in his parents' eyes, and their position in his eyes; or the preschool child's position in the eyes of his peers and their position for him. The following dimensions of current or changing position in a social system are found in peer relations among older children: emotional acceptance (liking-disliking), personal competence ("being good at the things you do") and social power (ability to influence others) (Glidewell et al., 1966). These variables lend themselves to study of the child's position with others and also of his attitudes toward others.

ATTITUDES TOWARD OTHERS.   Attitudes toward others have affective components, cognitive components and behavioral components (Proshansky, 1966). The affective components concern liking-disliking; the cognitive components concern knowing what the person does and how he influences others; and the behavioral components could be regarded as actions (effects on environment) reflecting organizational patterns or concepts which include these emotional and cognitive elements. These components in a particular social scene could be regarded as having deep-rooted bases in the dispositional systems of the individual (love-hostility, introversion-extroversion, power).

In the development of attitudes toward others the infant or child changes through processes of assimilation and accommodation. His social behavior shows differentiation, specialization, and organization on more complex planes as he grows older and has particular experiences. His *awareness*, *orientation* and *attitudes* are on simpler planes when he is very young and on more complex planes when he is older. This tends to be so whether the behavior selected for consideration is self-centeredness, attention to others, exchange of ideas, friendships, quarrels, sympathy, nurturance, aggression, dependence, masculine or feminine roles, intergroup attitudes, or withdrawal from the group.

These can be considered in family relations and in relations outside the family.

SELF-CENTEREDNESS. In the early close relations of the infant and the mother there are emotional attachments and also discoveries of a cognitive kind about the outside world. These early associations are significant for basic needs of warmth, security, dependence and independence and activity (Chaps. Four and Seven), as well as in sensory-motor and preoperational stages in concept formation (Chap. Ten). From the first few days of life the infant is adding schemata. Later he makes distinctions among people, things, self.

The self-absorption of the eighteen-month- to two-year-old reflects an earlier background of discoveries. As early as six or seven months of age he experiences feelings of conquest over his body in motor ways. He is sometimes so absorbed in his newly acquired control of eyes, head, arms and hands that he pays slight attention to other people, except for a moment at a time. When he has achieved upright locomotion, he spends prodigious amounts of energy getting into things, exploring, handling and manipulating everything he can lay his hands on, and seeming almost oblivious of the adult's, "No, no, don't touch." At this stage, in the pursuit of any objective he persists even as the adult tries to sidetrack or distract him.

By about eighteen months to two years "me," "mine" and "I want" begin to be outstanding in his language and in his action. It is as if he had suddenly discovered himself and is attempting to make a part of himself all that his expanding world includes. This self-absorption is modified somewhat as the child completes his mastery over elementary motor processes and intellectual learnings in the sense perception area. Despite the widening social horizons of the three-year-old, not until four or five years of age does the child seem to begin clearly to sense himself as part of a group.

Around four and thereafter, boasting may be a form of play and conversation. "Look at me, see me," and exaggerations which seem to be attempts to have more and be more occur frequently. Sometimes the child attempts to widen physical horizons, to break out of bounds, both physical and psychological, in his exploration of the new. Along with perception of his own size in reference to others, there seems to be an interest in growing up.

While becoming more aware of himself and of others, the child sometimes indicates a wish for a return to babyhood. He may say, "Let's play I'm a baby." Not infrequently this behavior develops at the time a new baby has been added to the household and expresses a desire to command his mother's full attention once more. It also occurs in only children and seems to express some aspect, as yet not quite understood, of the developing awareness of self. The child's interests in being independent and dependent conflict; he wants to be and is both (Beller, 1955; Heathers, 1955).

In the early preschool years the child is proceeding from a state in which his parents and others were more likely to respond to his wishes to one in which they are more likely to expect him to respond to theirs. This has been referred to as an "ego devaluation crisis" with a "satellizing solution." In accepting the will of others, even if he "feels assured in advance of their benevolent intentions," the child of two or three years of age may show negativistic reactions (Ausubel, 1958). Interest in autonomy seems to reflect this change in awareness of his own status and the expectations of others. Close attachments to some such possession as a soft doll or toy animal sometimes parallel adaptations to widening horizons.

ATTENTION TO OTHERS.   In his discoveries about his world and about himself the infant shows a trend from attentiveness to something in his environment (a sensory stimulation, at first not differentiated as to whether it is a person, thing, sound, or touch from one source or another) toward further differentiations, emotional and cognitive. Response to another person tends to proceed from passive attention to more active reaction. The infant two months of age or older tends to react actively when someone talks to him. His own vocalizations tend to increase when someone has been responsive to them. The mother's response to activity of the infant may encourage cognitive development.

An early study (Morgan and Morgan, 1944) provided "normative" information on ages at which active reactions of infants to the examiner's talking occurred. Data were provided from the age at which active reactions were first noted, through the increasing percentages as age increased, until all the subjects studied responded. By a little over two months of age most children were found to *react actively* to being talked to by the examiner. This active reaction consisted of smiling, cooing, laughing aloud or waving arms and legs excitedly. Some infants reacted in this way as early as twenty to thirty days of age; all children examined did so by three months. Most of the children reacted to being played with by a social smile before sixty days of age, and with cooing by seventy days.

Rheingold (1966) states principles concerning the development of social behavior in the infant as follows:

1. The infant is responsive to stimuli arising from social objects.
2. The infant is active in initiating social contacts.
3. The infant's social behavior is modified by the responses of others (social objects) to him.
4. The infant's social responses modify the behavior of others in his group.

Smiling behavior of the infant illustrates these principles. In his smiling and in other forms of behavior the infant is affected by the responsiveness of the other person. This sensitivity of the other person when he is active in various ways may have ramifications in many aspects of development.

By three or four months of age infants have begun to progress from a general reactivity to anyone at all who happens to be near them to the differential reactivity which depends on *discrimination between persons.* At this time most infants begin to discriminate between one familiar person and another. They give clear evidence that they recognize mother as different, for example, from father.

Social initiative on the part of the child himself may occur at four or five months, when he smiles a recognition of familiar persons, whether or not they have taken the initiative in playing with him. By five or six months he shows his resentment at being parted from a familiar person by crying; withdrawal from strangers may appear about this time.

"Sociable" behavior develops rapidly from nine or ten months on. By one year many children, if given sufficient previous social experiences, have developed a high degree of *social reciprocity* as compared with infants of three, six or nine months of age. Waving bye-bye, playing pat-a-cake, showing "how tall is baby" by patting his own head are usual at this time if the child has had a satisfactory kind of social experience. "Give Mamma the ball," or whatever else he happens to have in his hand, will receive a positive response around one year if she reaches toward the child gently and smiles encouragingly. At this time, too, a quick gesture of giving or handing something to other people is a favorite social action on the part of the infant himself. But the object proffered as a gesture of social behavior is more likely than not to be hung on to, and a howl will ensue if the adult or another child takes the gesture seriously and tries to part the infant from the proffered toy.

By the time most children are a year old they show definite preferences and dislikes for people. Uneasiness may be evident when the scene changes to one without a familiar person. A new place without a known person may seem too incongruous. The child may not remember people long, however, unless he has had some unusual emotional experience with them. Children may, as late as eighteen months, seem to forget even their mother if she is away for a week or more. Reacquaintance is rapid, however, when she returns.

Although evidence of effect of early personal associations on personality is not clear-cut, no one doubts the joy that the parents and the infant can have in their natural, easy response as they are sociable according to their temperaments. Figure 96 suggests that these social times of parents and children and the development of attitudes of trust of self and of others are related. Joy of this kind in early associations is evident in the following report:

Bob's mother believed that learning to be happy, resourceful and sociable began early. She patted and talked with Bob from the time she took over his care after arriving home from the hospital. As soon as she caught his first social smile she talked with him again, thus beginning in Bob the awareness that it is fun to communicate with people. Some suitable toy was always at hand when Bob was awake. His mother stopped by his crib as she went about her work, handing him the rattle he had let drop, rattling the string of wooden beads, or otherwise calling his attention to the toy. Thus he learned how to use and to enjoy toys. She talked with him, at first leaning over his crib, then from a greater distance as she worked, so that he could continue his smiling and wriggling reactions, and later could coo or babble in reply. This also added to his sense of nearness to her and kept him assured that he was not alone. Gradually she increased the length

FIGURE 96. Social responsiveness of parent and child seems interrelated.

Smiling behavior of this 7-month-old infant and of her father suggests trust of self and of others.

of time she left him alone with his toys, but she seldom failed to speak to him or to smile or to sing a snatch of song whenever she passed near him. Occasionally she changed the toy he was playing with or had dropped because of boredom. Thus she taught him how to be alone with his toys, yet gave him increasing experience in social relations. When she had to be away to shop or for relaxation, she left some congenial substitute person near. Thus Bob learned not to be too dependent on her presence, yet was never left without protection and a friendly presence. This also widened his circle of desirable acquaintances. He was never allowed to become a demanding baby who expected adults to respond to his every whim and to furnish amusement at all times.

By the time Bob was two years old his lively "Hi, Mummy!" "Hi, Daddy!" sent himself and his parents off to a good start in the morning. A firm, "That's all. Now we must do this," brought occasional resistance, but offered opportunity to teach Bob that the world of adults must sometimes move on despite his wish to keep on playing.

Bob greeted most people with a gay grin which won him innumerable friends. His alert interest in the things about him and his wide resourcefulness with even the simplest materials attracted the friendship of a wide variety of adults.

How much of Bob's personality is inborn and how much is due to experience is an open question.

Reactions to other children begin as early as three or four months, when one infant may react to others by brief notice, such as a smile at another baby's wrigglings. By six or seven months infants may show a brief interest in each other and will reach for each other's toys or poke a finger at each other playfully. By a year, if they have had previous experience with other children, they will offer each other playthings, but will usually hang on or cry if the other infant tries to take possession of the object. Around twenty-one to twenty-four months children will play briefly with each other.

Social interchange develops rapidly from two to four years of age. At four or five the socially experienced child shows much awareness of and ability to stimulate other children's reactions. They respond to distress in other children, make requests for assistance, and take social initiative in "Come on, let's play," and in making definite suggestions as to what to play. In response to other children they utilize varied techniques of acceptance, refusal, evasion or changing of the situation.

For reviews of research on social behavior, the reader is referred to Anderson and Anderson (1954), Campbell (1964) and Lambert (1960).

EXCHANGE OF IDEAS. As the young child ventures into a broader world beyond his family, his behavior suggests personality components of trust of self, of others, and of the immediate physical world, or a lack of them. His behavior also suggests interest in autonomy. In terms of cognitive development of the sensory-motor period, as early as four to eight months he has begun "to act toward objects and events outside his own body as though they have some permanence and stability"; at eight to twelve months "the beginnings of what are called 'means-ends

FIGURE 97. *Exploration of new social scenes, at early ages, seems more likely to occur when the parent is present.*

This 17-month-old child seems to be enjoying the experience with older children in their play area. It has novelty in it and also the reassurance of the mother's presence. For the young child, the mother and the older children, there seems to be exchange of ideas, although no one is talking at the moment.

relationships' are defined"; and at twelve to eighteen months he "begins to experiment, to search for new ways to solve problems; and he begins to get excited about novelty for its own sake." At eighteen months to approximately two years "he may invent solutions mentally; that is symbolically, rather than by trial and error" (Sigel, 1964). In his explorations, in new social settings, the presence of the mother and the early affectional ties with her seem to add to the young child's security (see p. 392). In Figure 97 the toddler, his mother and the older children are enjoying the novelty of the younger child's visit to the play area. In events such as this, each seems to be adding new details of information about the others.

In early associations with other children the infant may be attentive to another infant by looking or focusing his attention for relatively long or short periods of time. Later, if two or more children are together, after the first novelty of the association has worn off, the play becomes highly *individualistic*, each child occupying himself with his own activities in almost complete disregard of the other.

From eighteen months to two years the child continues to be absorbed in individual play, but is more influenced by the presence of another child. Characteristic play at this age is sometimes referred to as *parallel play*, for each child, although apparently playing by himself, usually plays at the same kind of activity that occupies the other children of the group. Not only does he play with the same material, but also he plays at it longer and has more resourceful ideas than if he were playing alone. A favorite situation at two years is digging in sand or dirt. One child fills his pail, carries it a short distance, and empties it. Another child, who has only been digging, adopts the idea and does the same. There has been no exchange of words, but simply an exchange of ideas. In Figure 98 a two-year-old has paused to watch another, who continues to be absorbed in her play.

Beginnings of *cooperative play* may come when the second child gets the idea of emptying the pail on the same pile of sand with the first child, thus changing the activity from a purely individualistic emptying of pails into a cooperative building of a mound of sand. This change may take place in silence or after an exchange of words, and may last for several minutes or relapse into individual activity almost immediately.

There is a gradual transition from solitary and parallel play to more cooperative forms of play. One child says, "I'll build a garage." Another answers, "All right. I'll build mine over here." Again separate projects will be undertaken with the blocks, but now there is an almost constant recognition of the presence of each other and a flow of conversation. "See, mine's big." "Oh, look, I made a roof." Perhaps there will be a temporary merging of projects. "Look out, my car's going to visit your garage."

A little later the *shifting group* is conspicuous (Fig. 99). Under this arrangement a fairly loosely organized interest group may grow up, lasting throughout a whole morning and embracing the activity of a number of children, but depending on the presence of no particular child. For

FIGURE 98. *Individual absorption in activity is frequent as young children play.*

Much of the play of these 2 children was parallel, each reacting in her own way, but near the other. Occasionally one paused to watch the other.

FIGURE 99. *Children go into and out of group activity according to their inclinations.*

This "spaceship" had children playing in it throughout the morning with different ones as astronauts at different times. Structures were added as a child thought of an addition he wished to make.

example, "operating a space ship" or playing store may go on with one child or with several, each coming or going at will.

From this shifting group play there develops *organized group play* (Fig. 100). During the preschool period these groups are never very complex or stable in their organization. Parten (1933) found a trend toward development of *leadership* throughout the year in a nursery school group, leaders excelling nonleaders in intelligence and occupational level of parents, but individual differences outweighing age differences. She corroborated the majority of studies in finding some children able to dominate for a time, but not retaining this status for long. She also found two types of leadership even in the preschool years: the "artful diplomat" and the child who attempts to lead by brute force.

In the preceding pages the child's attitudes toward others have been viewed in terms of his increased associations with them as he proceeds from self-centeredness toward further attention to others and then toward further exchange of ideas. In this progression relative proportions of these forms of behavior change, but each is likely to continue to be present. In the following pages particular attitudes in relations of the child with peers will be considered, i.e., friendship, aggression, sympathy, nurturance, dependence.

FIGURE 100. *Steps toward well-organized group play occur in preschool years.*

In the beginning of this group play 3 children are cooperating closely in a project which could not go on without them. One loads pine cones on a truck. Another "drives" the truck to the stationmaster. Two other children are watching the activity

FRIENDSHIP. Among variables influencing friendship contacts are chronologic age, developmental level, tendency to seek friendship, sex preferences, popularity, physical attractiveness. McCandless, Bilous and Bennett (1961) found that children who were most dependent on adults were least popular among their peers at preschool age. In addition to endogenous factors such as these, there are also numerous variables in the setting. Intermingling of group members over a period of time, group size, addition of new members, departure of "old" members, and personal qualities of group members are among the group characteristics considered significant in social behavior at later ages (Ziller, 1965), which also seem pertinent in preschool groups. According to Lambert (1960), "The area of inter-personal behavior in children has hardly been tapped."

Children have preferences. Northway and Weld (1956) say, "With children, there is considerable variation, but even at the nursery school level, there is some tendency for a child to maintain his sociometric level." Referring to "facts of social life" and emphasizing the importance of a person's finding his own situation satisfying, they say, "The child who has a low social potential can be just as satisfied and as satisfactory as the one who has a higher, provided he is not made to feel he should be more popular, or that he would be 'better off' if he were."

Subtleties contribute to influences of liked and disliked companions upon behavior. Disliked peers were more influential than liked peers (friends) in an experiment comparing effect of their praise on maintenance of a particular task (dropping marbles into holes and into a bin). According to Hartup (1965):

> Performance was better maintained in the group reinforced by disliked peers than in the group reinforced by liked peers, and by five-year-olds than by four-year-olds. . . . Performance was enhanced among five-year-old subjects reinforced by disliked peers, but in all other subgroups performance deteriorated during the session. . . . Ten of the eighteen nursery school subjects in the liked-peer group intensively attempted to converse with the reinforcing agent or to look at him during the six-minute response period; only five subjects reinforced by disliked peers did so. It is thus possible that differential performance in these two groups resulted from differential capacity of liked and disliked peers to elicit interfering dependency responses. . . . An alternative explanation of the results presented here is that the performance decrement with liked or popular peers reflects increasing boredom or fatigue (with the task), whereas other factors counteract this trend when the subject is reinforced by a disliked or unpopular peer.

AGGRESSION. It seems usual for two- to four-year-olds to show all types of social behavior, both constructive and friendly, and destructive and self-centered. One thing that puzzles many people who do not understand the beginnings of social development and do not appreciate the intellectual and emotional limitations of young children is their apparently contradictory behavior. Preschool children, for example, fight their best friends more than they fight other children (Isaacs, 1946; Murphy, 1937). This is not so contrary as it appears, since the child naturally more often "runs afoul" of the child he sees and plays with the most than he does of other children. The children's self-absorption and aggressive possessiveness run into each other in proportion as the children are exposed to each other in play.

The quarrels of preschool children, though frequent, are brief, and children recover from them quickly, seemingly harboring no resentment. Dawe (1934) showed that the average quarrel of a group of preschool children lasted only twenty-three seconds. The younger the child in this study, the more frequently he started quarrels, but the less aggressive he was. As the children in the preschool age group grew older, they quarreled less frequently, but were more aggressive when they did quarrel. The majority of the quarrels started with a struggle for possessions. Quarrels, as a rule, led to pushing, striking or other motor activities. Most quarrels settled themselves without adult interference, although some adult supervision was used to keep older and bigger children from bullying younger and smaller children.

Murphy's study (1937) revealed another apparent contradiction in social behavior. Children who had high scores in sympathetic behavior also showed considerable unsympathetic behavior and frequently had high scores in aggressive behavior. Here, again, the amount of social contact was high for some children who, in their many contacts, had wide opportunity to display the whole repertory of preschool social behavior, whereas less active children simply had fewer contacts.

Many of the conflicts or quarrels of the young child seem to arise from his intentness in pursuing his own purposes. This intention of accomplishing his own immediate aim is in contrast to the intention of hurting another. Although the surface behavior of a "brief encounter" and an expression of deep-rooted hostility may be similar, intentions of each differ.

Martin (1964) attempted to differentiate social behavior by the child's "goal response." Observers made distinctions among *aggression* (with goals of perceiving injury, discomfort, punishment or derogation of another, perceiving destruction to inanimate objects or constructions, having an object in one's own possession or having it back in possession), *control-dominance* (securing constructive, negative or authoritarian control) and *autonomous achievement* (seeking to carry out a task by oneself, securing removal of frustration or barrier to a goal). Dependency, nurturance, avoidance-withdrawal and friendship-affiliation were also differentiated. Percentage of agreement of two observers, observing simultaneously, on category and subcategory classification of behavior ranged from 68 to 74 per cent.

In another study (Gewirtz, 1948), when goal responses were classified into three categories, succorance (dependency), nurturance and aggression, percentage of agreement of two observers was 88 per cent. Thus it seems possible to make distinctions in social behavior according to intentions or goals of the individual, but with occasional disagreement.

Sears et al. (1953) were interested in considering frequency of aggressive acts as an index of strength of aggressive drive. The behavior was considered instrumental for goals of the child. They found aggression scores correlating with the rating of the activity level of the child.

Stability has been reported in the individual child's relative position in his nursery school group, according to frequency of observed aggressive behavior over a two-year period (Martin, 1964). Thus the child who perhaps was fourth in frequency of aggression, when scores of time-sampling observations were ranked from high to low for all in his group in the first semester, was likely to occupy a similar relative position in later semesters.

SYMPATHY. Awareness of and reaction to the feelings of others (sympathy) are beginning to emerge in the preschool years. Murphy (1937) found that the first awareness of the feelings of other children in a group she studied was shown in a tendency to help others when it was convenient or did not interfere with the given child's self-absorbed plans. The second stage was marked by a tendency to stop what one was doing in order to help another child or to respond to another's distress.

Bridges (1931) noted individual differences among children in this behavior. Some preschool children show sympathy only by staring or crying in sympathetic imitation. A more advanced stage of expression of sympathy is the attempt to comfort the distressed child by putting an arm around him, or saying, "Does it hurt?" or, "What are you crying for?" Only later in social development is sympathy expressed by more active measures to relieve the distressing situation, by such intuitive understanding as is shown by being kind to newcomers and helping them with their tasks, by offering to share materials, by getting a toy to give to a child or by defending the rights of smaller children.

Sympathetic behavior observed in very young children seems to arise from a number of different sources, such as warmth and friendliness, desire of a child to please a member of his group, projection of his own anxiety, realization that behavior such as fighting, which is usually forbidden by adults, may be permitted because it appears to be in defense of someone else (Murphy, 1937).

In an investigation of emotional sensitivity (Dimitrovsky, 1964) children five to ten years of age were asked to identify emotional meanings in recordings by adults. Five-year-olds were able to identify correctly, beyond the level of chance. They reported angry and sad responses more frequently than happy and loving ones. Correct identification increased with age.

NURTURANCE. Whereas sympathy is more allied with concern for distress, nurturance is more allied with a positive fostering of the well-being of another person. The two attitudes are closely related. In both, occurrence of this kind of behavior is comparatively rare, but certainly not completely absent, in the preschool child.

Hartup and Keller (1960) regard nurturance (giving affection, positive attention, reassurance and protection) as "basic to success in

"Making a building" (boy, 3 years 8 months)

"Building a hideout for him. Being quiet so he can build it" (girl, 4 years)

"Sitting down" (boy, 5 years 1 month)

"She is buckling her shoes. The little boy is watching it" (girl, 4 years 7 months)

"Blocks" (girl, 3 years 6 months)

"That is a boy. That is a girl" (girl, 4 years 2 months)

"They are making something. She is going in there, and he is putting the board there and she is holding it" (boy, 5 years)

FIGURE 101. The child's verbalizations provide information on development of awareness of people and relationships.

Children in a day-care center and in a nursery school were asked to "tell me about" these photographs (Halverson, 1967). Degree of attention to persons and to relations ranged from none, through enumeration, reference to action, singly or in a group, to comments on relations. The quotations beside the middle and lower photographs suggest different degrees of awareness (considered perhaps related to development of a concept of nurturance or of consideration for others). The verbalizations beside the upper photograph occurred when the investigator specifically asked what each child was "doing for" another.

some of an individual's most important roles, e.g., those of friend, spouse, parent, teacher, etc." It occurred relatively infrequently in nursery school children whom they studied. They found nurturance positively associated with seeking help and physical affection, considered to be more active and outgoing dependent responses, and negatively associated with being near, considered to be a more passive dependent response. "These results suggest some commonality in underlying motivation for both dependency and its seeming opposite, nurturance" (Hartup, 1963).

Figure 101 illustrates children's verbalizations when viewing photographs of nurturant or considerate behavior. Their comments were studied because sensitivity to people and their relationships seemed to be a preliminary step in development of a concept of nurturance. The children's remarks indicated awareness of detail, but rarely referred to relationships in a more general way.

DEPENDENCE. Studies of dependency in the sense of seeking attention, help or physical contact from others are related to attempts to discover why the child becomes anxious, and also to the effects of differing degrees of anxiety upon his behavior. Less information is available on dependency of the preschool child in his relations with his peers than on dependency in relations with adults (see Chap. Four). Among the behavioral correlates of dependency and independence (investigated in most instances with older children) are the following: responsiveness to social reinforcement, susceptibility to social influence, nurturance, sociometric status, aggression, orality, anxiety and defensiveness.

In an experimental study (Hartup, 1958) the learning of tasks rewarded by verbal approval was more efficient in the girls and dependent boys from whom nurturance by the adult (in the form of behavior which rewarded, encouraged, supported or showed affection) occurred for five minutes and was then withdrawn for five minutes before the learning of the new tasks. Boys with low dependency learned faster in the group for whom the nurturance was continuous (pp. 137-138 and 156). In a longitudinal study by Sontag, Baker and Nelson (1958) children who were very dependent on their parents in the years three to six were considered less likely to make contact with and to interact successfully with new aspects of their environment. They were described as less motivated by need for achievement; their intelligence quotients at later ages were less likely to be accelerated than those of children motivated by need for achievement (see p. 421).

In other research "direct positive maternal reactions to children's achievement behaviors were . . . predictive of young children's achievement behaviors in nursery school free play, while less direct maternal reactions such as general affection and the rewarding of dependence were not" (Crandall, Preston and Rabson, 1960). Mothers who were responsive to (rewarded) their children's achievement efforts were more likely to have children who made achievement efforts. Whether or not the mothers were affectionate was not associated either positively or negatively with the achievement behaviors of children. Futhermore, the children's achievement behaviors were not associated with whether or not the mothers rewarded the children's seeking help and emotional support (considered to be measures of independence training).

Distinctions need to be made between the child's caring enough about temporary changes in encouragement from others so that he tries harder to do well the tasks he undertakes, and the child's caring so much about long-time deprivations that his behavior in many situations is affected. Deep-seated anxiety and consequent dependence may be the result of basic needs not being met. For example, Freud and Burlingham (1944) described infants and children under the age of five who were away from their families in residential nurseries in England during World War II. The children enjoyed companionship of children their own age, but looked for objects toward whom to direct all the emotional interests they would normally have directed toward their parents.

MASCULINE AND FEMININE SEX ROLE IDENTITY. While the young child is developing attitudes toward others with affective, cognitive and behavioral components, he is also developing attitudes about his sex role, which include these components. Kagan (1964) asserts that the degree to which a person regards himself as masculine or feminine concerns his "sex role identity." This is but one part of a "complex interlocking set of beliefs the individual holds about himself. The complete set of attitudes is generally regarded as a self-concept or self-identity." As a background for regarding himself as masculine or feminine, the young child is developing concepts of behavior differences according to sex.

The child learns attributes of masculinity and femininity as he associates with the people of his world. As a part of cognitive development, children in the age period of three to seven years have concepts of sex roles (Kagan, 1964); sex-typing is beginning to occur. Children's behavior tends to be in agreement with cultural standards or expectations. For example, aggressive behavior is more frequent among boys (Bandura and Walters, 1963). "Data on sex differences in passivity and dependency are less consistent than those for aggression, but there are more studies reporting greater dependency, conformity and social passivity for females than for males at all ages" (Kagan, 1964). In play, boys are aware as early as age three "of some of the activities and objects that our culture regards as masculine. Among girls, however, preferences are more variable up to nine or ten years of age. Many girls between three and ten years of age show a strong preference for masculine games, activities and objects, whereas it is unusual to find many boys who prefer feminine activities during this period. Thus five-year-old boys show a clearer preference for masculine toys than girls show for feminine toys."

In a study considering ways in which children behaved like others in fantasy, girls seemed to be learning to be adults and boys seemed to be learning to be masculine (Emmerich, 1959).

In studies such as these there is variation in relative emphasis on biologic bases and on behavior learned through cultural influence.

Distinctions are sometimes made between the more frequent orientation of boys toward the "instrumental," getting tasks done, controlling, and the more frequent orientation among girls toward the "affective," a sensitivity for the feelings which are involved and nurturance. Here, again, variations within groups are evident. For example, among men who had creative achievements, affective qualities such as openness to feelings and emotions, sensitive intellect and wide-ranging interests were frequent (MacKinnon, 1962).

WITHDRAWAL FROM THE GROUP. Although our attention has focused on relations with others, recognition of the individual's liking to be by himself as well as with others is a part of our understanding of his social development. Participation in group activity and its form have a wide range among children, as a reflection not only of developmental pattern according to age, but also of constitution and experience. The tendency of the individual to turn his interests and attention toward a center inside himself, being more interested in ideas than in people or things (introversion), or to turn toward a center outside himself, being more interested in people and things than in ideas (extroversion), suggests the concept of a continuum. The individual is not to be labeled, but relative frequency of certain interests can be considered. Carrigan (1960) raises questions on extroversion-introversion as a unitary dimension and on its independence from adjustment. She calls the evidence on both issues equivocal. Persistence of the "dimension of outgoing responsiveness versus a retractive, inward looking response" over a span of years has been reported in several longitudinal studies (Honzik, 1965).

Our social culture seems to place a premium on the "go-getter" type. In contrast, many preschool children display shyness in social relations in the sense of wanting to make few contacts with people. Many children experience a period of shyness with strangers some time between nine months and two years of age; some experience it as late as three years of age. Many children are shy even with familiar persons.

Such behavior may change, depending on the reason for the shyness as well as on the treatment the child receives. When the child has an "easy setting" in which others are present and he can proceed according to his inclinations without being forced and without conflicting with others, sufficient adaptation is usually made, whether his shyness comes from an unfamiliar setting or from a wish for peace and quiet. Sometimes shyness is the result of inner tensions.

Barbara "ruled the roost" of her home during the first $2\frac{1}{2}$ years of her life, being coddled, shown off and made the center of attention not only of her parents, but also of visitors to the home. At the age of $2\frac{1}{2}$ she suffered two disasters within three months: her father went into the military service, and her mother became deeply absorbed not only in the loss of her husband's companionship, but also in tending to a new baby. When the baby sister reached six months of age, it became clear that she was a charmer socially. Barbara, in emotional bewilderment, passed through the stage of frantic bids for her mother's attention by toilet relapse, refusal to go to sleep at night and to eat, one device after another being adopted in an effort to focus her mother's attention upon herself, but abandoned as it failed to win her mother away from the baby. During this interval Barbara clung pathetically to other people, climbing on their laps and chattering feverishly to hold their attention. When the sister developed power to command the attention of visitors, Barbara began to sulk in dejected silence. Soon she began to withdraw and in time actually hid when visitors came. Some children at this point, or sooner, would have attacked the baby physically in an uncontrollable desire to dispose of the interloper, or at least to express some of the resentment felt, but Barbara at no time did this. Rather, she soon found that she could win a word of approval from her mother by being nice to the baby. Because the baby's smile eased her loneliness, she spent more and more time in the nursery.

When she began to hide, her behavior came sharply to her mother's attention and drew comment and was talked over thoroughly and frequently in the child's hearing. In time her silence spread to include her mother, and her conversation with her mother began only after several minutes of quiet, unconcerned social sharing, e.g., reading her a story.

The mother loved Barbara deeply and attempted to be understanding. With sincere thought on the subject and some quiet watching of the child's reactions, she realized much of what had happened. When she felt that she understood, she did two things. First, whenever visitors arrived, she quietly slipped her arm around Barbara and picked up a topic of conversation which would distract the visitors' attention from the fact that the child had not spoken to them. Thus Barbara began to feel less defeated by her social failure and to be less afraid that she would be forced to greet people when she could not find it in her power to do so. Second, the mother carefully planned her day to give the child more attention. Barbara, now four, could help her mother in many ways, thus creating a situation of relaxed companionship in which she could talk naturally. With each week the periods when she found it difficult to talk and to be with others shortened, and natural conversation became easier.

The mother also talked with one or two of her most understanding friends who came frequently to the house. These people, accepting Barbara's silence, quietly included her in the conversation from time to time, but always under circumstances which required no answer. In time Barbara began to feel at home with these friends and found conversation with them possible. It was over a year, however, before she could muster a social greeting even for these people when they first appeared or when they were leaving. It was two years before this carefully planned program produced ease of first greetings and farewells for most of the familiar persons in the social circle of the family. By that time Barbara had built inside herself the conviction that, although she did not charm people as her little sister did, she could have satisfying social contacts.

VALUES. Values, integrity, moral character, conscience or self-discipline are terms that seem imposing when referred to the young child. Much of what happens to him lets him know in one way or another what others value, as well as what he can or cannot do. In his social experience his own values begin to be formed. Much later he may be less influenced by others. As the child meets his contemporaries on an acceptable level, he progresses in the emotional weaning from his family and builds extensions of his social self. The period from three to five years of age is ordinarily one of rapid development in this respect. The child asserts himself as an individual with at least some degree of success. It is fairly usual for these independent strivings to take the form of boisterousness, of "showing off" and of fighting. Values of parents and other adults, as well as those of other children, come into focus as the child senses from them what is important in individuality and in conformity. It seems possible to encourage individuality without tolerating rudeness to adults or to other children or fundamental disrespect toward others.

Among the characteristics of young children which complicate measurement of their attitudes and values, Yarrow (1960) lists their narrow experience, ties to the concrete, less distinct boundaries in which "the real, the imagined, the wished for, the wished away may not always be distinguishable," and limited language skills.

The preschool child is in the process of discovering the rules of his society. His grasp of them is in accordance with his stage of cognitive development. Being oriented toward these rules cognitively is, at any age, different from practicing them. Selecting the basic rules to put first, i.e., elements to value, and being guided by internal as contrasted to external influences in living by them may, even at the age of five or six, as well as later, be on different planes for different individuals. Kohlberg (1964) differentiates between moral conduct (or behavior) and the development of moral ideology and judgment (as distinguished from moral knowledge or belief). For example, five-year-olds may show resistance to temptation to cheat or disobey. They may also be able to state the knowledge or belief that they should take turns or carry out the request of a teacher. In their ideology, however, or judgment or moral thought they are likely to be at a "premoral" stage.

Kohlberg (1963, 1964) distinguished three levels of morality. Level I is "premoral," with a punishment and obedience orientation or naive instrumental hedonism. As the individual talks about bases for decisions (moral judgment as contrasted to actual conduct), the quality of his underlying thought changes from level I through level II to level III. Level II is "morality of conventional role-conformity," with approval of others and authority as bases for decisions. Level III, "morality of self-accepted moral principles," has individual principles of conscience. In saying what he would or would not do in a particular situation the individual reveals his moral judgment. The levels do not classify his behavior. Development proceeds "from judging in terms of immediate external physical consequences to judging in terms of subjective or internal purposes, norms, or values."

Situational factors have been found to influence four-year-olds' resistance to temptation to cheat or disobey (Sears, Rau and Alpert, 1965). Positive and consistent relations between early parental practices, such as those emphasizing obedience, caring for property and performing chores, and resistance to temptation in four-year-olds have not been found (Burton, Maccoby and Allinsmith, 1961).

Variables in Emotional and Social Development

PERSONAL ATTRIBUTES AND SOCIALIZATION PROCESSES. In emotional and social development personal attributes such as age, sex

and activity level are somewhat predictive of particular forms of behavior. In addition, some stability of attributes (i.e., the tendency for an individual's distinctive combination of relative proportions of various forms of social behavior, intentions or goals to persist during the preschool years) may be noted. Martin (1964) commented on "the essence of the *individual* child—a pattern of social behavior which remains remarkably invariant in these early years (approximately two and one-half to five years) during which both the child as an organism and his social environment are constantly changing."

Socialization is the process by which the infant or child "is led to take on the way of life of his family and of the larger social groups in which he must relate and perform adequately in order ultimately to qualify for full adult status" (Clausen, 1966). Just how the child learns what to do and what not to do with family members, peers and others in his broader world is not completely known. Statement of ideas such as the following is to be considered tentative.

Focus of attention on social relations can vary in accordance *with adult suggestion.* For example, in one study it was observed that children of preschool age who were looking at photographs were more likely to note objects and persons in their spontaneous verbalizations. After an adult had inquired about nurturant relations, more of the children commented on them. Their spontaneous verbalizations, when the same photographs were shown three weeks later, more frequently concerned children in the photographs or their relationships (Halverson, 1967) (see Fig. 101).

Behavior brought out by liked or disliked peers is pertinent in study of *reinforcing effects of peers* (Hartup, 1965). In adult-child relations, *praise* can influence behavior; *criticism* or punishment can also influence it (Aronfreed, 1965; Hollenberg and Sperry, 1950).

Viewing an aggressive model in a movie can increase aggressive behavior in preschool children. Children of nursery school age studied by Bandura, Ross and Ross (1963) saw movies of adults aggressive in play with a doll and in their comments. After mild frustration at not being allowed to play with particular toys these children showed approximately twice as much aggression as children who had seen a nonaggressive model or had not seen the movie. They imitated the actions with the doll that they had seen in the movie; they were also more aggressive in nonimitative ways. Maccoby (1964) reported other variables in effects of mass media.

Effects of parent-child relations upon the child's behavior and thought are complex, and research continues to focus attention on early associations. *Affectional ties of the parent, the infant and the young child* influence social development. For example, Harlow and Harlow (1966) refer to influence on relations with age-mates; Sears, Maccoby and Levin (1967), Sears (1960b), and Sears, Rau and Alpert (1965) refer to influences on conscience.

The child's personal attributes influence his behavior, and this in turn influences reponse of others to him. In this *circular process* the competent child is more likely to have his own self-esteem and his acceptance by others increase; the reverse may occur for the less competent child. Glidewell et al. (1966) refer to a self-sustaining circular process as follows:

> Rejection breeds defensiveness, perceptual distortions, further aggression or withdrawal, and reduction in self-esteem. Further aggression or withdrawal and further counteraggression or passive rejection (in the teacher or peers) complete the circle, and symptoms of emotional conflict and disturbance appear. . . . This circular process model possesses some empirical support. For example, dominative behavior precipitates dominative behavior and integrative behavior stimulates integrative behavior.

Since social and emotional development includes elements of personality development, experience with self, experience with others and "awareness of the cosmos," information about sequence and interaction will come slowly. Attempts are being made to grasp the essence of the person as contrasted to meaningless figures.

The extent to which early emotional experiences make deep impressions which last into childhood and adult life, molding later ideas and behavior, requires scientific study. It would be helpful to have research on persistence of patterns in the individual which considers constitutional variables and both persistent and changing factors in the environment. "In the normal range of infant experience . . . we believe that events subsequent to the first year or two of life have the power to 'confirm or deny' the personality of the growing infant, to perpetuate or remake it, depending upon whether the situation of later childhood perpetuates or alters the situation in which the infant was reared" (Orlansky, 1949).

The concept of open-endedness of development seems to be sound (see pp. 5-6). Knowledge of some stability (as well as some change) in the individual's personality attributes over time suggests the following interesting possibility (Emmerich, 1966):

> Suppose that many more phases of personality development are found than any theory has thus far proposed. If this were the case, then each transformation could be small, so that the individual's link with his immediate past would be strong, and yet, if there were many such modifications in the course of development, personality could change markedly over long time spans.

In longitudinal studies in which some preschool aspects are predictive of later behavior, coefficients of correlation are not so high that change in later years is ruled out. According to Kagan and Moss (1962),

> Many of the behaviors exhibited by the child during the period 6 to 10 years of age, and a few during the age period 3 to 6, were moderately good predictors of theoretically related behaviors during early adulthood. . . . The preschool girl's involvement in achievement tasks predicted her concern with intellectual mastery in adulthood ($r = .44$; p .05). . . . (In boys) a tendency toward passivity during the first three years was linked to selected aspects of adolescent and adult personality. . . . Whether this tendency is the complete product of early learning or partly the indirect consequence of constitutional factors is a question that needs to be answered.

As for subtleties in influences, Caldwell (1964), reviewing effects of infant care, i.e., effects of particular parental practices, stated: "The relationship between parent attitudes and parent behavior is still insufficiently explored and imperfectly understood. In terms of the relative strength of either (in affecting infant behavior and later behavior), the weight of evidence . . . would appear to be on the side of the attitude."

STRESS AND PRESSURES.   When young children experience emotional difficulties, they may show loss of appetite, wakefulness, irritability or restlessness. Nightmares should raise questions about the child's emotional well-being (Josselyn, 1948). Release from emotional difficulties may be in imaginative play, through which the child can get rid of tension arising out of stress or anxiety (Henry, 1960; Levy, 1943; Moustakas, 1966; Murphy, 1956). Or accumulated emotional tensions may be released in explosions of temper or fear or in destructive play. Explosive behavior and retreat are symptoms that need to be studied to find out what the child is trying to say.

Emotional stress and inner anxiety as a cause of behavior difficulties in young children may come from a variety of sources. Some behavior problems occur simply as a result of growth, either from an inner disequilibrium in growth or from some error that we in our present culture are making in what we expect of children. Gesell and Ilg (1943) say:

> A developmental approach is of supreme importance in the management of those variations of conduct which are sufficiently atypical or pronounced to deserve the designation of behavior deviations. In infancy and early childhood it is especially difficult to draw a sharp line between normal and abnormal behavior. In a sense all children are problem children, because none can escape the universal problem of development which always presents some difficulties. On the other hand, there are few forms of malbehavior which are not in history and essence a variation or deflection of normal mechanisms. . . . Many behavior deviations have their inception at a specific age when a mild degree of manifestation is well nigh universal. The deviation is in the nature of an exaggeration, or an "overindividuation." Overindividuation means that in a period of normal disequilibrium, the behavior did not become duly subordinated to the total action system: it grew out of proportion.

Whether or not thumb-sucking (see Caldwell, 1964; Ridenour and Johnson, 1966; Spock, 1957) or stuttering is serious must be judged by its relation to the developmental pattern. In our culture most children suck their thumbs for longer or shorter periods. Also, transient speech defects such as stuttering often make their appearance at the stage of development when the child has more to say than he has words with which to express himself (see p. 356). Stuttering represents a disequilibrium in growth which occurs in many children by about $2\frac{1}{2}$ to three years of age.

Whenever a behavior problem is prolonged or severe, it is probably due to more than a temporary disequilibrium. For example, many six- to eighteen-month-old children rock themselves in bed, but some indulge in strenuous body rocking to the point of physical exhaustion. This is not to be regarded as a common aspect of growth, but rather as evidence of great inner tension. Likewise thumb-sucking which absorbs the child's attention over long periods in the daytime in competition with normal play interest raises questions about need for some change in routine or personal relations.

As the deeper meanings of the child's emotional and social development come to be understood, it becomes increasingly clear that aggressive attack upon such behavior as thumb-sucking, masturbation, nailbiting, stuttering and other such manifestations may not only be futile, but also can increase tensions. When the cause is of a deep-rooted emotional nature, mechanical devices, reminders and rewards are surface approaches which can increase strain. If children show emotional reaction clearly by negativism, defiant resistance, by sneaking under cover with the behavior, or by other signs of strain, they may be telling adults that they are not able, at that time, to change their behavior without undue strain. Among apparently corrected cases the breaking of one habit may mean the appearance of another.

On the other hand, readiness to proceed to another kind of response may reveal the child easily accepting new forms of behavior. Approaches with the child who is ready to proceed, but has not done so, may have a connection with the findings of Sears and others about weaning practice. Children who weaned themselves did not show any upset. When mothers took the initiative, the children were studied for signs of emotional upset or frustration. Variations were found according to age, with the reduction of upset among children weaned between eight and eleven months not yet explained. The more preparation a child had, and the more gradually his mother made the shift, the less disturbance he showed. Another factor was the mother's decisiveness. According to Sears, Maccoby and Levin (1957), the mother

. . . can be absolutely adamant about the process, never reversing herself, or she can be very sensitive to the child's expressions of discomfort, and go back to bottles over and over again. These two extremes in training would produce comparable differences in *the child's expectancies*. The former mother would create certainty for the child while the latter mother would create uncertainty. Her child would be placed in a greater state of conflict about what to expect from her. Since conflict is itself frustrating, we would expect such backing-and-filling by the mother to produce greater upset than a more direct approach to the matter. . . . Decisiveness is not to be confused with . . . preparation and gradualness.

Macfarlane et al. (1954) report information on *behavior problems* shown by one third or more of boys and girls whom they studied longitudinally:

Some problems were present early—at 21 months, diurnal and nocturnal enuresis and restlessness in sleep, and thumbsucking in girls at 21 months and three years—but never reached the one-third-of-the-children level again. Other problems started later—food finickiness, negativism, and lying—and were given up by the children after a relatively brief trial run and did not recur at the one-in-three level. These were largely coping devices which apparently outran their usefulness for most children relatively quickly.

Some problems were much later in appearing at the one-out-of-three level—reserve, . . . nailbiting, mood swings, disturbing dreams, and, in the boys, jealousy. Other patterns, once started, continued throughout most of the age span—tempers for boys (girls at age seven gave them up except for one age level), and oversensitiveness, the most continuous for girls and second to tempers for boys who largely dropped this pattern at age 12. Temper appears as both a coping technique and an expressive reaction, and oversensitiveness as largely a coping device although in a few children it was associated with real tension. Specific fears, though not lasting as long as either oversensitiveness or tempers, occurred in nine out of fourteen age levels for both the boys and the girls.

UNSTABLE AND INTEGRAL STAGES OF LEARNING.   Learning reaches an apparently smooth, finished result on the surface before it has been practiced in the nervous system long enough to make it truly automatic. This unstable stage, which is inherent in most, if not all, types of learning, is likely to come to light whenever the child is asked to make a new adjustment before given learnings are fixed. For example, children who seem to be trained for the toilet so that they no longer have accidents demonstrate this principle when they relapse if a baby is born into the family, or if they enter nursery school or if some other basic and demanding adjustment is required of them.

Each learning probably has this unstable stage, when strain will break up the not yet automatically fixed pattern. When, however, the pattern has had sufficient practice for it to function automatically, conscious attention to it or strain is no longer required. Change to another level of organization takes place; synthesis occurs. Psychological energy is then released to undertake new learnings or to produce a relaxed period of enjoyment of previous learnings.

In our culture, with the demands characteristically made on young children, there appears to be a period around eighteen months to three years of age when several basic learnings are in the unstable stage. Around three years (or if not at this chronologic age, then at the stage of learning which most children reach around this age) there seems to be a period in which fewer learnings are being newly mastered. At this time a total integration of previous learnings seems to occur. This is in many senses a breathing spell for the child, and, needless to say, for the mother as well. Four-year-olds are sometimes described as "bursting with powers." Entrance to kindergarten, and again to the first grade, may demand a great deal of attention and emotional energy.

Many of the most basic of human learnings have a long series of maturity levels. The more complex the ability, the longer the delay in the ultimate integration stage. Such learnings include social responsibility, the use of money, continued improvement in the use of language, constant refinement of self-controls, and so on. For example, one step in social responsibility pertains to whimsical demands upon other people. The baby learns not to fuss too much when he needs attention and to adapt his hunger and sleepiness to routines which fit into the larger routines of the family as a whole. A little later he learns to feed himself, still later to dress and undress himself and to take complete toilet responsibility, thus relieving his mother of much of his care. Along the way he makes a beginning toward doing his share in the running of the family machinery. He may pick up the newspapers in the daily

FIGURE 102. Differentiation, specialization and integration (on various planes of complexity) occur in social development as well as in other aspects of development.

This 2½-year-old girl helps to put away the table silver and thus takes one step in learning to assume responsibility.

housecleaning; he may dry the silver and the pans at dishwashing time. The child in Figure 102 enjoys helping her mother.

Each new task requires a learning process. Each learning will have a period of only apparent finish, which may be thrown off balance by distraction. Yet with practice (particularly if the practice is companionable and fun) each will eventually find integration and automatic smoothness as a part of the individual's social behavior.

Each stage of instability in the learning may produce some emotional repercussions; each stage of integration will result in freedom and rest. Some children absorb the emotional repercussions of new learning in stride, showing, in periods of strain, little more maladjustment than slight extra fatigue. Others, less phlegmatic and more excitable, take each of the new learnings required by life in a way that makes them seem constantly upset emotionally. Such children require a longer time in which to integrate or stabilize learnings before adaptations to new demands are made easily. Almost every person has some areas of learning in which integration comes more easily than in others. For example, some children take to intellectual learnings with great ease, yet take unusually long periods to stabilize motor learnings. Other children find the reverse. For some children social adjustments make no demand to speak of, yet every routine-training adjustment is difficult to make.

METHODS OF STUDYING EMOTIONAL AND SOCIAL DEVELOPMENT

The measurement of emotional and social development, including concepts of self and of others, presents problems of even greater complexity than the measurement of physical growth. Emotional and social growth data are far less definite than height, weight, the appearance of teeth, or even an x-ray film of bones. Children's behavior varies from situation to situation and depends on the form of stimulation, the state of physical fatigue and many other factors. It is particularly difficult to secure information on affective components of behavior. Still more difficult to identify are the motivations which underlie the particular intentions a child seems to have. When procedures for collection of data and classification of them are standardized, there is still the question of their reliability and validity. How much agreement from one time of study of behavior to another (reliability of the data) and how much the item noted pertains to the aspect of the individual it is intended to measure (validity of the measure) are important questions when particular procedures and the findings they provide are considered. Because of these factors it is difficult to standardize procedures for the description of behavior, and even more difficult to evaluate such a description accurately.

The devices for studying observable behavior are defended by some workers as being the only methods for studying social and personality development that can be counted on. These workers feel that what can be seen and heard one can be sure of, whereas one can only guess at what goes on inside the child. Others scoff at this idea, saying that it is exactly what is seen and heard that cannot be counted on, since one has no idea what the child meant to say or do, or what inner feelings and attitudes are being expressed in any given behavior, no matter how obvious it may appear on the surface.

There is something to be said for both points of view, as there is something to be said for most of the devices used by both groups. In fact, most of the methods developed for the observation of outward behavior and for the study of inner feelings and attitudes have something of the other point of view in them. Observers of outward behavior know that they cannot be sure, but must, nevertheless, be aware of the inner aspects of the person. Conversely, inner meanings can be discovered only by observation and study of what the child does and says.

Devices for Study of Outward Behavior

For many years attempts have been made to obtain data as definite as a height or weight figure that could be handled statistically. There are now available a number of *check lists* or *rating scales* of personality characteristics, or descriptions of behavior, on which a teacher or parent may check or report on those traits or reactions which apply to the particular child under consideration. These are useful for reminding the adult to look for and observe certain behaviors or situations which, in a free-running description of the child, he might forget to mention.

Some of these check lists have been weighted numerically, thus giving a rough estimate of the degree of the behavior present. For example, a five-point or seven-point scale can be used for indications from rare to frequent for incidence of aggression in the child's play with other children.

Justification of methods which convert detail observed to a score lies in the fact that detail can be sufficiently quantitative to be used in statistical studies, or for objective camparison of one child with another or for comparisons of the same child at different ages. Check lists, ratings, a count of some kind, permit groupings of items to be studied, and give a short and readily visible summary of material which in descriptive case studies often takes up many pages. (Examples are in Bridges, 1931; Sontag, Baker, and Nelson, 1958; Stott, 1967.) Information can be considered according to the same yardstick. The methods are sufficiently convenient, however, that they may tempt investigators to an indiscriminate overuse or misuse of the device.

Observational records in which detail of behavior is recorded at the time, instead of the rating, may be used in a structured situation or in a natural setting (Rafferty, Tyler and Tyler, 1960). This record provides information which is then rated. Interviews of parents and questionnaires involve recollection of detail.

In a *time-sampling observation,* behavior, as it occurs in a given period of time and setting, provides information to be recorded. A tally or check mark may be used to indicate occurrence of a particular response or sign of a particular intention. Occurrence and duration of responses within a category provide data for study (Kessen, Williams and Williams, 1961).

Another device which has a good deal of use in studying the social group relations of children is the *sociometric technique.* In this method *groups* of children are watched closely, and each contact any child makes with any other child is recorded. With these observations a sociogram can be sketched, revealing the number of contacts made by a given child, as well as which children he sought and which children sought him. Another way of studying group interrelations involves the naming of children preferred. It can also indicate, as can the sociogram, which children tend to cluster into small play groups or prefer cliques. (Examples of use of sociometric methods and discussion of them are in Jennings, 1947; Marshall and McCandless, 1957; Northway, 1967.) These devices and many others have helped our understanding of group formation and of associates the child seeks, or is sought by, as well as our knowledge of how individual children adapt to group associations.

Devices for Study of Inner Emotional Life

The behavior of a child, even the part we can see and hear, is extremely complex and therefore hard to measure. Still more complex and harder to assess is the vitally important inner aspect of behavior which we cannot see. This is the child's inner world that he creates for himself in terms of the meanings and feelings which his experiences produce inside himself. Until we understand these inner meanings and feelings, we cannot truly understand him. More and more we are realizing the deep and significant relation between the inner world of the child and his outward behavior.

A number of methods have been tried in the attempt to understand and to interpret this inner or private world of childhood. There are the methods used in a *natural setting* which, like those used to study the outward behavior of the child, consist of careful observations of free play of children. Trained observers can often gain valuable clues to inner behavior and feelings in this way. Another method is study of children's spontaneously produced creative products, such as paintings or drawings, spoken or written stories, or models made in clay.

In viewing these expressions of the child in a natural setting, particular frames of reference, or categories for classification of detail, are used which concern the child's feeling tone about himself, others, and his "life space." Attention is likely to focus on the individual rather than on scores which meet requirements of a well standardized testing procedure (Hartley, Frank, and Goldenson, 1952; Alschuler and Hattwick, 1947).

In addition to these and other nonschematic approaches to interpretation of children's inner life, there are devices for studying children under more *systematic and controlled conditions. Play with selected materials* or under standardized conditions has been investigated as a means of revealing inner thoughts and feelings. The materials or methods can be set up so that they stimulate and call out responses in specially selected areas of thought and feeling. For example, a set of dolls which includes, in miniature, adults and children comparable to the composition of the child's own family may be given to a child in an attempt to study his relations to and hence his feelings about his father, mother, himself and his sister. In his spontaneous dramatic play with these dolls he may, in some instances, reveal his feelings, and express pent-up emotion which has been denied outlet in his family life. Among the techniques now in use are play with puppets or dolls, with housekeeping toys, and with clay, paints and other creative materials.

Another device is to ask the child to name three or more wishes. Still another device is to start a story for the child, asking him to complete it, e.g., "Once there was a little girl who lived with her mother and her daddy. She had a little brother. Now you tell me the rest of the story." In instances such as these, fantasies of the child provide additional information in study of personality.

These *projective techniques*, as they are called, permit the child to project outward some of the thoughts and feelings he does not reveal in ordinary situations. In correctional treatment the play situations have been used not only to reveal the source of the difficulty, but also to help the child to express pent-up emotion and to replace destructive feelings with constructive ones. Used as a treatment device, the procedure is referred to as *play therapy*. When used simply as a means of investigating personality development or emotional reaction, it is usually referred to as the play technique or the projective technique. For discussions of projective techniques and illustrations of records of children's responses, the reader is referred to Levin and Wardwell (1962) and Murphy (1956).

Only well-trained observers should attempt to interpret the inner life of children as revealed in play, in creative products or in controlled situations. Even trained specialists need to be warned against the temptation to overgeneralize about the personality of the subject from the application of a projective technique. All projective methods should be subjected to careful validating studies to test the findings against the results of all available descriptions and general information about any child being studied. One session with a child in which one or several projective methods are used is not an adequate basis on which to draw sweeping conclusions about that child.

One test of personality, the Rorschach test, studies personality through the reactions of the subject to a series of ink-blot cards. Longitudinal studies of children from two to ten years suggest that the test (first standardized on adults) can be used effectively with children as young as three years if scored by child norms (Ames et al., 1952). Different scoring systems for Rorschach responses have been developed in an attempt to measure different emotional aspects (Levine, 1966).

The World Test * is also being used with young children. In it the child's arrangement of miniature parts of the world, such as people, houses, fences, animals and trees, is scored.

IMPLICATIONS OF EMOTIONAL AND SOCIAL DEVELOPMENT

In any discussion of emotional development the presence of conflicting feelings (ambivalence) should be mentioned. For example, a child may seem hostile and affectionate toward the same person within a comparatively short time. Our knowledge of patterns, gradients or stages is incomplete; variations with age are not clear.

Expression of Feelings

What is known about emotional behavior and its development suggests that the child's expressing his feelings instead of keeping them bottled up inside him can have advantages for him and for those associated with him. Many adults have wished that they knew what an aloof, restrained, silent and tense child was concerned about. If he talked, played, expressed himself through creative activities, or "exploded," he might ease the tension and also straighten out his own thoughts in the process. Also, in so doing, he might reveal to the adult what it was that bothered him, or what he needed a better grasp of. On the other hand, many have wished for more restraint, for his own sake and the sake of others, in the child whose frequent intense emotional reactions have jeopardized the safety and well-being of others. In children with extreme responses of these kinds, and in children who seem to be getting along very well, *insight is gained by considering feelings beneath the surface responses.* Furthermore, acceptance of the premise that the expression of feelings and

---

* Copyright by Charlotte Bühler, Los Angeles, California.

consideration for other people are not incompatible decreases the confusion that current emphasis on expressiveness sometimes produces.

An adult's understanding and acceptance of the way a child feels can encourage the child's expression of his feelings—a step toward handling them. Read (1966) says:

> A child may want the attention of the teacher and, not getting it, may attack the child who he feels is his rival or the teacher who he feels is deserting him. A child like this needs to have his confidence built up so that he will see others as less of a threat to him. He needs help in accepting and finding better outlets for his feeling. When it is all right to admit the feeling of wanting the teacher all to yourself, it becomes easier to work out a better solution than attacking others.

The child's realization that his feelings are understood may come about in different ways. Baruch (1949) tells of a child who clung to his mother. She tried mirroring his feeling (thinking what he was feeling and saying it aloud).

> Ronnie was nodding soberly each time she mirrored his feelings and in a subdued whisper he was repeating, "Ronnie want his mommie. Ronnie doesn't want his mommie to go 'way." Came a day when his voice was no longer small and subdued.... And then, suddenly,... "Mommie knows now.... Now Ronnie go play." Without another glance in her direction, he turned and trudged out to the yard and his sandbox, secure in his mind that his mother did know and understood.

Balance in use of the point of view which stresses expression of feelings comes through reference to other points of view also. The child's growth in self-discipline is discussed in the following chapter. Possibilities of assisting in the child's development of feelings of confidence through use of his abilities were suggested in discussions of learning through play in the chapters on motor and intellectual development.

Indications of Feelings

The term "emotional tone" was used in Chapter One to describe an aspect of the individual to be recognized in study of processes of development. It involves feelings about oneself and one's world not entirely of the obvious intensity that anger, fear, affection and other emotions often are. It may be described in terms of personality components, such as a sense of trust. Feeling secure, confident, adequate, competent, belonging, are other terms sometimes used. Agreement on the importance of understanding these feelings is general, but knowledge of how to do so is limited.

Everyday behavior of the child is one source of information about his feelings. Read (1966) says that characteristic attitudes "may be seen in such things as in the way the child walks, runs, holds his hands, in his posture, etc."

Responses in free play may also be revealing of emotional tone. The following example suggests the happy tone which those associated with this particular three-year-old sensed repeatedly.

Jerry comes in from another nursery school room. Drops down on his knees and begins to play with Don's train. Don has left it to put blocks away and pays no attention. Jerry straightens the train. It has an engine in front and a caboose in back; he puts on another engine in back of the caboose. He begins to choo choo in a very low tone. Goes from front to back engine. Makes each one choo choo in its turn. Gets very close to the teacher and Don who are putting blocks away on the shelves. When the blocks are all up, Don begins to straighten toys on the shelves. Looks at the train Jerry is pushing and says, "I'm going to put that away," and begins taking the train up, car by car. Jerry continues ch! ch! ch! Then helps put the train away. Jerry continues his ch ch ch after the train is put up and he has begun work on a puzzle. As he succeeds with the puzzle, the ch sounds become very loud and he smoothes the finished puzzle hard with both hands.

Sometimes a child's brief statements suggest uneasiness about plans beyond his grasp. The child who said, "I'll buy it," several times could reveal some of her thoughts when her mother inquired further. They were connected with the fact that their house was for sale and several people had come to look at it—many hours before the comment was made.

Expressions of imagination, such as dramatization, and creative activities, such as painting, may sometimes reveal feelings in less direct ways than actions of the previous descriptions seem to reveal them. For example, one may wonder what it means, if anything, for a particular child when she always wants to be the mother in housekeeping play, when hospital play occupies a large portion of her play time, or when she always covers over fresh bright colors in a painting until they become dark. Thought about actions such as these may lead to further understanding of the child.

Without venturing into a professional field involving use of projective techniques for which he is not qualified, a person seeking to understand a child's feelings can interest himself in what the child seems to be responding to, what he seems to be needing and seeking. This is a warm and human response, not an analytical one. There is no intention of studying every action and word to discover feelings they reveal, but there is genuine respect and concern for the feelings of another individual, i.e., of the child.

Consideration for Others

What is known about social behavior and its development suggests that the child's learning of consideration for others will reflect his motivations, behavioral events, joys and sorrows in immediate situations and in his long-term relations with members of his family and others. The broad basis of the child's learning to share is implicit in statements such as the following.

"Sensitiveness to the needs and desires of others and a willingness to adjust one's own needs and desires to them" (Chittenden in National Society for Study of Education, 1947) are elements of sharing. Chittenden says that the first responsibility is to create an environment in which young children can feel secure and happy. The second responsibility is to introduce physical and social factors conducive to the child's learning to share.

Even the secure and happy child may not seem generous at first. Young children are self-absorbed; their insight into other people's feeling is limited. Time concepts are also limited. When a young child is asked to lend his toy for five minutes, he may not realize that this is a short time. If he gets it back soon, he may be more willing to part with it the next time. It may be a painful period if the child is nagged to "be nice to your guest," or to give up precious possessions. Having to stand aside and see a favorite doll or truck or other cherished possession broken by another child does not result in a desire to share or even to have other children around.

When two or more very young children play together, it seems in accordance with their stage of development to have a tricycle or wagon, doll or pail available for each at the time when the sense of "mine" is acute. Grasping the difference between "mine" and "yours" usually precedes the stage of taking turns.

Social situations can include the rather obvious and also the rather subtle sensitivities to others. For example:

> Some children were running toward a steam shovel. Nicoli stood by a swing, holding her toy animal. Laura came close to her and said, "Come on, let's go see the shovel." Nicoli took Laura's hand, and together they went to the fence to watch the steam shovel go by. The driver waved.

Or this:

> "La, la, la, la, I'm taller than you. La, la, la, la, I'm taller than you." John is at the top of a slide. Later, "Hi, Mother Hubbard, I'm up in the tree cupboard," he calls to his mother from the tree.

Understanding Individual Differences

Understanding of the individual is an element in the adult's attitude toward the child. It occurs in varying degrees in relations of people, whatever their ages. The child's social growth suggests his potentiality for understanding and respecting each person if he is given the opportunity to reflect such a point of view from other people. Many parents and nursery school teachers can report illustrations of these potentialities in the responses of a child to another who is younger or slower, who is different physically or whose race or religion is different.

An illustration will serve to suggest, and probably to raise questions about, potentialities and influences of a given situation.

> In a nursery school a Chinese child entered a group of three-year-olds who had never seen a Chinese person. Two children looked at her closely, and one said, "Her eyes look sleepy." The teacher explained that her eyelids looked different; the three children looked at theirs in the mirror. Then the teacher said, "She is Chinese." Twice during the morning and later at the luncheon table with her, the two children repeated this statement. At the table when they said it, the Chinese child smiled and said, "I am Chinese."

Potentialities for Spiritual Development

Emotional and social development has a connection with spiritual growth. The way in which the individual views these experiences, which are close at hand, is one part of his spiritual growth. Another part concerns his beginning to have feelings about, and to seek knowledge of, what lies beyond his immediate experience or beyond his grasp in a tangible sense. At a simple level the young child begins to acquire what man has always sought: not only some understanding of a world which is big and beyond his immediate or complete comprehension, but also some understanding of his relation to it in the sense of the spirit and of the material.

Spiritual growth suggests something in addition to growth of a more material kind. Quality of thought and feeling is involved. For some, *spiritual growth in a broad sense* means appreciation and understanding of, and participation in, the good, the beautiful and the true. To some it concerns appreciation and understanding of one's immediate world, the broader world and the cosmos. These references to the spirit with which one views his world and has feelings about it suggest that the terms "spiritual growth" and "religious growth" are related.

Being religious, in a broad sense, concerns a person's way of living, his way of looking at his world, acting in it, viewing and feeling what is beyond his complete comprehension. Or, *in a more traditional sense,* being religious concerns a person's acceptance of a particular religion; allegiance is to organized statements of man's place in the world or his relation to the Infinite, as formulated in a particular religion and adhered to through its organization or church. Not only attitudes toward God, prayer, the source of order or power in the world, immortality and the Church, traditionally thought of as religious, but also attitudes of appreciation in everyday living are involved. Views in these fields, whether personal or in accordance with a particular religion, are spiritual or religious.

In the young child's spiritual or religious growth individual families will put emphases in accordance with their own conviction. Reflection of these family attitudes is a significant part of the child's spiritual growth. Consequently, discussion here will not deal with attitudes, but rather with the child's potentialities for many different attitudes, and with methods appropriate for his stage of development. Reference will be to responses which seem to be of a spiritual nature in infancy and preschool years and to methods of the adult which seem to warrant consideration, whatever the aims of guidance may be.

For the infant the understanding loving care of his family can mean the beginning of his spiritual growth. He has a feeling of harmony with his world. A sense of trust and a realization of the lawfulness of the universe can have their foundations laid early. For the child who is walking around, talking or playing in a group, there are many additional possibilities for spiritual growth.

The child's use of vocabulary concerning particular religious concepts often reveals his interest. An example is the following conversation of four-year-old boys.

> Dickie: There isn't really any sky. The air just goes up and up. I can touch the sky.
> Paul: I can see the sky. There is a sky and it is blue. That is heaven.
> Jimmie: If there was no sky, what would God sit on?

Inclination to state the familiar rather than the unknown is illustrated by the Iowa children whose teacher listened carefully to what they were singing and found that it was "Oh East Des Moines" instead of "Oh Eastern Morn." Signs of reverence, whatever the words, signs of interest, confusion, and clarification about the world, heaven, God, and days of particular religious significance are part of the potentialities of the preschool child for spiritual growth.

A group of parents kept a record of their children's questions because they, the minister and the teacher were interested in studying their Church School program (Murray and Tyler, 1937; Smart, 1939). Their three- to four-year-olds asked the following questions: Who is God? Where does God live? What does God look like? Where is heaven? Where did Daddy go? (asked after his father's death). Who made the hills? Who made the trees? The four- to five-year-olds asked: Where is God? Where did Jesus live? Will you die? What is an angel?

Anyone aware of social and spiritual potentialities such as those suggested here would respond to them according to his own convictions. Methods emphasized here could be appropriate, whatever the convictions of the adult. One point of emphasis is on the importance of recognition of signs of interest and readiness with regard to spiritual growth which appear at the preschool age. The second point of emphasis is on the importance of adaptation of experience to the child's stages of development. Both approaches stress thought on the adult's part as to what is done and why. This thought about meaning of experience provided may or may not mean following of tradition and convention, but, if it does, it will be with insight. A few illustrations of these approaches, rather than a more complete discussion, will be presented here.

John, $3\frac{1}{2}$ years old, had two visitors, Stanley and Sue. While the children were drinking milk and eating crackers, Stanley spilled a few drops of milk on the linoleum floor. Sue told him to wipe it up with his paper napkin. When he sat doing nothing, she began to push him, saying, "You spilled your milk, you must wipe it up." John began to imitate the pushing. His mother said, "Everybody spills things sometimes. Stanley knows about wiping things up. It's all right if he doesn't feel like doing it now. We might think about his wanting to decide things for himself. We could also think about our helping by saying nothing, or by wiping it up for him."

This mother considered respect for the dignity of each person important in her child's spiritual growth.

In another family, in which the parents considered a concept of God and of the Bible important, the four-year-old child began to ask questions about them. The parents answered his questions simply.

They found books that would aid their discussion. They tried to consider values of pictures and stories with simple phrasing and specific statements meaningful in terms of the child's experience. Values of Biblical language were also considered.

In a Church School where meaningful experience and happy associations were stressed, the children had activities such as the following: sharing toys, sharing news (telling of experiences of the preceding week), going into the church to look at the colors in the stained glass windows, having the minister tell them a story in their playroom, hearing the organist play songs they knew, watching the recessional, planting flower bulbs, dramatizing stories, having a few of the choir members visit them in their room, going with the sexton when he fired the furnace. Some of the more usual Church School experiences were also included. A variety of resources were used.

The illustrations presented here concern traditional religious concepts and experiences, i.e., the dignity of man, God, the Church, not because the aspect of spiritual growth called appreciation is less important. Other appreciations have already been referred to in considerations of the child's intellectual, emotional and social development.

Ability to Meet Situations

Emphases on development of ability combine several points of view. They stress importance of the child's own abilities to cope with his world with increasing competence, adult encouragement of learning, as well as indications of acceptance and understanding. Brody (1962) made the following suggestions to teachers of young children:

Basically, the task is to evaluate whether the child is using his school experience to practice ways to avoid, or ways to master, the realistic demands that every child meets in the normal course of school events. We should not be overly impressed by signs of inner conflict or inner anxiety in themselves. Rather we should try to determine the extent to which the conflicts and anxieties . . . may be snuffing out potentials, or impelling the child toward acquiring strength.

Brody suggests "signs by which to appraise a child's current state of emotional health" with the thought that additions may be made individually. These signs concern the following: attitudes of the child toward his own body, unspoken attitudes toward himself, relation to other persons, range of activities, quality of productions, quality of play, toleration of frustration, curiosity and moods.

TOPICS FOR STUDY AND DISCUSSION

1. As a focus for study, select several forms of emotional and social behavior about which to state orderly trends. Indicate your speculations on relation of these to development of a concept of self and of others.
2. Study an individual child and keep a record of
   (a) behavior which seems related to his sense of trust, autonomy, initiative and achievement

    (b) expressions of affection, anger or fear

    (c) social behavior illustrative of exchange of ideas

    (d) responses considered to reveal aggression, sympathy, nurturance

    (e) responses indicative of interest in and appreciation of the immediate world, a broader world and that beyond comprehension.

    Attempt placement of the child on the continua of love-hostility and introversion-extroversion according to the behavior recorded. Recall points of view and facts from this chapter which seem useful in understanding the behavior recorded.

3. Select a particular aspect of a child's behavior about which there are questions, such as hesitancy to join a group, use of force, seeking attention. Discuss references in the following list in terms of their usefulness to parents.

4. Students may wish to pretend to take the roles of a mother, father, child and teacher in a discussion of a particular situation concerning emotional, social or spiritual growth.

5. Select from this chapter a reference to research to consider thoroughly. Report on it in terms of its connection with a particular area, point of view or question.

SELECTED READINGS

Anderson, H., and Anderson, G.: Social Development; in L. Carmichael: Manual of Child Psychology. New York, John Wiley & Sons, Inc., 1954. Chap. 19.

Bro, M.: When Children Ask. New York, Harper & Brothers, 1956.

Brody, S.: Mental health and the capacity for nursery education. J. Nursery Education, 17:2, 58-63, 1962.

Chittenden, G.: Experiences in Which Young Children May Learn to Share. Chap. 7, Part II, pp. 179-193. Forty-sixth Yearbook, Part II, National Society for Study of Education. Chicago, University of Chicago Press, 1947.

Fahs, S. L.: Today's Children and Yesterday's Heritage. Boston, Beacon Press, Inc., 1952.

Goodman, M.: Race Awareness in Young Children. New York, Crowell-Collier, 1964.

Hartup, W. W.: Peers as agents of social reinforcement. Young Children, 20:176-184, 1965.

Kohlberg, L.: The development of children's orientation toward a moral order. Vita Humana, 6:11-33. 1963.

Moore, S. G.: Correlates of peer acceptance in nursery school children. Young Children, 22:281-297, 1967.

Proceedings of the XIV International Congress of Applied Psychology, 1961, General editor, G. S. Nielsen: Volume III: Child and Education. Vulnerabilities, sources of strength, and capacity to cope in the "normal" child by Grace Heider, pp. 79-93. Copenhagen, Einar Munksgaard Forlag, 1962.

Read, K. H.: The Nursery School. Philadelphia, W. B. Saunders Co., 1966. Chaps. 7 and 8.

Ridenour, N., and Johnson, I.: Some Special Problems of Children Aged Two to Five Years. Rev. ed. New York, Child Study Association of America, 1966.

Sears, R. R.: Reporting research to parents. J. Nursery Education, 16:1, 25-32, 1960.

Wenar, C.: Competence at one. Merrill-Palmer Quarterly, 10:329-342, 1964.

Yarrow, M. R.: The Measurement of Children's Attitudes and Values; in P. Mussen (Ed.): Handbook of Research Methods in Child Development. New York, John Wiley & Sons, Inc., 1960. Chap. 16.

Also current issues of Children, Childhood Education, Parent's Magazine and Young Children, all of which usually contain articles related to the content of this chapter.

CHAPTER TWELVE

Philosophy of Adult-Child Relations

VIEWS CONCERNING THE CHILD AND THE ADULT

Coordination in Adult Attitudes

The importance of adult attitudes for the child's development is suggested by current thinking and knowledge. Listing and describing five attitudes in the following way represent one of many possible formulations of point of view. Attitudes are regarded as including affective, cognitive and behavioral components. The ones indicated here overlap and are interrelated, and their order could be rearranged, but separate statement of them seems to suggest balance in the adult's perspective of child development.

USE OF A DEVELOPMENTAL-DYNAMIC CONCEPT. This concept suggests *attention to the child's sequential changes and the processes contributing to them.* Such an outlook (or angle of viewing in a perspective) has a particular connection with Chapter One, which refers to intrinsic factors responsible for the child's unfolding as well as extrinsic factors responsible for his use of his potentialities. It is applicable in every aspect of growth and development referred to in all the other chapters, because these factors not only limit what is to be expected, but also give cues to resources for new learning.

RECOGNITION OF THE HOME AND FAMILY AS A SETTING FOR GROWTH AND DEVELOPMENT. This attitude suggests *consideration of the child's family and interactions of its members with reference to emotional climate, environmental stimulation of intellectual development, and physical conditions of the present, as well as heritages from the past.* The fashioning of a family life together, its immediate exchanges and its community scene have many aspects and processes which such an attitude would attempt to view. Some of these are referred to in Chapter Two.

429

FIGURE 103. Children's behavior
suggests the diversity of avenues
of influence and the diversity of
responses.

PROVISION FOR MEETING THE CHILD'S BASIC NEEDS.   An attitude concerning basic needs includes *consideration of conditions in the child requiring supply or relief for physical well-being and development and for psychological well-being and development.* The adult's sensitivities to the child's needs may concern physical ones such as temperature regulation, health protection, nutrition, eating habits, toilet habits, and rest and activity, and psychological ones such as warmth, meeting situations without extreme stress or apathy, dependence and independence, and social contact or other needs. Quandaries may occur in attempting to differentiate basic needs from whims.

THOUGHT CONCERNING INTERRELATION OF VARIOUS ASPECTS AND PROCESSES IN THE INDIVIDUAL CHILD.   *Attempting to know what the child is like* may include being aware of details about his physical growth, health, motor ability, language, concept formation, problem-solving abilities and thought, creativity, emotional and social behavior, concepts of self, of others and of his world. In addition to his knowledge of attributes such as these, and of how they develop, the adult can also sense the uniqueness of their interrelations in the individual (the particular child's personality) and can appreciate it.

PROVISION OF OPPORTUNITY FOR THE CHILD (AND THE ADULT) TO ENJOY HIS USE OF HIS EMERGING ABILITIES.   In this listing of attitudes (particular elements of which would be reflections of the individual adult) it seems appropriate to refer to enjoyment. *Enabling the child to assimilate and accommodate with some zest* as he takes in certain aspects of his environment and makes adjustments to these new assimilations is related to motivations and processes of learning considered in various chapters.

Bases for Attitudes

These attitudes of the adult toward the child were regarded as growing out of, or receiving some support from, the content of previous chapters. Ways in which attitudes might be "brought to life" would vary with individual adults and the children with whom they were associated. Their focus would also vary according to the particular values, aims or goals of the adult.

Philosophy, as referred to in the title of this chapter, concerns not only attitudes of the adult, in the sense of outlook used in association with a particular child, but also hopes for the child toward which it is believed procedures will contribute. Both aims and methods are included in a philosophy. Reference to aims, goals or hopes of the adult for the child, and to the methods or ways in which the adult contributes to the child's development, may be misunderstood. It is a misconception to think of them as being fixed instead of flexible, or similar from one child to another or from one adult to another, instead of being unique for each.

Health, in the sense of physical well-being, has long been recognized as an important aim in child development. In the Children's Charter of the White House Conference Report of 1930 (1932) a number of the items refer to health and its protection. Emphases on the child's physical health and growth, his being well nourished and well cared for physically, are a reflection of the recognition of the importance of this aim. Goals of democracy were stressed in the 1940 White House Conference. Healthy personality was the theme in 1950. Components of a healthy personality, which is a growing personality, as the individual develops from infancy into childhood and adulthood were described in Chapter Seven. The Golden Anniversary White House Conference of 1960 placed particular emphasis on adjustments in a changing world.

In attempting to formulate his own body of principles or conceptions underlying his associations with children, the adult finds a wide range of content from research and theory upon which to draw. In making an effort to use these in his decision making, instead of relying upon personal opinion and experience only, he realizes that the research and theory have a tentative quality as part of a progression in concept formation. He also realizes that in his efforts to clarify beliefs and to look for supporting evidence for them, his thoughts frequently turn to immediate situations, the face-to-face associations or events in which the child is adding "schemata." These events, in which the particular practice is not considered influential alone and the intent which the child senses is considered especially important, often fall into categories such as affection, discipline and expectancies.

In discussions of these in the following pages an approach is suggested of weighing ideas on many sides and of identifying knowledge from research and theory, from which support for or opposition to various ideas might be provided. Emphasis is on thought and exploration of a possible procedure, or point of view, with the child, as contrasted to a fixed or irrefutable conclusion. Such an approach would have, as a basis, a review of general principles concerning personality. For related theories, see Chapter One. The following pages include ideas (many of them tentative) intended to encourage thought about the philosophy of adult-child relations.

USE OF IDEAS ABOUT PERSONALITY DEVELOPMENT

Expectations of Development

Physical growth brings about conspicuous changes which can be detected by everyone and, as a phenomenon of human life, is recognized and accepted by everyone. Cognitive growth, in terms of what the individual knows, being somewhat less conspicuous in its manifestations, is nevertheless fairly evident. That personality grows, however, is not so evident to many people. The "thinking, feeling, acting, human being," with his uniqueness, is also growing. According to knowledge in various fields, including child development, personality grows and develops in the sense of the continuous integration of various aspects which are changing with age and experience. Growth of this kind can continue over a long period of time and can follow certain clearly defined patterns.

Continuous growth, as contrasted to almost reaching a so-called ceiling of development early in life, varies from one person to another. Some persons become rather fixed or static early in life; others continue to grow, continuously acquiring additional integrations of personality. The 99 per cent maturity level for such continuously developing personalities is achieved only very late in life, after the person has met the vicissitudes of life as they occur, taking from each the richness and meaning which enable him to meet each successive stage more fully.

Development of personality in the sense of change of abilities and attitudes is rapid in childhood. The individual is then in a malleable or formative stage. Particular ways of responding, ideas and feelings are in the making in infancy and the preschool years. Everything is new; first experiences are many, and important first emotional overtones are being laid in. Although these important firsts will be added to and changed as time goes on, the fact remains that they *are* firsts and therefore can color reactions to later experiences and influence behavior as later happenings change them.

Personality is, in important ways, the result of experience. It is also the result of the child's own tendencies of exchange with his surroundings, since each child takes from his environment the things which fulfill his needs, and each reacts to events in his environment in his own way. Figure 104 suggests the complexities in the child's constitution and his setting which these exchanges involve.

The child's experiences cannot be determined entirely by parents and teachers, but they are in many ways outlined and steered into certain general channels. Just as the child's physical development can be directed by the nutritive quality or inadequacy of his food, by the full-

FIGURE 104. *Central orientations of the individual's personality affect his interactions with his environment.*

This 4-year-old girl's attention to something alive in the water, her controls of many different kinds as she stands to look at it, her thoughts which draw upon earlier experience and add the new, are a few of the responses here.

ness or the restrictions of his activities and other factors, so other aspects of development are affected by the stage set for him, the variety and quality of his experiences with people and with things, and by the way the adults in his environment deal with him in the routines and experiences of his day. Loved and cared for, he is, in turn, more likely to love others; denied love and security, he may either seek it frantically or withdraw into an inner world where he cannot be hurt. Varied and rich experiences shared with enthusiastic adults can encourage him to seek experiences and to be enthusiastic about learning. Forbidden activity, scolded and punished for adventuring into new learnings, he may rebel or withdraw, becoming overaggressive in his seeking of adventure or coming to dread and fear new experiences.

In trying out an approach which looks for illustrative supporting evidence for or against particular statements, knowledge from Chapters One, Ten and Eleven will be especially pertinent to the preceding statements.

Constitutional Factors in Personality Development

What a child will take out of his environment will, in a measure, be determined by the basic or constitutional personality he happens to have.

Ausubel (1957), discussing early manifestations of individuality, refers to six main categories of distinct and stable *individual differences identified in infants during the early months of life:* placidity and irritability; activity level; tone, length and vigorousness of crying; tolerance of frustration or discomfort and reaction to stress situations and over-stimulation; differential sensitivity to stimulation in various sense modalities; and social responsiveness. He continues: "The demonstration of differences such as these does not . . . preclude the existence of other genically conditioned differences in temperament (e.g., intro-version-extroversion) which can first be manifested after a certain stage of maturity is reached."

Among *sources of vulnerability* to which Heider (Proceedings of the XIV International Congress of Applied Psychology, 1962) referred are a tendency to instability in bodily functioning, low energy reserves and low sensory threshold.

Individual differences in behavior in infancy and sources of vulner-ability such as these seem related to dimensions used in classifying re-sponse tendencies over a wide age range. In the search for "central orientations" affecting the individual's interactions with his environ-ment, several with stability over time have been identified. In lon-gitudinal research, *expressive-outgoing* versus *reserved-withdrawn* and *placid-controlled* versus *reactive-explosive* dimensions have been reported as having stability between the ages of five and sixteen years and as being predictors of other behavior (Bronson, 1966; Honzik, 1965). Interrelations of the two dimensions were particularly predictive of adult behavior. Referred to as "emotional expressiveness," the first dimension concerns reserved-expressive, shy-socially easy and somber-gay behavior. The second dimension, referred to as "reactivity control," concerns reactive-phlegmatic, explosive-calm and resistive-compliant behavior.

In another report on social development *interpersonal* versus *im-personal orientation, positive* versus *negative attitude* and *active* versus *passive mode* are dimensions having continuity in children of nursery school age (Emmerich, 1964). *Passivity* in terms of "the degree to which the child acquiesced or withdrew in the face of attack or frustrating situ-ations, in contrast to an active attempt to overcome and deal with environmental frustrations" has been reported "highly stable for boys and girls during the first 10 years of life" (Kagan and Moss, 1962). The constitutional orientations and others, including some probably not yet identified, which the child brings to his everyday associations with his world have implications for adults who are with him.

Variations in adaptations of the individual child according to his response tendencies or central orientations will be suggested here by reference to a *phlegmatic-excitable* contrast and an *introversion-extroversion* contrast. The term "phlegmatic," with its easy-going implication, seems to have a physiological and neurological connotation which contrasts with the quick-triggered, low threshold connotations of the term "ex-citable." Introversion versus extroversion, as used in the following discussion, refers to a tendency toward involvement with ideas (turning in) as contrasted to a tendency toward involvement with an outside world of people or things (turning out). (In some research these terms are used with the social and emotional connotation of turning toward self-contained activities versus turning toward people [Schaefer, 1961; Emmerich, 1964].) In the following descriptions of personality, dimension extremes of a continuum are suggested. Position of the individual on a continuum would reflect study of a number of manifestations.

Each child is complex and cannot be labeled; however, he is likely to show more responses of one kind and less of another. Some children are phlegmatic, taking changes and adjustments to routines, accidents and other events in stride. Others tend to be more excitable and to be more easily thrown off balance by changes and the need to adjust to new situations. Some stability of these inclinations as the child grows beyond the preschool years provides a basis for thinking of them as constitutional (see pp. 463-464).

Tendencies of the individual show in both physical and psychological reactions. The more phlegmatic child tends to be stabilized in total metabolic reaction; he sleeps well, tends not to run a high temperature when ill and adapts to routines readily. As a baby he is the so-called good baby. He does not cry easily, takes the breast or bottle easily, has slight trouble learning to drink from a bottle or to eat from a spoon and is not easily upset by changes in food or in light or temperature. He sleeps soundly through ordinary noises or distractions, is not particularly upset by physical pain, and is not especially liable to disturbances of digestion. As he grows older he is steady, adaptable and usually happy.

The more excitable or less steady child is likely to have trouble in learning to take the breast or bottle, is inclined to be upset easily by change of any kind, cries easily, tires easily, runs a temperature with slight cause and is susceptible to digestive disturbances. As he grows older he gives evidence of overexcitability and hyperactivity which often lead to excessive fatigue. This fatigue is of the sort that deceives parents, since an overexcitable child when tired does not as a rule become sleepy, but is likely to run faster, shout more loudly and appear unusually alert. When finally put to bed, he may, if overtired, take a long time to go to sleep and, after the first exhaustion is slept away, spring into action again, driven by an overexcited nervous system to seek activity at four or five o'clock in the morning. It is sometimes hard for parents to realize that these symptoms point to a need of more rather than less rest. The unsteady child is likely to be changeable in mood and particularly likely to overreact to any nervous strain or emotional tension in the family atmosphere.

The foregoing does not necessarily imply that the child with more of the steady responses has a more desirable personality than the less steady child. Stability may or may not amount to flaccid indifference and to stolid lack of imagination. Excitability may or may not include increasing discrimination and competence in the child who reacts keenly to sensory stimuli, who sees and hears things that others fail to do and has an alert and fertile imagination.

The excitable child may or may not find in his environment an ally in helping him to adjust easily. Tension can continue to mount in the child who, needing more than most children a quiet, stable environment, is surrounded by persons who are often tense. In need of regularity in routine and most easily disturbed by irregularity of feeding, of sleep hours and of elimination, he may find himself in situations which provide many interruptions in routine.

Charles and Sally illustrate this point. Charles, a tense, high-strung boy of three, is constantly on the move. He runs about, seldom slowing his movements down to a walk, is likely to shriek with excitement every few moments in his play, cries easily when hurt and finds it almost impossible to relax at nap time. He is never ready to go to bed at night, often lying awake until 10 or 11 o'clock, even though put to bed early. In spite of this he is usually jumping about in his bed or running about his room, ready for action, at 5 o'clock in the morning. His family seems unable to help him to achieve rest. His father and his mother are quick-moving, high-strung people whose voices are inclined to shrillness and whose presence adds tension and excitement rather than relaxation and quietness to the family atmosphere. The mother has tried rubbing Charles's back at night in order to help him to relax, but her own tenseness serves only to key him to a still higher pitch. The remedy for Charles's excitability is not to be found in rigorous insistence that he sit quietly for certain periods of the day or spend more hours in bed, although this might help. The real solution lies in a change of family atmosphere — a reorganization of family routine to minimize hurry and fatigue and to build up more of a feeling of leisure.

Sally, on the other hand, is a child who plays hard, but stops to sit quietly when she becomes tired. She alternates quiet periods of handiwork or looking at books with periods of vigorous play. Her voice has the quiet pitch of a rested child and is seldom shrill or whiny. She is hungry at mealtime, eating her meal with dispatch, and trots off quietly to nap or to bed, where she drops to sleep within five to ten minutes. She wakens refreshed and smiling. Sally's parents are relaxed people who have a great deal of pleasure, but seldom become over-fatigued to the point of irritability and tension. The mother plans the day's routine so that breakfast can be unhurried and so that there is ample time for dressing, toilet and other essentials, thus minimizing the feeling of tension and hurry which plays so large a part in Charles's life.

Charles and Sally represent extremes of personality. Most children lie somewhere between these extremes in their reaction to the usual stimulations of life.

Whether the child tends to be phlegmatic or excitable, having some things to count on (in people and in routines) and having some variety (distinctive stimuli upon which attention can focus) seem to facilitate development. The child does not tend to grow well in a setting which is overroutinized or overprotected to the extent that he becomes habit-bound or inflexible in a changing world. A fairly safe guide for any child, phlegmatic or excitable, seems to be to let him settle into his own routine and to see that this routine remains adaptable to his growth needs as he changes and develops. (See Chapter Six for self-regulatory schedules.)

Also, just as some children may have too many routines and others not enough, some children, again, whether excitable or phlegmatic, may have too little or too much stimulation. A "dull" setting, or one with so many stimuli that selective attention is not likely to occur, does not facilitate development (see pp. 335-340 on attention, and pp. 278-279 on relation of experience to intellectual development). Children can have a fairly regular life, yet one which is not devoid of interest. Protection from exposure to nervous strain, emotional tension or over-stimulation seems sound. Yet life which is interesting and intellectually stimulating can offer enough demands for adaptation and adjustment to encourage the ability to meet difficulties when they arise.

Another way of viewing personality is to think of persons as tending toward introversion or extroversion (see p. 409). These words mean to *turn in* or to *turn out,* and, when applied to people, mean that some have a tendency to turn their attention and interests toward a center inside themselves, and some toward a center outside themselves. Those whose predominating attitudes and feelings turn in are more often interested in ideas than in people or things. Persons whose attitudes and feelings turn outward are more often interested in people and things than in ideas. Most people are neither completely one nor completely the other, but have some traits of both. So far as the child leans in one direction or another, he is likely to react to specific situations in his way.

To use this discussion as an indication of a basis for diagnosing personality types would be to presume too greatly upon the scientific knowledge now available about personality. The aim of such a discussion is to emphasize that specific situations in family life will not give rise to specific and predictable behavior reactions in all children. Not all children react to given situations in the same way, but differ at least somewhat in accordance with the tendency to turn inward or outward.

Before considering implications of the child's tendency to turn inward or outward, it seems pertinent to note the frequency with which longitudinal research has identified dimensions of this kind. Honzik (1965) refers to the social interaction anxiety-spontaneity continuum studied by Kagan and Moss (1962) at the Fels Research Institute, spontaneity versus inhibition studied by Tuddenham (1959) in the Oakland Growth Study, the active, extroverted versus inactive, introverted continuum of the Berkeley Growth Study (Bayley and Schaefer, 1964) and the introversion versus extroversion and excessive reserve-spontaneity dimensions of the Berkeley Guidance Study (Honzik and Macfarlane, 1965) (see p. 464 for further information on stability of these and other dimensions at later ages). "Despite the great variation in variable description, findings of the different longitudinal studies suggest that this dimension of outgoing responsiveness versus a retractive, inward-looking response may be one of the truly stable personality dimensions" (Honzik, 1965).

Behavior concerning imaginary companions might serve as an illustration of differences in reaction according to these response tendencies. If a child has, for lack of companionship, developed imaginary companions, the more introverted child may find such companions so satisfying that he will be inclined to cling to them even when there are children with whom he might play. The more extroverted child, however, seems more likely to find imaginary companions a pale substitute for live children and, when exposed to other children, is inclined to abandon his shadows promptly in favor of substance.

The more introverted child may respond to nagging by becoming submissive in action while withdrawing to his world of ideas and dreams for interest and satisfaction in life. The more extroverted child is likely to resist actively, to fight others, since he finds interest and satisfaction in the outside world, a world in which he finds himself so constantly intruded upon that he must resist. It seems that the effects of "sitting and thinking" after an adult-child clash of wills would differ according to whether the child had already thought a great deal or very little on the issue.

The child who is quiet and withdrawn may slip past his parents and teachers without attracting much attention or causing much anxiety. He may not be troublesome, meeting his problems alone and unaided, burying his difficulties within himself or retreating from them to his daydreams. On the other hand, in the child who meets his troubles in the open, symptoms of conflict or of unsolved problems are immediately evident. If he finds life unchallenging or unsuccessful, he responds in an active way by investigating—perhaps in forbidden places—or seeks success in mischief. He finds something to do which, although perhaps producing trouble, at least provides a growing mind with something substantial to feed upon or permits an outlet for emotion. The more introverted child, unchallenged or unsuccessful, retreats quietly. He is no trouble, and so we miss the fact that he may be feeding his mind on shadows or gathering steam from unsatisfied longings which occasionally burst forth in explosions or resentments.

Only a few of the many ways of thinking of personality have been mentioned here. To use these terms alone in describing an individual would be an oversimplification. Again, uniqueness of the child in his particular combination of qualities should be stressed. This uniqueness includes the child's own relative frequencies of various responses. The adult, in his attempts to understand a particular child, can note tendencies and accept them as important in producing behavior and determining reaction to events.

Motivations as Factors in Personality Development

Explanations of behavioral tendencies of the individual, in terms of heredity and the interplay of endowment and experience, await further research. Recognition of this interplay is implied in use of the term "constitutional factors." The child brings to each new event the products of exchanges of his endowment and his experience. His motivations reflect these exchanges. Rosenblith and Allinsmith (1966) refer to "motivational and perceptual attributes as 'resultants' because they clearly are caused or affected by a combination of . . . determinants."

Among these determinants they include biological bases, learning, interpersonal experiences, settings and specific stimuli, group memberships, age or developmental stage, sex and intelligence. Among the motivational and perceptual attributes they include "conscience and conscientiousness; level of aspiration and need for achievement; intellectual efficiency (ability to use one's intelligence rather than degree of intelligence); capacity for sublimation in resolution of inner conflict; tendency to experience anxiety and its effect on school performance; and various other personality traits." The infant and the young child proceed toward conditions such as these, building *motivational resultants.*

Situations in which the infant or child finds himself play an important part in the development of motivational and perceptual attributes. Hunt (1965), discussing *situational influence,* says, "It is neither the individual differences among subjects, *per se,* nor the variations among situations, *per se,* that produce the variations in behavior. It is, rather, the interactions among these which are important." In the information processing of the child's exchange with his setting, optimal incongruity, too little or too much, may occur. "Motivation inheres within the organism's informational interaction with its environmental circumstances. . . . Whatever the essential character of this informational organism-environment interaction and its relationship to arousal turns out to be, there appears to be an optimum amount of it for each organism at any given time" (see pages 443-448).

Possibilities of motivational and perceptual attributes, as resultants of the child's own dimensions and of situations, are suggested in the following illustrations. Again, reference is to extremes.

In the *seeking of food* and the *seeking of rest* after activity, one infant or young child may be satisfied by a small amount; another may be satisfied by a large amount. In either instance, whether the situation lets him know there is enough food or enough time for rest presents a basis for associations. In the *seeking of physical and psychological activity* one infant may be quietly attentive to a moving toy hung above his crib; another may reach out for involvement with it. The stimulation of something to look at, something with distinctiveness prompting attentive reactions, adds schemata; otherwise they are not added. The child who is in a situation in which he is expected to use words, or in which he hears reference to ideas in conversation, or in looking at books, will have these stimulations whether he tends to be a talkative child or not. In the child's *seeking of relatedness to others,* whether he is very sociable or not, if he is in a situation in which others are responsive to him, he is adding associations different from those added when others are not responsive to him.

In the *seeking of some order without too much uncertainty, but with some variety,* the child is beginning to organize in thought the schemata which his experiences provide. In behavior with others he may seem to seek a steady discipline which helps him to adjust his needs and wishes to those of other people and to the facts and situations of the work-a-day world.

This can be a step toward the internalizing of standards; whether the child finds the steadiness in his situation or not, again, affects his development. Senn (in Gruenberg, 1951) said: "Discipline is seen first as something which reaches the infant from the external world, yet early in life becomes incorporated within the child. This point marks the beginning of self discipline, which is necessary for the happy and creative life of the individual in the social group." Further discussion of discipline follows on pages 443 to 448.

In the illustrations above, perceptual attributes of the child related to motivations would differ according to situations he had experienced. Futhermore, affect (or feeling) in his exchanges with his environment would differ according to constitutional factors and qualities of the situation. For example, in beginning to use words, or to be attentive to ideas suggested in conversation or books, the child could be beginning to internalize these particular standards of behavior. This internalization could occur whether he received signs of pleasure in the adult for the expected behavior or signs of displeasure when the behavior was not forthcoming. His perception of the adult and his feeling about him would not automatically reflect the positive or negative method; this would be one part of a more complex relationship. Furthermore, reference to complexities also seems appropriate when motivations pertaining to identification with others and imitation of models are being considered.

Conditions of Learning as Factors in Personality Development

Insight into learning may be furthered by consideration not only of tendencies such as those above, but also of immediate goals and settings. Thought concerns such questions as the following: What impels the child to respond? What situations produce what responses? What seems rewarding or satisfying to him? What strengthens the probability of his responding in a similar way another time? What lessens the probability? Ausubel (1949, 1957) suggested that attempts to answer such questions will follow different patterns, according to whether the person is secure or insecure.

Rewarding or satisfying experience has been described in many different ways. Stendler's (1952) discussion of the child's learning related to dependence and independence includes reference to various aspects of the mother to which the child reacts. Among these are physical contact, proximity, paying attention, verbal praise, helping when the child has begun a task and has encountered difficulties in repeating it. Thus a mother may let her three-year-old put on his shoes, but may help by pointing out which shoe goes on which foot and may tie the laces.

Such associations with an adult are conditions of practice, under which change in performance can occur. In other conditions of practice satisfying experience does not have immediate connections with other people. For example, fitting together a nest of boxes, graduated in size, may give the child a sense of achievement; being rewarded in this way may be a factor in his wanting to put the boxes together again. Likewise, dissatisfying experiences, perhaps with shoes or with boxes, may or may not have immediate connections with people. Nevertheless, especially for the infant and the young child, any recognition of his broader setting for personality development includes recognition of the subtleties of emotional relations between parents and children and a realization of the great significance of how the person feels, as well as of what he says or does.

Affection, discipline and ambition, or expectations, have long been considered key parts of the relations of parents and children and consequently parts of the child's growth and development. Such a concept includes the idea that qualities in parents' affection, discipline and expectations are related to qualities in the child's behavior.

Brief references to constitutional factors, motivational factors and conditions of learning tend to suggest many issues about the child's personality development. The following discussion of adult attitudes, for which thought or personality development provides a background, also suggests many issues. Issues concern evidence from research and theory, for or against ideas stated. Ideas may or may not seem well enough supported for inclusion in a philosophy of adult-child relations. Cross references suggest related evidence for use when the question is raised: What is illustrative content supporting or rejecting ideas such as these?

ATTITUDES OF THE ADULT

Affection Conducive to Growth

The emotional climate in many homes is, fortunately for the children in them, one in which more experience is on the side of warmth, understanding and mutual support than on the side of coldness, misunderstanding and lack of support. Some homes, unfortunately for the development of the children in them, create an atmosphere of antagonism, suspicion, distrust, selfishness and mutual competition that is not conducive to growth and development.

So much has been said about the importance of loving children enough that it also seems advisable to realize that too much of some forms of love is hampering. In some families, affection may take the form of constant deference to the child, showering him with gifts, protecting him too much from the ordinary hardships of life.

DEMONSTRATIVENESS. At one time, advocates of the behavioristic school of psychology (Watson, 1928) recommended that children be given no physical demonstrations of affection at all. There was to be no kissing, petting, rocking or holding of the child. The danger, they claimed, was that of making the child too dependent upon the parent, with the possibility that the child would become emotionally fixed upon the parent and unable to free himself later from this "silver cord." At present the adult's ease with the baby and the young child is emphasized. Adults, as well as children, differ in demonstrativeness. Some children need little more than kind treatment, interest, and an accepting tone of voice; they are busy with their own affairs, and too much caressing becomes an interference with their activities which they tend to brush off in a self-sufficient manner. Other children seem more dependent upon outward demonstrations of affection.

INDICATIONS OF AFFECTION WHICH MEETS NEEDS. Deviation from the usual in a particular child's emotional expression suggests to the parent, teacher or clinical examiner at least the possibility that his environment needs investigation. Apathy, extreme instability, excessive shyness or boldness, negativism, feelings of inadequacy, excessive demands for attention, jealousy and too great or too little dependence on adults may indicate difficulty. To judge affectional relations by watching for such symptoms is, of course, a negative approach. Well-loved children are busy with their own affairs, yet reach out for adult support when in difficulty; they tend to be happy, reasonably calm, accept physical routines, and give evidence of enthusiasm for life.

Abuse of the love relation between parents and children can come through the use of love as a disciplinary measure. "Mother loves you when you're good," "Daddy can't love you if you're bad," raise questions for the following reasons: if we love a child at all, we must of necessity lie to him when we say that a single bit of behavior can win or destroy that love. He may gain from such statements either an example of dishonesty or a false notion that love is something to be given or withdrawn as a reward or punishment for trivial bits of behavior. Confusion may occur. On the other hand, the child may sense what we really mean, which is different from our particular choice of words.

RESPONSIVENESS, CARE AND WARMTH. The infant's responses, stimulating for him in sensory and motor ways, are a part of an early affectional relation. Responsiveness of the adult to his behavior affects the infant's use of these abilities. Physical care also affects him. Particular practices cannot be singled out as the only effective or the most effective ones for parents to use. The uniqueness of the child, his parents and his own setting makes different practices warranted. Nevertheless agreement on the importance of constancy for the child of his particular type of care seems general. The child who was a "good" baby may be a very different $2\frac{1}{2}$-year-old if a situation such as the illness of his mother separated him from her at a crucial time.

Thinking not only of the infant, but also of years beyond the first one or two, one can attempt to clarify what the adult does to make the child feel sure of his affection. One observer, trying to identify in adults the factors that lead to the child's sense of trust, autonomy, initiative, achievement and other personality components, noted the following behavior in children of preschool age in a short period of time.

A child about to go down a slide asked an adult to stand near her. When a child discovered that his teacher, who had been absent, had returned, he came and stood beside her; she picked him up and held him on her lap as they both sat watching two other children build with blocks. When a boy heard other children talking about Hallowe'en, he turned to his mother and seemed reassured by her answer to his question, "Will it be Hallowe'en for me, too?"

Agreement on the importance of warmth as an attitude different from provision of stimulation or physical care is general. For detail concerning its description and for an attempt to summarize meaning of it and of other elements in affection for the child, see pages 135 to 138.

Discipline Leading to Self-Discipline

LOVE AND DISCIPLINE. In beginning to think about aspects of discipline on which questions are frequently raised, it is useful to review a range of ideas (see pp. 152-156). The fact that the words "discipline" and "punishment" are not interchangeable is clarified if it is recognized that discipline can come from outside the self or from within. It is control, toward which a variety of methods may contribute. Some parents seem to think that if one loves a child, one cannot or must not exert authority, expecting behavior contrary to the child's inclination or wish, or, vice versa, that if one is firm with a child, one cannot love him. This is a different assumption from the one in which the parent believes that he can love his child through any and all vicissitudes, yet provide reasonable discipline whenever it is needed. It is not a question of love *or* discipline; it is, rather, a question of love *and* discipline.

Growth in the direction of self-discipline is the adult's aim for the child. As the child grows older, it is hoped that he will assume more responsibility for his actions and will rely less on authority outside himself. Effective methods encouraging growth in this direction fit the child's stage of maturity, his personality and temperament, his particular actions and the situation of the moment. The parent who loves his child and observes him enough to see the effect of various methods can usually provide for continuous growth in which self-discipline is increasing.

FREEDOM AND CONTROL. One of the most frequently discussed topics of parents concerns obedience in relation to growth in self-discipline. "How can I make my child mind me?" "When should I insist?" Some parents do not stop to think about the matter at all, but live with their children from moment to moment, exacting behavior or excusing it by whim rather than by principle. If a discussion on the subject arises, however, there usually develop two extreme points of view and all grades of variations in between. On the one hand, some parents will say that they expect instant and unquestioning obedience from their children, on the ground that obedience is a difficult but necessary life lesson which must be learned early and thoroughly. On the other hand, some parents will say that the most important thing for children to learn is to make intelligent and independent decisions and to express their thoughts freely. Obedience as such, they say, has no place in adult-child relations and should never be exacted; all behavior should flow freely from within outward. Self-expression, in other words, would be supreme.

In general, it can be said that *extreme views about authority in self or in others raise many questions.* In this case neither extreme has the advantage of reasonable limits. Parents represent authority to the young child. The attitudes he develops toward them can be bases for attitudes toward authority in other situations and at later ages. Parents and others provide standards of one kind or another as the child develops a super-ego, or conscience, with which to discipline or control his own behavior.

If extreme rigidity in discipline trains the child to depend on other judgments than his own, he is not developing ability to think for himself. The freshman who enters college unable to decide where to live, what courses to take, what clothes to buy and which friends to make might reflect this background. On the other hand, if the child experiences very little discipline, he is not developing ability to consider judgments made by others. When he meets authority he might be one to be "handled with kid gloves," one who "flies off the handle" when given orders, or who "simply can't stand to be bossed."

WISDOM IN UNDERSTANDING REASONS. Discussion of questions on discipline sometimes concerns extent to which the child can understand reasons for a particular action. Ability to grasp reasons which are not immediately evident changes with age. The eighteen-month-old child and the four-year-old differ greatly in this respect. Furthermore, the child may learn that if parents are ready to explain reasons, they may be sidetracked from carrying out a particular procedure. Children may use "why" as a means of postponing adherence once they really understand the nature of the request given. There are certain emergency occasions when commands must be obeyed instantly for the sake of safety, as well as other occasions when the reasons behind requests would be incomprehensible to the child. Implied in both these cases is a habit of acceptance of an authority which the child has learned from experience is reasonable, consistent and interested in his welfare. In some instances the reasonableness of the authority may be based, not on the child's own safety and well-being, but rather on the welfare of others or, occasionally, on convention.

Attempts are sometimes undertaken to make specific certain elements in relations with authority. The following items, suggested by a group of parents, are of interest, since each lends itself to the question, *Why does the adult practice seem sound, or unsound, in the light of our present knowledge of child development?*

Before telling the child what is wanted, take care to gain his attention.
Use language the child can understand. A four-year-old, for example, does not understand, "In the upper right-hand drawer you'll find so-and-so."

Enunciate slowly enough and clearly enough to be sure that he follows you. Children of preschool age are still learning to distinguish the meanings of individual words.

Do not give too many suggestions at once. To execute three exceedingly simple directions in order, even if they are repeated at least once under concentrated attention before he sets out to obey, may be beyond the ability of the child under five.

Be consistent. Do not tell the child to do one thing today and a contrary thing tomorrow (but have flexibility as the occasion varies).

Tell him to do only the things you consider important and really intend to have him do. Do not, because you have not stopped to think, or simply to show your authority, give needless commands which you do not carry to completion or which you lightly withdraw when you realize their uselessness.

Be sure that you are reasonable and fair in your requirements; then see that they are carried out.

Try not to make demands or allot punishment in anger.

Do not use threats or bribes as a means of gaining compliance.

Do not make misbehavior interesting by making it exciting or profitable.

Differentiate behavior in which the child has a choice of action and behavior in which compliance is important.

ATTITUDES TOWARD AUTHORITY.   The child has experiences which can contribute to independent judgment of authority. The very young child, as well as the older person, seeks autonomy; each also finds in his living that he is constantly making adjustments to physical and to social law. He eventually recognizes that, no matter how much he may wish to place his hand on a hot stove without burning it, he may not do so because physical law dictates that he will be burned.

He learns that society has organized itself according to a mutually agreed upon set of traffic rules and that, even though as an individual he may wish to disregard a red traffic light, he may not do so without danger to his own life and the lives of other people because the rest of society regards the green light as a go signal. He discovers that there are certain rules for friendship—rules of fair play, of generosity, of respect for other people's wishes as well as for one's own—which can be broken only at the cost of loss of friendship. Thus infringement on social law or rule, like infringement on physical law, entails specific consequences.

Learning what constitutes a desirable adjustment to authority includes learning what constitutes a sound authority: what kind of law it is wise to obey; what kind of superior wisdom and experience it is desirable to consult. It also includes learning what constitutes an unsound authority: what kind of opinion it is wise to disregard; what kind of advice is worthless or vicious. The child who is proceeding toward self-discipline can include in this compliance with a "good" authority.

Wisdom in judgment of authority and action in accordance with it can come as the result of practice. Children whose thought processes have developed sufficiently assume such responsibility as rapidly as they have achieved enough experience to make their judgment sound; they can weigh facts and wisdom of others, yet value their own experience for whatever those experiences may be worth.

VARIATION OF AMOUNT OF SELF-DISCIPLINE WITH AGE AND ABILITY. In the process of growing up, situations involving adjustments to authority are always present. Control by nature, society, another person and oneself is always a part of the situation. On the other hand, decision to act in acceptable or responsible ways, whether or not authority in the form of another person or an immediate consequence is present, can increase with age. Ability of this kind is allied to the sense of integrity. It is also allied to conscience, i.e., internalized standards to which the individual conforms, regardless of pressures and regardless of whether he will be discovered (see p. 410). Even before the young child's thoughts have the breadth and depth which these terms imply, he is proceeding toward self-discipline in particular situations.

For example, in handling a book appropriately, a young child may at first have his hand guided by an adult's; later he may respond to verbal suggestions, a glance, the mere presence of the adult. Still later his response is correct even when the adult is not present. One observer looking for illustrations of different stages of self-discipline in a group of preschool children found the following in a short period of time: a child throwing a piece from a puzzle into the sandbox, then walking with an adult to get it to put back into the puzzle; a child pushing a doll buggy without bumping into others; a child hanging up wraps without reminder; a child playing in accordance with suggestions of another child, taking tickets for a train ride.

Whenever *methods which adults use in encouraging specific learnings* are the subject of research, there is the wish that particular practices could be identified which would be predictive of the child's development. But, understandably, highly correlated antecedent-consequent relations have not been found. Nevertheless many variables somewhat suggestive of trends have been identified. In research on information from interviews, Sears, Maccoby and Levin (1957) found a patterning of maternal behavior into "love-oriented techniques" (praise as a means of reward, isolation as a punishment, withdrawal of love as a punishment) and "object-oriented techniques" (tangible rewards as incentives and rewards, deprivation of privileges as a punishment, physical punishment). They reported "some relationship between the mother's high use of love-oriented techniques and the occurrence of confession and guilt about misbehavior in her child . . . and . . . apparent relevance of the dimension or trait to conscience development." Their reference to these dimensions as "fallible indicators" of deeper dimensions is a useful point in thinking of implications of this finding.

When a further distinction is made between positive love-oriented methods (such as praise and reasoning) and negative love-oriented methods (those which threaten the love relation to the parent, such as isolation, showing disappointment and withdrawing love), and other qualities of the parent, differences in development of the children have been noted. Becker (1964), reviewing consequences of parental discipline, says:

The negative love-oriented disciplines . . . relate to signs of conscience only when mother has a warm relation with the child. . . . Sears and associates (1957) found no correlation between withdrawal of love and conscience. However, when only warm mothers were considered, use of withdrawal of love related positively to signs of conscience.

For one of a number of ways of formulating suggestions for encouragement of growth in self-discipline, see page 156.

The idea that adult methods which are not severe can encourage learning at early ages gains support from much of the experimental research on learning with human subjects.

There is also evidence from animal experiments that punishment can have the effect of inhibiting behavior. When effects of physical punishment were investigated in attempts to relate procedures reported by parents to development of children, many complexities emerged. Becker (1964), referring to physical punishment (pain or discomfort), reports children's aggression as one consequence of a punitive approach to discipline:

In trying to understand the meaning of this relationship, we are faced with difficulties. First, a series of studies . . . provide rather overwhelming evidence that hostile parents have aggressive children. . . . Hostile parents also tend to use more physical punishment and less reasoning and praise. We are faced with a situation where certain techniques of discipline and certain emotional attitudes of the parent tend to occur jointly and have similar consequences for the child.

For information on interrelations of these variables and their opposites, further research is needed.

Another distinction to be made in studying effects of "power-assertive" techniques is between their immediate use with the child and their use after more positive methods have been tried without success. In a study by Hoffman (1960), mothers and fathers were interviewed about their interactions with the child on the day before the interview. Lack of a consistent pattern of relations was reported between certain dimensions of the child's behavior as observed in nursery school and either the father's immediate assertion of pressure or his use of it when the child did not comply initially. For the mothers, their assertion of pressure when the child did not comply initially was correlated with the child's hostility and assertion of power toward other children, but not toward the teacher.

When behavior of adults and children during a short period of time is studied, certain forms of behavior of the adult seem more likely to be paralleled by certain forms of behavior in the child. For example, after on-the-scene observations of mothers and their children of preschool age at home, Lafore (1945) made the following tentative generalizations:

The parents who presented the smallest number of affectionate advances to their children received the largest number of affectionate advances from their children.

The parents who presented the largest number of instances of dictating and interfering with their children received the largest number of expressions of hostility from their children.

Parents who showed large numbers of instances of blaming, hurrying, punishing, threatening, and interfering had children who presented large numbers of instances of crying.

The parents who represented many instances of ignoring the child and diverting the child received many instances of teasing or nagging from the child.

The parents who interfered most often with their children encountered large numbers of instances of resistance by them.

This detail is included here because the items lend themselves to thought on the question: *What knowledge concerning autonomy, dependence and independence seems pertinent in considering statements such as these?*

Material included in this section on discipline suggests some of the responses in the child to which the adult may give thought as he explores effects of particular methods. Information on parent-child relations* is varied partly because of the wide range of possibilities from which particular elements have been selected for particular studies. Furthermore, equally satisfactory adjustment of children in different families can be the outcome of entirely different practices (Langdon and Stout, 1952).

Expectations Adapted to the Child's Own Pattern

Every child has a unique pattern of growth and development. If parents try to force growth into a more rapid pace or into a pattern different from the child's own, it may be because the child is an extension of the parents' egos. In this sense the child is sometimes allied to the most intimate thoughts and secret ambitions of his parents. This may involve the parents' unwillingness to grant the child a personality of his own. It may mean that the parents are self-effacing and make every sacrifice that their child may have possessions and privileges denied them in their own childhood. We hear these parents say, "Bob will never have to work as I had to," or, "Betty is going to have all the good times I missed when I was a girl."

So far as work and suffering are a detriment to growth, children should, of course, be protected from them. It is also recognized, however, that a certain amount of striving for achievement, of struggle for fulfillment, is satisfying as well as fundamental to development. Overprotected children, like overindulged children, may be denied the opportunity for strength and satisfactions which struggle gives.

REASONS FOR EXPECTATIONS. Less specific than the urge to live vicariously a previously missed detail of joy or disappointment through the child is the general urge to find success through the child in no matter what form. In this case the parents do not force any specific career on the child, but insist on success wherever the child seems most

---

* Methodological problems are discussed and illustrations of theory and research on parent-child relations are included in Glidewell (1961) and Medinnus (1967).

likely to achieve it. When parents, refusing to recognize mediocre or inferior ability or ability in other directions in the child, drive him to specific performances, this may produce great strain for him. Or, if a particular accomplishment cannot materialize for him, the child's feeling that he has failed to meet the expectations of his parents can be distressing. Continued disappointment of the parents in the child can produce a decrease in self-esteem.

The urge of parents for a feeling of success through their child may take another form. "He is mine. How well I am preparing him for the complex modern world," may be an overgratification. It is a natural accompaniment of parental love to wish to see the child succeed. It is not this wish or intention that hampers development; often the very wish for success and the faith that it will come contribute to it in the child. Difficulty arises when the intention or orientation behind the wish is gratification of the parent.

Illustrations of the influence of external factors on the mother's behavior in an experimental situation are given in Bishop (1951) and Merrill (1946). After being told that the child had not realized his full capacities during a play period, the mother, in the next session, showed an increase in the following responses: directing the child's activity, interfering, criticizing, making changes in his activity. Mothers in the control group who did not receive the mild criticism did not show changes. A positive relation between specific control by the mother and reluctant cooperation by the child was reported.

The complexity of distinctions between encouragement and over-influence of parental expectations implied in the previous discussion is also evident when thought concerns the child's interest in achievement. The parent's interest in the child's achievement has an influence on his accomplishment. Encouragement of self-reliance, of learning to learn, contributes to accelerated performance.

There is, of course, a contrast to the parent, or other adult, who seems to be pressing the child for greater achievement than he is able to have, or for accomplishments in areas not in accordance with the child's interests. At the other extreme is the parent, or other adult, whose disinterest or inability does not encourage development of a potentiality the child has (see pp. 352-357).

Adult expectations adjusted to the capacity and the interest of the child are not easily accomplished even by the person whose attitude or intention is of this kind. Interest in discovering what the child manages without undue stress, which also develops his capacities, seems to be an attitude appropriate for a wide range of background and abilities. Attention of the adult and the child can be oriented toward effort as well as product, and toward a concept of success broadened to include disposition, and individual and social points of view, and not limited to prowess in motor, cognitive or social situations.

DEVELOPMENT THROUGH EXPECTATION OF USE OF ABILITY. It can be seen that parent-child relations change as the child grows. In early infancy the child is completely dependent on the parent for every-thing—his physical well-being, psychological stimulation, emotional security. As he grows he gradually takes over for himself his own physical care, his pursuit of interest and his social contacts; his emotional security passes gradually from being centered in his parents to being centered in others and in things and situations under his own control. As he develops he becomes less dependent on his parents for support, for thinking and decision-making, and for security.

Socially, his exposure to other people's standards and ideas beyond those of his family comes by around two years or even sooner. It progresses as he is exposed to other children and the patterns of behavior and standards the parents of these other children hold for them. In school he is under the supervision of the teacher; he is deeply influenced by the ideas and ideals of his peers. Ultimately he must live economically, socially and emotionally as an adult, influenced by qualities in his affectional ties with his parents, yet independent in his decisions and his behavior and in his choice of friends and of his mate. Parents can think of their children at all stages of development as proceeding in these directions.

Any reference to dimensions of behavior of adults and their associations with behavior of children would tend to be qualified by saying that this dimension is one of many and that relative proportions among various dimensions seem pertinent. With this in mind, there are many variables in considering the adult's expectations of the child's use of his abilities. A few clues to dimensions in the adult and the child can be illustrated as follows.

Adult *encouragement of expression of ideas, the fostering of social development,* and *absence of overprotection* seem related to children's behavior. Grant (1939) found that parental overprotection was related to children's dependent behavior, submissiveness and withdrawal from the group. Encouragement of expression of ideas was related to cooperative, self-reliant behavior, perseverance and resourcefulness on the part of children.

Subtle factors in parents' attitudes, as contrasted to specific practices of one kind or another, can influence behavior. For example, Brody (1956), after studying mothers and infants as the infants were fed, said:

> Direct observation may not reveal the presence of conflict, but a mother's capacity to make the early feeding experience of her child satisfying can probably be assessed if the observer bears in mind the three sets of criteria that have been brought forward: the first relates to the mother's *sensitivity to the infant's needs;* the second, to her *use of physical space, time and communication* during feeding; and the third, to her choice of feeding methods and the *motives for her choice.* The three sets of criteria . . . contain overlapping features.

These dimensions have implications for situations other than the feeding situation.

The adult's being *relaxed* instead of tense seems related to behavior of the child. For example, Macfarlane (1943, 1954) reported that fewer problems were found among children of relaxed mothers than among those of mothers who were worrisome, uneasy or tense in their relations to their children.

It is important to recall the complexity of relations of parents and children and also the variations in ways of behaving and believing in different social groups. No simple cause-and-effect connections can be established. Sanford's (1943) emphasis on syndromes seems important. He considers different patterns of "family press" in terms of different personality structures of the children. Again, the interrelation of many factors is the pertinent point.

A parents' acceptance of and confidence in both himself and his mate can be related to expectations of behavior in the child in many ways. Sears, Maccoby and Levin (1957) referred to this dimension in the mother as important in general family adjustment. Wanting her child to develop toward mature status is referred to as a part of responsible child-training orientation. Achieving further independence need not mean that the child is weaned away from the love of parents and home. Quite the contrary. The child who can gradually become an independent personality within his home has a strong basis for devotion and loyalty to parents.

Encouraging the child's use of his abilities seems related not only to his becoming an adult who earns a living and adjusts to other people, but also to his becoming an adult who *lives happily with himself*. In doing this he accepts himself with all the assets and liabilities which he, along with everyone else, has. (See Chapter Eleven for concepts of self and of others and of the world.) He discovers and trusts his talents and capacities, somehow fitting his own peculiar special skills and talents to the life demands around him. He also accepts whatever liabilities or handicaps there are in his particular make-up. From his earliest adventures in living the infant can learn joy in using whatever ability he has and can, at the same time, learn to accept the fact that he is not all-perfect or all-powerful. He can find pleasure in the exercise of his capacities, yet accept the fact that there are some things in which he cannot "be the best in the whole world."

High standards which require genuine hard work to accomplish have a function; yet these standards can be so high that the child develops a constant sense of failure and inadequacy. (See Chapter Four for information on need for security, dependence and independence.) One of the greatest skills in parents and other adults can be the ability to gauge expectations of the child to fit the child's readiness (see Chap. One) and yet to set the stage in such a fashion that the child learns early the joy of success achieved through genuine effort.

TOPICS FOR STUDY AND DISCUSSION

1. As a focus for study, phrase several of your beliefs about adult-child relations concerning each of the following: personality development, affection, discipline, expectations adapted to the child's pattern. Indicate content related to your selections by illustrative references to theory, research and observation.

Affection

1. Consider several publications of a popular type in an attempt to discover how suggestions to parents represent use of knowledge from theory and research concerning child development.
   For example:
   Children's Bureau Publication. A Creative Life for Your Child, by Margaret Mead. Washington, D.C., U.S. Government Printing Office, 1962.
   Children's Bureau Publication. Infant Care. Washington, D.C., U.S. Government Printing Office, 1963.
   Children's Bureau Publication. Your Child from One to Six. Washington, D.C., U.S. Government Printing Office, 1962.
   Ginott, H. G. Between Parent and Child. New York, Macmillan Company, 1965.
   Hymes, J. L.: The Child Under Six. Washington, Educational Services, 1961.
2. In observing relations of children and adults look for illustrations of a sensitive attitude concerning an individual child on the part of an adult and for illustrations of a sensitive attitude concerning an individual adult on the part of a child.

Discipline

1. Read several types of articles concerning discipline in an attempt to decide what you agree or disagree with in their points of view, and why.
   For example:
   Discipline (Bulletin of Association for Childhood Education). Washington, D.C., Association for Childhood Education.
2. In observing a group of preschool children note illustrations of self-discipline in children of two, three and four years. Note effect of different adult methods, such as explaining, using force, arranging for logical sequence of events, example, expectation of a cooperative spirit, connection with reward, bribe, threat, deprival of privilege.
3. Report a situation or incident with a child and an adult in which you were a participant or observer, and attempt to decide what the child was seeking, what the adult was seeking, and the effects of their behavior.

Expectations Adapted to the Child's Pattern

1. Have a panel discuss ways of deciding whether a child is using his abilities well. What are signs that standards are too high, too low, appropriate?
2. Select a reference to research to consider thoroughly. Report on it in terms of its connection with a particular area, point of view or question of interest to parents.

SELECTED READINGS

Association for Childhood Education: Theme of December, 1967, issue of Childhood Education is "Teaching Is Growing."

Becker, W. C.: Consequences of Different Kinds of Discipline; in M. L. Hoffman and L. W. Hoffman (Eds.): Review of Child Development Research, Vol. 1. New York, Russell Sage Foundation, 1964, pp. 169-176.

Burton, R. V., Maccoby, E. E., and Allinsmith, W.: Antecedents of resistance to temptation in four-year-old children. Child Development, 32:689-710, 1961.

Crandall, V. J., et al.; Maternal reactions and the development of independence and achievement behavior in young children. Child Development, 31:243-251, 1960.

Gewirtz, J. L., and Baer, D. M.: The effect of brief social deprivation on behaviors for a social reinforcer. J. Abnorm. Soc. Psychol., 56:49-56, 1958.

Read, K. H.: The Nursery School. Philadelphia, W. B. Saunders Co., 1966. Chap. 9, Defining and Maintaining Limits for Behavior.

Sears, R. R., Maccoby, E. E., and Levin, H.: Patterns of Child Rearing. Evanston, Ill., Row, Peterson & Company, 1957. Chap. 13, The Sum and Substance.

CHAPTER THIRTEEN

Early Years: Foundation for Later Growth and Development

There was a child went forth every day,
And the first object he look'd upon, that object he became,
And that object became part of him for the day or a certain
*   part of the day,*
Or for many years or stretching cycles of years.

The early lilacs became part of this child,
And grass and white and red morning-glories, and white and
*   red clover, and the song of the phoebe-bird,*
. . . . .
And the fish suspending themselves so curiously below
*   there, and the beautiful curious liquid,*
And the water-plants with their graceful flat heads, all became
*   part of him.*
— Walt Whitman: Leaves of Grass *— There Was a Child Went*
*   Forth.*

This is a poet's way of saying that a child is the sum of his life's transactions.

With the directing force of his genetic make-up the individual utilizes his experiences to make himself the person he is. This is also demonstrated in Figure 1 (p. 6), in which are indicated the ongoing processes and the interaction of the aspects of life all being affected by, and in turn affecting, the environment. This is true of an infant, a preschooler, a school-age child or an adolescent. Changes take place as the child develops, expands his abilities, both physical and psychological, and reacts with greater maturity to his experiences.

For example, the newborn's activity is involuntary. Later he is able to direct his movements and can reach for something; still later, distance is no longer an obstacle and he can go and get the object. He can use that object for a variety of purposes. From birth he has sensory and motor behavior with accompanying satisfactions in the activity; these occur along with his associations with the people of his family. The newborn has very limited means of communication, and seemingly does not differentiate between himself and his environment. He gradually becomes aware of what is himself and what is outside himself. He increases his means of communication, first in nonverbal ways, and later by verbalization and increasing competence in the use of language. He begins with sensory behavior in response to stimulus sources. He gets information from his surroundings and develops perceptions of dimensions of difference in the objects and sounds of his world. His concepts and thoughts grow in complexity. In the course of these changes immediate satisfactions and dissatisfactions influence behavior. Change is also brought about by attachments to people and the modeling of behavior. Through his interactions with his world the child's personality, with its unique attributes, develops. His feelings and his knowledge serve as a basis for meeting the familiar and the new of each day. His life provides abundantly or meagerly for the needs which are fundamental for his development.

These transactions take place on different levels and with different aspects. There is the interaction in the cell between the nuclear material, the chromosomes and the cytoplasm. There is also the interaction between cells, between larger units of the body, the organs and systems which make up the biological unit. This biological aspect of life, which never operates alone, interacts with the psychological aspects to produce behavior. Both the biological and psychological systems operate in, are affected by, and affect the environment, both material and personal.

This book has dealt with a segment of life, the first five or six years and the preceding nine months of development, i.e., from the time of conception to the child's entrance into school. Development during these years lays foundations for later development. It portrays basic principles of development: namely, continuity, sequential patterns, tempo, individuality, interrelatedness and plasticity. It also depicts basic needs of an individual and effects of abundant or meager fulfillment. This fulfillment varies with age, not in the needs themselves, but in the manner and degree of fulfillment commensurate with developmental level.

What happens to the child in these early years not only is vital to his welfare at the moment, but also provides constitutional attributes he brings to the next span of years of his life. The search has been for explanations and, thus, for insight into the powers, or competences, of the individual in preschool years, in later childhood, adolescence and adult life. Early experiences have been explored to find possible antecedents of later consequences in physical, emotional, intellectual and social areas. Some of the pressing concerns include mental health, sufficient knowledge of the modern world, juvenile delinquency, obesity, heart disease in middle life. Through research on the early years and of a longitudinal nature there is hope of learning about the roots of the developmental sequences and the ramifications of these conditions.

This chapter will summarize the developmental achievements of this period and, so far as is known, suggest how much an individual's development and behavior at this early age can foretell the future.

SUMMARY OF DEVELOPMENT

The Newborn

The newborn in the United States generally weighs between $5\frac{1}{2}$ and $9\frac{1}{2}$ pounds, is around 19 to 21 inches long, and has a large head and small trunk and legs. The head may be temporarily misshapen as a result of molding during passage through the pelvic outlet at birth. The cranial part of the head predominates, and the mandibular section of the face is less developed than the maxillary. The skin is red and wrinkled. Hair may be abundant on the head, but is no indication of the amount and texture of later hair. The infant lies with arms, legs and fingers flexed. Legs are bowed. His abdomen is large. The eyes produce no tears. He has a repertory of activities—sucking, perhaps even his thumb; grasping so firmly that he can support his weight if suspended by his hands, making stepping movements when his body is firmly supported and feet touch ground; making primitive crawling movements; coughing; sneezing; yawning; crying; sleeping.

Birth, with its adjustments to extrauterine life, tests the integrity of all the systems of the body. It is the final test of the success of the development which took place during the nine months of intrauterine life. These adjustments in breathing, circulation, digestion and elimination of waste begin promptly at birth, but become perfected only gradually. For example, the expansion of lungs begins with the first breath, but is completed days later. During this process the infant may breathe irregularly. Also, the homeostatic mechanisms by which the stabilization of biochemical substances and physiologic activities are maintained are immature, as is easily observed in the newborn's inability to maintain a constant body temperature under changing conditions.

Nevertheless the newborn is equipped with the necessary development of structure and function to meet immediate needs. He breathes and thus takes in oxygen and releases carbon dioxide. A sucking reflex and activities of the digestive tract assure nourishment; urination and defecation provide for the elimination of other wastes.

In sensory equipment, the sense of touch is developed, with special sensitivity around the mouth. The newborn responds to bright light and to loud sound. In visual behavior he looks often or longer toward one object or pattern than toward another, thus suggesting differentiation of stimuli. He is relatively insensible to small differences in environmental temperature. Although responses of taste and smell are minimal when compared with those of adults, the newborn responds positively to the taste of sweetness, but negatively to salt, bitter and sour. Smell is developed to a degree which enables him to differentiate odors. With repetition of sensory stimulation, response diminishes, and then, with novel stimulation, recovery of response occurs, thus suggesting some central process of the nervous system, i.e., learning process. Orienting reactions are indicated by autonomic and other involuntary responses during response to stimuli of the external environment.

The newborn's behavior is dominated by the subcortical centers of the brain. It consists mainly of diffuse mass activity and reflexes. This diffuse mass activity is generalized and random, as can be seen during sucking and crying. It is incited more from within the body than from without. It is noticed, for example, when the infant is hungry or is having a bowel evacuation. There are also some specific movements, such as head movements, flexion, extension, rotation and the like of arms and legs. Reflexes which are specific, stereotyped and involuntary are numerous and important. They can be classified according to the region of the body involved (Ausubel, 1957): (1) eyes, (2) upper respiratory and gastrointestinal tracts, (3) abdominal and pelvic viscera, (4) head and neck, (5) arm and hand, (6) trunk, (7) leg and foot, (8) coordinate responses. These types of behavior form the dominant patterns of the newborn's behavior, i.e., crying, feeding, sleeping, and response to pain. Response to sensory stimulation of the outside world is also a part of the newborn's behavior.

Patterned emotions are absent. At this time there seems to be a generalized reaction suggestive of pleasantness or unpleasantness. For further details about the newborn, the student is referred to Ausubel (1957), Lipsitt (1966), Pratt (1954), Smith (1959), Thomas et al. (1963), and Vaughan (1964).

Physical Achievement

Much has happened in the life of a five-year-old as development progressed from a single cell to a highly differentiated and integrated organism which can function with considerable independence. In size he will have more than doubled his height; increased his weight a little more than fourfold; achieved about two-thirds of his adult height, 62.35 and 67.35 per cent for boys and girls, respectively (Bayley, 1962), and about one-third of his weight at eighteen (Stuart and Stevenson, 1959). Growth rate has changed from a rapid to a slower tempo. With this reduced tempo of growth and his growing absorption in his activities and the world about him, appetite often decreases during the second year and throughout the preschool years.

Body proportions are changing. Legs have tripled their length, while stem length has less than doubled. Components of weight change. At five years of age the subcutaneous fat layer is half as thick as it was at nine months (Stuart and Stevenson, 1959). Muscle has a similar pattern of growth, but a slower tempo than growth in size. Greater muscle development comes in early adolescence. The physique which will be characteristic of the child has begun to emerge. The tendency for leanness or muscular solidarity is evident. All deciduous teeth have erupted for most children. Bones have not only grown in size, but also have matured. All but one of the bones of the wrist have appeared, and all the epiphyses of the hand and wrist are present. The child of five has achieved a body balance in accordance with his development. The knock-knees and pronation which are characteristics of many young children are beginning to disappear. The abdomen is still prominent. Adult posture does not appear until adolescence.

The growth of the nervous system has been so rapid that it has achieved 90 per cent of its adult size. Changes in functioning from that of a reflex and less differentiated level (newborn) have been to more and more functioning under cortical control. This means that more behavior containing a planned element in the mode of reaction, a latency of response and a fertile variety of responses are observed during this period. Changes in the functioning of the brain are indicated by changes in brain waves. By five years the smaller, faster waves which replace the earlier, slow waves predominate most of the time.

The five-year-old shares family foods at mealtime. He has acquired habits and feelings about food from his experiences with it from the very beginning of his life. Elimination, defecation and urination are under voluntary control, and he has become aware of the social customs relating to them. His sleep habits and attitudes have developed according to his needs and experiences and reflect family attitudes and relations.

Some differences between boys and girls are apparent from infancy; others emerge as the children develop. In the physical aspect the dichotomy becomes most pronounced at early adolescence. From birth girls tend to be more mature than boys. This is indicated in skeletal maturation and in the percentage of adult height achieved at any age. There is generally a small difference in height and weight at birth in favor of boys, but this difference is relatively small and does not tend to increase in these early years. The height and weight of boys and girls at five years of age tend to be similar. Stuart and Stevenson (1959) give two sets of height and weight for five-year-olds from two sources. The fiftieth percentile for height of boys and girls, respectively, from one source is 42.8 and 42.9 inches, and from the other is 43.8 and 43.2 inches. The fiftieth percentile for weight is 40.5 and 40.5 pounds from one source and 42.8 and 41.4 from the other. In the time of eruption of deciduous teeth we see no sex differences.

Personality Achievements

In study of the thinking, feeling and acting of the child of five or six, i.e., his personality, one is aware of the tremendous contrast with the newborn. Areas in which change has occurred include the following: general use of the body in skillful coordination; eye-hand coordination in precise movements; accurate sensory perceptions; a variety of uses of language; complexity of problem solving, concepts and thoughts; self-expression in many forms of creativity. Intellectual activities have these resources. Furthermore, concepts of self, of others and of the world have not only greater objectivity, but also many personal connotations which emotional and social behavior of the individual add. The child during infancy and the preschool years incorporates within himself his sense of trust in others, in self and in things, a sense of autonomy and initiative at a time when they are especially important. His sense of accomplishment, identity, closeness to others and integrity are in their early forms. These are his foundations for later development.

Kagan (1966), discussing psychological development of the child, suggests "salient responses" associated with different chronologic periods and "environmental events that appear to be most influential in shaping the form of the final response." In the early period from birth forward,

. . . learning to expect nurturance from human agents, associating positive affect (or emotion of pleasure) with adults, and learning to display facial and vocal reactions to adults are primary dispositions acquired during the first 18 months. This 18 month period is regarded as critical because of the belief that absence of a regularly nurturant caretaker leads the child to withdraw from the social environment. . . .

Among biologically based differences in infancy Kagan includes vigor of activity, threshold for attention to external stimuli, and irritability threshold. "At our present level of knowledge it is reasonable to suggest that these and others are *unlearned* behavioral dispositions . . . present at birth, that some of these are stable over time and facilitate or impede the acquisition of particular motives, anxieties, and actions as a result of the special behaviors the child elicits in the caretaker."

In the period from eighteen months to three years when the child is developing locomotion, perceptions and language, he is also experiencing "socialization demands by the parents." He is "learning to inhibit responses that have strong motivational qualities." He is also developing "the capacity to experience anxiety at mother's absence or signs of maternal withdrawal of nurturance." The years three to six include "increasingly important interactions with the father and siblings. Moreover, the acquisition of new beliefs and actions, previously determined solely by patterns of reward and punishment, is powered by a uniquely human motive — *the desire to increase behavioral similarity to a model.*" Processes in identification (including feelings, beliefs, desires, imitation) contribute to changes in the child's behavior.

FORECASTING THE FUTURE

What has happened up to five or six years of age will affect later development. This is true in all aspects of development and is expressed in the basic concept of continuity or orderliness of development. How the future will be built on the past will depend, of course, on the interplay of intrinsic and extrinsic forces. Individuality in potential, pattern and speed of development will be responsible for variety in developmental trends.

There is great interest in forecasting or predicting from a present developmental status into the future. What kind of personality will the child have? Will he change? How intelligent will he be? How tall or heavy? What motivations or goals will influence him? These questions are raised for both theoretical and practical reasons.

Forecasting Physical Development

In physical development the interest may focus on size and maturation. Studies have been done on the relation of size in the early and later years and in predicting adult stature. Bayley (1954) showed that there is a fair degree of stability in height after the first year by correlations between height at eighteen years and one month as 0.64 for boys and 0.37 for girls, at one year 0.72 and 0.65, and at five years 0.86 and 0.84, respectively. Bayley stated that these correlations indicate that tall infants tend to be tall adults, and short infants, short adults, but the relation is not perfect. There will be those who change their status.

Bayley (1962) also explored methods of prediction using percentage of mature height and skeletal age to increase precision. Prediction of mature height can be made using skeletal age with a good degree of accuracy later than the preschool years (Bayley, 1946; Bayley and Pinneau, 1952). She found that the error in prediction from one year on is reduced for all except the young boys if skeletal age is taken into account. For the first four years the use of skeletal age does not improve prediction for the boys. She concluded from data from the Berkeley Growth Study and from the Harvard Longitudinal Study (Stuart) "that growth is not exactly predictable from the early years, whatever method we use. In many children we can predict fairly closely, but for an occasional child our predictions could be off as much as eight to twelve cm., or three to five inches." Bayley further stated that this error is probably inevitable in view of the present knowledge of the processes of growth.

Studies of growth show three periods: steady growth from three to nine years preceded and followed by periods of more rapid growth. Individual growth curves indicate these periods, but vary in timing and intensity of growth.

About the factors responsible for this pattern, Bayley (1962) states:

> It appears as though growth in the first three years is directed primarily by one set of factors, perhaps a combination of genetic and thyroid, during midchildhood by another, e.g., pituitary growth hormone, and at puberty by the steroid hormones that also accelerate the epiphyseal closure in the skeleton with concurrent termination of growth in height.

Reed and Stuart (1959) also gave evidence about the relation of growth in the early years to later growth. In the Harvard Longitudinal Growth study they classified the patterns of growth in height and weight by dividing the entire age period into three intervals: under six years, six to twelve years, and twelve to eighteen years. Individuals were classified in accordance with the magnitude of increment in each age interval as having slow, rapid or moderate growth. "The rate of growth during early childhood, i.e., before six years of age, is associated with, but not specifically predictive of, size at maturity and timing of the adolescent growth spurt. Individuals with rapid growth before six years of age tend to have large mature size and early adolescent growth spurt."

Use of skeletal age instead of chronologic age increases the degree of accuracy of prediction of adult stature, especially as the steroid phase of growth is approached.

Information on parental size also increases degree of accuracy of prediction, especially for children of tall or short parents. In recently constructed parent-specific age-size tables for boys and girls (Garn, 1966; Garn and Rohmann, 1966) parental size categories are included; the midparent value is the average of the paternal and maternal statures at age thirty. "Even at one year of age, the children so categorized [as having short (163 cm), median (169 cm) or tall (175 cm) midparent value] are a centimeter or more apart. At age eighteen the difference is 2.4 cm (approximately one inch) or more" (Garn, 1966).

Maresh (1959) examined the sequential picture of the relative length of bones of the arms and legs as a measure of linear body proportions. This study of linear body proportions in terms of length in relation to height in the longitudinal growth study at the Denver Child Research Council revealed shifts in percentile levels from one year to early adulthood. Less than one-third of the individuals maintained a constant percentile level in relative bone lengths or sitting height during this period. In general, shifts to higher or lower percentiles occurred in infancy and adolescence. From four years to adolescence the percentile positions were usually stable with only minor deviations. Changes were rarely of extreme magnitude. A very short-legged infant might have median length legs, but not relatively long legs in adolescence.

Just as there are fast, slow or moderate growers in height and weight, so there are those who are on a fast, slow or moderate schedule of physical maturation. One measure of physical maturation is that of the skeleton (see Chap. Eight). Here, as in the case of height and weight patterns, we find individuals who are consistently fast, slow or moderate in maturation from early childhood and those who change in tempo.

Pyle et al. (1959) reported on patterns of skeletal development of the hand, as assessed by the Greulich-Pyle atlas, of 133 children of the Harvard Growth Study followed periodically from birth to eighteen years of age. The patterns were classified as moderate, slow, fast or irregular, and the changes noted from one category to another. Thirty-five of the 133 children were consistent throughout, thirty-five changed to a faster rate, fifteen to a slower rate, thirty changed twice, eighteen had irregular patterns. Thus it was found (1) that individuals varied in their rate of progress, (2) that some were consistent, (3) that few were very irregular, (4) that many made one or two "substantial shifts" in rate from one period to another and (5) that the most common shift occurred between childhood and adolescence.

Further study of these same cases relating to the onset, completion and span of ossification, using the bone growth centers of the hand and the wrist, indicated that completion of ossification does not follow the same time order as onset. This study revealed that the time order of onset differs significantly from the time order of completion. Correlation between onset and completion ages shows that onset age does not forecast completion age. Therefore one cannot predict completion of ossification of bones by the time of the onset of ossification.

These studies of growth and skeletal maturation indicate that the concept of orderliness or continuity is demonstrated, but to the degree of association rather than accurate prediction of later development from development in the early years.

Forecasting Personality Development

In personality development the interest may focus on cognition, including concept formation, problem solving and creativity. It may also focus on behavioral intentions, motivations or goals as relations to a world of people, of things and of ideas are considered. Early choices among stimuli selected by the individual for attentive response may be the point of departure for a look from the early years toward later ages. In a number of these areas it is agreed that knowledge is limited or not even available. Ways of attempting to measure them are just beginning to be devised as a first step in collection of data which may have possibilities for study of predictions. In many instances in which methods of measurement have been devised and findings have been reported, conclusions are stated tentatively, and the wish for more satisfactory means of assessment is expressed.

More longitudinal detail is available for intelligence than for other areas. Sontag, Baker and Nelson (1958) showed some stability in intelligence test performance by correlation of 0.64 between intelligence quotients at three years and at seven years, and of 0.46 between intelligence quotients at three years and at twelve years. When the first test was at four years, correlation of intelligence quotients of that age with those at seven years is 0.70, and at twelve years is 0.43. When acceleration and deceleration in mental growth rate from three to six years and from six to ten years were investigated, certain personality factors were predictive. From three to six years, if the child was not overdependent on his parents and was learning to meet some of his needs through individual problem solving, this was reported to be a groundwork for motivation in need for achievement. In elementary years a high need for achievement was related to an accelerated mental growth rate. Need for achievement, competitive striving and curiosity were included in another report (Kagan et al., 1958) as predictive of intelligence quotient gain from age six to age ten.

According to Pinneau (1961), predictions of intelligence test scores can be more accurate if the scores are transformed into deviation intelligence quotients to take into account variations in size of standard deviations of the Stanford-Binet test at different ages. This would mean recognition of age changes in variability for the Stanford-Binet test scales. For subjects of the Berkeley Growth Study tested at two years and at subsequent ages, the median intelligence quotient score change is 14 from two to seven years and 20 from two to seventeen years. By use of another scoring procedure the deviation intelligence quotient score change has a median of 13 from two to seven years and 14 for two to seventeen years. For subjects tested at three years the median score change is 10 from three to seven years, 16 from three to seventeen years; the median deviation intelligence quotient score changes for these ages are 13 and 13. Thus 50 per cent of the subjects change as little, or as much, as the value specified (the median). Using information on quartiles, 25 per cent of subjects change as little as 4 points and 25 per cent as much as 17 points or more in intelligence quotient scores from three to seven years (6 and 24 are the figures for deviation score changes).

Jones (1960), in a discussion of the longitudinal method of study of personality, referred to a study of patterns of emotional expression and their relation to other aspects of personality. A physiologic reaction, the galvanic skin response, was used as a measure of autonomic activity, *inner or visceral response in emotional disturbance.* Crying in the infant is an example of an external sign, as contrasted to an internal sign, of emotional disturbance. The galvanic skin response in infants was of smaller magnitude and less easy to arouse than in older children. It was elicited in the first few weeks of life by "emotionally disturbing or mildly unpleasant" physical stimuli.

At nursery school age some individuals had fairly consistent patterns. "These patterns are of at least three sorts, as represented by the 'externalizer,' who displays a somewhat infantile pattern of marked overt but reduced or infrequent galvanic responses; the 'internalizer,' who reverses this relationship; and the 'generalizer,' who tends to respond with a total discharge both overt and internal."

At ages eleven to eighteen, on the basis of repeated testing, 20 per cent of the subjects at each extreme were selected for study. The two extremes were high and low reactives on the galvanic skin response. "Perhaps the most striking fact about the 'high reactive' group is the overt characteristic that may be termed *motor restraint.* In general, they were quiet, reserved, and deliberative. . . . The 'low reactives,' relatively unresponsive in the galvanometer records, present a very different picture in motor, emotional, and social traits." Their talkativeness, animation and motor activity were high. Bossiness, attention-seeking and irritable impulsiveness "not always compatible with smooth social relationships" were more frequent.

When information at ages thirty-three to thirty-seven years was compared to adolescent records, the higher reactive group on the galvanic skin response was more symptom-free in the sense of having fewer problems that could be traced to a psychological origin.

Jones (1960), referring to a repetition of this galvanic skin response experiment, said; "Our purpose is to learn something about long-term consistency in emotional patterns, and also to test the prediction that trends in one variable, such as a moderately increasing galvanic skin response, will be accompanied by trends in another, such as an increased socialization and impulse control."

Promising leads for further study of prediction from early to later ages come from information reported by Escalona and Heider (1959). Escalona read detailed records of infants first observed with their mothers at four to thirty-two weeks of age, and then wrote predictions in the form of clinical and inferential rating judgments for preschool behavior. These predictions were later compared with outcomes, i.e., records based on actual behavior when the majority of subjects were four years to five years eleven months of age. Correct predictions were more frequent in some areas than in others. Variables which their explorations suggested as promising for future research included activity level, for which predictions were among the most successful. *Amount and vigor of physical movement*, i.e., *activity level*, were considered of particular interest because of psychoanalytic theory that it may be predictive of balance between impulse and control, with capacity for control or delay of impulse expression allied with capacity for abstract thinking and verbal symbol formation.

Escalona and Heider found that most of the subjects for whom high perceptual sensitivity had been predicted in infancy actually showed this behavioral characteristic at preschool age. *Sensory thresholds* were of particular interest because of the theory that they are possible codeterminants (play a predisposing role) in development of later psychological functioning in expressive behavior (such as gestures, voice quality), intensity and quality of fantasy and imaginative life, and "social sensitivity."

Early *bodily orientation to space* was also considered a promising lead for prediction of a wide range of behavior and personality characteristics. "Many developmental theories have proposed that there exists a direct relationship between mental development (or ego development) and the growing sense of a constant environment (or reality testing) on the one hand, and very early bodily experience and bodily orientation to space on the other." Reference to this is found in Piaget's point of view and in ideas independently developed by others, such as Schilder (1951).

According to Escalona and Heider (1959):

> A cluster of variables, designated "availability of energy" . . . proved highly related to the success with which behavior was predicted. This factor included such related variables as activity level, zest, the ability to resist stress, and the capacity to draw upon energy reserves while under stress. The term energy here referred not only to bodily arousal but also to the mobilization of outwardly directed "psychic energy." . . . One could infer that there exists something like a characteristic amount of available energy which is of central importance for the child's total pattern of growth and adaptation.

Stability and change of particular personality dimensions at various periods of development have been investigated. Kagan and Moss (1962) report that

. . . the continuity between child and adult behavior generally became manifest during the first four years of school (six to ten years of age). This relation was clearest for the behavior of withdrawal (from stressful situations) (for women), involvement in task mastery, social spontaneity, and degree of adoption of traditional sex-typed interests. . . . A few (of the behaviors) during the age period 3 to 6 were moderately good predictors of theoretically related behaviors during early adulthood.

For example, the preschool girl's *involvement in achievement tasks* was somewhat predictive of her "concern with intellectual mastery in adulthood. . . . Passivity was highly stable for girls over the first 10 years of life . . . (but) a passive orientation during the first three years did not have any clear derivatives in the adult behavior of women."

A tendency toward *passivity* in boys during the first three years was somewhat predictive of qualities such as being nonaggressive and socially inhibited in adolescence. Kagan and Moss felt that "early passivity (with related variables of lack of hyperkinesis and fear of harm) and its potential relation to constitutional variables warrant intensive study."

In another investigation of stability and change (Honzik and MacFarlane, 1965; Honzik, 1965) *introversion versus extroversion* was the most consistent or stable variable over the period twenty-one months to eighteen years, and excessive *reserve-spontaneity* a second highly consistent dimension (see pp. 433-438). In ratings

. . . based on interviews with the parents and children, girls showed a greater consistency than boys on the dependent-independent continuum during the age period 4 to 16 years. Futhermore, when as 30-year-old women they checked themselves as "dependent," there was a high probability that they had been considered dependent during the middle years of childhood, and again at 15 and 16 years [Honzik, 1965].

Bronson (1966) investigated antecedents of degree of *emotional expressiveness* (expressive-outgoing versus reserved-withdrawn) and of *reactivity control* (placid-controlled versus reactive-explosive), which had been found to persist between the ages of five and sixteen. As to early preschool behavior, she found that "as far as problem behavior is concerned, for boys the presence of many problems, particularly in the first 21 months, tends to be increasingly predictive of later emotional expressiveness, achieving significance by adolescence." Among the specific problems were early food finicalness and temper tantrums. For boys, early placidity control was related to lack of problem behavior. For girls, the presence of many problems in the first twenty-one months was predictive of later expressiveness; the presence of problems at all preschool stages was predictive of early childhood reactivity explosiveness. "The total problem score may be taken as an index of a tendency to overrespond."

Schaefer and Bayley (1963) summarized their study of maternal behavior, child behavior and their intercorrelations from infancy through adolescence as follows:

Paternal behavior as well as maternal behavior should be investigated to obtain information on the interaction of sex of child and sex of parent as they relate to parent-child correlations. . . . [The] findings strongly suggest that the relations of maternal behavior to child behavior vary with sex and age of the child. . . . The data reported here, if interpreted from the viewpoint of social psychological theory, support hypotheses about maternal influence upon the development of the child. An analysis of progressive changes in parent-child correlations suggests that the child's social, emotional, and task-oriented behaviors, are, to some extent a reaction to the parental behaviors he has received throughout the period of childhood. . . . The consistency of a dimension of activity-passivity, and its relative independence of parent-child relationships, also supports the hypotheses that the human infant is not completely plastic but responds to his environment in accordance with his innate tendencies. . . . The early infancy ratings of *activity and rapidity*, which were interpreted as relating to the dimension of extraversion, have the highest correlations with behavior at subsequent age levels. Activity and rapidity are significantly negatively correlated with ratings of positive task-oriented behavior of boys through the age of 12 years. For girls, activity and rapidity during infancy are negatively correlated with task-oriented behaviors throughout childhood and are positively correlated with extraverted aggressive behaviors at adolescence. . . . Positive versus negative social adjustment during the first two years of life shows very little correlation with later behavior for either sex. More enduring patterns of adjustment develop at later ages since both social and task-oriented behaviors are relatively consistent for both boys and girls from about 4 to 12 years.

Again, in reporting this research on some of the subjects of the Berkeley Growth Study, Schaefer and Bayley (1963) indicate limitations of their data and analyses and suggest that the "findings may make certain hypotheses more probable" and that verification from further research is important.

In considering any of the attempts at predictions which have been mentioned here, understanding of particular measures of personality which were used is important.

From a study of older children reported by Anderson (1960) come statements about predictions of adjustment over time which are reminders pertinent to our interest in predictions from preschool to later years:

Predictors vary in their effectiveness in forecasting good and poor outcomes. In terms of the various criteria used for measuring later adjustments, groups are significantly separated on the predictors. Viewed, however, in terms of individuals, the possibilities of prediction are more limited. . . . The prediction of outstanding adjustment seems to be done much more readily than is the prediction of inadequate or poor adjustment. Every predictor separates out the outstanding persons at later ages. The patterns of measures that separate out inadequately- and poorly-adjusted children show much more variation. . . . Factors that present difficulty in interpreting our data arise out of the changes within the person with age and the changes in the life situation the person faces.

List of Films

This list presents films about infants and young children which may be used with this text. Additional films may be found by consulting annotated lists.* It is advisable that films be previewed before use and that an introduction to the film be given to the class before the showing, for the purpose of guiding the students' observations of the material shown in the film.

All films are 16 mm., sound film, and in black and white unless otherwise noted. The list is arranged alphabetically; the annotations are all taken from various lists of films.

The films listed here can be obtained from the producer or the distributor named for each title. Films frequently may be obtained from local libraries or borrowed from universities that maintain large film libraries.

Ages and Stages Series

> Produced by National Film Board of Canada, 1950

> Distributed by McGraw-Hill Book Company

He Acts His Age. 14 min., color, 1949
> Pictures how a child's emotional development keeps pace with his physical growth and the behavior he exhibits at certain ages. Examines the play habits of children 1 to 15 years of age and shows some characteristics of each age group.

> Introduction to the series.

Terrible Twos and Trusting Threes. 20 min., color, 1951
> Presents a close examination of the years between two and four.

Frustrating Fours and Fascinating Fives. 25 min., color, 1952

---

* United States Department of Health, Education, and Welfare: Selected Films on Child Life. A list of 16 mm. films. Compiled by Inez D. Lohr, Children's Bureau, Publication No. 376, Rev. 1965. Superintendent of Documents, Government Printing Office, Washington, D. C.

Journal of Nursery Education, March 1962, Suggested Films for Early Childhood Education, p. 88-90. National Association for The Education of Young Children, 1629 21st St. N. W., Washington, D.C.

The Detroit Public Library: Educational Films. Annotated catalogs of films on "Child Care and Development" in the collection of the Educational Film Department of the Detroit Public Library, 1965.

Sherburne, E. G. Science and Television. Science, 1964 (Feb. 21), 143, 792-793. Also reprinted in American Psychologist, 1964, 19:685-687. Ten twenty minute films in a series, "Focus on Behavior," produced for National Educational Television under the auspices of the American Psychological Association, are listed. Six of the films are discussed.

Depicts characteristic behavior of four- and five-year-old children.

Produced by Crawley Films for the National Film Board of Canada

And Gladly Learn.   Two sections of 40 minutes each, 1967

Part I.   Development of the Self Concept
Starts with the child's introduction to nursery school and shows his "explorations" as he gradually becomes better acquainted with a new setting away from home. Scenes concerning development of assurance in use of play materials, motor behavior, speech, and group associations are included. Self-control, assistance from the teacher for success if needed, cooperation in the group, opportunity for a realistic and positive concept of self, are among the situations shown.

Part II.   Language Development and Concept Formation
Use of stories in nursery school, the child's expression of his ideas, which receive the sympathetic attention of an adult, and informal conversations are shown. Also, experimentation, incidental learning, and carefully planned experiences suggest ways in which perceptions and concepts develop. Water play, puzzles, baby chickens, weights and balance, the planting of seeds, are among the aspects of a stimulating environment.

Produced by the Department of Family and Child Development, Utah State University with direction by Dorothy Lewis, in cooperation with the Utah State Research Foundation

Distributed by Audio-Visual Aids Library, Utah State University, Logan, Utah

Baby Meets His Parents.   11 min., 1948

Points out how differences in personality can be accounted for, not only by heredity, but also by the human relationships and environmental factors experienced during the first year of life.

Produced and distributed by Encyclopaedia Britannica Films in collaboration with Lawrence K. Frank, Director, Caroline Zachry Institute of Human Development

A Chance at the Beginning.   29 minutes, 1966

A glimpse of the work being done with four-year-olds in poorer New York public schools under the direction of Martin Deutsch. Shows ways of preparing preschool children for public school, suggesting social and psychological aspects of preparation. Also indicates ways of including mothers in the experiment.

Produced by Anti-Defamation League of B'nai B'rith

Distributed by New York University Film Library

Children Without.   29 minutes, 1966

Filmed at the Franklin School in Detroit, pictures preschool children of families newly migrated from rural areas, for whom urban living is new. Suggests ways of preparation for participation in later school experiences.

Produced by National Educational Association

Distributed by New York University Film Library

Focus on Behavior: The Conscience of a Child. 29 minutes

> Shows some of the ways in which psychologists are studying the growth and development of personality and emotional behavior in children, under the direction of Robert Sears. Explores the interaction between parental behavior and attitudes and the emotional development of children.

> Produced for National Educational Television under the auspices of the American Psychological Association

Design for Happy Mealtimes. 48 frames, 1954

> Ways by which a preschool child develops food habits and attitudes. Discussion guide included.

> Produced by The Merrill-Palmer Institute. Direction and script by Muriel G. Wagner. Photography by Donna Harris.

Emergence of Personality. 30 min., 1948

> A combined version of the three films "Baby Meets His Parents," "Helping the Child to Accept the Do's," and "Helping the Child to Face the Don'ts."

> Produced and distributed by Encyclopaedia Britannica Films

Fears of Children. 29 min., 1951

> How parents, eager to rear their five-year-old correctly, learn to handle a particular situation. Paul, frightened with false warnings from the mother, is timid, sulky and fearful. Father is impatient; he wants to encourage his son to do things for himself. These parents learn through similar experiences in another family that it is normal for children to become angry with their parents and that some rebellion should be tolerated.

> Produced by Julien Bryan for the National Association for Mental Health. Third in a series *Emotions of Everyday Living.*

> Distributed by International Film Bureau

Focus on Children. 26 min., 1961

> Shows children in many kinds of activities at home, at nursery school and day-care center learning to satisfy their curiosity, to express themselves, to cope with their own feelings and to get along with others. Stresses cooperation between home and nursery school.

> Produced by Department of Child Development, Iowa State University

Four Families, Parts I and II. 60 min., 1960

> Portrays family life in four countries, India, Japan, France and Canada, centering attention in each case on a one-year-old infant in a farm family of average income. Dr. Margaret Mead discusses the rearing of children in these four countries.

> Produced by the National Film Board of Canada

> Distributed through New York University Film Library

From Generation to Generation. 30 min., color, 1960

Illustrates the basic facts of human reproduction, showing childbirth as an emotional and spiritual experience as well as a physical one. The story of a young farm couple. By means of animation the creation and development of a new life are shown.

Produced and distributed by McGraw-Hill Book Company

Helping the Child to Accept the Do's.   11 min., 1948

Portrays the child learning to live in a world defined by the "do's" and explains how his personality is influenced by the extent to which they are accepted.

Produced and distributed by Encyclopaedia Britannica Films in collaboration with Lawrence K. Frank, Director, Caroline Zachry Institute of Human Development

Helping the Child to Face the Don'ts.   11 min., 1948

Reveals how the young child meets a world of "don'ts" and how he reacts in his own distinctive ways, thus forming his own individual personality.

Produced and distributed by Encyclopaedia Britannica Films in collaboration with Lawrence K. Frank, Director, Caroline Zachry Institute of Human Development

Human Beginnings.   22 min., color, 1950

Portrays what a group of young children believe about the origin of human life as expressed in their own drawings. Their teacher skillfully answers questions, and one of the children explains how his parents prepared him for the coming of a new baby into the family.

An Eddie Albert Production

Distributed by Association Films, Inc., Broad at Elm, Ridgefield, N.J. Area exchanges: 561 Hilgrove Ave., Lagrange, Ill.; Allegheny and Delaware Avenues, Oakmont, Pa.; 1621 Dragon St., Dallas, Texas; 25358 Cypress Avenue, Hayward, Calif.

Human Reproduction.   22 min., 1950

A film intended for college audiences which discusses the imminent birth of a child in a relative's household. The son approaches his father with the familiar question about the origin of babies. The film reviews for the benefit of the parents the basic facts of human reproduction, making use of models and animated drawings.

Produced and distributed by McGraw-Hill Book Company

It's a Small World.   38 min., 1951

Activities and routine of a day in a London day nursery photographed by a hidden camera. In detailed and leisurely fashion recounts all the events of the child's day—painting, building, sailing boats, cooking, playing games, eating and departure in the afternoon.

Produced by International Realist, 1950

Distributed by British Information Service

Language.   28 min., 1967

Children's response to direct teaching is demonstrated by one class of four-year-olds who have never been in school. Two other classes of children disadvantaged in cognitive learning, in the program for seven months, show the results of direct teaching. Intensive remedial classes using methods developed by Carl Bereiter and Siegfried Engelmann at the Institute for Research on Exceptional Children at the University of Illinois.

Distributed by Anti-Defamation League of B'nai B'rith

Learning While They Play. 28 min., black and white, color, 1966

Portrays young children involved in a variety of play activities – from spontaneous dramatic play with sand, water and mud to more formal situations in which children are exploring literature with an adult – appropriate for children at home as well as in play groups.

The focus is the value of play to the child, and the specific learnings which result from various experiences are presented by the narrator.

The film provides a brief introduction to child development research and demonstrates several research techniques which help the scientist learn more about the ways in which children learn through their play.

Produced by Department of Child Development and Family Relationships, New York State College of Home Economics, Cornell University, and distributed by Film Library, Cornell University, Ithaca, New York

Life with Baby. 18 min., 1946

Shows how children grow mentally and physically. A popular version and condensation of the Gesell Child Development Series.

Produced by March of Time Forum Films and distributed by McGraw-Hill Book Company

A Long Time to Grow. A series of three, 35 min. each, 1951, 1954, 1957

Shows in a series of incidents taken in a nursery school what children are like while they are learning and growing. The ways in which teachers help set limits, the effect of the variety and suitability of play equipment, and how student teachers assist are also pictured. Designed to show school experiences in the period of early childhood, intended for teachers and parents.

I. Two- and Three-Year-Olds in Nursery School
II. Four- and Five-Year-Olds in School
III. Six-, Seven- and Eight-Year-Olds – Society of Children.

Produced by the Department of Child Study at Vassar College

Distributed by New York University Film Library

Meeting Emotional Needs in Childhood: The Groundwork of Democracy. 33 min., 1947

Attempts to help children develop positive attitudes toward other people and toward the community.

Produced by Department of Child Study at Vassar College

Distributed by New York University Film Library

Ordinal Scales of Infant Development. 1967

Titles of the six films are as follows:
1) Visual Pursuit and the Development of Permanence of Objects
2) The Development of Means for Obtaining Desired Environmental Events
3) The Development of Imitation, Gestural and Vocal
4) The Construction of Operational Causality
5) The Construction of Object Relations in Space
6) The Development of Schemas for Relation to Objects

Produced under the direction of J. McVicker Hunt, Department of Psychology, University of Illinois

Distributed by University of Illinois Motion Picture Service

Preface to Life. 30 min., 1951

The story of a boy and two dreams. The boy is Michael Thompson, son of a typical young couple living in a small town or suburb. One dream is that of his father, a vision of Michael rising to be a strong and successful leader. The other dream is the mother's, the hope that Michael will always be her baby. It shows how attitudes may influence adult's actions in everyday situations and how trivial-seeming incidents may make a difference in the way a child develops. It promotes the basic idea that children must be understood and respected as individuals — growing personalities with their own emotional needs and rights.

Produced by National Institute of Mental Health

Distributed by New York University Film Library

Preschool Incidents (No. 1): When Should Grown-ups Help? 13 min., 1951

Shows four episodes in which an adult may not have intervened to assist the child. Intended to stimulate discussion on the issue and to provide an exercise in the observation and recording of behavior.

Produced by Department of Child Study, Vassar College

Distributed by New York University Film Library

Preschool Incidents (No. 2): And Then Ice Cream. 10 min., 1951

Presents episodes to stimulate discussion on the parental supervision of children's meals.

Produced by Department of Child Study, Vassar College

Distributed by New York University Film Library

Principles of Development. 15 min., 1950

Outlines the fundamentals of growth and change from early infancy.

Produced by Crawley Films

Distributed by McGraw-Hill Book Company

They Learn from Each Other. 29 min., color, 1959

"A film depicting some of the ways in which children in a nursery group may learn primarily from their spontaneous interactions with other children and with materials, when adult intervention is minimized."

Produced by The Merrill-Palmer Institute, 71 East Ferry Avenue,

Detroit, Michigan. Film may be rented from Visual-Auditory Center, Wayne State University, Detroit, Michigan.

A Two-Year-Old Goes to Hospital. 45 min., 1952

A little girl's reaction to an 8-day stay in the hospital shows some of the effects of her temporary separation from her parents. Because this film was part of a research project the child was photographed at the same time every day to secure a "daily time sample." The English hospital procedures depicted are in many respects different from those in American hospitals.

Produced by James Robertson, at the Tavistock Clinic, London, England, in the course of a research project directed by John Bowlby, M.D.

Distributed by New York University Film Library

Going to Hospital with Mother. 40 min., 1958

A counterpart to *A Two-Year-Old Goes to Hospital,* 1952, showing a child in the hospital when her mother remains with her.

Produced by James Robertson, at the Tavistock Clinic, London, England, in the course of a research project directed by John Bowlby, M.D.

Distributed by New York University Film Library.

Understanding Children's Play. 10 min., 1948

Shows how adults can understand and help children through observation of their use of toys and play materials. By increasing parents' awareness of children's play activities, they can function more effectively in guiding children.

Produced by Caroline Zachry Institute of Human Development

Distributed by New York University Film Library

Why Won't Tommy Eat? 19 min., color, 1948

Uncovers both physical and mental causes of the problem of the child who refuses to eat.

Produced by Crawley Films for Canadian Department of National Health and Welfare.

Distributed by Sterling Educational Films

Your Children's Sleep. 23 min., 1947

Discusses common causes of sleeplessness in adults: worry, overfatigue, unfortunate incidents during the day. Focusing upon the child, the film analyzes his difficulties in going from active play to sleep and explains the role which dreams play in the child's developing mind. Gives many good suggestions for helping children to relax and accept sleep.

Produced by Realist Film Unit

Distributed by British Information Service

DISTRIBUTORS OF FILMS LISTED

British Information Service, 30 Rockefeller Plaza, New York, N.Y. 10029, or 39 South LaSalle, Chicago, Ill. 60603.

Encyclopaedia Britannica Films, 1150 Wilmette Avenue, Wilmette, Illinois. 60091

International Film Bureau, 332 South Michigan Avenue, Chicago, Ill. 60604.

McGraw-Hill Book Company, Text-Film Department, 330 West 42nd Street, New York, N.Y. 10036.

New York University Film Library, 26 Washington Place, New York, N.Y. 10003.

Sterling Educational Films, 241 East 34th Street, New York, N.Y. 10016.

Bibliography

The numbers in boldface type following each entry refer to pages in this volume on which the material is either quoted or cited.

Acheson, R. M. 1954. A method of assessing skeletal maturity from radiographs. A report from the Oxford Child Health Survey. Brit. J. Anat., *88:*498-508. **270**

Acheson, R. M. 1966. Maturation of the Skeleton. Chap. 16, in F. Falkner (Ed.): Human Development. Philadelphia, W. B. Saunders Company. **8, 268, 269, 270**

Ackerman, N. W. 1958. The Psychodynamics of Family Life. New York, Basic Books, Inc. **34, 35**

Adler, A. 1924. Practice and Theory of Individual Psychology (translated by P. Radin). New York, Harcourt, Brace and Co. **41**

Aisensone, M. R. 1950. Closing of anterior fontanelle. Pediatrics, *6:*223-226. **271**

Aitken, F. C., and Hytten, F. E. 1960. Infant feeding: comparison of breast and artificial feeding. Nutrition Abst. and Rev., *30:*341-371. **183, 187, 188**

Aldrich, C. A., 1939. A role of gratification in early development. J. Pediat., *15:*578-582. **148**

Aldrich, C. A., 1947. Advisability of breast feeding. J.A.M.A., *135:*915-916. **188**

Aldrich, C. A., and Aldrich, M. M. 1954. Babies Are Human Beings. 2nd ed. New York, Macmillan Company. **157, 219**

Aldrich, C. A., and Hewitt, E. S. 1947. Self-regulating feeding program for infants. J.A.M.A., *135:*340-342. **205, 208**

Aldrich, C. A., Sung, C., and Knop, C. 1945a. The crying of newly born babies; the community phase. J. Pediat., *26:*313-326. **148, 232**

Aldrich, C. A., Sung, C., and Knop, C. 1945b. The crying of newly born babies; the individual phase. J. Pediat., *27:*89-96. **148, 204**

Allen, W., and Campbell, D. 1948. The Creative Nursery Center, a Unified Service to Children and Parents. New York, Family Service Association. **78**

Allinsmith, W. 1954. The Learning of Moral Standards. Doctoral Dissertation Series Publication No. 8266. Ann Arbor, Michigan, University of Michigan Microfilms. **17**

Almy, M. 1959. Ways of Studying Children. New York, Bureau Publications, Teachers College, Columbia University. **2**

Almy, M. 1967. Spontaneous play: an avenue for intellectual development. Young Children, *22:*265-277. **388**

Alschuler, R. H., and Hattwick, L. W. 1947. Painting and Personality, a Study of Young Children. Chicago, University of Chicago Press. Two volumes. **381, 420**

American Academy of Pediatrics. 1961. Report of the Committee on the Control of Infectious Diseases. Evanston, Ill., American Academy of Pediatrics. **141**

American Academy of Pediatrics and American Society of Dentistry for Children. 1959. Report of the joint committee of the American Academy of Pediatrics and the American Society of Dentistry for Children. Dental caries and a consideration of the role of diet in prevention. Pediatrics, *23:*400-407. **144, 145**

American Home Economics Association. 1967. Concepts and Generalizations: Their Place in High School Home Economics Curriculum Development. Washington, D.C., American Home Economics Association. **60**

Ames, L. B. 1946. Development of sense of time in the young child. J. Genet. Psychol., *68:*97-125. **364**

Ames, L. B. 1949. Bilaterality. J. Genet. Psychol., *75:*45-50. **309**

Ames, L. B., and Learned, J. 1946. Imaginary companions and related phenomena. J. Genet. Psychol., *69:*147-167. **375**

Ames, L. B., and Learned, J. 1948. Development of verbalized space in the young child. J. Genet. Psychol., *72:*63-84. **363**

Ames, L. B., et al. 1952. Child Rorschach Responses. New York, Harper & Brothers. **421**

Anand, B. K. 1960. Nervous regulation of food intake. Am. J. Clin. Nutrition, *8:*529-534. **204**

Andersen, H. 1966. The Influence of Hormones on Human Development. Chap. 8, in F. Falkner (Ed.): Human Development. Philadelphia, W. B. Saunders Company. **89, 291**

Anderson, A. 1953. Some observations on birth weights. Med. Officer, *89:*15-17. **254**

Anderson, H. 1939. Measurement of domination and of socially integrative behavior in teachers' contacts with children. Child Development, *10:*73-89. **372**

Anderson, H., and Anderson, G. 1954. Social Development. Chap. 19, in L. Carmichael (Ed.): Manual of Child Psychology. 2nd ed. New York, John Wiley & Sons, Inc. **399, 428**

Anderson, H. H. (Ed.) 1965. Creativity in Childhood and Adolescence. Palo Alto, Calif., Science and Behavior Books. **388**

Anderson, J. E. 1948. Personality organization in children. American Psychologist, *3:*409-416. **19**

Anderson, J. E. 1949. Psychology of Development and Personal Adjustment. New York, Henry Holt & Co., Inc. **366**

Anderson, J. E. 1956. Child Development; an historical perspective. Child Development *27:*181-196. **5**

Anderson, J. E. 1957. Dynamics of Development: Systems in Process, in D. B. Harris (Ed.): The Concept of Development: An Issue in the Study of Human Behavior. Minneapolis, University of Minnesota Press. **29**

Anderson, J. E. 1960. The prediction of adjustment over time, in I. Iscoe and H. W. Stevenson (Eds.): Personality Development in Children. Austin, University of Texas Press. **465**

Anderson, M., et al. 1956. Growth of the normal foot during childhood and adolescence. Length of the foot and interrelations of foot stature and lower extremities as seen in serial records of children between 1-18 years of age. Am. J. Phys. Anthropol., 14 ns: 287-308. **273**

Antonov, A. N. 1947. Children born during siege of Leningrad in 1942. J. Pediat., *30:*250-259. **106**

Arbuthnot, M. H. 1964. Children and Books. Chicago, Scott, Foresman & Co. **357**

Armstrong, E. M., and Wagoner, L. C. 1928. Motor control of children as involved in the dressing process. J. Genet. Psychol., *35:*84-97. **317**

Armstrong, W. D. 1955. Radiotracer studies of hard tissues, in Recent Advances in the Study of the Structure, Composition and Growth of Mineralized Tissue. Ann. New York Acad. Sc., *60* (art 5):670-684. **117**

Aserinsky, E., and Kleitman, N. 1955. A mobility cycle in sleeping infants as manifested by ocular and bodily activity. J. Appl. Physiol., *8:*11-18. **227, 231**

Association for Childhood Education. 1961. Literature with Children. Washington, D.C., Association for Childhood Education. **357**

Association for Childhood Education. 1965. Bibliography of Books for Children. Washington, D.C. Association for Childhood Education. **357**

Association for Childhood Education. Discipline, Bulletin 99. Washington, D.C., Association for Childhood Education. **452**

Association for Childhood Education. December, 1967. Theme of issue is "Teaching Is Growing." **452**

Arnstein, H. S. 1962. What to Tell Your Child about Birth, Illness, Death, Divorce and Other Family Crises. New York, Pocket Books, Inc. **78**

Aronfreed, J. 1965. Internalized behavioral suppression and the timing of social punishment. J. Pers. and Soc. Psychol., *1:*3-16. **412**

Ast, D. B., et al. 1956. Newburgh-Kingston caries-fluorine study. XIV. Combined clinical and roentgenographic dental findings after ten years of fluoride experience. J. Am. Dent. A., *52:*314-325. **145**

Ausubel, D. P. 1949. Ego-development and the learning process. Child Development *20:*173-190. **440**

Ausubel, D. P. 1957. Theory and Problems of Child Development. New York, Grune & Stratton, Inc. **90, 106, 213, 220, 225, 303, 314, 394, 396, 434, 440, 456**

Aznar, R., and Bennett, A. E. 1961. Pregnancy in the adolescent girl. Am. J. Obst. & Gynec., *81:*935-940. **83**

Bain, K. 1948. The incidence of breast feeding in hospitals in the United States. Pediatrics, *2:*313-320. **183**

Baird, D., et al. 1958. Age and reproduction. J. Obst. & Gynaec. Brit. Emp., *65:*865-876. **81**

Baker, S. J. 1925. Child Hygiene. New York, Harper & Brothers. **131**

Bakes, F. P. 1966. Speech, Language, and Hearing. Chap. 14, in F. Falkner (Ed.): Human Development. Philadelphia, W. B. Saunders Company. **352, 356**

Bakwin, H. 1949. Emotional deprivation in infants. J. Pediat., *35:*512-521. **131**

Bakwin, H. 1961. The overuse of vitamins in children. J. Pediat., *59:*154-161. **179, 190**

Bakwin, H. 1964. Feeding programs for infants. Fed. Proc., *23:*66-68. **180, 181, 185**

Bakwin, H. (Ed.). 1968. Developmental Disorders of Motility and Language. Pediat. Clin. N. Amer., 15, No. 3. **322, 352, 356**

Baldwin, A. L. 1955. Behavior and Development in Childhood. New York, Holt, Rinehart and Winston, Inc. **9, 12, 156, 241, 242**

Baldwin, A. L. 1961. The Parsonian Theory of Personality, in M. Black (Ed.): The Social Theories of Talcott Parsons. Englewood Cliffs, N. J., Prentice-Hall, Inc. **39, 40**

Baldwin, A. L. 1967. Theories of Child Development. New York, John Wiley & Sons, Inc. **4, 20, 29**

Balfour, M. L. 1944. Supplementary feeding in pregnancy. Lancet, *246:*208-211. **106**

Bamba, J. K. 1961. Longitudinal cephalometric roentgenographic study of face and cranium in relation to body height. J. A. Dent. A., *63:*776-779. **177**

Bandura, A. 1963. The role of imitation in personality development. J. Nursery Education, *18:*207-215. **246**

Bandura, A., Ross, D., and Ross, S. 1963. Imitation of film-mediated aggressive models. J. Abnorm. Soc. Psychol., *66:*3-11. **238, 412**

Bandura, A., and Walters, R. H. 1963. Aggression. Chap. 9, in H. W. Stevenson, J. Kagan and C. Spiker (Eds.): Child Psychology. Sixty-Second Yearbook of the National Society for the Study of Education. Chicago, University of Chicago Press. **408**

Barker, R. G. 1955. Midwest and Its Children: The Psychological Ecology of an American Town. Evanston, Ill., Row, Peterson & Co. **63**

Barker, R. G., and Barker, L. S. 1961. Research Symposium Report, in National Association for Nursery Education Digest of Conference, October 18-21, 1961. Washington, D.C. National Association for the Education of Young Children. **63**

Barker, R. G., Barker, L. S., et al. 1963. The Stream of Behavior: Explorations of Its Structure and Content. New York, Appleton-Century-Crofts. **63**

Barker, R. G., and Wright, H. F. 1951. One Boy's Day. New York, Harper & Brothers. **63**

Barnes, G. R., Jr., et al. 1953. Management of breast feeding. J.A.M.A., *151:*192-199. **183**

Barnes, R. H., Cunnold, S. R., Zimmermann, R. R., Simmons, H., MacLeod, R. B., and Krook, L. 1966. Influence of nutritional deprivation in early life on learning behavior of rats as measured by performance in a water maze. J. Nutrition, *89:*399-410. **159**

Barness, L. A. 1966. The evolution of infant feeding practices—consequences and problems. Proceedings Western Hemisphere Nutrition Congress. A.M.A. pp. 48-50. **159**

Barton, M., and Wiesner, B. P. 1945. Waking temperature in relation to fetal fecundity. Lancet, *2:*663-668. **109**

Baruch, D. 1937. Study of reported tension in interparental relationships as co-existent with behavior adjustment in young children. J. Exper. Educ. *6:*187-204. **44**

Baruch, D. 1939. Parents and Children Go to School. New York, Scott, Foresman & Co. **44, 349**

Baruch, D. 1949. New Ways in Discipline. New York, McGraw-Hill Book Co., Inc. **422**

Bayley, N. 1933. Mental growth during the first three years; developmental study of 61 children by repeated tests. Genet. Psychol. Monogr. *14:*1-92. **346, 384**

Bayley, N. 1935. Development of Motor Abilities during the First Three Years. Washington, D.C., Society for Research in Child Development, National Research Council. **300**

Bayley, N. 1936. California Scale of Motor Development. University of California Syllabus Series 259. **299, 329, 383**

Bayley, N. 1946. Tables for predicting adult height from skeletal age and present height. J. Pediat., *28:*49-64. **459**

Bayley, N. 1954. Some increasing parent-child similarities during the growth of children. J. Educ. Psychol., *45:*1-21. **249, 250, 254, 255, 459**

Bayley, N. 1955. On the growth of intelligence. American Psychologist, *10:*805-818. **28, 314, 384**

Bayley, N. 1956a. Growth curves of height and weight by age for boys and girls, scaled according to physical maturity. J. Pediat., *48:*187-194. **256**

Bayley, N. 1956b. Individual patterns of development. Child Development, *27:*45-74. **253, 262**

Bayley, N. 1962. The Accurate Prediction of Growth and Adult Height. Mod. Prob. Pediat., *7:*234-255. Basle, Switzerland, S. Karger. **248, 456, 459**

Bayley, N. 1965. Comparisons of mental and motor test scores for ages 1-15 months by sex, birth order, geographical location, and education of parents. Child Development, *36:*379-411. **299, 311**

Bayley, N. 1968. Behavioral correlates of mental growth: birth to thirty-six years. American Psychologist, *23:*1-17. **351**

Bayley, N., and Davis, D. C. 1935. Growth changes in bodily size and proportion during the first three years. Biometrika, *27:*26-87. **252**

Bayley, N., and Espenschade, A. 1941. Motor development from birth to maturity. Rev. Educ. Research, *11:*562-572. **303**

Bayley, N., and Espenschade, A. 1944. Motor development from birth to maturity. Rev. Educ. Research, *14:*381-389. **303**

Bayley, N., and Espenschade, A. 1950. Motor development and decline. Rev. Educ. Research, *20:*367-374. **303**

Bayley, N., and Pinneau, S. R. 1952. Tables for predicting adult height from skeletal age: Revised for use with the Greulich-Pyle Hand Standards. J. Pediat., *40:*423-441. **459**

Bayley, N., and Schaefer, E. S. 1964. Correlations of Maternal and Child Behaviors with the Development of Mental Abilities: Data from the Berkeley Growth Study. Monographs of the Society for Research in Child Development, 29, No. 6 (Serial No. 97). **437**

Bayley, N., and Stolz, H. R. 1937. Maturational changes in rectal temperatures of 61 infants from 1 to 36 months. Child Development, *8:*195-206. **134**

Beach, V., and Bressler, M. H. 1944. Phases in development of children's painting. J. Exper. Educ., *13:*1-4. **380**

Beal, V. A. 1953. Nutritional intake of children. I. Calories, carbohydrate, fat and protein. J. Nutrition, *50:*223-234. **194, 196**

Beal, V. A. 1954. Nutritional intake of children. II. Calcium, phosphorus and iron. J. Nutrition, *53:*499-510. **194, 196**

Beal, V. A. 1955. Nutritional intake of children. III. Thiamine, riboflavin and niacin. J. Nutrition, *57:*183-192. **194, 196**

Beal, V. A. 1956. Nutritional intake of children. IV. Vitamins A and D and ascorbic acid. J. Nutrition, *60:*335-347. **194, 196**

Beal, V. A. 1957. On the acceptance of solid foods, and other food patterns, of infants and children. Pediatrics, *20:*448-457. **192, 194, 195, 196**

Beal, V. A. 1961. Dietary intake of individuals followed through infancy and childhood. Am. J. Pub. Health, *51:*1107-1117. **194**

Beal, V. A. 1965. Nutrition in a longitudinal growth study. J. Am. Dietet. A., *46:*457-461. **194, 196**

Beaton, G. H. 1961. Nutritional and physiological adaptations in pregnancy. Fed. Proc. 20, No. 1, Part III: 196-201. **113**

Becker, W. C. 1962. Developmental Psychology; in P. R. Farnsworth et al. (Eds.): Annual Review of Psychology, Vol. 13. Palo Alto, Cal., Annual Reviews, Inc. **4**

Becker, W. C. 1964. Consequences of Different Kinds of Parental Discipline. Chap. in M. L. Hoffman and L. W. Hoffman (Eds.): Review of Child Development Research, Vol. 1. New York, Russell Sage Foundation. **155, 157, 446, 447, 452**

Bell, N. W., and Vogel, E. F. (Eds.) 1968. A Modern Introduction to the Family. New York, The Free Press. **79**

Beller, E. K. 1955. Dependency and independence in young children. J. Genet. Psychol., *87:*25-35. **156, 395**

Bellugi, U., and Brown, R. (Eds.) 1964. The Acquisition of Language. Monographs of the Society for Research in Child Development, 29, No. 1 (Serial No. 92). **388**

Benson, D. F., and Geschwind, N. 1968. Cerebral dominance and its disturbances. Pediat. Clin. N. Amer., *15:*759-769. **310**

Benzinger, T. H. 1961. The human thermostat. Scient. Amer., *204:*134-147. **133**

Bernard, J., and Sontag, L. W. 1947. Fetal reactivity to tonal stimulation: a preliminary report. J. Genet. Psychol., *70:*205-210. **103**

Bernstein, B. 1962. Social class, linguistic codes and grammatical elements. Lang. and Speech, *5:*221-240. **353**

Bernstein, B. 1964. Elaborated and restricted codes: their social origins and some consequences. Amer. Anthropologist, 66, Part II:55-69. **353**

Beyer, G. H. 1960. Future explorations in home economics. Housing. J. H. Econ., *52:*643-646. **62**

Bibby, B. G. 1961. Cariogenicity of foods. J.A.M.A., *177:*316-321. **144, 145, 198**

Bijou, S. W., and Baer, D. M., 1960. The Laboratory-Experimental Study of Child Behavior. Chap. 4, in P. Mussen (Ed.): Handbook of Research Methods in Child Development. New York, John Wiley & Sons, Inc. **366**

Bilodeau, E. A., and Bilodeau, I. McD. 1961. Motor-Skills in Learning; in P. R. Farnsworth et al. (Eds.): Annual Review of Psychology, Vol. 12. Palo Alto, Cal., Annual Reviews, Inc. **312**

Bishop, B. M. 1951. Mother-child interaction and the social behavior of children. Psychol. Monograph 65, No. 11. **449**

Blattner, R. J. 1959. Rubella during pregnancy. J. Pediat., *54:*257-260. **106**

Blayney, J. R. 1960. A report of thirteen years of water fluoridation in Evanston, Ill. J. Am. Dent. A., *61:*76-79. **145**

Bleiberg, N., and Forrest, S. 1959. Group discussions with mothers in the child health conference. Pediatrics, *24:*118-125. **74**

Blood, R. O., and Wolfe, D. 1960. Husbands and Wives. New York, The Free Press. **63**

Blum, A. 1957. The value factor in children's size perception. Child Development, *28:*5-14. **339**

Bossard, J. H. S., and Boll, E. S. 1966. The Sociology of Child Development. 4th ed. New York, Harper & Brothers. **36, 37**

Bowlby, J. 1951. Maternal Care and Mental Health. New York, Columbia University Press. **149**

Bowlby, J. 1958. The nature of the child's tie to his mother. Internat. J. Psycho-Analysis, *39:*350-373. **148, 393**

Bradley, C. 1957. Characteristics and management of children with behavior problems associated with organic brain damage. Pediat. Clin. N. Amer., *4:*1049-1060. **35**

Brady, J. V. 1964. Behavioral stress and physiological change: a comparative approach to the experimental analysis of some psychosomatic problems. Trans. N. Y. Acad. Sci., 26. **390**

Brady, J. V. 1966. Lecture at Purdue University, Lafayette, Indiana. **390**

Braestrup, C. B., and Mooney, R. T. 1959. X-ray emission from television. Science, *130:*1071-1074. **142**

Braine, M. D. S. 1962. Piaget on reasoning: a methodological critique and alternative proposals; in W. Kessen and C. Kuhlman (Eds.): Thought in the Young Child. Monographs of the Society for Research in Child Development, 27, No. 2. **358**

Brandenburg, J., and Brandenburg, G. C. 1919. Language development during the fourth year. Ped. Sem., *26:*27-40. **347, 348**

Bridges, K. M. B. 1931. Social and Emotional Development of Preschool Child. London, Geo. Routledge & Sons, Ltd. **391, 405, 419**

Brieland, D. 1959. Adoption research. Child Welfare, *38:*1-5. **78**

Brim, O. G. 1958. Family structure and sex role learning by children: a further analysis of Helen Koch's data. Sociometry *21:*1-16. **45, 79**

Brim, O. G. 1960. Personality Development as Role Learning; in I. Iscoe and H. W. Stevenson (Eds.): Personality Development in Children. Austin, University of Texas Press. **39**

Bro, M. 1956. When Children Ask. 2nd ed. New York, Willett, Clark and Company. **428**

Brobeck, J. R. 1960. Regulation of Energy Exchange; in T. C. Ruch and J. R. Fulton (Eds.): Medical Physiology and Biophysics. Philadelphia, W. B. Saunders Company. **132, 134**

Brody, S. 1956. Patterns of Mothering: Maternal Influence during Infancy. New York, International Universities Press, Inc. **18, 22, 148, 157, 393, 450**

Brody, S. 1962. Mental health and the capacity for nursery education. Journal of Nursery Education, *17*, 2, 58-63. **427, 428**

Broderick, C. B. 1967. Reaction to familial development, selective needs, and predictive theory. Journal of Marriage and the Family, *29:*237-240. **31**

Bronfenbrenner, U. 1958. Socialization and Social Class through Time and Space; in E. E.

Maccoby, T. Newcomb, and E. Hartley (Eds.): Readings in Social Psychology. New York, Henry Holt & Co., Inc. **64**

Bronson, W. C. 1966. Early antecedents of emotional expressiveness and reactivity control. Child Development, *37:*793-810. **434, 464**

Brown, R. W. 1958. How shall a thing be called? Psychol. Rev., *65:*14-21. **346**

Brown, R. W., and Fraser, C. 1964. The acquisition of syntax; in U. Bellugi and R. W. Brown (Eds.): The Acquisition of Language. Monographs of the Society for Research in Child Development, *29,* No. 1:43-79. **345, 348, 351, 388**

Brozek, J. 1961. Body composition. Science, *134:*920-930. **35**

Bruch, H. 1957. The Importance of Overweight. New York, W. W. Norton & Company, Inc. **55**

Bruner, J. S. 1964. The course of cognitive growth. American Psychologist, *19:*1-15. **370**

Bryan, E. S. 1930. Variations in responses of infants during first ten days of postnatal life. Child Development, *1:*56-77. **329**

Bryan, M. S., and Lowenberg, M. E. 1958. The father's influence on young children's food preferences. J. Am. Dietet. A., *34:*30-35. **197**

Bühler, C. 1930. The First Year of Life. New York, John Day Co., Inc. **326, 330, 391**

Bullowa, M., Jones, L. G., and Bever, T. G. 1964. The Development from Vocal to Verbal Behavior in Children; in U. Bellugi and R. W. Brown (Eds.): The Acquisition of Language. Monographs of the Society for Research in Child Development, 29, No. 1:101-107. **344**

Burch, E. P. 1966. Diseases of the Eye. Conditions with which the pediatrician and general practitioner should be familiar, Chap. 38 (Vol. IV); in I. McQuarrie and V. C. Kelley (Eds.): Brenneman's Practice of Pediatrics. Hagerstown, Md., W. F. Prior Co., Inc. **332**

Burchinal, L. G., and Bauder, W. W. 1965. Decision-making and role patterns among Iowa farm and nonfarm families. J. Marriage and the Family, *27:*525-532. **63**

Burgess, E. W., and Cottrell, L. S. 1939. Prediction of Success or Failure in Marriage. New York, Prentice-Hall, Inc. **44**

Burke, B. S. 1965. Nutrition in Pregnancy, in Greenhill, J. P.: Obstetrics. 13th ed. Philadelphia, W. B. Saunders Company. **116**

Burke, B. S., et al. 1943. The influence of nutrition during pregnancy upon the condition of the infant at birth. J. Nutrition, *26:*569-583. **105**

Burke, B. S., et al. 1949. Nutrition studies during pregnancy. V. Relation of maternal nutrition to condition of infant at birth: study of siblings. J. Nutrition, *38:*453-467. **105**

Burke, B. S., et al. 1959. Caloric and protein intakes of children—between one and eighteen years of age. Pediatrics, 24, Suppl.:922-940. **194**

Burke, B. S., et al. 1962. A longitudinal study of the calcium intake of children from one to eighteen years of age. Am. J. Clin. Nutrition, *10:*79-88. **194**

Burton, R. V., Maccoby, E. R., and Allinsmith, W. 1961. Antecedents of resistance to temptation in four-year-old children. Child Development, *32:*689-710. **411, 452**

Burton, R. V., and Whiting, J. W. M. 1961. The absent father and cross-sex identity. Merrill-Palmer Quarterly, *7:*85-95. **78**

Buxton, C. L. 1962. A Study of Psychophysical Methods for Relief of Childbirth Pain. Philadelphia, W. B. Saunders Company. **125**

Caldwell, B. M. 1964. The Effects of Infant Care. Chap. in M. L. Hoffman and L. W. Hoffman (Eds.): Review of Child Development Research, Vol. 1. New York, Russell Sage Foundation. **16, 154, 203, 208, 220, 223, 413, 414**

Caldwell, B. M., and Richmond, J. B. 1962. The impact of theories of child development. Children, *9:*73-78. **30**

Call, J. D. 1959. Emotional factors favoring successful breast feeding of infants. J. Pediat., *55:*485-496. **183**

Campbell, J. D. 1964. Peer Relations in Childhood. Chap. in M. L. Hoffman and L. W. Hoffman (Eds.): Review of Child Development Research, Vol. 1. New York, Russell Sage Foundation. **399**

Cannon, W. B. 1933. Wisdom of the Body. New York, W. W. Norton & Co., Inc. **19, 132**

Caplan, G. 1960. Emotional Implications of Pregnancy and Influences on Family Relationships, in H. C. Stuart and D. G. Prugh (Eds.): The Healthy Child. Cambridge, Harvard University Press. **117, 118**

Caplan, G. (Ed.) 1961. Prevention of Emotional Disorders in Children. New York, Basic Books. **23**

Carbonara, N. T. 1961. Techniques for Observing Normal Child Behavior. Pittsburgh, University of Pittsburgh Press. **2**

Carlson, A. J., Johnson, V., and Calvert, H. M. 1961. The Machinery of the Body. 5th ed. Chicago, University of Chicago Press. **163, 168, 217, 279, 326**

Carmichael, L. 1954. Onset and Early Development of Behavior. Chap. 2, in L. Carmichael (Ed.): Manual of Child Psychology. 2nd ed. New York, John Wiley & Sons, Inc. **312, 334**

Carothers, J. C. 1953. The African Mind in Health and Disease. WHO Monogr. Series No. 17. Geneva, World Health Organization. **90**

Carrigan, P. M. 1960. Extraversion-introversion as a dimension of personality: a reappraisal. Psychol. Bull., *575:*329-360. **409**

Carson, R. 1966. So You Want to Adopt a Child. Public Affairs pamphlet. 381 Park Avenue South, New York, Public Affairs Committee. **78**

Casler, L. 1961. Maternal Deprivation: A Critical Review of the Literature. Monographs of the Society for Research in Child Development, 26, No. 2. **4, 18, 148, 149, 279, 337**

Cazden, C. B. 1965. Environmental Assistance to the Child's Acquisition of Grammar. Unpublished doctoral dissertation, Harvard Graduate School of Education. (Reviewed in S. Ervin Tripp, 1966.) **356**

Child Study. 1957. The Man in the Family, *34:*No. 3. **79**

Child Welfare League of America. 1959. Standards for Adoption Service. 345 E. 46th St., New York, Child Welfare League of America. **78**

Child Welfare League of America. 1960. Standards for Day Care Service. 345 E. 46th St., New York, Child Welfare League of America. **76, 78**

Chomsky, N. 1964. Discussion of a paper in U. Bellugi and R. Brown (Eds.): The Acquisition of Language. Monographs of the Society for Research in Child Development, 29, No. *1:*35-39. **388**

Chow, B. F., and Lee, C. J. 1964. Effect of dietary restriction of pregnant rats on body weight gain of offspring. J. Nutrition, *82:*10-18. **158**

Christensen, H. (Ed.) 1964. Handbook of Marriage and the Family. Chicago, Rand McNally, 1964. **79**

Church, J. 1961. Language and the Discovery of Reality. New York, Random House, Inc. **387**

Clark, D. W. 1961. The Family and the Physician, in I. Galdston (Ed.): The Family. A Focal Point in Health Education. New York, International Universities Press, Inc. **75**

Clausen, J. A. 1966. Family Structure, Socialization, and Personality. Chap. in L. W. Hoffman and M. L. Hoffman (Eds.): Review of Child Development Research, Vol. 2. New York, Russell Sage Foundation. **40, 45, 46, 79, 412**

Clements, F. W. 1961. Nutrition in maternal and infant feeding. Fed. Proc. 20, No. 1, Part III:165-168. **110, 112**

Comar, C. L. 1959. Radioactivity in foods. J.A.M.A., *171:*1221-1223. **143**

Committee on Nutrition. 1958. On feeding of solid foods to infants. Pediatrics, *21:*685-692. **191, 192**

Committee on Nutrition. 1960. Composition of milks. Pediatrics, *26:*1039-1047. **180, 185**

Committee on Nutrition, American Academy of Pediatrics 1965. Vitamin D intake and the hypercalcemic syndrome. Pediatrics, *35:*1022-1023. **158, 190**

Cooke, R. E. 1952. Behavioral response of infants to heat stress. Yale J. Biol. & Med., *24:*334-340. **179**

Corbin, H., Brown, I. K., and Hughes, H. H. (Ed.) 1962. Meeting the Child-bearing Needs of Families in a Changing World. Report of a Work Conference sponsored by Maternity Center Association. 48 East 92nd St., New York. **123**

Corner, G. W. 1944. Ourselves Unborn. New Haven, Yale University Press. **108**

Coursin, D. B. 1965. Effects of undernutrition in central nervous system function. Nutrition Rev., *23:*65-68. **158**

Crandall, V. J., and Preston, A. 1955. Patterns and levels of maternal behavior. Child Development, *26:*267-278. **156**

Crandall, V. J., Preston, A., and Rabson, A. 1960. Maternal reactions and the development of independence and achievement behavior in young children. Child Development, *31:*243-251. **407, 452**

Cravioto, J., De Licardie, E. R., and Birch, H. E. 1966. Nutrition, growth and neurointegrative development: an experimental and ecologic study. Pediatrics, *38:*319-372. **158**

Cuthbertson, D. P. 1958. The Adolescent, in Proceedings of The Borden Centennial Symposium on Nutrition, April 12, 1958. The Borden Company Foundation, Inc., 350 Madison Ave., New York. **82**

Darby, W. J., et al. 1955. The Vanderbilt Cooperative Study of Maternal and Infant Nutrition. IX. Some obstetric implications. Obst. & Gynec., *5:*528-537. **105**

Dargassies, S. Saint-Anne. 1966. Neurological Maturation of the Premature Infant of 28-41 Weeks Gestational Age. Chap. 11, Part V., in F. Falkner (Ed.): Human Development. Philadelphia, W. B. Saunders Company. **298**

Darner, C. B., and Hunter, G. W. 1943. Importance of rest in initiation of breast feeding. Am. J. Obst. & Gynec., *45:*117-120. **127**

Daughaday, W. H. 1962a. The Adenohypophysis. Chap. 2, in R. H. Williams (Ed.): Textbook of Endocrinology. 3rd ed. Philadelphia, W. B. Saunders Company. **289**

Daughaday, W. H. 1962b. The Neurohypophysis. Chap. 3, in R. H. Williams (Ed.): Textbook of Endocrinology. 3rd ed. Philadelphia, W. B. Saunders Company. **289**

Davis, A., and Havighurst, R. 1947. Father of the Man. How Your Child Gets His Personality. Boston, Houghton Mifflin Co. **51**

Davis, C. M. 1928. Self-selection of diet by newly weaned infants. Am. J. Dis. Child., *36:* 651-679. **209, 210**

Davis, C. M. 1933. Practical application of some lessons on self-selection diet study to feeding of children in hospitals. Am. J. Dis. Child., *46:*745-750. **210**

Davis, M. E., and Rubin, R. 1962. DeLee's Obstetrics for Nurses. 17th ed. Philadelphia, W. B. Saunders Company. **124**

Dawe, H. C. 1934. Analysis of two hundred quarrels of preschool children. Child Development, *5:*139-157. **404**

Dawe, H. C. 1947. The Child's Experiences in Communication; in Forty-sixth Yearbook of the National Society for the Study of Education, Part II. Chicago, University of Chicago Press. **350**

Dawe, H. C. 1952. Environmental Influences on Language Growth, in R. Kuhlen and G. Thompson (Eds.): Psychological Studies in Human Development. New York, Appleton-Century-Crofts, Inc. **355**

Day, E. 1932. Development of language in twins: comparison of twins and single children. Child Development, *3:*179-199. **354**

Dean, R. F. A. 1951. XXVIII. The size of the baby at birth and the yield of breast milk. Studies of Undernutrition, Wuppertal 1946-1949. Special Report Series Medical Research Council, No. 275. London, Her Majesty's Stationery Office. **105**

Dean, R. F. A. 1960. The Effects of Malnutrition on the Growth of Young Children; in F. Falkner (Ed.): Modern Problems in Pediatrics. V. Child Development, an International Method of Study. New York, S. Karger. **23**

Dearborn, G. V. N. 1910. Motor-Sensory Development. Baltimore, Warwick & York, Inc. **328**

DeCoursey, R. M. 1961. The Human Organism. 2nd ed. New York, McGraw-Hill Book Co., Inc. **275, 276**

DeHaas, J. H., and Posthuma, J. H. 1946. Nederlandsche kinderen in Japansche interneerings kampen op Java. Nederl. tijdschr. v. geneesk., *90:*1530-1541. **255**

Dekaban, A. 1959a. Neurology of Infancy. Baltimore, Williams & Wilkins Company. **276**

Dekaban, A. 1959b. The outcome of pregnancy in diabetic women. II. Analysis of clinical abnormalities and pathologic lesions in off-spring of diabetic mothers. J. Pediat., *55:*767-776. **107**

Dekaban, A., and Baird, R. 1959. The outcome of pregnancy in diabetic women. J. Pediat., *55:*563-576. **107**

Dell, P., Bonvallet, M., and Hugelin, A. 1960. Mechanisms of Reticular Deactivation; in G. E. W. Wolstenholme and M. O'Connor (Eds.): Ciba Foundation Symposium on The Nature of Sleep. June 27-29, 1960. Boston, Little, Brown and Company. **226**

Dement, W. 1960. The effect of dream deprivation. Science, *131:*1705-1707. **231**

Deming, J., and Washburn, A. H. 1935. Respiration in infancy; method of studying rates, volume, and character of respiration. Am. J. Dis. Child., *49:*108-124. **170**

Despert, J. L. 1949. Sleep in preschool children: preliminary study. Nerv. Child, *8:*8-27. **227, 231**

Deutsch, C. 1964. Auditory discrimination and learning: social factors. Merrill-Palmer Quarterly, *10:*277-296. **355, 388**

Deutsch, M. 1964. Facilitating development in the preschool child: social and psychological perspectives. Merrill-Palmer Quarterly, *10:*249-263. **79**

Deutsche, J. M. 1937. Development of Children's Concept of Causal Relations. Institute of Child Welfare Monograph No. 13. Minneapolis, University of Minnesota Press. **368**

Dewey, E. 1935. Behavior Development in Infants. New York, Columbia University Press. **303**

Dicks-Bushnell, M. W., and Davis, K. C. 1967. Vitamin E content of infant formulas and cereals. Am. J. Clin. Nutrition, *20:*262-269. **191**

Dieckmann, W. J., et al. 1951. Observations on protein intake and the health of the mother and baby. I. Clinical and laboratory findings. J. Am. Dietet. A., *27:*1046-1052. **105**

Diercks, E. C., and Morse, L. M. 1965. Food habits and nutrient intakes of preschool children. J. Am. Dietet. A., *47:*292-296. **197**

Dietrich, H. F. 1966. Accidents in Childhood. Chap. 18, Section I (Vol. I), in I. McQuarrie and V. C. Kelley (Eds.): Brennemann's Practice of Pediatrics. Hagerstown, Md., W. F. Prior Co., Inc. **146**

Dimitrovsky, L. 1964. The ability to identify the emotional meaning of vocal expressions at successive age levels. Chap. 6 in Davitz, J. R. (Ed.): The Communication of Emotional Meaning. New York, McGraw-Hill Book Co., Inc. **405**

Dollard, J., and Miller, N. M. 1950. Personality and Psychotherapy. New York, McGraw-Hill Book Co., Inc. **13**

Doss, C., and Doss, H. 1957. If You Adopt a Child. New York, Henry Holt & Co., Inc. **78**

Douglas, J. W. B. 1950. The extent of breast feeding in Great Britain in 1946, with special reference to health and survival of children. J. Obst. Gynaec. Brit. Emp., *57:*335-361. **183, 188**

Downer, D. B., Smith, R. H., and Lynch, M. T. 1968. Values and housing—a new dimension. J. Home Econ., *60:*173-176. **62**

Dreger, R. M., and Miller, K. S. 1960. Comparative psychological studies of Negroes and whites in the United States. Psychol. Bull., *57:*361-402. **311**

Dublin, T. D., and Fraenkel, M. 1949. A plan for health services for the family, in The Family as a Health Unit. New York, Milbank Memorial Fund. **75**

Dudley, D. T., Moore, M. E., and Sunderlin, E. M. 1960. Children's attitude toward food. J. Home Econ., *52:*678-681. **197**

Duff, A. 1944. Bequest of Wings. New York, The Viking Press, Inc. **357**

Duff, A. 1956. "Longer Flight," a Family Grows Up with Books. New York, The Viking Press, Inc. **357**

Dukes, W. F., and Bevan, W. 1952. Accentuation and response variability in the perception of personally related objects. J. Personality, *20:*457-465. **339**

Dunbar, F. 1954. Emotions and Bodily Changes. 4th ed. New York, Columbia University Press. **19**

Dunn, P. M., Fisher, A. M., and Kohler, H. G. 1962. Phocomelia. Amer. J. Obstet. Gynec., *84:*348-354. **107**

Dupertuis, C. W., and Michael, N. B. 1953. Comparison of growth in height and weight between ectomorphic and mesomorphic boys. Child Development, *24:*203-214. **262**

Duvall, E. M. 1967. Family Development. 3rd ed. Philadelphia, J. B. Lippincott Company. **32, 33, 65, 79**

Eastman, N. J. 1944. Effect of interval between births on maternal and fetal outlook. Am. J. Obst. & Gynec., *47:*445-466. **81**

Ebers, D. W., et al. 1956. Gastric acidity on the first day of life. Pediatrics, *18:*800-802. **164**

Egli, G. E., et al. 1961. The influence of the number of breast feedings on milk production. Pediatrics, *27:*314-317. **183**

Eichorn, D. H. 1963. Biological Correlates of Behavior. Chap. 1 in H. W. Stevenson, J. Kagan and C. Spiker (Eds.): Child Psychology. The Sixty-Second Yearbook of the National Society for the Study of Education. Chicago, University of Chicago Press. **331**

Ellenwood, J. 1940. There's No Place Like Home. New York, Charles Scribner's Sons. **50**

Emmerich, W. 1959a. Parental identification in young children. Genet. Psychol. Monographs, *60:*257-308. **39**

Emmerich, W. 1959b. Young child's discrimination of parent and child roles. Child Development, *30:*403-419. **39, 409**

Emmerich, W. 1964. Continuity and stability in early social development. Child Development, *35:*311-332. **434, 435**

Emmerich, W. 1966. Stability and change in early personality development. Young Children, *21:*233-243. Also in W. W. Hartup and N. L. Smothergill (Eds.). 1967. The Young Child—Reviews of Research. Washington, D.C. National Association for the Education of Young Children. **413**

Erikson, E. H. 1950. Childhood and Society. New York, W. W. Norton & Co., Inc. 2nd ed. 1963. **242**

Erikson, E. H. 1956. The problem of ego identity. Journal of the American Psycho-analytic Association, IV, No. 1: 58-121. Also in M. R. Stein et al. (Eds.). Identity and Anxiety. Chicago, The Free Press of Glencoe. **38**

Erikson, E. H., and Close, K. 1960. The life cycle, in Golden Anniversary White House Conference on Children and Youth. Reference Papers on Children and Youth, pp. 19-26. **246**

Ervin, S. M., and Miller, W. R. 1963. Language Development. Chap. 3 in H. W. Stevenson, J. Kagan and C. Spiker (Eds.): Child Psychology. The Sixty-Second Yearbook of the Study of Education, Part One. Chicago, University of Chicago Press. **343, 344, 345, 348**

Ervin-Tripp, S. 1966. Language Development. Chap. in L. W. Hoffman, and M. L. Hoffman (Eds.): Review of Child Development Research, Vol. Two. New York, Russell Sage Foundation. **343, 344, 351, 354, 355, 356**

Escalona, S. 1953. Emotional development in the first year of life; in M. J. Senn (Ed.): Problems of Infancy and Early Childhood. Transactions of the Sixth Conference, pp. 11-92. Josiah Macy, Jr., Foundation. **148**

Escalona, S. 1968. The Roots of Individuality: Normal Patterns of Development in Infancy. Chicago, Aldine. **36**

Escalona, S., and Heider, G. M. 1959. Prediction and Outcome: A Study in Child Development. New York, Basic Books, Inc. **312, 314, 463**

Espenschade, A. 1947. Motor development. Rev. Educ. Research, *17*:354-361. **303**

Fahs, S. 1952. Today's Children and Yesterday's Heritage. Boston, Beacon Press, Inc. **428**

Falk, J. L. 1960. The physiological basis of thirst. Nutrition Rev., *18*:289-291. **179**

Falkner, F. 1957. Deciduous tooth eruption. Arch. Dis. Child., *31*:386-391. **174, 175**

Falkner, F. 1958. Skeletal maturation: An appraisal of concept and method. Am. J. Phys. Anthropol., *16*:381-396. **270**

Falkner, F. 1962. Some physical growth standards for white North American children. Pediatrics, *29*:467-474. **247, 249**

Falkner, F. 1966. General Considerations in Human Development. Chap. 2 in F. Falkner (Ed.): Human Development. Philadelphia, W. B. Saunders Company. **30, 88, 251, 311**

Falkner, F. (Ed.). 1966. Human Development. Philadelphia, W. B. Saunders Company. **3, 251**

Fanshel, D. 1966. Foster Parenthood, a Role Analysis. Minneapolis, University of Minnesota Press. **78**

Fantz, R. L. 1961. The origin of form perception. Scient. Amer., *204*:66-72. **331**

Fantz, R. L. 1963. Pattern vision in newborn infants. Science, *140*:296-297. **331**

Feeney, M. C., Dodds, M. L., and Lowenburg, M. E. 1966. The sense of taste of preschool children and their parents. J. Am. Dietet. A., *48*:399-403. **173, 199, 224**

Ferguson, A., et al. 1956. Growth and development of Negro infants. VI. Relationship of certain environmental factors to neuromuscular development during the first year of life. J. Pediat., *48*:308-313. **311**

Filer, L. J. 1966. Current problems in pediatric nutrition. Borden's Review of Nutrition Research, *27*:1-11. **202**

Finn, S. B. 1952. Prevalence of Dental Caries, in Survey of the Literature of Dental Caries. Food and Nutrition Board, National Research Council Publ. No. 225. Washington, D.C., National Academy of Sciences – National Research Council. **144**

Fischer, A. E., and Moloshok, R. E. 1960. Diabetic and prediabetic pregnancies with special reference to the newborn. J. Pediat., *57*:704-714. **107**

Fitzsimmons, C., and Manning, S. L. 1962. Purchases of Non-food Items in Selected Indiana Retail Stores. Lafayette, Indiana, Purdue University, Agricultural Experiment Station. **54**

Flanagan, G. L. 1962. The First Nine Months of Life. New York, Simon and Schuster, Inc. **128**

Flavell, J. H. 1963. Developmental Psychology of Jean Piaget. Princeton, N.J., Van Nostrand. **339, 360**

Flory, C. D. 1936. Osseous Development in Hand as Index of Skeletal Development. Monographs of the Society for Research in Child Development, 1, No. 3. **269**

Follis, R. H., and Park, E. A. 1952. Some observations on bone growth, with particular reference to zones and lines of increased density at the metaphysis. Amer. J. Roentgenol., *68*:709-724. **267**

Fomon, S. J. 1960. Comparative study of adequacy of protein from human milk and cow's milk in promotive nitrogen retention by normal full-term infant. Pediatrics, *26*:51-61. **185**

Fomon, S. J. 1966. Body Composition of the Infant. Chap. 10, Part 1, in F. Falkner (Ed.): Human Development. Philadelphia, W. B. Saunders Company. **279**

Fomon, S. J., Younoszai, M. K., and Thomas, L. N. 1966. Influence of Vitamin D on linear growth of normal full-term infants. J. Nutrition, *88:*345-350. **190**

Foote, N. N. (Ed.) 1960. Consumer Behavior: Models of Household Decision Making. New York, New York University Press. **54**

Foote, N. N., and Cottrell, L. S. 1955. Identity and Interpersonal Competence: A New Direction in Family Research. Chicago, University of Chicago Press. **38**

Forbes, G. B. 1957. Overnutrition for the child: Blessing or curse? Nutrition Rev., *15:*193-196. **180**

Forbes, G. B. 1958. Do we need a new perspective in infant feedings. J. Pediat., *52:*496-498. **180**

Forbes, G. B. 1960. The radioactive "fall-out" problem. A Commentary. Pediatrics, *26:*929-931. **142, 143**

Forbes, G. B. (Ed.) 1961. Symposium on overnutrition. Am. J. Clin. Nutrition, *9:*525-572. **180**

Ford, C. E. 1960. Chromosomal Abnormality and Congenital Malformations, in Ciba Foundation Symposium on Congenital Malformations, Jan. 19-21, 1960. **89**

Forsham, P. H. 1962. The Adrenals. Chap. 5, in R. H. Williams (Ed.): Textbook of Endocrinology. 3rd ed. Philadelphia, W. B. Saunders Company. **291, 292**

Foss, B. M. (Ed.) 1961. Determinants of Infant Behavior. Proceedings of a Tavistock study group on mother-infant interaction. London, Methuen & Company, Ltd.; New York, John Wiley & Sons, Inc.

Foss, B. M. (Ed.) 1963. Determinants of Infant Behavior II. London, Methuen & Company, Ltd.

Fowler, W. 1962. Cognitive learning in infancy and early childhood. Psychol. Bull., *59:*116-152. **303, 338**

Fowler, W. 1962. Teaching a two-year-old to read: an experiment in early childhood learning. Genetic Psychology Monographs, *66:*181-283. **12, 338**

Frank, J. 1960. Your Child's Reading Today. Garden City, Doubleday & Company, Inc. **357**

Frank, L. K. 1951. Working toward Health Personality; in M. J. Senn (Ed.): Problems of Infancy and Childhood. Transactions of Fourth Conference, March 6-7, 1950. New York, Josiah Macy, Jr., Foundation. **200**

Frank, L. K. 1966. The Cultural Patterning of Child Development. Chap. 13 in F. Falkner (Ed.): Human Development. Philadelphia, W. B. Saunders Company. **37**

Fraser, D. 1966. Nutritional problems in North America. Proc. Western Hemisphere Nutrition Congress. A.M.A. pp. 57-59. **158, 179**

Freud, A., and Burlingham, D. T. 1944. Infants without Families. New York, International Universities Press, Inc. **408**

Fries, M. E., and Lewi, B., 1938. Interrelated factors in development. Amer. J. Orthopsychiat., *8:*726-752. **312, 314**

Funkenstein, D. H. 1955. The physiology of fear and anger. Scient. Amer., *192:*74-80. **292**

Galdston, I. (Ed.) 1961. The Family: A Focal Point in Health Education. New York, International Universities Press, Inc. **74**

Garn, S. M. 1952. Individual and group deviations from "channelwise" grid progression in girls. Child Development, *23:*193-206. **258**

Garn, S. M. 1958. Fat, body size and growth in the newborn. Hum. Biol., *30:*265-280. **262**

Garn, S. M. 1962. An annotated bibliography on bone densitometry. Am. J. Clin. Nutrition, *10:*59-67. **264**

Garn, S. M. 1966. Body Size and Its Implications. Chap. in L. W. Hoffman and M. L. Hoffman (Eds.): Review of Child Development Research, Vol. 2. New York, Russell Sage Foundation. **250, 251, 259, 293, 460**

Garn, S. M., and Rohmann, C. G. 1966. Interaction of nutrition and genetics in the timing of growth and development. Pediat. Clin. N. Amer., *13:*353-379. **460**

Garn, S. M., and Shamir, Z. 1958. Methods for Research in Human Growth. Springfield, Ill., Charles C Thomas. **8**

Garn, S. M., et al. 1951. Stature, body build and tooth eruption in Aleutian children. Child Development, *22:*261-270. **250**

Garn, S. M., et al. 1956. Fat thickness and growth progress during infancy. Hum. Biol., *28:*232-250. **262**

Garn, S. M., et al. 1960. Sibling similarities in dental development. J. Dent. Res., *39:*170-175. **174**

Genné, W. H. 1956. Husbands and Pregnancy: the Handbook for Expectant Fathers. New York, Association Press. **128**

Gentry, E. F., and Aldrich, C. A. 1948. Toe reflexes in infancy and development of voluntary control. Am. J. Dis. Child., *76:*389-400. **277**

Gesell, A. 1925. Mental Growth of Preschool Child. New York, Macmillan Company. **299, 329, 345, 346, 366, 383**

Gesell, A., in collaboration with Amatruda, C. S. 1945. The Embryology of Behavior. New York, Harper & Brothers. **228, 229, 230, 246**

Gesell, A., and Amatruda, C. S. 1947. Developmental Diagnosis. New York, Paul B. Hoeber, Inc. **299, 306, 383**

Gesell, A., and Ames, L. 1947. Development of handedness. J. Genet. Psychol., *70:*115-175. **309**

Gesell, A., and Ilg, F. L. 1937. Feeding Behavior of Infants. Philadelphia, J. B. Lippincott Company. **163**

Gesell, A., and Ilg, F. L. 1943. Infant and Child in Culture of Today. New York, Harper & Brothers. **205, 228, 302, 363, 374, 414**

Gesell, A., et al. 1940. The First Five Years of Life. New York, Harper & Brothers. **277, 299, 305**

Gesell, A., and Thompson, H. 1941. Twins T. and C. from infancy to adolescence. Genet. Psychol. Monogr., *24:*3-121. **10, 311**

Getzels, J. and Jackson, P. 1962. Creativity and Intelligence. New York, John Wiley & Sons, Inc. **376, 388**

Gewirtz, J. L. 1948. Succorance in young children. Unpublished doctoral dissertation. Iowa City, State University of Iowa. **404**

Gewirtz, J. L. 1961. A learning analysis of the effects of normal stimulation, privation and deprivation on the acquisition of social motivation and attachment; in B. M. Foss (Ed.): Determinants of Infant Behaviour. Proceedings of a Tavistock study group on mother-infant interaction. London, Methuen & Company, Ltd. **41, 42, 138, 233**

Gewirtz, J. L., and Baer, D. M. 1958. The effect of brief social deprivation on behaviors for a social reinforcer. J. Abnorm. & Social Psychol., *56:*49-56. **452**

Gibson, E. J. 1963. Perceptual Development. Chap. 4 in H. W. Stevenson, J. Kagan and C. Spiker (Eds.): Child Psychology. The Sixty-Second Yearbook of the National Society for the Study of Education. Chicago, University of Chicago Press. **331, 332, 334, 339**

Gibson, E. J., Gibson, J. J., Pick, A. D., and Osser, H. 1962. A developmental study of the discrimination of letter-like forms. J. Comp. Physiol., Psychol., *55:*897-906. **334**

Gibson, E. J., and Olum, V. 1960. Experimental Methods of Studying Perception in Children. Chap. 8, in P. Mussen (Ed.): Handbook of Research Methods in Child Development. New York, John Wiley & Sons, Inc. **332, 333, 339, 340, 387**

Gibson, E. J., Pick, A. D., Osser, H., and Hammond, M. 1962. The role of grapheme-phoneme correspondence in the perception of words. Amer. J. Psychol., *75:*554-570. **334**

Gibson, E. J., and Walk, R. D. 1960. The "Visual Cliff." Scient. Amer., *202:*64-71. April. **332**

Gibson, J. J. 1963. The useful dimensions of sensitivity. American Psychologist, *18:*1-15. **325**

Ginott, H. G. 1965. Between Parent and Child. New York, Macmillan Company. **452**

Glass, B. 1956. The hazards of atomic radiation to man. British and American reports. J. Hered., *47:*260-268. **143**

Glidewell, J. C. (Ed.) 1961. Parental Attitudes and Child Behavior. Springfield, Ill., Charles C Thomas. **448**

Glidewell, J. C., Kantor, M. B., Smith, L. M., and Stringer, L. A. 1966. Socialization and Social Structure in the Classrooms. Chap. in L. W. Hoffman and M. L. Hoffman (Eds.): Review of Child Development Research, Vol. 2. New York, Russell Sage Foundation. **394, 413**

Golden Anniversary White House Conference on Children and Youth. 1960a. Children and Youth in the 1960's; Survey Papers. Washington, D.C., Golden Anniversary White House Conference on Children and Youth. **79, 431**

Golden Anniversary White House Conference on Children and Youth. 1960b. Children in a Changing World, a Chart Book. Washington, D.C. Golden Anniversary White House Conference on Children and Youth. **66-72**

Golden Anniversary White House Conference on Children and Youth. 1960c. Reference

Papers on Children and Youth. Washington, D.C., Golden Anniversary White House Conference on Children and Youth. **79, 181**

Goldsmith, G. A. 1965. Intestinal flora, nutrition, and metabolism. Am. J. Digestive Diseases, *10:*829-835. **169**

Gonzaga, A. J., Warren, R. J., and Robbins, F. C. 1963. Attenuated poliovirus infection in infants fed colostrum from poliomyelitis immune cows. Pediatrics, *32:*1039-1045. **188**

Goodenough, F. L. 1931. Anger in Young Children. Inst. Child Welfare Monograph Series, No. 9. Minneapolis, University of Minnesota Press. **197, 392**

Goodman, M. E. 1952. Race Awareness in Young Children. Reading, Mass., Addison-Wesley Publishing Co., Inc. Also, 1964, Collier Books paper back edition, New York, Collier-Macmillan. **428**

Goodrich, D. W. 1961. Possibilities for Preventive Intervention during Initial Personality Development; in G. Caplan (Ed.): Prevention of Emotional Disorders in Children. New York, Basic Books. **33**

Goodrich, F. W. 1950. Natural Childbirth. New York, Prentice-Hall, Inc. **126**

Graber, T. M. 1966. Craniofacial and dentitional development; in F. Falkner (Ed.): Human Development. Philadelphia, W. B. Saunders Company. **165, 166, 167, 174, 177, 178**

Graham, F. K., et al. 1957. Anoxia as a significant perinatal experience: A critique. J. Pediat., *50:*556-569. **108**

Grant, E. 1939. Effect of Certain Factors in Home Environment upon Child Behavior. Studies in Child Welfare, 17. Iowa City, State University of Iowa. **450**

Graubard, M. 1943. Man's Food, Its Rhyme or Reason. New York, Macmillan Company. **55**

Gray, L. A. 1960. Gynecology in Adolescence, in Symposium on Adolescence. Pediat. Clin. N. Amer., *7:*43-57. **82**

Gray, S. W., and Klaus, R. A. 1965. An experimental preschool program for culturally deprived children. Child Development, *36:*887-898. **12, 338**

Green, J. D. 1962. Basic Neuroendocrinology. Chap. 13 in R. H. Williams (Ed.): Textbook of Endocrinology. 3rd ed. Philadelphia, W. B. Saunders Company. **288**

Greenhill, J. P. 1965. Obstetrics. 13th ed. Philadelphia, W. B. Saunders Company. **82, 97, 105, 109, 110, 111, 124**

Greenwaldt, E., et al. 1960. The onset of sleeping through the night in infancy. Relation to introduction of solid food in the diet, birth weight and position in the family. Pediatrics, *26:*667-668. **228**

Greulich, W. W. 1957. A comparison of the physical growth and development of American-born and native Japanese children. Am. J. Phys. Anthropol., *15:*489-515. **90, 250**

Greulich, W. W., and Pyle, S. I. 1959. Radiographic Atlas of Skeletal Development of Hand and Wrist. Stanford, Stanford University Press. **21, 266-270**

Griffith, W. H. 1967. The scope of nutrition. Fed. Proc., *26:*153-157. **159**

Griffiths, R. 1954. The Abilities of Babies. A Study in Mental Measurement. New York, McGraw-Hill Book Co., Inc. (Also University of London Press.) **298, 299, 300**

Gross, I. H. 1959. Research in home management. J. H. Econ., *51:*260-263. **60**

Gross, R. T., and Moses, L. E. 1956. Weight gains in the first four weeks of infancy: A comparison of three diets. Pediatrics, *18:*362-368. **187**

Gruenberg, S. M., and the Child Study Association (Eds.). 1951. Our Children Today. New York, The Viking Press, Inc. **440**

Gryboski J. D. 1965. The swallowing mechanism of the neonate. I. Esophageal and gastric motility. Pediatrics, *35:*445-452. **163**

Gutelius, M. F. 1948. Modified self-selection method of feeding preschool children in the home. Am. J. Pub. Health, *38:*1118-1125. **210**

Gutheim, F. 1948. Houses for Family Living. New York, The Woman's Foundation. **59, 60, 63**

Guthrie, H. A. 1966. Effect of early feeding of solid foods on nutritive intake of infants. Pediatrics, *38:*879-885. **191**

Guthrie, H. A. 1967. Introductory Nutrition. St. Louis, C. V. Mosby Company. **180, 185, 186, 189, 191, 198, 202**

Gutteridge, M. 1939. Study of motor achievements of young children. Arch. Psychol., No. 244. **302**

Gutteridge, M. 1947. The Child's Experiences in Bodily Activity; in Forty-sixth Yearbook of the National Society for the Study of Education. Part II. Chicago, University of Chicago Press. **302**

Guttmacher, A. F. 1957. Pregnancy and Birth: A Book for Expectant Parents. New York, The Viking Press, Inc. Pocket ed., Signet Key Books. The New American Library of World Literature, Inc., New York. **128**

Guy, L. P., et al. 1956. The possibility of total elimination of retrolental fibroplasia by O_2 restriction. Pediatrics, *17:*247-249. **104**

Gyllenswärd, C. 1960. Reported in F. C. Aitken and F. E. Hytten: Infant feeding: comparison of breast and artificial feeding. Nutrition Abst. & Rev., *30:*341-371. **187**

György, P. 1961. Orientation in infant feeding. Proc. 5th International Congress of Nutrition. Fed. Proc. 20 Part III: 169-176. **185, 187, 218**

Haber, R. N. (Ed.) 1966. Current Research in Motivation. New York, Holt, Rinehart and Winston, Inc. **387**

Haer, J. L. 1957. Predictive utility of five indices of social stratification. American Sociological Review, *22:*541-546. **64**

Halverson, H. M. 1933. Acquisition of skill in infancy. J. Genet. Psychol., *43:*3-48. **305**

Halverson, H. M. 1937. Studies of the grasping responses of early infancy. J. Genet. Psychol., *51:*371-449. **103, 305**

Halverson, H. M. 1943. The Development of Prehension in Infants; in R. G. Barker, J. S. Kounin and H. F. Wright (Eds.): Child Development and Behavior. New York, McGraw-Hill Book Co., Inc. **103, 305**

Halverson, V. B. 1967. Concepts of Nurturance in Young Children. Master's thesis. Lafayette, Indiana, Purdue University. **406, 412**

Ham, A. W., and Leeson, T. S. 1965. Histology. 5th ed. Philadelphia, J. B. Lippincott Company. **162, 264, 270, 275, 276, 288, 289, 291, 292**

Hamburger, W. W. 1960. Appetite in man. Am. J. Clin. Nutrition, *8:*569-586. **204**

Hamilton, W. J., Boyd, J. D., and Mossman, H. W. 1952. Human Embryology. Cambridge, England, W. Heffer & Sons, Ltd. **101**

Hansen, A. E., and Bennett, M. 1964. Nutritional Requirements, in W. E. Nelson (Ed.): Textbook of Pediatrics. 8th ed. Philadelphia, W. B. Saunders Company. **179**

Hansman, C. F., and Maresh, M. M. 1961. A longitudinal study of skeletal maturation. Am. J. Dis. Child., *101:*305-321, **268**

Hardy, J. D. 1961. Physiology of temperature regulation. Physiol. Rev., *41:*521-606. **133**

Harlow, H. F. 1963. The maternal affectional systems; in B. M. Foss (Ed.): Determinants of Infant Behavior II. London, Methuen & Company, Ltd. **392**

Harlow, H. F., and Harlow, M. K. 1966. Learning to love. American Scientist, *54:*244-272. **12, 157, 390, 392, 412**

Harris, D. B. (Ed.) 1957. The Concept of Development. Minneapolis, University of Minnesota Press.

Harris, D. B., and Harris, E. S. 1946. Study of fetal movements in relation to mother's activity. Hum. Biol., *18:*221-237. **103**

Harris, F. R., Wolf, M. M., and Baer, D. M. 1964. Effects of adult social reinforcement on child behavior. Young Children, *20:*8-17. Also in W. W. Hartup and N. L. Smothergill (Eds.) 1967. The Young Child—Reviews of Research. Washington, D.C., National Association for the Education of Young Children. **312, 322**

Hartley, R. E. 1959. Children's concepts of male and female roles. Merrill-Palmer Quarterly, *6:*153-164. **58**

Hartley, R., Frank, L. K., and Goldenson, R. 1952. Understanding Children's Play. New York, Columbia University Press. **2, 376, 378, 381, 388, 420**

Hartley, R. E., and Goldenson, R. M. 1957. The Complete Book of Children's Play. New York, Thomas Y. Crowell. **322**

Hartup, W. W. 1958. Nurturance and nurturance-withdrawal in relation to the dependency behavior of preschool children. Child Development, *29:*191-201. **137, 138, 156, 407**

Hartup, W. W. 1963. Dependence and Independence. Chap. 8 in H. W. Stevenson, J. Kagan and C. Spiker (Eds.): Child Psychology. Sixty-Second Yearbook of the National Society for the Study of Education. Chicago, University of Chicago Press. **407**

Hartup, W. W. 1965. Peers as agents of social reinforcement. Young Children, *20:*176-184. Also in W. W. Hartup and N. L. Smothergill (Eds.): The Young Child—Reviews of Research. Washington, D.C., National Association for the Education of Young Children, 1967. **403, 412, 428**

Hartup, W. W., and Keller, E. D. 1960. Nurturance in preschool children and its relation to dependency. Child Development, *31:*681-689. **405**

Hassan, H., Hashim, S. A., Van Italli, T. B., and Sebreth, W. H. 1966. Syndrome in premature infants associated with low plasma vitamin E levels and high polyunsaturated fatty acid diet. Am. J. Clin. Nutrition, *19:*147-157. **191**

Hatfield, J. S., Ferguson, L. R., and Alpert, R. 1967. Mother-child interaction and the socialization process. Child Development, *38:*365-414. **155, 156**

Havighurst, R. J. 1950. Developmental Tasks and Education. New York, Longmans Green & Co., Inc. **33, 139**

Havighurst, R. J., and Davis, A. 1955. A comparison of the Chicago and Harvard studies of social class differences in child rearing. Am. Sociol. Rev., *20:*438-442. **64**

Haynes, H., White, B. L., and Held, R. 1965. Visual accommodation in human infants. Science, *148,* 3669:528-530. **331**

Heathers, G. 1955. Emotional dependence and independence in nursery school play. J. Genet. Psychol., *87:*37-57. **395**

Hebb, D. O. 1966. A Textbook of Psychology. 2nd ed. Philadelphia, W. B. Saunders Company. **9, 13, 20, 30, 150, 275, 277, 278, 279, 293, 311, 324, 392**

Hechinger, F. M. (Ed.) 1966. Pre-school Education Today. Garden City, N.Y., Doubleday & Company, Inc. **386**

Heilbroner, R. L. 1960. The Future as History. New York, Harper & Brothers. **65**

Heiner, D. C., Wilson, J. F., and Lahey, M. E. 1964. Sensitivity to cow's milk. J.A.M.A., *189:*563-567. **189**

Henry, W. E. 1960. Projective Techniques. Chap. 15 in P. Mussen (Ed.): Handbook of Research Methods in Child Development. New York, John Wiley & Sons, Inc. **414**

Herdan, G. 1954. The relation between birth weight and subsequent weight in childhood. Arch. Dis. Childhood, *29:*220-223. **254**

Hess, R. D. 1964. Maternal Teaching Styles, Social Class and Educability. Paper read at the Midwestern Association for Nursery Education Conference, May 2, 1964, Minneapolis, Minnesota. Mimeographed. **12, 353**

Hess, R. D., and Handel, G. 1959. Family Worlds: A Psychosocial Approach to Family Life. Chicago, University of Chicago Press. **31, 32, 38, 39, 79**

Hess, R. D., and Shipman, V. C. 1965. Early experience and the socialization of cognitive modes in children. Child Development, *36:*869-886. **23, 43, 353**

Hewitt, D. 1957. Some familial correlations in height, weight and skeletal maturity. Ann. Hum. Genet., *22:*26-35. **250**

Hicks, S. P. 1953. Developmental malformations produced by radiation: a time table of their development. Am. J. Roentgenol., *69:*272-293. **142**

Hildreth, G. H. 1948. Manual dominance in nursery school children. J. Genet. Psychol., *72:*29-45. **309, 310**

Hildreth, G. H. 1949. Development and training of hand dominance: characteristics of handedness; developmental tendencies in handedness; origins of handedness and lateral dominance. J. Genet. Psychol., *75:*197-275. **309, 310**

Hildreth, G. H. 1950. Development and training of hand dominance: developmental problems associated with handedness; training of handedness. J. Genet. Psychol., *76:*39-144. **309, 310**

Hill, R. 1949. Families Under Stress; Adjustment to Crises of War Separation and Reunion. New York, Harper & Brothers. **78**

Hill, R. 1966. Contemporary developments in family theory. J. Marriage and the Family, *28:*10-26. **31**

Hill, R., and Hansen, D. A. 1960. The identification of conceptual frameworks utilized in family study. Marriage and Family Living, *22:*299-311. **77**

Hillman, R. W. 1964. Nutrition in Pregnancy; in M. G. Wohl and R. S. Goodhard (Eds.): Modern Nutrition in Health and Disease. 3rd ed. Philadelphia, Lea & Febiger. **128**

Hirsch, M. 1931. Mütterschaftsfürscorge. Arch. Gynakol., *144:*34-85. **106**

Hochberg, J., and Brooks, V. 1962. Pictorial recognition as an unlearned ability: a study of one child's performance. Amer. J. Psychol., *75:*624-628. **334**

Hoeflin, R. 1954. Child-rearing practices and child-care resources used by Ohio farm families with preschool children. J. Genet. Psychol., *84:*271-297. **63**

Hoerr, N. L., Pyle, S. I., and Francis, C. C. 1962. Radiographic Atlas of Skeletal Development of the Foot and Ankle. Springfield, Ill., Charles C Thomas. **275**

Hoffman, L. W., and Hoffman, M. L. (Eds.) 1966. Review of Child Development Research, Vol. 2. New York, Russell Sage Foundation. **3**

Hoffman, L. W., and Lippitt, R. 1960. The Measurement of Family Life Variables. Chap. 22 in P. Mussen (Ed.): Handbook of Research Methods in Child Development. New York, John Wiley & Sons, Inc. **64, 79**

Hoffman, M. L. 1960. Power assertion by the parent and its impact on the child. Child Development, *31:*129-143. Also in G. R. Medinnus (Ed.): Readings in the Psychology of Parent-Child Relations. New York, John Wiley & Sons, Inc., 1967. **447**

Hoffman, M. L., and Hoffman, L. W. (Eds.) 1964. Review of Child Development Research, Vol. 1. New York, Russell Sage Foundation. **3**

Holcomb, A. E., and Meredith, H. V. 1956. Width of the dental arches at the deciduous canines in white children 4 to 8 years of age. Growth, *20:*159-177. **26, 27**

Hollenberg, E., and Sperry, M. 1950. Some antecedents of aggression and effects of frustration on doll play. Personality, *1:*32-43. **392, 412**

Holway, A. 1949. Early self-regulation of infants and later behavior in play interviews. Am. J. Orthopsychiat., *19:*612-623. **208**

Honzik, M. P. 1965. Prediction of behavior from birth to maturity, a book review of *Birth to Maturity:* a study in psychological development, by Jerome Kagan and Howard Moss (New York: Wiley, 1962). Merrill-Palmer Quarterly, *11:*77-88. **409, 434, 437, 464**

Honzik, M. P. 1967. Mother-child interaction and the socialization process. Child Development, *38:*337-364. **22**

Honzik, M. P., and Macfarlane, J. W. 1965. Prediction of specific behaviors and personality characteristics from 21 months to 30 years. (MS, referred to in M. P. Honzik, 1965.) **437, 464**

Hooker, D. 1952. The Prenatal Origin of Behavior. Porter Lectures, Series 18. Lawrence, Kansas, University of Kansas Press. **102**

Horney, K. 1942. Self-Analysis. New York, W. W. Norton & Co., Inc. **41, 148**

Horney, K. 1950. Neurosis and Human Growth. New York, W. W. Norton & Co., Inc. **41**

Howorth, B. 1946. Dynamic posture. J.A.M.A., *131:*1398-1404. **281**

Hubert, M. A. G., and Britton, J. H. 1957. Attitudes and practices of mothers rearing their children from birth to the age of two years. J. H. Econ., *49:*208-219. **209, 214, 222, 232**

Hummel, F. C., et al. 1937. Consideration of nutritive status in metabolism of women during pregnancy. J. Nutrition, *13:*263-277. **84**

Hunt, E. F. 1966. The Developmental Genetics of Man. Chap. 4 in F. Falkner (Ed.): Human Development. Philadelphia, W. B. Saunders Company. **89, 251, 310**

Hunt, J. McV. 1960. Experience and the development of motivation: some reinterpretations. Child Development, *31:*489-504. **13, 18, 150, 233, 246**

Hunt, J. McV. 1964. The psychological basis for using preschool enrichment as an antidote for cultural deprivation. Merrill-Palmer Quarterly, *10:*209-248. **12**

Hunt, J. McV. 1965. Traditional personality theory in the light of recent evidence. American Scientist, *53:*80-96. **439**

Hunt, J. McV. 1966. The Epigenesis of Intrinsic Motivation and Early Cognitive Learning; in R. N. Haber (Ed.): Current Research in Motivation. New York, Holt, Rinehart and Winston, Inc. **13, 387**

Huschka, M. 1942. The child's response to coercive bowel training. Psychosom. Med., *4:*301-308. **219**

Hymes, J. L. 1961. The Child Under Six. Washington, D.C., Education Service. **452**

Hytten, F. E., et al. 1958. Difficulties associated with breast feeding: a study of 106 primipara. Brit. Med. J., *i:*310-315. **82**

Illingworth, R. S., et al. 1949. Relation of birth weight to physical development in childhood. Lancet, *2:*598-602. **254**

Illingworth, R. S., and Lister, J. 1964. The critical or sensitive period, with special reference to certain feeding problems in infants and children. J. Pediat., *65:*839-848. **192**

Illingworth, R. S., and Stone, D. G. H. 1952. Self-demand feeding in a maternity unit. Lancet, *262:*683-687. **182**

Ingalls, T. H. 1950. Anoxia as a cause of fetal death and congenital defect in the mouse. Am. J. Dis. Child., *30:*34-45. **108**

Ingalls, T. H. 1953. Preventive Prenatal Pediatrics; in S. Z. Levin (Ed.): Advances in Pediatrics. Vol. VI. Chicago, Year Book Publishers, Inc. **108**

Ingalls, T. H. 1956. Causes and prevention of developmental defects. J.A.M.A., *161:* 1047-1051. **108**

Ingalls, T. H. 1960. Environmental Factors in Causation of Congenital Anomalies; in G. E. W. Wolstenholme and C. M. O'Connor (Eds.): Ciba Foundation Symposium on Congenital Malformations. Boston, Little, Brown and Co. **104**

Inhelder, B. 1962. III. Some aspects of Piaget's genetic approach to cognition; in W. Kessen and C. Kuhlman (Eds.): Thought in the Young Child. Monographs of the Society for Research in Child Development, 27, No. 2. **14, 314, 325, 359, 360**

Irwin, O. C. 1930. The amount and nature of activities of new-born infants under constant external stimulating conditions during the first ten days of life. Genet. Psychol. Monogr., *8:*1-92. **314**

Irwin, O. C. 1952. Speech development in the young child; some factors related to the speech development of the infant and young child. J. Speech and Hearing Disorders, *17:*269-279. **344**

Irwin, O. C. 1960. Language and Communication. Chap. 12 in P. Mussen (Ed.): Handbook of Research Methods in Child Development. New York, John Wiley & Sons, Inc. **347, 352, 355**

Irwin, O. C., and Weiss, L. A. 1934. The effect of darkness on the activity of newborn infants. Studies in Child Welfare, *9:*163-175. Iowa City, University of Iowa. **298**

Isaacs, S. S. 1946. Social Development in Young Children; Study of Beginnings. London, Geo. Routledge & Sons, Ltd. **41**

Isaacs, S. S. 1952. The Nature and Function of Phantasy. Developments in Psychoanalysis. London, Hogarth Press, Ltd. **375**

Iscoe, I., and Stevenson, H. (Eds.) 1960. Personality Development in Children. Austin, University of Texas Press.

Ivy, A. C., and Gibbs, G. E. 1966. Physiology of the Gastro-intestinal Tract. Chap. 20 (Vol. I) in I. McQuarrie (Ed.): Brennemann's Practice of Pediatrics. Hagerstown, Md., W. F. Prior Co., Inc. **164, 165, 168**

Ivy, A. C., and Grossman, M. I. 1952. Digestive System. Chap. 20 in A. I. Lansing (Ed.): Cowdry's Problems of Aging. 3rd ed. Baltimore, Williams & Wilkins Company. **164, 165**

Jackson, E. B. 1956. Childbirth Patterns in the United States, in Mental Health and Infant Development; in K. Soddy (Ed.): Proceedings of the International Seminar held by the World Federation for Mental Health at Chichester, England. Vol. I. New York, Basic Books, Inc. **127**

Jackson, E. B., et al. 1956. Statistical report on incidence and duration of breast feeding in relation to personal-social and hospital maternity factors. Pediatrics, *17:*700-715. **184**

Jackson, R. L. 1966. Effect of malnutrition on growth of the pre-school child, in Pre-school child malnutrition primary deterrent to human progress. National Academy of Sciences—National Research Council. Publication 1282, Washington, D.C. **158**

Jackson, R. L., and Kelly, H. G. 1945. Growth charts for use in pediatric practice. J. Pediat., *27:*215-229. **256, 257**

Jackson, R. L., Westerfield, R., Flynn, M. A., Kimball, E. R., and Lewis, R. B. 1964. Growth of "well-born" American infants fed human and cow's milk. Pediatrics, *33:*642-652. **187**

Jacobzinger, H. 1959. Causation, prevention and control of accidental poisoning. J.A.M.A., *171:*1769-1777. **146**

Jacobzinger, H., et al. 1960. A study of nonfatal accidents in children under supervision in Child Health Stations of New York City, Department of Health (1952-1959). Pediatrics, *26:*415-431. **146**

Jeans, P. C., and Stearns, G. 1938. Effect of vitamin D on linear growth in infancy; effect of intake above 1800 U.S.P. units daily. J. Pediat., *13:*739-740. **190**

Jeans, P. C., et al. 1955. Incidence of prematurity in relation to maternal nutrition. J. Am. Dietet. A., *31:*576-581. **105**

Jelliffe, D. B. 1962. Culture, social changes and infant feeding. Current trends in tropical regions. Am. J. Clin. Nutrition, *10:*19-45. **183**

Jennings, H. H. 1947. Sociometry of Leadership. New York, Beacon House, Inc. **419**

Jersild, A. T. 1931. Influence of training on vocal ability of three-year-old children. Child Development, *2:*272-291. **382**

Jersild, A. T. 1954. Emotional Development. Chap. 14 in L. Carmichael (Ed.): Manual of Child Psychology. 2nd ed. New York, John Wiley & Sons, Inc. **390, 392**

Jersild, A. T., and Bienstock, S. 1934. Study of development of children's ability to sing. J. Educ. Psychol., *25:*481-503. **381**

Jersild, A. T., and Holmes, F. B. 1935. Children's Fears. Child Development Monograph, No. 20. New York, Teachers College, Columbia University. **150, 391**

Johnson, W. 1955. Stuttering in Children and Adults: Thirty Years of Research at the University of Iowa. Minneapolis, University of Minnesota Press. **356**

Johnson, W., et al. 1959. The Onset of Stuttering: Research Findings and Implications. Minneapolis, University of Minnesota Press. **356**

Jones, H. E. 1949. Motor Performance and Growth. Berkeley, University of California Press. **314**

Jones, H. E. 1954. The Environment and Mental Development. Chap. 10 in L. Carmichael (Ed.): Manual of Child Psychology. 2nd ed. New York, John Wiley & Sons, Inc. **385**

Jones, H. E. 1960. The Longitudinal Method in the Study of Personality; in I. Iscoe and H. Stevenson (Eds.): Personality Development in Children. Austin, University of Texas Press. **462**

Jones, M. C. 1965. Psychological correlates of somatic development. Child Development, *36*:899-911. **314**

Jordan, W. A. 1960. Anticaries technics in nonfluoride areas: topical fluoride treatment. J. Am. Dent. A., *60*:181-192. **145**

Journal of Marriage and the Family. February 1967. Special Issue: Government Programs and the Family. Vol. 29, Number 1. **78**

Jundell, I. 1959. Cited in C. A. Smith: The Physiology of the Newborn Infant. 3rd ed. Springfield, Charles C Thomas. **134**

Kagan, J. 1964. Acquisition and Significance of Sex Typing and Sex Role Identity; in M. L. Hoffman and L. W. Hoffman (Eds.): Review of Child Development Research, Vol. 1. New York, Russell Sage Foundation. **408**

Kagan, J. 1966. Personality, Behavior, and Temperament. Chap. 12, Part I, in F. Falkner (Ed.): Human Development. Philadelphia, W. B. Saunders Company. **458**

Kagan, J. 1967. On the need for relativism. American Psychologist, *22*:131-142. **336, 337**

Kagan, J., Henker, B. A., Hen-Tov, A., Levine, J., and Lewis, M. 1966. Infants' differential reactions to familiar and distorted faces. Child Development, *37*:519-532. **336**

Kagan, J., and Moss, H. A. 1962. Birth to Maturity, a Study in Psychological Development. New York, John Wiley & Sons, Inc. **2, 3, 312, 413, 434, 437, 463, 464**

Kagan, J., Sontag, L. W., Baker, C. T., and Nelson, V. L. 1958. Personality and I. Q. Change. J. Abnorm. & Social Psychol., *56*:261-266. **386, 461**

Kahl, J. A., and Davis, J. A. 1955. A comparison of indexes of socio-economic status. American Sociological Review, *20*:317-325. **64**

Kaiser, A. D. 1966. The Tonsil and Adenoid Problem. Chap. 4 (Vol. 2) in I. McQuarrie (Ed.): Brennemann's Practice of Pediatrics. Hagerstown, Md., W. F. Prior Co., Inc. **140**

Kawi, A. A., and Pasamanick, B. 1959. Prenatal and Paranatal Factors in the Development of Childhood Reading Disorders. Monographs of the Society for Research in Child Development, 24, No. 4. **104**

Keeney, A. H. 1966. Development of Vision. Chap. 15 in F. Falkner (Ed.): Human Development. Philadelphia, W. B. Saunders Company. **331**

Keister, M. E. 1950. Relation of mid-morning feeding to behavior of nursery school children. J. Am. Dietet. A., *26*:25-29. **197**

Keister, M. E., and Updegraff, R. 1937. Study of children's reactions to failure and experimental attempt to modify them. Child Development, *8*:241-248. **392**

Kelley, V. C., and Bosma, J. F. 1966. Basal Metabolism in Infants and Children. Chap. 22 (Vol. 1) in I. McQuarrie (Ed.): Brennemann's Practice of Pediatrics. Hagerstown, Md., W. F. Prior Co., Inc. **171**

Kellogg, W. N. 1941. Method for recording activity of human fetus in utero with specimen results. J. Genet. Psychol., *58*:307-326. **103**

Kendall, H. O., Kendall, F. P., and Boynton, D. A. 1952. Posture and Pain. Baltimore, Williams & Wilkins Company. **284**

Kennedy, C. 1959. Biological Characteristics of Brain Development, in Maryland Child Growth and Development Institute, June 1-5. Baltimore, Md., Maryland State Department of Health. **276**

Kessen, W., Williams, E. J., and Williams, J. P. 1961. Selection and test of response measures in the study of the human newborn. Child Development, *32*:7-24. **308, 312, 322, 419**

Kessen, W., and Kuhlman, E. (Eds.) 1962. Thought in the Young Child. Monographs of the Society for Research in Child Development, 27, No. 2. **18**

Keys, A., et al. 1950. Biology of Human Starvation. Vol. II. Minneapolis, University of Minnesota Press. **84, 254**

Kinsey, V. E., et al. 1956. Retrolental fibroplasia. A.M.A. Arch. Ophth., *45*:481-543. **104**

Kirk, S. A. 1962. Educating Exceptional Children. Boston, Houghton Mifflin Co. **386**

Kirkpatrick, C. 1967. Familial development, selective needs, and predictive theory. J. Marriage and the Family, *29:*229-236. **31**

Klaus, R. A., and Gray, S. W. 1968. The Early Training Project for Disadvantaged Children: A Report after Five Years. Monographs of the Society for Research in Child Development, 33, No. 4 (Serial No. 120). **338**

Klein, H. 1935. Effects of pregnancy on incidence of tooth decay. Dental Cosmos, *77:*864-867. **117**

Klein, H. 1946. The family and dental disease. Dental disease (D.M.F.) experience in parents and offspring. J. Am. Dent. A., *33:*735-743. **145**

Klein, H. 1947. The family and dental disease; caries experience among parents and offspring exposed to drinking water containing fluoride. Pub. Health Rep., *62:*1247-1253. **145**

Kleitman, N. 1944. Sleep and Wakefulness, in O. Glasser (Ed.): Medical Physics. Vol. 1. Chicago, Year Book Publishers, Inc. **134**

Kleitman, N. 1957. Sleep, wakefulness and consciousness. Psychol. Bull., *54:*354-359. **228**

Kleitman, N. 1960a. The Nature of Dreaming; in G. E. W. Wolstenholme and M. O'Connor (Eds.): Ciba Foundation Symposium on The Nature of Sleep, June 27-29. Boston, Little, Brown and Co. **227**

Kleitman, N. 1960b. Patterns of dreaming. Scient. Amer., *203:*82-88. **227, 231**

Kleitman, N. 1963. Sleep and Wakefulness. Rev. ed. Chicago, University of Chicago Press. **134, 226, 227**

Kleitman, N., and Engelmann, T. G. 1953. Sleep characteristics of infants. J. Appl. Physiol., *6:*269-272. **227, 228**

Kluckhohn, F. R., and Strodtbeck, F. L. 1961. Variations in Value Orientations. Evanston, Ill., Row, Peterson & Co. **37**

Knobloch, H., and Pasamanick, B. 1960. Environmental factors affecting human development before and after birth. Pediatrics, *26:*210-218. **90**

Knowles, J. A. 1965. Excretion of drugs in milk. A review. J. Pediat., *66:*1068-1082. **189**

Koch, H. L. 1955. The relation of certain family constellation characteristics and the attitudes of children toward adults. Child Development, *26:*13-40. **45**

Koch, H. L. 1956a. Attitudes of young children toward their peers as related to certain characteristics of their siblings. Psychol. Monogr. 70, No. 19 (whole No. 426). **45**

Koch, H. L. 1956b. Children's work attitudes and sibling characteristics. Child Development, *27:*289-310. **45**

Koch, H. L. 1956c. Emotional attitudes of the young child in relation to characteristics of his sibling. Child Development, *27:*393-426. **45**

Koch, H. L. 1956d. Sissiness and tomboyishness in relation to sibling characteristics. J. Genet. Psychol., *88:*231-244. **45**

Koch, H. L. 1957. The relation in young children between characteristics of their playmates and certain attributes of their siblings. Child Development, *28:*175-202. **45**

Koch, H. L. 1960. The Relation of Certain Formal Attributes of Siblings to Attitudes Held Toward Each Other and Toward Their Parents. Monographs of the Society for Research in Child Development, 25, No. 4. **23, 45**

Koffka, K. 1925. Growth of the Mind. New York. Harcourt, Brace and Company. **329**

Kohlberg, L. 1963. The development of children's orientation toward a moral order. Vita Humana, *6:*11-33. **411, 428**

Kohlberg, L. 1964. Development of Moral Character and Moral Ideology; in M. L. Hoffman and L. W. Hoffman (Eds.): Review of Child Development Research, Vol. 1. New York, Russell Sage Foundation. **411**

Koos, E. L. 1954. The Health of Regionville. New York, Columbia University Press. **30, 65**

Korslund, M. K., and Eppright, E. S. 1967. Taste sensitivity and eating behavior of preschool children. J. Home Economics, *59:*168-170. **199, 329**

Krogman, W. M. 1950a. The concept of maturity from a morphological viewpoint. Child Development, *21:*25-32. **9**

Krogman, W. M. 1950b. Handbook of Measurement and Interpretation of Height and Weight, in the Growing Child. Monographs of the Society for Research in Child Development, 13, No. 3. **247, 250, 258, 293**

Krogman, W. M. 1956. The Physical Growth of Children: An Appraisal of Studies 1950-1955. Monographs of the Society for Research in Child Development, 20, No. 1. **258**

Kuenne, M. 1946. Experimental investigation of the relation of language to transposition behavior in young children. J. Exper. Psychol., *36:*471-490. **371, 372**

Lacey, J. I., Kagan, J., Lacey, B. C., and Moss, H. A. 1963. Situational determinants and behavioral correlates of autonomic response patterns; in P. H. Knapp (Ed.): Expression of Emotions in Man. New York, International Universities Press. **35**

Lacey, J. I., and Van Lehn, R. 1952. Differential emphasis in somatic response to stress: An experimental study. Psychosom. Med., *14:*71-81. **139**

Lafore, G. 1945. Practices of Parents in Dealing with Preschool Children. Child Development Monograph No. 31. New York, Teachers College, Columbia University. **447, 448**

Laird, D. A., and Breen, W. J. 1939. Sex and age alteration in taste preference. J. Am. Dietet. A., *15:*549-550. **173**

Lambert, W. W. 1960. Interpersonal Behavior. Chap. 20 in P. Mussen (Ed.): Handbook of Research Methods in Child Development. New York, John Wiley & Sons, Inc. **399, 403**

Landreth, C. 1958. The Psychology of Early Childhood. New York, Alfred A. Knopf, Inc. **208, 322**

Langdon, G., and Stout, I. 1952. The Discipline of Well-adjusted Children. New York, John Day Co., Inc. **448**

Lantis, M. 1962. The child consumer. J. H. Econ., *54:*370-375. **57**

Lark-Horowitz, B., and Norton, J. 1960. Children's art abilities: the interrelations and factorial structures of ten characteristics. Child Development, *31:*453-462. **381**

Larroche, J. 1966. The Development of the Central Nervous System during Intrauterine Life. Chap. 11, Part II in F. Falkner (Ed.): Human Development. Philadelphia, W. B. Saunders Company. **276, 277, 296**

Law, F. E., et al. 1961. Topical applications of fluoride solutions in dental caries control. Pub. Health Rep., *76:*287-290. **145**

Lee, D. 1957. Cultural factors in dietary choice. Am. J. Clin. Nutrition, *5:*166-170. **56**

Lee, D. 1962. American Home Economics Association Conference on Aging (talk). Lafayette, Indiana. **37**

Leeper, S. H., Dales, R. J., Skipper, D. S., and Witherspoon, R. L. 1968. Good Schools for Young Children. New York, Macmillan Company. **78**

Lenneberg, E. H. 1964. Speech as a motor skill, with special reference to nonaphasic disorders: in U. Bellugi and R. W. Brown (Eds.): The Acquisition of Language. Monographs of the Society for Research in Child Development, 29, No. 1 (Serial No. 92). **342, 351**

Lenneberg, E. H., Rebelsky, F., and Nichols, I. 1965. The vocalization of infants born to hearing and deaf parents. Human Development, *8:*23-37. **344**

Leslie, G. 1955. Parent-Teacher Institute (talk). Lafayette, Indiana. **72**

Leslie, G. 1967. The Family in Social Context. New York, Oxford University Press. **73**

Leverton, R. M. 1967. Basic nutrition concepts for use in nutrition education. J. H. Econ., *59:*346-348. **57, 58**

Leverton, R. M., and Clark, G. 1947. Meat in the diet of young infants. J.A.M.A., *134:* 1215-1216. **192**

Leverton, R. M., et al. 1952. Further studies of use of meat in diet of infants and young children. J. Pediat., *40:*761-766. **192**

Levin, B., et al. 1959. Weight Gains, Serum Protein Levels and Health of Breast Fed and Artificially Fed Infants. Med. Res. Council Spec. Rep. Ser. No. 296. London, Her Majesty's Stationery Office. **187**

Levin, H., and Wardwell, E. 1962. The research uses of doll play. Psychol. Bull., *59:*27-56. **420**

Levine, M. 1951. A modern concept of breast feeding. J. Pediat., *38:*472-475. **189**

Levine, M. 1966. Psychological Testing of Children; Chap. in L. W. Hoffman and M. L. Hoffman (Eds.): Review of Child Development Research, Vol. 2. New York, Russell Sage Foundation. **421**

Levy, D. 1943. Maternal Overprotection. New York, Columbia University Press. **414**

Lewis, A. B., and Garn, S. M. 1960. The relationship between tooth formation and other maturational factors. Angle Orthodontist, *30:*70-77. **174**

Lewis, M. 1967. Infant attention: response decrement as a measure of cognitive processes, or What's New Baby Jane. Paper presented at the Society for Research in Child Development Symposium on the Role of Attention in Cognitive Development, New York, March 1967. **22**

Lewis, M. M. 1959. How Children Learn to Speak. (First published in Great Britain in 1957.) New York, Basic Books, Inc. **388**

Lewis, M. M. 1951. Infant Speech: A Study of the Beginnings of Language. 2nd ed. New York, Humanities Press, Inc.; London, Routledge & Kegan Paul, Ltd. **344, 345, 351**

Lilienfeld, A. M., and Pasamanick, B. 1954. The association of maternal and fetal factors with the development of epilepsy. Abnormalities of the prenatal and paranatal periods. J.A.M.A., *155:*719-724. **104**

Ling, B. C. 1941. Form discrimination as a learning cue in infants. Comp. Psychol. Monogr. 17, No. 2. **333**

Linzell, J. L. 1959. Physiology of the mammary glands. Physiol. Rev., *39:*534-576. **182**

Lipsitt, L. P. 1966. Learning processes of human newborns. Merrill-Palmer Quarterly *12:*45-71. **12, 41, 215, 298, 328, 337, 388, 456**

Lipsitt, L. P., Engen, T., and Kaye, H. 1963. Developmental changes in the olfactory threshold of the neonate. Child Development, *34:*371-376. **327**

Lipsitt, L. P., and Kaye, H. 1964. Conditioned sucking in the human newborn. Psychonomic Sci., *1:*29-30. **329**

Lipsitt, L. P., and Levy, N. 1959. Electro-tactual threshold in the neonate. Child Development, *30:*547-554. **326**

Lipton, E. L., Steinschneider, A., and Richmond, J. B. 1966. Psychophysiologic Disorders in Children; Chap. in L. W. Hoffman and M. L. Hoffman (Eds.): Review of Child Development Research, Vol. 2. New York, Russell Sage Foundation. **19, 35**

Lloyd, C. W. 1962. The Ovaries. Chap. 7 in R. H. Williams (Ed.): Textbook of Endocrinology. 3rd ed. Philadelphia, W. B. Saunders Company. **182, 292**

Lombard, O. M. 1950. Breadth of bone and muscle by age and sex in childhood. Child Development, *21:*229-239. **260, 261, 262**

Lowenberg, M. E. 1959. Between Infancy and Adolescence; in Food, The Yearbook of Agriculture. Washington, D.C., U.S. Department of Agriculture, 1959. **202**

Lowenberg, M. E. 1965. Philosophy of nutrition and application in maternal health services. Am. J. Clin. Nutrition, *16:*370-373. **201**

Lowenfeld, V., and Brittain, W. L. 1964. Creative and Mental Growth. 4th ed. New York, Macmillan Company. **380**

Lowery, L. G. 1940. Personality distortion and early institutional care. Amer. J. Orthopsychiat., *10:*576-585. **131**

Maccoby, E. E. 1958. Children and working mothers. Children, 5, (No. 3):83-89, May-June, 1958. **47**

Maccoby, E. E. 1964. Effects of the Mass Media; in M. L. Hoffman and L. W. Hoffman (Eds.): Review of Child Development Research, Vol. I. New York, Russell Sage Foundation. **239, 241, 412**

Maccoby, E. E., Dowley, E. M., and Hagen, J. W. 1965. Activity level and intellectual functioning in normal preschool children. Child Development, *36:*761-770. **314, 322**

Macfarlane, J. W. 1943. Study of Personality Development. Chap. 18 in R. G. Barker et al. (Eds.): Child Behavior and Development. New York, McGraw-Hill Book Co., Inc. **450**

Macfarlane, J. W., et al. 1954. A Developmental Study of the Behavior Problems of Normal Children Between Twenty-one Months and Fourteen Years. Berkeley, University of California Press. **415, 416, 450**

MacKinnon, D. W. 1962. The nature and nurture of creative talent. American Psychologist, *17:*484-495. **383, 388, 409**

MacKinnon, D. W. 1965. Personality and the realization of creative potential. American Psychologist, *20:*273-281. **383**

Macleod, K. I. E. 1961. Toward solving the accident problem. Pub. Health Rep., *76:*606-617. **61**

McCall, A. 1966. This Is Music. Boston, Allyn and Bacon, Inc. **386**

McCandless, B. R. 1967. Children, Behavior and Development. 2nd ed. New York, Holt, Rinehart and Winston. **30, 154, 157, 203**

McCandless, B. R., Bilous, C. B., and Bennett, H. L. 1961. Peer popularity and dependence on adults in preschool-age socialization. Child Development, *32:*511-518. **403**

McCarthy, D. 1954. Language Development in Children. Chap. 9 in L. Carmichael (Ed.): Manual of Child Psychology. 2nd ed. New York, John Wiley & Sons, Inc. **343, 346, 351**

McCarthy, D. 1961. Affective aspects of language learning, in Newsletter, Division of Developmental Psychology, American Psychological Association, Fall, 1961. Washington, D.C., American Psychological Association. **343, 354**

McGanity, W. J., et al. 1954. The Vanderbilt Cooperative Study of Maternal and Infant

Nutrition. VI. Relationship of obstetric performance to nutrition. Am. J. Obst. and Gynec., *67:*501-527. **84, 105, 106**

McGanity, W. J., et al. 1955. The Vanderbilt Cooperative Study of Maternal and Infant Nutrition. VIII. Some nutritional implications. J. Am. Dietet. A., *31:*582-588. **84**

McGanity, W. J., et al. 1958. Vanderbilt Cooperative Study of Maternal and Infant Nutrition. XII. Effect of reproductive cycle on nutritional status and requirements. J.A.M.A., *168:*2138-2145. **113**

McGeoch, J. A., and Irion, A. L. 1952. The Psychology of Human Learning. New York, Longmans, Green & Co., Inc. **12**

McGraw, M. B. 1939. Later development of children specially trained during infancy. Child Development, *10:*1-19. **11, 311, 312**

McGraw, M. B. 1941. Neural maturation as exemplified in reaching—prehensile behavior of human infant. J. Psychol., *11:*127-141. **306**

McGraw, M. B. 1943. Neuromuscular Maturation of Human Infant. New York, Columbia University Press. **11**

McGraw, M. B. 1946. Maturation of Behavior; Chap. 7 in L. Carmichael (Ed.): Manual of Child Psychology. New York, John Wiley & Sons, Inc. **334**

McKay, R. J., Jr., and Smith, C. A. 1964. Physiology of the newborn infant; in W. E. Nelson (Ed.): Textbook of Pediatrics. 8th ed. Philadelphia, W. B. Saunders Company, pp. 331-337. **170, 297**

McMorris, R. O. 1961. Faulty Posture. Pediat. Clin. N. Amer., *8:*213-224. **282**

Macy, I. G. 1942. Nutrition and Chemical Growth in Childhood. Vol. 1. Springfield, Ill., Charles C Thomas. **168, 198, 199**

Macy, I. G. 1958. Metabolic and biochemical changes in normal pregnancy. J.A.M.A., *168:*2265-2271. **112**

Macy, I. G., Kelley, H., and Sloan, R. 1950. Composition of Milks. Bulletin No. 119. Washington, D.C., National Academy of Science—National Research Council. **185**

Macy, I. G., and Kelley, H. J. 1959. Food for Expectant and Nursing Mothers; in Food, The Yearbook of Agriculture (Washington, D.C.) U.S. Department of Agriculture, 1959. **202**

Macy, I. G., et al. 1930. Human milk flow. Am. J. Dis. Child., *39:*1186-1204. **182**

Macy, I. G., et al. 1931. Human milk studies. Am. J. Dis. Child., *42:*569-589. **184**

Maier, H. W. 1963. Three Theories of Child Development. New York, Harper & Row. **4**

Mann, D., Woodward, L. E., and Joseph, N. 1961. Educating Expectant Parents. 107 East 70 Street, New York, Visiting Nurse Service of New York. **88**

Marcus, I. M., et al. 1960. An Interdisciplinary Approach to Accident Patterns in Children. Monographs of the Society for Research in Child Development, 25, No. 2. **146**

Maresh, M. M. 1940. Paranasal sinuses from birth to late adolescence. Am. J. Dis. Child., *60:*55-78. **272**

Maresh, M. M. 1959. Linear bone proportions. J. Am. Dis. Child., *98:*27-49. **253, 460**

Maresh, M. M. 1961. Bone, muscle and fat measurements. Longitudinal measurements of the bone, muscle and fat widths from roentgenograms of the extremities during the first six years of life. Pediatrics, *28:*971-984. **260, 261, 262**

Marquis, D. P. 1931. Can conditioned responses be established in the newborn infant? J. Genet. Psychol., *39:*479-492. **329**

Marquis, D. P. 1941. Learning in the neonate: modification of behavior under three feeding schedules. J. Exper. Psychol., *29:*263-282. **227**

Marshall, H., and McCandless, B. 1957. A study of prediction of social behavior of preschool children. Child Development, *28:*148-159. **419**

Martin, W. E. 1957. Effects of early training on personality. Marriage and Family Living, *19:*39-45. **23**

Martin, W. E. 1964. Singularity and Stability of Profiles of Social Behavior; in C. B. Stendler (Ed.): Readings in Child Behavior and Development. 2nd ed. New York, Harcourt, Brace & World, Inc. **28, 404, 405, 412**

Masland, R. L. 1958. The prevention of mental retardation. Am. J. Dis. Child., *9:* Part II: 3-105. **90**

Masland, R. L., Sarason, S. R., and Gladwin, T. 1958. Mental Subnormality. New York, Basic Books, Inc. **35**

Massler, M. 1958. Dental Caries in the Growing Child, in Dentistry for Children. 4th ed. New York, McGraw-Hill Book Co., Inc. **144**

Massler, M., and Schour, I. 1958a. The Endocrine Glands, in Dentistry for Children. 4th ed. New York, McGraw-Hill Book Co., Inc. **174**

Massler, M., and Schour, I. 1958b. Nutrition and Oral Disease, in Dentistry for Children, 4th ed. New York, McGraw-Hill Book Co., Inc. **174**

Maternal and Child Health and Food and Nutrition Section 1966. Economy in nutrition and feeding of infants. Am. J. Pub. Health, *56:*1756-1784. **185, 188, 202**

Mattson, M. 1933. The relation between the complexity of the habit to be acquired and the form of the learning curve in young children. Genet. Psychol. Monogr., *13:* 299-398. **312**

Mead, G. H. 1934. Mind, Self and Society. Chicago, University of Chicago Press. **38**

Mead, M. 1950. Cultural context of nutritional patterns. Centennial Collected Papers presented at the Centennial Celebration, September 13-17, 1948. Washington, D.C., American Association for the Advancement of Science. **56**

Mead, M., and Wolfenstein, M. (Eds.) 1955. Childhood in Contemporary Cultures. Chicago, University of Chicago Press. **79**

Medinnus, G. R. 1967. Readings in the Psychology of Parent-Child Relations. New York, John Wiley & Sons, Inc. **448**

Mellander, O., et al. 1960. Reported in The Nornbotten Study. Nutrition Rev., *18:*6-8. **187, 188**

Meredith, H. V. 1946. Order and age of eruption for deciduous dentition. J. Dent. Res., *25:*43-66. **175**

Meredith, H. V. 1948. Body size in infancy and childhood; comparative study of data from Okinawa, France, South Africa and North America. Child Development, *19:*180-195. **250**

Meredith, H. V. 1950. Birth order and body size; neonatal and childhood materials. Am. J. Phys. Anthropol., *8:*195-224. **247, 253**

Meredith, H. V. 1951a. A chart on eruption of the deciduous teeth for the pediatrician's office. J. Pediat., *38:*482-483. **175**

Meredith, H. V. 1951b. Relation between socio-economic status and body size in boys seven to ten years of age. Am. J. Dis. Child., *82:*702-709. **250**

Meredith, H. V. 1957. A Descriptive Concept of Physical Development; in D. B. Harris (Ed.): The Concept of Development. Minneapolis, University of Minnesota Press. **8**

Meredith, H. V., and Knott, V. B. 1938. Changes in body proportions during infancy and preschool years; Skelic Index. Child Development, *9:*49-62. **252, 253**

Merrill, B. 1946. A measurement of mother-child interaction. J. Abnorm. & Social Psychol., *41:*37-49. **449**

Metraux, R. W. 1950. Speech profiles of the pre-school child — 18-54 months. Journal of Speech and Hearing Disorders, *15:*37-53. **347**

Meyer, H. F. 1958. Breast feeding in the U. S.: extent and possible trend. Pediatrics, *22:* 116-121. **183**

Meyer, H. F. 1960. Infant Foods and Feeding Practice. Springfield, Ill., Charles C Thomas. **191, 192, 202**

Michaels, R. H., and Mellin, G. W. 1960. Prospective experience with maternal rubella and the associated congenital malformations. Pediatrics, *26:*200-207. **106**

Midcentury White House Conference on Children and Youth. 1951a. Chart Book. Raleigh, N. C., Health Publications Institute. **48**

Midcentury White House Conference on Children and Youth. 1951b. Fact-finding Report. Raleigh, N. C., Health Publications Institute. **242-245**

Midcentury White House Conference on Children and Youth. 1951c. Proceedings. Raleigh, N. C., Health Publications Institute. **65, 73**

Milbank Memorial Fund. 1954. The Family Health Demonstration, Proceedings of a Round Table at the 1953 Annual Conference of the Milbank Memorial Fund. New York, Milbank Memorial Fund. **75**

Millar, P. L. 1961. Home management patterns of three generations. J. H. Econ., *53:* 95-99. **58**

Miller, D. R., and Swanson, G. E. 1958. The Changing American Parent. New York, John Wiley & Sons, Inc. **64, 79**

Miller, D. S. 1962. Changes in the consumer food market since World War II. J. H. Econ., *54:*9-14. **57**

Millis, J. 1952. A study of the effect of nutrition on fertility and the outcome of pregnancy in Singapore in 1947 and 1950. Med. J. Malaya, *6:*157-179. **84**

Millis, J. 1956. The influence of breast feeding on weight gain in infants in the first year. J. Pediat., *48:*770-775. **187**

Montague, A. 1964. Human Heredity. 2nd ed. New York, The World Publishing Co. **128**

Montessori, M. 1912. The Montessori Method. Translated by Anne E. George with introduction by H. W. Holmes. New York, Frederick A. Stokes Company, 1912. Republished by Robert Bentley, Inc., Cambridge, Mass., in 1964, with original photographs and Introduction by Martin Mayer. Republished in paperback by Schocken Books, Inc., New York, in 1964, with Introduction by J. McV. Hunt. **333, 340**

Montessori, M. 1913. Pedagogical Anthropology (translated by F. F. Cooper). New York, Frederick A. Stokes Co. Republished in paperback by Schocken Books, Inc., New York, in 1965, with Introduction by Nancy Rambusch. **333**

Montessori, M. 1920. Dr. Montessori's Own Handbook. London, William Heinemann, Ltd. **333**

Moore, S. B., and Richards, P. 1959. Teaching in Nursery School. New York, Harper & Bros. **78**

Moore, S. G. 1967. Correlates of peer acceptance in nursery school children. Young Children, *22*:281-297. Also in W. W. Hartup and N. L. Smothergill (Eds.): The Young Child—Reviews of Research. Washington, D.C., National Association for the Education of Young Children, 1967. **428**

Moorrees, C. F. 1959. The Dentition of the Growing Child: A Longitudinal Study of Dental Development between 3 and 18 years of age. Cambridge, Harvard University Press. **176**

Morgan, R. H. 1961. Radiation control in public health. Pub. Health Rep., *76*:571-581. **143**

Morgan, S. S., and Morgan, J. J. B. 1944. Adaptive behavior patterns in infants. J. Pediat., *25*:168-177. **396**

Moustakas, C. E. (Ed.) 1966. Existential Child Therapy: the Child's Discovery of Himself. New York, Basic Books, Inc. **414**

Mowrer, O. H. 1952. Speech development in the young child. The autism theory of speech development and some clinical applications. J. of Speech and Hearing Disorders, *17*:263-268. **354**

Mowrer, O. H. 1960. Learning Theory and Behavior. New York, John Wiley & Sons, Inc. **240**

Moyers, R., and Hemrend, B. 1953. The growth of the cranio-facial skeleton. Toronto, privately printed. **271**

Muellner, S. R. 1958. The voluntary control of micturition in man. J. Urol., *80*:473-478. **218, 220**

Muellner, S. R. 1960. Development of urinary control in children. Some aspects of the cause and treatment of primary enuresis. J.A.M.A., *172*:1256-1261. **218, 219, 221**

Munro, N. 1954. Between meal feedings for preschool children. J. H. Econ., *46*:724-728. **198**

Murphy, G., and Murphy, L. B. 1960. The Child as Potential; in E. Ginzberg (Eds.): The Nation's Children. Vol. 2. Development and Education. Published 1960 for the Golden Anniversary White House Conference on Children and Youth. New York, Columbia University Press. **24, 30**

Murphy, L. B. 1937. Social Behavior and Child Personality; Exploratory Study of Some Roots of Sympathy. New York, Columbia University Press. **393, 403, 404, 405**

Murphy, L. B. 1956. Personality in Young Children. Two volumes. New York, Basic Books, Inc. **414 ,420**

Murphy, L. B. 1962. The Widening World of Childhood, Paths toward Mastery. New York, Basic Books, Inc. **41, 208**

Murray, B. F., and Tyler, D. 1937. Study of religious education for young children. Relig. Educ., *32*:55-61. **426**

Murray, J., and Blake, E. 1959. What Do We Eat, in Food. The Yearbook of Agriculture. 1959. Washington, D.C. Government Printing Office. **56**

Mussen, P. (Ed.) 1960. Handbook of Research Methods in Child Development. New York, John Wiley & Sons, Inc. **4**

Mussen, P., and Distler, L. 1959. Masculinity, identification, and father-son relationships. J. Abnorm. & Social Psychol., *59*:350-356. **236**

Mussen, P., and Rutherford, E. 1963. Parent-child relations and parental personality in relation to young children's sex-role preferences. Child Development, *34*:589-607. Also in J. Rosenblith and W. Allensmith (Eds.). 1966. The Causes of Behavior II: Readings in Child Development and Educational Psychology. 2nd ed. Boston, Allyn and Bacon, Inc. **236, 237, 238, 246**

Nanda, R. S. 1960. Eruption of human teeth. Am. J. Orthodont., *46*:363-378. **175**

National Academy of Sciences—National Research Council. 1964. Recommended Dietary

Allowances. Report of the Food and Nutrition Board. Revised 1964. Publication 1146. Washington, D.C., National Academy of Sciences–National Research Council. **115, 182, 187, 190, 199**

National Association for the Education of Young Children, 1948. Essentials of Nursery Education. Washington, D.C., National Association for the Education of Young Children. **76, 78**

National Association for the Education of Young Children 1962. The Cooperative Nursery School: Educational Responsibility. Washington, D.C., National Association for the Education of Young Children. **78**

National Association for the Education of Young Children 1963. Bibliography for Cooperative Schools: Nursery and Kindergarten. Washington, D.C., National Association for the Education of Young Children. **78**

National Association for the Education of Young Children. 1964. Distributor of Space for Play: the Youngest Children, by Lady Allen of Hurtwood, F.I.L.A., et al. Published by World Organization for Early Childhood Education. **322**

National Conference on Family Life. 1948. Dynamics of Family Interaction. Report of committee, edited by E. Duvall and R. Hill. Mimeographed. **33, 37**

National Society for Study of Education. 1940. Thirty-ninth Yearbook. Intelligence, Its Nature and Nurture. Bloomington, Ill., Public School Publishing Co. **385**

National Society for the Study of Education. 1947. Forty-Sixth Yearbook, Part II Early Childhood Education. Chap. 6, Practices and Resources in Early Childhood Education, by E. Fuller et al. Chap. 7, Part II, Experiences in Which Young Children May Learn to Share, by G. Chittenden. Chicago, University of Chicago Press. **78, 423, 428**

Navarra, J. G. 1955. The Development of Scientific Concepts in a Young Child. New York, Bureau of Publications, Columbia University. **368**

Neel, J. V. 1958. A study of major congenital defects in Japanese infants. Am. J. Hum. Genet., *10:*398-445. **142**

Neel, J. V., and Schull, W. J. 1956. The Effect of Exposure to the Atomic Bombs on Pregnancy Termination in Hiroshima and Nagasaki. Washington, D.C., National Academy of Science–National Research Council. **142**

Nelson, W. E. (Ed.) 1964. Textbook of Pediatrics. 8th ed. Philadelphia, W. B. Saunders Company.

Nesbitt, M. 1943. Student and child relationships in the nursery school. Child Development, *14:*143-166. **372**

Nesbitt, R. E. L. 1966. Perinatal Development. Chap. 5 in F. Falkner (Ed.): Human Development. Philadelphia, W. B. Saunders Company. **104, 278**

Newberry, H. 1941. Studies in fetal behavior; measurement of three types of fetal activity. J. Comp. Psychol., *32:*521-530. **103, 312**

New Cambridge Modern History 1957-61. Vol. 12, The Era of Violence, 1898-1945. Cambridge, England, Cambridge University Press.

Newton, N. R. 1955. Maternal Emotions. A Study of Women's Feelings toward Menstruation, Pregnancy, Childbirth, Breast Feeding, Infant Care and Other Aspects of Their Femininity. A Psychosomatic Medicine Monograph. New York, Paul B. Hoeber, Inc., Medical Book Department of Harper & Brothers. **118, 119**

Newton, N. R. and Newton, M. 1950a. Relation of let-down reflex to ability to breast feed. Pediatrics, *5:*726-733. **183**

Newton, N. R., and Newton, M. 1950b. Relationship of ability to breast feed and maternal attitudes toward breast feeding. Pediatrics, *5:*869-875. **183**

Nice, M. M. 1920. Concerning all day conversations. Ped. Sem., *27:*166-177. **347**

Nitowsky, H. M., Cornblath, M., and Gordon, H. H. 1956. Studies of tocopherol deficiency in infants and children. Am. J. Dis. Child., *92:*164-174. **191**

Northway, M. L. 1967. A Primer of Sociometry. 2nd ed. Toronto, University of Toronto Press. **419**

Northway, M., and Weld, L. 1956. Children and their contemporaries, what has been learned from sociometric studies. Bulletin of the Institute of Child Study, University of Toronto, *18:*8-16. **403**

Novack, C. R. 1954. The appearance of ossification centers and the fusion of bones. Am. J. Phys. Anthropol., *12:*63-69. **267**

Nye, R. I., and Hoffman, L. W. (Eds.) 1963. The Employed Mother in America. Chicago, Rand McNally.

Olmsted, R. W., and Jackson, E. B. 1950. Self-demand feeding in the first week of life. Pediatrics, *6:*396-401. **205**

Orlansky, H 1949. Infant care and personality. Psychol. Bull., *46:*1-48. **22, 149, 413**

Osborn, J. J., Dancis, J., and Juan, F. J. 1952. Studies of immunology of newborn infant. Pediatrics, *9:*736-744. **141**

Owen, G. M., and Brozek, J. 1966. Body Composition during Childhood and Adolescence. Chap. 9 in F. Falkner (Ed.): Human Development. Philadelphia, W. B. Saunders Company. **280**

Owen, G. M., Filer, L. J., Maresh, M., and Fomon, S. J. 1966. Sex Related Differences in Body Composition in Infancy. Chap. 10, Part II, in F. Falkner (Ed.): Human Development. Philadelphia, W. B. Saunders Company. **260**

Paiva, S. L. 1953. Pattern of growth of selected groups of breast fed infants in Iowa City. Pediatrics, *11:*38-47. **187**

Palmer, A. 1942. Basal body temperature in disorders of ovarian function and pregnancy. Surg. Gynec. & Obst., *75:*768-778. **109**

Paolucci, B. 1966. Contributions of a framework of home management to the teaching of family relationships. J. Marriage and the Family, *28:*338-342. **60**

Park, E. A. 1954. Bone growth in health and disease. Arch. Dis. Childhood, *29:*269-281. **267**

Parmelee, A. H., et al. 1961. Sleep patterns of the newborn. J. Pediat., *58:*241-250. **227**

Parsons, T., and Bales, R. F. 1955. Family, Socialization, and Interaction Process. Chicago, The Free Press of Glencoe. **31, 39**

Parten, M. L. 1933. Leadership among preschool children. J. Abnorm. & Social Psychol., *27:*430-442. **402**

Patten, B. M. 1953. Human Embryology. 3rd ed. New York, McGraw-Hill Book Co., Inc. **21, 94, 95, 96, 101, 265**

Patton, H. D. 1965. Higher Control of Autonomic Outflows: The Hypothalamus; in T. C. Ruch and H. D. Patton (Eds.): Medical Physiology and Biophysics. 19th ed. Philadelphia, W. B. Saunders Company. **133, 275**

Paynter, K. J., and Grainger, R. M. 1961. Influence of nutrition and genetics on morphology and caries susceptibility. J.A.M.A., *177:*306-307. **145**

Payton, E., et al. 1960. Growth and development. VII. Dietary habits of 571 pregnant southern Negro women. J. Am. Dietet. A., *87:*129-136. **113**

People's League of Health. 1946. Nutrition of expectant and nursing mothers in relation to maternal and infant mortality and morbidity. J. Obst. & Gynaec., Brit. Emp., *53:*498-509. **105**

Phelps, W. M., Kiphuth, R. J. H., and Goff, C. W. 1956. The Diagnosis and Treatment of Postural Defects. 2nd ed. Springfield, Ill., Charles C Thomas. **283, 293**

Piaget, J. 1926. Language and Thought of the Child. New York, Harcourt, Brace and Company. **349**

Piaget, J. 1952. The Origins of Intelligence in Children. New York, International Universities Press, Inc. **150, 234**

Piaget, J. 1954. Construction of Reality in the Child. New York, Basic Books, Inc. **150, 314, 335, 358, 360, 375**

Pick, H. L. 1963. Some Soviet research on learning and perception in children; in J. C. Wright and J. Kagan (Eds.): Basic Cognitive Processes in Children. Monographs of the Society for Research in Child Development, 28, No. 2 (Serial No. 86). **327**

Pinneau, S. R. 1950. Critique on articles by Margaret Ribble. Child Development, *21:*203-228. **17, 148**

Pinneau, S. R. 1955a. The infantile disorders of hospitalism and anaclitic depression. Psychol. Bull., *52:*429-452. **17**

Pinneau, S. R. 1955b. Reply to Dr. Spitz. Psychol. Bull., *52:*459-462. **18, 148**

Pinneau, S. R. 1961. Changes in Intelligence Quotient, Infancy to Maturity. Boston, Houghton Mifflin Co. **385, 461, 462**

Plant, J. S. 1950. The Envelope. New York, The Commonwealth Fund. **36**

Platt, B. S. 1961. Digestion in infancy. Fed. Proc., 20, Part III:188-195. **168**

Plummer, G. 1952. Anomalies occurring in children exposed in utero to the atomic bomb in Hiroshima. Pediatrics, *10:*687-693. **107**

Pond, M. A. 1946. How does housing affect health? Pub. Health Rep., *61:*665-672. **62**

Population Reference Bureau. 1962. Population Profile: The Teen-Age Mother. Population Reference Bureau, Inc. **81**

Pratt, K. C. 1954. The Neonate, Chap. 4, in L. Carmichael (Ed.): Manual of Child Psychology. 2nd ed. New York, John Wiley & Sons, Inc. **296, 327, 328, 335, 456**

Pratt, K. C., Nelson, A. K., and Sun, K. H. 1930. Behavior of the Newborn Infant. Ohio State University Studies, Contrib. Psychol. No. 10. **298, 326**

Preyer, W. 1893. The Senses and the Will (translated by H. W. Brown). New York, D. Appleton-Century Company, Inc. **328**

Price, D. E. 1958. Radiation as a public health problem. Pub. Health Rep., *73:*197-202. **143**

Proceedings of the XIV International Congress of Applied Psychology, 1962. Vol. III: Child and Education. Copenhagen, Einar Munksgaard Forlag. (General editor, G. S. Nielsen.) **428, 434**

Proshansky, H. M. 1966. The Development of Intergroup Attitudes. Chap. in L. W. Hoffman and M. L. Hoffman (Eds.): Review of Child Development Research, Vol. 1. New York, Russell Sage Foundation. **90, 394**

Prugh, D. G. 1960. Personality Development Throughout Childhood. Chap. VII in H. C. Stuart and D. G. Prugh (Eds.): The Healthy Child. Cambridge, Harvard University Press. **168, 204, 219, 222**

Prugh, D. G. 1964. Clinical Appraisal of Infants and Children in W. E. Nelson (Ed.): Textbook of Pediatrics. 8th ed. Philadelphia, W. B. Saunders Company. **133**

Pyle, S. I., and Hoerr, N. L. 1955. Radiographic Atlas of Skeletal Development of the Knee. Springfield, Ill., Charles C Thomas. **267**

Pyle, S. I., and Sontag, L. W. 1943. Variability in onset of ossification in epiphyses and short bones of extremities. Am. J. Roentgenol., *49:*795-798. **268, 269, 274**

Pyle, S. I., et al. 1959. Patterns of skeletal development in the hand. Pediatrics, 24, No. 5. Part II: 886-903. **268, 460**

Pyles, M. 1932. Verbalization as factor in learning. Child Development, *3:*108-113. **371**

Rabinovitch, R. D., and Fischhoff, J. 1952. Feeding children to meet their emotional needs. J. Am. Dietet. A., *28:*614-621. **55**

Rafferty, J. E., Tyler, B. B., and Tyler, F. B. 1960. Personality assessment from free play observations. Child Development, *31:*691-702. **419**

Rasmussen, H., and Reifenstein, E. C., Jr. 1962. The Parathyroid Glands. Chap. 11 in R. H. Williams (Ed.): Textbook of Endocrinology. 3rd ed. Philadelphia, W. B. Saunders Company. **291**

Rathbone, J. L. 1957. Teach Yourself to Relax. Englewood Cliffs, N. J., Prentice-Hall, Inc. **116**

Read, K. H. 1966. The Nursery School. 4th ed. Philadelphia, W. B. Saunders Company. **78, 224, 349, 422, 428, 452**

Reed, R. B., and Stuart, H. C. 1959. Patterns of growth of height and weight from birth to eighteen years of age. Pediatrics, *24:*904-921. **249, 250, 459, 460**

Reed, S. C. 1963. Counseling in Medical Genetics. 2nd ed. Philadelphia, W. B. Saunders Company. **85**

Reichert, A. 1961. The homemaker as employed worker. J. H. Econ., *53:*18-22. **47**

Reisen, A. H. 1960. Receptor Functions. Chap. 7 in P. Mussen (Ed.): Handbook of Research Methods in Child Development. New York, John Wiley & Sons, Inc. **328**

Review 1958a. Genetic aspects of metabolic disease in childhood. Part I. Nutrition Rev., *16:*323-325. **90**

Review 1958b. The regulation of thirst. Nutrition Rev., *16:*302-304. **179**

Review 1958c. The role of breast-feeding in immunity. Nutrition Rev., *16:*261-263. **188**

Review 1959a. Genetic aspects of metabolic disease in childhood. Part II. Nutrition Rev., *17:*3-5. **90**

Review 1959b. Inborn errors of metabolism. Nutrition Rev., *17:*325-328. **90**

Review 1960a. Nutritional excess in infancy and childhood. Nutrition Rev., *18:*255-256. **179**

Review 1960b. Refractory rickets as a sex-linked congenital anomaly. Nutrition Rev., *18:*232-233. **89**

Review 1961a. Effects of meal eating vs. nibbling on body composition. Nutrition Rev., *19:*9-11. **57**

Review 1961b. Nutrition, health and longevity. Nutrition Rev., *19:*305-306. **180**

Review 1965. Breast-feeding and polio susceptibility. Nutrition Rev., *23:*131-133. **188**

Review 1966a. The safe level of vitamin D intake for infants. Nutrition Rev., *24:*230-232. **190**

Review 1966b. Rampant caries in the pre-school child. Nutrition Rev., *24:*297-299. **144, 198**

Reynolds, E. L. 1945. Bony pelvic girdle in early infancy; roentgenometric study. Am. J. Phys. Anthropol., *3:*321-352. **273**

Reynolds, E. L. 1947. Bony pelvis in prepuberal childhood. Am. J. Phys. Anthropol., *5:*165-200. **273**

Reynolds, E. L. 1960. Irradiation and human evolution. Hum. Biol., *32:*89-108. **142**

Reynolds, E. L., and Grote, P. 1948. Sex differences in distribution of tissue components in human leg from birth to maturity. Anat. Rec., *102:*45-53. **262**

Rheingold, H. L. 1966. The development of social behavior in the human infant; in H. W. Stevenson (Ed.): Concept of Development. Monographs of the Society for Research in Child Development, 31, No. 5 (Serial No. 107). **137, 157, 298, 391, 396**

Rheingold, H. L., and Bayley, N. 1959. The later effects of an experimental modification of mothering. Child Development, *31:*363-372. **354**

Rheingold, H. L., Gewirtz, J. L., and Ross, H. W. 1959. Social conditioning of vocalizations in the infant. J. Comp. Physiol. Psychol., *52:*68-73. **18, 137, 157**

Ribble, M. 1943. The Rights of Infants. New York, Columbia University Press. **148**

Richards, T. W. 1936. The relationship between bodily and gastric activity of newborn infants: I. Correlation and influence of time since feeding. Human Biol., *8:*368-380. **314**

Richards, T. W., and Irwin, O. C. 1935. Studies in Infant Behavior: Plantar Responses of Infants and Young Children: Examination of Literature and Reports of New Experiments. Studies in Child Welfare 11 (1). Iowa City, University of Iowa. **297**

Richards, T. W., and Newberry, H. 1938. Studies in fetal behavior. Can performance on test items at six months postnatally be predicted on basis of fetal activity? Child Development, *9:*79-86. **106, 314**

Richards, T. W., et al. 1938. Studies in fetal behavior. II. Activity of the human fetus in utero and its relation to other prenatal conditions particularly the mother's basal metabolic rate. Child Development, *9:*69-78. **103**

Richmond, J. B. and Massler, M. I. 1964. The Digestive System: The Oral Cavity, in W. E. Nelson (Ed.): Textbook of Pediatrics. 8th ed. Philadelphia, W. B. Saunders Company. **174**

Ridenour, N., and Johnson, I. 1966. Some Special Problems of Children Aged 2 to 5 Years. New York, Child Study Association. **414, 428**

Riley, C. M., et al. 1954. Further observations in familial dysautonomia. Pediatrics, *14:*475-480. **35**

Roberts, K. E. 1932. Ability of preschool children to solve problems in which a simple principle of relationship is kept constant. J. Genet. Psychol., *40:*118-133. **371**

Roberts, K. E., and Schoelkopf, J. A. 1951. Eating, sleeping, and elimination; practices of group of two-and-one-half-year-old children. Am. J. Dis. Child., *82:*121-152. **169, 218, 220, 222, 228**

Robinow, M., Johnston, M., and Anderson, M. 1943. Feet of normal children. J. Pediat., *23:*141-149. **275**

Robinow, M., Richards, T. W., and Anderson, M. 1942. Eruption of deciduous teeth. Growth, *6:*127-133. **174, 175**

Robinow, M., and Silverman, F. N. 1957. Radiation hazard in the field of pediatrics. Pediatrics, *20:*921-940. **142, 143**

Rock, J., and Loth, D. 1949. Voluntary Parenthood. New York, Random House, Inc. **80**

Rodgers, R. 1964. Toward a theory of family development. J. Marriage and the Family, *26:*262-270. **31**

Rose, A. M. (Ed.) 1962. Human Behavior and Social Processes, An Interactionist Approach. Boston. Houghton Mifflin Co. **40**

Rose, M. S. 1929. Feeding the Family. 3rd ed. New York, Macmillan Company. **200**

Rosenblith, J. F. 1959. Learning by imitation in kindergarten children. Child Development, *30:*69-80. **374**

Rosenblith, J. F. 1961. Imitative color choices in kindergarten children. Child Development, *32:*211-223. **374**

Rosenblith, J. F. 1966. Prognostic value of neonatal assessment. Child Development, *37:*623-631. **384**

Rosenblith, J. F., and Allinsmith, W. (Eds.) 1966. The Causes of Behavior: Readings in Child Development and Educational Psychology, II. Boston, Allyn & Bacon, Inc. **438, 439**

Ross, Pediatric Research Conference. 1957. Psychological Implications of Current Pediatric Practice. Report of the 24th Ross Pediatric Research Conference, March 1-2, 1957. Columbus, Ohio, Ross Laboratories. **231**

Rowntree, G. 1950. Accidents among children under two years of age in Great Britain. J. Hygiene, *48:*322-337. **147**

Ruch, T. C., and Patton, H. D. (Eds.) 1965. Medical Physiology and Biophysics. 19th ed. Philadelphia, W. B. Saunders Company. **275**

Rudolph, S. H. 1963. Notes from a maternity ward. Atlantic Monthly, March, pp. 122-125. **128**

Russell, D. 1956. Children's Thinking. Boston, Blaisdell Publishing Company. **378, 388**

Rutledge, A., 1960. Marriage and divorce; in Golden Anniversary White House Conference on Children and Youth, Children and Youth in the 1960's; Survey Papers. **48, 49, 78**

Salber, E. J., and Fernleib, M. 1966. Breast-feeding in Boston. Pediatrics, *37*:299-303. **183**

Salber, E. J., et al. 1958. Patterns of breast feeding. I. Factors affecting the frequency of breast feeding in the newborn period. N. Eng. J. Med., *259*:707-713. **183**

Salber, E. J., et al. 1959. Patterns of breast feeding in a family health clinic. II. Duration of feeding and reasons for weaning. N. Eng. J. Med., *260*:310-315. **183**

Sampson, E. E. 1965. The study of ordinal position: antecedents and outcomes; in B. Mahar (Ed.): Progress in Experimental Personality Research, Vol. II. New York, Academic Press. **45**

Sanford, R. N. 1943. Personality Patterns in School Children. Chap. 32, in R. G. Barker et al. (Eds.): Child Behavior and Development. New York, McGraw-Hill Book Co., Inc. **451**

di Sant' Agnese, P. 1949. Combined immunization against diphtheria, tetanus, and pertussis in newborn infants. Pediatrics, *3*:20-33. **141**

Sargent, D. W. 1961. An evaluation of Basal Metabolic Data for Children and Youth in the United States. Home Economics Research Report No. 14. Human Nutrition Research Division, Agricultural Research Service, United States Department of Agriculture. Washington, D.C., November. **171**

Sargent, D. W. 1962. An Evaluation of Basal Metabolic Data for Infants in the United States. Home Economics Research Report No. 18. Human Nutrition Research Division, Agricultural Research Service, United States Department of Agriculture, Washington, D.C. **171**

Schaefer, E. S. 1961. Converging conceptual models for maternal behavior and for child behavior; in J. C. Glidewell (Ed.): Parental Attitudes and Child Behavior. Proceedings of the Second Annual Conference on Community Mental Health Research. Social Science Institute, Washington University, 1960. Springfield, Ill., Charles C Thomas. **40, 155, 393, 435**

Schaefer, E. S., and Bayley, N. 1963. Maternal Behavior, Child Behavior, and Their Intercorrelations from Infancy through Adolescence. Monographs of the Society for Research in Child Development, 28, No. 3 (Serial No. 87). **22, 136, 137, 155, 464, 465**

Scheibel, M. E., and Scheibel, A. B. 1964. Some Neural Substrates of Postnatal Development. Chap. in M. L. Hoffman and L. W. Hoffman (Eds.): Review of Child Development Research, Vol. 1. New York, Russell Sage Foundation. **277, 324**

Schilder, P. 1951. The Image and Appearance of the Human Body. New York, International Universities Press, Inc. **38**

Schlesinger, B. 1966. The one-parent family: recent literature. J. of Marriage and the Family, *28*:103-109. **78**

Schlesinger, E. R., et al. 1956. Newburgh-Kingston caries fluorine study. XIII. Pediatric findings after ten years. J. Am. Dent. A., *52*:296-306. **145**

Schmeidler, G. 1941. The relation of fetal activity and the activity of the mother. Child Development, *12*:63-68. **103**

Schour, I., and Massler, M. 1958. Development of the Teeth, in Dentistry for Children. New York, McGraw-Hill Book Co., Inc. **174**

Schramm, W., Lyle, J., and Parker, E. 1961. Television in the Lives of Our Children. Stanford, Cal., Stanford University Press. **65**

Scott, E. M., Verney, E. L., and Morissey, P. D. 1950. Self selection of diet; appetites for calcium, magnesium and potassium. J. Nutrition, *41*:187-201. **209**

Scott, R. B., et al. 1950. Growth and development of Negro infants; growth during first year of life as observed in private pediatric practice. J. Pediat., *37*:885-893. **250**

Sears, R. R. 1960a. Reporting research to parents. J. of Nursery Education, *16*:1, 1960-61, pp. 25-32. **428**

Sears, R. R. 1960b. The growth of conscience; in I. Iscoe and H. W. Stevenson (Eds.): Personality Development in Children. Austin, University of Texas Press. **412**

Sears, R. R., Maccoby, E., and Levin, H. 1957. Patterns of Child Rearing. New York, Harper and Row. **22, 45, 47, 128, 136, 138, 150, 153, 154, 155, 181, 189, 208, 209, 213, 220, 221, 224, 231, 246, 412, 415, 446, 451, 452**

Sears, R. R., Rau, L., and Alpert, R. 1965. Identification and Child Rearing. Stanford, Cal., Stanford University Press. **411, 412**

Sears, R. R., et al. 1946. Effect of father-separation on preschool children's doll play aggression. Child Development, *17*:219-243. **49**

Sears, R. R., et al. 1953. Some child-rearing antecedents of aggression and dependency in young children. Genet. Psychol. Monogr., *47*:135-234. **156, 404**

Selye, H. 1950. Stress—The Physiology and Pathology of Exposure to Stress. Montreal, Acta, Inc. **139, 291, 292**

Selye, H. 1956. The Stress of Life. New York, McGraw-Hill Book Co., Inc. **19, 139, 291, 292**

Shanas, E., and Streib, G. F. (Eds.) 1965. Social Structure and the Family: Generational Relations. Englewood Cliffs, New Jersey, Prentice-Hall, Inc. **54**

Shaw, J. H. 1961. Symposium: Nutrition in tooth formation and dental caries. Introduction—Factors controlling the incidence of dental caries. J.A.M.A., *177*:304-305. **144, 145**

Sherry, S. N., and Kramer, I. 1955. The time of passage of the first stool and first urine by the newborn infant. J. Pediat., *46*:158-159. **169**

Shirley, M. M. 1931. The First Two Years; a Study of Twenty-Five Babies. Minneapolis, University of Minnesota Press. **298, 300, 306, 326, 334, 346**

Shock, N. W. 1952. Aging of Homeostatic Mechanisms. Chap. 18, in A. I. Lansing (Ed.): Cowdry's Problems of Aging. 3rd ed. Baltimore, Williams & Wilkins Company. **132**

Sigel, I. E. 1956. The need for conceptualization in research on child development. Child Development, *27*:241-252. **4**

Sigel, I. E. 1964. The Attainment of Concepts. Chap. in M. L. Hoffman and L. W. Hoffman (Eds.): Review of Child Development Research, Vol. 1. New York, Russell Sage Foundation. **298, 332, 359, 360, 361, 388, 400**

Sigel, I. E., Jarman, P. D., and Hanasian, H. 1962. Some correlates of styles of categorization for young children. Mimeographed report. **365, 366, 367**

Sillman, J. H. 1942. Malocclusion in deciduous dentition: serial study from birth to five years. Am. J. Orthodontia & Oral Surg., *28*:197-209. **176**

Sillman, J. H. 1951. Thumbsucking and the oral structures. J. Pediat., *39*:424-443, 515-516. **176, 177, 178**

Silver, G. A. 1961. Family Health Maintenance: A Perspective on the Ailing Family; in I. Galdston (Ed.): The Family. A Focal Point in Health Education. New York, International Universities Press, Inc. **75**

Simmons, K. 1944. Brush Foundation Study of Child Growth and Development; Physical Growth and Development. Monographs of the Society for Research in Child Development, 9, No. 1. **249, 254**

Skinner, B. F. 1953. Science and Human Behavior. New York, Macmillan Company. **366**

Smart, M. S. 1939. Child development and religious education. Childhood Educ., *16*:159-164. **426**

Smith, C. A. 1947. Effects of maternal undernutrition upon the newborn infant in Holland. J. Pediat., *30*:229-243. **84, 105**

Smith, C. A. 1959. Physiology of the Newborn Infant. 3rd ed. Springfield, Ill., Charles C Thomas. **102, 132, 164, 165, 169, 170, 185, 188, 190, 217, 326, 456**

Smith, C. A., et al. 1953. Maternal-fetal nutritional relationships. Effect of maternal diet on size and content of the fetal liver. Obst. & Gynec., *1*:46-58. **105**

Smith, C. A., et al. 1955. Persistence and utilization of maternal iron for blood formation during infancy. J. Clin. Invest., *34*:1391-1402. **185**

Smith, D. W., et al. 1957. The mental prognosis of hypothyroidism of infancy and childhood. Pediatrics, *19*:1011-1022. **290**

Smith, G. J. 1962. The hospital is where they take care of you. Parents' Magazine, October, p. 56. **350**

Smith, H. T. 1953. A comparison of interview and observation measures of mother behavior. Unpublished doctoral dissertation, Harvard University. **156**

Smith, M. E. 1926. Investigation of Development of the Sentence and Extent of Vocabulary in Young Children. Studies in Child Welfare 3 (5). Iowa City, University of Iowa. **346**

Smith, M. E. 1933. Grammatical errors in speech of preschool children. Child Development, *4*:183-190. **348**

Smith, N. J., and Vaughan, V. C., III. 1964. Diseases of the Blood, in W. E. Nelson (Ed.): Textbook of Pediatrics. 8th ed. Philadelphia, W. B. Saunders Company. **107**

Smith, R. T. 1960. Immunity in Infancy; in V. C. Kelley (Ed.): Symposium on Recent Clinical Advances. Pediat. Clin. N. Amer., *7*:233-456. **141**

Soddy, K. (Ed.) 1956. Mental Health and Infant Development; Proceedings of the International Seminar held by the World Federation for Mental Health at Chichester, England. Vols. I and II. New York, Basic Books, Inc. **148, 393**

Sontag, L. W. 1941. Significance of fetal environmental differences. Am. J. Obst. & Gynec., *42*:996-1003. **106, 107**

Sontag, L. W., Baker, C. T., and Nelson, V. L. 1958. Mental Growth and Personality Development: A Longitudinal Study. Monographs of the Society for Research in Child Development, 23, No. 2. **22, 42, 385, 407, 419, 461**

Sontag, L. W., and Wallace, R. F. 1935. The movement response of the human fetus to sound stimuli. Child Development, *6*:253-258. **103**

Spiker, C. C. 1956a. Experiments with children on the hypotheses of acquired distinctiveness of equivalence of cues. Child Development, *27*:253-263. **332**

Spiker, C. C. 1956b. The stimulus generalization gradient as a function of the intensity of stimulus lights. Child Development, *27*:85-98. **332**

Spiker, C. C. 1960. Research Methods in Children's Learning. Chap. 9 in P. Mussen (Ed.): Handbook of Research Methods in Child Development. New York, John Wiley & Sons, Inc. **358**

Spiker, C. C. 1966. The Concept of Development: Relevant and Irrelevant Issues; in H. W. Stevenson (Ed.): Concept of Development: A Report of Conference Commemorating the Fortieth Anniversary of the Institute of Child Development, University of Minnesota. Monographs of the Society for Research in Child Development, 31, No. 5 (Serial No. 107). **15**

Spiker, C. C., and White, S. H. 1959. Differential conditioning by children as a function of effort required in the task. Child Development, *30*:1-7. **15, 16, 332**

Spock, B. 1950a. Round table discussion on present day attitudes toward breast feeding. (Smith, C. A., Chairman) Pediatrics, *6*:656-659. **189**

Spock, B. 1950b. In Symposium on the Healthy Personality, M. J. E. Seen (Ed.). New York, Josiah Macy, Jr., Foundation, p. 74. **83**

Spock, B. 1957. The Common Sense Book of Baby and Child Care. 2nd ed. New York, Duell, Sloan and Pearce, Inc. Also in pocket book edition. New York, Pocket Books, Inc. **41, 224, 414**

Srole, L., Langner, S., Michael, S., Opler, M., and Rennie, T. 1962. Mental Health in the Metropolis: The Midtown Manhattan Study. New York, McGraw-Hill Book Co., Inc. **65**

Staples, R. 1932. Responses of infants to color. J. Exper. Psychol., *15*:119-141. **332**

Stearns, G. 1939. Mineral metabolism of normal infants. Physiol. Rev., *19*:415-438. **180**

Stearns, G. 1951. Human Requirement of Calcium, Phosphorus and Magnesium. Chap. IV, in Handbook of Nutrition; a Symposium. 2nd ed. American Medical Association, published by Blakiston Co. **84, 197**

Stearns, G. 1952. Nutritional health of infants, children and adolescents, in Proceedings of Food and Nutrition Institute, Agriculture Handbook No. 56. Washington, D.C., U.S. Department of Agriculture. **196**

Stearns, G. 1958. Nutritional state of the mother prior to conception. J.A.M.A., *168*:1655-1659. **83, 106**

Stearns, G. 1959. Infants and Toddlers; in Food, The Yearbook of Agriculture. Washington, D.C., U.S. Department of Agriculture, 1959. **202**

Stearns, G., Jeans, P. C., and Vandecar, V. 1936. Effect of vitamin D on linear growth in infancy. J. Pediat., *9*:1-12. **190**

Stein, K. F., et al. 1956. Influence of heredity in the etiology of malocclusion. Am. J. Orthodontics, *42*:125-141. **176**

Stendler, C. B. 1952. Critical periods in socialization and overdependency. Child Development, *23*:1-12. **149, 440**

Stendler, C. B. (Ed.) 1964. Readings in Child Behavior and Development. 2nd ed. New York, Harcourt, Brace & World, Inc.

Stern, C. 1960. Principles of Human Genetics. 2nd ed. San Francisco, W. H. Freeman & Co. **21, 35, 89, 90, 142, 250**

Stevenson, H. W. 1962. Piaget, behavior theory and intelligence. In W. Kessen and C. Kuhlman (Eds.): Thought in the Young Child. Monographs of the Society for Research in Child Development, 27, No. 2. **388**

Stevenson, H. W. (Ed.) 1966. Concept of Development: A Report of Conference Commemorating the Fortieth Anniversary of the Institute of Child Development, University of Minnesota. Monographs of the Society for Research in Child Development, 31, No. 5 (Serial No. 107).

Stevenson, H. W., Kagan, J., and Spiker, C. (Eds.) 1963. Child Psychology. The Sixty-second Yearbook of the National Society for the Study of Education. Chicago, University of Chicago Press. **4**

Stevenson, S. S. 1947. Adequacy of artificial feeding in infancy. J. Pediat., *31:*616-630. **185, 188**

Stewart, A., and Westropp, C. 1953. Breast-feeding in the Oxford Child Health Survey. 2. Comparison of bottle-fed and breast-fed babies. Brit. Med. J. *2:*305-308. **187, 188**

Stiebling, H. K. 1959. Food in Our Lives, in Food: The Yearbook of Agriculture, 1959. Washington, D. C., Government Printing Office. **56**

Stitt, P. G. 1960. Progress During Infancy; in H. C. Stuart and D. G. Prugh (Eds.): The Healthy Child. Cambridge, Harvard University Press. **309, 329**

Stitt, P. G., et al. 1960. Pediatric experience in a family health clinic; A research project offering multi-professional services for the continuum of pregnancy and early childhood. Pediatrics, *26:*1024-1030. **74**

Stolz, L. M., et al. 1954. Father Relations of War-Born Children. Stanford, Stanford University Press. **50**

Stone, A. A., and Onqué, G. C. 1959. Long'tudinal Studies of Child Personality. Cambridge, Harvard University Press. **3**

Stott, L. H. 1945. Research in family life in Nebraska. J. H. Econ., *37:*80-83. **63**

Stott, L. H. 1967. Child Development, An Individual Longitudinal Approach. New York, Holt, Rinehart and Winston, Inc. **419**

Strang, R. 1951. Introduction to Child Study. 3rd ed. New York, Macmillan Company. **215**

Stuart, H. C., and Prugh, D. G. (Eds.) 1960. The Healthy Child. Cambridge, Harvard University Press. **126, 157, 202, 224, 293, 330**

Stuart, H. C., and Sobel, E. H. 1946. Thickness of skin and subcutaneous tissue by age and sex in childhood. J. Pediat., *28:*637-647. **262**

Stuart, H. C., and Stevenson, S. S. 1959. Physical Growth and Development; in W. E. Nelson (Ed.): Textbook of Pediatrics. 7th ed. Philadelphia, W. B. Saunders Company. **261, 456, 457**

Stutsman, R. 1930. Scale of Mental Tests for Preschool Children. New York, World Book Company. **317, 318, 319, 332**

Sullivan, H. S. 1953. The Interpersonal Theory of Psychiatry. New York, W. W. Norton & Co., Inc. **38**

Sussman, M. B. (Ed.) 1968. Sourcebook in Marriage and the Family. 3rd ed. Boston, Houghton Mifflin Co. **79**

Swift, J. W. 1964. Effects of Early Group Experience. Chap. in M. L. Hoffman and L. W. Hoffman (Eds.): Review of Child Development Research, Vol. 1. New York, Russell Sage Foundation. **78**

Talbot, N. B., Sobel, E. H., McArthur, J. W., and Crawford, J. D. 1952. Functional Endocrinology from Birth Through Adolescence. Cambridge, Harvard University Press. **289, 291, 292**

Tanner, J. M. 1958. The Evaluation of Physical Growth and Development, in Modern Trends in Pediatrics. London, Butterworth & Co., Ltd. **250**

Tanner, J. M. 1961. Education and Physical Growth. London, University of London Press, Ltd. **277**

Tanner, J. M. 1962. Growth at Adolescence. 2nd ed. Oxford, Blackwell Scientific Publications. **90, 180, 260, 262**

Tanner, J. M. 1963. The regulation of human growth. Child Development, *34:*817-847. **251, 293**

Tanner, J. M. 1965. Radiographic studies of body composition in children and adults. In Brozek, J. (Ed.): Human Body Composition. Oxford, England, Pergamon Press. **279**

Tanner, J. M., and Whitehouse, R. H. 1962. Standards for subcutaneous fat in British children. Brit. Med. J., *1:*446-450. **261**

Tanner, J. M., et al. 1956. Aberdeen Growth Study I The prediction of adult body measurements from measurements taken each year from birth to 5 years. Arch. Dis. Children, *31:*372-381. **248, 249, 250, 254**

Taussig, H. B. 1962. Thalidomide—a lesson in remote effects of a drug. Am. J. Dis. Child., *104:*111-113. **107**

Taylor, K. W. 1954. Parent Cooperative Nursery Schools. New York, Bureau of Publications, Columbia University. **78**

Templin, M. C. 1952. The development of certain language skills in children. J. Speech and Hearing Disorders, *17:*280-285. **330, 347**

Templin, M. C. 1957. Certain Language Skills in Children. Minneapolis, University of Minnesota Press. **347**

Terman, L. M., and Merrill, M. A. 1960. Stanford-Binet Intelligence Scale: Manual for the Third Revision Form L-M. Boston, Houghton Mifflin Company. **332, 363**

Terman, L. M., et al. 1938. Psychological Factors in Marital Happiness. New York, McGraw-Hill Book Co., Inc. **44**

Teuber, H. L. 1964. Formal discussion, in U. Bellugi and R. Brown (Eds.): The Acquisition of Language. Monographs of the Society for Research in Child Development, 29, No. 1, pp. 131-138. **342**

Thomas, A., Chess, S., Birch, H., Hertzig, M., and Korn, S. 1963. Behavioral Individuality in Early Childhood. New York, New York University Press. **216, 456**

Thomas, A., Chess, S., and Birch, H. G. 1968. Temperament and Behavior Disorders in Children. New York, New York University Press. **36**

Thoms, H. 1950. Training for Childbirth. New York, McGraw-Hill Book Co., Inc. **116**

Thoms, H., in collaboration with L. G. Roth. 1950. Understanding Natural Childbirth. New York, McGraw-Hill Book Co., Inc. **116, 128**

Thomson, A. M. 1957. Technique and perspective in clinical and dietary studies of human pregnancy. Proc. Nutrition Soc., *16:*45-51. **82, 106**

Thomson, J. 1955. Observations on weight gain in infants. Arch. Dis. Childhood, *30:*322-327. **187**

Tischler, H. 1957. Schreien, Lallen und erstes Sprechen in die Entwicklung des Säuglings. Z. Psychol., *160:*210-263. (Referred to in Ervin-Tripp, 1966.) **344**

Todd, T. W., et al. 1937. Atlas of Skeletal Maturation. St. Louis, C. V. Mosby Company. **264, 269, 270**

Todd, V. E., and Heffernan, H. 1964. The Years before School; Guiding Preschool Children. New York, Macmillan Company. **78**

Toman, W. 1961. Family Constellation. New York, Springer Publishing Company. **78**

Tompkins, W. T., and Wiehl, D. G. 1955. Maternal and Newborn Nutrition Studies at Philadelphia Lying-in Hospital. Maternal Studies III. Toxemia and maternal nutrition, in The Promotion of Maternal and Newborn Health. New York, Milbank Memorial Fund. **84**

Tompkins, W. T., et al. 1955. The underweight patient as an increased obstetric hazard. Am. J. Obst. & Gynec. *69:*114-123. **84, 105, 110**

Torrance, E. P. 1962. Guiding Creative Talent. Englewood Cliffs, New Jersey, Prentice-Hall, Inc. **379**

Toverud, K. U., Stearns, G., and Macy, I. G. 1950. Maternal Nutrition and Child Health; Interpretative Review. Bulletin No. 123, Washington, D.C. National Academy of Science–National Research Council. **181**

Trainham, G., et al. 1945. A case history of twins breast fed on a self-demand regime. J. Pediat., *27:*97-108. **206, 207**

Traisman, A. S., and Traisman, H. S. 1958. Thumb and finger sucking: a study of 2650 infants and children. J. Pediat., *52:*566-572. **177**

Tucker, W. E. 1960. Active Alerted Posture. Edinburgh & London, E. & S. Livingstone, Ltd. **281**

Tuddenham, R. D. 1959. The constancy of personality ratings over two decades. Genet. Psychol. Monogr., *60:*3-29. **437**

Turner, C. D. 1966. General Endocrinology. 4th ed. Philadelphia, W. B. Saunders Company. **181**

Turner, N. C. 1960. A biochemical pattern basic to tooth decay. J. Am. Dent. A. *61:*20-31. **145**

United States Bureau of the Census. 1961. Statistical Abstract of the United States: 1961. Ed. 82. Washington, D.C. **122**

United States Bureau of the Census. Pocket Data Book, U.S.A. 1967. U.S. Government Printing Office. **66, 67, 68, 70, 72, 122**

United States Department of Agriculture. 1959. Food in Our Lives: The Yearbook of Agriculture. Washington, D.C., Government Printing Office.

United States Department of Agriculture. 1964. Food for Fitness, Leaflet 424. Agricultural Research Service, U.S. Department of Agriculture. **196**

United States Department of Health, Education, and Welfare. 1952. A Healthy Personality for Your Child. Children's Bureau Publication No. 337. Washington, D.C., United States Department of Health, Education, and Welfare. **242**

United States Department of Health, Education, and Welfare. 1961a. Care Services, Form and Substance. Children's Bureau Publication No. 393. (Also, U.S. Department of

Labor Publication, Women's Bureau Bulletin No. 281). Washington, D.C., U.S. Department of Health, Education, and Welfare. **78**

United States Department of Health, Education, and Welfare. 1961b. Public Health Service, National Vital Statistics Division, 1961. Infant Mortality: United States and Each State and Hawaii, Puerto Rico and the Virgin Islands (U.S.) 1959. Vital Statistics Special Reports. National Summaries, 54, No. 7. December. **141**

United States Department of Health, Education, and Welfare. 1962a. Services in Public and Voluntary Child Welfare Programs. Children's Bureau Publication No. 396. Washington, D.C., U.S. Department of Health, Education, and Welfare. **78**

United States Department of Health, Education, and Welfare. 1962b. Your Child from One to Six. Children's Bureau Publication No. 30. Washington, D.C., U.S. Department of Health, Education, and Welfare. **452**

United States Department of Health, Education, and Welfare. 1962c. A Creative Life for Your Child. Children's Bureau Headliner Series number 1, by Margaret Mead. Washington, D.C., U.S. Department of Health, Education, and Welfare. **452**

United States Department of Health, Education, and Welfare. 1963. Infant Care. Children's Bureau Publication No. 8. Washington, D.C., U.S. Department of Health, Education, and Welfare. **452**

United States Department of Health, Education, and Welfare. 1965. When You Adopt a Child. Children's Bureau Publication No. 33N. Washington, D.C., U.S. Department of Health, Education, and Welfare. **78**

United States Department of Health, Education, and Welfare. 1966. Nursery-Kindergarten Enrollment of Children under Six: October 1965. Office of Education Publication. U.S. Department of Health, Education, and Welfare. **76**

United States Department of Labor. 1966. Who Are the Working Mothers? Leaflet 37. U.S. Department of Labor. **48, 49**

Updegraff, R. 1930. The visual perception of distance in young children and adults: A comparative study. Studies in Child Welfare, 4 (4). Iowa City, University of Iowa. **362**

Updegraff, R., et al. 1937. Effect of Training upon Singing Ability and Musical Interest of Three-, Four-, and Five-Year-Old Children. Studies in Child Welfare, 14 (1), Part III. Iowa City, University of Iowa. **382**

Valquist, B. 1958. The transfer of antibodies from mother to offspring. Advances Pediat. *10:*305-310. **188**

Valadian, I. 1960. General Features of Illness by Age, in H. C. Stuart and D. G. Prugh (Eds.): The Healthy Child. Cambridge, Harvard University Press. **140**

Van Riper, C. 1950. Teaching Your Child to Talk. New York, Harper & Brothers. **344, 347**

Van Riper, C. 1963. Speech Correction Principles and Methods. New York, Prentice-Hall, Inc. **352, 355**

Vaughan, V. C. 1964. Growth and Development in the Infant and Child, in W. E. Nelson (Ed.): Textbook of Pediatrics. 8th ed. Philadelphia, W. B. Saunders Company. **247, 253, 254, 256, 261, 285, 456**

Velten, H. V. 1943. The growth of phonemic and lexical patterns in infant language. Language, *XIX:*281-292. **343**

Via, W. F., and Churchill, J. A. 1959. Relationship of enamel hypoplasia to abnormal events of gestation. J. Am. Dent. A., *59:*702-707. **174**

Walker, J. S., Margolis, F. J., Teate, H. L., Jr., Weil, M. L., and Wilson, H. L. 1963. Water intake of normal children. Science, *140:*890-891. **179**

Walker, R. N. 1962. Body Build and Behavior in Young Children: I. Body Build and Nursery School Teachers' Ratings. Monographs of the Society for Research in Child Development, 27, No. 3 (Serial No. 84). **262, 263**

Wallace, B., and Dobzhansky, T. 1959. Radiation, Genes and Man. New York, Henry Holt & Co., Inc. **142, 157**

Wallach, M. A., and Kogan, N. 1965. A new look at the creativity-intelligence distinction. J. of Personality, *33:*348-369. **379**

Waller, H. 1946. The early failure of breast feeding; clinical study of its causes and their prevention. Arch. Dis. Child., *21:*1-12. **183**

Waller, W. 1951. The Family. Revised by R. Hill. New York, Holt, Rinehart and Winston, Inc. **79**

Walters, C. E. 1965. Prediction of postnatal development from fetal activity. Child Development, *36:*801-808. **314**

Walters, J. 1962. A review of family research in 1959, 1960, and 1961. Marriage and Family Living, *24:*158-178. **79**

Walters, R. H., Parke, R. D., and Cane, V. A. 1965. Timing of punishment and the observation of consequences to others as determinants of response inhibition. J. Exp. Child Psychol., *2:*10-30. **240, 241**

Wann, K. D., Dorn, M. S., and Liddle, E. A. 1962. Fostering Intellectual Development in Young Children. New York, Teachers College, Columbia University. **386**

Warkany, J., Roth, C. B., and Wilson, J. G. 1948. Multiple congenital malformations; considerations of etiologic factors. Pediatrics, *1:*462-471. **84**

Warner, W. L. 1953. American Life: Dream and Reality. Chicago, University of Chicago Press. **64**

Warren, J. 1952. Personal communication concerning data from New York State College of Home Economics. **58, 59**

Warren, R. J., Lepow, M. L., Bartsch, G. E., and Robbin, F. C. 1964. The relationship of maternal antibody, breast feeding, and age to the susceptibility of newborn infants to infection with attenuated polioviruses. Pediatrics, *34:*4-13. **188**

Washburn, A. H. 1966. Appraisal of Health Growth and Development from Birth to Adolescence. Chap. 8 (Vol. 1), in I. McQuarrie and V. C. Kelley (Eds.): Brennemann's Practice of Pediatrics. Hagerstown, Md., W. F. Prior Co., Inc. **172, 270, 272**

Watson, E. H., and Lowrey, G. H. 1967. Growth and Development of Children. 5th ed. Chicago, Year Book Publishers, Inc. **133, 164, 168, 170, 171, 173, 174, 202, 217, 218, 224, 272, 279, 293**

Watson, J. B. 1928. Psychological Care of Infant and Child. New York, W. W. Norton & Co., Inc. **41, 219, 441**

Watterson, R. L. (Ed.) 1959. Endocrines in Development. Chicago, University of Chicago Press. **21**

Weber, F. J., and Hetznecker, W. H. 1961. Radiation and child health. Pediatrics, *28:* 147-158. **142, 143**

Wehrle, P. F., et al. 1961. The epidemiology of accidental poisoning in the urban population. III. The repeater problem in accidental poisoning. Pediatrics, *27:*614-620. **146**

Weisberg, P. 1963. Social and nonsocial conditioning of infant vocalizations. Child Development, *34:*377-388. **137**

Welbourn, H. F. 1958. Bottle feeding: a problem of civilization. J. Trop. Pediat., *3:*157-170. **188**

Wellman, B., et al. 1931. Speech Sounds of Young Children. Studies in Child Welfare. V (2). Iowa City, University of Iowa. **347**

Wells, H. L. 1959. Financial management practices of young families. J. H. Econ., *51:* 439-444. **54**

Wenar, C. 1964. Competence at one. Merrill-Palmer Quarterly, *10:*329-342. **428**

Wenger, M. A. 1936. An investigation of conditioned responses in human infants. Studies in Child Welfare, *12:*1-90. Iowa City, University of Iowa. **329**

Werner, E. E., and Bayley, N. 1966. The reliability of Bayley's Revised Scale of Mental and Motor Development during the first year of life. Child Development, *37:*39-50. **299, 383, 384**

Wetzel, N. C. 1941. Physical fitness in terms of physique, development and basal metabolism. J.A.M.A., *116:*1187-1195. **258**

Wetzel, N. C. 1943. Assessing physical condition of children; components of physical status and physical progress and their evaluation. J. Pediat., *22:*329-361. **258**

Wetzel, N. C 1944. Growth; in O. Glasser (Ed.): Medical Physics. Vol. I. Chicago, Year Book Publishers, Inc. **258**

Wetzel, N. C. 1946. The baby grid. J. Pediat., *29:*439-454. **258**

White, B. L. 1967. An experimental approach to the effects of experience on early human behavior. Minnesota Symposia on Child Psychology, Vol. *1:*201-225. **322**

White, B. L., and Held, R. 1966. Plasticity of sensorimotor development in the human infant; in J. Rosenblith and W. Allinsmith (Eds.): The Causes of Behavior II. Boston, Allyn and Bacon, Inc. **12, 22, 306, 307, 308, 311, 322, 331, 338**

White, R. W. 1960. Competence and the psychosexual stages of development. Nebraska Symposium on Motivation, 97-104, 106-108, 133-138. Lincoln, Neb., University of Nebraska Press. Also in J. Rosenblith and W. Allinsmith (Eds.): 1966. The Causes of Behavior: Readings in Child Development and Educational Psychology II. Boston, Allyn & Bacon, Inc. **14, 234**

White, S. H. 1963. Learning. Chap. 5 in H. W. Stevenson, J. Kagan and C. Spiker (Eds.): Child Psychology. Sixty-Second Yearbook of the National Society for the Study of Education. Chicago, University of Chicago Press. **14**

White House Conference on Child Health and Protection. 1932. Growth and Development of the Child. Part I. New York, The Century Co. **431**

White House Conference Report. 1940. Children in a Democracy. Washington, D.C., Superintendent of Documents. **431**

Widdowson, E. M. 1955. Reproduction and obesity. Am. J. Clin. Nutrition, *3:*391-396. **83, 105**

Widdowson, E. M., and McCance, R. A. 1963. The effect of finite periods of undernutrition at different ages on the composition and subsequent development of the rat. Proc. Roy. Soc. Series B., *158:*329-342. **158**

Wiegand, E. 1954. Use of Time by Full-Time and Part-Time Homemakers in Relation to Home Management. Memoir 330. Ithaca, N. Y., Cornell University Agricultural Experiment Station. **59**

Wiehl, D. G., and Tompkins, W. L. 1954. Size of babies of obese mothers receiving nutrient supplements. Milbank Mem. Fund Quarterly, *32:*125-140. **247, 253**

Wilkins, L. 1960. Masculinization of female fetus due to use of orally given progestine. J.A.M.A. *172:*1028. **108**

Wilkins, L. 1965. The Diagnosis and Treatment of Endocrine Disorders in Childhood and Adolescence. 3rd ed. Springfield, Ill., Charles C Thomas. **288, 290, 292**

Williams, H. H. 1961. Differences between cow's and human milk. J.A.M.A., *175:*104-107. **185, 187**

Williams, R. B., and Matson, M. 1942. Effect of social groupings upon language of preschool children. Child Development, *13:*233-245. **355**

Williams, R. H. 1962a. General Principles of the Physiology of the Endocrines. Chap. 1 in R. H. Williams (Ed.): Textbook of Endocrinology. 3rd ed. Philadelphia, W. B. Saunders Company. **287, 288**

Williams, R. H. 1962b. The Pancreas. Chap. 9 in R. H. Williams (Ed.): Textbook of Endocrinology. 3rd ed. Philadelphia, W. B. Saunders Company. **291**

Williams, R. H., and Bakke, J. L. 1962. The Thyroid. Chap. 4 in R. H. Williams (Ed.): Textbook of Endocrinology. 3rd ed. Philadelphia, W. B. Saunders Company. **290**

Williams, R. J. 1951. Biochemical Institute Studies. IV. Individual metabolic patterns and human disease: an exploratory study utilizing predominantly paper chromatographic methods. Austin, University of Texas Publication No. 5109. **36, 90**

Williams, R. J. 1956. Biochemical Individuality. The Basis for the Genetotrophic Concept. New York, John Wiley & Sons, Inc. **24, 90**

Williams, R. J., and Siegel, F. L. 1961. Editorial: "Propetology," a new branch of medical science? Am. J. Med., *31:*325-327. **35**

Willis, N. H. 1964. Basic Infant Nutrition. Philadelphia, J. B. Lippincott Company. **158**

Wilner, D. M., et al. 1960. Housing as an environmental factor in mental health. The Johns Hopkins Longitudinal Study. Am. J. Pub. Health, *50:*55-63. **61**

Wilner, D. M., et al. 1961. The Housing Environment and Family Life. A Longitudinal Study of the Effects of Housing on Morbidity and Mental Health. School of Public Health. Los Angeles, University of California. Prepared for WHO Expert Committee on the Public Health Aspects of Housing. Geneva, Switzerland. May. **61**

Wilson, B. A. 1952. The Development and Evaluation of a Speech Improvement Program for Kindergarten Children. Doctoral thesis, Purdue University. **355**

Windle, W. F. 1960. Effects of asphyxiation of the fetus and the newborn infant. Pediatrics, *26:*565-569. **108**

Winitz, H., and Irwin, O. C. 1958. Syllabic and phonetic structure of infants' early words. J. Speech Dis., *1:*250-256. **344**

Wishik, S. M. 1959. Nutrition in pregnancy and lactation. Fed. Proc. 18 No. 2 Part II: 4-8. **113**

Witmer, H., and Kotinsky, R. (Eds.) 1953. Personality in the Making: Fact-finding Report of Midcentury White House Conference on Children and Youth. New York, Harper & Brothers. **4, 152**

Wohlwill, J. F. 1962. VI. From perception to inference: a dimension of cognitive development, in W. Kessen and C. Kuhlman (Eds.): Thought in the Young Child. Monographs of the Society for Research in Child Development, 27, No. 2. **363**

Wolff, H. G. 1952. Stress and Disease. Springfield, Ill., Charles C Thomas. **139**

Wolff, P. H. 1959. Observations on newborn infants. Psychosom. Med., *21:*110-118. **314**

Wolman, I. J. 1944. Major motility patterns of the child's digestive tract: a review. Am. J. M. Sc., *207:*782-804. **169**

Wolman, I. J. 1946. Does milk between meals hamper the appetite or food intake of the child? J. Pediat., *28:*703-712. **198**

Woodhill, L. M., et al. 1955. Nutrition studies of pregnant Australian women. Part II.

Maternal diet and the duration of lactation. Am. J. Obst. & Gynec., *70:*997-1003. **182**

Wright, J. C. 1966. Cognitive Development. Chap. 12, Part II, in F. Falkner (Ed.): Human Development. Philadelphia, W. B. Saunders Company. **327, 335, 372**

Wright, S. W. 1957. Phenylketonuria. J.A.M.A., *165:*2079-2083. **35**

Yamazaki, J. N., et al. 1954. Outcome of pregnancy in women exposed to the atomic bomb in Nagasaki. Am. J. Dis. Child., *87:*448-463. **107**

Yankhauer, A., et al. 1958. Social stratification and health practices in child-bearing and child-rearing. Am. J. Pub. Health, *48:*732-741. **183**

Yarrow, L. J. 1961. Maternal deprivation: toward an empirical and conceptual re-evaluation. Psychol. Bull., *58:*459-490. **354**

Yarrow, M. R. 1960. The Measurement of Children's Attitudes and Values. Chap. 16 in P. Mussen (Ed.): Handbook of Research Methods in Child Development. New York, John Wiley & Sons, Inc. **411, 428**

Yarrow, M. R., Scott, P., DeLeeuw, L., and Heinig, C. 1962. Child rearing in families of working and non-working mothers. Sociometry, *25:*122-140. **47**

Young, P. T. 1967. Affective arousal: some implications. American Psychologist, *22:*32-40. **14**

Young, W. O. 1961. Dental Health, in The Survey of Dentistry. The final report. Commission on the Survey of Dentistry in the United States, B. S. Hollinshead, Director. Washington, D.C., American Council of Education. **144**

Zigler, E. 1966. Mental Retardation: Current Issues and Approaches. Chap. in L. W. Hoffman and M. Hoffman (Eds.): Review of Child Development Research, Vol. 2. New York, Russell Sage Foundation. **350, 383**

Ziller, R. C. 1965. Toward a theory of open and closed groups. Psychological Bulletin, *64:*164-182. **403**

Ziskin, D. E., and Hotelling, H. 1937. Effects of pregnancy, mouth acidity and age on dental caries. J. Dent. Res., *16:*507-519. **117**

Zubek, J. P., and Solberg, P. A. 1954. Human Development. New York, McGraw-Hill Book Co., Inc. **334**

Index

In this index, *italic* page numbers indicate illustrations; page numbers followed by (t) indicate tables.

Ability(ies), of child, adult attitudes and, 430, 449
  differences in, family relations and, 46
  language, 344
  self-discipline and, 446
  to meet situations, 427
Accident(s), 146
Accommodation, definition of, 14, 325
  to incongruities, 149, *151*, 325
  visual, intellectual development and, 331
Accomplishment, sense of, 244
Achievement, autonomous, aggression and, 404
  warmth and, *135*
  expectations and, 449
  in five-year-old, personality, 457
    physical, 456
  involvement in, in forecasting personality, 464
ACTH, 139, 289
Active reaction, social behavior and, 396
Activity, 232
  bodily, in newborn and infant, 298
  fetal, 102
  level of, in forecasting personality, 463
  motivation for, 233
  motor development and, 310, 314, 316
  reflex. See *Reflex(es)*.
  need for rest and, 225-235
  sensory, warmth and, 148
Adaptability, human, 23
Adaptation, to stress, 292
Adaptation syndrome, 395
Adenoids, 140
Adolescence, pregnancy during, 81
Adopted child, 46
Adrenal glands, 287, 291
Adrenocorticotropin (ACTH), 139, 289
Adult, developmental tasks of, 33
Adult-child relations, 429-451
  emotional development and, 16, 422
  intellectual development and, 371, 378
  motor development and, 312
  personality development and, 441-451
  social development and, 407, 412
Affection, in adult-child relations, 135, 235, 236, 412, 441, 442

Affection (*Continued*)
  trends in, 390, 392
Affectional ties, 235. See also *Affection*.
  language development and, 353
  social development and, 412
Affective behavior, 389
Age, ability and, self-discipline and, 446
  as variable, in language development, 351
Aggression, in peer relations, 403, 412
  model in, 235, 412
Aggressiveness, maternal, 154
Alimentary canal, 161, 314
Allergy, breast feeding vs. bottle feeding and, 189
Ambidextrous period, 310
Ambivalence, 421
Amniotic fluid, 97
Amniotic sac, 97, *100*
Amylase, 164
Analgesia, during childbirth, 125
Androgens, cortical, 291
  gonadal, 292
Anemia, radiation and, 142
Anesthesia, during childbirth, 125
Anger, 391
  hunger and, 197
Anoxia, effect on fetus, 108, 278
Anxiety, behavior problems and, 414
  in infancy, 149
Apathy, stress and meeting situations without, 129, 138-151, *151*, 427
Appetite, 204
  age and, 194, *195*, 204
  individuality in, 197, 200
  neurological control of, 275
Arm, motor development in, *301*
Arousal, reticular formation in, 276
Articulation, in language development, 347
Ascorbic acid, requirement for, 190, 196
Aspects, definition of, 7
Assimilation, definition of, 14, 325
Attention, contrast and distinctiveness and, 336, *336, 339, 340*
  selective, 335
  visual, 331

513

Attitudes, adult, balance in, 429
  bases for, 431
    personality development and, 441-451
  as need in mature person, 241
  toward authority, 445
  toward new baby, 119-122
  toward others, social development and, 394
Authority, attitudes toward, 445
Autonomous achievement, *135*, 404
Autonomy, 152, *152*
  achievement and, aggression and, 404
    warmth and, *135*
  eating procedures and, *214*
  feeding schedule and, 208
  sense of, healthy personality and, 243
Autonomy-control, 40
  child behavior and, *135*, 155
  love-hostility and, 155

Babinski reflex, 277, 297
Baby Grid, 258
Back, muscle control of, 299, *299*
Balance, body, growth and, 283
  motor development and, 302, *302, 303, 304*
  muscle and bone condition in, 282
  play materials and, 321
Basal metabolism, 171
  in pregnancy, 113
Basic need, definition of, 130
Bathing, health protection and, 143
Bayley curves, for height and weight assessment, 256
Bedtime, 231
  routines of, 228
Behavior, affective, 389
  as indication of feelings, 422
  biological functioning and, 35
  body form and, 262
  change in, imitation and, 238, *238, 239*
    orderly trends in, 21
  conscience as internalized control of, 17
  diversity of influences and responses in, *430*
  eating, 203-216
  effective, 390
  fetal, 102
  learned, neurological development and, 277
  linguistic, language development and, 343
  motor and sensory, problem-solving and, *313*
  pleasure and displeasure and, 240
  problems with, 414
  sleep, orderly trends in, 227
  social, development of, 396
  speech and language in regulation of, 350
  study of, 418
Behavioral dispositions, 389-427, 453-465
  definition of, 458

Berkeley Growth Study tests, 462
Biological system(s), definition of, 20
  language development and, 351
  motor development and, 310
Birth. See also *Childbirth.*
  answering child's questions about, 121
  reflexes present at, 296
Birth date, calculation of, 91
Birth order, behavior and, 44
Birth rate, United States, *66*
Biting reflex, 161
Bladder, in pregnancy, 109
Bladder control, 219, 221. See also *Toilet training.*
Blastocyst, 94, *95, 96*
Block play, 317
Blood cells, count in infancy, 172
  formation of, 264
Blood pressure, in infancy, 172
Blood-vascular system, nutrition and, 172
Bodily activity. See *Activity.*
Body, child's perception of, 364
  development of control over, 295-304, *299-305, 313, 317, 318, 320*
  form (physique) of, 262
  growth of, variations in, 251
  maturity of, skeletal status and, 270
  movement of, systems involved in, 247
  orientation of to space, personality and, 463
  proportions of, 251, *252, 253, 274*
  temperature regulation of, 132. See also *Temperature.*
  weight of, 253. See also *Weight.*
Body dynamics, 281-287
  concept of, 281
  individual differences in, 284
  variables in, 282
Body rocking, 414
Bone(s), body dynamics and, 282
  development of, 264, *265, 266*
  formation of, parathyroid glands and, 290
  functions of, 263
  methods of assessment of, 267
Bone scars, 267
Books, language development and, 357
Bottle-feeding, 181
  vs. breast feeding, 185
Bowel control, 219, 220. See also *Toilet training.*
Bowel movements, 169
Brain, in sleep-wakefulness cycle, 226
Brain waves, 277
Breast, in pregnancy, 108, 111
Breast feeding, 180
  vs. bottle feeding, 185
Budget, family orientation and, 59

Calcium metabolism, parathyroid glands and, 290
Calories, need for, 191

Candy, 198
Carbohydrate, in diet, 198
  caries and, 144, 198
  metabolism of, 291
Caries, dental, 144
  carbohydrate in diet and, 198
Categorization, in concept formation, 365, *371*
  perception and, 339
Cause and effect, problem solving and, 367
Caution, fear and, 391
Central nervous system, 275
  in pregnancy, 117
  nutrition and, 158, 275
Cerebellum, 276
  movement and, 275
Cerebral cortex, 275
Chairs, posture and, 285
Channel of development, 26, *27, 28*
Cheating, 411
Check lists, for behavior study, 418
Chemoreceptors, 172
Chewing, 161
  learning of, 192
Child, adopted, 46
  development of. See *Child development* and specific type of development.
  gifted, 383
  newborn. See *Newborn.*
  preschool. See *Preschool child.*
Child development, definition of, 3
  theories of, 19
Childbirth, 122-128. See also *Labor.*
  hospitalization for, 123
  natural (cooperative), 126
Chorionic vesicle, 97, *98, 100*
Chromosomes, 88, 91, *92*
Church, attitudes toward, 425
City, family orientation and, 63
Class, social, family orientation and, 64
Clavicle, 273
Climate, emotional, 40
  physical, 51
Clothing, body dynamics and, 285
  motor development and, 316
  temperature regulation and, 134
Cognition, 335
  cultural differences and, 43
  development of, 358
    concepts of self and others and, 389-417
  motor development and, 314
Cognitive style, of categorization, 365
Coldness, maternal, warmth vs., 136, 148
Color, perception of, 332, *341*
Colostrum, as infant's first food, 180
  secretion of, 111
Comfort devices, bedtime routines and, 228
Communication, as language use, 349
  restricted vs. elaborated, 352
Community, 65-77
  facilities, planning for parenthood and, 85

Community (*Continued*)
  services, day care, 75
    family use of, 73
    health, 74
    trends in, *66-72*
Competence, 14
  interpersonal identity and, 38
  maturation and, 9
Comprehension, language development and, 344
Concept formation, 358-373, *361, 362*
  emotional and social development and, 389-427
  perception and, 339, *340*
  trends in thought on, 358-361
Concrete thinking stage, 359, *340, 341, 361, 362*
Congenital malformations, causes of, 104, 106, 107, 108
Conscience, as internalized control of behavior, 17
  development of, 411, 444
  initiative and, in healthy personality, 244
Consideration of others, 423
Consonants, in early vocalization, 344
Constitution, definition of, 4
  emotional tone and, 19
  orderly development and, 21
  personality development and, 433
  types of, 434
Contrast, in perceptual learning, 336, *336, 339, 340*
Control, bowel and bladder, 219. See also *Toilet training.*
  democratic-autocratic, 156
  freedom and, in personality development, 443
  motor, development of, 295-304
Control-dominance, aggression and, 404
Cooperative play, 400, *401, 402*
Coordination, eye-hand, 305
  hand-mouth, 308
  maturation and, 9, *10*
  muscular and nervous systems and, *280*
  play materials and, 319
Correlates, definition of, 29
Correlation coefficient, 138
Cortex, cerebral, 275
  of adrenal glands, 291
Counting, learning of, 363
Courage, motor development and, 316
Courtesy, imitation in teaching of, 374
Cow's milk, content of, vs. human, 185, *186*
Crawling, 301
Creativity, 373-383
  assessment of, 376
  definition of, 376
  individual differences in, 382
Creeping, 301
  play materials and, 321
Cretinism, 290
Criticism, social development and, 412
Crying, hunger and, 204
  language development and, 343

Crying (*Continued*)
  sleep and, 228
Culture, cognition and, 43
  definition of, 36
  early training and, 337
  family differences in, 42
  language development and, 353
  social, breast-feeding and, 183
Cup, learning use of, 211, *211*
Curiosity, as motivation for learning, 233

Dallying, concept of time and, 364
Darwinian (grasp) reflex, 103, 296
Dawdling, at meals, 200
Day-care services, 75
Deafness, word, 352
Death rates, maternal and infant, 122
Decidua, 94
Deciduous teeth, 27, 175(t). See also *Teeth.*
Decision making, 370
  in home management, 60
Decisiveness, maternal, stress and, 415
Defecation, 163, 169
Defects, physical, anoxia and, 108, 278
  early recognition of, 144
  posture and, 284
Deficiency, iodine, 290
  nutritional, maternal, fetus and, 105
Deglutition. See *Swallowing.*
Delinquency, rates of, in slum areas, *61*
Demineralization, of bone, 291
Democratic-autocratic control, 156
Demonstrativeness, 441
Dental caries, 144, 198
Dentition. See *Teeth.*
Dependence. See also *Independence-dependence.*
  achievement and, 42, 407
  independence and, 129, 151-157, *152*, 447
  learning and, 137
  nurturance-withdrawal and, 137, 155
  parental control and, 155
  physical and psychological, 155
Deprivation, perceptual development and, 337
Depth discrimination, 331
Development, child, definition of, 3
  channels of, 26, *27, 28*
  current concepts of, 3-29
  emotional-social, 389-427. See also *Emotional development* and *Social development.*
  forecasting of, 458-465
  intellectual, 323-386. See also *Intellectual development.*
  motor, 294-322. See also *Motor development.*
  perceptual, 324-342. See also *Perceptual development.*
  personality. See *Personality, development of.*

Development (*Continued*)
  physical, 247-293. See also *Physical development.*
  spiritual, 425
Developmental stage (phase, step), 11
Developmental tasks, of family members, 33
Developmental-dynamic concept, of child development, 5-21
  adult attitudes and, 429
  basic needs and, 130
Diabetes mellitus, 291
Diet, carbohydrate in, 198
  in lactation, 115(t), 182
  in pregnancy, 115, 115(t)
  maternal, influence on fetus, 105
  of child, 195
  tooth care and, 145
Differentiation, behavioral and motor, 303
  cellular, 91
  emotional, 390
Digestion, mechanism of, 161
Digestive system, 161
Diphtheria immunization, 141
Discipline, 153, 443
  age and ability and, 446
  love and, 442, 443
  self-discipline and, 443
Discrimination, between persons, 396
  depth, 331
  of shapes, 333
  sound, 330
Disease, incidence of, breast feeding vs. bottle feeding and, 188
  protection against, 139, 141
Disobedience, 411
Disposition(s), behavorial, 389-427, 453-465
  definition of, 458
Dispositional systems, 14, 393, 463
Dissonance. See *Incongruity-dissonance.*
Distance, learning judgment of, 362
  perception of, 331
Distinctiveness, in perceptual learning, 336, *336, 339, 340*
Dominance, lateral, 309
Dramatic play, 376, *377*
Drive(s), definition of, 13. See also *Motivation.*
Drooling, 164
Drugs, during childbirth, 125
  excretion of, in breast milk, 189
  in pregnancy, effect on fetus, 107
Dwarfism, pituitary, 288
Dynamics, body, 281-287. See also *Body dynamics.*

Ear, 329
Eating behavior, 203-216, *212, 214, 216*
  digestive system and, 161
  motor development and, 11
  self-regulation of, 182, 204, *206-208*

Eating behavior (*Continued*)
variables in, 215
Economic factors, family climate and, 53
Ectoderm, formation of, 94
Ectomorphy, 262
Effectance, motivation and, 13
Effective behavior, 390
Electroencephalogram, 275
Elimination, 203, 216-223
in infant, 169
in pregnancy, 116
neurological control of, 219
Embryo, development of, 91-108, 91(t), *95, 96*
Emotion(s), behavior problems and, 414
body dynamics and, 284
definition of, 389
food practices and, 55
galvanic skin response and, 462
in pregnancy, 106, 117-119
motor development and, 316
Emotional climate, 40
sleep behavior and, 232
Emotional development, 389-427
expressiveness in, 435, 464
implications of, 421-427
methods of study of, 417-421
speech and language in, 350
Emotional-social development, 389-427
"Emotional temperature," 135
Emotional tone, definition of, 16
indication of feelings and, 422
Endocrine glands, 287-293
fetal, 102, 107
lactation, 111, *112,* 181
in pregnancy, 107, 111, 112, *112*
stress and, 139
Endomorphy, 262
Enrichment, language development and, 355
perceptual development and, 337
Entoderm, formation of, 94
Environment, body dynamics and, 284
body weight and, 254
definition of, 251
exogenous, definition of, 21
heredity and, 88-90
intelligence test performance and, 385
language development and, 350, 352
motor development and, 310
motor skills and, 318
perceptual development and, 335
protection against disease and, 140
responsiveness to, activity and, 233, *233, 234*
safety of, 147
stimulation from, in family, 41
Enzymes, in digestion, 164
Epinephrine, 293
Estrogen, 292
Excitable constitution, vs. phlegmatic, 434
Excretory system, 217
Exercise, in pregnancy, 116
of teeth and jaws, 178

Expectations, individual child and, 448
personality development and, 432
Experience(s), definition of, 4
early, mental development and, 278
perceptual development and, 337
real vs. vicarious, 340
general, vs. specific training, 12
language development and, 354
personality development and, 432, *433*
sensory, 149, 337
Exploration, as motivation for activity, 233
Expressiveness, emotional, 421, 464
Expressive-outgoing constitution, 434
Extremities, development of, 273
Extroversion. See *Introversion-extroversion.*
Eye(s), development of, intellectual development and, 330
Eye-hand coordination, *301,* 305, *318*
enrichment and, 338
play materials and, 321

Face, development of, *177,* 271
Family, 31-78
attitudes in, adult, 429
toward new baby, 119-122
bilingual, language development in, 355
community and, *61,* 65-77, *66-72*
complexity of, 31-32
composition of, 40
concept of, developmental, 31, 40
structural, 31
crises in, 78
cultural differences of, 42
employment of mother and, 47, 48(t)
food practices of, 55, 56
heritage of, 35
income of, *69, 70*
methods of study of, 77-78
nuclear, 31
number of children per, *67*
orientations of, 51-65
position in, 43
relations among members of, 40-51
responsibility in, division of, 46
roles in, 39, *59,* 78, *121*
rural and urban, 63
sequences of, 32
Farm, family orientation and, 63
Fat, as component of weight, 260, *261*
Father, absence of, 49
status of, children receiving Social Security payment and, *71*
Father nurturance, sex role identification and, 236, 237(t)
Fatigue, 226
Fear, 391
incongruity-dissonance and, 150
Feces, 163
Feeding. See also *Eating behavior.*
breast and bottle, 180, 185
infant's jaw movements in, *165*
mother-child relations and, 180, 183, 189

Feeding (*Continued*)
  practices, changes in, 179
  schedule, self-regulation of, 204, *206-208*
Feelings. See also *Emotions.*
  expression of, 421
  in emotional development, 389
  indications of, 422
Feminine role identity, 39, 121, 236, 237(t), 408
Fertilization, 93
Fetal membranes, development of, 97, *98-100*
Fetus, behavior of, 102
  development of, 91-108, *100, 101*
  maturity of, survival and, 103
  nervous system in, 276
  physiological functions of, 102
  prenatal influences on, 104
  susceptibility to radiation of, 142
Films, models to imitate and, 238, 240
Finances, pregnancy and, 86
Fingers, motor development and, 304, *305*, 307(t)
Five-year-old, summary of achievement in, 456
Fluid, amniotic, 97
Fluoridation, water, tooth care and, 145
Follicle-stimulating hormone, 289
Fontanelles, 270
Food(s), attitudes to, *216*
  daily intake of, adequacy of, 193
    for infants and young children, 195, 199, 199(t)
    in pregnancy, 115, 115(t)
    neurological control of, 275
  digestion of, mechanism of, 161
  family practices and, 55. See also *Food practices.*
  first, for infant, 180
  introduction of, 191, 211
  maturing child's needs for, 193
  preferences for, 201
  refusal of, in preschool child, 200
  self-selection of, 209
  sense of taste and, 328
Food practices, 55, 56
  early experiences and, 193
  in preschool child, 200
Foot, development of, 273
  pronation of, 283
Forecasting, of future development, 458-465
Form, perception of, 332, *341*
Formal thinking stage, 359
Free play, as indication of feelings, 422
  perceptual development and, 340, *341*
Freedom, control and, personality development and, 443
Friendship, 403
FSH, 289

Galvanic skin response, 462
Gene(s), 89

Gene(s) (*Continued*)
  in lateral dominance, 310
  radiation injury to, 142
Generalization, problem solving and, 367
Genetics, definition of, 251
  growth and development of family and, 35
  stature and, 250
Germ cells, maturation of, 91, *92*
German measles, in pregnancy, 106
Gesell Developmental Scale, 383
Gifted child, 383
Glands, adrenal, 287, 291
  endocrine, 287-293. See also *Endocrine glands.*
  in digestive system, 161
  mammary, in pregnancy, 111
  parathyroid, 287, 290
  pituitary, 139, 287, 289
  sex, 287, 292
  thyroid, 287, 290
Goals, discipline and, 156
  of family, 34
Goal response, aggression and, 404
Gonads, 287, 292
Gonadotropin, 289
Grandparents, 50
Grasp reflex, in fetus, 103
  in newborn, 296
Grasping, enrichment and, 338
  motor development and, 304, *305*, 307(t)
  play materials and, 320
Gratification of parent, child's success and, 449
Gravity, body dynamics and, 282
Grid graphs, for height and weight assessment, 258
Group, withdrawal from. See *Introversion-extroversion.*
Group play, 400, *401, 402*
Growth, current concepts of, 3-29
  definition of, 8
  child's equipment for, 247-293
  early years as foundation for, 453-465
  forecasting of, 459
  home and family and, 31-78
  in height, 247. See also *Height.*
  in weight, 253. See also *Weight.*
  nutrition and, 158
  variations in, 251
Growth hormone, 289
GSR, 462

Habits, breaking of, 415
  food. See *Food practices.*
  living, pregnancy and, 87
  sleeping, 231. See also *Sleep.*
Habituation, 327
Hand(s), motor development in, *301*
  letting go of objects and, 308
  skeletal development of, 273
  in forecasting future growth, 460

Hand(s) *(Continued)*
  skeletal maturation in, 267
  washing of, health protection and, 144
Hand-eye coordination, 305. See also *Eye-hand coordination.*
Hand-mouth coordination, 308
Hand-mouth inhibition, 309
Hand preference, 309
  stuttering and, 356
Hand skills, development of, 304-310, *305,* 307(t)
Head, neck and, muscle control of, 298, *299*
  skull and, development of, 270, *271*
Health, adult attitudes and, 431
  definition of, 54
  maternal, effect on fetus, 104
  planning for parenthood and, 81
  protection of, 139
  radiation hazard to, 107, 142
Health practices, and, 54
Health services, community, 74
Healthy personality, components of, 242-245
Hearing, intellectual development and, 329
  language development and, 352
Heart, fetal, function of, 102
Heart rate, 172
Heartbeat, fetal, as sign of pregnancy, 109
Heat, physiological production and loss of, 132
Height, 247, *248, 249*
  assessment of, 255, *256, 257*
  environment and, 250
  forecasting of, 459
  heredity and, 250, 259, 259(t)
  racial differences in, 250
  sex differences in, 247
  size and behavior and, 251
Hemoglobin, level of, in infancy, 172
Heredity, 35
  environment and, 88-90
  height and, 250, 259
Home management, family orientation and, 58
Homeostasis, definition of, 132, 139
  endocrine glands and, 288
  health protection and, 139
Hormones, in pregnancy and lactation, 111, *112*
  interaction of, 288
  pituitary, 289
Hospitalization, for childbirth, 123
  return home after, 127
Hostility, love vs. See *Love-hostility.*
Housing, family orientation and, 60
  healthful principles of, 62
Human development concept, *6*
Human milk, content of, vs. cow's, 185, *186*
Hunger, 204
  anger and, 197
  motor development and, 314
Hunger contractions, 164, 204
Husband, role of, during childbirth, 126

Hypothalamus, appetite control and, 204, 276
  endocrine gland function and, 292
  temperature regulation by, 133

Ideas, exchange of, in social development, 399
Identification, role learning and, 235, 458
Identity, definition of, 38
  interpersonal, competence and, 38
  sense of, 244
Illness, motor development and, 315
Image, family interactions, and, 38
Imagination, creativity and, 375
  emotional expression and, 421
  language use and, 349
Imitation, behavior change and, 238, *238, 239*
  creativity and, 373
  language development and, 352
  motivation and, 235
  observation of films and, 238, 240
  posture and, 285
Immunity, breast feeding vs. bottle feeding and, 188
  disease and, 141
Immunization, 141
Implantation, of ovum, 94
Incentive(s), 13. See also *Motivation.*
Income, *69, 70*
  adjustment to pregnancy and, 86
  food patterns and, 56
Incongruity-dissonance, 13
  accommodation to, 149, *151, 325*
  contrast and distinctiveness and, 336, *336*
  fear and, 150
  personality development and, 439
Increment, 25, *25*
Independence-dependence, 129, 151-157, *152,* 447. See also *Dependence.*
  achievement and, 42, 407
  learning and, 137
Individual, uniqueness of, 24
Individualistic play, 400, *401*
Individuality, adaptation of expectations to, 448
  adult attitudes and, 430
  basic needs and, 130
  in activity, 225
  in body dynamics, 284
  in creativity, 382
  in intelligence, *28*
  in motor development, 312
  in personality development, 434
  in skeletal development, 268
  in sleep-wakefulness cycle, *229, 230,* 231
  in social development, 412
  values and, 410
  position in family and, 43
  understanding of, 424

Individuality (*Continued*)
  ways of viewing, 25-29
Infant care, classes in, 88
Infantile swallowing, *166*
Infections, incidence of, breast feeding vs.
    bottle feeding and, 188
  viral, maternal, effect on fetus, 106
Information, processing of, learning and,
    13
  seeking of, language use and, 349
Inhibition, hand-mouth, 309
  of activity, motor development and, 314
Initiative, sense of, 244
  social, 397
Instrumental learning, 235
Insulin, secretion and function of, 291
Integration, behavioral and motor, 303,
    304
  of learning, 416, *417*
  of personality, 432
Integrity, sense of, 245
Intellectual development, 323-386, *323*
  concept formation and problem-solving
    and thought in, 358-373, *361, 362*
  sensitivity and perception in, 324-342
Intelligence, individual patterns of, *28*
  language development and, 351
  measurement of, 383-386
  motor development and, 314
  predicting of, 461
Intelligence quotient, 384
Intelligence test(s), 379, 383, 461
  performance in, enrichment and, 338
    factors influencing, 385
Interaction(s), 5, *6*, 37, 389
Interpersonal identity, competence and,
    38
Intestinal flora, in digestion, 169
Intimacy, sense of, 244
Introversion-extroversion, personality de-
    velopment and, 434, 437, 464
  social development and, 393, 409
Iodine, deficiency, 290
Iowa curves, for height and weight assess-
    ment, 256, *257*
I.Q., 384
Islets of Langerhans, 291

Jaw(s), development of, *176, 177*
  movement of, in infant feeding, *165*
  nutrition and, 173
Joy, definition of, 392
  in creativity, 378
Judging distance, 362

Kidneys, 217
Kinesthetic sensitivity, intellectual devel-
    opment and, 334

Labor, 124
  husband's role during, 126

Labor (*Continued*)
  mother's role during, 125
Lactation, 181
  diet during, 115(t), 182
  hormones in, 111, *112*
Laissez-faire-involvement, 155
Langerhans, islets of, 291
Language, definition of, 342, 346
  development of, 342-358
    variables in, 351
  enjoyment of, 357
  enrichment, 355
  hearing and, 330
  restricted vs. elaborated, 352
  uses of, 348
Lateral dominance, 309
Leadership, development of, 402
Learning, complexity of, *15*
  conditions of, in personality develop-
    ment, 440
  definition of, 12
  instrumental, 235
  maturation and, 10
    motor development and, 311
  neurological development and, 277
  of eating procedures, 211, *212, 214*
  social influence on, *18*
  unstable and integral stages of, 416, *417*
Leg, motor development in, *301*
Letter-like forms, discrimination of, 334
Letting go, of objects, 308
Leukemia, radiation as cause of, 142
LH, 289
Life cycle, family, role functions in, *59*
  stages in, 32
Linguistics, 343
Lipase, in digestion, 164
Liver, indigestion, 161, 162, 164
Locomotion, bone function in, 263
  motor development and, *297, 299, 300,
    301, 301-303*
Love, discipline and, 442, 443
  personality development and, 441
Love-hostility, 155
  in social development, 393
  maternal, 136
Love-oriented techniques, self-discipline
    and, 446
Loving care, 131
Luteinizing hormone, 289
Lymphatic system, in protection against
    disease, 140

Malformations, congenital, causes of, 104,
    106, 107, 108
Mammary glands, in pregnancy, 111
Management, home, 58
Manners, table, 215
Masculine role identity, 39, 121, 236, 237(t),
    408
Mass media, 239
Mastication, mechanism of, 166
Maternal mortality rates, 122

Maturation, definition of, 8
  forecasting of, 459
  motor development and, 311
  of germ cells, 91, *92*
  of nutriture, 159, 160(t)
  orderly trends in, 21
  pace and pattern in, 9, *10*
  physical and psychological, 9, 311
  skeletal, *267, 268,* 459
Maturity, concept of, behavorial, 10
    biological, 9
  fetal, survival and, 103
  in swallowing, *167*
  nutritive, 195
  parenthood and, 81
  skeletal status and, 270
Meals, dawdling at, 200
Measles, German, in pregnancy, 106
Meconium, excretion of, 169
  formation of, 102
Media, mass, 239
Mediation (mediating processes), 279, 324, 372
  verbal, 350
Medical care, in childbirth, 122
Medulla, of adrenal glands, 291
Meeting situations, stress and apathy and, 129, 138-151, *151,* 427
Membranes, fetal, development of, 97, *98-100*
Menstruation, cessation of, in pregnancy, 108
  uterine mucosa in, *94*
Mental retardation, language development and, 351
Merrill-Palmer Scale of Mental Tests, 384
Mesoderm, formation of, 94
Mesomorphy, 262
Metabolism, basal, 171
  definition of, 159
  endocrine glands in, 288
  in pregnancy, 112
  inborn errors of, 89
Milk, human, as infant's first food, 180
    vs. cow's, content of, 185, *186*
  requirement for, in preschool period, 197
Minerals, bone as reservoir of, 263
  infant's need for, 191
Minnesota Preschool Scales, 384
Mobility, rates of, in United States, *68*
Model, aggressive, social development and, 412
  behavior change and, 238, *238, 239*
  in teaching courtesy, 374
  language development and, 352
Mongolism, 89
Montessori Method, 339
Mood(s), 241
  constitution and, 19
  in pregnancy, 117
Moral ideology, 411
Moro reflex, 297, *297*
Mortality rates, in slum areas, *61*
  maternal and infant, 122

Morula, formation of, 94, *95*
Mother(s), aggressiveness and punitiveness of, 154
  as language model, 353
  attitude of, sleep habits and, 232
  decisiveness of, stress and, 415
  emotional involvement of, 136, 148
  emotional tone of infant and, 16
  employment of, 47, 48(t), *69*
    day care services and, 75
  health of, influence on fetus, 104
  hospitalization of, for childbirth, 123
  nutrition of, for lactation, 182
    in pregnancy, 83, 113
  postpartum care of, 126
  presence of, in new social experiences, *399,* 400
  role of, during labor, 125
  self-esteem of, child rearing and, 47
Mother nurturance, sex role identification and, 236, 237(t)
Motility, of digestive tract, 165
  pattern of, in sleep, 231
Motivation, activity and, 233
  learning and, 13
  motor development and, 316
  need vs., 131
  personality development and, 438
Motor development, 294-322, *295*
  assessment of, 298
  finger and thumb in, 304, *305,* 307(t)
  hand and arm and leg movement in, *301*
  implications of, 315-322
  in infant, 298, *299, 300*
  in preschool child, *299-305, 313, 314, 317, 318, 320*
  speech and, 342
  variables in, 310-322
Motor restraint, 462
Mouth-hand coordination, 308
Movement, body systems for, 247
  coordinated, muscular and nervous systems and, *280*
  motor development and, *295, 303, 304*
  muscle growth and, 279, *280*
  voluntary, neurological control of, 277
Muscle, as component of weight, 260, *261*
  body dynamics and, 282
  coordinated movement and, *280*
  tone of, *280*
    in newborn, 298
  voluntary and involuntary, 279
  perceptual development, and, *341*
Muscular system, 279-281, *280*
Music, creativity and, 381
Mutations, radiation as cause of, 142
Myelination, of nerves, 276

Naps, 228
Narration, language use and, 349
Natural childbirth, 126
Nausea, in pregnancy, 109

Neck, head and, muscle control of, 298, *299*
Need(s), basic, 129-245
    adult attitudes toward, 430
    definition of, 130
    meeting of, as developmental task, 34
        personality development and, 442
    varieties of, 241
Nervous system, 275-279
    central, 117, 158, 275. See also *Central nervous system.*
    control of elimination and, 219
    development of, 276
        early experiences and, 278
        hand dominance and, 310
    endocrine glands and, 288
    in pregnancy, 117
    resistance to stress and, 139
New foods, 211
Newborn, activity in, 298
    body weight of, 253
    brain waves in, 277
    development in, summary of, 455
    eating behavior in, 215
    extremities in, 273
    hand-mouth coordination in, 308
    head and skull in, 270, *271*
    hunger and appetite in, 204
    immunity to disease in, 141
    muscular system in, 279
    nervous system in, 276
    reflex behavior in, 296, *297*
    respiration in, 170
    sense of touch in, 326
    skeletal development in, *265*, 267
    sleep behavior in, 227, 232
    water consumption of, 179
Norepinephrine, secretion and function of, 293
Novelty, social development and, *399*, 400
Nuclear family, 31
Numbers, concepts of, 363
Nursery school, 75
Nursing care, in childbirth, 122
Nurturance, dependence and, 156
    sex role identification and, 236, 237(t)
    social acts and, in infant, 137
    social development and, 405, *406*
Nurturance-withdrawal, 137, 155
Nutrients, absorption of, 162
    in human milk vs. cow's, 185, *186*
    recommended daily allowances of, 199(t)
Nutrition, 178-201
    as basic need, 158-201
    basic concepts of, 56, 158, 178
    body weight and, 254
    family food patterns and, 56
    maternal, during pregnancy, 113, 115, 115(t)
        for lactation, 115(t), 182
        influence on fetus, 104
    needs, 159-161
        of child, 192
        of infant, 179
    physical equipment for, 161-178

Nutrition *(Continued)*
    preconceptional, 83
Nutriture, maternal, during pregnancy, 113
    maturation of, 159, 160(t)
        endocrine glands in, 288

Obedience, 443
Obesity, 179
    maternal, influence on fetus, 105
Object-oriented techniques, self-discipline and, 446
Objectives, as need in mature person, 242
Observation, as social contact, *234*
    behavior change and, 238, *238, 239*
Observational records, in behavior study, 1, 419
Occlusion, 176, *176, 177*
Orderly trends, in child development, 21-23
    in concept formation, 358
    in sleep behavior, 227, *229, 230*
Organs, special sense, 324
Orientations, central, in personality development, *433, 434*
    family, 51-65, *61*
Orienting responses, 296, 326, 334
Overdependence, 156
Overprotection, 448, 450
Overweight, in pregnancy, 114. See also *Obesity.*
Ovum, *92*, 93, *94, 96*
Oxygen, in neurological development, 278
    in nutrition, 178
    in prematurity, 104
    lack of, in pregnancy, effect on fetus, 108
    respiration and, 170
Oxytocin, secretion of, 289

Pace, in maturation, 9, *10*
Pain, sense of, 326
Painting, creativity and, 379, *380*
Pancreas, function of, 291
    in digestion, 161, 162, 164
Parallel play, 400, *401*
Parathyroid glands, 290
Parent(s), absence of, 47
    creativity and, 378
    democratic-autocratic practices of, 156
    developmental task of, 33
    emotional tone of infant and, 16
    expectations of, 448
    gratification of, child's success and, 449
    identification of child with, 235
    permissiveness-strictness of, 153
    presence of, in new social experiences, *399*, 400
    stature of, height and weight of child and, 259, 259(t)
    separation from, anxiety and, 149
Parental sense, 245
Parenthood, preparation for, 80-85

Passivity, personality development and, 434, 464

Pattern, in maturation, 9, *10*

Peers, social development and, 403, 412

Pelvis, development of, 273

Pepsin, in digestion, 164

Percentile statistics, 26

Perception, definition of, 324
of body, 364
of distance, 331
of form, 332, *341*
of numbers, 363
of shape, 333
of size, 332
of weight, *341*, 364

Perceptual development, 324-342
early sensory experience and, 340
in play, *339*
variables in, 335

Peristalsis, 168

Permanence, concept of, 360

Permissiveness-strictness, 153
feeding schedule and, 208

Personality, changes in, in pregnancy, 117
components of, 242-245
continuous integrations of, 432
definition of, 242
development of, conditions of learning and, 440
constitution and, 433
expectations of, 432
in five-year-old, summary of, 457
motivations in, 438
siblings and, 45
use of ideas about, 432-441
early personal associations and, 397, *398*
eating behavior and, 203
forecasting of, 461
motor development and, 314
toilet training and, 203, 220

Persons, discrimination between, 396

Phenylketonuria, 89

Phlegmatic-excitable constitution, 434

Phonemes, of speech, 325, 334

Phosphorus metabolism, 290

Physical climate, of family, 51

Physical defects, anoxia and, 108, 278
early recognition of, 144
posture and, 284

Physical development, 247-293
forecasting of, 459
in five-year-old, summary of, 456

Physical needs, 129-245

Physician, child's health supervision and, 143

Physiological warmth, 132

Physique, 262

Pituitary dwarfism, 288

Pituitary gland, 287, 289
resistance to stress and, 139

Placenta, development of, 97, *100*
functions of, 111

Placid-controlled constitution, 434

Plantar reflex, 297

Play, block, 317
concept of, 233
dramatic, 376, *377*
free, as indication of feelings, 422
perceptual development and, 340, *341*
social development and, 400, *401, 402*

Play materials, in study of emotions, 420
sensory-motor development and, 317, *317*, 318

Play therapy, 420

Poisoning, accidental, 146

Poliomyelitis, 141

Population, U.S., changes in, *66-68*

Position sense, intellectual development and, 334

Postpartum care, of mother, 126

Posture, 281, *282*
assessment of, 283
contrasts in, 285, *286, 287*
environment and, 284
in pregnancy, 110
neurological development and, 277
variables in, *282*, 284

Poverty, 53

Power relationships, 38
dispositional systems and, 393
weaning and, 213

Power-assertive techniques, self-discipline and, 447

Practice, learning and, *15*
language development and, 355
motor development and, 315

Praise, social development and, 412

Preconceptional preparation, for parenthood, 83

Pregnancy, adjustment to, 86-88
age of mother and, 81
diet in, 115, 115(t)
during adolescence, 81
emotions in, 117-119
hard work in, prematurity and, 106
health of mother in, 81, 104
maternal changes during, 109-113
nutrition in, 83, 105, 113
obstetrical period in, 122-128
physical needs during, 113-117
recognition of, 108-109
uterine mucosa in, *94*

Prehension, enrichment and development of, 338
motor development and, 305, *305*, 307(t)

Prematurity, maternal hard work and, 106
maternal nutrition and, 105
oxygen in, 104
weight gain in pregnancy and, 110

Prenatal influences, 104

Preschool child, body weight of, 254
eating behavior in, 196, 215
imitative behavior in, 239
motor development in, *299-305, 313*, 314, *317, 318, 320*
perceptual and intellectual development in, 326
sleep behavior in, 227

Pressure. See *Stress.*
Probability statistics, 16, 138
Problem-solving, 358-373, *369*
　definition of, 366
　sensory-motor, *313*, 314, 366, 372
　steps in, *369*, 370
　thought and, 358, 372
　verbal, 366, 371
Processes, definition of, 7
　learning, 12
　mediating, 279, 324, 372
Progesterone, secretion and function of,
　292
Projective techniques, in study of emo-
　tions, 420
Prolactin, 289
Pronation, 283
Proportions, body, 251, *252, 253*
　relative, individual differences and, 28
Proprioception, 335
Protection, from accidents, 146
　of health, 139
Psychological needs, 129-245
Psychological responsiveness, 147, 442
Psychological system(s), definition of, 20
　motor development and, 310
Psychological warmth, 135, *135*, 442
Psychosocial interaction, 38, 393
Pulse rate, in infancy, 172
Punishment, 240
　self-discipline and, 447
Punitiveness, 154

Quarrels, 404
Questions, language use and, 348

Race, height differences and, 250
　heredity and, 90
　motor and skeletal development and, 311
　understanding differences of, 424
Radiation, health protection and, 142
　in pregnancy, effect on fetus, 107
Rating scales, for behavior study, 418
Reaching, motor development and, 305
　enrichment and, 338
　play materials and, 320
Reactive-explosive constitution, 434
Reactivity control, 435
　in forecasting personality, 465
Reading, enrichment and, 338
　eyes and, 331
　form perception and, 334
Reasoning, language use and, 349
　problem solving and thought and, 366
Receptors, skin, 326
Reciprocity, social, 397
Records, observational, in behavior study,
　1, 419
Red cell count, in infancy, 172
Reflex(es), 277, 297
　biting, 161

Reflex(es) (*Continued*)
　Darwinian (grasp), 103, 296
　fetal development of, 102, 103
　in newborn, 296, *297*
　Moro, 297, *297*
　neurological development and, 277
　plantar, 297
　rooting, 161, 163
　salivary, 162
　sucking, 102, 161, 163
　swallowing, 161, 163, *166, 167*
Reinforcement, 13
　activity and, 232
　definition of, 14
　positive and negative, 240
　social relations and, 136, 147
Relaxation, lactation and, 182
Religion, 425
　food practices and, 55
　understanding differences of, 424
Reserve-spontaneity, personality develop-
　ment and, 434, 464
Respiration, 159
　nutrition and, 170
Respiratory movements, fetal, 102
Respiratory system, 170
Response(s), 13
　in infant, emotional tone and, 16
　orienting, 296, 326, 334
　smiling, in infant, 137
　startle, 298, 330
Responsibility, division of, in family, 46
Responsiveness, psychological, warmth and,
　　147, 442
　social, 235, 393, 396, *399*
　to environment, activity and, 233, *233,
　234*
Rest, activity and, 225-235
　　motor development and, 310
　in pregnancy, 116
　lactation and, 182
　sleep and, 226
　　individual differences in, 231
Restraint, motor, 462
Retardation, mental, language develop-
　ment and, 351
Reticular formation, arousal, 276
　early activation of, 148, 278, 337
　in sleep and wakefulness, 226
Reward, 240
Rh factor, 107
Ribs, development of, 272
Rickets, vitamin D-resistant, 89
Role(s), child's concept of, attitude toward
　　new baby and, 120, *121*
　in family, 38, *59*
　of husband, during childbirth, 126
　of mother, during labor, 125
　sex, 39, 121, 236, 408
　　learning of, 121, 235, 237(t), *238, 239*
　variety of, 39
Rolling over, 299
Rooming-in, for childbirth, 127

Rooting reflex, 161, 163
Rorschach test, 421
Routines, bedtime, 228
Rubella, 106

Sac, amniotic, 97, *100*
Safety, 147
Salivary glands, 161, 164
Salivary reflex, 162
Salivation, 161
Satiety, infant feeding and, 181
    mechanism of, 163
    neurological control of, 275
Scales, rating, for behavior study, 418
Scars, bone, 267
Schedule, feeding, self-regulation of, 204,
    206-208
    lactation and, 182
   home management, 59
Schema, 325, 335, 359
Schemata, 14, 323, 359
School, enrollment in, increase in, *72*
   nursery, 75
Science, 378, *378, 379*
Security, physical and psychological, 139
   physiological functioning and, 147
   signs of, *135,* 148, *151, 152*
Selective attention, 335
Self, concept of, 38
      emotional and social and cognitive de-
      velopment and, 389-427
Self-centeredness, 395
Self-control, independence and, 152, 243
Self-discipline, adult procedures and, 156
   age and ability and, 446
   discipline and, 443
   growth toward, 153
   in motor development, 315
   independence-dependence and, 153
Self-esteem, maternal, child rearing and, 47
   security and, 150
Self-regulation, of feeding schedule, 204,
    206-208
    lactation and, 182
Self-selection, of food, 209
Senses, special, organs of, 324
Sensitivity, intellectual development and,
   324-342
   kinesthetic, 334
Sensory activity, warmth and, 148
Sensory experience, 149, 337
Sensory-motor development, activity change
   in, 316
   play materials and, 317, *317,* 318
Sensory-motor period, 325
Sensory-motor stage, in intellectual devel-
   opment, *299, 301, 305, 336, 339, 359*
Sensory thresholds, personality and, 463
Sentences, building of, 348
Separation, from parent, anxiety and, 149

Sequence(s), in growth of family, 32
   interaction and, 5, *6*
   emotional-social, 389-427
Services, community, day-care and nursery
   school, 75
Sex, determination of, *92,* 93
   height differences and, 247
   language development and, 351
   weight differences and, 260
Sex education, 121, 144, 151
Sex role(s), affectional ties and, 236, 237(t)
   learning of, 39, 121, 236, 237(t), *238, 239,*
   408
Sex glands, function of, 287, 292
Sex-linked characteristics, 89
Shape, perception of, 333
Sharing, 423
Shifting group, in play, 400, *401*
Shoes, body dynamics and, 285
   motor development and, 316
Showing off, 411
Shyness, 409
Siblings, child's personality and, 45
Sight, sense of, 330, *341*
"Silver cord," 442
Sinuses, development of, 271
Sitting up, in infant, 299, *300*
Situations, influence of, personality devel-
   opment and, 439
   meeting of, stress and apathy and, 129,
   138-151, *151,* 427
Size, perception of, 332
Skeletel system, 263-275
   assessment of, *266*
   body maturity and, 270
   bone function in, 263
   bone scars in, 267
   development of, individual differences
   in, 268
   maturation of, *267, 268*
   in forecasting future growth, 459, 460
   indicators of, 269
Skills, hand, 304-310, *305,* 307(t)
Skin, 140
   receptors in, 326
Skin response, galvanic, 462
Skull, development of, 270, *271*
Sleep, 226
   brain waves in, 278
   individual differences in, 228, *229, 230,*
   231
   neurological control of, 276
   orderly trends in, 227
Slums, delinquency and mortality rates
   and, *61*
Smallpox, 141
Smell, sense of, 172, 327
Smile, social, 137, 235, 396
Snacks, 197
Social acts, in infant, 137
Social class, family orientation and, 64
   food practices and, 55
Social contact, need for, 235-241

Social development, 389-427
  attention to others in, 396
  exchange of ideas in, 399
  implications of, 421-427
  initiative in, 397
  methods of study of, 396, 417-421
  responsiveness in, 235, 393, 396, *399*
  self-centeredness in, 395
  variables in, 411
Social Security Act, *71*
Socialization, 235
  definition of, 412
  personal attributes and, 411
Socioeconomic variation in families, *61,* 64
Sociometric technique, in behavior study, 419
Solid food, introduction of, 191
Somatotropin, 289
Sound, discrimination of, 330
Space, bodily orientation to, personality and, 463
  motor development and, 316
  physical climate of family and, 52
Spacing of children, 81
Speech. See also *Language.*
  articulation of, 347
  definition of, 342
  phonemes of, 325, 334
Sperm, maturation of, *92*
Spiritual development, potentialities for, 425
Spontaneity, reserve vs., personality development and, 434, 464
Spoon, learning use of, 211
Standard deviation statistics, 28
Standing, motor development and, 300
  neurological development and, 277
Stanford-Binet intelligence test, 384, 461
Startle response, 298, 330
Statistics, correlation coefficient, 138
  percentile, 26
  probability, 16, 138
  standard deviation, 28
Stature, 247, *248, 249*
  forecasting of, 459
  genetics in, 250
Stepping movements, 300
Stimulation, environmental, 41
  learning and, 13
  maturation and, 12
  sensory, security and, 149
  tactile, fetal response to, 103
Stomach, capacity of, 163
Stories, language development and, 357
Stress, adaptation to, hormones in, 292
  emotional, in pregnancy, 119
  health and, 139
  maternal, effect on fetus, 106
  meeting situations without, 129, 138-151, *151,* 427
  variations in, development, 414
Strictness, permissiveness and, 153, 208
Stuttering, language development and, 356
  stress and, 414

Suburb, family orientation and, 63
  population expansion in, *67*
Sucking, mechanism of, 165, *165*
Sucking reflex, 161, 163
  fetal, 102
Sugar, in diet, 198
Supplements, dietary, in pregnancy, 116
Survival, fetal, maturity and, 103
Sutures, of skull, 270
Swallowing, 161, 163
  mechanism of, *166,* 167, *167*
Swallowing reflex, fetal development of, 102
Sweets, in diet, 198
Sympathy, 405
Syntax, comprehension of, 345
System(s). See also name of specific system.
  biological and psychological, 20

Table manners, 215
Taste, sense of, 172, 197, 328
Taste buds, 173
Teeth, care of, 144, 145
  caries in, 144, 198
  deciduous, calcification and eruption and shedding of, 175(t)
    nutrition and, 173
    variations in spacing of, *27*
  in digestion, 162
  in pregnancy, 116
  jaws and, development of, *176*
Television. See *Mass media.*
Temperature, diurnal change in, 134
  in pregnancy, 109
  physiological regulation of, 132
Tension, language development and, 356
Test(s), Berkeley Growth Study, 462
  biological, for pregnancy, 109
  of creative thinking, 379
  of intelligence, 383, 461
    factors influencing performance in, 383, 385
  Rorschach, 421
  Stanford-Binet, 384, 461
  World, 421
Testosterone, secretion and function of, 292
Tetanus, 141
Tetany, 291
Texture, perception of, *341*
Thalidomide, 107
Thorax, development of, 272
Thought, 358-373, *371*
  conscious, cerebral cortex and, 275
  creative, tests of, 379
  expression of, language use and, 349
  problem-solving and, 366, *371*
  sequence of, 359
  variables in development of, 371
Thresholds, sensory, personality and, 463
Thumb, fingers and, apposition of, 304, *305,* 307(t)

Thumb-sucking, in newborn, 308
  occlusion and, 177
  stress and, 414
Thyroid gland, 287, 290
Thyrotropin, 289
Thyroxin, secretion and function of, 290
Time, concept of, 363
  home management and, 58
Time-sampling observation, in behavior study, 419
Timidity, motor development and, 316
Tocopherol, infant requirement for, 191
Toilet training, neurological control of elimination and, 219
  parental variables and, 138
  personality development and, 203, 220
Tongue, control of, *165-167*
  in digestion, 162
Tonsils, 140
Toothbrushing, 145
Torso, motor control of, 299, *299*
Touch, sense of, 326, *341*
Toxemia, in pregnancy, effect on fetus, 104
Toys. See *Play materials.*
Tradition, family food practices and, 55
Training, intelligence test performance and, 385
  specific, vs. general experience, 12
  perceptual development and, 337
  toilet. See *Toilet training.*
Traits, origin of, 90
  sex-linked, 89
Trophoblast, formation of, 94
Trust, sense of, 243
Trypsin, 164

Umbilical cord, development of, 97, *100*
Understanding, of individual differences, 424
Underweight, in pregnancy, 114
United States, birth rate, *66*
  family food patterns in, 56
  mobility rates in, *68*
Urban family, expenditure of income of, *69*
  orientation of, 63
Urination, 218
Urine, excretion of, 217, 218
Uterus, in menstrual cycle and in pregnancy, *94*
  in pregnancy, 109

Values, definition of, 34
  in social development, 410
  variations in, 34, 35, 36
Vasopressin, 289
Verbal mediation, 350
Verbalization, concept formation and problem-solving and thought and, 371
  development of nurturance and, *406,* 407

Vernix caseosa, formation of, 97
Vertebral column, development of, 272
Vesicle, chorionic, 97, *98, 100*
Vicarious life, of parent, through child, 448
Viral infections, breast feeding vs. bottle feeding and, 188
  maternal, effect on fetus, 106
Visceral swallow, *166*
Vision, intellectual development and, 330
Visual attention, in infants, 331
Vitamin(s), infant's need for, 191
Vitamin C, infant requirement for, 190, 196
Vitamin D, infant requirement for, 189
  excess, 190
Vitamin D-resistant rickets, 89
Vitamin E, infant requirement for, 191
Vocabulary, active, language development and, 346
  hearing and, 330
  in expression of spiritual growth, 425
Vocalization, 137
  early, language development and, 343
  emotional tone and, 18, *18*
Vomiting, in pregnancy, 109
Vowels, consonants and, use of, 344
Vulnerability, personality development and, 434

Wakefulness, 226
  brain waves in, 278
Walking, motor development and, 297, *299, 300-303,* 301
  neurological development and, 277
  variations in development of, *10*
Warmth, 129, 132-151
  child behavior and, 136
  maternal, 136, 148
  physiological, 132
  psychological, 135, *135*
  personality development and, 442
Washing, health protection and, 143
Water, as component of weight, 260
  in nutrition, 179
Water fluoridation, 145
Weaning, 212
  stress and, 415
  time of, 213
Weight, 247, 253
  assessment of, 255, *256, 257, 259*(t)
  breast feeding vs. bottle feeding and, 187
  components of, 260, *261*
  in pregnancy, 110
  learning concept of, 364
  perception of, *341*
  of human embryo, 91, 91(t)
  sex differences in, 260
Wetzel Grid, 258

White cell count, in infancy, 172
Whooping cough, 141
Withdrawal, nurturance and, 137, 155
  social, 409
Word deafness, 352
Work, hard, in pregnancy, 106

Working mothers, 47, 48(t), *69,* 75. See
  also *Mother(s), employment of.*
World Test, 421

X-ray, radiation hazard from, 107, 142